T0181810

Lecture Notes in Computer Science 13304

More information about this series at https://link.springer.com/bookseries/558

Masaaki Kurosu (Ed.)

Human-Computer Interaction

User Experience and Behavior

Thematic Area, HCI 2022
Held as Part of the 24th HCI International Conference, HCII 2022
Virtual Event, June 26 – July 1, 2022
Proceedings, Part III

 Springer

Editor
Masaaki Kurosu
The Open University of Japan
Chiba, Japan

ISSN 0302-9743   ISSN 1611-3349 (electronic)
Lecture Notes in Computer Science
ISBN 978-3-031-05411-2   ISBN 978-3-031-05412-9 (eBook)
https://doi.org/10.1007/978-3-031-05412-9

This Springer imprint is published by the registered company Springer Nature Switzerland AG
The registered company address is: Gewerbestrasse 11, 6330 Cham, Switzerland

Foreword

Human-computer interaction (HCI) is acquiring an ever-increasing scientific and industrial importance, as well as having more impact on people's everyday life, as an ever-growing number of human activities are progressively moving from the physical to the digital world. This process, which has been ongoing for some time now, has been dramatically accelerated by the COVID-19 pandemic. The HCI International (HCII) conference series, held yearly, aims to respond to the compelling need to advance the exchange of knowledge and research and development efforts on the human aspects of design and use of computing systems.

The 24th International Conference on Human-Computer Interaction, HCI International 2022 (HCII 2022), was planned to be held at the Gothia Towers Hotel and Swedish Exhibition & Congress Centre, Göteborg, Sweden, during June 26 to July 1, 2022. Due to the COVID-19 pandemic and with everyone's health and safety in mind, HCII 2022 was organized and run as a virtual conference. It incorporated the 21 thematic areas and affiliated conferences listed on the following page.

A total of 5583 individuals from academia, research institutes, industry, and governmental agencies from 88 countries submitted contributions, and 1276 papers and 275 posters were included in the proceedings to appear just before the start of the conference. The contributions thoroughly cover the entire field of human-computer interaction, addressing major advances in knowledge and effective use of computers in a variety of application areas. These papers provide academics, researchers, engineers, scientists, practitioners, and students with state-of-the-art information on the most recent advances in HCI. The volumes constituting the set of proceedings to appear before the start of the conference are listed in the following pages.

The HCI International (HCII) conference also offers the option of 'Late Breaking Work' which applies both for papers and posters, and the corresponding volume(s) of the proceedings will appear after the conference. Full papers will be included in the 'HCII 2022 - Late Breaking Papers' volumes of the proceedings to be published in the Springer LNCS series, while 'Poster Extended Abstracts' will be included as short research papers in the 'HCII 2022 - Late Breaking Posters' volumes to be published in the Springer CCIS series.

I would like to thank the Program Board Chairs and the members of the Program Boards of all thematic areas and affiliated conferences for their contribution and support towards the highest scientific quality and overall success of the HCI International 2022 conference; they have helped in so many ways, including session organization, paper reviewing (single-blind review process, with a minimum of two reviews per submission) and, more generally, acting as goodwill ambassadors for the HCII conference.

This conference would not have been possible without the continuous and unwavering support and advice of Gavriel Salvendy, founder, General Chair Emeritus, and Scientific Advisor. For his outstanding efforts, I would like to express my appreciation to Abbas Moallem, Communications Chair and Editor of HCI International News.

June 2022   Constantine Stephanidis

HCI International 2022 Thematic Areas and Affiliated Conferences

Thematic Areas

- HCI: Human-Computer Interaction
- HIMI: Human Interface and the Management of Information

Affiliated Conferences

- EPCE: 19th International Conference on Engineering Psychology and Cognitive Ergonomics
- AC: 16th International Conference on Augmented Cognition
- UAHCI: 16th International Conference on Universal Access in Human-Computer Interaction
- CCD: 14th International Conference on Cross-Cultural Design
- SCSM: 14th International Conference on Social Computing and Social Media
- VAMR: 14th International Conference on Virtual, Augmented and Mixed Reality
- DHM: 13th International Conference on Digital Human Modeling and Applications in Health, Safety, Ergonomics and Risk Management
- DUXU: 11th International Conference on Design, User Experience and Usability
- C&C: 10th International Conference on Culture and Computing
- DAPI: 10th International Conference on Distributed, Ambient and Pervasive Interactions
- HCIBGO: 9th International Conference on HCI in Business, Government and Organizations
- LCT: 9th International Conference on Learning and Collaboration Technologies
- ITAP: 8th International Conference on Human Aspects of IT for the Aged Population
- AIS: 4th International Conference on Adaptive Instructional Systems
- HCI-CPT: 4th International Conference on HCI for Cybersecurity, Privacy and Trust
- HCI-Games: 4th International Conference on HCI in Games
- MobiTAS: 4th International Conference on HCI in Mobility, Transport and Automotive Systems
- AI-HCI: 3rd International Conference on Artificial Intelligence in HCI
- MOBILE: 3rd International Conference on Design, Operation and Evaluation of Mobile Communications

List of Conference Proceedings Volumes Appearing Before the Conference

1. LNCS 13302, Human-Computer Interaction: Theoretical Approaches and Design Methods (Part I), edited by Masaaki Kurosu
2. LNCS 13303, Human-Computer Interaction: Technological Innovation (Part II), edited by Masaaki Kurosu
3. LNCS 13304, Human-Computer Interaction: User Experience and Behavior (Part III), edited by Masaaki Kurosu
4. LNCS 13305, Human Interface and the Management of Information: Visual and Information Design (Part I), edited by Sakae Yamamoto and Hirohiko Mori
5. LNCS 13306, Human Interface and the Management of Information: Applications in Complex Technological Environments (Part II), edited by Sakae Yamamoto and Hirohiko Mori
6. LNAI 13307, Engineering Psychology and Cognitive Ergonomics, edited by Don Harris and Wen-Chin Li
7. LNCS 13308, Universal Access in Human-Computer Interaction: Novel Design Approaches and Technologies (Part I), edited by Margherita Antona and Constantine Stephanidis
8. LNCS 13309, Universal Access in Human-Computer Interaction: User and Context Diversity (Part II), edited by Margherita Antona and Constantine Stephanidis
9. LNAI 13310, Augmented Cognition, edited by Dylan D. Schmorrow and Cali M. Fidopiastis
10. LNCS 13311, Cross-Cultural Design: Interaction Design Across Cultures (Part I), edited by Pei-Luen Patrick Rau
11. LNCS 13312, Cross-Cultural Design: Applications in Learning, Arts, Cultural Heritage, Creative Industries, and Virtual Reality (Part II), edited by Pei-Luen Patrick Rau
12. LNCS 13313, Cross-Cultural Design: Applications in Business, Communication, Health, Well-being, and Inclusiveness (Part III), edited by Pei-Luen Patrick Rau
13. LNCS 13314, Cross-Cultural Design: Product and Service Design, Mobility and Automotive Design, Cities, Urban Areas, and Intelligent Environments Design (Part IV), edited by Pei-Luen Patrick Rau
14. LNCS 13315, Social Computing and Social Media: Design, User Experience and Impact (Part I), edited by Gabriele Meiselwitz
15. LNCS 13316, Social Computing and Social Media: Applications in Education and Commerce (Part II), edited by Gabriele Meiselwitz
16. LNCS 13317, Virtual, Augmented and Mixed Reality: Design and Development (Part I), edited by Jessie Y. C. Chen and Gino Fragomeni
17. LNCS 13318, Virtual, Augmented and Mixed Reality: Applications in Education, Aviation and Industry (Part II), edited by Jessie Y. C. Chen and Gino Fragomeni

Preface

Human-Computer Interaction is a Thematic Area of the International Conference on Human-Computer Interaction (HCII). The HCI field is today undergoing a wave of significant innovation and breakthroughs towards radically new future forms of interaction. The HCI Thematic Area constitutes a forum for scientific research and innovation in human-computer interaction, addressing challenging and innovative topics in human-computer interaction theory, methodology, and practice, including, for example, novel theoretical approaches to interaction, novel user interface concepts and technologies, novel interaction devices, UI development methods, environments and tools, multimodal user interfaces, human-robot interaction, emotions in HCI, aesthetic issues, HCI and children, evaluation methods and tools, and many others.

The HCI Thematic Area covers three major dimensions, namely theory, technology, and human beings. The following three volumes of the HCII 2022 proceedings reflect these dimensions:

- Human-Computer Interaction: Theoretical Approaches and Design Methods (Part I), addressing topics related to theoretical and multidisciplinary approaches in HCI, design and evaluation methods, techniques and tools, emotions and design, and children-computer interaction
- Human-Computer Interaction: Technological Innovation (Part II), addressing topics related to novel interaction devices, methods and techniques, text, speech and image processing in HCI, emotion and physiological reactions recognition, and human-robot interaction.
- Human-Computer Interaction: User Experience and Behavior (Part III), addressing topics related to design and user experience case studies, persuasive design and behavioral change, and interacting with chatbots and virtual agents.

Papers of these volumes are included for publication after a minimum of two single-blind reviews from the members of the HCI Program Board or, in some cases, from members of the Program Boards of other affiliated conferences. I would like to thank all of them for their invaluable contribution, support, and efforts.

June 2022

Masaaki Kurosu

39. CCIS 1582, HCI International 2022 Posters - Part III, edited by Constantine Stephanidis, Margherita Antona and Stavroula Ntoa
40. CCIS 1583, HCI International 2022 Posters - Part IV, edited by Constantine Stephanidis, Margherita Antona and Stavroula Ntoa

http://2022.hci.international/proceedings

Human-Computer Interaction Thematic Area (HCI 2022)

Program Board Chair: **Masaaki Kurosu,** The Open University of Japan, Japan

- Salah Ahmed, University of South-Eastern Norway, Norway
- Valdecir Becker, Federal University of Paraiba, Brazil
- Nimish Biloria, University of Technology Sydney, Australia
- Zhigang Chen, Shanghai University, China
- Yu-Hsiu Hung, National Cheng Kung University, Taiwan
- Yi Ji, Guangdong University of Technology, China
- Tsuneo Jozen, Osaka Electro-Communication University, Shijonawate, Japan
- Masanao Koeda, Okayama Prefectural University, Japan
- Hiroshi Noborio, Osaka Electro-Communication University, Neyagawa-shi, Japan
- Michiko Ohkura, Shibaura Institute of Technology, Japan
- Katsuhiko Onishi, Osaka Electro-Communication University, Shijonawate, Japan
- Vinícius Segura, IBM Research, Rio de Janeiro, Brazil
- Mohammad Shidujaman, American International University-Bangladesh, Bangladesh

The full list with the Program Board Chairs and the members of the Program Boards of all thematic areas and affiliated conferences is available online at

http://www.hci.international/board-members-2022.php

HCI International 2023

The 25th International Conference on Human-Computer Interaction, HCI International 2023, will be held jointly with the affiliated conferences at the AC Bella Sky Hotel and Bella Center, Copenhagen, Denmark, 23–28 July 2023. It will cover a broad spectrum of themes related to human-computer interaction, including theoretical issues, methods, tools, processes, and case studies in HCI design, as well as novel interaction techniques, interfaces, and applications. The proceedings will be published by Springer. More information will be available on the conference website: http://2023.hci.international/.

General Chair
Constantine Stephanidis
University of Crete and ICS-FORTH
Heraklion, Crete, Greece
Email: general_chair@hcii2023.org

http://2023.hci.international/

Contents – Part III

Persuasive Design and Behavioral Change

Interacting with Chatbots and Virtual Agents

Design and User Experience Case Studies

A Study on How Users Choose Apps

Adel Alhejaili[1,2]([✉]) and James Blustein[1][iD]

[1] Dalhousie University, Halifax, NS, Canada
adel.alhejaili@dal.ca, jamie@ACM.org
[2] Taibah University, Medina, Saudi Arabia

Abstract. Smartphone apps are part of daily life for many people. It is essential for app developers' success to understand how users choose which apps to install.

Before choosing which apps to install, users may consider the app description, screenshots, ratings, and reviews. When users evaluate the information cues presented by the app stores, they tend to apply shortcuts to reduce the cognitive burden. These shortcuts lead to quicker decisions but ignore some available information.

We conducted an observational lab study with semi-structured interviews of 26 participants who viewed 84 apps using the Google Play Store during app selection tasks.

We created a model based on 13 information cues and four factors that influenced users when choosing which apps to install. Using data mining approaches, we created two models using Weka and Rapidminer to discover the frequent itemsets or patterns among the dataset using Apriori and FP-Growth algorithms.

Our findings indicate that users do not usually rely on a single cue or factor but instead consider a combination of cues and factors. We found that some cues are used as a starting point in the decision process, and the core of these cues is the app reviews. After viewing multiple app, in 8% of instances, participants concluded that the first app they viewed was ultimately the best option to download.

Keywords: HCI theories and methods · Apps · Decision-making · Information cues · Laboratory experiment · Data mining · Association rules

1 Introduction

Understanding why, and how, people choose which apps to install is important for several reasons: to help developers make apps that will be installed, and to help companies sell their apps.

The vast amount of information available in most of the search queries are considered to be overwhelming. It is increasingly important to consider essential aspects of using the available tools by understanding "how users manage to orient themselves and retrieve relevant information" [30, p. 778]. Given the enormous

M. Kurosu (Ed.): HCII 2022, LNCS 13304, pp. 3–22, 2022.
https://doi.org/10.1007/978-3-031-05412-9_1

number of apps in app selection platforms (such as the Google Play Store), it appears unreasonable to expect consumers to regularly use their cognitive abilities and detailed evaluations of the available apps [16].

Evaluation of available information (cues and factors in the app platform) is necessary to make decisions [1,4]. *Cues*, such as ratings, can be observed in the app platform. *Factors* are related to users, not the app selection platform. An example of a factor is the user's motive to install an app, e.g. the problem that creates the need which the app would fulfill.

It is crucial to understand what drives people's decisions of downloading apps since it impacts the benefits and usefulness of such technologies [26]. The key source of providing the required information for consumers lies with app developers since they are the ones who incorporate that information (e.g., cues) into their apps. The provided app description "represents a key channel to inform consumer choice" [21, p. 1].

In recent years, mobile app ecosystems have developed rapidly in which the number of mobile apps and categories have increased significantly. DataReportal recorded as of October of 2021 that there are 5.29 billion unique mobile phone users, accounting for 67.1% of the global population [7]. The worldwide increase of mobile apps has also led to fierce competition, resulting in some apps' disappearance. To succeed in this highly competitive app market, app developers need to understand their users' experiences and make strategic decisions for app survival and sales [23]. App stores owners, developers and marketers need to attract users' attention by improving the app store interface to improve app downloads further [3,31]. With a better understanding of users' behaviour, devices, services and applications can be improved [32].

Our research aims to illustrate how users choose which app to install, and further investigate their importance using data mining approaches to find meaningful relationships, "interesting patterns," and "useful insights." Also, to explore the decision making strategies employed by users when searching for apps.

This work contributes to the understanding of the 'app search space' in the following ways: First, we extend the app model created by Huang and Bashir [14] by identifying multiple stages that users go through before installing an app and determining which information cues are used as a starting point in the app selection process. Second, we corrected a misconception reported in earlier work that the information cues that users initially viewed are important. Our result showed that the importance of these cues was determined later in the search process. Third, we found that users tended to consider a combination of cues and factors when searching for apps. Based on their experience of evaluating other apps, they may gradually develop a substantially different view of the importance of various cues. Fourth, our study shows the importance of certain cues, e.g. app reviews, and their role in the app selection process. Fifth, we show that users use different strategies when searching for apps. Sixth, we identified a new heuristic called "Return to the First."

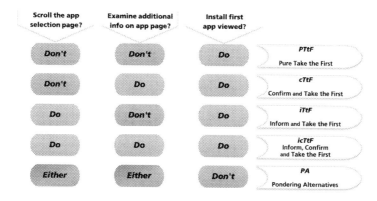

Fig. 1. Dogruel et al. Classification of decision-making methods [8].

2 Background and Related Work

We outline previous research by providing theoretical aspects from a general heuristic perspective, heuristics from an app selection perspective, along with app selection studies.

Also, we briefly describe the data mining approaches and the measures used to assess the relationships between the itemsets "patterns."

2.1 Heuristics

Even since the early days of research on decision-making, "it has been argued that humans do not always use their cognitive abilities extensively before they make a decision or execute an action" [30, p. 779]. Users tend to rely on heuristics as a result of "time deficit and insufficient skills," applying shortcuts and ignoring some of the available information to facilitate quicker decisions [22, p. 59].

Such heuristics support people's primary objectives when looking for information by finding it "quickly, conveniently, and without any substantial engagement with the information or source itself" [22, p. 62].

2.2 App Selection Studies

We first address heuristics from an app selection perspective. Then, we describe related app selection studies.

Dogruel et al. [8] studied heuristic decision-making strategies users incorporate during the app selection process. Figure 1 summarizes their finding of five decision-making heuristics when users search for apps. Four of these heuristics are "variants of 'TtF' Take the First heuristics".

They concluded that the most used heuristics was "Take the First (TtF)", used by 80% of their participants and involved installing the first app that users encountered without looking for or examining other apps [8, p. 139]. Note that they did not investigate the Pondering Alternative heuristic due to the low frequency of occurrence among their participants.

Bowman et al. [2] and Joeckel et al. [16] conducted studies similar to Dogruel et al. [8] but both used think-aloud protocols and had their participants watch recorded footage of their app selection tasks. Bowman et al. found that 42% of their participants chose only to look for games that they had "either previously owned or had some specific familiarity with" [2, p. 4]. Joeckel et al. [16] concluded that users relied on the familiarity of an app, ratings and reviews.

Huang and Bashir [14] created an adoption flow model of anxiety-related apps in the mental health domain and collected eight types of what they called "metadata cues" ("app prices, ratings, reviews, installs, categories, permissions, ranking, and title") [14, p. 4]. Their method did not include users.

2.3 Data Mining

Due to the increasing amount of data collected, many domains are using data mining techniques to extract valuable information and hidden interesting patterns through the process of knowledge discovery for further use [17].

Frequent itemsets and association rules mining are approaches for discovering transactions and interesting rules in the dataset. *Frequent itemsets*, are itemsets that frequently appear in a dataset that satisfy the given minimum support threshold. *Association rules*, is the task of uncovering relationships of itemsets or patterns that come together among large datasets that have a strong association between the discovered items. Mining all the rules are based on different measures such as confidence that would potentially find the relationships between these patterns to analyze the data better and help any domain with the decision-making process (e.g., the product placement) [12,25]. Antecedent (or Premises) is the left-hand side of the rule LHS. Consequent (or Conclusion) is the right-hand side of a rule RHS.

Interesting Measures. We describe a few of the most used measures to evaluate the generated rules.

Support is a measure that gives the percentage of the transactions that include items X and Y to the total number of transactions in a dataset. It shows how frequently the items or combinations of itemsets are bought together [25].

Confidence measures the percentage of the transactions that contain both X and Y to the number of transactions that include only X. It shows how frequently items X and Y appear together in a transaction, given the number of times that X occurs [25].

Lift measures the "frequency of X and Y together if both are statistically independent of each other" [25, p. 21]. It shows the strength of a rule over the random occurrences of X and Y.

3   Research Objective

Prior research has identified multiple information cues when searching for apps [8,9,14,15,19]. The research conducted by Dogruel et al. [8], and Huang and Bashir [14] is the most relevant to our work, despite having different objectives and slightly different methods.

Dogruel et al. [8] did not address the use of multiple heuristics among their participants, and they did not investigate the Pondering Alternative heuristic. Dogruel et al. [8] assumed that the cues that were looked at first by users were important. Moreover, search terms were stored on the phone to "keep specific search terms consistent" among their participants [8, p. 131]. We note that users may not necessarily know the exact name of the app that they were looking to find in actual practice.

Huang and Bashir [14] work was limited to apps in the anxiety category.

We adopted the heuristic-decision strategies of Dogruel et al. [8] and adapted Huang and Bashir's [14] model as the base to develop our model of how users choose which apps to install.

Following earlier work, we present the following research questions:

- What type of information influences users when searching for apps?
- Are the information cues that were looked at first important?
- Do users follow the same heuristics while selecting an app?
- What is the role of the "Pondering Alternative" heuristic?

4   Method

4.1   Participants

According to Creswell and Clark [5], the sample size recommended for using the thematic analysis approach to provide proper codes and themes is 20–30 participants.

The study data was collected as a convenience sample on the campus of a Canadian university with a total of twenty-six participants (25 males and 1 female). Twelve participants were 18–22 years of age, twelve were 23–30, one was 31–40, and one was older than 40. Of the sample, 34% were undergraduate students, 65% were graduate students, 11% were PhD students, 50% were Master's students, and one participant had two Master's degrees but was studying for Bachelor's degree. Participants were recruited through the university e-mail lists. Two restrictions were applied to be eligible to participate: the participant's age was at least 18 years old and should own an Android smartphone. Participants received $10 compensation for their participation.

4.2   Procedure

The study procedure was modified from that of Felt et al. [9] and Kelley et al. [18, 19]. It is an observational lab study with semi-structured interviews. It consisted of five parts as presented in the Supplementary Details (Table A1). After the participants signed the consent, they were asked to think aloud while installing two apps. Also, they completed a short questionnaire to collect demographic data. Moreover, they were interviewed to elaborate on why they either considered or ignored some factors/information cues during the search task. The study took about 30 min to complete.

It is important to note that five participants spent more time on the given app search task, and due to the time restriction of our study, they were only able to engage in one app search task. Also, paid apps were not considered in this study.

4.3   Measures Used for Data Preparation and Analysis

Some steps were taken to prepare the data for analysis [6]: (1) The participants' interactions with the smartphone were video-recorded during the lab study using built-in software. We found that video-recording without eye-tracking provided sufficient data [8] as all interactions and touches were recorded. The phone has a 5.5-inch (1080×1920 pixel) screen. (2) All interviews were transcribed. (3) Video recordings were coded using the rules guide adapted from the work of Dogruel et al. [8] with modifications as shown in the Supplementary Details (Table A2). (4) Thematic analysis was used by identifying main themes based on participants' observations and responses. Codes representing each theme were generated, and some of these codes were later merged into higher-level codes as shown in the Supplementary Details (Table A2). (5) The letter N represents the overall frequency of occurrences. (6) We created two visual matrices as shown in Fig. 4. (7) The first visual matrix, in Fig. 4a, depicts the total combination of cues and factors employed by participants and it shows the participants' ID numbers and the task order (1 for first, and 2 for second) with the number of attempts made for each task. It is organized by the number of cues and factors based on frequency of occurrences, from the most used to the least (nine to zero). Zeroes are represented when participants moved between apps during the app selection tasks without considering any cues/factors. Note that because some participants viewed multiple apps during their first and second tasks, there are many occurrences of 1 and 2 in the chart. For example, ID10 viewed five apps (that is, that participant made five attempts) during the first task and viewed three apps during the second task. The second visual matrix is organized by participants' ID numbers for easier interpretations is shown in Fig. 4b. (8) Each row/record of the factors/cues considered by participants is treated as a transaction coded as 1 (for true) or 0 (for false). An *itemset* is a subset of items within a transaction, e.g. {ratings, reviews} from {ratings, reviews, number of downloads, full description}. (9) We used tools such as Rapidminer and Weka to create models of the Apriori and FP-Growth algorithms to find the frequent itemsets (patterns) to generate the association rules. (10) We used different techniques to interpret some of the derived association rules such as: table-based technique, and graph-based visualization.

5   Results

First, we describe the model we created of how users choose which apps to download. Second, we identify decision-making patterns, along with the use of multiple heuristics and the Return to the First heuristic. Third, we outline the installation cues/factors considered by participants. Fourth, we describe our models for patterns discovery. Lastly, we detail some of the derived association rules and show the importance of the app reviews cue in particular and some other cues.

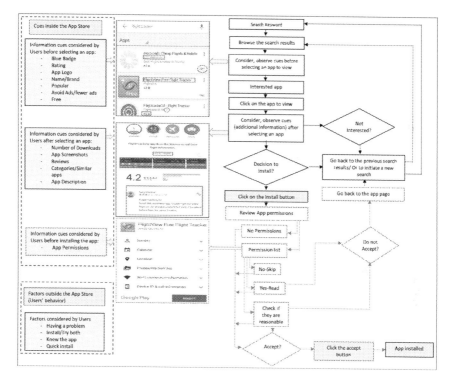

Fig. 2. A model of how users choose which apps to install.
The dotted-red cue and its corresponding behaviour (namely permissions) are not available after Android 6. (Color figure online)

5.1   A Model of How Users Choose Apps

Based on our observations during the app selection process we created a model of how users choose apps to install. Figure 2 is an extended version of the model created by Huang and Bashir [14].

From 41 instances, we identify the cues used by participants as a starting point in the search process. Figure 2 shows three stages that participants go through before installing an app. It also shows the cues that are available in the app selection platform. Moreover, as can be see on the bottom left, there is a list of factors that are considered by users that are not part of the app selection platform.

In the first stage participants initiate the search process after typing a keyword for the desired app. They observe or consider the following available cues on the search results screen of the app selection platform: blue badge (a mark given by Google to the "top developers" in a particular field)[1], app ratings, app logo, app name/brand, app popularity, whether the app is free and avoiding ads or fewer ads before making their decision to view the app for more information.

If the participants were interested in viewing the app they proceeded to the second stage, where they examined and evaluated the cues of app description, categories, number of downloads, screenshots, and reviews.

There were two possibilities in the third stage: if participants were not interested in their initial options, they could (1) again browse the app search results or (2) initiate another search; or, if they decide to go ahead with the app installation, they would be presented with either (1) no permissions or (2) a list of permissions.

Note that the following factors in our model: having a problem, quick install, knowing the app, and install/try both are not directly related to the observed cues available on the app selection platform. Instead, they are related to the participants' app search behaviour criteria or actions, where some participants indicated that they would have an issue and that the app would solve it. Some of our participants explained that they would quickly install the app rather than look for cues, as they wanted to experience the use of the app first-hand before making a decision to keep it. Similarly, some expressed that they would install more than one app to get a better sense when comparing two or more apps.

5.2   Identifying Decision-Making Patterns

Overall, the "Pondering Alternatives" heuristic has the highest percentage, garnering 70% ($N = 59$) of our sample. Only 17% ($N = 14$) of participants chose the "Confirm Take the First heuristic", while the "Inform and Confirm and Take the First" heuristic came third at 8% ($N = 7$). The least-used heuristics were "Inform and Take the First" and "Pure Take the First" with 1% ($N = 1$) and 4% ($N = 3$), respectively.

5.3   The Use of Multiple Heuristics and the Return to the First Heuristic

In terms of the use of multiple heuristics, we found that 65% ($N = 17$) of participants adhere to using only one type of heuristic, whereas 23% ($N = 6$) used two different types of heuristics (simple and complex), and 11% ($N = 3$) employed two variant of "Take the first" heuristic (two instances of cTtF and icTtF, one instance of iTtF and icTtF).

---

[1] Blue badges recognize high levels of downloads [11].

We found that 54% ($N = 25$) of our participants viewed only one app per search task, 24% ($N = 11$) viewed two apps, 11% ($N = 5$) viewed three apps, 7% ($N = 3$) viewed four apps, and 4% ($N = 2$) viewed five apps.

Investigating the "Pondering Alternatives" heuristic, led us to some intriguing results in terms of the decision-making strategies used by some of the participants. We found that 8% ($N = 7$), after evaluating other apps, returned to their initial first chosen app they had already viewed. Based on the heuristic literature [27,29], we call this the "Return to the First" heuristic. In our study ID10 and ID25 returned to their first chosen app in both tasks, while ID16, ID22 and ID24 returned to their first chosen app in one of the tasks.

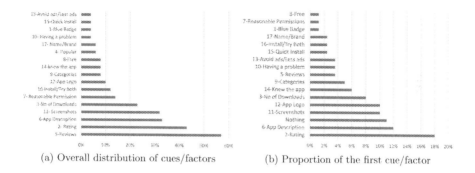

(a) Overall distribution of cues/factors   (b) Proportion of the first cue/factor

Fig. 3. Distribution of all cues & factors and first ones considered during search.

5.4   Cues and Factors Influencing App Selection

We report the overall distribution of cues, factors and the first ones considered.

Figure 3a suggests what influenced our participants to select some apps rather than others. Figure 3b shows the first cues/factors chosen among participants.

Overall, 57% ($N = 48$) considered reviews, 43% ($N = 36$) looked at ratings, 33% ($N = 28$) read the app full description, 32% ($N = 27$) noted the app screenshots, and 23% ($N = 19$) looked for the number of downloads. For permissions, 67% of participants skipped them, 7% read them, and 26% checked if the permissions requested seemed reasonable to them.

Most of the cues and factors shown in Fig. 3 are self-explanatory. However, the nothing item as shown in Fig. 3b represents 11% ($N = 9$) of our cases where some participants moved quickly between apps during the selection tasks apparently without considering anything. Lastly, Fig. 3b show that 18% ($N = 15$) of our participants had determined that the app ratings was the most important first cue when selecting an app (discussed in Sect. 6.1).

5.5   Models for Patterns Discovery

We report first our initial finding of the combination of cues and factors. Then, we describe our models for finding frequent itemsets "patterns" and the derived association rules.

Combinations of Cues and Factors. Our findings show that participants had considered different combinations of cues and factors during the app search process as shown in Fig. 4.

Correlations of the combinations that are significant, according to the Spearman's Rho test, are presented in the Supplementary Details (Table A3). We elaborate more on this behaviour and provide some examples. ID10 viewed five apps in the first task. His search path was: (1) He chose the Smart Receipts app and considered four cues: free, ratings, number of downloads, and reviews. (2) Then, he viewed the Cash Receipts app and considered app reviews and read the app's full description. (3) He went back and chose the Receipts app as his third choice and considered only the app's full description cue. (4) Then, he decided to view another app called Receipts Bank. He considered app reviews and reading the full app description in his fourth choice, similar to what he did when viewing the second app. (5) Finally, for the fifth app, he decided to return to his first choice and viewed the Smart Receipts app and considered three different cues and factors from his first time viewing the app. He considered the full app description, install/try both, and reasonable permissions.

Participant ID25 took a slightly different approach where he viewed three apps in total for the second task. He considered five cues at first, then viewed another app, and he decided to return to his first choice without considering any additional cues or factors.

In summary, when participants searched for apps in the selection platform, they considered different combinations of cues and factors. Most participants did not rely solely on individual cues or factors (in 60 of 84 instances). We found that some participants might consider additional cues and factors or disregard them while searching for apps.

Frequent Itemsets or Patterns. After our initial analysis of discovering the combinations of cues and factors as shown in Fig. 4, we used the data mining approaches shown in Fig. 5 and created two models using Weka [10] and Rapidminer [13].

The Weka model used both Apriori and FP-Growth algorithms, while the Rapidminer used only the FP-Growth algorithm.

We present the most frequent itemsets using the Apriori algorithm in Weka. We chose minimum support of 3% to show the items that occurred three times, the lowest frequency in our dataset as seen in Table 1, which is similar to Fig. 4.

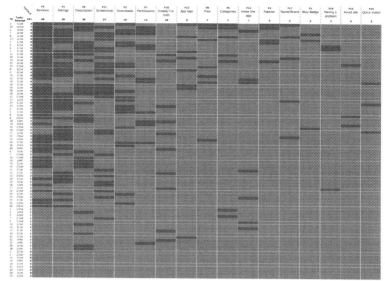

(a) Matrix 1 organized by the number of cues & factors considered by participants (e.g. ID3 considered 9 factors during their first attempt of their first task.

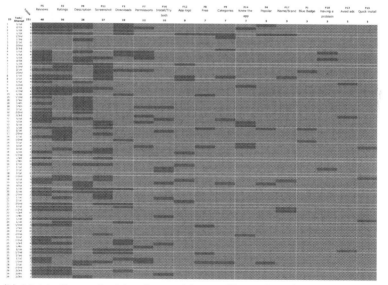

(b) Matrix 2 organized by the participants ID numbers (e.g. ID1 had one attempt for task 1 and task 2.

Fig. 4. Combinations of cues & factors employed by each participant while completing their tasks organized by number of cues & factors and by the participants ID numbers.

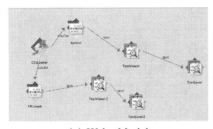

(a) Weka Model

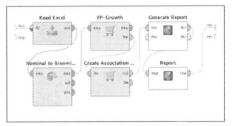

(b) Rapidminer Model

Fig. 5. Weka and Rapidminer Models for (Apriori and FP-Growth algorithms).

Table 1. The frequency of the frequent itemsets of one item.

Frequent Itemsets $L(1)$	Count	Frequent Itemsets $L(1)$	Count	Frequent Itemsets $L(1)$	Count
F5-Rev	48	F16-Try	10	F17-Brand	5
F2-Rat	36	F12-Logo	8	F1-Badge	3
F6-Full	28	F8-Free	7	F10-Prob	3
F11-Scre	27	F9-Cat	7	F13-Ads	3
F3-Num	19	F14-Knew	7	F15-Quick	3
F7-Perm	12	F4-Pop	5		

Table 2. The frequency of some frequent itemsets of two, three and four itemsets.

Frequent Itemsets $L(2)$	Count	Frequent Itemsets $L(3)$	Count	Frequent Itemsets $L(4)$	Count
F5-Rev F2-Rat	28	F5-Rev F2-Rat F3-Num	12	F5-Rev F2-Rat F11-Scre F3-Num	4
F5-Rev F6-Full	22	F5-Rev F2-Rat F11-Scre	11	F5-Rev F2-Rat F11-Scre F12-Logo	4

Overall, we found 60, 73, 35, and 4 cases of two, three, four and five frequent itemsets of cues and factors, respectively.

Tables 2 displays a few examples which show the relative importance of the different combinations of cues that occurred together.

5.6 The Derived Association Rules

We briefly describe the differences between the Weka and Rapidminer tools in terms of finding the rules. We report some interesting rules with preliminary interpretations.

Weka [10] shows the overall frequency of each cue and factor, but does not display the percentage of the support measure as shown in Table 3. For the first rule, 36 means the overall frequency of the rating cue, and 28 means the overall frequency of the reviews cue that appeared with the rating cue. Interestingly,

Table 3. App ratings and reviews association rules with minimum support of 33%.

No.	Rules	Confidence	Lift	Leverage	Conviction
1	F2-Rat 36⇒ F5-Rev 28	0.78	1.22	0.07	1.44
2	F5-Rev 48⇒ F2-Rat 28	0.58	1.22	0.07	1.19

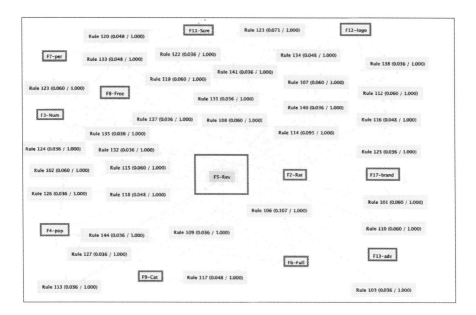

Fig. 6. A graph showing the links between some of the association rules of some cues.

the first rule has higher confidence of 78% than the second rule, which means that for rule one, the consequent, app reviews, is more likely to be present in a transaction containing the rating cue as an antecedent.

In Rapidminer [13], Table 4 does not display the frequency of the occurrence of each cue. However, it does show the actual percentage of the support measure.

It was interesting to see that the reviews cue appeared as a consequent in 20 rules (highlighted in **bold**) out of 32 as shown in Table 4. Moreover, in 3 instances (highlighted in *italic*), app reviews appeared with other cues as a consequent (RHS), which brings a total of 23 instances of the app reviews cue out of 32. This shows how important is app reviews to users.

Figure 6 shows the links between some of the association rules with some cues. The app review (F5-Rev) is the most important cue in the graph because even if the users considered other cues, most of the rules show that app review is the core of those rules. Also, it shows that almost all of the rules are headed towards the app reviews cue. It was mostly considered as the consequent (RHS) in the rules except in three cases when reviews were used as the first cue for three participants. Two of them viewed the app review cue in their second or third

Table 4. The derived rules using the FP-Growth algorithm. The app reviews cue was highlighted using **bold** and *italic* text on the right side of the rule (Consequent). **Bold**: for the app reviews cue only; *Italic* for the app reviews appeared with other cues.

No.	Rules	Support	Conf*	LaPlace	Gain	p-s	Lift	Conv†
1	F2-Rat⇒ **F5-Rev**	0.333	0.778	0.933	-0.524	0.088	1.361	1.929
2	F6-Full⇒ **F5-Rev**	0.262	0.786	0.946	-0.405	0.071	1.375	2.
3	F11-Scre⇒ **F5-Rev**	0.226	0.704	0.928	-0.417	0.043	1.231	1.446
4	F3-Num⇒ **F5-Rev**	0.202	0.895	0.981	-0.250	0.073	1.566	4.071
5	F3-Num⇒ F2-Rat	0.167	0.737	0.951	-0.286	0.070	1.719	2.171
6	F5-Rev, F3-Num⇒ F2-Rat	0.143	0.706	0.950	-0.262	0.056	1.647	1.943
7	F2-Rat, F3-Num⇒ **F5-Rev**	0.143	0.857	0.980	-0.190	0.048	1.500	3.
8	F7-Perm⇒ **F5-Rev**	0.107	0.750	0.969	-0.179	0.026	1.312	1.714
9	F2-Rat, F6-Full⇒ **F5-Rev**	0.107	1.	1.	-0.107	0.046	1.750	∞
10	F6-Full, F11-Scre⇒ **F5-Rev**	0.095	1.	1.	-0.095	0.041	1.750	∞
11	F12-Logo⇒ **F5-Rev**	0.083	0.875	0.989	-0.107	0.029	1.531	3.429
12	F8-Free ⇒ **F5-Rev**	0.071	0.857	0.989	-0.095	0.024	1.500	3.
13	F12-Logo⇒ F11-Scre	0.071	0.750	0.978	-0.119	0.041	2.333	2.714
14	F5-Rev, F12-Logo⇒ F11-Scre	0.071	0.857	0.989	-0.095	0.045	2.667	4.750
15	F11-Scre, F12-Logo⇒ **F5-Rev**	0.071	1.	1.	-0.071	0.031	1.750	∞
16	F12-Logo⇒ *F5-Rev, F11-Scre*	0.071	0.750	0.978	-0.119	0.050	3.316	3.095
17	F9-Cat ⇒ **F5-Rev**	0.060	0.714	0.978	-0.107	0.012	1.250	1.500
18	F4-Pop⇒ **F5-Rev**	0.060	1.	1.	-0.060	0.026	1.750	∞
19	F17-Brand⇒ **F5-Rev**	0.060	1.	1.	-0.060	0.026	1.750	∞
20	F8-Free ⇒ F2-Rat	0.060	0.714	0.978	-0.107	0.024	1.667	2.
21	F17-Brand⇒ F2-Rat	0.060	1.	1.	-0.060	0.034	2.333	∞
22	F5-Rev, F12-Logo⇒ F2-Rat	0.060	0.714	0.978	-0.107	0.024	1.667	2.
23	F2-Rat, F12-Logo⇒ **F5-Rev**	0.060	1.	1.	-0.060	0.026	1.750	∞
24	F5-Rev, F8-Free⇒ F2-Rat	0.060	0.83	0.989	-0.083	0.029	1.944	3.429
25	F2-Rat, F8-Free⇒ **F5-Rev**	0.060	1.	1.	-0.060	0.026	1.750	∞
26	F8-Free ⇒ *F5-Rev, F2-Rat*	0.060	0.714	0.978	-0.107	0.032	2.143	2.333
27	F5-Rev, F17-Brand⇒ F2-Rat	0.060	1.	1.	-0.060	0.034	2.333	∞
28	F2-Rat, F17-Brand⇒ **F5-Rev**	0.060	1.	1.	-0.060	0.026	1.750	∞
29	F17-Brand⇒ *F5-Rev, F2-Rat*	0.060	1.	1.	-0.060	0.040	3.	∞
30	F6-Full, F3-Num⇒ **F5-Rev**	0.060	1.	1.	-0.060	0.026	1.750	∞
31	F11-Scre, F3-Num⇒ **F5-Rev**	0.060	1.	1.	-0.060	0.026	1.750	∞
32	F3-Num, F7-Perm ⇒ **F5-Rev**	0.060	1.	1.	-0.060	0.026	1.750	∞

* Confidence   † Conviction

attempt when searching for apps and while moving between apps to evaluate them before their final decision to install the app.

What stands out in Fig. 6 is that some cues are used by users as a starting point (antecedents) when searching for apps such as app rating (F2), app logo (F12), app name/brand (F17), avoid ads (F13), app popularity (F4) and free (F8), which validates our model. Those who consider the app logo, for example, as shown in Fig. 7 are 3.8 times more likely to view app screenshots, reviews and

Fig. 7. A heat map plot showing the importance of the association rules of some cues based on the Lift measure.

ratings. Moreover, the heat map plot of Lift measures (Fig. 7) shows the relative importance of cues.

Another interesting aspect was the number of downloads (F3), the full app description (F6), and the app screenshot (F11) cues. Figure 6 indicates that users tend to consider them and move on to other cues.

Table 5. A few association rules of some participants that shows their behaviour.

No.	Antecedents	Consequents	Support	Confidence	Lift	Conviction
1	ID3	F9-Cat	0.036	0.500	6	1.833
2	ID7	F2-Rat F11-Scre	0.036	0.750	3.938	3.238
3	ID20	F5-Rev F11-Scre	0.036	1	4.421	∞
4	ID25	F5-Rev F2-Rat F3-Num	0.036	0.429	3	1.500

Lastly, Table 5 show the behaviour of a few participants that stands out when generating the association rules. According to the Lift measure, ID20 is 4.4 times more likely to consider the app reviews and screenshots.

6   Discussion

In this section, we discuss and elaborate on some of the results.

6.1   The Assumptions of the Importance of First Information Cues

One of the assumptions made by Dogruel et al. [8] work was that the cues that were considered first were important to users.

However, based on the model we created (Fig. 2) and results (Table 4, Fig. 6, Fig. 7), the importance of cues was determined later in the search process, i.e., after viewing apps and looking at different combinations of cues at the same time. The use of different combinations was in line with what was reported by Todorov et al., who stated that "people consider all relevant pieces of information, elaborate on these pieces of information, and form a judgment base on these elaborations." [28, p. 196].

We reported earlier that the two most influential cues were app reviews and ratings. We found that the app rating cue came first (18%) when we looked at the first cue chosen by participants. However, the reviews cue came in eighth place (4%).

This does not necessarily mean that the first cue is always important, which contradicts the work of Dogruel et al. [8]. These cues may play an important role individually because they were treated or associated with other cues/factors. Still, they were not used as the primary reason for participants to make the final decision to install apps. Instead, they were considered to be a "starting point" or "just a place to start" the search process [9, p. 6].

7   Limitations

We provide an overview of some of the limitations of our work. We must first address one of the flaws of the conducted study, which is gender imbalance. In our study sample, we had only one female participant.

As a result of that, our results cannot be considered as representative of how users, in general, install apps from the Google Play Store, and it is only applicable in a very limited sample of mainly male participants.

On the other hand, it can still determine what kind of behaviour users may be exhibited when searching for apps.

It was also important to note that a few participants could only download one app, and we did not encounter the role of considering paid apps.

8   Future Work

Our initial research effort was an attempt to understand and observe how users choose which apps to install.

Therefore, future work should look at integrating multiple settings, such as moving from a laboratory setting to "real-world" settings or letting participants use their phones, which could make it more realistic rather than an artificial task [2, p. 7]. Researchers should also consider the individual differences and the domain knowledge (i.e., level of expertise). Everyone has their own internal ranking of what matters that might be related to the knowledge acquired about the alternatives when making the decision [20,24] since some "apps might be more personally or situationally relevant to users" [16, p. 13].

Furthermore, since our study sample is small, future work should address this issue by incorporating a larger and more representative sample.

Lastly, we aim to refine our model by incorporating the changes made to the Google Play Store. For example, the blue badges popularity indicator was replaced with the "editors' choice" badge.

Perhaps most importantly, the store now supports filtering results by rating and badge status. We stress that although our study used the Google Play Store, we are trying to create a general model for every app selection platform.

9   Conclusion

We conducted an observational lab study with semi-structured interviews to understand better how users search for apps in the Google Play Store. Our work expands and contributes to the app search domain, validated by our models and the analysis of the different combinations of cues and factors.

Using data mining approaches, we found that there are influential cues that are used as a starting point in the process of searching for apps, and that certain cues are used by users temporarily before moving on to other cues, and the most influential cues are used are the app reviews. We found that while participants were searching for apps in the app selection platform, they sometimes changed the cues they were attending to (considering additional cues or disregarding cues they had used previously).

Surprisingly, we also found that in 8% of the instances ($N = 7$), after evaluating other apps, participants ultimately returned to the app they had first viewed, a process which we named the "Return to the First" heuristic.

In conclusion, our work showcase the importance of certain information cues that may help app developers to understand their users.

Acknowledgments. The first author gratefully acknowledges a scholarship from Taibah University, Saudi Arabia.

A   Supplementary Details

The study protocol, coding rules, and correlation table associated with this article can be found, in the online version, at https://drive.google.com/file/d/1-3-ZLjREu6gGuwkCw-UPhy4cxSIRrzhP/view.

References

1. Bellur, S., Sundar, S.S.: How can we tell when a heuristic has been used? Design and analysis strategies for capturing the operation of heuristics. Commun. Methods Measures **8**(2), 116–137 (2014). https://doi.org/10.1080/19312458.2014.903390

2. Bowman, N.D., Jöckel, S., Dogruel, L.: "The app market has been candy crushed": observed and rationalized processes for selecting smartphone games. Entertainment Comput. **8**, 1–9 (2015). https://doi.org/10.1016/j.entcom.2015.04.001

3. Burgers, C., Eden, A., de Jong, R., Buningh, S.: Rousing reviews and instigative images: the impact of online reviews and visual design characteristics on app downloads. Mobile Media Commun. **4**(3), 327–346 (2016). https://doi.org/10.1177/2050157916639348

4. Chaiken, S., Liberman, A., Eagly, A.H.: Heuristic and systematic information processing within and beyond the persuasion context. In: Unintended Thought. The Guilford Press, NY (1989)

5. Creswell, J.W., Clark, V.L.P.: Designing and Conducting Mixed Methods Research. SAGE (2018)

6. Creswell, J.W., Creswell, J.D.: Research Design: Qualitative, Quantitative & Mixed Methods Approaches, 5th edn. SAGE, Los Angeles (2018)

7. Datareportal: Digital Around The World (2021). https://datareportal.com/global-digital-overview

8. Dogruel, L., Joeckel, S., Bowman, N.D.: Choosing the right app: an exploratory perspective on heuristic decision processes for smartphone app selection. Mobile Media Commun. **3**, 125–144 (2015). https://doi.org/10.1177/2050157914557509

9. Felt, A.P., Ha, E., Egelman, S., Haney, A., Chin, E., Wagner, D.: Android permissions: user attention, comprehension, and behavior. In: SOUPS '12: Proceedings of the Eighth Symposium on Usable Privacy and Security. ACM, NYC (2012). https://doi.org/10.1145/2335356.2335360

10. Frank, E., Hall, M.A., Holmes, G., Kirkby, R., Pfahringer, B., Witten, I.H.: Weka: a machine learning workbench for data mining. In: Maimon, O., Rokach, L. (eds.) Data Mining and Knowledge Discovery Handbook, pp. 1305–1314. Springer, Boston (2005). http://researchcommons.waikato.ac.nz/handle/10289/1497

11. Grush, A.: Play store introduces colorful badges denoting number of app downloads, August 2014. https://www.androidauthority.com/play-store-badges-417072/

12. Hassani, H., Huang, X., Ghodsi, M.: Big data and causality. Ann. Data Sci. **5**(2), 133–156 (2017). https://doi.org/10.1007/s40745-017-0122-3

13. Hofmann, M., Klinkenberg, R.: RapidMiner: Data Mining Use Cases and Business Analytics Applications. Chapman & Hall/CRC (2013)

14. Huang, H.Y., Bashir, M.: Users' adoption of mental health apps: examining the impact of information cues. JMIR Mhealth Uhealth **5**(6) (2017). https://doi.org/10.2196/mhealth.6827

15. Janse Van Rensburg, W., Thomson, K.-L., Futcher, L.: Factors influencing smartphone application downloads. In: Drevin, L., Theocharidou, M. (eds.) WISE 2018. IAICT, vol. 531, pp. 81–92. Springer, Cham (2018). https://doi.org/10.1007/978-3-319-99734-6_7

16. Joeckel, S., Dogruel, L., Bowman, N.D.: The reliance on recognition and majority vote heuristics over privacy concerns when selecting smartphone apps among German and US consumers. Inf. Commun. Soc. **20**, 621–636 (2017). https://doi.org/10.1080/1369118X.2016.1202299

17. Kantardzic, M.: Data-Mining Concepts, chap. 1, pp. 1–31. Wiley (2019). https://doi.org/10.1002/9781119516057.ch1

18. Kelley, P.G., Consolvo, S., Cranor, L.F., Jung, J., Sadeh, N., Wetherall, D.: A conundrum of permissions: installing applications on an android smartphone. In: Blyth, J., Dietrich, S., Camp, L.J. (eds.) FC 2012. LNCS, vol. 7398, pp. 68–79. Springer, Heidelberg (2012). https://doi.org/10.1007/978-3-642-34638-5_6

19. Kelley, P.G., Cranor, L.F., Sadeh, N.: Privacy as part of the app decision-making process. In: Proceedings of the SIGCHI Conference on Human Factors in Computing Systems. pp. 3393–3402. CHI 2013, Association for Computing Machinery, New York (2013). https://doi.org/10.1145/2470654.2466466

20. Kleinmuntz, D.N.: Human decision processes: heuristics and task structure. Adv. Psychol. **47**(C), 123–157 (1987). https://doi.org/10.1016/S0166-4115(08)62308-0

21. Larsen, M.E., et al.: Using science to sell apps: evaluation of mental health app store quality claims. NPJ Digital Med. **2**(1), 18 (2019). https://doi.org/10.1038/s41746-019-0093-1

22. Materska, K.: Information heuristics of information literate people. In: Kurbanoğlu, S., Špiranec, S., Grassian, E., Mizrachi, D., Catts, R. (eds.) ECIL 2014. CCIS, vol. 492, pp. 59–69. Springer, Cham (2014). https://doi.org/10.1007/978-3-319-14136-7_7

23. Ouyang, Y., Guo, B., Guo, T., Cao, L., Yu, Z.: Modeling and forecasting the popularity evolution of mobile apps: a multivariate Hawkes process approach. Proc. ACM Interact. Mob. Wearable Ubiquitous Technol. **2**(4), 1–23 (2018). https://doi.org/10.1145/3287060

24. Payne, J.W.: Heuristic search processes in decision making. Adv. Consum. Res. **3**(1), 321–327 (1976). https://scholars.duke.edu/display/pub1057867

25. Prajapati, D.J., Garg, S., Chauhan, N.: Interesting association rule mining with consistent and inconsistent rule detection from big sales data in distributed environment. Future Comput. Inform. J. **2**(1), 19–30 (2017). https://doi.org/10.1016/j.fcij.2017.04.003

26. Schueller, S.M., Neary, M., O'Loughlin, K., Adkins, E.C.: Discovery of and interest in health apps among those with mental health needs: survey and focus group study. J. Med. Internet Res. **20**(6) (2018). https://doi.org/10.2196/10141

27. Shah, A.K., Oppenheimer, D.M.: Heuristics made easy: an effort-reduction framework. Psychol. Bull. **134**(2), 207–222 (2008). https://doi.org/10.1037/0033-2909.134.2.207

28. Todorov, A., Chaiken, S., Henderson, M.D.: The heuristic-systematic model of social information processing. In: The Persuasion handbook: Developments in theory and practice. Sage Reference, Thousand Oaks, CA, USA (2002). https://doi.org/10.4135/9781412976046

29. Van der Pligt, J.: Decision making, psychology of. In: Wright, J.D. (ed.) International Encyclopedia of the Social & Behavioral Sciences), 2nd edn, pp. 917–922. Elsevier, Oxford (2015). https://doi.org/10.1016/B978-0-08-097086-8.24014-2

30. Wirth, W., Böcking, T., Karnowski, V., Von Pape, T.: Heuristic and systematic use of search engines. J. Comput. Mediat. Commun. **12**(3), 778–800 (2007). https://doi.org/10.1111/j.1083-6101.2007.00350.x

31. Zhang, C., Ha, L., Liu, X., Wang, Y.: The role of regulatory focus in decision making of mobile app download: a study of Chinese college students. Telematics Informatics **35**(8), 2107–2117 (2018). https://doi.org/10.1016/j.tele.2018.07.012

32. Zhao, S., et al.: Mining user attributes using large-scale app lists of smartphones. IEEE Syst. J. **11**(1), 315–323 (2017). https://doi.org/10.1109/JSYST.2015.2431323

Create More Than One Design: A Case Study of Applying Ethnographic Approach to Explore the Potential Information Application in Senior Karaoke Community

Wan-Ling Chang(⊠), Ting-Yi Wu, and Yu-Hsiu Hung

Industrial Design, National Cheng Kung University, Tainan, Taiwan, R.O.C.
{WanLingChang,p38081041}@gs.ncku.edu.tw,
idhfhung@mail.ncku.edu.tw

Abstract. In the commercial world, design ethnographers look into people's behaviors and thoughts to discover the broad patterns of everyday experiences that are specifically relevant for the conception, design and development of new products and services. An understanding of the social and cultural contexts generated through an ethnographic approach usually contributes to better product or service designs. However, compared to the classic ethnographic study, the design ethnography usually has a short duration and a quick investigation of the field sites without many details. Also, since the application of technology or potential technology is central to many modern design ethnography studies, those studies had a technology application target in the first place of researchers arriving at the field sites. In this paper, we argued for a more "classic" way of doing design ethnography, which means appropriating the open attitudes and immersive engagements with the field with a longer design ethnography research period than the common quick-and-dirty ethnography. This approach makes it possible to get an in-depth understanding of the field for better design that addresses the actual needs of users in their everyday lives. This paper reported a nine-month design ethnography study with a senior karaoke community, and the researchers kept their attitude open while collecting qualitative data. The research findings indicated the importance of researchers' immersion with the community and being natural to the data collection. Applying this ethnographic design approach in field study revealed some hidden patterns of social phenomena and inspired various perspectives of product designs.

Keywords: Design ethnography · Elderly

1 Introduction

Through ethnography, the researchers attempt to make sense of people's perspectives by observing and participating in day-to-day life activities and then understanding the local culture. In the commercial world, design ethnographers look deeper into people's behaviors and thoughts to discover the broad patterns of everyday experiences that

M. Kurosu (Ed.): HCII 2022, LNCS 13304, pp. 23–35, 2022.
https://doi.org/10.1007/978-3-031-05412-9_2

are specifically relevant for the conception, design, and development of new products and services (Salvador, Bell and Anderson 1999). Design ethnography has been widely applied in the HCI field. The theoretical base of situated action enables design ethnographers to understand the social organization of action, the interactional work of a setting, and methods that members in the setting organize action and interaction (Crabtree et al. 2009). An in-depth understanding of the social and cultural contexts, generated through an ethnographic approach, usually contributes to better product or service designs (e.g., Wood and Mattson 2019).

Compared to the classic ethnographic study, the design ethnography usually has a short duration and a quick investigation of the field sites without many details (Müller 2020, a). It usually takes a couple of weeks to collect as much field data as possible. Sometimes, ethnographic investigation for commercial purposes may take even a shorter period to a day or even half a day (Salvador et al. 1999). In addition to the feature of short research duration of design ethnography, the researchers and designers usually applied ethnography to explore the practical implication for a single design goal (e.g., Carbajal and Baranauskas 2019). Unlike typical ethnographic works, the time design ethnographers spend in the field is short, and the focus is narrow. While the classic ethnography collects intensive data regarding devoting time and immersive experience, design ethnography appropriate ethnographic field study approach concentrating on the themes surrounding technology (or product) implementation (Müller 2020, b). Applying technology or potential technology is central to many modern ethnographic studies. Usually, those studies had a technology application target in the first place of arriving at the field sites. The single focus of the design ethnography study appropriates a data-intensive approach to efficiently collect data in a short time (Müller 2020, b). However, the quick and dirty approach of design ethnography may hinder understanding the social and cultural patterns behind those observed phenomena. At the same time, there is no built trust between the researchers and the field participants. To collect an in-depth understanding of the field, in this paper, we argued that the design ethnography should be conducted in an extended research period.

Prior design ethnographic studies tended to specify specific technology implications or use contexts. They led to the overlook of other critical themes, which contribute to our understanding of the users and the fields as well as inspire design ideas in response to other potential users' needs. In this paper, we argue that applying design ethnography in understanding users' everyday practices shall stay open in collecting the data. Instead of concentrating on circumstances of the interested technology implementation, we suggest a recall of the curiosity and open attitude toward people and the social contexts as the principal of design ethnography (Müller 2020, b). The immersion of the field sites can always teach designers more things about users than what the designers were initially interested in.

In this paper, we review the development of design ethnography and ethnographic research in information technology study and elderly technology users to offer contextual information about the prior works on similar research topics. Later, to support our argument of the open attitude and long-term study in design ethnography, we report a case study of ethnographic work with a senior karaoke community in Tainan city, Taiwan. The case illustrated how the curiosity and open attitude and the long-term engagement enabled the design researchers to immerse in the elderly community members' social lives and dig deep into their extended daily routines after they left the community activities. The in-depth field data provided designers references of redefining the users' needs and designing a technology application relating to the karaoke activity, which the technology developing team was interested in. Moreover, the insights generated from those immersive field data also inspired the designers to propose another technology application design, the mobile exercise app, which the developing team was excited about.

2   Related Works

2.1   Design Ethnography

Ethnographic methods are designed to gain cultural insights from human behaviors and activities in natural settings. As Spradley noted, ethnographers understand the human experience from "what people do, what people know, and the things they make and use" (Spradley 1980, p. 5). In addition to the focus on humans, ethnography also concerns the "things" relating to human activities. This perspective is appropriated by design ethnography to develop the practices surrounding humans and things (Müller 2020, b). Ethnography is the methodology of studying culture developed in anthropology, and design ethnography, a form of focused ethnography, is widely practiced by other fields, such as Human-computer interaction (HCI) and Computer Supported Cooperative Work (CSCW) (Müller 2020, b). HCI and CSCW applied ethnography to better capture human interaction with and relation to the information technology and how people's use of "things" is situated in the social contexts (Suchman 2002). From the design ethnography perspective, people in the field should not be treated as technology users solely; a comprehensive socio-cultural understanding of people should be approached in the field (Suopajärvi 2015). At the same time, the design ethnographer gave up the separation between the technical and the social. They recognized that the social and technical contexts were co-constructed; a design ethnography research starts with the unseparated mixture of technology within people's everyday life (Suopajärvi 2015). Different from the classic ethnographic study, in design ethnography, researchers are immersed in not just the field study of observation and interviews but also the design practices (Baskerville and Myers 2015). With active engagement with people in the field, design ethnography provides designers a new approach to investigate user problems and gain insights into user unaddressed needs (White and Devitt 2021). Sometimes, because of the short research time of ethnographic fieldwork, Design ethnography is also known as "quick and dirty ethnography" (Knoblauch 2001; Vindrola-Padros and Vindrola-Padros 2018). However, unlike those short-term design ethnographic studies, this research argues for an extended research time to leverage the advantages of classic ethnographic study and concentrate on the social contexts of people in the field and the "things".

2.2   Design Ethnography in HCI

Design ethnography has usually been treated as "implications of design in the HCI field." The ethnographers are responsible for understanding users' behaviors and thoughts and digging into their needs, and the designers are responsible for leveraging that knowledge to create technological implications (Khovanskaya et al. 2017). The (Müller 2020, b). Different from the mainstream definition of design ethnography, Baskerville and Myers (2015) redefined the term design ethnography. They called the practices of employing ethnographic techniques to support the design activities design as Ethnography for Design (E4D) and the ethnographic study of the complete design process, including the E4D of studying the context of design, the design activities, and the testing of design intervention, as Design Ethnography. In this study, we would take the more widely accepted definition of design ethnography, the field research approach to understanding targeted users' social and cultural contexts and the use of technology.

Since Suchman firstly apply ethnography in studying HCI (1987), design ethnography is widely used in HCI, especially for those information technology application designs. McDonald et al. (2007) applied design ethnography to explore the impact of financial incentives on clinical autonomy and internal motivation in primary care. Cerna et al. (2020) used design ethnography to understand nurses' work practices about the design process of a self-monitoring application. Design ethnography is usually adopted in the early stages of the design process when it is necessary to inspire or inform designers of the potential application of new technologies (Zimmerman et al. 2007). Applying design ethnography to discover successful design elements can also inspire novel features across varied applications (Rapp 2021). In this study, we also adopted design ethnography in the early stage of technology innovation. Instead of finding design elements, we applied a more comprehensive aspect of exploring the field sites and users' extended life outside the targeted site, the community center.

2.3   Design Ethnography and the Technology Design for the Elderly

As discussed in the previous section, design ethnography is often used in technology research and the study of technology designed for senior users. The ELDer project is one of the early design ethnographic studies of older adults and the technology for their independent livings (Hirsch et al. 2000). In this project, the researchers conducted a four-month design ethnographic study in an elderly community in the United States to capture the elderly experience and the psychological and social factors of their lives with various stakeholders and identify potential technology implications for the elderly. As the early promoter of applying a design ethnography approach, Hirsh et al. called for attention to understanding older adults from a broad social, emotional, and environmental perspective. Doyle et al. (2013) applied an ethnographic assessment of independent living technology with over 200 elderly households. The research intended to provide the finding of ethnographic studies and recommendations of the deployment of independent living technologies into the homes of older adults. Talamo et al. (2017) conducted another ethnographic research of forty-one participants aged over 65 in Italy to interstage the suitable domestic technologies which fit into seniors' homes. Unlike the ELDer project, they concentrated more on the older adults' meaning-making of products relating to their lives. In a design ethnographic study of 390 participants, Righi et al. (2017) gain first-hand knowledge of the older adults' information and communication technology (ICT) practices concerning their functional capability. Their findings argued for attention to community-based ethnographic study to understand older people's interaction with it.

Those studies of older people with technology implications indicated a research focus of particular technology use. The ethnographic research findings also revealed the design suggestions in response to the research focus. In this study, we intended to appropriate an open mindset of traditional ethnography and explore the senior people's live activities regarding technology outside the target we set prior to our field study, which is different from previous design ethnographic study with the older people.

3 Contexts of the Design Ethnography Study

3.1 Research Design

We conducted a nine-month-long ethnographic study in a local community center in Tainan city, Taiwan, to study the weekly karaoke activities of a senior group. This study was initiated by a technology developing team whose goal was to apply Taiwanese natural language technology to support the elderly singing activities. They planned to design a new karaoke system that applied automatic speech recognition for users to select songs they wanted to sing. The design research team was involved in this design project and assisted the developing team in exploring the karaoke community's social contexts and user experiences, identifying the needs of the users, and creating the potential design applications of the karaoke theme. This study adopted the classic ethnography features of open attitude and long-term engagement with the targeted field site to collect intensive qualitative data. In addition to observing how people sang in the community karaoke activity, we attempted to know about the everyday practices of the elderly community participants, the organization of singing spaces, the process and events surrounding the singing activities, and the culture of the local community.

The community karaoke activities took place twice a week, on Wednesdays and Thursdays, from two to five in the afternoon. In this study, we visited the senior karaoke community at least once a week and observed and participated in the community activities for around two hours of each visit. There were nineteen senior members in the karaoke group, and around ten to fifteen seniors regularly participated in the weekly singing activities. All the participants were over their sixties. Most of them were female, and the oldest member was a 93-year-old gentleman. The social combination of activity participants on Wednesday and Thursday differed slightly, but most of the regular activity members attended both singing activities every week.

We usually observed what happened in the karaoke activities and chit-chatted with some community members. We had casual conversations with them not only about singing but also about their everyday life and routines. The long-term engagement with the community activity and those relaxing conversations built up trust between the researchers and the community members. In addition to the regular observational study, the karaoke members revealed more critical information in the informal chatting.

3.2 The Field Sites

The karaoke activities were held in the local community center. This regular activity was planned by the village chief and supported by other community volunteers. The community center building had a long rectangle open space on the first floor, and the karaoke activity was on the western side of the room. The karaoke system was equipped in a cart with a computer monitor and a hardware system for selecting songs. The volunteers usually took the cart out of the storage room 30 to 60 min before the activity started. The karaoke cart was usually placed in front of the stage, and participants sat in lines facing the computer monitor in front of the karaoke cart.

The other side of the room was almost empty, and there were some unused and piled tables and chairs placed against the room's walls. In addition to the physical configuration of the karaoke activities, the community center was commonly equipped with reading materials, such as newspapers and magazines, and other health or exercise-related equipment, such as blood pressure machines and table tennis.

4 Findings of the Field Studies

The intensive engagement with the field sites for an extended period established the trust between the researchers and community members. It enabled the researchers to get a comprehensive and profound understanding of hidden patterns behind what we have seen.

4.1 Karaoke Singing Activities

In the early stage of this study, we found that the community center had a karaoke machine offered by the city government. The system required inputting the corresponding number of the song while selecting what users wanted to sing. A couple of months before we entered the field, the city government provided a new karaoke system to the village community center. The city government intended to have all the village community centers in Tainan city use the same karaoke system to have easy and better maintenance. Usually, people find the song they want to sing in the song catalogs and its corresponding song number. The singer gave the song number to the volunteers, and they would input the song number with a remote controller of the karaoke system. The change of the karaoke system urged the member to learn the new song number system since the song numbers of one song were different in various karaoke systems.

To adopt the new karaoke system, the community members had to search the song number of the new karaoke system even though they had sung it in the old system. Some members knew the song's title they wanted to sing and searched the corresponding song numbers in the vast song number catalog. They browsed the pages according to how many characters were in the song title. But some members just browsed the song catalog to search through the updated pages with a list of lastly uploaded songs or casually looked through pages to see whether there were songs that interested them. When the community members found songs they were looking for, they usually checked whether more than one version of the song music usually had different song numbers. They would check the song music version they preferred by inputting varied song numbers to the karaoke system and testing them. Even though searching the song numbers in the song catalog was problematic to them, they still prefer to use the existing karaoke system and not spend extra money to purchase a fancy one without the city government's support.

In the field, we found that the karaoke community members usually kept a private "songbook" of their loved song collections. The songbook contained a list of song titles and their corresponding song numbers in the karaoke system. Some members used a notebook to arrange their songbooks, and the others had clipped paper notes of song lists. The members usually categorized their songbooks by the language of the songs. Most of them had two separate songbooks of Mandarin and Taiwanese songs. Some people who enjoyed singing Japanese or English songs had an independent songbook for that language (Fig. 1). The community members were always interested in singing "new" songs. The "new" songs did not mean the latest songs in the music market but the songs they had never heard before, which included those songs updated to the karaoke system every month.

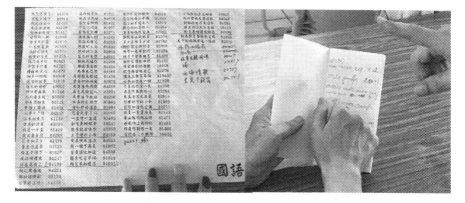

Fig. 1. Community seniors' songbooks

4.2   The Community Karaoke Activities as Events of Performing Singing

With an extended duration of the field study, we found some hidden behavioral patterns behind the karaoke activities. We usually assumed that the seniors practiced singing in the community karaoke activities. However, our extensive finding indicated that, for those senior members, the karaoke activities were not for practicing singing but events of personal singing performance (Fig. 2). The senior community members prepared and practiced three to five songs at home before participating in the weekly karaoke activities to avoid lousy performances. They searched the songs they liked to sing on YouTube and practiced songs repeatedly by following the singers' voices and the melody of the YouTube videos. If the seniors could not find the song numbers of the prepared songs in their songbooks, they searched the song number catalog for their song numbers at the beginning of the karaoke activity. They added the songs to their songbook with the found numbers. They were also greatly concerned about singing in tone and sometimes changing the pitch of a song based on their voice range. If they changed the pitch, they took notes in their songbooks.

From the informal interviews, some community members also reported that the repeated practices of singing songs and remembering the rhythms and lyrics helped strengthen their mental and cognitive capability. For them, singing was not just for fun but a cognitive exercise for their brain.

Fig. 2. Karaoke activity

4.3 Exercising While Waiting for Their Turns of Singing

With the extended field observation and participation in the whole karaoke activity, we found that community members often did various physical exercises to fill up the intervals between their singing turns. It usually took more than twenty minutes to sing again for the community members. The senior community members did various things while waiting for their songs. In the early karaoke activities, people tended to check their songbook or song number catalog or listen to other people's singing while waiting. In the second half of the karaoke activity, people were more likely to stand up and do some simple exercise, such as stretching, shaking their hands near the seat, walking around to chat with others. They shared the health messages they received on their smartphones with each other and demonstrated a strong interest in health-related topics, especially the information on exercise for specific health purposes (e.g., exercise for reducing the risk of heart attack). Later, the community members were not satisfied with the simple exercises and tried something more intensive, such as playing hula hoops, dancing, playing table tennis. They usually enjoyed exercising together and shared information about doing exercises. The community members also enjoyed playing mahjong. For them, mahjong was one cognitive exercise that prevented them from getting dementia. In-between singing activities and notes collected in the informal interviews revealed a strong interest in health and well-being among those karaoke community seniors.

The senior community members' tendency to exercise was also demonstrated in their everyday activities. Most seniors participated in community physical activities and had regular exercise habits, such as yoga, Tai Chi, aerobic dance, hiking. The exercises they chose were very diverse, and if they did not engage in intensive exercise, they usually walked for at least half an hour daily. Some active community members also served as exercise group leaders and taught other members doing exercises.

5   Discussion

5.1   A Complete User Experience of Singing

The original focus of this study was on the karaoke activity in the community center. We expected to gather the complete user experience in the karaoke activities in the early stage of this study. Unexpectedly, the engagement with the community and the extended research of community seniors' life experiences outside the field site enabled us to dig deep into what was going on behind the karaoke activities. We found that the singing experience occurred not only in the field site but also in community members' daily lives after they left the community center. The senior community members practiced songs they wanted to sing for the next karaoke activity as part of their domestic life. The awareness of the social and performing qualities of the karaoke activity triggered the senior community members to practice their singing after going home. A cycle of one community member's singing experience usually started with choosing the songs for the karaoke activity next week. S/he searched the YouTube video to practice singing the song and repeatedly listened, sang, and advanced the singing skill of that song. Preparing for the performing in the karaoke activity, the community member commonly took notes of the title and corresponding song number of the interesting song in her/his songbook and then highlighted the pitch which worked best for her/him. Based on the notes in the songbook, the community member could quickly provide the song numbers to volunteers who input the song number to the karaoke system to order the song for her/him and set the pitch while s/he was singing. The cycle of singing experience would be completed while the community member finished singing that song in the community karaoke activity.

According to the in-depth design ethnographic investigation, we recognized the continuity of singing behaviors that the senior members sang after they left the karaoke activities. At the beginning of the fields study, we identified superficial needs. Finding the corresponding song numbers was critical to the users when selecting songs in the karaoke system. However, the extended research time and immersive participation in the field richened the behavioral patterns we identified in the field study. The data revealed a complete journey of the community member's singing experience. This design ethnography approach allowed us to redefine the problem spaces of design exploration, uncover more insights regarding the continuous singing experience of the community members, and redesign the proposed technology applications which addressed the needs concerning the entire user experience. We proposed a personal songbook app design for the senior community members to collect song lists with corresponding song numbers based on those findings. The songbook was primarily used to practice singing with YouTube song videos and provided song number references while users selected songs in the karaoke system. The Taiwanese and Mandarin natural language system will serve users to search songs in their songbook and YouTube videos for practicing singing. In the prototype testing with the community members, they appreciated the design of the songbook phone app and thought the design fit into their life routines.

5.2   Generate More Than One Focus in the Field: The Benefits of Maintaining an Open Attitude Toward the Field Sites

This study intended to utilize the open attitude toward the people and the field site in classic ethnography. Before starting the ethnographic study, the technology developing team tended to target issues relating to karaoke singing. However, trying to maintain an open attitude toward the field sites, we collected as much data as possible. We did not concentrate solely on the singing processes and singers' behavioral patterns. This approach enabled the researchers to recognize the significant attention to the physical and mental well-being of the karaoke community. For example, for those community members, singing was a pleasant hobby as well as a cognitive training for mental health. The substantial consideration of health and well-being was also illustrated in those behavioral patterns of community members while they were waiting for their songs in the karaoke activities. They did varied types of physical exercises across the waiting intervals. Even though they had individual preferences of doing exercises, which strongly depend on their energy and physical functionality, they still tried their best to train their bodies and maintain their physical health. In addition to the physical exercise, the community members engaging with mahjong playing demonstrated their attention to maintain cognitive well-being. Since the news and medical research all reported the benefits of playing mahjong in slowing the cognitive declines, the community members intended to exercise their brains by playing this game. The informal interviews with those community members showed that the seniors were afraid of functional and mental declines along with the aging process. They would like to stay healthy to enjoy their lives.

Besides the attention to the health issues, the community members were also concerned about the sociality in the karaoke community. The karaoke community served as a social gathering for them. They looked to attend the activities and prepared songs for singing in front of friends during the week. It was easy to recognize how much they enjoyed the activities in the field observation and researchers' causal chatting with them. Also, the community members enjoyed sharing and doing things together. They played mahjong together and laughed. They did exercise together while waiting their turn to sing. They shared health information with others and taught others the exercise they had just learned. Sociality played an essential role in this karaoke community.

We propose a mobile exercise app with social functions to the technology developing team based on the finding. The app design provided exercise suggestions and plans for the seniors to leverage their health concerns and the desire to be social in the community. They can do the suggested exercises when waiting for their turns of singing in the karaoke activities. The senior community members would follow the demonstration of the movements to exercise and share their exercise progress with friends through playing games. Since the exercise apps significantly applied the natural language technology to support fluent exercise interactions with the users, the technology developing team was surprised and excited about the additional findings in the field site and the proposed exercise design. The proposal of low fidelity prototypes will be tested in the field later in this project.

5.3 The Importance of Immersion

Even though immersion in the field is critical to both classic ethnography and design ethnography (Müller 2020), it is always difficult for the design ethnographer to immerse in the field in a short research period. The long-term engagement with the community activities and interaction with the people allowed the ethnographers to build up intimate and trustful relationships with the participants in the field. The close relationships encouraged people in the field site to talk more and uncover more thoughts that they would never tell strangers. In this study, the researchers recognized the importance of building trustful relationships with the field participants. In the early stage of this study, the researchers collected data remarkably relied on the field observation and the small talks with active community members. Most people in the field did not talk a lot about their personal lives. After long-term regular participation in the karaoke community activities, those who were more silent in the early stage of the study started to have more conversations with the researchers and talk about something related to their lives outside the karaoke community. The information collected through casual talks was aggregated while the increasing familiarity between the researchers and community members. Those aggregated data authorized us to identify the continuity of the singing experience of the community members and their strong interest in staying healthy and maintaining cognitive well-being. Also, some behavioral patterns of what people did between their singing turns did not show in the early stage of this study. We got a more comprehensive picture of how people exercise in the karaoke activities until the later stage of the study. The extended research time and engagement with the community are critical to our research findings. For this reason, we argued for a more "classic" way of doing design ethnography, which means appropriating the open attitudes and immersive engagements with the field with a more extended design ethnography research period than the quick-and-dirty ethnography. This approach makes it possible to get an in-depth understanding of the field for better design that addresses the actual needs of users in their everyday lives.

6   Conclusion

In the commercial world, design ethnography appropriates the ethnographic approach. It attempts to understand the social and cultural contexts, which usually contribute to better product or service designs. However, unlike the traditional way of doing an ethnographic study, design ethnography usually has a short duration and a quick investigation of the field sites without many details. Also, the design ethnography studies usually have a technology application target. In this paper, we argued for a more "classic" approach to design ethnography with longer research time and an open attitude toward data collection. This paper reported a nine-month long-term ethnography study with a senior karaoke community. The research findings indicated that the long-term and immersive participation with the community enabled the researchers to find out the hidden patterns of the continuity of community members' singing experience and their strong focus on maintaining physical and mental well-being. This study supported our primary argument of calling for a classic ethnographic approach in design ethnography and showed the benefits in the design field of finding the actual needs of the users and generating various design concepts based the in-depth insights.

References

Baskerville, R., Myers, M.D.: Design Ethnography in information systems. Inf. Syst. J. **25**(1), 23–46 (2015)

Carbajal, M.L., Baranauskas, M.C.C.: Using ethnographic data to support preschool children's game design. In: Proceedings of the 18th Brazilian Symposium on Human Factors in Computing Systems, pp. 1–10, October 2019

Crabtree, A., Rodden, T., Tolmie, P., Button, G.: Ethnography considered harmful. In: Proceedings of the SIGCHI Conference on Human Factors in Computing Systems, pp. 879–888, April 2009

Cerna, K., et al.: Nurses' work practices in design: managing the complexity of pain. J. Workplace Learnong **32**(2), 135–146 (2020)

Doyle, J., Bailey, C., Ni Scanaill, C., van den Berg, F.: Lessons learned in deploying independent living technologies to older adults' homes. Univ. Access Inf. Soc. **13**(2), 191–204 (2013)

Hirsch, T., Forlizzi, J., Hyder, E., Goetz, J., Kurtz, C., Stroback, J.: The ELDer project: social, emotional, and environmental factors in the design of eldercare technologies. In: Proceedings on the 2000 Conference on Universal Usability, pp. 72–79, November 2020

Knoblauch, H.: Fokussierte Ethnographie. Sozialer Sinn **1**, 123–141 (2001)

Khovanskaya, V., Sengers, S., Mazmanian. M., Darrah, D.: Reworking the gaps between design and ethnography. In: CHI 2017extended abstracts on Human Factors in Computing Systems, Denver, Colorado, USA, pp. 5373–5385 (2017)

Müller, F.: Introduction: design as a discipline of alternation. In: Müller, F. (ed.) Design Ethnography: Epistemology and Methodology, pp. 1–6. Springer International Publishing, Cham (2021). https://doi.org/10.1007/978-3-030-60396-0_1

Müller, F.: Methods and aspects of field research. In: Müller, F. (ed.) Design Ethnography: Epistemology and Methodology, pp. 31–76. Springer International Publishing, Cham (2021). https://doi.org/10.1007/978-3-030-60396-0_5

McDonald, R., Harrison, S., Checkland, K., Campbell, S.M., Roland, M.: Impact of financial incentives on clinical autonomy and internal motivation in primary care: ethnographic study. BMJ-Br. Med. J. **334**(7608), 1357–1359 (2007)

Rapp, A.: In search for design elements: a new perspective for employing ethnography in human-computer interaction design research. Int. J. Human-Comput. Interact. **37**(8), 783–802 (2021)

Righi, V., Sayago, S., Blat, J.: When we talk about older people in HCI, who are we talking about? Towards a 'turn to community' in the design of technologies for a growing ageing population. Int. J. Hum Comput Stud. **108**, 15–31 (2017)

Talamo, A., Camilli, M., Di Lucchio, L., Ventura, S.: Information from the past: how elderly people orchestrate presences, memories and technologies at home. Univ. Access Inf. Soc. **16**(3), 739–753 (2017)

Vindrola-Padros, C., Vindrola-Padros, B.: Quick and dirty? A systematic review of the use of rapid ethnographies in healthcare organisation and delivery. BMJ Qual. Saf. **27**(4), 321–330 (2018)

Suchman, L.A.: Plans and Situated Actions: The Problem of Human-Machine Communication. Cambridge university press, New York, USA (1987)

Spradley, J.P.: Participant Observation. Wadsworth, Belmont (1980)

Suchman, L.: Located accountabilities in technology production. Scand. J. Inf. Syst. **14**(2), 91–105 (2002)

Salvador, T., Bell, G., Anderson, K.: Design ethnography. Design Manage. J. (Former Series) **10**(4), 35–41 (1999)

Suopajärvi, T.: Past experiences, current practices and future design: Ethnographic study of aging adults' everyday ICT practices — And how it could benefit public ubiquitous computing design. Technol. Forecast. Soc. Chang. **93**, 112–123 (2015)

Wood, A.E., Mattson, C.A.: Quantifying the effects of various factors on the utility of design ethnography in the developing world. Res. Eng. Design **30**(3), 317–338 (2019). https://doi.org/10.1007/s00163-018-00304-2

White, P.J., Devitt, F.: Creating personas from design ethnography and grounded theory. J. Usability Stud. **16**(3), 156–178 (2021)

Zimmerman, J., Forlizzi, J., Evenson, S.: Research through design as a method for interaction design research in HCI. In: Proceedings of the SIGCHI Conference on Human Factors in Computing Systems. pp. 493–502, April 2007

Designing to Fight Pandemics: A Review of Literature and Identifying Design Patterns for COVID-19 Tracing Apps

Isaac Criddle[1], Amanda Hardy[1], Garrett Smith[1], Thomas Ranck[1], Mainack Mondal[2], and Xinru Page[1(✉)]

[1] Brigham Young University, Provo, UT 84602, USA
{stapl,xinru}@cs.byu.edu
[2] Indian Institute of Technology, Kharagpur, India

Abstract. Throughout the pandemic, digital contact tracing using smartphone applications (or apps) has been endorsed by many authorities across the globe as a tool to limit the spread of COVID-19. Consequently, to deploy contact tracing in large populations, multiple contact tracing apps have been developed and deployed globally. However, due to the relative recency of the COVID-19 pandemic as well as the suddenness of the need for contact tracing at this scale, app designers are often left with no systematic guidelines. Designers today lack guidelines on what factors might affect perceptions and adoption of their apps. They also lack a knowledgebase of features that could be appropriate to include in their app for a given context. To address this gap, we conducted a review of the academic literature on attitudes towards and adoption of COVID-19 response apps, as well as a feature review of a diverse set of international tracing apps. Our investigation yielded a set of design patterns which can be used readily by designers of contact tracing apps. Our work lays the foundation to identify opportunities for new contextual feature design and use.

Keywords: Contact tracing · Human-Computer Interaction · Coronavirus apps · Design patterns

1 Introduction

On March 11, 2020, the World Health Organization declared the COVID-19 as a global pandemic. Nearly 2 years later, the world is still fighting variants of the disease. Since the beginning of 2020 [54], over 407 million people have been infected and there have been 5.8 million fatalities due to this disease. Consequently, a wide variety of measures have been taken by authorities across the world to limit the spread of COVID-19. One primary preventive measure has been contact tracing.

Contact tracing is a method used by health professionals to fight epidemics by notifying individuals that they have been exposed. Exposed individuals can then take additional protective measures. This has historically been done through call centers and public health officials conducting interviews with potentially infected citizens. In recent

M. Kurosu (Ed.): HCII 2022, LNCS 13304, pp. 36–49, 2022.
https://doi.org/10.1007/978-3-031-05412-9_3

years, governments and other organizations have created a host of systems to automate contact tracing primarily by leveraging mobile applications (i.e., apps) for this purpose. These apps often work by checking the proximity of other app-installed phones so that they can be notified when they have been in close proximity with an infected user. These contact tracing apps also automatically send notifications to notify users about exposures.

However, the designs of these apps did not come without its own set of problems. Towards the beginning of the COVID-19 pandemic, tech privacy advocates raised concerns about data privacy in early COVID-19 contact tracing apps due to its obvious potential to surveil citizens at large [1]. Consequently, developers started designing contact tracing applications with better privacy guarantees to address these concerns. For example, tech giants Google and Apple have come together to design and deploy a Bluetooth-based contact tracing protocol that allows for more privacy-preserving contact tracing in apps by allowing users to store their data on their own devices [50]. Even so, different apps are developed and used in different jurisdictions for contact tracing.

For the most part, contact tracing apps are not interoperable and so the effectiveness of automated contact tracing depends on the proportion of a population that uses a given contact tracing app [20] Thus, to have the best chance of reaching majority adoption (and consequently being more useful), contact tracing apps should be seen by users as both private and effective [12, 40, 43].

To achieve these goals, governments and research institutions around the world have developed their own contact tracing apps. These apps are often developed independently and so there exists a wide design diversity among them. Recent research has explored public perceptions regarding contact tracing apps in general, but little has been done in understanding the design paradigm of these apps. There is no comprehensive documentation of the variety of features that are found in contact tracing apps. In this paper we bridge this gap and provide designers a set of design patterns that are used today to support contact tracing. To achieve our goal of providing designers with guidance on the design of contact tracing apps for the pandemic, we conducted a literature review to summarize the results of previous research, followed by an app review to describe the variety of design patterns and features within contact tracing apps deployed in the context of COVID-19. These can serve as guidance for designing such apps and understanding what factors may affect adoption and utilization.

Specifically, our work makes the following contributions to the field of Human-Computer Interaction:

- We synthesize a taxonomy of the factors that have been found to affect adoption of contact tracing apps for COVID-19. We found that the literature has identified the most influential factors shaping adoption of contact tracing apps are the perceived privacy of the app, the perceived trustworthiness of the organization sponsoring the app, and finally the perceived effectiveness of the app.
- Our analysis of existing contact tracing apps around the world reveals four categories of features found in contact tracing or Coronavirus apps: contact tracing features, educational features, statistical features, and personal health management features.

- For each of these categories, we present a set of design patterns based on analysis of existing contact tracing features. These design patterns can help app designers consider which features to incorporate into their contact tracing apps.

2 Methods

In this section, we first present how we aggregated and synthesized the existing work on contact tracing apps, and how we judged the relative importance of the factors that affect the adoption of these apps. We then present our method to analyze the contact tracing app features.

2.1 Literature Review

We used the keywords "COVID" and "contact tracing perceptions" to search research databases (EBSCO and Google Scholar). Next, we screened the resultant articles by reviewing the abstracts to find the articles which are most directly relevant to perceptions towards and adoption of COVID-19 contact tracing apps. We then performed a content analysis of the final 51 identified articles.

Our analysis of these 51 research papers primarily centered around perceptions and acceptance of COVID-19 contact tracing apps. Specifically, we extracted the results from each paper and performed a thematic analysis of the text to uncover factors impacting the adoption of contact tracing apps. Our analysis revealed how demographics, life experiences, and the design of the features all affect attitudes and adoption.

2.2 App Review

After reviewing the literature, we analyzed contact tracing apps found in a widely recognized database maintained by MIT researchers and which contains COVID-19-related apps used in multiple countries and in almost all 50 United States [53]. Using this database, we identified a total of 78 applications and ultimately studied 46 of the 78 applications. (The remaining 32 were not found in the Google nor Apple stores or needed authentication in the apps' country of deployment). We downloaded to our local devices as many of these 46 apps as possible to examine their features and collect screenshots. For the small number where we could not download the app (e.g., due to geographical restrictions), we collected screenshots of the app's page in the app store. When available, we also reviewed the corresponding application support website and the history of the app's release in the Google Play Store and Apple App Store.

3 Results

3.1 Factors Affecting Adoption

Through our literature review, we identified several factors that drive COVID-19 app adoption. Table 1 summarizes these factors. We found that two factors were much more frequently mentioned than the others: Privacy and Trust in the Organization.

Table 1. Taxonomy of the factors shown to affect adoption and usage of contact tracing or other COVID-19 apps with the relevant sources from the literature.

Factors	Characteristic & Impact on Adoption (+ Increase or − Decrease Adoption)	Reference to prior work
Technology design	More private +	[12, 23, 24, 26, 29, 32, 35, 38–40, 43, 44]
	More accurate +	[12, 23, 40, 45]
	Easier to use +	[12, 24, 40, 43, 45]
	Includes contact tracing functionality +	[28, 32]
	Software compatible with cell phone +	[12, 23]
Health status	Believes oneself to already have been infected with the virus -	[31]
	Higher perceived personal health risk from the virus +	[27, 35, 36, 38, 44, 45]
Social or cultural concerns	Knows someone who has died from COVID-19 +	[1]
	Health company or research institution hosts the app +	[12, 23, 27–29, 32, 34, 35, 38–41, 43–45]
	Government or private company hosts the app −	
Demographic	Age has conflicting evidence in both directions	[23, 29, 31]
	Higher level of education +	[34]

The factors driving adoption of contact tracing apps fall into four themes: Technology design, health status of the user, social/cultural concerns, and demographics. Users generally report being willing to adopt privacy-preserving and usable solutions of contact tracing. Feeling like they were at higher health risk due to the virus also drove adoption of these apps. People also appear to trust health organizations and research institutions with the data more than governments and industry. The relationship between age and adoption is inconclusive: in some studies, being older was associated with increased adoption while other studies found the opposite.

We next turn to the question of which design elements are used in these apps to support contact tracing.

3.2 The Design Patterns

Most apps had a simple bottom navigation bar with 3 to 5 tabs, with tab names including "Home," "Settings," "Health," "Symptoms," "News," "Contact," and "Scan QR code." These navigation bars allow users to quickly peruse the app and develop a locational memory for where to find each feature (Fig. 1).

Fig. 1. Kuwait's app "Shlonik" has a 5-tab bottom navigation bar. The "Home" tab primarily includes statistical and educational features.

Our analysis of the features implemented in 46 contact-tracing apps from around the globe revealed that they fell into four design paradigms. Each paradigm is designed to protect public health in a different way. These are:

- Contact tracing features
- Educational features
- Statistical features
- Personal health management features

Next, we will describe each of the four design paradigms and enumerate the design patterns that fall under each paradigm.

Contact Tracing Features in Contact Tracing App Design. Contact tracing features alert users about exposures to people who test positive for COVID-19. In many of the apps, the contact tracing functionality uses a very simple feature design, often just a small text box or bubble indicating whether an exposure has been reported (See Fig. 2 and 3). Contact tracing features are typically found on the homepage of the app near the top. The design patterns for automatic contact tracing through apps include the following:

- *Location Services*: Location services tracing features track a user's physical location through GPS or other systems. The physical location of the user is recorded, and when a location and time is matched with someone who has a positive COVID-19 test result, the user is notified that they have been near someone else who was likely contagious at the time. Location-based contact tracing is often paired with a centralized database, which carries more privacy risks.
- *Bluetooth:* The Bluetooth features allow a user's phone to keep track of the identifiers of other nearby phones. Unlike the location services tracing features, the Bluetooth system does not require knowledge of a user's absolute location. Many of these text boxes include a button or switch to toggle the Bluetooth feature on and off. These are sometimes found with additional text boxes that confirm to the user that the Bluetooth exposure detection is active or inviting users to report positive test results.

At least 23 of the applications surveyed with a Bluetooth tracing API utilized the Google-Apple Bluetooth Tracing API, which preserves the anonymity of users through a decentralized system. Another 16 used some other Bluetooth proximity-based contact tracing protocol, including the Google-Apple API's precursor, DP3-T [22].

- *Check-in to a Location:* The app is used to log the amount of time spent at a public location. For example, in China's health code system, establishments post a QR code at the front of the store which is then used by customers to log time spent there. The app can then later notify those simultaneously present at the establishment if one receives a positive test result. Figure 4 shows an example of this feature in New Zealand's NZ COVID Tracer app.

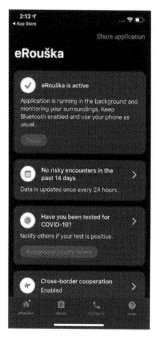

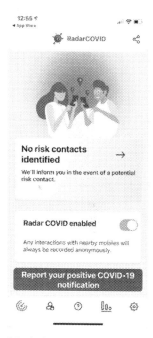

Fig. 2. The Czech Republic's contact tracing app eRouška. A small button toggles the Bluetooth sensing.

Fig. 3. Mexico's RadarCOVID app also follows the simple contact tracing homepage design pattern. Three boxes 1) toggle the functionality, 2) report possible exposures, and 3) offer option for reporting a positive COVID-19 test.

Each of these contact tracing features is paired with a feature that allows the user to declare a positive COVID-19 test result. The system then notifies those who may have been exposed.

Fig. 4. New Zealand's NZ COVID Tracer app allows users to log when they go to public places, enabling later contact tracing for those present at the venue.

Fig. 5. Poland's ProteGOSafe app has a separate important information tab with a variety of simple, reliable articles.

Educational Features in Contact Tracing App Design. Educational features provide accurate and actionable information for users about the status of the pandemic in their area, best practices for protecting health, and resources made available to the public. The following design patterns were commonly used:

- *News Articles:* The app either links to reliable news about the state of the pandemic or provides a view of news articles in the app itself. In France's TousAntiCovid, this entails a simple text box with a "Read all news" button that opens a small newsfeed.
- *General Information Pages:* 19 of the apps had other curated articles with reliable health information, including lists of common symptoms of COVID-19, how to protect oneself in public and what to do if exposed. These articles are commonly found in a menu found low on the homepage or dashboard below the contact tracing feature. Figure 5 shows example of Poland's ProteGOSafe app which presents such a general information page.
- *Test or Vaccine Locator:* A simple map showing testing or vaccination sites.

Fig. 6. Utah's Healthy Together app uses a choropleth map to display the risk levels of exposure by county.

Fig. 7. Ghana's GH COVID-19 Tracker contains a symptom questionnaire with its own icon on bottom navigator bar.

Fig. 8. In Qatar's Ehteraz app, the color of a user's QR Code personal identifier indicates their recorded health status. The app is mandatory for all citizens of Qatar.

Statistical Features. Educational features provide accurate and actionable information for users about the status of the pandemic in their area, best practices for protecting one's health, or resources made available to the public. the following design patterns are used to create such features:

- *Numeric Info Boxes.* At their most basic, statistical features in these apps simply displayed a number. Some common indicators include the number of users of the app, total number of cases in a country or state, total deaths in an area, and the total number of people vaccinated in an area.
- *Trend Graphs.* A line graph shows the trend of number of cases in the locality.
- *Maps.* Often a choropleth map where color indicates severity or risk of the pandemic in an area. Users have reported that maps of hotspot locations are perceived as useful [40]. An example of maps included in an interface is shown in Fig. 6 for Utah's Healthy Together app.

Personal Health Management Features. Personal health features provide tools for users to manage their own health. they do not typically provide curated information for users, but rather allow the users to take action for their own health. these personal health features are usually found as individual pages separate from the homepage and any informational features, although there may be buttons to access personal health management features found on the dashboard or homepage. The design patterns we found:

- *Test Result Report.* Allows a user to see new COVID-19 test results inside the app.
- *Health Diary.* Users can type or otherwise log their contacts with people and places. Health diaries help to facilitate later contact tracing done by humans through call centers.
- *Symptom Questionnaire.* A brief set of questions can help a user identify their own symptoms or monitor changes in their health. In most cases, this takes the form of a linked text box on the home page, but in some cases the questionnaire has a tab on the navigator bar. Figure 7 shows Ghana's GH COVID-19 Tracker which presents a symptom questionnaire to the users.
- *Risk Evaluation Questionnaire.* Questions identifying the age and health history of an individual can allow a user to learn about their risk of more serious symptoms if infected.
- *Vaccination Tracker or Card.* Certifies or at least tracks the user's vaccination status. This feature is usually accessed with a simple button on a dashboard.
- *QR Code Personal Identifier.* Four of the apps we reviewed assigned each user a unique personal QR code displayed within the app. The code allows a third party to assess the user's risk of exposure. Interestingly, adoption of three of the four apps that implement a QR code personal identifier (from China, the United Arab Emirates, and Qatar) is enforced by national law. Figure 8 shows an example of a QR code identifier in Qatar's Ehteraz app.

3.3   Prevalence of Identified Design Patterns

Finally, we detail the prevalence of the identified design patterns on the apps we investigated. The result is shown in Table 2. We found that while nearly all the apps used some form of contact tracing functionality, especially Bluetooth proximity-based contact tracing, a minority of the apps implemented statistical or educational features.

In total only 15 out of the 46 apps attempted to show the statistical features to the users, increasing transparency and objectivity, and less than half (22 out of 46) of the apps attempted to make the user experience educational. Consequently, we asked how many features are implemented per app. Figure 9 shows the distribution of the number of features falling under each design pattern among the 46 apps.

Figure 9 demonstrates that the apps identified for our study are simple in design, with few tabs and little interactivity, despite there being a wide spectrum of design choices that they could have leveraged (as identified in this work). While our sample of apps had a wide variety of features among them, each individual app only utilized a few – the median application utilized only four design patterns. No single educational, statistical, or personal health feature predominated. Thus, we identify an opportunity to have contact tracing apps that support a wider range of features.

Table 2. This table indicates which of the 46 apps reviewed have features that implement a design pattern. Some features may be underreported due to language or other barriers.

Type of feature	Feature	Count (from 46)
Contact tracing	Bluetooth-based proximity	40
	Location-based	9
	QR code for venue	14
	Ability to self-report test results	31
	Any contact tracing feature	*46*
Educational	News and alerts	8
	General information and health best practices	19
	Test or vaccine locator	7
	Any educational feature	*22*
Statistical	Trend graphs	3
	Numeric info boxes	12
	Geographic data	4
	Any statistical feature	*15*
Personal health	Symptom or risk questionnaire	14
	Test result report	6
	Vaccine tracker	5
	QR code personal identifier	4
	Quarantine day counter	2
	Any personal health management feature	*25*

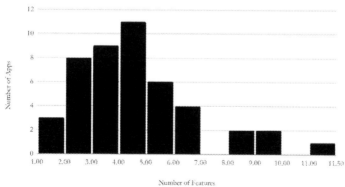

Count of Feature Categories Found per App

Fig. 9. Of all the features listed in Table 2 above, the median app only possessed 4 features. This histogram includes all 46 apps that we reviewed.

4   Discussion

The perceived privacy of a user's data has been shown to be the most influential obstacle to a user adopting a contact tracing app. There is some evidence that an individual becomes less concerned with the privacy of the application as trust in the institution behind the app increases [38], sometimes even preferring a centralized architecture that trades a degree of personal privacy for an increased ability of the organization hosting the app to reach out to people who are exposed to the virus [40]. In the app review, most of the apps were built directly by governments, however designers should consider the perceived status of their organization. Research and health organizations tend to be much more trusted than governments themselves. Since this is one of the most influential factors shown to affect the adoption of Coronavirus apps, having some degree of partnership with a research or health organization could help encourage adoption of government mandated contact tracing apps.

Another powerful factor affecting adoption of Coronavirus apps is the perceived privacy of an app. The vast majority of the apps surveyed use Bluetooth-based contact tracing, primarily through use of the Google-Apple API or other DPT-3 protocol [22]. Both the Google-Apple API and DPT-3 are markedly decentralized in hopes of maintaining a higher degree of privacy. However, it has been shown that many people do not understand how the technology functions, leading to a lower degree of trust in the privacy of these applications, and likely to a lower adoption rate. As people more fully understand the process behind Bluetooth proximity-based contact tracing, they may be more likely to favor a decentralized system [29].

We found that a surprisingly low proportion of contact tracing apps offered substantial informational or educational features. Since experiments have shown that certain statistical features are seen as useful, designers of Coronavirus or similar apps should seriously consider integrating reliable and simple informational features into their designs to encourage adoption [40]. This would also have the added benefit of providing another reliable information source for app users, leading to better public awareness of the status of the epidemic.

From our literature search, we found a considerable amount of information about the aspects of contact tracing features which might affect adoption. On the other hand, we found little information describing how the exact design of educational, statistical, and other features may impact a user's willingness to download and use a contact tracing app. By detailing the various design patterns of these features, we are helping designers understand the various ways a given functionality can be supported. It remained for future research to understand at a more detailed level exactly how the different design patterns affect user's attitudes towards and willingness to adopt contact tracing apps.

5   Conclusion

We conducted a literature review of 51 articles and a feature review of 46 apps. We found that the literature shows that the two most important factors for adoption of Coronavirus apps are the perceived privacy of the application and the perceived trustworthiness of the organization. We also found four major categories of features in the apps: contact tracing features, educational features, statistical features, and personal health management features.

References

1. Wired Opinion: The Success of Contact Tracing Doesn't Just Depend on Privacy. Wired. Conde Nast, 23 May 2020. https://www.wired.com/story/the-success-of-contact-tracing-doesnt-just-depend-on-privacy/
2. Miller, S., Smith, M.: Ethics, public health and technology responses to COVID-19. Bioethics **35**(4), 366–371 (2021). Res. Lib. Sci. Technol. https://doi.org/10.1111/bioe.12856
3. Abueg, M., et al.: Modeling the effect of exposure notification and non-pharmaceutical interventions on COVID-19 transmission in Washington State. NPJ Digit. Med. **4**(1) (2021). SCOPUS. https://doi.org/10.1038/s41746-021-00422-7.www.scopus.com
4. Shu Wei, T.D., Lawrence, C., Victor, D., Wong, T.Y.: Digital technology and COVID-19. Nat. Med. **26**(4), 459–461 (2020). https://doi.org/10.1038/s41591-020-0824-5
5. Jobie, B., et al.: Digital technologies in the public-health response to COVID-19. Nat. Med. **26**(8), 1183–1192 (2020). https://doi.org/10.1038/s41591-020-1011-4
6. Halan, D.: Trends: Role of Information Technology in Covid-19 Research. Electronics for You, 01 Mar 2021. ProQuest
7. Rapid Implementation of Mobile Technology for Real-Time Epidemiology of COVID-19. Science **368**(6497), 1362–1367 (2020). https://doi.org/10.1126/science.abc0473. https://www.proquest.com/scholarly-journals/rapid-implementation-mobile-technology-real-time/docview/2414833342
8. Tong, A., Sorrell, T.C., Black, A.J., et al.: Research priorities for COVID-19 sensor technology. Nat. Biotechnol. **39**, 144–147 (2021). https://doi.org/10.1038/s41587-021-00816-8
9. Yusuke, Y., Shelby, K.L., Makoto, I.: Human–automation trust to technologies for naïve users amidst and following the COVID-19 Pandemic. Hum. Fact. **62**(7), 1087–1094 (2020). https://doi.org/10.1177/0018720820948981
10. Gemma, N., et al.: Innovation under pressure: Implications for data privacy during the Covid-19 Pandemic. Big Data & Society **7**(2) (2020). https://doi.org/10.1177/2053951720976680
11. Mokbel, M., Abbar, S., Stanojevic, R.: Contact tracing: beyond the apps. SIGSPATIAL Special 12, **2**, 15–24 (2020). https://doi.org/10.1145/3431843.3431846
12. Utz, C., et al.: Apps against the spread: Privacy implications and user acceptance of COVID-19-related smartphone apps on three continents. In: Proceedings of the 2021 CHI Conference on Human Factors in Computing Systems, May 2021. https://doi.org/10.1145/3411764.3445517
13. Robertson, E., et al.: Predictors of COVID-19 vaccine hesitancy in the UK household longitudinal study. Brain Behav. Immun. **94**, 41–50 (2021). https://doi.org/10.1016/j.bbi.2021.03.008
14. Caserotti, M., et al.: Associations of COVID-19 risk perception with vaccine hesitancy over time for Italian residents. Soc. Sci. Med. **272**, 113688 (2021). https://doi.org/10.1016/j.socscimed.2021.113688
15. Perry, S.L., et al.: Culture wars and COVID-19 conduct: Christian nationalism, religiosity, and Americans' behavior during the coronavirus pandemic. J. Sci. Study Religion **59**(3), 405–416 (2020). https://doi.org/10.1111/jssr.12677
16. Gokmen, Y., et al.: The impact of national culture on the increase of COVID-19: A cross-country analysis of European countries. Int. J. Intercult. Rel. **81**, 1–8 (2021). https://doi.org/10.1016/j.ijintrel.2020.12.006

17. Opratko, B., et al.: Cultures of rejection in the Covid-19 Crisis. Ethnic Racial Stud. **44**(5), 893–905 (2021). https://doi.org/10.1080/01419870.2020.1859575
18. Grishina, N.V., Lupulyak, P.V.: The COVID-19 experience: Features of culture and belonging in the context of peoples native to a country and migrants. Psychol. Russia State Art **13**(4), 119–33 (2020). https://doi.org/10.11621/pir.2020.0408
19. Help Speed up Contact Tracing with Trace Together. http://www.gov.sg/article/help-speed-up-contact-tracing-with-tracetogether
20. Hinch, R., et al.: Effective configurations of a digital contact tracing app: A report to nhsx
21. PEPP-PT: Data Protection and Information Security Architecture (2020). GitHub, 20 Apr 2020. https://github.com/pepp-pt/pepp-pt-documentation/blob/master/10-data-protection/PEPP-PT-data-protection-information-security-architecture-Germany.pdf
22. Troncoso, C. et al.: Decentralized Privacy-Preserving Proximity Tracing. 25 May 2020. https://github.com/DP-3T/documents/blob/master/DP3T%20White%20Paper.pdf
23. Thomas, R., Michaleff, Z.A., Greenwood, H., Abukmail, E., Glasziou, P.: Concerns and misconceptions about the Australian government's Covidsafe app: Cross-sectional survey study. JMIR Pub. Health Surveill. **6**(4), e23081 (2020)
24. Simko, L., Chang, J.L., Jiang, M., Calo, R., Roesner, F., Kohno, T.: Covid-19 contact tracing and privacy: A longitudinal study of public opinion. arXiv preprint arXiv:2012.01553 (2020)
25. Walrave, M., Waeterloos, C., Ponnet, K.: Ready or not for contact tracing? investigating the adoption intention of covid-19 contact-tracing technology using an extended unified theory of acceptance and use of technology model. Cyberpsychology Behav. Soc. Networking (2020)
26. Altmann, S., et al.: Acceptability of app-based contact tracing for covid-19: Cross-country survey study. JMIR Mhealth Uhealth **8**(8), e19857 (2020)
27. Guillon, M., Kergall, P.: Attitudes and opinions on quarantine and support for a contact-tracing application in France during the covid-19 outbreak. Public health, **188**:21–31 (2020). https://www.ncbi.nlm.nih.gov/pmc/articles/PMC7550094/
28. Buder, F., et al.: Adoption rates for contact tracing app configurations in Germany (2020). https://www.nim.org/sites/default/files/medien/359/dokumente/2020_nim_report_tracing_app_adoption_fin_0.pdf
29. Kostka, G., Habich-Sobiegalla, S.: In times of crisis: Public perceptions towards covid-19 contact tracing apps in China, Germany and the US, 16 September 2020. https://papers.ssrn.com/sol3/papers.cfm?abstract_id=3693783
30. Washington Post-University of Maryland National Poll, 21–26 April 2020. Washington Post. https://www.washingtonpost.com/context/washington-post-university-of-maryland-national-poll-april-21-26-2020/3583b4e9-66be-4ed6-a457-f6630a550ddf/
31. Bachtiger, P., Adamson, A., Quint, J.K., Peters, N.S.: Belief of having had unconfirmed covid-19 infection reduces willingness to participate in app-based contact tracing. NPJ Digital Med. **3**(1), 1–7 (2020)
32. Wiertz, C., Banerjee, A., Acar, O.A., Ghosh, A.: Predicted adoption rates of contact tracing app configurations-insights from a choice-based conjoint study with a representative sample of the UK population. Available at SSRN 3589199 (2020)
33. Baumgärtner, L., et al.: Mind the gap: Security & privacy risks of contact tracing apps. arXiv preprint arXiv:2006.05914 (2020)
34. Hargittai, E., et al.: Americans' Willingness to Adopt a COVID-19 Tracking App: The Role of App Distributor. First Monday, Oct 2020. firstmonday.org. https://doi.org/10.5210/fm.v25i11.11095
35. Hassandoust, F., Akhlaghpour, S., Johnston, A.C.: Individuals' privacy concerns and adoption of contact tracing mobile applications in a pandemic: A situational privacy calculus perspective. J. Am. Med. Inf. Assoc. (2020)
36. Horstmann, K.T., Buecker, S., Krasko, J., Kritzler, S., Terwiel, S.: Who does or does not use the "corona-warn-app" and why? Euro. J. Pub. Health (2020)

37. Horvath, L., Banducci, S., James, O.: Citizens' attitudes to contact tracing apps. J. Exp. Polit. Sci. 1–13 (2020)

38. Kaptchuk, G., Hargittai, E., Redmiles, E.M.: How good is good enough for covid19 apps? The influence of benefits, accuracy, and privacy on willingness to adopt. arXiv preprint arXiv: 2005.04343 (2020)

39. Li, T., et al.: What makes people install a covid-19 contact-tracing app? Understanding the influence of app design and individual difference on contact- tracing app adoption intention. arXiv preprint arXiv:2012.12415 (2020)

40. Li, T., et al.: Decentralized is not risk-free: Understanding public perceptions of privacy utility trade-offs in covid-19 contact-tracing apps. arXiv preprint arXiv:2005.11957 (2020)

41. O'Callaghan, M.E., et al.: A national survey of attitudes to COVID-19 digital contact tracing in the Republic of Ireland. Irish J. Med. Sci. (1971 -) **190**(3), 863–887 (2020). https://doi.org/10.1007/s11845-020-02389-y

42. Redmiles, E.M.: User concerns & Tradeoffs in technology-facilitated COVID-19 response. Digit. Gov.: Res. Pract. **2**(1), Article 6, 12. https://doi.org/10.1145/3428093(2021)

43. Trang, S., Trenz, M., Weiger, W.H., Tarafdar, M., Cheung, C.M.K.: One app to trace them all? Examining app specifications for mass acceptance of contact-tracing apps. Eur. J. Inf. Syst. **29**(4), 415–428 (2020). https://doi.org/10.1080/0960085X.2020.1784046

44. Nakamoto, I., et al.: A QR code–based contact tracing framework for sustainable containment of COVID-19: Evaluation of an approach to assist the return to normal activity. JMIR MHealth and UHealth **8**(9), e22321 (2020). mhealth.jmir.org. https://doi.org/10.2196/22321

45. von Wyl, V., et al.: Drivers of acceptance of COVID-19 proximity tracing apps in Switzerland: Panel survey analysis. JMIR Pub. Health Surveill. **7**(1), e25701. https://doi.org/10.2196/25701

46. Williams, S.N., et al.: Public attitudes towards COVID-19 contact tracing apps: A UK-based focus group study. Health Expect. Int. J. Pub. Participation Health Care Health Policy **24**(2), 377–385 (2021). https://doi.org/10.1111/hex.13179

47. Zhang, B., et al.: Americans' perceptions of privacy and surveillance in the COVID-19 pandemic. PLOS ONE **15**(12), e0242652 (2020). https://doi.org/10.1371/journal.pone.024 2652

48. Peng, W., et al.: A qualitative study of user perceptions of mobile health apps. BMC Public Health **16**(1), 1158 (2016). https://doi.org/10.1186/s12889-016-3808-0

49. Imran, A., et al.: AI4COVID-19: AI enabled preliminary diagnosis for COVID-19 from cough samples via an app. Inf. Med. Unlocked **20**, 100378 (2020). https://doi.org/10.1016/j.imu.2020.100378

50. Privacy-Preserving Contact Tracing - Apple and Google. Apple. https://www.apple.com/covid19/contacttracing

51. Davalbhakta, S., et al.: A systematic review of the smartphone applications available for corona virus disease 2019 (COVID19) and their assessment using the mobile app rating scale (MARS). medRxiv, 4 July 2020, p. 2020.07.02.20144964. medRxiv, https://www.medrxiv.org/content/10.1101/2020.07.02.20144964v1

52. Servick, K.: Can phone apps slow the spread of the Coronavirus?" Science, June 2020. www.science.org, https://doi.org/10.1126/science.368.6497.1296

53. The Covid Tracing Tracker: What's Happening in Coronavirus Apps around the World. MIT Technology Review. https://www.technologyreview.com/2020/12/16/1014878/covid-tracing-tracker/

54. COVID Live - Coronavirus Statistics - Worldometer. https://www.worldometers.info/coronavirus/

Educational AGV Design by AHP and DFX Methods

Yu-Xuan Hsueh, Jui-Hung Cheng[✉], Jia-Hong Shen, Zih-Ling He,
and Bai-Chau Chen

Department of Mold and Die Engineering, National Kaohsiung University of Science and
Technology, Kaohsiung, Taiwan
rick.cheng@nkust.edu.tw

Abstract. In response to the current trend of Industry 4.0, the general academic community has not kept up with the changes. The biggest reason is that the current AGV trucks are expensive. It is difficult to exert the educational effect, and it is difficult for students to do it or even modify it. Stimulate the imagination of students. Some manufacturers try to cut into this area in the current teaching aid market, but due to the lack of processing knowledge and the unfamiliarity with the actual application environment, it is not easy to make a car body that meets the education market. Many details cannot notice, and the user experience will be accompanied by various immaturities, resulting in users who want to try AGV trucks having a wrong understanding of the AGV truck. The unsuitable processing method will also increase the processing cost so that the terminal price is also lower. In this study, DFX is used as the front-end design analysis, making up for the processing and actual application environment information. Before the design, the user needs to be understood, and the product can be entirely modular. The advantage of the design is that it is easy to replace parts and the expansion or modifying replacement of functions according to the use environment. Even if the parts are damaged, only need to replace and debug the problem quickly. After officially producing the product, the link between industry and academia strengthens. To make up for the technical gap between the two, students can get started more quickly after entering the industry, reducing the time for employee training to become an immediate force.

Keywords: AGV · Modular design · AHP · DFX · Technical and vocational education

1 Introduction

AGV (Automated Guided Vehicle) provides chemical factories for handling and material transportation. It has a laser, magnetic tape, ultrasonic, rail, infrared, et cetera., and has an automated vehicle body that automatically avoids obstacles and patrols tracks. According to different fields, select the corresponding [1, 2]. The car body can also equip with various transportation functions, such as inspection type, plug-in type, handling type,

M. Kurosu (Ed.): HCII 2022, LNCS 13304, pp. 50–60, 2022.
https://doi.org/10.1007/978-3-031-05412-9_4

jack-up type, traction type, shallow escape type, roller type, et cetera [3, 4]. Special-purpose models developed for special needs in the face of the current trend of industrial transformation automation are an inevitable development direction. Automated management saves human errors and obtains longer working hours, bringing more stable quality [5–7]. It has become the leading indicator of Industry 4.0. This research mainly focuses on developing modularized AGV teaching aids by AHP (Analytic Hierarchy Process) and DFX (Design for Excellence) methods to help teachers with low-cost and low learning disabilities and help technical and vocational education students quickly learn professional knowledge and skills.

2 Methodology

2.1 AHP (Analytic Hierarchy Process)

For Modular Design Processes of AGV [8], AHP is to classify system elements into multiple groups, divide each group into various sub-groups, and put them into a hierarchical structure according to the rank order. It divides into the first layer: final project, the second layer: evaluation project, the third layer: evaluation project, and the fourth layer: alternative plan. Generally, there are no more than seven groups in the first layer [9, 10]. The establishment of hierarchies is beneficial to dividing labor at each level and sorting the importance. The final purpose will not be affected when fine-tuning each level. The evaluation scale divides into nine categories, "1" means equally essential, "3" means slightly important, "5" means quite essential, "7" means extremely important, "9" means essential, 2, 4, 6, 8 are the median value of jobs on adjacent scales as shown in Table 1. Finally, the results made by the group classification are assessed, according to the number, to select the best design.

Table 1. Analytic hierarchy process scale description

Evaluation scale	Definition	Instruction
1	Equally important	The contribution of the two ICPs is of equal importance
3	Slightly important	Experience and judgment tend to favor a certain program slightly
5	Important	Experience and judgment have a strong tendency to prefer a program
7	Quite important	The actual display shows a very strong tendency to prefer a certain scheme
9	Very important	There is enough evidence to definitely prefer a certain scheme
2, 4, 6, 8	Median value of adjacent scales	Eclectic straight

AHP Step 1. Based on 6 SIGMAs, perform the DMAIC steps. First, each component module is defined and discusses all shallow refactor problems, and then the AHP statistical method is used to calculate [11, 12]. By establishing a focus hierarchy and limiting the factors to no more than seven, the number of effective hierarchies can estimate by n/7. Hierarchical structures allow for efficient comparison and matching, and better consistency goals can achieve. Then, take the key elements of each level as the evaluation benchmark, conduct surveys, and comparisons, and make judgments on the scale of 1-9. The relationship between the upper and lower levels should not be too far-fetched. Both are 1), and the value of the lower triangle part is the overall value of the relative position of the upper triangle, for example, $a_{ji} = \frac{1}{a_{ij}}$.

Furthermore, $a_{ij} = \frac{w_i}{w_j}$, w_1, w_2 k, w_n represent the influence weight of each factor of level i on a factor of level i-1.

$$A = \begin{bmatrix} 1 & a_{12} & L & a_{1n} \\ a_{21} & 1 & L & a_{2n} \\ L & L & L & L \\ a_{n1} & a_{n2} & L & 1 \end{bmatrix} = \begin{bmatrix} 1 & a_{12} & L & a_{1n} \\ 1/a_{21} & 1 & L & a_{2n} \\ L & L & L & L \\ 1/a_{n1} & 1/a_{n2} & L & 1 \end{bmatrix} = \begin{bmatrix} w_1/w_1 & w_1/w_2 & L & w_1/w_n \\ w_2/w_1 & w_2/w_2 & L & w_2/w_n \\ L & L & L & L \\ w_n/w_1 & w_n/w_2 & L & w_n/w_n \end{bmatrix} \quad (1)$$

AHP Step 2. In the next step, compute the priority vector and maximum eigenvalue. In order to obtain the advantage vector, four approximation methods can use to obtain the advantage vector, and the geometric mean of the vector is a better evaluation method of the advantage vector. The methods are as follows:

Normalization of the Geometric Mean of Column Vectors as:

$$w_1 = \frac{\left(\prod_{j=1}^{n} a_{ij}\right)}{\sum_{i=1}^{n}\left(\prod_{j=1}^{n} a_{ij}\right)} \quad I, j = 1, 2, k \ldots n \quad (2)$$

In order to find the maximum eigenvalue (λ_{max}), it is necessary to multiply

$$\frac{uv}{A} \times \frac{uv}{W} = \frac{uuv}{w'} \begin{bmatrix} 1 & a_{12} & L & a_{1n} \\ 1/a_{21} & 1 & L & a_{2n} \\ L & L & L & L \\ 1/a_{n1} & 1/a_{n2} & L & 1 \end{bmatrix} \begin{pmatrix} w_1 \\ w_2 \\ L \\ W_4 \end{pmatrix} = \begin{pmatrix} w_1 \\ w_2 \\ L \\ W_4 \end{pmatrix} \quad (3)$$

Then the maximum eigenvalue λ_{max} can be obtained by the following as:

$$\lambda_{max} = \frac{1}{n}\left(\frac{w_1}{w_1} + \frac{w_2}{w_2} + \ldots + \frac{w_n}{w_n}\right)$$

AHP Step 3 Then calculate the consistency indicators at all levels, confirm the suitability, carry out the consistency test on the feature vector, and calculate each level's consistency ratio (C.R.) and the whole level's consistency ratio (CHR). Its consistency value must be less than 0.1. Otherwise, there is a problem with the association of hierarchical elements and recalculation.

(1) consistency index, C.I.

$$C.I. = \frac{\lambda_{max} - n}{n - 1} \tag{4}$$

(2) consistency ratio, C.R.

$$C.R. = \frac{C.I.}{R.I.} \tag{5}$$

Among them, the random index (R.I.) evaluation scale is a positive reciprocal value matrix generated by 1–9, and the consistency index value generated under different numbers, the random index is shown in the Table 2.

Table 2. Random Index (R.I.)

Factorial	1	2	3	4	5	6	7	8	9	10	11	12	13	14	15
R.I.	0	0	0.58	0.9	1.12	1.24	1.32	1.41	1.45	1.49	1.51	1.48	1.56	1.57	1.58

Consistency ratio hierarchy (C.R.H.), when the importance of the hierarchy is different, the hierarchy consistency needs to be tested. To calculate the overall hierarchy consistency ratio by dividing the consistency index of the hierarchy, C.I.H. passes the random index of the hierarchy, R.I.H. Its mathematical formula:

$$C.H.I. = \sum (Per - level\ priority\ vector)/(C.I.\ Values\ per\ Tier) \tag{6}$$

$$R.I.H. = \sum (Per - level\ priority\ vector)/(R.I.\ Values\ per\ Tier) \tag{7}$$

$$C.R.H. = \frac{C.I.H.}{R.I.H.} \tag{8}$$

If the final C.R.H. value is <0.1, the overall consistency is within a reasonable range. After the hierarchy passes the consistency check, the overall weight can calculate the plan priority vector. The decision-maker can choose the plan according to the final result.

2.2 DFX (Design for Excellence)

When we talk about the methodology and technology of remanufacturing, we have to consider the disassembly of the product and the need for reassembly. Both aspects need to consider during the design process. Remanufacturing has become an essential aspect of environmental sustainability. The main goal is to restore a product or part to its useful life. Easily assembled with fewer parts, products, parts, and materials can easily recycle for reuse. Implementing this concept and philosophy becomes attractive to the industry when saving costs increases the sustainability of everyday items. Hence, for AGV structure design and modular design, especially in less is more design trends, the DFX

(Design for Excellence) is the design method that focuses on excellent design, hoping for a perfectly designed product. Assemble (DFA, Design for Assembly), Manufacturability (DFM, Design for Manufacturability), Inspection (DFT, Design for Inspection), Testability (DFT, Design for Testability), Repairability (DFR, Design for Repairability), Cost (DFC, Design for Cost), Recycle (DFR, Design for Recycle), which means the requirements of each aspect in the product life cycle. The design front-end operation is thoroughly analyzed the customer needs and production costs [13, 14]. After comparison, the production cost and customer needs can balance. Then the production costs can reduce as much as possible and satisfy customer needs. The methods can maximize the design capabilities.

3   AGV Body Design and Evaluation

According to the AHP experimental method, the most suitable parts are selected for each module, as shown in Fig. 1 and the weight ratio distribution used for comparison, and the most relevant features selected according to the use requirements or all selected to

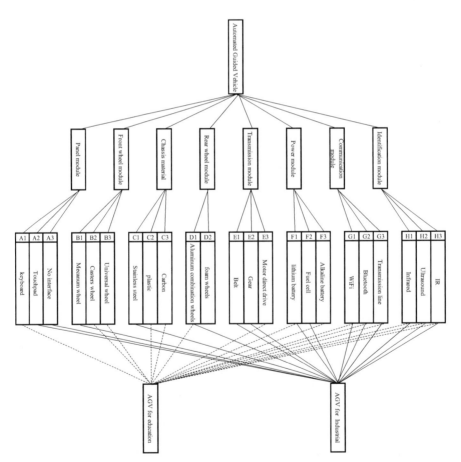

Fig. 1. Body design architecture diagram

increase the functional diversity, without affecting the difficulty of use and maintenance cost (Table 3). The premise is to optimize the AGV body design with AHP processes, as shown in Fig. 2.

Table 3. Design selection project index summary description

Evaluation Items	Definition	Attributes
Panel module	Interface for controlling car body functions and switching machines	Qualitative
Front wheel module	The front wheel of the car body supports and guides the wheel set of the car body to turn	Qualitative
Rear wheel module	The rear wheel support of the car body guides the wheel set of the car body to rotate and move	Qualitative
Chassis material	Common base for all body objects	Qualitative
Transmission module	Motor gearbox can modify speed by gear ratio	Qualitative
Power module	The system in which the motor assembly drives the gearbox and then drives the rear wheel module	Qualitative
Communication module	Signal transmission through wireless transmission, traffic control system and task assignment	Qualitative
Identification module	Mainly responsible for the function of vehicle body visual recognition and obstacle avoidance	Qualitative

3.1 Panel Module

According to QFD analysis, the user experience optimizes so that the subsequent design of the product is more in line with the actual use situation, and the design makes from the user's point of view. Because the average user uses it for the longest time, this part needs to be evaluated before the design starts with intuitive operation easily is the development direction, giving users the best experience. After comparison, the mechanical button with display effect is better. The simple mechanical button can quickly eliminate the fault in case of failure, the maintenance cost is low, and the welding process can practice. It is a relatively suitable design as a teaching aid. Although the touch screen has a high degree of freedom, the high maintenance threshold cannot improve students' basic abilities. In contrast, the mechanical button with display is the most suitable.

3.2 Front-Wheel Module

Disassemble the AGV left and suitable dual modules and assemble them separately. Although the assembly steps will increase, the rotational torque generation will reduce, and the middle connection part will omit so that the user can effectively use the space and the car body layout can be denser. The module adopts double H-shaped brackets with a locking top plate and 360° wheels, coping with various movement modes. We only need

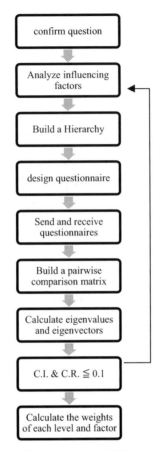

Fig. 2. AHP Process for AGV Body Design

to replace the H-shaped frames of different specifications to lift the body. Evaluating the Mecanum wheel, casters wheel, and universal wheel, all three, can meet the basic needs of teaching aids, and melanic is expensive to equip the most AGV mainstream. Although the price of universal ball wheels is competitive, the structural changes are relatively limited, and it is not easy to adjust the vehicle. Body height, after comparison, 360° casters are the most suitable for educational AGV design.

3.3 Rear-Wheel Module

The aluminum wheel frame covers the super rubber tire skin, which provides grip and more stable support when the load is loaded. The coupling and the body are combined to make the whole more stable.

3.4 Chassis Module

Corresponding holes cut out for all electronic parts, the effective mistake-proof combination is more intuitional, the overall assembly layout is clear, and the distance is reserved in advance to ensure that the wires will not be bent. Fast parts maintenance does not require the dismantling of the whole vehicle. Only the dismantling and troubleshooting of the faulty parts are required. Select the stainless steel, ABS plastic, and carbon fiber as AGV bodies for cost issues. Although the ABS plastic chassis is light in weight, it needs to be produced by mold opening, and the material strength will limit subsequent modifications. If want increases the chassis strength, the thickness will also increase excessively, making the car body configuration very difficult. Although carbon fiber has excellent strength and weight, its impact resistance is not good enough, and the cost is higher than that of stainless steel. Finally, we use a 2mm stainless steel plate as the chassis material.

3.5 Transmission System

In this educational AGV transmission system, the motor is equipped with a gearbox so that the axis of the motor and the motor body is at a right angle of 90°, and the overall configuration is more symmetric than the traditional design. Compared with the horizontal motor, the advantage of the vertical configuration is that the transmission wheels are all placed on the rear wheel, and no belt or chain is required. For power transmission, to prevent power loss and parts wear, and other hidden dangers, the speed can be adjusted according to the needs of the field, need to replace the gear ratio of the gearbox, the left and suitable motors connected by tie rods, and the wheels will not be skewed due to the influence of torque when the load is loaded. Robust body design. For Belt, gear, and motor direct drive to avoid transmission loss, wear adjustment or gear chipping, and other problems, the direct motor drive is the most efficient way without worrying about damage, and the motor is converted with a gearbox to achieve deceleration. The gearbox also can adjust the effect of the machine.

3.6 Power Module

Although we can use Lithium batteries, fuel cells, and alkaline batteries, fuel cells are not suitable for educational AGV because of safety and difficulty. Although alkaline batteries are very convenient to obtain, they have a very high replacement rate and cause recycling and environmental protection problems. Lithium-ion batteries can provide long-term battery life stably. When the power is exhausted, the batteries can quickly replace to continue use, which can meet the needs of one-day courses or exhibitions. Moreover, it can be recharged repeatedly and can last for a long time, so this study selected the lithium battery as the power source.

3.7 Communication Module

Wi-Fi and Bluetooth connection for signal transmission and external remote control with electronic devices, and internal line transmission to cooperate with the communication system and cope with different working environments, the above three methods all can connect AGV operation. Using the Wi-Fi function of the mobile phone or computer to control the AGV when it needs enormous data uploading does not require special equipment to operate with only one transmission line to shorten the connecting time.

3.8 Identification Module

For transport management, this educational AGV uses Infrared, ultrasonic, and IR tracking sensors, of which infrared and ultrasonic for obstacle avoidance. Considering the characteristics of the two systems, they choose to load these two devices at the same time to make up for each other's shortcomings, while the IR tracking sensor is mainly responsible for vehicle body navigation and cooperate with the dispatching system to receive tasks and cooperate with the traffic control system. Integrating three systems of RFID, infrared and visual recognition, It can walk on a line or trackless and make different adjustments according to the site, as shown in Table 4.

Table 4. Design evaluation and program index weights

Evaluation Items	Plan	Relative Weight	Overall Weight	Sort	I.R
Panel module	Keyboard	33.5%	5%	7	0.02
	Touchpad	35.7%	3.3%	16	
	No interface	30.8%	2.7%	20	
Front wheel module	Mecanum wheel	35.2%	4.1%	11	0.01
	Casters wheel	34.6%	4.4%	10	
	Universal wheel	30.2%	3.5%	16	
Rear wheel module	Aluminum combination wheels foam wheels	52.3% 47.7%	4.5% 3.2%	9 17	0
Chassis material	Stainless steel	34.8%	4%	12	0.02
	Plastic	29.5%	2.9%	19	
	Carbon	35.7%	5.1%	6	
Transmission module	Belt	29.6%	5.2%	6	0.01
	Gear	34.5%	6.3%	2	
	Motor direct drive	35.9%	6.5%	1	
Power module	Lithium battery	35.8%	3.8%	14	0.02
	Fuel cell	29.5%	3.1%	18	
	Alkaline battery	34.7%	3.7%	15	
Communication module	WiFi	33.6%	5.6%	4	0
	Bluetooth	34.3%	5.8%	3	
	Transmission line	32.1%	5.4%	5	
Identification module	Infrared	27.3%	3.2%	17	0.01
	Ultrasound	42.1%	4.8%	8	
	IR	30.6%	3.9%	13	

3.9 DFX Verifications with DFA & DFM

This educational AGV design assembly direction is one-way assembly, which can reduce repeatedly turning the components over and avoid various accidental factors such as workpiece collisions or falls. Moreover, use the implanted nails as the assembly positioning to reduce the number of screws, reduce the number of parts, shorten the assembly SOP, and minimize the number of shared screws between the parts. Although the number of screws will increase slightly, it will not remove due to the removal of screws during maintenance and disassembly afterward. If there are too many parts, only the required parts need to be disassembled and assembled, and the use of the unfolded design provides a high degree of freedom for subsequent modifications or expansions. The DFM part is because of the need for effective restrictions. Meanwhile, to facilitate manufacturing and reduce the difficulty of processing and production, all parts use 2D plane design. Because the 3D form design team will have specific requirements for processing equipment if the 2D plane design can use laser cutting, 3D three-dimensional design needs to use three axes for the above processing tools. The advantages of laser cutting are lower processing costs and faster processing speeds. However, laser cutting will produce some burrs and then sandblasting to finish the surface after anodizing. The overall appearance is indecent compared to the finished product of CNC machining tools. Design all screw holes are to be the same size, which reduces the tedious process of processing steps, and there will be no hole positions that do not match.

4   Results and Contributions

This study uses DFX as the front-end design analysis and verifies the AHP questionnaire. Design products from users' perspectives so that the output products are closer to actual needs. In order to provide users with a convenient and straightforward operating experience, integrating the vehicle body into a modular design, users can replace parts according to the use environment. Moreover, in response to Industry 4.0, automation equipment has become an inevitable development direction. However, what is currently lacking is a complete educational system to provide users with correct concepts and experiences. This design can strengthen the link between industry and academia, give students the feeling of applying what they have learned, make up for the technological gap between the industry and academia, promote industrial development and reduce education and training costs. Because the body design is highly simplified, even students with essential abilities can easily understand it. Students can use the processing knowledge to process the car body, which has good variability and stimulates the younger generation's imagination in the process of matching and combining. Formulate the most suitable models for different field environments, and achieve electromechanical integration. One more thought before the design so that more details can notice in the design process, which improves the design foundation and improves the ability of electromechanical integration. Coupled with the competition of AGV crewless trucks, students can arouse their desire to improve through the competition mode. Participating in the competition, whether they win or lose, they can learn from it, and even the industry can see new design methods or discoveries in the competition. The available talent produces a win-win situation.

References

1. Tang, H., et al.: Research on equipment configuration optimization of AGV unmanned warehouse. IEEE Access **9**, 47946–47959 (2021)
2. Zou, W.Q., Pan, Q.K., Tasgetiren, M.F.: An effective iterated greedy algorithm for solving a multi-compartment AGV scheduling problem in a matrix manufacturing workshop. Appl. Soft Comput. **99**, 106945 (2021)
3. Zhong, M., et al.: Multi-AGV scheduling for conflict-free path planning in automated container terminals. Comput. Ind. Eng. **142**, 106371 (2020)
4. Digani, V., et al.: Ensemble coordination approach in multi-AGV systems applied to industrial warehouses. IEEE Trans. Autom. Sci. Eng. **12**(3), 922–934 (2015)
5. Tang, G., Tang, C., Claramunt, C., Hu, X., Zhou, P.: Geometric a-star algorithm: an improved a-star algorithm for AGV path planning in a port environment. IEEE Access **9**, 59196–59210 (2021)
6. Theunissen, J., Xu, H., Zhong, R.Y., Xu, X.: Smart AGV system for manufacturing shopfloor in the context of industry 4.0. In: 2018 25th International Conference on Mechatronics and Machine Vision in Practice (M2VIP) IEEE, pp. 1–6 (2018)
7. Lynch, L., Newe, T., Clifford, J., Coleman, J., Walsh, J., Toal, D.: Automated Ground Vehicle (AGV) and sensor technologies-a review. In: 2018 12th International Conference on Sensing Technology (ICST) IEEE, pp. 347–352 (2018)
8. Barros, L.: Modelling modular design processes for automated production facilities. Int. J. Logist. **6**(1–2), 63–81 (2003)
9. Lin, H.-H., Cheng, J.-H.: USR combined with PBL, fuzzy analytical hierarchy process special-oriented curriculum research. In: Education and Awareness of Sustainability: Proceedings of the 3rd Eurasian Conference on Educational Innovation 2020 (ECEI 2020). (2020)
10. Li, Y., et al.: An integrated method of rough set, Kano's model and AHP for rating customer requirements' final importance. Expert Syst. Appl. **36**(3), 7045–7053 (2009)
11. Rehman, S.T., et al.: Supply chain performance measurement and improvement system: a MCDA-DMAIC methodology. J. Model. Manage. (2018)
12. Mishra, P., Sharma, R.K.: A hybrid framework based on SIPOC and Six Sigma DMAIC for improving process dimensions in supply chain network. International J. Quality Reliab. Manage. (2014)
13. Holt, R., Barnes, C.: Towards an integrated approach to "Design for X": an agenda for decision-based DFX research. Res. Eng. Design **21**(2), 123–136 (2010)
14. Benabdellah, A.C., Bouhaddou, I., Benghabrit, A., Benghabrit, O.: A systematic review of design for X techniques from 1980 to 2018: concepts, applications, and perspectives. Int. J. Adv. Manuf. Technol. **102**(9–12), 3473–3502 (2019)

Research on Auditory Performance of Vehicle Voice Interaction in Different Sound Index

Wenhao Hu[✉], Xiang Li, and Zehua Li

Nanjing University of Science and Technology, Nanjing 210094, China
1748733630@qq.com

Abstract. In recent years, voice interaction has gradually become a hot topic in the field of artificial intelligence. Due to the portability and stability of voice, voice interaction is gradually applied to various human-computer interaction scenes in recent years. As one of the connected core hardware, the construction of voice interaction platform in the automotive field has also entered a white hot stage. The vehicle interaction scene is gradually becoming the scene where users are most used to using voice interaction. In order to determine which voice environment causes the least driving command cognitive errors and propose the optimization design strategy of vehicle voice environment. This study conducted repeated experiments on the set independent variables, analyzed the experimental data, studied the correlation between the independent variables and the error rate, and reached a reliable conclusion.

Keywords: Voice interaction · Car compass · Job performance · Auditory performance

1 Introduction

In the design process of on-board voice environment, the safety and stability of the interaction process should be focused. In this process, the driver transmits instructions to the intelligent hardware through voice signals, and the intelligent hardware transmits information to the driver through voice interaction. In this process, The legibility of voice information will directly affect the driver's work performance and even driving safety. This paper aims to evaluate the driver's performance in different voice environments through repeated experiments, and finally analyze the experimental data to obtain the design strategy of vehicle voice environment.

2 Literature Review

2.1 Research Background

In the design process of on-board voice environment, the safety and stability of the interaction process should be focused. In this process, the driver transmits instructions to the intelligent hardware through voice signals, and the intelligent hardware transmits

© The Author(s), under exclusive license to Springer Nature Switzerland AG 2022
M. Kurosu (Ed.): HCII 2022, LNCS 13304, pp. 61–69, 2022.
https://doi.org/10.1007/978-3-031-05412-9_5

information to the driver through voice interaction [1]. In this process, The legibility of voice information will directly affect the driver's work performance and even driving safety. This paper aims to evaluate the driver's performance in different voice environments through repeated experiments, and finally analyze the experimental data to obtain the design strategy of vehicle voice environment.

2.2 The Process of Voice Interaction

Voice interaction process the product features or interaction processes of intelligent voice products may be different, but the voice interaction process between people and intelligent hardware is roughly as follows. Firstly, the intelligent hardware product converts the user's voice instructions into words, and then the device starts to understand and define these words. Then, if the user wants to complete the dialogue, the man-machine dialogue mode will be started. Finally, the interaction results will be returned to the user in the form of voice signal output [2].

2.3 The Status of Relevant Research

Auditory cognitive errors are usually caused by users' own memory cognitive errors or hearing impairment, as well as defects or faults in given working conditions. Under the market background of increasingly mature voice interaction technology, some scholars have studied the voice interaction interface of intelligent devices. Liao Qingyun et al. Concluded that the anthropomorphism degree of intelligent voice assistant is directly proportional to user experience through emotional experimental research, subjective questionnaire survey, data analysis and other experimental methods [3]. Zhou Wenxiang studied the characteristics of interpersonal communication and put forward the strategies of emotional intelligent voice interaction design: one is to detect the user's psychological state, such as anxiety and depression, and the other is to make different feedback for unused situations to provide users with appropriate content services to meet the user's personalized needs, so as to optimize the user experience [4].

In addition, some scholars have conducted in-depth research on voice interaction feedback time. Li Yue et al. Evaluated the speed related information in the process of voice interaction through experiments, and concluded that reasonable control of voice interaction feedback time can guide the change of users' emotion and experience in the process of human-computer interaction, Therefore, it is proposed to add the speech speed real-time monitoring function module into the interaction process between intelligent devices and users, so as to facilitate users' understanding and experience [5].

3   Methodology

3.1   Design

The task of this experiment focuses on the driver's auditory performance in the vehicle voice environment, so it should consider eliminating the potential impact of external background sound. Since the initial focus is on auditory performance, a method that only simulates auditory performance tasks is designed, which is to make corresponding operations through eliminating operations and cognitive tasks, such as receiving driving instructions, Participants were only asked to repeat the voice commands they heard while performing an operation task.

3.2 Participant

In the previous literature research, there was no theoretical basis for the difference of auditory performance caused by gender differences. Therefore, this experiment did not take gender as the reference factor for the selection of subjects, and the gender ratio of subjects was 1:1. In order to avoid the possible influence of the subjects' driving experience on the final experimental results, the subjects in this experiment are limited to the veterans who have obtained the driving license and have passed the internship. In the North District of Nanjing University of technology, the subjects were found through on-the-spot invitation and inquiry. A total of 20 volunteers participated, with certain economic compensation.

Due to the differences in the hearing level of randomly selected subjects, in order to avoid interference with the experimental results, the subjects need to have a hearing test before the experiment. The test tool is Mimi hearing test software in the app store. After wearing a Bluetooth headset, the tester gives operation feedback according to the text instructions in the app, and the test results are displayed in the form of medical report, The specific test process is shown in the figure below (Fig. 1). Finally, the hearing level of the subjects is graded. The subjects with binaural hearing levels of 90%–100% are set as ha3 level, 80%–90% are set as HA2 level, and 70%–80% are set as HA1 level. The relevant personnel whose listening level is less than 70% will not participate in the experiment and will be given some economic compensation.

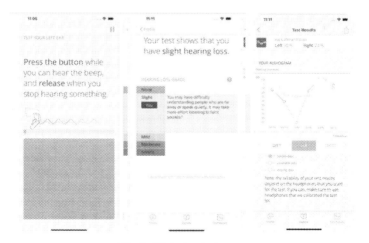

Fig. 1. Listening test process

As the human hearing level tends to decline with the increase of age, considering the possible impact of age on the experimental results, the participants in this experiment are students of Nanjing University of technology, aged between 20 and 30, and there are no participants in other age ranges.

4 Materials

Background Sound and Normal Sound. In recent years, the voice instruction mainly adopts the form of artificial synthetic voice, and mainly adopts TTS Technology (text to speech conversion technology), which outputs the spoken text in the computer into standard and high-quality voice. In the process of testing the legibility of voice, we found that the voice volume (DB) has a relevant impact on the user's understanding. Too high or too low voice volume will cause discomfort or difficulty in understanding [6]. The sound open source data in the vehicle environment shows that the volume range of the vehicle voice environment is between 45 db-100 db. In addition, due to the interference of different sounds, the background sound in the on-board environment is related to the driver's understanding efficiency of speech [7]. During driving, the volume of background sound in getting off at different speeds is different. The research data shows that the background diagram in getting off at different speeds is shown in the figure below (see Fig. 2–1), In the experiment, the wind sound or motor vehicle motor vibration sound is simulated by voice simulation software. Because the energy of sound wave will decay with the propagation distance, the experimental distance should be controlled at the specified value. In this study, a head holder is used to ensure that the experimental distance remains unchanged. During the experiment, a portable decibel meter shall be used to monitor and measure the volume.

Speech Rate. Some scholars have conducted in-depth research on voice interaction feedback time. Li Yue et al. Evaluated the speed related information in the process of voice interaction through experiments, and concluded that reasonable control of voice interaction feedback time can guide users to change their work efficiency and experience in the process of human-computer interaction. In order to continue to further explore the impact of voice speed on drivers' work efficiency, This study uses Windows media player to play MP3 audio with the same text content at different speeds. In order to ensure that the text content is related to the driving environment, this study creates a format by imitating the text content of vehicle voice navigation content, and then changes and replaces its key information, such as "please turn to (XX) direction after (XX) meters to reach (XX) location", The key information is replaced by random numbers or places to avoid the participants' memory of the text content in the later stage. There are three possibilities for each key information, and there are 27 different content texts.

We input the predetermined text content and export MP3 audio on iFLYTEK's online speech synthesis website. Throughout the experiment, the default speech speed is set to two bytes per second (normal). In addition to the normal level, the speech speed in this experiment is also divided into slow (0.5x default speech speed - 1.0x default speech speed), slightly fast (1.0x default speech speed - 1.5x default speech speed) and extremely fast (1.5x default speed - 2.0 default speed) In order to avoid the influence of fatigue factors on the experimental data, the experiment was conducted by two subjects in the same voice environment at the same time. The auditory performance of the subjects did not change during the experiment, and the duration of the experiment was 10 min. In the experiment, the degree of sleepiness of the subjects in different voice environments was evaluated by Epworth Sleepiness Scale Points to monitor the possible effects of fatigue.

4.1 Procedures

Before starting the experiment, the researchers gave a brief explanation of the procedure and collected signed informed consent. After that, a hearing test was conducted to determine the participants' hearing ability. The experiment starts with a "virtual" test, which allows participants to get used to the experiment []. After the virtual test, the voice environment is changed and the real test begins.

The whole experiment took 30 min for each subject, including subjective questionnaire evaluation. During the experiment, the subjects operate the driving simulation game "off road 4 * 4 car driving mountain" on the iPad in silent mode, and broadcast the voice text content at random. After playing a single voice text content, the subjects are required to repeat the voice content orally, record its accuracy and score manually. There are 8 experimental voice texts to be tested in one experiment, After each experiment, change a single independent variable and repeat the experiment again. The experiment needs to be repeated 15 times. During the interval of the experiment, the subjects are required to fill in a questionnaire to ask about their satisfaction with the current speech conditions and sleepiness.

In the whole experiment, the independent variables are voice volume, speech rate and listening level. The experiment is divided into three parts. The first part is set for voice volume, the second part is set for speech rate and the third part is set for listening level.

Participants were asked to complete two questionnaires. The first questionnaire was set according to the Karolinska sleep scale KSS to determine the degree of sleepiness and fatigue of the subjects. The second questionnaire was aimed at the users' subjective feelings about different experimental voice environments. The contents of the questionnaire are shown in the table below (see Table 1).

Table 1. Questionnaire

Number	Question
1	How do you feel about the whole experimental environment?
2	Do you think the voice quality of this experiment is clear?
3	Is it difficult for you to understand the voice content of this experiment?
4	What situations can lead to distraction in this experiment?
5	Which phonetic conditions do you think are most convenient for memory and understanding?

In the experimental methods of evaluating performance, most of them take the accuracy and reaction time as the main reference. In this experiment, because the reaction time is very short (less than 3S) and different subjects have different reaction speeds, this experiment only takes the accuracy as the measurement of auditory performance.

In order to determine the error rate and type of subjects, the staff need to compare the records in real time in the control table designed in advance. This control table contains the sequence of key information that the subjects need to repeat. When the participants repeat the key information they hear, the staff will compare the correct number of key information at the same time. When the subjects have cognitive errors, the staff will mark it as a number between 1 and 5, indicating the type of error. Numbers 1 to 5 refer to the following:

- Participants skip a key message.
- Participants repeat incorrect information.
- Participants exchange two duplicate key information.
- Participants cannot repeat any text content.
- Any combination of the above contents.

4.2 Experimental Data Analysis

All data is recorded in Microsoft Excel 2016. The data is organized in such a way that the letters of all labels of each participant are read incorrectly plus the error type are recorded. The data from the survey are recorded in the same file. The statistical analysis is completed by using the software program IBM SPSS.

The relevant independent variables of this experiment are nine speech volume conditions, four levels of speech speed and three listening levels. The expected statistical analysis is mixed analysis of variance. However, due to the non normality and the randomness of sample size, the final experimental data adopts one-way repeated measurement analysis of variance.

The analysis of experimental data is used to verify the following assumptions:

- H1: The volume condition has no effect on the error rate.
- H2: The volume condition has an effect on the error rate.
- H3: The speed condition has no effect on the error rate.
- H4: the speed condition has an effect on the error rate.
- H5: listening level has no effect on error rate.
- H6: listening level has an impact on the error rate.

According to the previous research, the voice volume conditions in this test are divided into 9 types: background sound 40 dB, indication sound 60 dB; The background tone is 40 dB and the indication tone is 70 dB; The background tone is 40 dB and the indication tone is 80 dB; Background sound 50 dB, indication sound 70 dB; Background sound 50 dB, indication sound 80 dB; Background sound 60 dB, indication sound 90 dB; Background tone, indication tone 100 dB. In this round of experiment, the hearing level of the subjects was controlled at ha3, and the speaking speed condition was controlled to two bytes per second. The results of single factor repeated measurement variance showed that different voice volume conditions had a significant impact on the error rate of participants ($P = 0.0236 < 0.05$).volume (60 db−80 db) is negatively correlated with the error rate; when the background volume is at 50 dB, the average error rate (6.73%) is higher than 40 dB, and the indicated volume (70 db−80 db) is negatively correlated with the error rate, but The indicated volume (80 db−90 db) is positively correlated with the error rate; when the background tone is 60 dB, the average error rate is 8.0%, and the indicated volume (80 db−100 db) is positively correlated with the error rate.

In this round of experiment, participants' auditory ability level is all at ha3 (greater than 90%), and they adopt 0.5x default speed, 0.75x default speed, 1.0x default speed, 1.25x default speed, 1.5x default speed, 1.75x default speed and 2.0x default speed. The results of single factor repeated measurement variance show that different speed conditions have a significant impact on participants' error rate results (P = 0.0128 < 0.05).

The mean error rate of subjects under different speech speed conditions is shown in the table below (see Fig. 2). In a single experiment, the speech speed conditions are positively correlated with the error rate of subjects. In nine rounds of experiments, the speech speed conditions are positively correlated with the error rate of subjects. The difference between the mean error rate of 1.5x-2.0x and the mean error rate of 1.0x-1.5x is more significant than that of 1.0x-1.5x and 0.5x-1.0x.

4.3 Experiment Results

This study focuses on the impact of vehicle voice conditions on drivers' auditory performance. In this study, the auditory error rate related to voice volume, voice speed and auditee's auditory perception under controlled conditions is discussed.

At the level of voice volume, the results of this study confirm the hypothesis: voice volume conditions have an impact on the performance of subjects' listening awareness. At the level of environmental volume, the higher the environmental volume, the higher the subjects' error rate. When the environmental volume is at 40 dB (human voice environment), the subjects' interference degree is the lowest; At the level of voice volume, when the difference between voice volume and ambient volume is 40 dB, the subjects' auditory error rate is the lowest and the subjects' subjective feeling is the most comfortable. At the same time, when the voice volume exceeds 80 dB, the subjects' auditory error rate will increase and their satisfaction will decrease.

At the level of sound speed, the results of this study confirm the hypothesis (see Fig. 3): sound speed conditions have an impact on the performance of subjects' auditory awareness. When the speed is two bytes per second, the subjects' auditory error rate is the lowest. After slowing down the speed, the subjects' auditory error rate does not change significantly, but the subjects' satisfaction with the voice environment decreases. After accelerating the default speed, The error rate of auditees' perception increases, and the difficulty of users' understanding also increases.

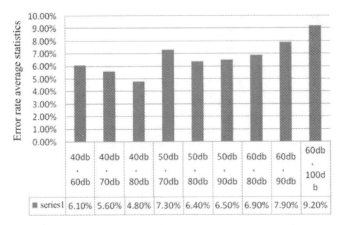

Fig. 2. Comparison chart of Error rate experiment data

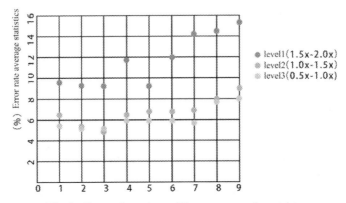

Fig. 3. Comparison chart of Error rate experiment data

At the level of auditory ability, the results of this study(see Fig. 4) confirm the hypothesis that subjects' auditory ability has an impact on their auditory performance. The stronger their auditory ability, the lower their error rate.

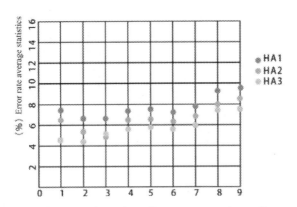

Fig. 4. Comparison chart of Error rate experiment data

5   Conclusion

This study focuses on the impact of vehicle voice conditions on drivers' auditory performance. In this study, the auditory error rate related to voice volume, voice speed and auditee's auditory perception under controlled conditions is discussed.

At the level of voice volume, the results of this study confirm the hypothesis: voice volume conditions have an impact on the performance of subjects' listening awareness. At the level of environmental volume, the higher the environmental volume, the higher the subjects' error rate. When the environmental volume is at 40 dB (human voice environment), the subjects' interference degree is the lowest; At the level of voice volume, when the difference between voice volume and ambient volume is 40 dB, the subjects' auditory error rate is the lowest and the subjects' subjective feeling is the most comfortable. At the same time, when the voice volume exceeds 80 dB, the subjects' auditory error rate will increase and their satisfaction will decrease.

At the level of sound speed, the results of this study confirm the hypothesis: sound speed conditions have an impact on the performance of subjects' auditory awareness. When the speed is two bytes per second, the subjects' auditory error rate is the lowest. After slowing down the speed, the subjects' auditory error rate does not change significantly, but the subjects' satisfaction with the voice environment decreases. After accelerating the default speed, The error rate of auditees' perception increases, and the difficulty of users' understanding also increases.

At the level of auditory ability, the results of this study confirm the hypothesis that subjects' auditory ability has an impact on their auditory performance. The stronger their auditory ability, the lower their error rate.

References

1. Jin-Hua, D.O.U., Ruo-Xuan, Q.I.: Elderly-adaptability voice user interface design strategy of smart home products based on context analysis. Packaging Eng. **42**(16), 202–210 (2021). https://doi.org/10.19554/j.cnki.1001-3563.2021.16.028. (in Chinese)
2. Guzman, A.L.: Voices in and of the machine: source orientation toward mobile virtual assistants. Comput. Human Behav. (2018)
3. Lee, B., Kwon, O., Lee, I., Kim, J.: Companionship with smart home devices: the impact of social connectedness and interaction types on perceived social support and companionship in smart homes. Comput. Human Behav. **75**, 922–934 (2017)
4. Qin-Lin, L., Mei, W., Zhan, F.: Voice interaction design of smart home products based on emotional interaction. Packaging Eng. **40**(16), 37–42 (2019) https://doi.org/10.19554/j.cnki.1001-3563.2019.16.006 (in Chinese)
5. Yue, L.I., Jun-fen, W.A.N.G., Wen-Jun, W.A.N.G.: Optimization of VUI feedback mechanism based on the time perception. Art & Design **07**, 100–103 (2019). https://doi.org/10.16272/j.cnki.cn11-1392/j.2019.07.023(inChinese)
6. Stein, J.-P., Ohler, P.: Venturing into the uncanny valley of mind—the influence of mind attribution on the acceptance of human-like characters in a virtual reality setting. Cognition **160**, 43–50 (2017)
7. Niculescu, A., Dijk, B., Nijholt, A., Li, H., See, S.L.: Making social robots more attractive: the effects of voice pitch, humor and empathy. Int. J. Social Robot. **5**(2), 171–191 (2013)

Study on Experience Design of Elderly Online Learning Interface Based on Cognitive Load

Tianyu Huang and Jiaqi Zhang[✉]

College of Design Art and Media, Nanjing University of Science and Technology,
Nanjing 210094, China
2522043912@qq.com

Abstract. This paper analyzes and summarizes the evaluation indicators that affect the online learning of elderly users, effectively alleviates the cognitive load of the elderly group with a medium or above education degree in online learning, and improves their user experience. The subjective and objective methods were combined. First, eye movement experiments were carried out on the three kinds of layout of geriatric learning interface and three kinds of fonts at different levels by eye movement tracking technology. Then, the cognitive load and user experience were scored respectively by using Pass subjective scale and Likert five-point scale. The realization of online learning for the elderly is an important part of future learning, which is conducive to the "active retirement" model. In the design of relevant interfaces, it is suggested to simplify the layout, highlight the main content, retain the navigation function, and increase the font size, so as to effectively reduce the cognitive load of elderly users during online learning and improve their experience.

Keywords: Elderly online learning interface · Cognitive load · Experience design · Eye movement experiment

1 Introduction

With the rapid development of science and technology and the advent of 5G era, the concept of "Internet+" has penetrated into all aspects of People's Daily life and learning. Especially in recent years, all kinds of intelligent electronic products have been updated and iterated rapidly, and people are faced with more diversified choices to improve their life quality.

However, for most elderly people, "Internet+" is still a brand new field that has not yet been involved, and they are experiencing a process of cognitive aging with the growth of age [1], which is mainly manifested in changes in memory, attention, spatial perception and reaction time. The objective physical limitations will inevitably affect their experience when they interact with the product, although a small percentage of the elderly can skillfully use WeChat chat with relatives and friends, but they are generally of similar online banking registration such as difficult to master operation is not good, makes the elderly user groups is not easy to enjoy the developed mobile Internet brings convenience [2]. At present, the elderly population in China continues to increase, and the fertility rate continues to decline, which lead to the shortage of labor population, forming a huge social pension pressure. In the face of this problem, it is of great social significance to guide new media and other advanced technologies to provide services for the elderly, to make the aging society develop in a positive direction, and to make the elderly enjoy the convenience brought by the development of science and technology and the Internet.

This paper mainly discusses the influence of cognitive load on the experience of using online learning websites for the elderly. Cognitive load theory is based on studies on attention and working memory. Relevant studies have shown that when using the same interface, the elderly are more prone to cognitive overload than the young, and their average operating performance is lower than that of the young [3]. In addition, this paper conducts user market segmentation for the existing elderly group, focusing on the elderly group with a medium or above education level, thinking about how to improve their Internet life and learning mode, and believes that focusing on the study of related aspects of the elderly online learning interface is an effective method. Compared with traditional classroom learning, online education for the elderly, as a teaching form that follows the trend of The Times, has many characteristics, such as flexibility, complementarity and autonomy [4]. These characteristics will increase the cognitive load of user groups to a certain extent, and have a certain negative impact on the learning effect of users. Therefore, the research focus of this paper is to analyze the relevant evaluation indicators of the elderly learning interface, so as to effectively relieve the cognitive load of the elderly group with a medium degree or above in online learning and improve their use experience.

2 Determine Evaluation Indicators

2.1 Determine the Evaluation Index of Cognitive Load

Theories related to cognitive load are further studied on the basis of studies on psychological load or mental load. Cognitive load refers to the total amount of psychological cognitive resources occupied by people in the process of processing external or internal information in the body [5].

The relationship between cognitive load and user experience is complicated. If cognitive load is too high or too low, user experience will decrease correspondingly. When cognitive load is overloaded, users tend to give up tasks. When the cognitive load is too low, attention will be distracted, which increases the error rate of completing relevant tasks. Compared with traditional learning mode, the amount of information that learners need to receive and process in online learning increases exponentially, and the information structure is more complex, which may lead to excessive cognitive load of users in the process of online learning, thus affecting the learning efficiency. It has even become the main reason why many students cannot complete online learning without supervision [6]. The cognitive load problems encountered by the elderly in online learning are more obvious.

The reason is that visual effort is one of the reasons for cognitive load. In the context of online learning of elderly groups, interface layout, text size, color scheme, pattern background, online help, etc., all determine the degree of visual effort to a certain extent. In this paper, the interface layout and font size were selected as the factors of the study, and eye movement experiments were carried out. Eye movement indicators related to cognitive load, such as fixation times and fixation duration, were taken as important bases to evaluate cognitive load. The effects of interface layout and font size on cognitive load were studied respectively.

2.2 Determine User Experience Evaluation Indicators

User experience studies interaction from the perspectives of product structure, functional performance, quality, emotion and experience. Generally speaking, it refers to the feeling of using a product and the design made to improve the experience of users when using a product or enjoying a service. In today's era of increasingly strong emotional needs of users, the concept of user experience has attracted the attention of researchers in many fields since it was proposed, and has been introduced into many different fields, continuously expanding, enriching and applying [7].

At present, relevant researches on user experience mainly involve two parts. One is system, which mainly includes system availability, ease of use, function and purpose. On the other hand, people's needs, emotions, motivations and tendencies are involved. After preparing the literature research, found that most of the literature selection according to the specific research questions to determine their own study required by the relevant factors of user experience, such as Morville and Rosenfield [8] the user experience is divided into seven aspects, respectively is: availability, usefulness, ease of use, reliability, easy to find, purpose, value, etc. Broadly speaking, any design can be evaluated from the dimension of user experience. Combined with the interface object studied in this paper, the subjective index of comfort and the objective index of task completion time are selected to measure the experience of elderly users.

Likert five-point scale was used to measure comfort, and task completion time was measured by setting relevant search terms and recording the time when users found the target search terms.

3   Eye Movement Experiment of Interface Layout

3.1 Experimental Design

Based on the population orientation of this project, 20 elderly subjects aged 60–80 with medium or above knowledge level were selected, including 10 males and 10 females, mainly family members of residents in Nanjing University of Science and Technology community, as shown in Table 1. All of them have used online learning sites or attended senior university. Tobii eye tracker was used in the experiment.

In terms of experimental materials, due to the large number of elderly learning websites at present, ten typical learning websites are selected from them through comprehensive comparison and screening. They are: ① Jilin Province distance education learning network for the elderly; ② Shandong University for the Elderly distance education network; ③ Jiaxing Education and Learning Network for the Elderly; ④ Fujian Elderly

Table 1. Composition of subjects

The participants	Gender	Age	Education background	Former professional
The participant 01	Male	67	Junior high school	Office clerk
The participant 02	Female	75	Senior high school	Teacher
The participant 03	Male	76	Junior high school	Office clerk
The participant 04	Female	65	Primary school	Freelance work
The participant 05	Female	78	Primary school	/
The participant 06	Male	67	Senior high school	Doctor
The participant 07	Male	69	Junior high school	Office clerk
The participant 08	Male	71	Senior high school	Office clerk
The participant 09	Female	72	Junior high school	Nurse
The participant 10	Female	68	Junior high school	Office clerk
The participant 11	Male	68	Junior high school	Accountant
The participant 12	Male	75	Senior high school	Teacher
The participant 13	Male	63	Primary school	Freelance work
The participant 14	Female	74	Junior high school	Office clerk
The participant 15	Female	64	Senior high school	Doctor
The participant 16	Male	69	Junior high school	Office clerk
The participant 17	Female	65	Primary school	/
The participant 18	Female	71	Junior high school	Nurse
The participant 19	Male	72	Senior high school	Civil servant
The participant 20	Female	66	Junior high school	Accountant

learning Network; (5) Distance Education network of Hubei University for the Aged; ⑥ Guangdong University for the Elderly; ⑦ Taiyuan Open College for the Elderly; ⑧ Xiyanghong Elderly learning network; ⑨ Wenzhou Education network for the Elderly; ⑩ Tianjin Distance Learning network for the elderly.

In this experiment, a single control variable was used to keep the text size, color scheme, pattern background, online help and other related factors unchanged. Only the layout of the above ten elderly learning web pages was summarized, and the three most commonly used layout forms were the independent variables of this experiment. They are: the same font layout; Corner layout; Modular layout. The same font layout has an AD banner at the top, a main content area in the middle of the page, navigation areas on both sides, and information about the site at the bottom. The same font layout is common in some of the most informative sites. A corner layout is a page with a logo and banner at the top of the header, a content body at the bottom of the header, navigation on the left of the body, and specific content on the right. This type of layout is similar to the structure of the same font layout, but simplified in form, omitting the navigation part on the right. Modular layout page structure is simple, but its information content is very rich, compared with the traditional interface layout may bring new visual experience to the user group. Figure 1, 2 and 3 shows the experimental samples of the above three layouts.

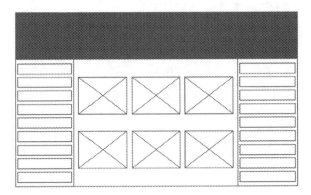

Fig. 1. The same font layout

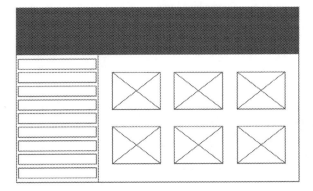

Fig. 2. Corner layout

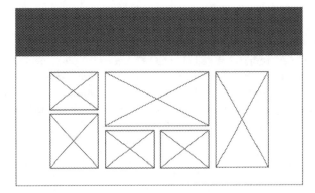

Fig. 3. Modular layout

3.2 Experimental Process

Before the experiment, the tester should explain the specific experimental requirements to the subjects and clarify the experimental tasks. The subjects entered the laboratory one by one to ensure that each subject saw the experimental sample for the first time and did not learn relevant experimental information in advance, so as to improve the experimental accuracy. The specific experimental process is as follows:

(1) The tester explains the testing process to the subjects and starts the experiment when the subjects correctly understand the tasks needed to be completed;
(2) The subject sat on a chair in front of the monitor with a distance of about 60cm from the screen for eye movement calibration;
(3) The picture of "experiment start" is displayed at first, lasting for 2s to provide a buffer for the subjects to adapt to the experiment;
(4) Play three experimental samples in turn. Each image is browsed for 5 s, and the interval between the image and the next image is 2 s. During this process, the instrument will record relevant experimental data such as fixation times and fixation time by itself (Fig. 4).

Fig. 4. Test scenario of the participant 01

3.3 Analysis of Experimental Results

After the completion of the experiment, the number of valid samples was 17, excluding a few extreme data caused by eye diseases or errors.

Hotspot Map Analysis
A hotspot map means an individual's focus on the area of interest and can provide more intuitive visualization results than data. Different color depths reflect the attention degree

of the subjects. The red area represents the area with the hottest fixation, that is, the area with the longest fixation time, followed by yellow, green and blue. No color represents the area without fixation. From the hot spots of the three interface layouts (as shown in Fig. 5), it can be seen that the subjects' eyes mainly focused on the main part of each

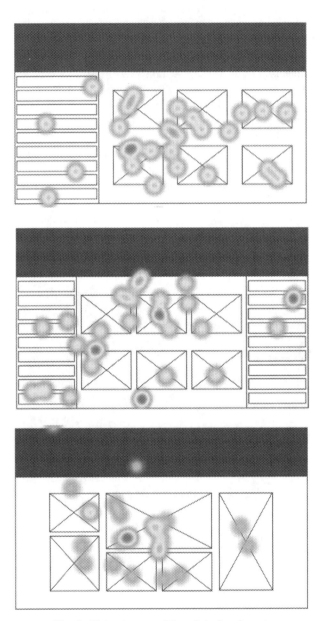

Fig. 5. Hotspot maps of three interface layouts

interface layout, while they paid less attention to the side navigation part of the same-font layout and corner layout. This suggests that we should highlight the main content as much as possible and simplify the interface to some extent when designing the elderly learning interface.

Fixation Sequence Analysis

As can be seen from the sequence diagrams of fixation points of the corner layout and the modular layout in Fig. 6, the eye track of the subjects was relatively clear when they looked at the corner layout, showing a general trend of first left then right, first up then down. However, the sequence of fixation points in modular layout was more chaotic, and the subjects' sight was not guided. This shows that the navigation bar on the left of the corner layout interface can play a guiding role, and the simplification of the navigation bar should be carefully considered when designing the interface.

In addition, found that within a certain range of the module area, the greater the appeal of participants, the greater the type in the module interface layout, the line of sight of subjects back after scanning the global module with the largest area, older subjects more attention to this part, the enlightenment we can in the interface design appropriately

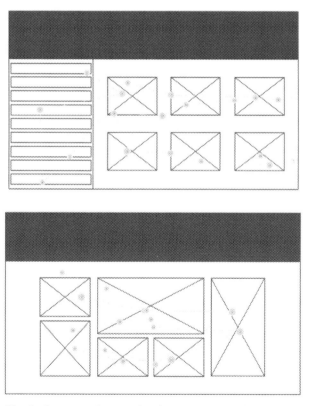

Fig. 6. Sequence of gaze points for corner and modular layouts

increase the area of the existing module, It can attract the attention of middle-aged and elderly users to a certain extent, thus reducing their cognitive load.

4   Eye Movement Experiment of Font Size

4.1   Experimental Design

Experiment subjects and equipment same as above.

In terms of experimental materials, according to the research conclusion of Zhou Aibao et al. [9], the adoption of different common fonts will not have a significant impact on the cognition of Chinese characters. Therefore, the Microsoft Yahei font was used in the experimental sample. According to the relevant research results and the font size statistics of the existing online learning interface for the elderly, three levels of font size: 12 pixels, 14 pixels and 16 pixels were used as independent variables. The same old course name text content (freehand flower and bird painting professional course; Calligraphy courses; Specialized courses of traditional nutrition; Taiji soft ball professional courses; Taijiquan, fan professional courses; Dietary nutrition professional course) is placed in the main area of the three different interface layouts of the above experiment with three font sizes. Figure 7, 8 and 9 shows an experimental sample.

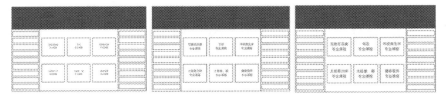

Fig. 7. Interface of three font sizes of the same font

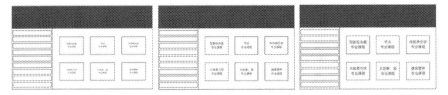

Fig. 8. Interface of three font sizes of corner type

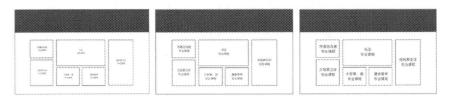

Fig. 9. Interface of three font sizes of modular type

4.2   Experimental Design

(1) The tester explains the testing process to the subjects and starts the experiment when the subjects correctly understand the tasks needed to be completed;

(2) The subject sat on a chair in front of the monitor with a distance of about 60cm from the screen for eye movement calibration;

(3) The picture of "experiment start" is displayed at first, lasting for 2s to provide a buffer for the subjects to adapt to the experiment;

(4) The tester spoke the target search words and required the subjects to search for the target words in the experimental sample interface. After completing the search task, the tester was informed that the time of task completion was recorded by the eye tracker, and press the space bar to switch to the next interface and complete the search task of the target words in the 9 interfaces successively (Fig. 10).

Fig. 10. Test scenario of the participant 02

4.3   Analysis of Experimental Results

Task Search Time Analysis

Based on the analysis of the above interface layout, the AOI area was set in the main content area of the interface to analyze and compare the effects of three different levels of font size on users' cognitive load and user experience under the same font layout, corner layout and modular layout (See Fig. 11).

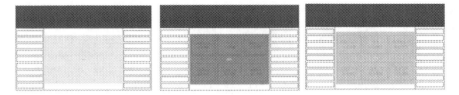

Fig. 11. The Same font layout with three sizes of AOI area R1R2R3

Table 2. Average task search time of the three layouts

Task search time (s)	16 pixels	14 pixels	12 pixels
The same font layout	9.78	16.06	20.64
Corner layout	8.56	15.37	19.96
Modular layout	7.89	15.23	19.98

By Table 2 shows, when the other factors unchanged, only size changes, also will try to be the search task caused great influence, when text is 16 pixels, the participants search target vocabulary spent an average time of 9.78 s, when text is 14 pixels, the participants search target vocabulary spent an average time of 16.06 s, It was about 61% slower than text at 16 pixels, and when text was set to 12 pixels, the task took 20.64 s, or 2.2 times as long as text at 16 pixels. This indicates that the size used in many online learning interfaces for the elderly is not enough to meet the visual characteristics of the elderly, and the size can be appropriately increased without losing the aesthetic.

As can be seen from Table 2, when using the corner and module interface layouts, the time to complete the target word search task is reduced under the three different horizontal fonts compared with the same font layout, and the reduction is more obvious when the font size is larger. For the same 16-pixel text, the average time to complete the task for the corner layout was 8.56 s, about 12% faster than that for the same font layout. The average time for the modular layout was 7.89 s, about 19% faster than the average time for the same type of layout, but it was notable that the modular layout was only about 7% faster than the average time for the corner layout. This indicates that when the interface is simplified to a certain extent, the impact on the cognitive load of the user is somewhat reduced. Therefore, we do not need to be extremely simple when designing the interface, because too simple interface may increase the cognitive load of the user. Should consider the function, beauty and other factors in the realization of the scope of simplification can achieve better results.

Two-Factor Variance Analysis of Eye Movement Data
This paper mainly studied the effects of layout and font size on cognitive load and user experience of elderly users. The intra-group factor was font size, and the inter-group factor was layout. Based on previous experience, the variance of fixation times and fixation time ratio of different horizontal fonts in the same font layout group, corner layout group and modular layout group was compared. Table 3 shows the mean value

of eye movement data of subjects. The experimental data were processed and analyzed by SPSS software.

Table 3. Mean value of eye movement data

AOI	The same font layout	Corner layout	Modular layout
Fixation count			
R_1(12 pixels)	37.721	36.227	35.208
R_2(14 pixels)	23.398	21.293	19.431
R_3(16 pixels)	14.504	12.323	12.309
Ratio of fixation time to total time/%			
R_1(12 pixels)	82.140	67.632	75.744
R_2(14 pixels)	6.689	11.060	7.329
R_3(16 pixels)	6.556	9.003	10.754

Table 4 for eye movement experiment of two-factor variance analysis results, which is analyzed according to the variance of fixation times: the layout shows a significant relationship ($F = 281.650$, $P = 0 < 0.05$), indicating that the layout has a different relationship to fixation times, which is mainly reflected in that the fixation times of the same font layout are higher than the fixation times of the other two layouts. The size is significant, $F = 17464.974$, $P = 0 < 0.05$, indicating that the size also has a different relationship with fixation times. The main effect of the interaction between font size and layout was significant ($F = 10.491$, $P = 0 < 0.05$), which was mainly reflected in the higher fixation times for the R1 interest area of the same-font layout with font size of 12 pixels.

Analysis was made based on the variance of the ratio of fixation time to total time: the font size showed significant, $F = 78548.785$, $P = 0 < 0.05$, which was mainly reflected in that the subjects fixated on the 12-pixel text with the same font layout for a longer time, and the ratio of fixation time to total time was much higher than that of the 14-pixel and 16-pixel text. At the same time, the main effect of layout is also significant, $F = 97.538$, $P = 0 < 0.05$, indicating that layout has a different relationship with the ratio of fixation time to total time. The main effect of the interaction between font size and layout was significant ($F = 507.909$, $P = 0 < 0.05$), which was mainly reflected in the longer fixation time for the 12-pixel text under the three different layout modes.

The analysis of the above experimental data showed that subjects had significant differences in the two eye movement indicators in different interest zones, mainly reflected in the ratio of fixation times and fixation time to the total time. The indicator of R_1 interest zone was significantly higher than that of other interest zones. This means that the difficulty of the layout of the interface and whether the font size is appropriate have a great impact on the observation, cognition and experience of elderly users when they learn online.

Table 4. Two-factor variance analysis of eye movement data

Sources of variation	Sum of squares	DOF	Mean square error	F	P
Fixation count					
Word size	136.174	2	4222.052	17464.974	0.000**
Layout	8444.104	2	68.087	281.650	0.000**
Word size * Layout	10.145	4	2.536	10.491	0.000**
Ratio of fixation time to total time/%					
Word size	88731.947	2	44365.973	78548.785	0.000**
Layout	110.183	2	55.092	97.538	0.000**
Word size * Layout	1147.510	4	286.878	507.909	0.000**

5   Cognitive Load and Subjective Evaluation Scale of User Experience

5.1   Cognitive Load Was Evaluated with Pass Subjective Scale

The commonly used measurement methods of cognitive load include physiological mea-surement, subjective measurement and task performance measurement. Because when using physical measurement, has nothing to do with the cognitive load of the other factors (such as environment, attention, mental stress or emotion, etc.) can also cause some changes, and physiological measurement method on the experiment and testing of equipment used process requirements are relatively high, so many researchers more praise highly subjective measurement method, more simple and practical and easy to use.

Pass et al. made statistics of previous studies on cognitive load and found that most researchers chose subjective measurement to measure the cognitive load level of sub-jects. Because of its operability, subjective measurement method still has significant advantages in many measurement crimes. Among them, the subjective assessment scale designed by Pass et al., referred to as Pass scale, was adopted most by researchers.

The scale included two aspects: mental effort and task difficulty. The first item involved mental effort, and the second and third items involved task difficulty. In the specific study of this paper, the subjects need to answer two questions: "How difficult do you think the online learning content is" and "how much mental effort did you put into the learning process". Subjects were asked to rate the learning process on a subjective scale from 1 to 9, with 1 indicating that the learning material was very easy and required minimal effort, 5 indicating that the learning material was moderately difficult and required moderate effort, and 9 indicating that the material was very difficult and required the greatest effort. The subjects studied the diet and nutrition course with the same difficulty for 10 min on Tianjin Distance Learning Network for the Elderly (the same font layout), Shandong University distance Learning Network for the Elderly (corner layout) and Taiyuan Open College for the Elderly (modular layout). After online learning, the scores of the 20 subjects on the Pass subjective scale are shown in Table 5.

Table 5. Pass subjective scale

Score	Tianjin Distance Learning Network for the Elderly (The same font layout)	Shandong University for the Elderly Distance Education Network (Corner layout)	Taiyuan Open College for the Elderly (Modular layout)
The participant 01	8	5	5
The participant 02	7	5	4
The participant 03	7	6	3
The participant 04	8	4	4
The participant 05	9	6	6
The participant 06	5	7	3
The participant 07	5	7	3
The participant 08	6	3	2
The participant 09	8	3	7
The participant 10	8	2	6
The participant 11	8	2	7
The participant 12	8	7	2
The participant 13	5	7	3
The participant 14	6	3	3
The participant 15	5	3	6
The participant 16	9	6	5
The participant 17	8	5	4
The participant 18	7	6	6
The participant 19	8	4	4
The participant 20	7	5	3
The average	7.1	4.8	4.3

As can be seen from Table 5, the overall task difficulty and mental effort of the subjects in learning typical websites with corner layout and modular layout were much lower than those with the same font layout, both of which were below 5 points. This also verifies the results of the above eye movement experiment from another dimension.

5.2   Likert Five-Point Scale Was Used to Evaluate User Experience

Likert five-point scale is the most common summative scale, which was formed by social psychologist Likert according to the modification and optimization of the summative scale. This scale is usually composed of a group of statements, which in this study are: "very comfortable", "comfortable", "not necessarily comfortable", "not comfortable", "very uncomfortable", and the score is 5 points, 4 points, 3 points, 2 points, and 1 points in sequence.

Elderly subjects in tianjin distance learning network (the same font layout), shandong university of elderly distance education (corner layout), taiyuan open old college (module layout) for 10 min respectively the same difficulty of dietary nutrition course learning, task is completed using Likert five-point scale on the user's subjective experience mainly evaluate the comfort, Data integration of subjective evaluation of comfort is shown in Table 6. The user experience evaluation indexes determined above include subjective comfort evaluation and objective task completion time analysis. Therefore, these two factors should be taken into comprehensive consideration when evaluating and analyzing the experience of font design on user interface.

The subjects rated the comfort of modular layout the highest, with an average of 3.8 points, which was not much different from that of corner layout, with an average of 3.6 points. It was difficult to evaluate the advantages and disadvantages of the two

Table 6. Comfort evaluation of Likert five-point scale

Score	Tianjin Distance Learning Network for the Elderly (The same font layout)	Shandong University for the Elderly Distance Education Network (Corner layout)	Taiyuan Open College for the Elderly (Modular layout)
The participant 01	2	4	5
The participant 02	2	5	4
The participant 03	1	3	4
The participant 04	3	3	5
The participant 05	3	4	3
The participant 06	4	4	3
The participant 07	2	3	4
The participant 08	3	5	2
The participant 09	1	4	4
The participant 10	2	3	4
The participant 11	1	3	5
The participant 12	3	4	3
The participant 13	4	2	3
The participant 14	2	3	2
The participant 15	3	3	4
The participant 16	2	5	4
The participant 17	2	3	5
The participant 18	3	4	4
The participant 19	1	4	3
The participant 20	2	3	5
The average	2.3	3.6	3.8

interface layouts only from the aspect of comfort. However, the comfort evaluation of the same font layout differs greatly from that of the other two simpler interface layouts, with an average value of 2.3. So we found that the subjects of the corner type layout and module type generally received a good layout, and the same font layout experience, may with font layout there is certain relationship between the amount of information is more complicated, about the contents of the navigation bar configuration is closely, can cause interference with the older users group gives on the vision, not quick access to key information. Combined with the above analysis of eye movement experiments, it is found that the cognitive load and sensory experience of the same font layout are relatively poor in both subjective and objective aspects.

6 Conclusion

Transferring elderly learning to online platforms is not only conducive to enriching the leisure life of elderly users after retirement, but also helps them actively integrate into the rapidly developing modern society, effectively alleviating some problems caused by population aging to a certain extent, facilitating the mode of "active pension" and realizing sustainable development.

Therefore, the realization of online learning for the elderly is an important part of future learning, and how to effectively reduce the cognitive load encountered by the elderly in online learning, so as to improve their user experience has become a problem worthy of our consideration. After the research and analysis of this paper, some preliminary suggestions on interface optimization are obtained, which can be started from the following two aspects:

(1) Layout: the existing interface layout is simplified to a certain extent, highlighting the important information of the main part of the page, appropriately increasing the area of the module area, and the title bar of the advertising banner, navigation part of the text are brief. However, it should not be too simplified, and the guidance function of the navigation part should be retained to prevent the occurrence of low cognitive load, which will increase the error rate during operation, thus reducing the user experience.

(2) Font size: The text size used by the existing learning websites for the elderly should be added as appropriate. In the experiment of this paper, the font size with the best user experience is 16 pixels, while the current common text size of web pages is 12 pixels, which can be optimized in the subsequent design. It is worth noting that the text size should not be too large, otherwise it will lose the aesthetics of the interface, and the user experience will be reduced.

Of course, the conclusions drawn in this study are necessarily limited. First of all, there are certain difficulties in defining the elderly users with secondary education and above studied in this paper, and their ability to use online websites for learning also has certain differences. Secondly, the number of subjects involved in the experiment is too small. In the future, it is necessary to continue to analyze the specific needs of the whole elderly user group based on big data, so as to better guide the interaction design in this aspect and provide better online learning services for the elderly user group with a medium degree or above.

References

1. Papalia, D.E.: Experience Human Development. MIT Press, New York (1997)
2. Ying, X.L.: Research on mobile application design of goal-oriented online learning for the elderly. Southwest Jiaotong University, Sichuan (2018)
3. Ronsenfield, M., Jahan, S., Nunez, K., et al.: Cognitive demand, screens and blink rate. Comput. Hum. Behav. **51**(13), 403–406 (2015)
4. Zhu, Y.Q.: Research on distance education for the elderly in China under the background of aging. J. High. Contin. Educ. **29**(3):48–53 (2016). (in Chinese) DOI:https://doi.org/10.3969/j.issn.1006-7353.2016.03.011
5. Luo, X., Xie, Q.: Research on reducing product cognitive load based on goal-oriented design theory. Design (16), 119–120 (2015)
6. Xue, Y., Li, Z.: Research on quantitative model of cognitive load in online learning based on eye movement tracking technology. Mod. Educ. Tech. **29**(7), 60–66 (2019). https://doi.org/10.3969/j.iSSN.1009-8097.2019.07.009
7. Ding, Y., Guo, F., Hu, M., et al.: Industrial engineering and management (4), 92–97, 114 (2014)
8. Morville, P., Rosenfield, L.: Information Architecture for the World Wide Web. Tsinghua University Press, Beijing (2003)
9. Zhou, A., Zhang, X., Shu, H., et al.: The effects of font size and part of speech on cognitive processing of Chinese characters. J. Appl. Psychol.**11**(2) :128–132 (2005)

Design Study and User Evaluation of an Application Model for Self-management and Rehabilitation Training for Users with Hearing Loss

Qiqi Huang, Fanghao Song[(✉)], Yan Liu, and Xiaomin Ma

School of Mechanical Engineering, Shandong University, Jinan 250061, China
{202014428,202014430}@mail.sdu.edu.cn, {songfanghao,
liuyan2008}@sdu.edu.cn

Abstract. Nowadays hearing rehabilitation training has the disadvantages of single training method and low compliance. We constructed a Chinese tongue-twister-based hearing rehabilitation training to improve users' auditory sensitivity through repetitive combination training of similar phonemes, thus helping users to recover their hearing level. An application model was developed, for which user assessments of demand and satisfaction were conducted, followed by principal component analysis to further explore the correlation between principal components and ratings. The tongue twister rehearsal training is the feature with the highest ranking in terms of user demand and satisfaction. The mean (SD) score of demand for the five core functions is 6.24 (0.16), and the mean (SD) score of the satisfaction is 6.17 (0.2). The average (SD) demand and satisfaction scores for this overall application model are 6.62 (0.56) and 6.52 (0.64). The proposed application model of self-hearing health management, which integrates assessment and training, bridges the gap between assessment and training in traditional hearing health management software, and achieves high overall scores in user demand and satisfaction surveys. The application model we developed will make up for the current deficiency of hearing rehabilitation training and provide a new reference solution for future rehabilitation training of related diseases.

Keywords: Hearing loss · Rehabilitation training · m-Health · Applied model · User assessment

1 Introduction

1.1 Research Status

The first World Hearing Report calls on the relevant authorities to take measures and summarize the key points about the current state of hearing health, the causes of hearing loss, and prevention. Currently, more than 1.5 billion people in the world are affected by hearing loss. Among them, 430 million people have moderate or severe hearing loss in the better-hearing ears. It is estimated that the number of hearing loss will increase by more than 1.5 times in the next 30 years, and more than 700 million people may

M. Kurosu (Ed.): HCII 2022, LNCS 13304, pp. 87–105, 2022.
https://doi.org/10.1007/978-3-031-05412-9_7

suffer from moderate of severe hearing loss [1]. In addition to normal medication, some timely and effective rehabilitation training can benefit people at risk of hearing loss or those with hearing loss. The common causative factors of hearing loss can be broadly classified as pathological and non-pathological, and pathological hearing loss requires professional medical diagnosis and pharmacological intervention, wearing appropriate hearing aid instruments, etc. However, a larger proportion of hearing impaired people stop using hearing aids after the purchase of hearing aids and after the end of fitting [2, 3]. Some studies have shown that the main reason why hearing impaired people refuse to wear hearing aids is that the effect brought by hearing aids is small and they do not achieve satisfactory results in different conversational situations. In addition to pathological conventional treatments, some timely and effective non-pharmacological and device-based interventions can restore hearing in people at risk of hearing loss or with hearing loss. These interventions mainly include behavioral interventions and rehabilitation training. Chen and Zhang [4] proposed the IKAP management model of "information-knowledge-belief-behavior", which can effectively improve disease perception, anxiety and depression and promote hearing recovery in elderly patients with sudden deafness compared with drug treatment alone. Zhu et al. [5] concluded through clinical trials that conventional drug treatment based on The intensive gaze stability training for patients with bilateral vestibular hypofunction on top of conventional medication can help improve the patients' systemic inflammatory state, promote the improvement of clinical symptoms, and facilitate hearing recovery. Tao [6] proposed a model of care application for patients with sudden deafness from the perspective of positive psychology, which can significantly reduce patients' anxiety. Li and Chen [7] investigated the effects of therapeutic play on preschool sudden deafness The effect of therapeutic play on the psychological stress and hearing recovery of preschool children with sudden deafness, and concluded that the combination of therapeutic play intervention and medication can effectively reduce anxiety and isolation and improve compliance with examination and treatment in preschool children with sudden deafness. It also improves the child's compliance with examination and treatment, promotes the recovery of hearing function, and increases the satisfaction of the child's family with the care provided. The above study is a clinical study in a relatively fixed population, and although it confirms that behavioral interventions can effectively help improve hearing, their application is not suitable for widespread dissemination.

Hearing training is one of the effective means to rehabilitate non-pathological hearing loss, mainly through repetitive, focused listening activities to improve hearing levels. Murray [8] proposed four stages of auditory skill development, stating that the improvement of auditory skills can be divided into several stages, the most important and most neglected of which is the auditory discrimination stage. One of the most frequently used methods in listening training is speech tracking, and a study in Korea applied the principle of speech tracking to the perception of Korean sentences in a noisy environment [9], and Chang & Lee also applied the principle of speech tracking, and they developed a sentence inventory for improving communication in hearing impaired people They developed a sentence inventory for speech tracking training to improve communication of hearing impaired people and created a CD audio source for hearing impaired people to use according to their needs [10]. Based on the characteristics of Chinese speech structure and phonological acoustics, Liu et al. [11] constructed a decomposition training model suitable for the development of auditory abilities of hearing impaired people in the Mandarin system. In addition to comparative studies between normal populations, the effects of auditory training between musicians and non-musicians have received extensive attention, and the brains of musicians have been used in many studies as a model to study the plasticity of this auditory system and to demonstrate that the increase in hearing levels during this audio training is related to experience-related training. Kraus and Chandrasekaran [12] investigated the effects of music training on arousal-induced brain plasticity and explored the development of music in influencing brain hearing. Herholz et al. [13] reviewed studies of music training-induced brain plasticity, highlighted common patterns and possible underlying mechanisms of this plasticity, and integrated these studies with the development and models of plasticity mechanisms in other domains. Wang et al. [14] have emphasized the importance of stimulus frequency otoacoustic emissions in clinical hearing screening and diagnosis, and the use of music training to enhance auditory rehabilitation.

According to the International Telecommunication Union [15], by the end of 2019, there will be about 4 billion Internet users, representing 51% of the global population. This trend comes just in time to work with mobile health apps (m-Health) to update the traditional healthcare model. As reported in 2018, there are 325,000 m-Health apps available for download via the Internet [16]. The smartphone app market has seen the emergence of many audiometry-enabled apps, which are more convenient and easy to use than traditional forms of hearing health management, and their reliability and validity have been demonstrated [17]. Hearing screening [18, 19], diagnosis [20, 21], training [22, 23], and counseling [24] have all shifted to online applications for development and application. lycke et al. [25] studied an app called uHear, which uses speech perception tests with acceptable noise levels to assess subjects' hearing impairment. The results of the study showed an accuracy of 94.6% compared to traditional audiometric methods in hospitals. Corry et al. [26] studied the accuracy and time consumption of an APP called Audiogram Mobile versus clinical pure-tone audiometry and found that the APP was significantly different from clinical pure-tone audiometry at all audiometric frequencies except 500 Hz; the time consumption was significantly shorter than clinical Yeung et al. [27] studied the effectiveness of ShoeBox audiometry for screening mild hearing loss and above, with negative predictive value and sensitivity of 89.7% and 91.2%, respectively.

Kwak et al. [28] and others developed an auditory rehabilitation APP for older adults with suspected or known hearing loss, complete with four customized exercises for the elderly auditory system and a self-report questionnaire for determining the degree of hearing loss in older adults.

In addition, a variety of similar APPs were studied on the app platform, including Hearing Test, Baysound Hearing Test, Hearing Ability, Hood Hearing, Ear Doctor Hearing, and Hearing Pro. Similar to uHear, Audiogram, and ShoeBox, they all use automated hearing detection technology to provide users with a self-test for the degree of hearing impairment. Some of these apps also include an online consultation function. Hearing knowledge popularization, scenario hearing aids and other functions.

In summary, we found that the current hearing health management apps do not systematically integrate audiometric and rehabilitation training functions, and there are few hearing rehabilitation training models for hearing impaired patients. There is a single training model and more training restrictions, which may lead to lower compliance with treatment and thus affect their recovery.

1.2 Pure-tone Hearing Threshold Test Theory

As an existing clinical diagnostic standard for the degree of hearing loss, the pure-tone hearing threshold test has been widely used by major testing institutions. Although the pure-tone hearing testing technique is inexpensive, the lack of appropriate testing technicians has severely limited the clinical application of this technique [29]. With the development of technology, hearing detection technology using smartphones as a carrier has emerged, making it possible to achieve remote detection through smartphones. There are three main principles of pure-tone hearing threshold detection. The first one is the "adjustment method" proposed by Bekesy and G.V. [30], in which the subject adjusts the intensity of the stimulus sound emitted by an automatic audiometer to the minimum audible level, and we finally take the average value as the hearing threshold at the frequency. The second is the "qualifying method", which is the most commonly used method. The research of Mahomed et al. [31] and Swanepoel et al. [32] showed that pure-tone audiometry using the qualifying method is reliable, accurate and less time-consuming, and can be applied to normal hearing and patients with pure-tone hearing thresholds testing. There is another method called the "adaptive method" [33], which is similar to the "qualifying method", but the intensity of the stimulus sound emitted by the audiometer vibrates around the predicted threshold, making it possible to obtain the threshold more quickly than the "qualifying method". Technologies such as pure-tone hearing threshold detection, remote hearing rehabilitation, and the application of sound isolation and noise reduction technologies will change the current structural composition of hearing detection departments [34]. Hearing tests no longer need to take up space and bulky traditional soundproof rooms. The remote hearing test technology allows subjects to obtain reliable pure-tone hearing threshold tests without going to professional institutions. In addition, the risk of cross-contamination due to crowding and confined booths highlights the advantages of remote hearing testing. Smart terminal pure-tone hearing threshold detection technology allows subjects to have their hearing tested anytime and anywhere [35–37], and patients can go to a hospital terminal for further treatment based on the smart terminal pure-tone hearing threshold testing results. The advantage of this method is that it takes less time, and the problem of low-frequency threshold deviation can be solved by using noise-cancelling headphones.

1.3 Principle of Listening Rehabilitation Training

The ambiguity of the words used in the existing rehabilitation training is still insufficient, and the user's ability to distinguish words that are close to each other is still weak. Besides, the design of the language level that is easily confused in daily life is lacking. Therefore, we choose to use ambiguous words for recovery training, which mainly relies on phoneme-based acoustic contrast training protocols to strengthen the brain's ability to distinguish between different phoneme, psychoacoustic adaptive speech noise protocols to improve the listening ability in daily life, and simulated "real-world" listening environment to enhance the user's hearing sensitivity, thus building the function of hearing rehabilitation.

The medical evaluation of auditory ability includes: spatial hearing (positioning and distance), the speech perception (in quiet and noisy environments), and other auditory characteristics (speech discrimination, comprehension). In the design of this application model, we achieve control of sound in the spatial dimension by adjusting the radio distance. At the speech perception level, we simulated typical life scenes, such as watching TV, shopping, and outdoor scenes to help the user return to normal life scenes as soon as possible after training. We choose to use Chinese tongue-twister aural rehabilitation training to enhance the user's auditory discrimination ability and hearing sensitivity. The user selects the content heard to complete the hearing recovery training to achieve the needs of the indicators at the level of speech recognition and comprehension ability. We choose to use tongue twister listening selection training to improve the user's discrimination ability and listening sensitivity, and the user selects what he has heard to complete the listening recovery training, so as to meet the index requirements of speech recognition and comprehension.

1.4   Difficulty Level of Chinese Tongue Twister

To the best of our knowledge, there is no exact method of defining the difficulty of tongue twisters. From the phonological point of view, the reason for the difficulty of tongue twisters is that they consist of the main vowels, rhymes and tones that appear repeatedly. The vowels and rhymes are arranged and combined according to the similarities and differences of the parts and methods of pronunciation, thus making the utterance roundabout. The tones are repeatedly changed by the yin and yang to achieve the tongue twister effect. According to the different dominant word sounds of different tongue twisters, we can divide the tongue twisters into two categories:

Vowels: repetition of the main vowel and repetition of similar vowel combinations. The main vowel repetition is characterized by the recurrence of a vowel with various rhymes in the tongue twister. This type of tongue twister makes it difficult by having repeated vowels. The main vowel repetition type of tongue twister is relatively a simple type of tongue twister. The vowel combinations in this type of tongue twister are mainly divided into two categories: those with the same pronunciation part but different pronunciation method and those with different pronunciation parts but same pronunciation method.

Rhymes: repetition of main rhymes and repetition of similar rhyme combinations. The main vowels are repeated in the same way as the initials, and the difficulty is increased by repeating a large number of vowels. The difficulty is similar to the repetition of the main initials. Similar rhyme combinations mainly repeat one or several similar compound rhymes and single rhymes. These similar compound rhymes increase the degree of difficulties by changing the rhyme head or rhyme end to increase the tongue movement. Similar single rhymes increase the degree of difficulties by changing the tongue position and lip shape. The difficulty of this kind is between the repetition of the main vowel and the recurrence of similar vowel combinations.

Based on the theoretical basis above, we divide the types of tongue twister questions within this application into two categories, one with major vowel repetition and similar vowel combination repetition, and the other with major rhyme repetition and similar rhyme combination repetition. The construction of the framework and the specific design of the program are described in detail in the following sections.

To address the problems of the above research, in this paper we construct a theoretical framework of hearing rehabilitation training, and design a new type of hearing rehabilitation training. We propose to develop an application model integrating audiometry, hearing rehabilitation training, and hearing aid functions, and conduct a user demand and satisfaction questionnaire survey for the five core functions of the application model to test its usability and rationality. The framework of this paper is shown in Fig. 1.

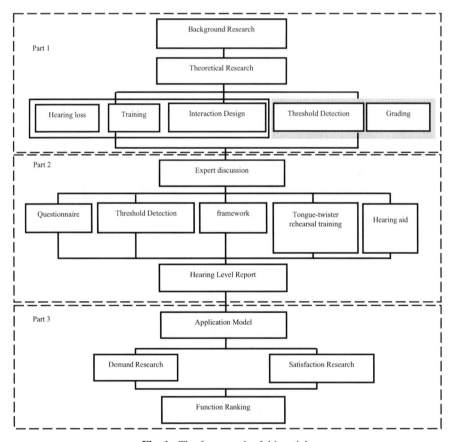

Fig. 1. The framework of this article

The research objectives of this paper are shown below:

Designing a new hearing rehabilitation training method.

By implanting a hearing detection function in the application model, we make sure that users can monitor their hearing health in real time.

The hearing aid function and online consultation module are added to the application model to realize the home care model of users' hearing health management.

2   Methods

2.1   Expert Team Discussion

Based on the research on the relevant applications and underlying principles mentioned above, an expert team consisting of application model developers and multidisciplinary researchers was formed to discuss and determine the specific functional modules of the application model. The team consists of two specialized researchers, three developers, and one programmer, half of the expert team members are women and half are men, four are under 30 years of age and two are under 50 years of age, all of whom have experience in the use and development of mobile health management applications for medical procedures.

In order to determine the basic functions of the Hearing Health Management and Rehabilitation App, the group of experts discussed it through an offline meeting, which lasted for one hour. Based on thorough research and validation of relevant studies, four questions were given and the experts were given 40 min to reflect and answer these four questions. What are the APPs related to hearing health management that you have come across? Which app do you prefer to use for what function of hearing health management? Which features do you think should be discarded in your known hearing health management APPs? What features do you think should be kept in your known hearing health management app? We have organized the results of the expert discussion in Fig. 2 and explained each requirement in detail below.

Fig. 2. Brainstorming poster (drawn by the author via miro)

Self-Hearing Testing and Obtaining Reports of Hearing Levels
Experts believe that the prerequisite for users to manage their hearing health is a basic understanding of their hearing health, so it is necessary to insert a pure-tone hearing

threshold test into the application model, and this function has been widely used as a standard paradigm in clinical diagnosis.

Hearing Rehabilitation Training at Home
Since the emergence of COVID-19, hospitals and other medical institutions are also facing unprecedented pressure, experts suggest that we should meet the needs of users to achieve hearing health management at home, so as to share the pressure of hospitals, but also according to the user's own needs at any time hearing health management.

The Hearing Level Report Can be Used as a Basis for Online Consultation
Experts believe that because different users have different knowledge of hearing health, users may face the situation of not being able to read the report after obtaining their own hearing level report through the application model, which may cause anxiety among users and is more detrimental to their hearing health management, so it will be helpful to cooperate with hospitals and other medical institutions through online platforms to achieve online consultation.

In case of severe hearing impairment, hearing aid service should be provided under the premise of medication.

After brainstorming, highlighters, tape and sticky notes were distributed to the experts. They were asked to write down their actions, needs and pains, touch points, and how customers felt at various stages of operating the application model, and the experts were encouraged to substitute themselves into specific usage scenarios as they created their journey maps, which are shown in Fig. 3.

Fig. 3. Journey map (drawn by the author via miro)

The experts were then asked to create a prototype of the application model based on the results of the brainstorming and journey map outputs above. The prototype was required to meet the user requirements discussed during the brainstorming, to avoid the issues raised during the discussion that interfered with the user experience, and to produce a smooth flow of operations in conjunction with the journey map. The prototype design of the application model is shown in Fig. 4.

Fig. 4. Prototype sketch

2.2 Application Model

Purpose

Hearing level loss is very common in modern society, but not enough attention has been paid to it. At the moment when the awareness of self-health management is still insufficient, there is little attention to the self-management of hearing health. Therefore, we need a scientific and integrated hearing health management application. In addition, in order to enhance the user loyalty and motivation, we have considered the ease of use and interactivity of the application model, almost all operations are done by user clicks. The interface will give certain prompts from a multimodal perspective when performing rehabilitation training to help users build confidence and improve their compliance.

The first category is for users with non-pathological hearing impairment, for which the application will mainly provide hearing sensitivity training based on tongue-twisters. The second group is the hearing impaired due to pathological factors, if the results of the preliminary questionnaire show that the user has a disease that affects hearing level, the user will be recommended to the hearing aid function.

The model is mainly used for two types of user groups. One is hearing impaired users caused by non-pathological factors. For this kind of users, the application will mainly provide users with hearing sensitivity training based on the tongue twister. The other one is hearing impaired users caused by pathological factors. If the previous questionnaire survey results show that the user has diseases affecting hearing, the hearing aid function is preferred for the user.

Introduction of Core Functions

The following are the five core functions of the application model, including the research of the basic information of users' personal hearing health, the hearing test based on medical theory, the report of personal hearing results, the new rehabilitation training method and the hearing aid function. The five core functions form a complete management process for users' self-hearing management in all aspects.

Questionnaire: Before the start of the hearing test, the user is required to fill out a questionnaire, the purpose of which is to initially grasp the user's hearing condition and determine whether the user has an ear disease that causes hearing loss.

Pure-tone hearing threshold detection: During the pure-tone hearing threshold test, the headset automatically emits the stimulus sound set by the instrument, while the audiometer adjusts the intensity of the stimulus sound according to the user's press of the response button. When the user presses "sound/hearing", the intensity of the stimulus sound is reduced by 10 dB; when the user presses "no sound/no hearing", the intensity of the stimulus sound is increased by 5 dB. The intensity of the stimulus is increased by moving the user from pressing "no sound/no hearing" to "sound/hearing" and then decreasing the intensity of the stimulus until the user presses "no sound/no hearing" five times. A certain intensity value is determined as the threshold by responding to "sound/hearing" three times.

Hearing level report: At the end of the pure-tone hearing threshold test, the application gives a score report on the user's listening level test. If the user uses the pure tone hearing threshold test function several times, then in the hearing level report module, the user can see their stage hearing level report. The user can send the hearing level report to the physician by using the online consultation function. We work with a team of professional physicians to set up an online consultation function in the application, so that users can choose to consult a physician online or book an appointment with a physician for offline treatment. Users who make an appointment through the application model can send their hearing level report to the doctor, who will give a medical diagnosis based on information such as user's hearing level report, diagnostic results. The user can download a report after the consultation and issue it at the next consultation, providing a multi-dimensional diagnosis reference for the physician.

Tongue twister rehab training: In the rehabilitation training module, the user will hear a total of 15 random tongue twister audios, each audio will play four tongue twisters. The user needs to answer the questions according to the content heard. For example, in response to the question "Please select the fourth phrase you hear", the user selects the four options given in the interface. The options are mostly confusing words in the tongue twister, and if these words can be identified, the users can gradually build up enough confidence for recovery. Each option is set up with an image prompt containing keywords, and each question contains two sets of the same keywords, as shown in Fig. 5. This allows the user to capture the focus of this training directly, and also helps the user to make basic judgments to some extent. The rehabilitation training module can adjust the categories of questions according to the user's training situation, thus meeting the user's individual training needs. If a user makes a mistake during training, the system will record whether the user's mistake is rhyme-driven or vowel-driven. Based on the type of mistake, the user is given focused training for the next test, thus forming a personalized training mechanism for the user. If the user makes a wrong choice due to a wrong touch, the user can choose to retest when the error box appears, and after choosing to retest, the content of the user's error will not be included in the personalized training.

Hearing aid: If the user is determined to be hearing impaired after the pure-tone hearing threshold detection, the application will automatically open the hearing aid page and ask if the user needs to turn on the hearing aid function or not, and the hearing aid function needs to be used with headphones. If the user needs to turn on the hearing aid function, there are three types of hearing aid environments can be chosen from: indoor, outdoor, and watching TV. After selecting the environment, users can choose the level of noise cancellation for their personal needs. In addition to the adjustable noise cancellation level, users can also choose the radio distance and the balance of the left and right channels according to the sound generation distance and the hearing level of the left and right ears respectively. The hearing aid function is provided for users with hearing impairment due to pathological factors to assist their normal medication, and to avoid the user's low self-esteem, anxiety and dissociation due to hearing loss.

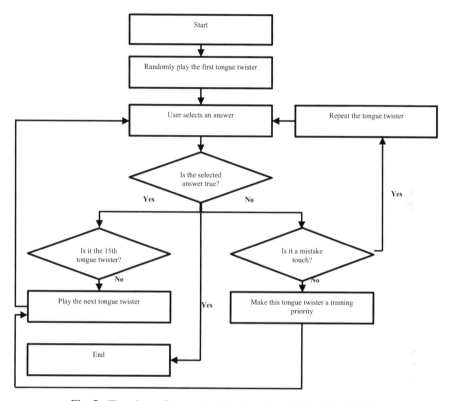

Fig. 5. Flowchart of tongue-twisting hearing rehabilitation training

2.3 User Evaluation

Experimental Design

In order to verify that our application model meets user needs and satisfies users, a user's demand and satisfaction test was designed and executed. The application prototype was first tested internally by the expert team to ensure that all features worked smoothly and that the interactive interface could respond to user actions in a timely manner. Next, we designed a questionnaire and invited the subjects to fill it out. Before the subjects filled in the questionnaire, we introduced the operation logic and the usage process of the application model to the users, and asked them to use the application model.

The questionnaire contains three parts. The first part asks for information about the subjects' use of smartphones and other related devices, and this part serves to understand the subjects' smart device usage. The second part consists of 12 (10 + 2) questions, 10 of which ask subjects about their demand for and satisfaction with each of the five core functions, while the other two questions ask subjects about their overall demand for and overall satisfaction with the application model. For example, "I think the questionnaire research function is necessary" and "I am satisfied with the questionnaire function", and users indicate the extent to which they agree with the current statement by selecting the numbers in the scale. The correspondence among the numbers in the scale and the level of agreement is shown in Table 1.

Table 1. Likert scale on demand and satisfaction

Presentation statements	I think the questionnaire function is necessary.						
Level of agreement	Strongly disagree	Disagree	Somewhat disagree	Neutral	Somewhat agree	Agree	Strongly disagree
Score	1	2	3	4	5	6	7
Presentation statements	I think the questionnaire function is satisfactory.						
Level of agreement	Strongly disagree	Disagree	Somewhat disagree	Neutral	Somewhat agree	Agree	Strongly disagree
Score	1	2	3	4	5	6	7

Where a score of 1 means strongly disagree and a score of 7 means strongly agree. The higher the score, the higher the degree of agreement and the lower the degree of disagreement. (1) strongly disagree; (2) disagree; (3) somewhat disagree; (4) neutral; (5) somewhat agree; (6) agree; and (7) strongly agree. In the third part of the questionnaire, we asked the subjects to rank the demand and satisfaction of each of the five core functions in a comprehensive manner, based on Eq. (1).

$$a = \frac{\sum (F \times \omega)}{i} \qquad (1)$$

In Eq. (1), a represents the average composite score of options, F represents the frequency, is the weight, and i represents the number of people filling in the question. The higher the score, the higher the ranking position. The weight value is determined by the position of the core function being ranked. For example, if there are four core functions in the ranking, the first position will have a weight of 4, the second position will have a weight of 3, the third position will have a weight of 2, and the fourth position will have a weight of 1.

Subject Recruitment

A total of 52 subjects were invited to participate in this study, including 28 males and

24 females, with an average age of 23.1 (SD $= 0.86$) years old, covering workers in various industries and school students. These subjects all had a mild hearing loss. All subjects had some experience in using smartphones and related devices, and all of them participated voluntarily and submitted a written informed consent. After the expert team explained the logic of the application model and the process of using it, the subjects were asked to experience the application model. After the operation, the subjects were asked to answer 12 questions in the questionnaire.

3 Result

3.1 User Statistics

A total of 52 questionnaires were distributed for this user assessment, and 52 valid questionnaires were returned. We import the questionnaire data into SPSS software for the reliability and validity analysis and the Cronbach coefficient Alpha value is $0.696 > 0.6$, which means that the questionnaire data reliability is acceptable. Kaiser-Meyer-Olkin (KMO) value is $0.581 > 0.5$, Bartlett's spherical test freedom value is 66, significant coefficient is $0 < 0.05$, which means that the questionnaire structural validity is acceptable.

3.2 Evaluation Outcomes

The mean (SD) score of demand for the five core functions is 6.25 (0.18), and the mean (SD) score of the satisfaction is 6.17 (0.18). The average (SD) demand and satisfaction scores for this overall application model are 6.62 (0.57) and 6.52 (0.61), respectively. The demand and satisfaction scores for each function is detailed in Table 2.

Table 2. Average demand and satisfaction scores for the five core functions and application model

Functions	Questionnaire objectives	
	Demand mean (SD)	Satisfaction mean (SD)
Questionnaire	6.35 (0.73)	6.33 (0.73)
Pure tone hearing threshold detection	6.38 (0.79)	6.31 (0.69)
Hearing level report	6.21 (1)	6.1 (0.95)
Tongue twister rehab training	6.35 (0.87)	6.29 (0.93)
Hearing aid function	5.94 (1.18)	5.81 (1.13)

According to Eq. (1), the results of the subjects' ranking of demand for the five core functions are obtained as follows: tongue-twister rehab training > pure-tone hearing threshold test > hearing test report > questionnaire > hearing aid, as shown in Table 3.

The results of the satisfaction ranking are: tongue-twister rehab training > pure-tone hearing threshold test > hearing test report > questionnaire > hearing aid, the specific ranking details can be seen in Table 4.

Table 3. Combined demand scores for the five core functions

Functions	Overall score
Questionnaire	3.94
Pure tone hearing threshold detection	3.37
Hearing level report	3
Tongue twister rehab training	2.71
Hearing aid function	1.98

Table 4. Combined satisfaction scores for the five core functions

Functions	Overall score
Questionnaire	4.18
Pure tone hearing threshold detection	3.47
Hearing level report	3
Tongue twister rehab training	2.61
Hearing aid function	1.75

The questionnaire contains a total of six questions, each question was answered for demand and satisfaction, and a total of twelve indicators were involved in the extraction of principal components, and four principal components were extracted by factor analysis, thus fusing multiple variables into a composite variable for further analysis in conjunction with the above questionnaire data.

After extracting the principal components with SPSS software, the KMO value was 0.58 and the Bartlett's sphericity test sig value was 0. According to the criteria, when the KMO value is greater than 0.5 and the Bartlett's sphericity test sig value is less than 0.05, the data are suitable for principal component analysis, so the data basically meet the conditions of principal component analysis, and the details are shown in Table 5.

Table 5. Suitability test

KMO and Bartlett's test		
KMO Sampling suitability quantity		0.581
Bartlett sphericity test	Approximate cardinality	299.180
	Degree of freedom	66
	Significance	0

Table 6. Total variance explained

Ingredients		f1	f2	f3	f4
Initial Eigenvalue	Total	2.946	2.818	1.589	1.330
	Variance %	24.547	23.487	13.244	11.085
	Cumulative %	24.547	48.034	61.277	73.362
Extraction of the sum of squares of loads	Total	2.946	2.818	1.589	1.330
	Variance %	24.547	23.487	13.244	11.085
	Cumulative %	24.547	48.034	61.277	73.362
Sum of squared rotating loads	Total	2.861	2.103	2.070	1.649
	Variance %	23.840	17.528	17.251	13.743
	Cumulative %	23.840	41.368	58.619	72.362

Table 6 shows the characteristic roots and variance contribution of the data, from which we can visualize the number and importance of the principal components.

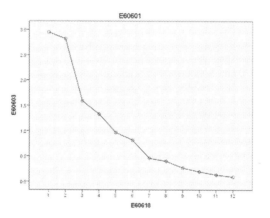

Fig. 6. Gravel plot

Figure 6 is the "gravel plot", which shows the magnitude of the extracted principal components' eigenvalues. In this analysis, we extracted four principal components, named f1, f2, f3, and f4, respectively. f1 has a root of 2.946, which explains 24.547% of the overall data; f2 has a root of 2.818, which explains 23.487% of the overall data; f3 has a root of 1.589, which explains 13.244% of the overall data. The characteristic root of principal component f4 is 1.330, which explains 11.085% of the overall data; the remaining components have characteristic roots less than 1, indicating that there is no need to extract them. It can be seen that the above four principal components have a strong explanatory power, explaining a total of 72.362% of the data, and they can be used as a comprehensive indicator to evaluate this application model and thus decipher the causes behind the results of these data.

4 Discussion

Table 7 reflects the extent to which information on each variable was extracted by the principal components. The principal component f1 is influenced by the demand and satisfaction scores of the hearing test report function and the hearing aid function. This is probably because users who focus on these two functions pay more attention to the instrumental characteristics of the application model, expecting the model to give feedback on its use and provide aids for their hearing improvement. The scores of overall demand and satisfaction of the application model in principal component f2 are the main variables, indicating a high overall acceptance of the application model by users. The demand and satisfaction scores for the pure tone hearing threshold test function and the tongue-twister rehabilitation training function in the f3 principal component are highly correlated, indicating that users have some general knowledge of hearing health and are able to understand the rehabilitation mechanism of rehabilitation training on this basis. The main variables of the F4 principal component are the demand and satisfaction scores of the questionnaire features, indicating that users who are concerned about this part of the features have a certain degree of knowledge about their hearing health. Given the above feedback, we can take into account the needs of users with non-pathological hearing impairment in the subsequent development process. Since they may know less about certain diagnostic functions than users with hearing impairment due to pathological factors, we can achieve better results by inserting appropriate explanations in the model before each function starts to help users understand the reason why we set up the function.

Table 7. Component matrix after rotation

	Principal components			
	f1	f2	f3	f4
Questionnaire demand score				0.799
Questionnaire satisfaction score		0.605		0.617
Pure tone hearing threshold detection demand score	0.410		0.498	
Pure tone hearing threshold detection satisfaction score	0.385	0.384	0.412	
Hearing level report demand score	0.747			0.427
Hearing level report satisfaction score	0.727			
Tongue twister rehab training demand score			0.914	
Tongue twister rehab training satisfaction score			0.844	
Hearing aid function demand score	0.840			0.316
Hearing aid function satisfaction score	0.843			0.314
Application model demand score		0.810		
Application model satisfaction score		0.819		

In previous studies, the training methods of listening rehabilitation are single, and the variability of the trained words is large, which cannot improve the ability of users to distinguish ambiguous words. The training format is boring, the frequency of user-initiated use is low, and the training effect is not very satisfactory. In this study, we explored the feasibility of designing a new approach to hearing rehabilitation through literature research, theoretical studies, and concrete practice to improve the efficiency and compliance of users' hearing rehabilitation. Based on the theoretical framework, we discussed and designed an application model in conjunction with an expert team, followed by a user's demand and satisfaction study.

The main limitation in this design study is that the age coverage of users in the user study needs to be extended. Access has been limited due to the epidemic, so it has not been possible to expand the user group to include the middle-aged and elderly population. The second is that the application model has not yet been fully developed as a standalone application. In the future, we will continue to deepen our research in this area so as to provide a richer case reference for hearing rehabilitation training application areas.

5   Conclusions

We change the current status quo of separating audiometric functions from rehabilitation training. At the same time, unlike the traditional training method of pure sound stimulation the application model we proposed to use the unique pronunciation pattern of Chinese tongue twisters to design a new training model based on the repetition of similar phonemes to improve the user's hearing sensitivity. The proposed application model of self-hearing health management with the integration of measurement and training has achieved a high overall score in the user's demand and satisfaction survey, which makes up for the loophole of the separation of measurement and training in traditional hearing health management software and helps users to establish a mindset of independent hearing health management.

References

1. Deafness and hearing loss. https://www.who.int/health-topics/hearing-loss#tab=tab_2
2. Kochkin, S.: MarkeTrak VII: Customer satisfaction with hearing aids in the digital age. Hear. J. **58**(9), 30–37 (2005)
3. Koo, S.M., Kim, J.S., Lim, D.H.: A summary of the census for the disabled in Korea- focusing on the hearing impaired. Audiology **2**(1), 52–57 (2006)
4. Chen, C.J., Zhang, W.: Effects of information-knowledge-belief-behavior model on anxiety, depression and self-efficacy in elderly patients with sudden onset deafness. China Drug Clini. **21**(05), 725–727 (2021)
5. Zhu, W.J., et al.: Analysis of the effect of gaze stability training on the intervention of patients with bilateral vestibular hypofunction. Shaanxi Med. J. **49**(11), 1476–1478 (2020)
6. Tao, P.: Positive psychology perspective on the effectiveness of care for patients with sudden onset deafness. Contemp. Nurse (Next issue) **27**(6), 88–90 (2020)
7. Li, Y., Chen, C.: Effects of therapeutic children's play on psychological stress response and hearing recovery in preschoolers with sudden deafness. Nurs. Res. **34**(10), 1774–1779 (2020)
8. Tye-Murray, N.: Foundations of Aural Rehabilitation: Children, Adults, and Their Family Members. Plural Publishing (2019)

9. De Filippo, C.L., Scott, B.L.: A method for training and evaluating the reception of ongoing speech. J. Acoust. Soc. America **63**(4), 1186–1192 (2021)

10. Chang, S., Lee, J.: Development of auditory training tool for adults using sentences. Audiol. Speech Res. **12**(2), 89–96 (2016)

11. Liu, Q.Y., et al.: The construction of a decomposed auditory skills training model for Chinese language. J. Clinical Otolaryngol. **12**, 574–576 (2006)

12. Kraus, N., Chandrasekaran, B.: Music training for the development of auditory skills. Nat. Rev. Neurosci. **11**(8), 599–605 (2010)

13. Herholz, S.C., Zatorre, R.J.: Musical training as a framework for brain plasticity: behavior, function, and structure. Neuron **76**(3), 486–502 (2020)

14. Wang, Y., et al.: Characteristic of stimulus frequency otoacoustic emissions: detection rate, musical training influence, and gain function. Brain Sci. **9**(10), 255 (2019)

15. International Telecommunications Union: Statistics. https://www.itu.int/en/ITU-D/Statistics/Pages/stat/default.aspx

16. mHealth App Economics 2017: Current Status and Future Trends in Mobile Health. www.research2guidance.com

17. Swanepoel, D.W., Hall, J.W., III.: A systematic review of telehealth applications in audiology. Telemedicine e-Health **16**(2), 181–200 (2010)

18. Bexelius, C., et al.: Evaluation of an internet-based hearing test—comparison with established methods for detection of hearing loss. J. Med. Internet Res. **10**(4), e32 (2008)

19. Smits, C., Merkus, P., et al.: How we do it: the Dutch functional hearing–screening tests by telephone and Internet. Clin. Otolaryngol. **31**(5), 436–440 (2006)

20. Choi, J.M., et al.: PC-based tele-audiometry. Telemedicine e-Health **13**(5), 501–508 (2007)

21. Yao, J., Wan, Y., Givens, G.D.: Using web services to realize remote hearing assessment. J. Clin. Monit. Comput. **24**(1), 41–50 (2010)

22. Lee, Y.: Mobile application development for improving auditory memory skills of children with hearing impairment. Audiology Speech Res. **13**(1), 50–61 (2017)

23. Sweetow, R.W., Sabes, J.H.: The need for and development of an adaptive listening and communication enhancement (LACE™) program. J. Am. Acad. Audiol. **17**(08), 538–558 (2006)

24. Laplante-Lévesque, A., et al.: Providing an internet-based audiological counselling programme to new hearing aid users: a qualitative study: provisión de un programa de consejería audiológica por Internet para nuevos usuarios de auxiliares auditivos: un estudio cualitativo. Int. J. Audiol. **45**(12), 697–706 (2006)

25. Lycke, M., et al.: The use of uHear™ to screen for hearing loss in older patients with cancer as part of a comprehensive geriatric assessment. Acta Clin. Belg. **73**(2), 132–138 (2017)

26. Corry, M., et al.: The accuracy and reliability of an app-based audiometer using consumer headphones: pure tone audiometry in a normal hearing group. Int. J. Audiol. **56**(9), 706–710 (2017)

27. Yeung, J.C., et al.: Self-administered hearing loss screening using an interactive, tablet play audiometer with ear bud headphones. Int. J. Pediatr. Otorhinolaryngol. **79**(8), 1248–1252 (2015)

28. Kwak, C., et al.: Development of the Hearing Rehabilitation for Older Adults (HeRO) healthcare mobile application and its likely utility for elderly users. Int. J. Environ. Res. Public Health, **17**(11), 3998 (2020)

29. Wang, J., Zhao, F.: Automatic pure tone hearing threshold detection technology. Chinese J. Hearing Speech Rehabil. Sci. **19**(1), 1–2 (2021)

30. Békésy, G.V.: A new audiometer. Acta Otolaryngol. **35**(5–6), 411–422 (1947)

31. Mahomed, F., et al.: Validity of automated threshold audiometry: a systematic review and meta-analysis. Ear Hear. **34**(6), 745–752 (2013)

32. Swanepoel, D.W., et al.: Hearing assessment—reliability, accuracy, and efficiency of automated audiometry. Telemedicine e-Health **16**(5), 557–563 (2010)
33. Margolis, R.H., et al.: AMTAS®: automated method for testing auditory sensitivity: validation studies. Int. J. Audiol. **49**(3), 185–194 (2010)
34. Jackler, R.K., et al.: The future of otology. J. Laryngol. Otol. **133**(9), 747–758 (2019)
35. McCaslin, D.L.: Rise of the machines: audiology and mobile devices. J. Am. Acad. Audiol. **30**(03), 168 (2019)
36. Thoidis, I., et al.: Development and evaluation of a tablet-based diagnostic audiometer. Int. J. Audiol. **58**(8), 476–483 (2019)
37. Fletcher, K.T., et al.: Audiology telemedicine evaluations: potential expanded applications. Otolaryngology-Head Neck Surg. **161**(1), 63–66 (2019)

Analysis of Responsiveness and Usability in Websites Serving Public Transparency in a Mobile Environment: Case Study in the State of Paraíba Through Heuristic Evaluation

Elias de Almeida Jácome Filho[1] 🆔 and João Marcelo Alves Macêdo[2](✉) 🆔

[1] Federal Savings Bank Brazil e Uniesp University Center, João Pessoa, Paraíba, Brazil
[2] Federal University of Paraíba (UFPB), Mamanguape, Paraíba, Brazil
joao.marcelo@academico.ufpb.br

Abstract. Technology is an important item nowadays, especially with regard to the popularization of the internet, but it still has restrictions, such as access mechanism, bandwidth speed and other limiting factors. Taking into account the need for continuous evolution of technology, especially to ensure effectiveness of citizen participation, with a satisfactory public transparency, allowing the majority of the population to have access to government information. Given this, this study aimed to verify, in a selection of electronic sites of public transparency in the State of Paraíba, the adequacy of accessibility from the perspect of visits through mobile devices (smartphones). The deductive method was used through the evaluation of mobile device interfaces using the heuristic evaluation strategy. Currently, this gadget is becoming the most common tool for access to information within popular reach. For this study, a usability was tested during visits to the websites, in order to evaluate the compatibility with responsiveness. Results were then assigned to a scale of compatibility, divided into "compatible", "partially compatible" and "incompatible". The results showed that most of the websites have responsiveness, but in more than half of the evaluations there was room for improvement. It is concluded that the lack of this compatibility has hindered the popularization of access, especially by limiting the population that has restrictions on access mechanisms, using solely mobile devices.

Keywords: Public transparency · Smartphones mobile devices · Responsiveness · Usability

1 Introduction

The Democratic State of Law establishes that the basic elements that promote a dignified life for all citizens will be met from a State governed democratically and submitted to the Law as the first foundation of its actions [1]. Democratic countries, whether republican or parliamentarian, must have their laws guaranteed by a Constitution. In Brazil, the

M. Kurosu (Ed.): HCII 2022, LNCS 13304, pp. 106–127, 2022.
https://doi.org/10.1007/978-3-031-05412-9_8

Federal Constitution of 1988 establishes in its 1st article that the Federative Republic of Brazil, formed by the indissoluble union of States and Municipalities and the Federal District, is constituted as a Democratic State of Law and, among its foundations, it lists citizenship. The sole paragraph of this article defines that "all power emanates from the people, who exercise it through elected representatives or directly, under the terms of this Constitution" [2]. Meanwhile, the Federal Constitution evokes the active participation of society in the management of the public thing and the express obligation of the state to create mechanisms to establish parameters of efficiency of public management, as well as criteria to make available information necessary for the full exercise of this citizenship.

Among these mechanisms are the Fiscal Responsibility Law (Complementary Law No. 101/2000), the Transparency Law (Complementary Law No. 131/2009), and the Access to Information Law (Law No. 12.527/2011), all of which meet the premise of providing specific information capable of ensuring citizens the timely monitoring and control of public affairs [3–5]. It is a broad act of inspection, "the right to inspect refers not only to spending, but also to whether the resources have been managed correctly" [6]. Thus, citizens can monitor various sorts of irregularities, such as the use of public goods with misuse of purpose, the designation to public positions and functions of people without proper qualification, also flaws in bidding or the adequacy of the type of works performed by public agencies.

According to the National Household Sample Survey (PNAD), conducted in 2019, three out of four Brazilians had access to the internet and, among them, the cell phone was the most used equipment for this access in 99.5% of households [7]. According to the Annual Survey of Information Technology Use, year 2020, by the São Paulo School of Business Administration of the Getúlio Vargas Foundation (FGV EAESP), we have 234 million smartphones in use in Brazil, representing more than one device per inhabitant, against 190 million computers [8] STRONG, D. M.; LEE, Y. W.; WANG, R. Y. Data quality in context. Communications of the ACM, v. 40, n. 5, p. 103–110, 1997.

To ensure the fundamental right of access to information, the Access to Information Law (Law No. 12.527/2011), determines in its article 8 that it is the duty of public agencies and entities to use all legitimate means and instruments available to them for the disclosure of information of collective or general interest produced or held in custody by them, being mandatory the disclosure on official websites. In addition, the quality of information can be defined as the composition of data that meet the needs of consumers [9].

The Brazilian Service of Support for Micro and Small Enterprises (SEBRAE) defines responsiveness as the ability of the website to adapt the size of its pages (layout change) to the size of the screens being displayed, such as mobile and tablet screens [10].

Aware of the growing profile of users accessing the Internet via smartphones, it is essential for public managers to seek ways to introduce responsiveness in websites aimed at transparency. It should be added that, according to Google, the lack of responsiveness in the electronic site is also a reason for the low ranking in searches in its platform through mobile devices, making it difficult to find pages that are not adapted.

Based on these observations, this study seeks to answer the question: Is the lack of responsiveness in electronic public information sites affecting the transparency of information in the State of Paraíba?

To obtain the answer, it was outlined as an objective to verify, in a selection of electronic sites of public transparency in the scope of Paraíba, the adequacy of accessibility via mobile devices (mobile) smartphones.

Thus, it is possible to observe, among the public entities that met the inclusion criteria for the study, which ones adapt their websites to accessibility via smartphones, as well as, at the end of the study, demonstrate the negative impacts on the effectiveness of public transparency in the absence of responsiveness.

This research is justified because it serves as a basis for the development of new research with this theme, fostering scientific production, as well as for public managers to use it to encourage public investments in information technology, aimed at the advancement of transparency policies.

2   Exercising Citizenship

The 1988 Federal Constitution sought not only to establish the basis of the Democratic State of Law, preaching the rights and duties of citizens, but also to educate society on the importance of the exercise of citizenship for the proper functioning of the state [2]. When presenting Chapter III, Section I, which deals specifically with Education, in its Article 205, it established the constitutional principles of Education, declaring it to be the right of all and the duty of the State and the family, further emphasizing that it aims at "the full development of the person, his preparation for the exercise of citizenship, and his qualification for work" [2]. The concept of educating for the exercise of citizenship is broad and supported by the perception that "citizenship is something that is not only learned from books, but from living together, in social and public life [11].

It became clear the need to prepare individuals for such a feat, where the Federal Constitution presents numerous expressions that declare the active character of the exercise of citizenship. In article 5, paragraph LXXIII, states the legitimacy of any citizen to propose popular actions to annul harmful acts by any public entity, and in paragraph XXXIII, evokes that everyone has the right to receive information of private or collective interest from public agencies [2]. In paragraph IV, §2°, of article 58, it clarifies that the legislative will receive, in it's formed commissions, petitions, complaints, representations or claims of any person against acts or omissions of the authorities or public entities [2]. In the caput of article 61, it defines that it is also up to citizens to initiate complementary and ordinary laws, and in the items of §3, paragraph XXII, of article 37, the attention of the public administration to the complaints of the users of the public service is provided, as well as the provision of access to administrative records and information of government acts, and also disciplines the form of representation against the negligent or abusive exercise of office, employment or function in the public administration [2]. Finally, §2, paragraph IV of article 74 provides that any citizen is a legitimate party to denounce irregularities or illegalities before the Federal Audit Court [2].

The citizen must be aware that, besides being the holder of rights, he is also part of a large and complex organism, which is the collectivity, the nation, the State, whose functioning, capable of providing the common good, is only achieved with the contribution of each citizen [11].

Ergo, the citizen is recognized as the main actor of the Democratic State of Law, exercising directly or through elected representatives the power provided by the people, as stated in Article 1 of the Federal Constitution.

3 Transparency in Public Administration

Transparency in the Public Administration is based on the Principle of Publicity, presented in the Federal Constitution in its Article 5, item XXXIII, which expresses the right of every citizen to obtain information of interest to him or her, or of collective interest, from public agencies, which have the duty to provide it within the period prescribed by law, under penalty of liability, with the exception of information whose secrecy is essential to the safety of society and the State [2].

The Public Administration must have its actions directed to the publicity of acts, respecting the principle of publicity, legality, impersonality, morality and effectiveness [12]. It should be added that the public administration should appreciate providing information that is easy to understand to every citizen, that is, clear, objective and structured information that is able to communicate the real meaning they express, provided to social control in a timely manner [13].

With the enactment of Complementary Law 101/2000, the Fiscal Responsibility Law (LRF), parameters to be followed regarding public spending in each Brazilian federative entity (states and municipalities) were established on a national basis. The Fiscal Responsibility Law reinforces the role of the planning activity and, more specifically, the link between the activities of planning and execution of public spending [14], guiding the responsibility of fiscal management and that transparency will be achieved through knowledge and participation of the society, as well as in the wide publicity that should surround all acts and facts related to the collection of revenues and the realization of expenditures by the government.

To this end, it provides for popular participation in the discussion and preparation of plans and budgets, the availability of the administrators' accounts, throughout the fiscal year, for consultation and appreciation by the citizens and institutions of society, as well as the issuing of periodic fiscal management and budget execution reports, also of public access and wide dissemination.

Next, the Complementary Law 131/2009 (Transparency Law), changes the wording of the Fiscal Responsibility Law (LRF) regarding the transparency of fiscal management. The text innovates and determines that detailed information about the budgetary and financial execution of the Union, the States, the Federal District, and the Municipalities must be available in real time. The Transparency Law obliges federal, state and municipal public agencies with more than 50,000 inhabitants to publish detailed budget information on the Internet, through transparency portals [13].

With the approval of Law No. 12,527/2011 (Access to Information Law), Brazil has taken another important step toward the consolidation of its democratic regime, expanding citizen participation and strengthening the instruments of control of public management. Therefore, the Law 12,527/2011 represents a paradigm shift in public transparency, since it establishes that access is the rule and secrecy the exception, any citizen may request access to public information, i.e., information not classified as confidential, according to a procedure that will observe the rules, deadlines, control instruments and resources provided [15].

In this context, we highlight the importance of the public manager's commitment to qualify the published data, so that they meet the constitutional principle of transparency, where the language and the structure transmit the information clearly and objectively and, consequently, allow the understanding of citizens.

4   Transparency Accessible by Smartphones

The Annual Survey of Information Technology Use, year 2020, of the Center for Applied Information Technology of the São Paulo School of Business Administration of the Getúlio Vargas Foundation (FGV), indicates that Brazil is experiencing a recent phenomenon of displacement of the use of the desktop computer to the smartphone [8]. This data is reinforced by the result of the National Household Sample Survey (PNAD), conducted in 2019, in which three out of four Brazilians had access to the internet and, among them, the cell phone was the most used equipment for this access in 99.5% of households [7].

The FGVcia survey also exposes that there is more than one smartphone per inhabitant in Brazil, which added to the mobility characteristic of the devices and the ease of access to the Internet, emerges as an important gateway of ordinary citizens to transparency data [8].

The use of mobile devices to access public transparency data requires that the website accessed has responsiveness, a term that the Brazilian Micro and Small Business Support Service (SEBRAE) defines as the website's ability to adapt the size of its pages (layout change) to the size of the screens being displayed, such as mobile and tablet screens.

The largest search platform on the internet, Google, promoted a change in its algorithm that promotes the ranking of searches, so that when a user performs searches from a smartphone or other mobile devices, the websites that do not present responsiveness or are adapted for these, will fall positions in the query result ranking [16].

Thus, aware of the growth in the use of smartphones as the first technological resource for Internet access and the importance of providing transparency data to the largest number of citizens, we realize the importance of the public manager to pay attention to the responsiveness of the site that provides transparency data, as a guarantee of the effectiveness of this service.

5   Evaluation Heuristics and the Transition from e-Government to m-Government

In the context of studies related to Human-Computer Interaction (HCI) arise the debates related to usability. In this historical context it is known that digital technologies have changed the relationship between voters and politicians [17]. It is known that the context of electronic government (e-gov) has streamlined and mediated this relationship between citizens and the governmental sphere, at this point, the debates about the impact of design and usability in the dialogue of the population with the public management are fostered [17].

Heuristic Evaluation (HE) has been based on computer systems, thus, they do not satisfactorily detect usability problems specific to mobile devices, so the authors propose a compilation of checklists based on the existing literature and focused on mobile [18]. A compilation of metrics and evaluation methodologies focused on e-gov solutions, highlighting the benefit of this tool supporting transparency, efficiency, trust and citizen participation and classifying poor usability as a barrier to these initiatives [19].

The OECD contextualized the evolution of government solutions and linked it to the explosion of wireless access points or wi-fi and the vertiginous increase of mobile devices, which promotes an ease of access to government services [20]. Moreover, the pressure initially from e-government motivates the access of mobile government (m-government), that is, a pattern of access to services through applications (app's) and not only the browser (web browser) [20].

Discussing the redesign, from the findings and the opinion of users and operators, of the *Portal del Empleo*, Mexican, using a methodology supported in the evaluation of effectiveness, when understood as managed to perform a request for information without problems and by the status in which the portal was intended, efficiency measured by the time of completion of tasks, user satisfaction, part of a subjective opinion focusing on likes and dislikes, appreciating technical criteria and users and, finally, the main improvements and recommendations, as suggested by respondents, that went candidates and recruiters [21].

The challenges and opportunities of the services available in mobile governments (m-government), adding the success of these projects given their almost ubiquitous availability, with the possibility of viable connection, usability and low cost of m-government infrastructure [22]. In the same vein, the OECD points to organizational, technical, governance, and social barriers to m-government implementation, among which are listed transparency and accountability in governance, and price and usability in social [20]. Once overcoming the economic issues (price) that prevent access to the technology, we get to the design or even the technical educational capacity for operation, even if intuitive (usability) and this culminates in a need for transparency by the government and consequently responsibilities for accountability to these citizens who have access to m-government.

Nielsen and Molich (1990) is a classic of heuristic evaluation, which they conceptualized as an informal method of usability analysis where a number of evaluators are presented with an interface design and asked to comment on it [23]. It refers back to Nielsen's idea (1989) with a simplified basis for evaluation focused on three lines: (a) Simplified user testing; (b) Narrowed-down prototypes; and (c) Heuristic evaluation. Here we will dedicate ourselves to the latter [24].

Enhanced through the studies [25] it is pointed out: (i) Simple and natural dialogue; (ii) Speak the user's language; (iii) Minimize user's memory load; (iv) Be consistent; (v) Provide feedback; (vi) Provide clearly marked exits; (vii) Provide shortcuts; (viii) Good error messages; (ix) Prevent errors; and (x) Help and documentation (Table 1).

Table 1. Association between the categories and Nielsen's heuristics

Category of problem	Nielsen's heuristic
Use of screen space, according to the orientation	HE6. Recognition rather than recall (approximated)
Consistency of the interface	HE4. Consistency and standards
Standardization of the interface	HE4. Consistency and standards
Visibility of the information presented on the screen	HE6. Recognition rather than recall (approximated)
Suitability of the component to the functionality	
Clarity of mapping between the component and information displayed	
Positioning of the interface components	HE8. Aesthetic and minimalist design (approximated)
Objectivity and clarity of the message	HE2. Match between system and the real world
User language	HE2. Match between system and the real world
Error prevention	HE9. Help users recognize, diagnose, and recover from errors
Recovery of the previous state of the system	HE3. User control and freedom 9. Help users recognize, diagnose, and recover from errors
Ease of data input	HE6. Recognition rather than recall (approximated)
Ease to access the functionality	HE6. Recognition rather than recall
Visibility of possible interactions	
Feedback easily interpreted and with local scope	HE1. Visibility of system status
Application must be self-restraint	
Help and documentation	HE10. Help and documentation
Minimization of the user's memory load	HE5. Error prevention HE6. Recognition rather than recall
Personalization	HE7. Flexibility and efficiency of use

Note. [26] based in Nielsen (1994); Williams (2005); Shneiderman and Plaisant (2009); Bertini, Gabrielli and Kimani (2006); Dix et al. (2004); Moraveji and Soesanto (2012);

Table 2 presents the data regarding the construction of heuristics for mobile device evaluation, based on Nielsen's findings.

Table 2. Heuristics for evaluating the usability of mobile device interfaces: second version.

Heuristic mobile	Description
HM1 - Use of screen space	The interface should be designed so that the items are neither too distant, nor too stuck. Margin spaces may not be large in small screens to improve information visibility. The more related the components are, the closer they must appear on the screen. Interfaces must not be overwhelmed with a large number of items
HM2 - Consistency and standards	The application must maintain the components in the same place and look throughout the interaction, to facilitate learning and to stimulate the user's short-term memory. Similar functionalities must be performed by similar interactions. The metaphor of each component or feature must be unique throughout the application, to avoid misunderstanding
HM3 - Visibility and easy access to all information	All information must be visible and legible, both in portrait and in landscape. This also applies to media, which must be fully exhibited, unless the user opts to hide them. The elements on the screen must be adequately aligned and contrasted
HM4 - Adequacy of the component to its functionality	The user should know exactly which information to input in a component, without any ambiguities or doubts. Metaphors of features must be understood without difficulty
HM5 - Adequacy of the message to the functionality and to the user	The application must speak the user's language in a natural and non-invasive manner, so that the user does not feel under pressure. Instructions for performing the functionalities must be clear and objective
HM6 - Error prevention and rapid recovery to the last stable state	The system must be able to anticipate a situation that leads to an error by the user based on some activity already performed by the user [8]. When an error occurs, the application should quickly warn the user and return to the last stable state of the application. In cases in which a return to the last stable state is difficult, the system must transfer the control to the user, so that he decides what to do or where to go

(continued)

Table 2. (*continued*)

Heuristic mobile	Description
HM7 - Ease of input	The way the user provides the data can be based on assistive technologies, but the application should always display the input data with readability, so that the user has full control of the situation. The user should be able to provide the required data in a practical way
HM8 - Ease of access to all functionalities	The main features of the application must be easily found by the user, preferably in a single interaction. Most-frequently-used functionalities may be performed by using shortcuts or alternative interactions. No functionality should be hard to find in the application interface. All input components should be easily assimilated
HM9 - Immediate and observable feedback	Feedback must be easily identified and understood, so that the user is aware of the system status. Local refreshments on the screen must be preferred over global ones, because those ones maintain the status of the interaction. The interface must give the user the choice to hide messages that appear repeatedly. Long tasks must provide the user a way to do other tasks concurrently to the task being processed. The feedback must have good tone and be positive and may not be redundant or obvious
HM10 - Help and documentation	The application must have a help option where common problems and ways to solve them are specified. The issues considered in this option should be easy to find
HM11 - Reduction of the user's memory load	The user must not have to remember information from one screen to another to complete a task. The information of the interface must be clear and sufficient for the user to complete the current task

Note. [26]

To this end, demonstrate that the heuristics used for mobile devices, extends the concepts and adapts, beyond the original ones, with aspects observed from contributions of other authors, as reported in the construction of Table 2. In this sense, the authors in their results suggest that the heuristics for mobile are more easily adapted to the evaluation of mobile devices [26].

6   Methodology

This study, according to the proposed objective, is classified as descriptive, as it proposes to validate the adequacy of the electronic site to responsiveness, establishing levels of usability of the same from smartphones, characterizing this aspect as compatibility. With a deductive method, and as to the approach, it is characterized as qualitative, since the results do not express quantity, but quality of the electronic sites. About qualitative research "unlike experimental research and surveys in which the analytical procedures can be defined in advance, there are no formulas or predefined recipes to guide researchers [27]. Thus, data analysis in qualitative research becomes very dependent on the ability and style of the researcher".

Regarding the procedures, the research is classified as documentary, with the characteristic that the source of data collection is restricted to primary sources and can be made concomitant to the fact or phenomenon or after.

Data collection was carried out in seven electronic sites that act as transparency portals of public entities with different administrative ties, as shown in Table 3:

Table 3. List of transparency portals for analysis

Addresses of the transparency portals	Link to
http://transparencia.fiepb.com.br/ https://www.fiepb.com.br/fiep/	Federation of Industries of the State of Paraíba - Parastatal entity. It is not part of the Public Administration
https://dados.pb.gov.br/ https://sic.pb.gov.br/ https://paraiba.pb.gov.br/ https://transparencia.pb.gov.br/	Paraíba State Government - State Executive
https://www.joaopessoa.pb.gov.br/ http://sic.joaopessoa.pb.gov.br/open.php https://transparencia.joaopessoa.pb.gov.br/	João Pessoa Municipal Government - Municipal Executive Board
http://www.al.pb.leg.br/ http://www.al.pb.leg.br/transparencia	Paraíba's Legislative House - State Legislative Branch
https://www.tjpb.jus.br/ https://www.tjpb.jus.br/transparencia	Paraíba's Court of Justice - State Judiciary System
https://tce.pb.gov.br/ https://tce.pb.gov.br/gestao https://tce.pb.gov.br/portal-da-transparencia/ portal-da-transparencia	Court of Audit of the State of Paraíba - Auxiliary body of the State and Municipal Legislative Branch

Note. Built for research

In order to obtain different experiences in accessibility, a vast range of administrative sources was accessed, reducing the risk of websites sharing information technology resources, and also to exclude portals that were limited to providing the result of queries by downloading files.

In the selected websites, the responsiveness was analyzed, verified by means of a Heuristic Evaluation, as proposed in the basic literature of this work. The Chrome browser was used to emulate the iPhoneX and Samsung Galaxy S5 mobile devices, and several screenshots were made in order to generate a flow of images for analysis. To clarify the flow of commands made or desired on the smartphone, arrows and circles were added to the images, with a yellow interior and red border, representing scrolling and clicking, respectively.

For the purposes of this study, smartphone usability compatibility was measured in severity levels, ranging from 0 to 4 as follows: 0) I do not agree that the problem encountered is a usability problem; 1) Cosmetic / superficial problem - needs to be fixed only if a time is available; 2) Small usability problem - this problem has a low severity to be solved; 3) Large usability problem - important to solve the problem, high priority; and, 4) Catastrophe - essential to solve this problem before the product is released for marketing.

7 Results

7.1 Federation of Industries of the State of Paraíba

The website Transparency Portal of the Federation of Industries of the State of Paraíba (FIEP/PB), accessed through the address < http://transparencia.fiepb.com.br/ >, has good responsiveness, easy viewing of content and handling, however, in one of the queries made it was only possible to fully view the data in the table presented with the smartphone in horizontal position. It was impossible to scroll the table horizontally when the device is in vertical position.

Figure 1 shows three screens captured, which represent in order the flow of consultation for bidding, in the invitation modality. The screens show the ease of locating the service and the good visibility of the query results.

Figure 2 shows five screens captured, which represent in order the flow for consultation of contracts and agreements of the Industry Social Service of the Paraíba. The screens show the ease of locating the service, however, the responsiveness of the website did not generate a lower scroll bar for the table presented in the query result, making it impossible to view the CNPJ and Contract Value columns vertically, making it mandatory to view it in the horizontal position whether operating as an iPhoneX device or as a Samsung Galaxy S5. On both devices devices in the horizontal position the table presents good visibility of its contents.

Fig. 1. Bidding consultation screens, invitation mode, of the Industry Social Service (SESI/PB). Note. Figure from the Transparency Portal of the Federation of Industries of the State of Paraíba <https://transparencia.fiepb.com.br/>

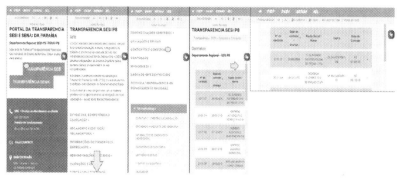

Fig. 2. SESI/PB contract consultation screenshots. Note. Figure from the Transparency Portal of the Federation of Industries of the State of Paraíba <https://transparencia.fiepb.com.br/>

By the classification proposed in this study, regarding usability on smartphones, it was concluded that the level of compatibility is partially compatible, because although the website has good responsiveness overall, one of the queries presented a limitation in data visibility, as the items are highlighted in Table 5, in reference to the visualization shown in Figs. 1, 2 (Table 4).

Table 4. Heuristic evaluation table model

Code of the violated heuristic	Problem description	Severity
HM 1. Use of screen space	Cutting at the bottom of information	2 - Small usability problem
HM 3. Visibility and easy access to all information	Information not layered requiring scrolling of the screen for better viewing	3 - Large usability problem

Note. Built for research

7.2   Transparency Portal of the Paraíba State Government

The Transparency Portal of the Government of the State of Paraíba (PARAÍBA, 2021), accessed through the address <https://transparencia.pb.gov.br/>, has good responsiveness, easy viewing of content and handling, however, in one of the consultation environments the fields to inform the consultation data and the button to perform the consultation, even in the horizontal position, trespass the limits of the screen.

Fig. 3. Payment Authorization query screens. Note. Figure from the Paraíba Government Transparency Portal. <https://transparencia.pb.gov.br/>

Figure 3 shows five screens captured, which represent, in order, the flow of queries for Payment Authorizations. The screens show the ease of locating the service, clicking on the "Expenses" button, and then on the "Payment Authorizations" option, however, the responsiveness of the website did not adjust in the layout the fields to inform the query data and the button to perform the query, being mandatory to scroll the screen to finish the query, even with the equipment horizontally, a situation verified operating with both devices, IphoneX and Samsung Galaxy S5.

Table 5. Heuristic evaluation table model

Code of the violated heuristic	Problem description	Severity
HM 1. Use of screen space	Cutting at the bottom of information	2 - Small usability problem
HM 3. Visibility and easy access to all information	Information not layered requiring scrolling of the screen for better viewing	3 - Large usability problem
HM 8. Ease of access to all functionalities	Query several search fields exceed the layout limits, impairing functionality and data return	3 - Large usability problem

Note. Built for research

By the classification proposed in this study, regarding the usability on smartphones it was concluded that the level of compatibility is partially compatible, because although the website has good responsiveness in general, in one of the query environments several search fields exceed the limits of the layout, even with the table presenting good visibility of its contents. Thus, there is a violation of Nielsen's Heuristics 1, 3 and 8, according to Table 5.

7.3 Transparency Portal of the João Pessoa Municipal Government

The website Transparency Portal of the João Pessoa Municipal Government, accessed through the address <https://transparencia.joaopessoa.pb.gov.br/>, has good responsiveness, easy viewing of content and handling, presenting satisfactorily the data of the query performed.

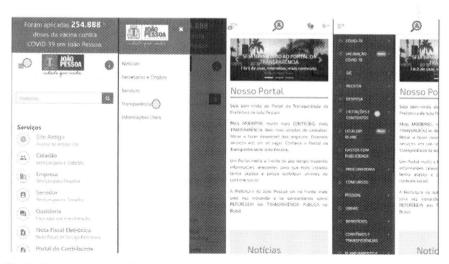

Fig. 4. Payment Authorization query screens. Note. Figure from the Transparency Portal of the João Pessoa Municipal Government. < https://transparencia.joaopessoa.pb.gov.br/>

Figure 4 shows three screens captured, which represent in order the flow for opening the page for consultation of bidding process and contracts. The screens demonstrate the ease of locating the service.

Figure 5 shows three screens captured, which represent in order the flow for performing the contract query. The screens show the ease of locating the service and the good visibility of the query result, being possible to scroll the table and view all its contents.

By the classification proposed in this study, regarding the usability on smartphones it was concluded that the level of compatibility is compatible, because the website presents good responsiveness, ease of locating the services and good visibility of the query results, with absence of Nielsen's Heuristics notes.

Fig. 5. Payment Authorization query screens. Note. Figure from the Transparency Portal of the João Pessoa Municipal Government. <https://transparencia.joaopessoa.pb.gov.br/>

7.4   Transparency Portal of the Paraíba's Legislative House

The website Transparency Portal of the Paraíba Legislative Assembly, accessed through the address <http://www.al.pb.leg.br/transparencia/>, does not present responsiveness, making its content unreadable and difficult to handle with the device in the vertical position. When used horizontally, part of the electronic site becomes legible, but its handling remains difficult.

Figure 6 presents four screens captured, which represent in order the flow for conducting a Payments query. The screens show the difficulty in reading the data and the use of a website that does not present responsiveness when accessed via a smartphone. The query in question was directed to be performed through the Transparency Portal of the State Government of Paraíba, already evaluated.

Fig. 6. Payment Lookup Screens. Note. Figure from the Paraíba's Legislative House. <http://www.al.pb.leg.br/transparencia/>

Figure 7 shows two screens captured, which represent in order the flow of access to query Payments, now with the mobile device in a horizontal position. The screens show that, even this way, the layout remains very small, making it difficult to manipulate.

Fig. 7. Horizontal payout query access screens. Note. Figure from the Paraíba's Legislative House. <http://www.al.pb.leg.br/transparencia/>

Fig. 8. Horizontal payout query access screens. Note. Figure from the Paraíba's Legislative House. <http://www.al.pb.leg.br/transparencia/>

Figure 8 shows a captured screen, which represents the last screen of the flow for consultation of Payments with the mobile device in horizontal position. The screens of Figs. 7, 8, show that even using the device in the horizontal position, either operating as an iPhoneX device or as a Samsung Galaxy S5 device, the difficulty in reading the data and handling to proceed the query remains.

Table 6. Heuristic evaluation table model

Code of the violated heuristic	Problem description	Severity
HM 1. Use of screen space	Cutting at the bottom of information	2 - Small usability problem
HM 3. Visibility and easy access to all information	Information not layered requiring scrolling of the screen for better viewing	3 - Large usability problem
HM 8. Ease of access to all functionalities	query several search fields exceed the layout limits, impairing functionality and data return	3 - Large usability problem

Note. Built for research

By the classification proposed in this study, regarding usability on smartphones, it was concluded that the level of compatibility is incompatible, because although the electronic site displays the content, the reading experience and usability of it is bad, given the absence of responsiveness. These points reveal that the site violated three Nielsen heuristics, namely, 1, 3 and 8, as presented in Table 6.

7.5 Transparency Portal of the Paraíba's Court of Justice

The website Transparency Portal of the Court of Justice of Paraíba, accessed through the address <https://www.tjpb.jus.br/transparencia/>, has good responsiveness, easy viewing of content and handling, however the consultation of data was directed to be performed through the Transparency Portal of the Government of the State of Paraíba, already evaluated.

By the classification proposed in this study, regarding usability on smartphones, it was concluded that the level of compatibility is incompatible. Although the electronic site displays the content, the reading and usability experience is poor, given the absence of responsiveness.

Figure 9 shows five screens captured, which represent in order the flow to perform the Expenses query. The screens show ease of locating the service and good visibility, however, the query in question was directed to be performed through the Transparency Portal of the Government of the State of Paraíba, already evaluated.

Fig. 9. Horizontal payout query access screens. Note. Figure from the Paraíba's Legislative House. <http://www.al.pb.leg.br/transparencia/>

By the classification proposed in this study, with regard to smartphone usability, it was concluded that the level of compatibility is compatible, since the website presents good responsiveness and ease of locating the services.

7.6 Transparency Portal of the Paraíba State Court of Audit (TCE/PB)

The home page of the website of the Paraíba State Court of Audit (TCE/PB), accessed at <https://tce.pb.gov.br/>, has good responsiveness, easy viewing of content and handling. However, the consultation of data was directed to be performed through the Transparency Portal of the State Government of Paraíba, already evaluated.

Figure 10 shows five screens captured, which represent in order the flow of two screens containing the access to the Transparency Portal, where from the portal of the State Audit Court you only click on the button "Transparency". The other screens show the ease of locating the service on the portal, clicking on the button "Expenses", and then on the button "Payments". Yet the responsiveness of the website did not adjust the layout of the objects properly and part of the items were not displayed in the layout. In order to visualize the missing menu items ("Conventions", "Revenues", "Accounting Information" and "Fleet of Vehicles") on either tested devices, horizontal page scrolling was required. The query in question was directed to be performed through the Transparency Portal of the State Government of Paraiba, already evaluated.

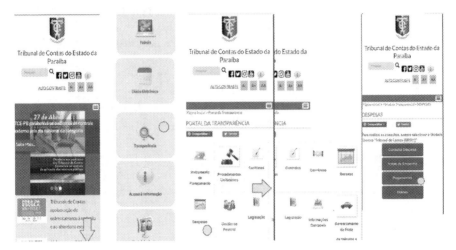

Fig. 10. Access screens to the Transparency Portal and consultation of Payments. Note. Figure from the Paraíba State Court of Audit (TCE/PB). <https://tce.pb.gov.br/>

By the classification proposed in this study, regarding usability on smartphones it was concluded that the level of compatibility is partially compatible, because although the website has good responsiveness overall, in one of the consultation environments several icons exceed the limits of the layout.

Table 7. Heuristic evaluation table model

Code of the violated heuristic	Problem description	Severity
HM 1. Use of screen space	Information at the bottom of the screen is cut off and this error affects the icons on the side of the screen	3 - Large usability problem
HM 3. Visibility and easy access to all information	Information not layered requiring scrolling of the screen for better viewing	3 - Large usability problem
HM 8. Ease of access to all functionalities	query several search fields exceed the layout limits, impairing functionality and data return	3 - Large usability problem

Note. Built for research

The severity of the problems are increased by the violations of Nielsen's Heuristics, as shown on Table 7 adjustment is recommended to make them available to the public.

8   Conclusions and Future Work

Transparency in public management is a link between the State and the citizen, allowing the latter to access information on public management, providing the effectiveness of social control of public affairs and the exercise of citizenship intended by the Federal Constitution.

In this sense, the improvement of legislation, notably highlighting the Law of Fiscal Responsibility, the Transparency Law and the Access to Information Law (Law No. 12.527/2011), have contributed to the real transparency of public actions taken by federal entities, forcing them to publish detailed budget information on the Internet, through transparency portals.

As proposed, the approach of this study would analyze a selection of seven electronic sites called Transparency Portals within the State of Paraíba, conferring compatibility criteria for use through smartphones. From the analysis of the websites, it was found that among the seven transparency websites evaluated, six promoted the adequacy of responsiveness for access by cell phones and tablets, but in three of these there is the possibility of making technical improvements in order to remedy the flaws in the layout adjustment verified in the study. The Transparency Portal of the Legislative Assembly of Paraíba, the only site evaluated to present the level incompatible with responsiveness, exposes the importance of constant investment in technologies by public managers, in order to ensure users the least possible difficulty when accessing data of public transparency.

Through the results of the study it was possible to verify gaps for public investment in the qualification of at least four transparency portals in the State of Paraíba. Thus, public managers must remain attentive to technological evolution and its urgent demands, as well as to the announced obsolescence of other technologies, always striving for the best user experience. It is worth clarifying that although the search for constant optimization is desirable, in view of the responsibility with the treasury, the manager must measure the investment, aware that the absence of responsiveness does not represent, today, direct non-compliance with the legal assumptions regarding transparency, since there is no express requirement for this.

In light of the facts, we conclude that the public administration, which is legally responsible for the effectiveness of public transparency, must accompany the technological evolution with greater effectiveness. In response to the growing presence of mobile devices with internet access on people's daily lives, administrators may seek to optimize, in its various spheres, the technological tools in service, or others that may be developed to facilitate the use of these means for the exercise of citizenship, through effective social control of public affairs.

For future research it is suggested to evaluate the benefits of the expansion of social control when providing transparency data through applications or websites aimed primarily at access through mobile devices. We emphasize that the tests performed in this study were conducted only under the perception of the researcher, and other studies may expand the data, collecting the perception of other users in the handling of electronic sites.

References

1. Porfírio, F.: Estado Democrático de Direito; Brasil Escola. Retrieved from https://brasilesc ola.uol.com.br/sociologia/estado-democratico-direito.htm. Accessed 1 May 2021
2. BRASIL: Constituição Da República Federativa do Brasil de (1988)
3. BRASIL: Lei Complementar N° 101, DE 4 DE MAIO DE 2000 – Lei de Responsabilidade Fiscal. Retrieved from http://www.planalto.gov.br/ccivil_03/Leis/LCP/Lcp101.htm. Accessed 29 Apr 2021
4. BRASIL: Lei Complementar N° 131, DE 27 DE MAIO DE 2009 – Lei da Transparência. Retrieved from http://www.planalto.gov.br/ccivil_03/leis/lcp/lcp131.htm. Accessed 29 Apr 2021
5. BRASIL: Lei N° 12.527, DE 18 DE NOVEMBRO DE 2011. – Lei de Informação Retrieved from http://www.planalto.gov.br/ccivil_03/_Ato2011-2014/2011/Lei/L12527.htm. Accessed 29 Apr 2021
6. Rebelo, M.: Fiscalizar o uso dos recursos públicos é direito da população e dos servidores: MEDIUM, 2016. Retrieved from https://medium.com/@mrebelo71/fiscalizar-o-uso-dos-rec ursos-públicos-é-também-dever-da-população-e-dos-servidores-319dbecee74a. Accessed 1 May 2021
7. IBGE: Pesquisa Nacional por Amostra de Domicílios Contínua: Acesso à internet e à televisão e posse de telefone móvel celular para uso pessoal 2019. Rio de Janeiro: IBGE, 2021. Retrieved from https://biblioteca.ibge.gov.br/index.php/biblioteca-catalogo?view=detalhes& id=2101794. Accessed 30 Apr 2021
8. Meireles, F.S.: Pesquisa Anual do Uso da TI - Tecnologia de Informação nas Empresas. 31 ed. São Paulo: FGV, 2020. Retrieved from https://eaesp.fgv.br/producao-intelectual/pesquisa-anual-uso-ti. Accessed 30 Apr 2021
9. Strong, D.M., Lee, Y.W., Wang, R.Y.: Data quality in context. Commun. ACM **40**(5), 103–110 (1997)
10. Sebrae: O que é um site responsivo. 2013. Retrieved from https://www.sebrae.com.br/sites/ PortalSebrae/artigos/o-que-e-um-site-responsivo,4a6ad1eb00ad2410VgnVCM100000b2 72010aRCRD. Accessed 1 May 2021
11. Madrigal, A.: O exercício da cidadania no desenvolvimento da sociedade. Revista Jus Navigandi, ISSN 1518-4862, Teresina, ano 21, n. 4673, 17 abr. 2016. Retrieved from https://jus. com.br/artigos/48124. Accessed 4 May 2021
12. Biazus, E.: Atuação dos municípios quanto à aplicação da lei da transparência e da lei de acesso à informação. Monografia (especialização) - Universidade Federal de Santa Maria, Centro de Ciências Sociais e Humanas, Curso de Especialização em Gestão Pública, EaD, RS, 2013. Retrieved from http://repositorio.ufsm.br/handle/1/180 Accessed 4 May 2021
13. Farias, L.A.C., Ceretta, P.S.: Análise da transparência na gestão pública: um estudo em cidades gaúchas. Florianópolis: UFSC, 2017. Retrieved from https://repositorio.ufsm.br/bit stream/handle/1/11815/Farias_Luis_Antero_Cavalheiro_de.pdf?sequence=1&isAllowed=y. Accessed 1 May 2021
14. Nascimento, E.R., Debus, I.: Lei Complementar N° 101/2000: Entendendo a Lei de Responsabilidade Fiscal. 2 ed. Brasília: Tesouro Nacional. 2000 Retrieved from https://sisweb.tes ouro.gov.br/apex/f?p=2501:9:::::9:P9_ID_PUBLICACAO:27789. Accessed 1 May 2021
15. CONTROLADORIA GERAL DA UNIÃO: Acesso à informação pública: uma introdução à Lei n° 12.527, de 18 de novembro de 2011. Brasília (DF), 2011. Retrieved from https://www. gov.br/acessoainformacao/pt-br/central-de-conteudo/publicacoes/arquivos/cartilhaacessoa informacao-1.pdf Accessed 1 May 2021
16. Carneti, K.: Google deixa de mostrar nas buscas sites não responsivos. EXAME, 2015. Retrieved from https://exame.com/tecnologia/google-deixa-de-mostrar-nas-buscas-sites-nao-responsivos/. Accessed 1 May 2021

17. Barbosa, S.D.J., et al.: Interação Humano-Computador e Experiência do Usuário. Auto publicação (2021)
18. Yáñez Gómez, R., Cascado Caballero, D., Sevillano, J.-L.: Heuristic evaluation on mobile interfaces: a new checklist. Sci. World J. **2014** (2014). https://doi.org/10.1155/2014/434326
19. Lyzara, R., et al.: E-government usability evaluation: insights from a systematic literature review. In: Proceedings of the 2nd International Conference on Software Engineering and Information Management, pp. 249–253 (2019)
20. Organisation for Economic Co-operation and Development: M-government: mobile technologies for responsive governments and connected societies. OECD Publishing, Paris (2011)
21. Rocha, M.A.M., et al.: Developing a usability study for Mexican Government Sites: the case study of the Portal del Empleo. In: Proceedings of the 5th Mexican Conference on Human-Computer Interaction, pp. 1–6 (2014) https://doi.org/10.1145/2676690.2676692
22. Abu Tair, H.Y., Abu-Shanab, E.A.: Mobile government services: challenges and opportunities. Int. J. Technol. Diffus. **5**(1), 17–25 (2014)
23. Nielsen, J., Molich, R.: Heuristic evaluation of user interfaces. In: Proceedings of the SIGCHI Conference on Human Factors in Computing Systems, pp. 249–256 (1990) https://doi.org/10.1145/97243.97281
24. Nielsen, J.: Usability engineering at a discount. In: Salvendy, G., Smith, M.J. (eds.) Designing and Using Human-Computer Interfaces and Knowledge Bused Systems, pp. 394–401. Elsevier Science Publishers, Amsterdam (1989)
25. Molich, R., Nielsen, J.: Improving a human-computer dialogue. Commun. ACM **33**(3), 338–348 (1990). https://doi.org/10.1145/77481.77486
26. Machado Neto, O., Pimentel, M.D.G.: Heuristics for the assessment of interfaces of mobile devices. In: Proceedings of the 19th Brazilian Symposium on Multimedia and the Web, pp. 93–96 (2013) https://doi.org/10.1145/2526188.2526237
27. Gil, A.C.: Métodos e técnicas de pesquisa social, 6 edn. Atlas, São Paulo (2008)

Reimagining "Space": An Approach to Increase Participants' Social Aspects During Online Conferencing

Tingting Jiang⬥, Zixuan Wang⬥, and Kostas Terzidis(✉)⬥

College of Design and Innovation, Tongji University, Shanghai 200092, China
{zixuanwang,kostas}@tongji.edu.cn

Abstract. Online conferencing has become a new normal after the COVID-19 pandemic. However, existing systems like ZOOM fall short of facilitating informal social aspects like chats, talks, discussions, dialogues, gatherings, secrets, or even gossip or quarrel, which often occur spontaneously during physical meetings. In this study, we design and prototype a novel system considering key spatial features that influence social interactions offline. The proposed system consists of three typical meeting modes: square mode for free social, room mode for split group discussion, stage mode for speech and presentation. Through Wizard-of-Oz testing with 10 participants, we summarize the design features that contribute to the richness of ambiance, the flexibility of distance, the serendipity of interaction of online conferences, and the effect of these aspects on social interaction. Together with the limitations and suggestions for future work, we hope this paper can inspire the design of spatial interaction on screen, with the aim to improve informal social aspects of online conferencing.

Keywords: Online conferencing · Social presence · Social interaction · Human-computer interaction

1 Introduction

The COVID-19 pandemic has expanded previous trends to use computer-based technologies for conferences, courses, workshops, and other social activities that formerly required physical gathering [23]. While existing conferencing platforms like ZOOM[1] might be effective for the formal part of a meeting, they fall short of facilitating unofficial encounters and social interactions between participants [1,10].

The design of space plays a crucial role in facilitating social interaction offline. Through the arrangement of rooms, walls, doors, openings, and separators, we can invite or inhibit interactions between people [5]. However, the most prevailing

---

[1] https://zoom.us/.

Supported by Shangxiang Lab.

online software people use to meet nowadays remain limited regarding these "space" features [10]. The hypothesis is that online social interaction is also implicitly affected by the style, dimension, and condition of the virtual meeting space. Thus, if these elements are handled in the right way, then social aspects during remote conferencing will be improved.

In this study, we propose a novel approach to express and experience "space" online, without conforming to preset frameworks, intending to facilitate social aspects in screen-mediated conferences. We first form our research model based on comparing the offline and online meeting spaces. We then design and prototype three typical modes of online conferencing (square mode, room mode, stage mode) and conducted Wizard-of-Oz testing with 10 participants, using a common online workshop as an example. Scale results show excellent user experience regarding our proposed system's attractiveness, stimulation, and novelty. Based on the interview, we further summarize the design features contributing to the richness of ambience, the flexibility of distance, and the serendipity of interaction in a screen-mediated conference, following the elaboration on the intriguing interplay between these spatial elements and social interaction. Our work contributes to screen-mediated spatial interaction and can inspire the design of virtual meeting tools as well as human-computer interaction in general.

2   Related Works

2.1   Social Aspects in Online Conferencing

The concept of social presence was originally referred to as the "realness" of other persons in the interaction [19], and later Gunawardena [6] linked social presence with community building and social cohesion among people in a conference, pioneering its importance in assessing the satisfaction of online education. In recent years, the definition of social presence has been developed due to the popularity of online teaching, real-time conferencing and other scenarios. Karel Kreijns [12] disentangled social presence theory and reformulated the "social interaction" concept, combining "social presence", "social space" and "sociability" (Fig. 1). This definition helps us clarify what socially relevant elements of online conferencing need to be taken into account and how these elements can be enabled at the platform design level.

Previous research shows positive effects of social interaction on remote working motivation, efficiency, and outcomes both at class and works [1,3,17,21]. Lahlou et al. [13] point out that successful interactive virtual conferencing applications must facilitate both functional information exchange and informal social interaction. Actually, the informal social and entertainment elements, such as receptions, dinners, and tours, can, in turn, facilitate formal meetings [18]. The study finds that small talks may have a function concerning the development of trustworthy interpersonal relationships during group work [12]. However, Bleakley et al. [1] found an increased formality in virtual meeting settings compared to offline ones. Support for meaningful social interaction and the personal connection remains underdeveloped in current conferencing platforms [13].

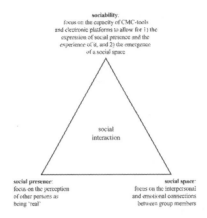

Fig. 1. The social presence, sociability, and social space triangle [12]

2.2 Influence of "Space" on Social Interaction

Studies in architecture and public space design have demonstrated the complex interplay between spatial configuration and social interactions. Anthropologist Edward T. Hall [7] gives an overview regarding the function of space dimension and human senses in connection with interpersonal contact. By changing the design of a space, it can assemble or disperse, integrate or segregate, invite or repel, open up or close in a social activity [5]. Occasionally, there is an implicit border that separates spaces that are more important than the space itself, such as porticos, corridors, or lobbies, where most substantial conversations happen (i.e. "lobbying").

When looking to the "online public space", studies have explored the relationship between social behaviors and interaction architectures [4,9]. The attempts trying to intervene the sense of "space" into remote meeting tools mainly fall into two groups. One type is approaches that utilize mixed reality technology [8,20] to project remote attendees into a real or authentic-like physical conference space. Numerous applications in both industrial (i.e. Facebook Horizon Workrooms[2], Spatial[3]) and academia [13–16] have been probing this area. However, the drawback lies in that people easily get lost or lack control (i.e. cybersickness [2]) and sometimes need a high-cost headset to obtain the best experience [22]. Another type is applications like Gather Town[4], Ohyay[5] and Mozilla Hubs[6], trying to create a virtual space on the two-dimensional screen by mimicking physical spacial infrastructure. Different from these approaches, the aim of this study is not to replicate physical spaces in the online setting but to re-imagine an abstracted

---

[2] https://www.oculus.com/workrooms.

[3] https://spatial.io.

[4] https://www.gather.town.

[5] https://ohyay.co.

[6] https://hubs.mozilla.com.

form of screen-mediated conferencing space and the social interactions it could facilitate.

3   Our Approach

3.1   Research Model

We summarize three limitations by comparing offline conferences with the most prevailing online conferencing platforms people use to meet nowadays. First is the *homogeneity* of the space depicted by online video meeting tools. The interfaces and atmospheres are monotonous across apps and types of meetings, without the intricacies of lighting, decoration, and spatial layout in physical rooms. Second is *isometricity*, the lack of differentiation regarding the distance and focus area of the online participants. It deprives the sense of intimacy fostered by physical proximity while the interplay between the intensity and distance of sensual impressions is widely used in human communication [5]. The third is the *rigidness* of the online meeting space. An essential feature of offline socializing is being able to move around the space, which inevitably leads to unplanned interactions [10]. Most existing conferencing systems fail to offer this kind of serendipity [24]. Based on these limitations, we form our research model (Fig. 2) and three research questions of the study.

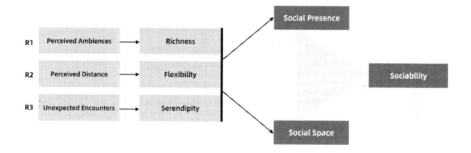

Fig. 2. Research model

R1. How online conferencing space can form various ambiances in different meetings or during different stages of a meeting, and how the perceived richness of the space will affect social interaction?

R2. How online meeting space can facilitate flexible distances between people and spaces, and how perceived changes of distance will affect social interaction?

R3. How online meeting space can support serendipitous encounters with unexpected topics and people, and how the perceived serendipity of the space will affect social interaction?

According to Karel Kreijns's social interaction theory, the sociability of the computer-mediated communication tool will be increased when the platform "allows for the expression of social presence and the experience of it, and the emergence of a social space" [12]. Thus, we hypothesize that with the improved richness, flexibility, and serendipity of the online space, the conferencing platform's sociability will be promoted.

3.2   Design

We design and prototype a conferencing system to explore the three research questions using Figma[7] and ProtoPie[8]. The design is based on previous arguments that, first, the space atmosphere should change according to the theme or phase of the meeting. Secondly, the user should be able to move around and change the space according to their needs. Thirdly, the platform should support the user to encounter unexpected topics or people when moving in the space.

The system consists of three typical conferencing modes: *square mode* (Fig. 3) for free social, *room mode* (Fig. 4, Fig. 5) for split group discussion, *stage mode* (Fig. 6) for speech and presentation. We will explain design features for each mode following serial orders in the figures. Of note that some features are across modes and will be described in the first mode they appear.

Square Mode. This mode refers to ice-breaking at the beginning, tea break in the middle, or happy hour at the end of the meeting. *Feature 1: Movable Avatar* Participants can wander around the square at will, and the live circular video avatar will follow their cursor, making them aware of the strong connection between the avatar and themselves. This direct mapping may give the user a sense of authenticity and increase their perception of the presence of others. *Feature 2: Sound Distance* When we get close enough to enter someone's audio range, we can initiate a private conversation that other attendees outside this range will not hear. The physical distance of sound will give physical properties to the virtual space and allow for free and flexible conversations, such as one-to-one and many-to-many, rather than being limited to the one-to-many format of existing software. *Feature 3: Surprise Egg* Eggs can be wrapped in any content and hidden anywhere in space, waiting to be opened by curious passers-by. For example, we can use an egg to hide our own photography, and if an interested attendee stumbles across my egg and views my work, we might start a random conversation. *Feature 4: Hobby Tag* When we hover over someone's avatar, we can view his/her hobby attributes, according to Cutler [11]: one's disclosure of personal information can help individuals know more about each other, then they are more likely to establish trust, build support, and thus find satisfaction.

---

[7] https://www.figma.com/.
[8] https://www.protopie.io/.

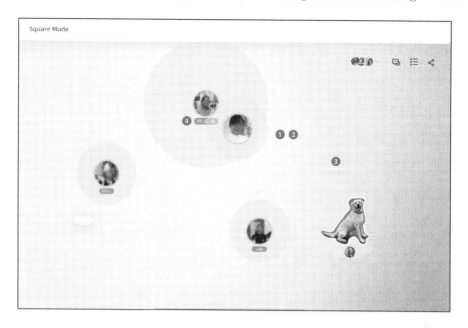

Fig. 3. A screenshot of the square mode in our design.

Room Mode. This mode is for the discussion within separated small groups. *Feature 5: Room Create* The user can drag and drop geometric shapes or draw closed shapes anywhere on the whiteboard to create a group room of any shape, and attendees who are included in the selected area will enter the room with their consent, participants who are not boxed into the selection area can also enter the room by moving their avatar. *Feature 6: Group Discussion Status Display* Members who are not in the group can see thumbnails of other groups' members and group documents' abbreviated content outside the group. *Feature 7: Listen In* When we leave our own group room and approach another room, we can get closer to listen to other groups' discussions without entering the room.

Stage Mode. This mode is needed when the presenter gives a keynote speech or when groups in a workshop need to present their outputs to all audiences. *Feature 8: Stage and Spotlight* The overall visual of stage mode is in the form of a spotlight to focus everyone's attention on the speaker. When the speaker starts the stage mode, audiences' real-time video avatars will come closer and surround the speaker, creating a more immersive presentation experience and real-time audience feedback.

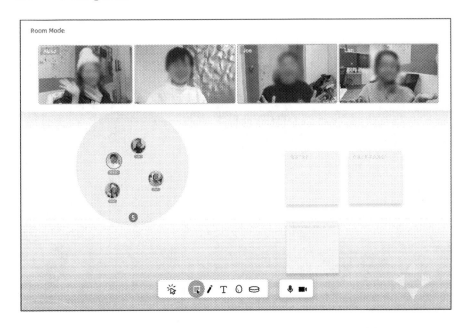

Fig. 4. A screenshot of the room mode in our design (1)

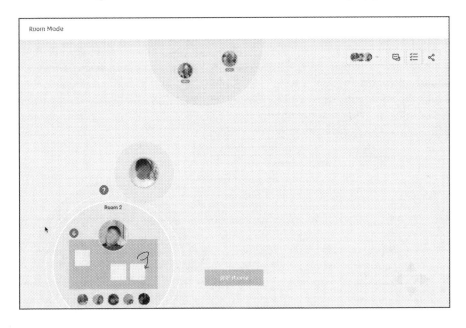

Fig. 5. A screenshot of the room mode in our design (2)

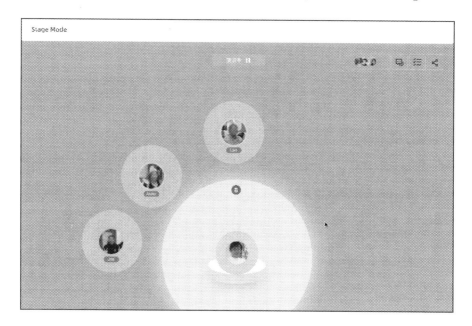

Fig. 6. A screenshot of the stage mode in our design

4   Experiment

With an interactive prototype, ten rounds of user tests were conducted to investigate the research questions: how the richness, flexibility, serendipity of the "space" will affect the social experience of attendees in the context of an online conference, and how to act upon with design elements.

4.1   Procedure and Tasks

The experiment took place in a pre-arranged space with a laptop for testing the prototype design and an iPad to show participants the task instructions (see Fig. 7). Each experiment lasted around 45 min with three parts: a 15-min prototype experience and task completion, a 5-min questionnaire filling, and a 20-min post-test interview. In the beginning, one researcher introduces the project's background, the online conference's three typical modes, and the steps that participants will go through. Then participants will explore the design following the task instructions on iPad independently. After that, participants will be asked to complete a standard user experience questionnaire[9], following a semi-structured interview.

---

[9] https://www.ueq-online.org/.

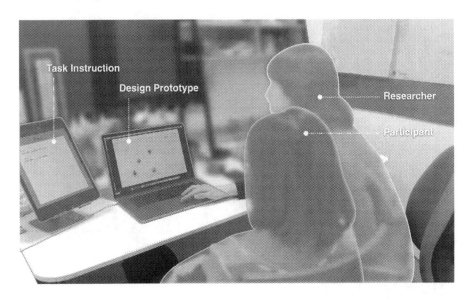

Fig. 7. A photo of our experiment set-up. The researcher is setting up the prototype, which the participant will then explore on their own according to the task instructions.

4.2 Data Collection

A total of 10 participants with prior offline and online conferencing experiences aged from 23 to 29 (mean = 25.20, SD = 1.72) from diverse fields took part in this study. Half of them identified as female, while the other half were male.

Before the experiment, the researcher asks each participant for a profile photo used as their avatar in the prototype for authenticity and immersion of the testing. Each participant was asked to provide consent for academic usage of the process photo, questionnaire results, and interview recordings.

Researchers will leave their seats while the participants fill in the questionnaire to minimize respondent bias. The interviews are recorded and transcribed for further coding in Atalas[10].

5   Results

5.1   User Experience Questionnaire

As shown in Fig. 8, overall, participants give positive ratings for all six aspects regarding the user experience of our designed artifact. Compared to the benchmark (Fig. 9), we can see that our prototype scores excellent in attractiveness (mean = 2.12, SD = 0.67), stimulation (mean = 2.18, SD = 0.47), and novelty

---

[10] https://atlasti.com/.

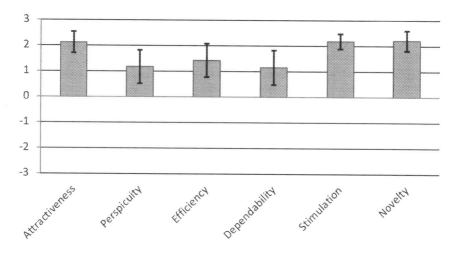

Fig. 8. UEQ result

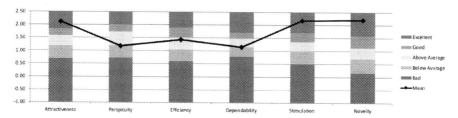

Fig. 9. UEQ benchmark

(mean = 2.20, SD = 0.63). This indicates that participants perceive our design as extremely attractive, innovative, and motivating to use.

However, when considering the pragmatic quality aspects of the design, participants show a less positive attitude. The score of efficiency (mean = 1.43, SD = 1.05) is above average, and the results of perspicuity (mean = 1.18, SD = 1.05) and dependability (mean = 1.15, SD = 1.07) are slightly below the average compared to the benchmark.

Of note is that some participants (P3, P5, P8, P9) think the interface is confusing (Q21, mean = 0.90, SD = 1.73). In particular, participant 5 regards the design as not so understandable (Q2, mean = 0.90, SD = 0.99) and can be complicated (Q13, mean = 1.10, SD = 1.37). The reasoning for these negative ratings in perspicuity aspects may be due to the fact that our design is a new form of online conferencing, which is completely different from what the participants are already familiar with using. As for some relatively low scores in dependability aspects, such as predictability (Q8, mean = 0.90, SD = 1.60) and sense of security (Q17, mean = 0.90, SD = 1.37), may be attributed to our aim of facilitating interactions with a sense of serendipity and uncertainty in the design.

The UEQ results summarized participants' experiences of the prototypes in general, but could not help us gain insight into the impact factors and impact outcomes of the social aspects, so we further organized semi-structured interviews for a more in-depth analysis.

5.2   Comparison with Existing Software

Previously Used Software. To compare our design with the existing applications, in the interview, we first ask participants to recall the conferencing and collaboration tools they often use. Their answers can be mainly grouped into three categories:

- video conferencing software: VooV Meeting[11] (N = 10), Zoom[12] (N = 9), Lark[13] (N = 5), WeCom[14] (N = 2));
- whiteboard collaboration software: Conferencing Table[15] (N = 9), Miro[16] (N = 7), Figma[17] (N = 6)).

Overall Feeling. In general, participants feel that the design is very innovative as it is different from any conferencing or collaboration tools they had used before (P2, P7, P8). In particular, although very abstract, they point out that the design gives them some sense of interaction in the offline space (P1, P2, P3, P4, P6).

Difference 1: Flexible Interaction. The most significant difference mentioned by most participants is more diverse and flexible interactions with the meeting space and other attendees (P1, P2, P3, P4, P6, P7, P9, P10). This is supported by the design that your live video is an avatar following the mouse (P1, P3, P6). In this way, the attendees are encouraged to move around the space and encounter other people. In contrast, attendees' live videos are stacked as fixed squares in most traditional conferencing applications. In addition, P4 and P7 also highlight the benefits of the feature in facilitating their interaction with other attendees.

Difference 2: Ambiguous Purpose. Participants felt that our design is more multi-functional, and the purpose of using it can be more ambiguous in a sense when compared with existing conferencing tools (P5, P8, P10). As P5 describes, "When I open a Zoom or VooV Meeting, I know exactly what I will be doing.

---

[11] https://meeting.tencent.com/.
[12] https://zoom.us/.
[13] https://www.larksuite.com.
[14] https://work.weixin.qq.com/.
[15] https://www.huiyizhuo.com/.
[16] https://miro.com/.
[17] https://www.figma.com/.

I enter when the meeting starts and leave when it ends. However, with this design, I'm not quite sure what I'm going to do when I enter, as there are so many interactions that can happen".

Difference 3: Informal Atmosphere. Some participants also mentioned that the design makes them feel that the meeting is more relaxing and informal (P5, P9, P10). P10 believes that you can even interact with others during breaks in our design, whereas people simply turn off the camera or leave the meeting in most online conferences' breaks. P5 describes it as a feeling of an "online community" rather than just a meeting. As such, it is also noted that it may not be suitable for formal business meetings.

5.3 The Richness of Ambience

For R1, we want to learn about participants' perceived difference in different ambiances as well as their influence on social interaction. To achieve this, we ask participants to describe the feeling and atmosphere of three modes, respectively. However, it is worth noting that some participants are more concerned with functional features and cannot express the atmosphere and feelings. Therefore, these answers have not been counted in this section.

Mode 1. Participants' general feelings of the first atmosphere are free (P4, P7, P9), vibrant (P2, P9), and interesting (P1, P2, P5), which makes them feel curious and intrigued to explore (P3, P7, P8, P9, P10). The majority of the participants believe that the ambiance in this scenario facilitates their social interaction with other attendees (P1, P2, P4, P6, P7, P8, P9, P10), while one participant expressed the concern for social phobia attendees.

Mode 2. Compared to the first scenario, participants think the atmosphere in scenario 2 is more formal (P4, P9). They also feel a stronger sense of boundaries (P3, P4, P8) since they are visually clustered inside a group circle. Some believe that this ambiance can help attendees focus more on the members and content inside the group (P4).

When comparing to traditional meeting software such as Zoom's breakout room, participants think the design of drawing to create a group, dragging to exit a group, and moving to observe other groups makes them feel that they can start a group discussion more flexibly and freely (P1, P4, P5). P4 likens it to the atmosphere of a small square where several small discussion groups happen at the same time. Two or three friends gather together and form a small discussion circle naturally where anyone passing by can join or leave at any time.

Mode 3. Many participants have the strongest feeling of the ambiance in this scenario due to the stage metaphor and the change of light (P8, P10). P6 believes that the interaction "stepping onto the stage to make a speech" creates a sense of ritual.

Most participants believe that the design helps them feel the audience's focus during the presentation (P3, P4, P5, P6, P7, P10). By referring to the previous online presenting experience, P5 regards this as positive feedback from the software, feeling that her efforts are being respected. P10 believes that feeling the audience's concentration will make him more engaged when presenting, while P9 feels more control as a speaker. Interestingly, not all people are eager for attention. P4 expressed the sense of safety as an audience in this scenario since all focus is on the host.

5.4   The Flexibility of Distance

For R2, we ask participants' perceived distance change during the experiment. Based on the interview answers, we summarized factors influencing the perception of distance into five categories and analyzed the influence on social interaction.

Aspect 1: Size. The first design feature that many participants report making them feel a closer distance is when their cursor moves near another user, the user's avatar circle will become larger (P1, P2, P3, P8). P3 specifically noted that while in collaboration software like Figma and Miro the user cursor can also be moved around the interface, our design make her feel a stronger change in interpersonal distance. She assumes this is because the interaction you can have with each other also changes when two cursors move closer that only two users within a certain distance can hear each other and chat in real-time audio.

Similarly, when entering a split group, the group member's cameras will become larger. P10 believes that this makes him feel people within the group are closer. This may indicate that online interaction is influenced by the physical metaphor of being nearer and larger.

Aspect 2: Movement. Another element that contributes to the sense of distance is the movement of the mouse in the interface. For the square mode, P9 argues that if someone moves in the same direction as her, she will feel psychologically closer to that person, even more so than if it keeps them fixed at a very close distance.

For the room mode, P3 and P5 both mentioned feeling a change in their distance to different groups when dragging their avatar out of one group and moving closer to another.

Aspect 3: Boundary. The majority of the participants feel their distance with group members reduced after they enter the same group circle (P1, P2, P6, P7, P8, P9, P10). The change of background is regarded as a visual indicator and a metaphor for physical boundaries. P9 mentions that this change in distance allows her to feel a stronger sense of cohesion within the group. P8 and P10 report a significantly more distance from the in-group members when they moved out of the circle.

Aspect 4: Stage. For the stage mode, participants show a disparate perception of distance. P2 and P5 argue that being on stage distanced the speaker from the audience, while P3 and P10 think that the surrounding of other participants' avatars reduced the audience-speaker distance compared to traditional conferencing tools like Zoom's presentation mode.

Aspect 5: Interest. Some participants reveal the feeling of special distance: relational distance changes when they find they share the same interest with another attendee (P4, P9, P10). This is facilitated by the design feature "surprise eggs" that attendees could discover the personal product other people hide. P4 describes that he feels a lot closer to on attendee when he finds the cat picture hidden by that attendee. P9 thinks that if someone is looking at the same object as she did, she will feel closer to that person and assume that they share the same interest.

5.5   The Serendipity of Interaction

For R3, we ask participants' experience of unexpected encounters with the environment and other attendees, focusing on features that inspire serendipitous and informal social interactions, as well as the effect of those behavior changes.

Aspect 1: Avatar. From participants' descriptions, serendipity appears in many features embedded in different modes. Firstly, avatar-related designs receive many comments enhancing the serendipity. For instance, P3 mentions that "avatar following the cursor makes me want to move around and explore new features. When the avatar is separated from the cursor (i.e., inside split group discussion), my desire to move is reduced." Moving brings a lot of incidental interaction with people and the environment. As the avatars get closer, the aperture of the avatars becomes larger, and one-to-one conversations become possible, which lowers the threshold for participants to interact and allows a more natural social interaction (P2, P4, P7).

Aspect 2: Interest. The hobby tags on each attendees' avatar, as well as the images representing their work, life, or interest" buried in the surprise eggs, provide participants with: "more personal information," "conversation starters," "common topics," and similarities. Those bring a sense of intimacy and trust, facilitating more dynamic interaction behaviors (P4, P5, P10).

Feature3: Listen in. The "listen in" feature of room mode can also lead to uncertain interactions, and P10 believes this can increase the level of group dynamics in the environment.

5.6   Limitations and Suggestions

Limitations. On the one hand, participants concern about the consistency of the existing online meeting product positioning, which is efficiency-driven and some of the novelty features we designed, for instance, "surprise eggs" may undermine the seriousness of the meeting (P6), too much social interaction oriented features may distract attendees from the content of the conference (P8), and those social functions' frequency of use would be low (P1). While there is a need to balance efficiency and social aspects to popularize the tool, our initial focus prioritized how to improve social factors, so these concerns are valid but not the central issue of this version of the design.

On the other hand, there are some limitations in the prototyping itself, mainly regarding the design of the interaction details, i.e., some interaction responses are missing or inappropriate. For example, due to the lack of feedback, it's hard for participants to know whether the group members they are spectating could sense their presence, which would give them a sense of shame (P5, P8). Due to the strong feedback when avatars approach each other, P3 feels social pressure. The moving background leads some participants to mistakenly believe that the change in the background is related to their own motor behavior (P1, P10).

Suggestions. Many participants expect more layers of communication: support for both synchronous and asynchronous communication (P6), support for socialization from pan-attention to focus interaction (P3) with different levels of visualization (P9), support for different modes of social status such as do not disturb mode (P4), support for low information communication such as text, emoji likes, handing business cards, etc. (P5, P6, P7), support for multi-sensory interactions such as using the vibration of the touch screen to indicate the proximity of the avatars, support for continuous communication after the meeting (P7).

Regarding the online meeting space backgrounds, P3 and P5 both suggest that the backgrounds could be kept abstract but provide more guidance, such as spatial zoning or scenes related to the theme. As for break-out rooms, participants expect enhanced feelings of entering the split group, such as zooming in to the group whiteboard content darkening of the surroundings (P1, P7). P9 is concerned about wrongly selecting members when creating the room and wants to confirm the members in a list format. In the presentation scenario, P10 expects more interaction with audiences as a speaker, such as hovering an avatar next to him to cue a particular audience. The above suggestions can be considered in future designs and would work well for product experience iterations.

6   Conclusion

A significant, yet often dismissed aspect of official meetings such as conferences, panel discussions, symposia, etc., whether offline or online, is the informal part of these meetings: chats, introductions, talks, conversations, discussions, dialogues, gatherings, reminders, secrets, or even gossip or quarrels. It is what we call "the backstage." These activities usually are not allowed, promoted, or empowered, let alone encouraged, and yet they comprise one of the main reasons people get interested in a meeting besides the topic. These activities online are hard to perform mainly because of the structure of the online systems, as well as the lack of tools that provide enough confidence to the users to engage in such activities. The proposed system, taking inspiration from physical spaces and meetings, sets out to empower the user not only with the means to perform but also to construct customized ways to interact informally with other users. The objective was to involve random users to get feedback and hopefully engage them in new behaviors we did not predict. This alone was an unexpected yet desirable effect of the proposed system that allowed us to evaluate the effectiveness and most, most notably, the dialectic relationship between the tool and its user.

References

1. Bleakley, A., et al.: Bridging social distance during social distancing: exploring social talk and remote collegiality in video conferencing. Hum. Comput. Interact. 1–29 (2021)
2. Chang, E., Kim, H.T., Yoo, B.: Virtual reality sickness: a review of causes and measurements. Int. J. Hum. Comput. Interact. **36**(17), 1658–1682 (2020)
3. Dahik, A., et al.: What 12,000 employees have to say about the future of remote work. Boston Consulting Group (2020)
4. Erickson, T., Kellogg, W.A.: Social translucence: Using minimalist visualisations of social activity to support collective interaction. In: Designing Information Spaces (2003)
5. Gehl, J.: Life between buildings, vol. 23. Van Nostrand Reinhold, New York (1987)
6. Gunawardena, C.N.: Social presence theory and implications for interaction and collaborative learning in computer conferences (1995)
7. Hall, E.T.: The hidden dimension, vol. 609. Doubleday, Garden City (1966)
8. tom Dieck, M.C., Jung, T.H., Loureiro, S.M.C. (eds.): Augmented Reality and Virtual Reality. PI, Springer, Cham (2021). https://doi.org/10.1007/978-3-030-68086-2
9. Harry, D., Donath, J.: Information spaces-building meeting rooms in virtual environments. In: CHI'08 Extended Abstracts on Human Factors in Computing Systems, pp. 3741–3746. ACM SIGCHI (2008)
10. Jacobs, N.J., Lindley, J.: Room for improvement in the video conferencing 'space'. AoIR Selected Papers of Internet Research (2021)
11. Joe, S.K.: Socioemotional use of CMC: factors related to self-disclosure in computer-mediated communication (1997)
12. Kreijns, K., Xu, K., Weidlich, J.: Social presence: conceptualization and measurement. Educ. Psychol. Rev. **34**(2), 139–170 (2021)
13. Lahlou, S., et al.: Are we 'beyond being there'yet? Towards better interweaving epistemic and social aspects of virtual reality conferencing. In: Extended Abstracts of the 2021 CHI Conference on Human Factors in Computing Systems, pp. 1–6 (2021)
14. Lee, C., Joo, H., Jun, S.: Social VR as the new normal? understanding user interactions for the business arena. In: Extended Abstracts of the 2021 CHI Conference on Human Factors in Computing Systems, pp. 1–5 (2021)

15. Manuel, M., Dongre, P., Alhamadani, A., Gračanin, D.: Supporting embodied and remote collaboration in shared virtual environments. In: Chen, J.Y.C., Fragomeni, G. (eds.) HCII 2021. LNCS, vol. 12770, pp. 639–652. Springer, Cham (2021). https://doi.org/10.1007/978-3-030-77599-5_44

16. McVeigh-Schultz, J., Isbister, K.: The case for "weird social" in VR/XR: a vision of social superpowers beyond meatspace. In: Extended Abstracts of the 2021 CHI Conference on Human Factors in Computing Systems, pp. 1–10 (2021)

17. Richardson, J.C., Maeda, Y., Lv, J., Caskurlu, S.: Social presence in relation to students' satisfaction and learning in the online environment: a meta-analysis. Comput. Hum. Behav. **71**(JUN), 402–417 (2017)

18. Rogers, B., Masoodian, M., Apperley, M.: A virtual cocktail party: supporting informal social interactions in a virtual conference. In: Proceedings of the 2018 International Conference on Advanced Visual Interfaces, pp. 1–3 (2018)

19. Short, J., Williams, E., Christie, B.: The Social Psychology of Telecommunications. Wiley, Toronto (1976)

20. Speicher, M., Hall, B.D., Nebeling, M.: What is mixed reality? In: Proceedings of the 2019 CHI Conference on Human Factors in Computing Systems, pp. 1–15 (2019)

21. Tu, C.H., Mcisaac, M.: The relationship of social presence and interaction in online classes. Am. J. Distance Educ. **16**(3), 131–150 (2002)

22. Wiederhold, B.K.: Connecting through technology during the coronavirus disease 2019 pandemic: avoiding "zoom fatigue" (2020)

23. Wiederhold, B.K.: Social media use during social distancing (2020)

24. Woods, M.: Serendipity in practice: a social state. In: Bite: Recipes for Remarkable Research, pp. 176–181. Brill Sense (2014)

Vulnerabilities and Secure Coding for Serverless Applications on Cloud Computing

Yonghwan Kim⬩, Jahwan Koo⁽✉⁾⬩, and Ung-Mo Kim⬩

Graduate School of Information and Communications, Sungkyunkwan University,
25-2 Sungkyunkwan-ro, Jongno-gu, Seoul, South Korea
`prokyhsigma@g.skku.edu`, {`jhkoo,ukim`}`@skku.edu`

Abstract. Cloud computing has enabled remarkable progress by providing many advantages such as low initial cost, high scalability and flexibility, and low maintenance cost. The success of cloud computing allows developers who want to make various microservices to get interested in serverless applications. However, although many studies have been conducted on the development of serverless applications based on cloud computing over the past few years, the focus is mainly on the security of the cloud computing infrastructure, thus there are few studies on serverless application security itself. In this paper, we analyze security vulnerabilities for serverless applications on cloud computing and present their secure coding techniques. To be effective in practice, the architecture for AWS based serverless applications is designed, and five major security vulnerabilities are identified using the STRIDE threat methodology. Moreover, we provide secure codes for the identified five major security vulnerabilities that will help make more secure serverless applications.

Keywords: Cloud computing · Serverless application · Security · Secure coding · Vulnerabilities

1 Introduction

As the huge popularity of cloud computing began a few years ago, the applications on the cloud computing are becoming more popular [1]. Various characteristics of the cloud environment, such as the scalability and fault tolerance, allow large Internet corporations (e.g., Google, Facebook, Microsoft and Amazon) to use a microservice architecture that can develop, test, deploy, operate, and manage their applications in serverless fashion that will improve development agility [2,3].

Serverless is a programming model and architecture that small pieces of codes are executed in the cloud without control over the running resources, and it is a

M. Kurosu (Ed.): HCII 2022, LNCS 13304, pp. 145–163, 2022.
https://doi.org/10.1007/978-3-031-05412-9_10

new cloud computing execution model that can change the composition of modern scalable applications [4,5]. This model allows cloud developers to develop, deploy, and operate their applications with more fine-grained service functionalities without the complexity of creating and managing (for example, to cope with inconsistent traffic patterns) the infrastructure resources necessary for their execution [3]. With these features, serverless applications on cloud computing make easier and more cost-effective to develop scalable microservices, and have evolved into the next step in the cloud computing architecture [5].

The transition to serverless in the cloud does not provide the only positive change. To use the cloud, data should be stored externally, and in serverless, even the source code should be stored externally, thus the security for preventing exposure of information and source code has become very important. Following these changes, various studies show that data security, user authentication and authorization, and logging and monitoring appear to be the representative security requirements of the cloud [6,7]. However, most of these research focused on the security properties of cloud computing infrastructure, and there are few security researches on serverless application development. Moreover, since the OWASP Top 10 [8] informs the most recently discovered vulnerabilities in general style, the problem arises that developers should understand a scope broadly. Also, there is a problem that the specificity of the cloud environment is not properly reflected.

In this paper, we identify major security vulnerabilities that developers need to check through STRIDE threat methodology and provide secure coding techniques to strengthen these vulnerabilities. To be effective in practice, we consider that the application architecture is based on AWS Lambda and WAS resources designed and built using the event-based and flow-based four use-cases presented in [5]. Next, five major vulnerabilities are identified through the threat methodology of the built application, and determined according to more important aspects in a serverless environment. Finally, we provide secure codes for the identified security vulnerabilities.

Our contributions will help developers to get new security knowledge competency that needs to be checked in a serverless environment other than a traditional web application, and it seems that they will be able to more safely protect their data, customer information, and source codes that have moved to cloud environment.

2   Related Work

Significant security researches are already underway on the cloud side. The following studies are summarized and presented only those relevant to our study.

Annanda Rath shows 5 security domains and 31 security patterns, from the system and data security to privacy protection, and provides case studies for solutions for each pattern to ensure a trusted environment when designing and developing Cloud SaaS applications [6].

Hamed Tabrizchi presents cloud security issues and challenges based on the OWASP attack classification to address the security issues facing the system after conducting and analyzing a survey of cloud users on various components of cloud computing such as policies, security, data storage, applications, and networks [7].

Wesley O'Meara point out that attackers focus on vulnerabilities in functional flows within serverless application architectures, with the intent of illegal access to sensitive data, denial of service to consumers, and illegal use of cloud resources, and the author also explains the scenarios that multiple attack vectors can be used to bypass secure function and directly access sensitive services. Therefore, to realize the benefits of serverless, the author mentions that these types of attacks should be considered when designing and implementing security strategies and application architectures [9].

John Michener introduces that the secure implementations targeting OWASP Top 10 vulnerabilities are common because cloud users are responsible for security issues related to the codes and data. Therefore, the author suggests that authentication and authorization for calling codes and callers, data transmission protection and verification, vulnerabilities checking in open sources and libraries, and encryption of sensitive information are necessary. Also, the author mentions that large-scale Function-as-a-Services (FaaS) applications require powerful processes conjunct with automation to reasonably ensure application security during the development and deployment process [10].

Moreover, the authors in [9, 10] point out about the necessity of applying Secure Software Development Life Cycle (SSDLC) along with threat modeling from the planning stage during serverless development as well as secure coding referring OWASP Top 10.

3   Application Vulnerabilities

Many existing studies [6, 7, 9, 10] related to cloud and serverless describe vulnerabilities and security requirements based on OWASP. However, since the vulnerabilities discussed in OWASP are broadly explained, there are difficulties in the implementation process for developers who need to do secure coding. Therefore, we identify and present major application-level vulnerabilities on cloud environments for developers.

3.1   Serverless Application Design

In order to identify common vulnerabilities in serverless applications, we present the architecture that includes the characteristics of serverless applications, referring to the four use-cases of serverless presented in [5], as shown in Fig. 1.

This architecture consists of a front-end (e.g., Browser, Object Storage and Mobile), cloud service (Key Manager), External/Internal Web APIs, data storage (e.g., Object Storage, Cache and Database), and several functions (Function 1-5). External/Internal Web APIs are included in the architecture so that some

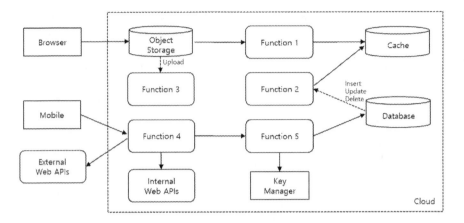

Fig. 1. Serverless application architecture for use-cases.

functions can call 3rd party APIs or access other Web APIs in the cloud. Also, there are Key Manager to restrict access to important information, and Cache, Object Storage, and Database for storing and managing data in service. Here, the Cache keeps the data fetched through the functions for a short period of time to reduce the I/O processing of data in the database. Object Storage not only stores data used for application but also stores source codes such as HTML and JavaScript to provide front-end service through hosting service. The arrow connecting each module means the calling direction. The straight line means direct call by the caller, and the dotted line means automatic call based on the event. Also, the content written next to the dotted line means the event content to which the function is connected.

3.2   Analysis of Possible Vulnerabilities in Serverless Application

To check out what vulnerabilities exist in the architecture established in the previous section (see Fig. 1), we perform threat analysis using the STRIDE threat methodology. Then, following the well-known CVE vulnerabilities [9], OWASP Top 10 vulnerabilities [8], CSA Security Guideline [12], and security vulnerabilities mentioned in [9,10,13], we identify what types of attacks can actually occur in the architecture. Table 1 shows the results.

As shown in Table 1, various vulnerabilities have been identified in the serverless application architecture. These vulnerabilities ranged from vulnerabilities commonly found in web applications to vulnerabilities that occur only in serverless or on-premises with different severity. In order to identify major vulnerabilities of serverless applications, vulnerabilities related to data security, authentication and authorization, logging and monitoring, which are described to be important in existing studies, were identified. And vulnerabilities that affect the cost of using the cloud when it occurs in the cloud were identified. Finally, vulnerabilities frequently seen in on-premises web applications were excluded. The main vulnerabilities of serverless applications identified in this way are as follows.

Table 1. Examples of possible vulnerable scenarios in serverless application.

Threat	Vulnerable scenario
Spoofing	Authenticate as another user through cookie modification
	Authenticate as another user through parameter modulation
	Absence of user re-authentication before performing important functions
	SSRF attack possible due to lack of validation on the calling API URL
	Lack of response in case of certificate error
Tampering	Possible to inquire, modify, and delete other user information through parameter tampering
	Possible to edit information that cannot be modified by adding parameters
	Function event can be forced through parameter tampering
	Possible to read, edit, and delete files upload-ed by others
	Possible to tamper the source codes in Repositories
Repudiation	No system logs for important functions, data and transactions
	No system log for authentication failure
	No log content to a level that can be tracked issues
	Log messages can be tampered with by logging without input validation
	No log by configuring a specific format in the log contents
Information disclosure	Sensitive information such as personal information, sensitive information, and identification information is exposed in response data
	Exposure of Instance Credential Information
	Exposure of sensitive information on the net-work
	Sensitive information is stored in the public repository
	Sensitive information is stored as plain text in the database
Denial of service	Lack of service restrictions when requesting a function more than a certain number of times
	No limit on the number of requests when dynamically allocating cloud resources
	Lack of verification of functions that can double the CPU consumption of the server
	Lack of verification of the ability to consume the server's resources
	Directly pass commands to allocate server resources
Elevation of privilege	Lack of verification of actions that users cannot perform
	Applications can access resources using the cloud user's account
	The account used by the application does not use least privilege
	Privilege elevation possible through tampering with authentication tokens
	Privilege Elevation through SQL Injection and Command Injection

1. Stealing instance credential information of cloud resources through Server-Side Request Forger (SSRF) attack
2. Exposure hard-coded important information written in the source codes
3. Tampering of log messages through logging without verification of input values
4. Infinite function event occurrence through incorrect path configuration
5. Information exposure due to the absence of encryption for sensitive information
6. Difficulty in event detection and analysis through insufficient log recording

In case number 3 (Log Forging), when receiving an input value by inserting Carriage Return/Line Feed (CR/LF) such as "\r\n" that can induce multiple log messages to be recorded, API Gateway throws an exception before starting Functions. So we confirmed that the log was not recorded in the Function. However, for the remaining 5 cases, we confirmed that actual vulnerabilities occurred, and a sample code was implemented to confirm each vulnerability. For more details on this, see the next section.

4   Secure Coding for Vulnerabilities in Serverless Application

A web security vulnerability is a kind of loophole that could allow an attacker to break into a web application and perform unwanted actions on a target website [14]. In this section, we examine which vulnerabilities can occur in cloud-based serverless applications. Next, we present vulnerabilities directly implemented at the code level for developers and provide safe coding techniques that can enhance security. Moreover, we provide examples of serverless applications developed in Node.js on the Amazon AWS cloud environment.

4.1   Server-Side Request Forgery (SSRF)

SSRF is recently mentioned as a vulnerability that is important enough to be identified as a major Top 10 vulnerability [8] in web applications. SSRF attacks occur when an application executes a URL with the server's privileges or obtains a remote resource without validating the URL received from the outside. In particular, if the URL points to an internal service and the server maintain a connection, it becomes very vulnerable to SSRF attacks and can be very destructive when exploiting the internal service [15]. And, in a cloud environment where serverless applications are running, if the metadata that stores the instance credentials of cloud resources is stolen through an SSRF attack, the attacker can directly access the cloud resource through the stolen credentials. So the SSRF attack in a cloud environment is much more destructive than SSRF in the on-premises environment.

Stealing Instance Credentials through SSRF Attack. In the AWS Cloud environment, if Lambda can access the internal web service using EC2, there is a possibility of stealing credential information through EC2 instance metadata. Here, instance metadata is instance-specific data that can be used to configure or manage running instances, including dynamic data such as instance credential documents that are created when an EC2 instance is launched [16]. The instance credential document is exposed in JSON format through the instance metadata service and can only be retrieved via a local IPv4 address (169.254.169.254) in AWS Cloud [17]. If the Lambda function that can access EC2 does not properly validate the received URL as shown in Listing. 1.1, attackers can steal the credential document by passing the URL that can check the credential document of EC2.

Listing 1.1. Example of a vulnerable Lambda function without validation

```
1  callURL = event["url"];
2  // Use the url parameter received from outside without
       verification
3  const option = {
4      uri: "http://abcd.compute.amazoneaws.com/call.php?
           url=" + callURL,
5      method: "GET"
6  };
7  request( option, function( err, response, body ) {
8      ...
9  }
```

To perform this attack, it is necessary to know the IAM role of EC2, but the IAM role information can also be easily checked through the SSRF attack. If the attackers successfully obtain the IAM role information, they can compose the URI to access the metadata and steal the EC2 credentials. Then, they can gain access to those services and resources through the stolen credentials. To respond to this issue, AWS also provides instance metadata service version 2 that allows access to metadata after a token is issued [18]. However, when creating EC2, the instance metadata service is set to version 1 by default, so if cloud users do not know these details when creating EC2, the vulnerability still could be occurring. Even if Amazon will select version 2 as the default value, since cloud users can select version 1 by themselves, the possibility of stealing instance credentials through an SSRF attack is open until version 1 is no longer available.

Secure Coding to Prevent SSRF. To prevent SSRF attacks, you need to verify the URL that you want to use. The best way to verify URL is to configure the logic to use only domains that have been verified in advance. First, after identifying the URLs to be allowed, the allowed URLs are stored in the same place as an array. Next, the client implements to deliver only the Index value instead of the URL or implements it to use after checking whether the URL input is included in the allowed URL list as shown in Listing. 1.2.

Listing 1.2. URL validation with white-list of allowed URLs

```
1  var allowed_url = [ "https://1234.amazoneaws.com/greeting
     " ];
2  callURL = event["url"];
3  // Check whether url parameter received from outside is
     included in allowed_url
4  if ( allowed_url.indexOf( callURL ) > -1 ) {
5     ...
6  }
```

However, if the URLs cannot be defined in advance because various domains must be allowed, validation logic can be implemented to at least restrict access to AWS internal IPs with a blacklist filter method, as shown in Listing. 1.3.

Listing 1.3. URL validation using not allowed URLs

```
1  function checkURL(url) {
2     var isValid = true;
3     // Check if url parameter received from the outside is
        the internal IP
4     if ( url.startsWith("//169.254.169.254") ||
        url.startsWith("http://169.254.169.254")
5        || url.startsWith("https://169.254.169.254") ) {
6        isValid = false;
7  }
8  return isValid;
9  }
10 ...
11 callURL = event["url"];
12 if ( checkURL( callURL) ) {
13    ...
14 }
```

When implementing the blacklist method, it is possible to find out whether the received URL includes internal IP using only IP, but if you want to include the HTTP protocol as in the sample code, you must include the URL starting with "//" because HTTP protocol can be omitted. As in the sample code, if a developer uses a whitelist or blacklist filter to prevent access to AWS internal IP, we can prevent stealing of AWS resources using internal IP authentication information by malicious users.

4.2   Hard-Coded Sensitive Information

When reviewing the source code of developers, one of the most frequently discovered vulnerabilities empirically is the exposure of hard-coded information. Developers often use test account information as comments or hard-coded variables for quick and convenient testing and debugging during the development process. Also, developers tend to think that this is not a problem because they are only exposed to the source code, and when developing internal services, the tendency to think like this is stronger. There is various information such as test account information, developer's personal information, database credential, and so on. However, in general, this information is not accessible to all developers. Also, if the credential information is hard-coded, it can create a serious loophole that can bypass authentication [19]. So that credentials should be replaced regularly according to the life-cycle, the source code may need to be modified. In this paper, if RDS account information in serverless application is hard-coded, we suggest what issues can arise and how to protect them.

Hard-coded RDS Credential Exposure. When you want to use RDS like MySQL in AWS Lambda, you need to connect RDS using the location of the RDS resource and account information. Then, if the credential information is hard-coded as shown in Listing. 1.4, RDS access information and account information can be exposed to all developers who can access the Lambda function.

Listing 1.4. Exposure of hard-coded RDS credential

```
1  // Exposed account ID and Password
2  var connection = mysql.createConnection( {
3      host : "database.ap-northeast-2.rds.amazonaws.com",
4      user: "aws_rds_admin",
5      password: "aws_rds_admin_password",
6      port: "3306",
7      database: "user_info"
8  });
```

However, RDS access information and account information must be implemented using a secure method instead of hard-coding since it should be exposed to only users with RDS rights at a minimum. In general, the developer keeps the password in a safe place so that credential information such as password is not exposed [20]. AWS provides environment variables [21] that can be used instead of hard-coding, but it cannot be said to be safe. Because all developers who can access the Lambda can check the environment variables, it is the same with exposure of credential information to every Lambda developer. When using environment variables, AWS provides a secure function to store them after encryption, depending on the type of information, even if it is encrypted information, exposure itself may arise an issue from laws or compliance, or information may be exposed through cracking.

Secure Coding to Prevent Hard-coded RDS Credential. The safe way to store and use credential information is to safely store and manage credential information using a separate service. Although there is a way to manage it using an open-source such as Vault [22] that allows to safely access important information, cloud service providers are already providing services that can safely store important information. In AWS, they provide a service called Secrets Manager. Developer can implement to retrieve credentials programmatically instead of hard-coding using Secrets Manager. Because the secret no longer exists in the source codes, you can prevent the security password from being compromised by someone examining the code [23]. You can also configure Secrets Manager to automatically rotate secrets on a schedule secret owners specify. Therefore, the long-term security password can be replaced with a short-term security password, which has the advantage of greatly reducing the risk of damage [23]. If this is applied, it can be implemented so that RDS can be accessed without the hard-coded credential information of RDS in the Lambda function as shown in Listing. 1.5. Through this, sensitive information cannot be unnecessarily exposed to developers who do not have permission for RDS Credentials.

Listing 1.5. Sample for using Secret Manager instead of hard-coding

```
1  var client = new AWS.SecretsManager({
2      region: "ap-northeast-2"
3  });
4  client.getSecretValue( {secretId: "prod/lambda/mysql"} ,
       function(err, data){
5      var secret = data.SecretString;
6  }
7  // Access database using the access information and
       account information obtained through SecretManager
8  var connection = mysql.createConnection( {
9      host: JSON.parse(secret).host,
10     user: JSON.parse(secret).username,
11     password: JSON.parse(secret).password,
12     port: JSON.parse(secret).port,
13     database: user_info
14 } );
```

4.3   Infinite Loop of Lambda Call

Cloud Providers, including AWS, provide codes to easily use Functions as event handlers and configure services [5]. if Lambda is set as event-based, it can be implemented so that Lambda can be invoked automatically even if the user does not directly call it. This function enables short and simple implementation because the developer does not need to implement all logic directly according to data and control flow. However, if it falls into a recursive call through incorrect settings or implementation during the implementation process, this lambda function can be called infinitely. In Cloud, cloud users pay only for what they use Lambda, and they are charged according to the number of Function requests and how long it takes to execute their codes [24]. Therefore, special attention is required when using this type of Function. In this paper, we describe infinite Lambda invocation according to recursion through an arbitrary Lambda Function connected to an S3 event in a serverless application.

Infinite Lambda Call through Incorrect Path. Let's take an example of a social media service that is used a lot these days. Suppose that a thumbnail is created to reduce the processing data of the picture list when a user uploads a picture taken. If developers implement all the logic by themselves, they will have to implement the logic to create and save a thumbnail for the uploaded image after waiting until the upload is complete. However, developers only need to create a Function that performs only the logic for saving the uploaded image by reducing the size of the uploaded image as shown in Fig. 2, and connect this Function to the path "/image".

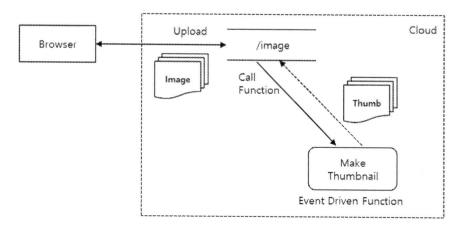

Fig. 2. Upload architecture using a Function on the Cloud.

Then, if the user just saves the file to be uploaded in the "/image" path, the thumbnail will be created automatically. What if the developer accidentally saves the thumbnail in the "/image" again as shown in Listing. 1.6.

Listing 1.6. Save the thumbnail file in the same path

```
1  var bucket_src = event.Records [0].s3.bucket.name;
2  var bucket_dst = bucket_src;
3  var key_src = event.Records [0].s3.object.key;
4  var key_dst = key_src;
5  ...
6  function uploadThumbnail(contentType, data, next) {
7      // Use the same Bucket and Path(Key) that Lambda is
           triggered
8      s3.putObject( {
9          Bucket: bucket_dst,
10         Key: key_dst,
11         Body: data,
12         ContentType: contentType
13     }, function( err, buffer ){
14         ...
15     } );
16 }
```

As you can guess, the "Make Thumbnail" Function will be called again. Then, if there is no special exit code, the Function will be called indefinitely, and accordingly, cloud users will have to pay a significant amount. Most developers would like to believe they won't make these mistakes, but anyone can make a mistake. Also, if the code implemented to receive the location of the storage path as a parameter is not verified separately, a malicious user may unnecessarily increase the cost of using the cloud through a parameter tampering attack.

Recently, DoS attacks are being used for the purpose of significantly increasing cloud usage fees rather than stopping service for the cloud-based application, and it is also called EDoS [6]. As can get to know from these attack trends, an incorrectly implemented Function can be used as a security vulnerability rather than a simple development mistake.

Secure Coding to prevent Infinite Loop Lambda Calls. To solve the above vulnerability, the simplest way is to save the newly created thumbnail in a path different from the path of the repository connected to the Lambda Function as shown in Listing. 1.7.

Listing 1.7. Save the thumbnail file in the separate path

```
1  var bucket_src = event.Records[0].s3.bucket.name;
2  var bucket_dst = bucket_src;
3  var key_src = event.Records[0].s3.object.key;
4  // Add "thumbnail/" to use different path than the
       triggered path
5  var key_dst = "thumbnail/" + key_src;
6  ...
7  function uploadThumbnail(contentType, data, next) {
8      s3.putObject( {
9          Bucket: bucket_dst,
10         Key: key_dst,
11         Body: data,
12         ContentType: contentType
13     }, function( err, buffer ){
14         ...
15     } );
16 }
```

In the Lambda code of Listing. 1.7, the bucket and Key(Path) value of the location where the file is newly stored is retrieved through the Event object from the S3 Repository where Lambda is connected, and the file is saved by adding the "thumbnail/" path. According to this, it will prevent the paths from overlapping when saving thumbnails. In this sample code, it does not receive the storage path and file name using external parameters in order the current sample code is very simple to help understand easily (The value stored in the event object is the value delivered by AWS.) However, if the location information where the thumbnail is to be stored needs to be imported as an external parameter due to business purposes, the logic must be implemented to save the file only when the Bucket or Key values are different after verifying Bucket and Key(Path) values.

4.4 Sensitive Information Encryption

In order to provide various services, companies collect the personal information of users and use them for services, or some services are provided only to users who have been authenticated through membership registration. In order to provide these services, it is necessary to store and use important information such as user personal information and account information in a database. Although cloud service providers protect the database themselves, it is the responsibility of the cloud users to protect the contents and data in databases [25]. Perhaps most developers and security operators already know that sensitive information stored in the database needs to be managed through encryption So a security configuration that can encrypt or protect the database itself is sometimes used as the security solution for the database.

Cloud providers also provide encryption configuration for resources in the database. In AWS, to protect data from unauthorized access to the database, instance encryption using Transparent Data Encryption (TDE) and connection encryption to the DB instance using SSL/TLS are supported [25]. However, this configuration cannot completely protect the data. By developing virtualization to the next level using a virtual machine, the cloud computing uses a multi-tenancy sharing model where multiple customers can share the same physical machine [26]. Because this multi-tenancy restricts logical access, it is the same as saying that you can access other users' data if you can bypass it.

Some developers may think that an attack that bypasses multi-tenancy is very difficult, so it may not happen very often. And they may have doubt whether data also should be encrypted when considering the cost of development. However, it is possible to access sensitive data through attacks such as SQL Injection, or direct access is also possible by stealing account information. Also, exposing users' personal information in plain text to database administrators can also arise a security issue from laws and compliance. Therefore, sensitive data stored in the database must be programmatically encrypted before storing it in the database. When data is encrypted, it must be stored through one-way encryption or two-way encryption according to the data type specified by laws or compliance. Also, when using AES for two-way encryption, data must be securely encrypted using GCM Mode to avoid padding oracle attacks.

Lack of Encryption Applied When Saving Password. There are various types of important information that require encryption when stored in a database. In the case of password, it is used after storage using one-way encryption such as Hash. Because Hash cannot be decrypted, to confirm a password that a user has forgotten, some developers and operators use two-way encryption that can be decrypted, or store it in plaintext as shown in Listing. 1.8. However, when stored in this way, the user's account information may be stolen by the database administrator, and if a SQL injection attack is possible on the service, the user's account information may be stolen by the attacker through this attack.

Listing 1.8. Save login password in plaintext

```
1   // Save the plained password received from outside
2   var param = {
3       TableName: "user_info",
4       Item: {
5           "id": event["userID"],
6           "password": event["userPassword"],
7           ...
8       }
9   };
10  ...
11  dynamoDB.putItem( param, function( err, data) {
12      ...
13  });
```

Secure Coding to Save Password with Encryption. The encryption algorithm used to encrypt and store the password must be careful not to use an encryption algorithm that is no longer secure, such as MD5 or SHA1. For one-way encryption, you must use a secure encryption algorithm of SHA-256 or higher as shown in Listing. 1.9. (SHA-512 is used in the sample code) Also, when applying the Hash algorithm, an arbitrary salt value should be used. If an arbitrary salt value is applied, password theft can be prevented because the original password cannot be accurately known even if the hash value is exposed.

Listing 1.9. Save login password after hashing

```
1   var userID = event["userID"];
2   var userPassword = event["userPassword"];
3   crypto.randomBytes(512, function(err, salt) {
4       ...
5       passwordSalt = salt.toString("base64");
6       // Hash and store the received password
7       crypto.pbkdf2(userPassword, passwordSalt, 4096, 512, "
            sha512", function(err, derivedKey) {
8           hashedPassword = derivedKey.toString("base64");
9           var param = {
10              TableName: "user_info",
11              Item: {
12              "id": userID,
13              "password": hashedPassword,
14              "salt: passwordSalt,
15              ...
16              }
17          };
```

```
18          . . .
19       dynamoDB.putItem( param, function( err, data) {
20          . . .
21       });
22   };
```

4.5 Insufficient Logging

Serverless applications can bring about additional complexity by development and support teams because it involves creating an application workflow by combining multiple cloud services, Functions, triggers, and events as a microservice architecture [9]. This complexity makes application security more difficult, and even if a security incident occurs, it is impossible to quickly identify the cause and solve the problem. Therefore, developers must establish a thorough security strategy from the application design stage. The most powerful force for this is logging and monitoring. Although logging has limitations as a pre-action method for hacking, it can become powerful when performing post-action measures. However, if the information recorded by such logging is not adequate or sufficient, it will be difficult to properly proceed with post-action. In this section, we will find out logging to serverless applications.

Difficulty in Event Detection due to Insufficient Logging. Log data is very important information in proceeding with follow-up actions. Especially when small units of Functions are automatically executed at a specific point in time, it will take a very long time to find a problem if you do not log enough data. Therefore, sufficient log data should be saved when using a Function, and in particular, when accessing important functions such as authentication/authorization or important information such as personal information, sufficient log data should be saved. The source code of Listing. 1.10 is the source code to initialize the password, and there is no logging for exceptions or failure reasons during the password initialization process.

Listing 1.10. Insufficient logging of password change failure

```
1   function getUser( email, function( err, token ) {
2       if (err) {
3           // No log when an error occurs
4           callback( "Error in getUser(): " + err);
5       } else if ( !token ) {
6           // No log when requested without token
7           callback( null, { password_changed: false });
8       } else {
9           cryptoUtil.computeHash( newPassword, function(
                err, newSalt, newHash ){
10              if (err) {
11                  // No log when an error occurs in the
                        hash process
```

```
12                       callback("Error in computeHash(): " + err
                             );
13                   } else {
14                       callback(null, { password_changed: true
                             });
15                   }
16               }
17           }
18   }
```

In this insufficient logging, even if a malicious user attempts to steal a specific user's account information, operators cannot know about it, and appropriate action cannot be taken. So, if the developer does insufficient logging like this, in addition to important functions and security functions, it is impossible to identify that the application has been damaged or that the service has been used for illegal purposes, then attackers will be able to go unnoticed by cyber attacks [9].

Sufficient Logging for Sensitive Services. Logging cannot protect against malicious attacks by itself, but it can detect an attack in progress, or even if an attack is successful, it helps to quickly respond to vulnerabilities and take post-action. In the source code of Listing. 1.10, even though an error occurred in authentication and authorization processing in the progress of changing the password, cloud operators cannot know that because proper logging is not recorded for this. Therefore, it is necessary to respond to security incidents by recording appropriate logs in each error situation as shown in Listing. 1.11.

Listing 1.11. Sufficient logging for password change failure

```
1    function getUser( email, function( err, token ) {
2        if (err) {
3            // Log when an error occurs
4            console.log("Error occurs    email: " + email +
                 ", err : " + err);
5            callback( "Error in getUser(): " + err);
6        } else if ( !token ) {
7            // Log when requested without token
8            console.log( "There is no token    mail" + email
                 );
9            callback( null, { password_changed: false });
10       } else {
11           cryptoUtil.computeHash( newPassword, function(
                 err, newSalt, newHash ){
12               if (err) {
13                   // Log when an error occurs in the hash
                         process
14                   console.log( "Failed for encryption: " +
                         err);
```

```
15               callback("Error in computeHash():  " + err
                    );
16           } else {
17               callback(null, { password_changed: true
                    });
18           }
19        }
20     }
21  }
```

In Lambda, objects passed through handlers are basically "event" and "context" objects. The "event" object records which external parameters are fetched or the requester's IP can be obtained by using the Mapping Template of the Method Integration Request. And the "context" object can check various information related to function invocation, such as Lambda function name, version, called Amazon resource name (ARN), request ID, user identity, and bucket information. Since the value delivered to the "context" object is different for each Function configuration, it is necessary to check this object information delivered to each Function, and then, save the necessary information in a log.

Additionally, it would be good that logging includes information such as who, when, where, what, and how for events that occur not only in important functions or security functions but also in input value validation, authentication/authorization validation, errors, and exceptions. And when constructing log messages using a specific format, in addition to more efficient log analysis, the automatic alert function can be used through the monitoring service.

5   Conclusion

We identified 5 major security vulnerabilities for cloud-based serverless applications that will become killer applications in the near future. We found vulnerabilities at the code level, such as (1) stealing instance credentials through SSRF attack, (2) hardcoded RDS credential exposure in source codes, (3) infinite loop of Lambda call, (4) lack of encryption applied when saving password, (5) difficulty in event detection due to insufficient logging. This will help developers to implement serverless applications more easily, quickly, and safely in cloud computing environments.

Even though major vulnerabilities are implemented with secure coding, it does not guarantee that an application is completely secure in terms of security. Since serverless applications are also web applications, it is also necessary to defend against traditional attacks such as SQL Injection, parameter tampering, authentication bypass attacks, and so on. Since the security configuration may be wrong in the cloud architecture, even if the developer alone applies the secure coding well, it cannot be said that the application is secure. Therefore, cloud operators and developers must collaborate organically, and periodically review and audit each Function that will become increasingly complex and the privileges and roles connected to the Functions so that the minimum privilege can be applied well. And it is necessary to minimize risks through preemptive responses to attacks by setting appropriate logs and monitoring through with alarms. In addition, if developers configure the pipeline to use a secure version that does not have vulnerabilities by checking the CVE for the libraries or open sources used in the serverless source code during the automatic deployment process, developers will be able to build a more secure serverless application.

Acknowledgment. This research was supported by Basic Science Research Program through the National Research Foundation of Korea (NRF) funded by the Ministry of Education (NRF-2021R1F1A1059650)

References

1. AWS Customer Story. https://aws.amazon.com/solutions/case-studies/. Accessed 16 Dec 2021
2. Villamizar, M., et al.: Infrastructure cost comparison of running web applications in the cloud using AWS Lambda and monolithic and microservice architectures. In: 2016 16th IEEE/ACM International Symposium on Cluster, Cloud and Grid Computing, IEEE, Cartagena, Colombia (2016)
3. Jamshidi, P., Pahl, C., Mendonça, N.C., Lewis, J., Tilkov, S.: Microservices: The journey so far and challenges ahead, IEEE Software, pp. 24–35 (2018)
4. Hendrickson, S., Sturdevant, S., Harter, T., Venkataramani, V., Arpaci-Dusseau, A.C., Arpaci-Dusseau, R.H.: Serverless computation with openlambda. In: 8th USENIX Workshop on Hot Topics in Cloud Computing (2016)
5. Baldini, I., et al.: Serverless computing: Current Trends and Open Problems. In: Chaudhary, S., Somani, G., Buyya, R. (eds.) Research Advances in Cloud Computing, pp. 1–20. Springer, Singapore (2017). https://doi.org/10.1007/978-981-10-5026-8_1
6. Rath, A., Spasic, B., Boucart, N., Thiran, P.: Security pattern for cloud SaaS: From system and data security to privacy case study in AWS and Azure. Computers **8**(2), 34 (2019)
7. Tabrizchi, H., Rafsanjani, M.K.: A survey on security challenges in cloud computing: Issues threats, and solutions. J. Supercomput. **76**, 9493–9532 (2020)
8. OWASP Top 10. https://owasp.org/Top10/. Accessed 16 Dec 2021
9. O'Meara, W., Lennon, R.G: Serverless computing security: Protecting application logic. In: 2020 31th Irish Signals and Systems Conference. IEEE, Letterkenny, Ireland (2020)
10. Michener, J.: Security Issues with Functions as a Service, IT Professional, pp. 24–31 (2020)
11. CVE. https://www.cve.org/. Accessed 16 Dec 2021
12. CSA Security Guideline. https://cloudsecurityalliance.org/artifacts/security-guidance-v4/. Accessed 16 Dec 2021
13. Securing Weak Point in Serverless Architectures: Risks and Recommendations. https://documents.trendmicro.com/assets/white_papers/wp-securing-weak-points-in-serverless-architectures-risks-and-recommendations.pdf. Accessed 16 Dec 2021
14. Nirmal, K., Janet, B., Kumar, R.: Web application vulnerabilities - The hacker's treasure. In: The International Conference on Inventive Research in Computing Application 2017, Coimbatore, India. IEEE (2018)

15. Jabiyev, B., Mirzaei, O., Kharraz, A., Kirda, E.: Preventing server-side request forgery attacks. In: 36th Annual ACM Symposium on Applied Computing, pp. 1626–1635. ACM, New York (2021)
16. AWS EC2 Instance Metadata. https://docs.aws.amazon.com/AWSEC2/latest/UserGuide/ec2-instance-metadata.html. Accessed 16 Dec 2021
17. AWS Instance Identity Document. https://docs.aws.amazon.com/ko_kr/AWSEC2/latest/UserGuide/instance-identity-documents.html. Accessed 16 Dec 2021
18. AWS IMDSv2. https://docs.aws.amazon.com/AWSEC2/latest/UserGuide/configuring-instance-metadata-service.html. Accessed 16 Dec 2021
19. CVE-798. htttps://cwe.mitre.org/data/definitions/798.html. Accessed 16 Dec 2021
20. Islam, M., Rahaman, S., Meng, N., Hassanshahi, B., Krishnan, P., Yao, D.D.: Coding practices and recommendations of spring security for enterprise applications. In: 2020 IEEE Secure Development, Atlanta, GA, USA (2020)
21. AWS Lambda Environment Variables. https://docs.aws.amazon.com/lambda/latest/dg/configuration-envvars.html. Accessed 16 Dec 2021
22. HashiCorp Vault Git. https://github.com/hashicorp/vault. Accessed 29 Dec 2021
23. AWS Secret Manager. https://docs.aws.amazon.com/secretsmanager/latest/userguide/intro.html. Accessed 16 Dec 2021
24. AWS Lambda Pricing. https://aws.amazon.com/lambda/pricing/. Accessed 16 Dec 2021
25. Data Protection in Amazon RDS. https://docs.aws.amazon.com/AmazonRDS/latest/UserGuide/DataDurability.html. Accessed 16 Dec 2021
26. Odun-Ayo, I., Misra, S., Abayomi-Alli, O., Ajayi, O. : Cloud multi-tenancy: Issues and developments. In: The 10th International Conference on Utility and Cloud Computing, pp. 209–214. ACM, New York (2017)

Prototyping the Virtual Reality-Based NIHSS Stroke Assessment Training System

Wei-Jung Li[1](✉) ⓘ, Chien-Hsu Chen[1,2] ⓘ, Pi-Shan Sung[3] ⓘ, and Yu-Ming Chang[3] ⓘ

[1] Industrial Design Department, National Cheng Kung University, Tainan, Taiwan
wjung9610@gmail.com, chenhsu@mail.ncku.edu.tw
[2] Hierarchical Green-Energy Materials Research Center, National Cheng Kung University, Tainan, Taiwan
[3] Department of Neurology, National Cheng Kung University Hospital, College of Medicine, National Cheng Kung University, Tainan, Taiwan

Abstract. This study is a prototype of the virtual reality-based NIHSS stroke assessment training system and its evaluation. The National Institutes of Health Stroke Scale (NIHSS) plays an important role in assessing acute ischemic stroke. However, it has always been a difficult task to train young doctors or medical students. Both educators and learners face different problems. The lack of practice opportunities causes a gap between verbal lectures and clinical practice. In this study, we try to overcome the difficulties of mastering NIHSS. After some investigation, we found that virtual reality (VR) has great potential in this case. We created a virtual reality system in which users will be provided with virtual stroke patients in the hospital. By the designed user and patient's movements and dialogues, the user can interact with the patient in person and learn through practice. The prototype currently takes a healthy adult as the virtual patient to find out major system usability problems, and actual cases in the real world can be imported into the VR system afterward to provide the learners with an adequate self-improvement space. It can also be a helpful tool for the educators to train professional clinical staff. Heuristic evaluation carried out by designers and neurologists was conducted throughout the development. The VR system is believed to be an effective way to learn NIHSS. It solved some of the current NIHSS training problems and showed its potential value of operating the clinical skill in person in a 3D immersive environment.

Keywords: NIHSS · Stroke scale · Virtual Reality · Medical education · Virtual patient

1 Introduction

According to the "Guidelines for the Early Management of Patients With Acute Ischemic Stroke" (The 2019 updated version), the National Institutes of Health Stroke Scale (NIHSS) is the recommended severity rating tool in the emergency evaluating stage [1]. After a stroke patient arrives at the hospital, NIHSS must be carried out as soon as possible regardless of the severity of the patient, and the treatment decision can be

M. Kurosu (Ed.): HCII 2022, LNCS 13304, pp. 164–181, 2022.
https://doi.org/10.1007/978-3-031-05412-9_11

made based on the assessment results. For example, thrombolytic agents (recombinant tissue plasminogen activator, rt-pa, alteplase), which is the first-line treatment within 4.5 h after acute ischemic stroke onset, can only be used when the patient's NIHSS score is between 4–25 [2, 3].

Nevertheless, the NIHSS is not easy to master. Like many other clinical skills, traditional medical education has mainly focused on written information and verbal lectures in the early stages. Medical students begin to conduct clinical practices after entering the hospital for internships. However, the patients' complex conditions make it difficult to convert their knowledge into skill. The clinical skills need to be gradually refined through experience and practical operations so that the medical students often need to spend much effort taking NIHSS into practice. Once the real patient comes, the tension also makes them feel stressed in such urgent conditions. Being under this situation makes it even more important to have a good learning and practice route for NIHSS training.

Therefore, a suitable simulation is important to train a learner into a qualified clinical staff for stroke assessment. Developing a good simulation system is arguably necessary to help medical students gain enough experience before implementing NIHSS on an actual patient, so we decided to develop the Virtual Reality-Based NIHSS Stroke Assessment Training System.

2 Literature Review

The content of the NIHSS should be fully understood to create a training system. Thus, we studied the use of NIHSS, observed related studies with different solutions for its learning difficulties as well as existing applications of VR in medical education.

2.1 The National Institutes of Health Stroke Scale (NIHSS)

Since some stroke symptoms are nonspecific and hard to recognize, different stroke scales are created to improve diagnostic accuracy, help with treatment decisions, check a patient's neurologic deficits, and predict the outcomes after treatments [4]. Among all the stroke scales, NIHSS is one of the most reliable, effective, and widely used [3].

In the assessment, the doctor provides instructions to the patient, including asking certain questions and requesting some specific movements. Each item will then be scored based on the patient's response. The 11 items in the NIHSS can be summed up to 0–42 points, as shown in Table 1.

2.2 Related Studies

The importance of NIHSS and the training difficulties are long-standing facts. Such clinical skills are difficult to be fully communicated in words. Previous studies have tried to solve this problem in different ways.

Video is a common and intuitive solution. However, for NIHSS, it would be better for the doctor to observe the patient in all directions within close distances. Therefore, the choice of the video shooting direction is crucial, but it is hard to control in clinical conditions. To record all the features that the physicians need to see during the

Table 1. The National Institutes of Health Stroke scale [5].

Tested item	Title	Score
1a	Level of consciousness	0–3
1b	Orientation questions	0–2
1c	Response to commands	0–2
2	Gaze	0–2
3	Visual fields	0–3
4	Facial Movement	0–3
5aL, 5bR	Motor function (Arm)	0–4
6aL, 6bR	Motor function (Leg)	0–4
7	Limb ataxia	0–2
8	Sensory	0–2
9	Language	0–3
10	Articulation	0–2
11	Extinction or inattention	0–2

assessment, Lyden et al. used two cameras to record the assessment process in different directions, one for the close-ups of the patient's facial expressions and another for the entire patient's performance (see Fig. 1) [5]. Recording the assessment process by video has been applied in studies, and it is still a commonly used teaching method.

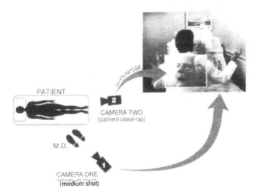

Fig. 1. Shooting teaching videos with two cameras by Lyden et al. [5].

However, learners watching videos only receive one-way information. The lack of interaction is considered an aspect that can be improved [6]. Therefore, Koka et al. created a screen-based interactive learning module using the internet, as shown in Fig. 2. By arranging a number of slides with characters and descriptions, users interact with the system by clicking the mouse. Clicking on different options will lead to different routes.

If a wrong answer is selected, the user would get a hint or be directed to an explaining page [7]. In a later version, Suppan et al. inserted videos as supplements for some of the items for the users to better understand the patient's performance (see Fig. 2) [8]. This module is supported in different aspects of verification, including learning performance, course satisfaction, and course recommendation [7, 8].

Fig. 2. The interactive learning module by Koka et al. [7] and the video supplements [8].

Although the above case is available online, the content was designed in French so that it cannot be applied to the training of Taiwanese students due to the language barrier. Studies suggest that teaching tools designed in English may still cause learning difficulties in non-English speaking areas [6]. Moreover, the learners cannot interact with the patient in person.

2.3 Application of VR in Medical Education

Simulation-based learning (SBL) has received more and more attention in the medical education of clinical skills. Lacking opportunities to practice causes a gap between verbal lectures and clinical practice. Current simulation technologies vary from screen-based platforms, partial-task trainers, to full environment simulation with high-fidelity mannequin simulators [9], all of which bring learners different simulating experiences for skill learning.

VR acts as a new method of delivering simulation for medical education [10]. Researches support the use of VR technology [10], and many indicate that the performance of VR training systems is no less than or even better than traditional education methods. Whether being in emergencies [11], clinical skills requires adequate practice [12], or high-risk treatments [13], if a proper simulation can be carried out as a practicing opportunity before implementation, the maturity of the clinical staff and the quality of patient care can be improved.

3 Design Methods

3.1 Stakeholders Interview

To further explore clinical pain points as well as understand the current situation of NIHSS education, stakeholder interviews were conducted in the early stage of this study.

We interviewed educators (experienced doctors) and learners (young doctors) about the current NIHSS training methods, difficulties from learning to practice, and problems encountered in teaching and learning.

In the current NIHSS teaching process, the educators mostly describe the situation and patient performance through verbal lectures and simple demonstrations by themselves since there is not always a suitable patient for demonstration. The lack of a good visualizing tool also makes it hard to pass their experiences down. On the other hand, even though the learners have already had the basic knowledge of the standardized patient performance in the assessment, it is still stressful when facing an actual patient for the first few times. If they are not coping with the case quickly and precisely, it might lead to a late treatment or a wrong decision. The NIHSS is often used in an emergency immediately after a stroke patient arrives, conducting the assessment within 5–10 min. A user journey map was created based on the background information and the interviews (see Fig. 3), which visualizes the training process and user pain points.

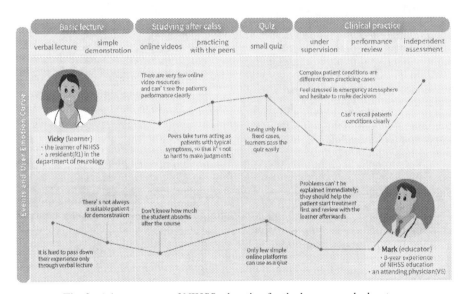

Fig. 3. A journey map of NIHSS education for the learners and educators.

As seen in Fig. 3, the pain points of the learners and educators lie in the autonomous learning stage after class and the time when the learners first enter clinical practice to face real patients. Based on the pain points, this study tried to provide opportunities for learners to practice independently and help educators with training difficulties.

3.2 Applying VR in NIHSS Training

After having a deep understanding of the expectations and pain points of the stakeholders, we believe that a suitable simulation and teaching tool can help ease the time-consuming and laborious teaching process, and eventually increase the number of reliable assessing staff.

There are some reasons why we decided to apply VR in NIHSS training. Firstly, VR shares many features with most screen-based multimedia teaching methods (videos or animations), including automatic records and analysis, the ability to practice repeatedly, as well as breaking the limitations of time and space. Moreover, VR has an immersive sense of presence, a multi-sensory experience, and more interaction possibilities. This allows the NIHSS assessment, which requires doctor-patient interactions, to enhance the practical experience when learning through VR. As mentioned above, some traditional training methods use pre-recorded videos. Having fixed directions when shooting a video easily causes difficulties in judgments. In VR, users can observe the patient in all directions in the virtual environment much more naturally. Secondly, studies offered a list of features for people to consider whether or not to use VR in their own cases [14]. Many of the features show that it is suitable to introduce VR to the education of NIHSS, including having difficulties teaching in the real world, the necessity of learning through experiences, trying in the real world could cause harm, and practicing tasks that need manual dexterity or physical movement.

VR is not appropriate for all education issues [10, 14]. For instance, since most VR is controlled by hand controllers, teaching abdominal palpation is not recommended because the need for haptic feedback is much more important than a complex simulation [10]. Although it is undeniable that lack of haptic feedback may affect the immersive experience, as NIHSS assessment mainly relies on the doctor's observations and not their haptic perception, it is less of a negative impact on providing a realistic haptic simulation.

Therefore, this study believes that the use of VR in NIHSS training has sufficient rationality, appropriateness, as well as many outstanding features. In Taiwan, residents in the neurology department are the main ones who have to face this practice, which means the target users of this system are the young doctors.

3.3 Storyboards and Flow Charts

Storyboards are used commonly in design and the human-computer interaction (HCI) field [15]. A lecture by a neurologist and a series of simulation videos were used to form a basic understanding of NIHSS. In order to have an efficient discussion of the scenario, at the beginning of the system design, a manual sketched storyboard of the assessment process in the VR system was created referring to the videos. Afterward, to better communicate the configuration of the system, we used opened 3D model resources with the rendering software, Keyshot, to simulate the expected effect. We added the user's possible operation scenarios in the real world along with the storyboard to show the relationship between the expected user action and the scene changes in the virtual world (see Fig. 4).

To go deeper into the differences between each item and connect with system programming, item-by-item system flow charts are created to clarify the flow and match with the original scale (see Fig. 5). After visualizing through storyboards and flowcharts, we extracted the process that each item must go through and sorted out a general pattern of the doctor-patient interaction in the VR system, including: (1) the instruction stage, (2) the interaction stage, and (3) the scoring stage.

Fig. 4. The storyboard with the expected user action of item 2 "Gaze".

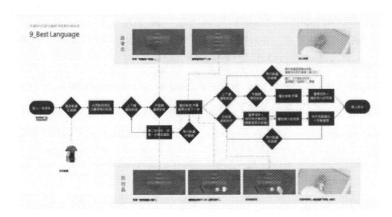

Fig. 5. The flow chart of item 9 "Best Language".

4   System Implementation

In this prototype, a healthy man was selected as the assessing object. He can complete all the tasks requested by the doctor. The NIHSS assessment requires doctor-patient interactions, that is, the interactions between the user and the virtual patient in the VR system. We divided the interactions into four parts and listed some problems to be solved, as shown in Fig. 6. Each problem was solved after finishing the prototype.

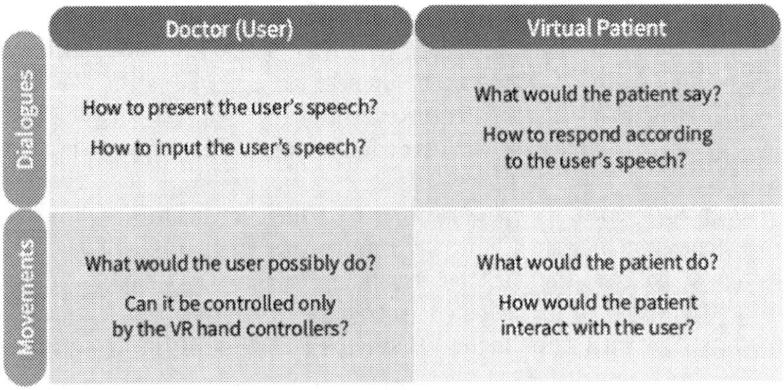

	Doctor (User)	Virtual Patient
Dialogues	How to present the user's speech? How to input the user's speech?	What would the patient say? How to respond according to the user's speech?
Movements	What would the user possibly do? Can it be controlled only by the VR hand controllers?	What would the patient do? How would the patient interact with the user?

Fig. 6. Questions about doctor(user)-patient interactions.

4.1   Construction of the Virtual Environment

The main virtual environment is a ward inclusive of a bed, hospital equipment, and a virtual patient (see Fig. 7). To achieve the required movements in the NIHSS assessment, there are many restrictions on the patient's 3D model selection. The patient needs to perform not only limb movements but also some subtle movements and facial expressions, such as raising eyebrows and turning eyeballs, so that multiple joints and facial features must be adjustable.

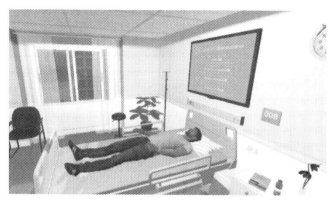

Fig. 7.   The main virtual environment.

4.2   The Whole Training Process in the VR System

At the beginning, users will enter the initial environment, a duty room, where they can familiarize themselves with the VR environment and the interaction through hand controllers. After being notified to assess a stroke patient, they will enter the ward following the designed instructions and start the assessment of the patient. In each item, the user will go through the three stages (see Fig. 8):

Fig. 8.   The training process.

(1) The Instruction Stage.   The doctor (the user) gives out instructions by choosing a sentence on the dialogue options.

(2) The Interaction Stage. After providing instructions by clicking on the dialogue options, some interactions between the user and the virtual patient may be needed in certain items. The user observes the virtual patient's response.

(3) The Scoring Stage. Every item ends up with the user scoring on the scoring screen.

4.3   Dialogues in the System

The assessment requires the doctor to give out instructions. However, natural language processing is not added to the system. A simple VR system cannot interpret the user's speech and allow the virtual patient to respond automatically. Therefore, we searched for others' practices.

A previous research created a VR system to train nursing students' communication skills with the instructor's manipulation for the patient's response [7]. Another research established an interactive webpage for nurse training, in which the user is allowed to interact with virtual patients through keyboard input [16].

In this study, a floating box is used to show the dialogue options since the instructions in each item were fixed in NIHSS (see Fig. 9). The options are designed based on the sentences offered by the doctors, which are often used when they assess a patient in the real world. When the user selects one of the dialogue options, the box will disappear, and the system will play the pre-recorded voice file to represent the user, and the response of the virtual patient will also be played via a pre-recorded patient voice.

Fig. 9. The floating dialogue options of item 1C "Response to commands".

4.4   The Doctor Movements

The user does not need to move around a lot since the assessment is completed mainly by the bedside. However, some items require the doctor's action to trigger the virtual patient's response. For example, in item 7 "Ataxia", the instruction to touch the doctor's finger requires him to point out his finger for the patient to achieve. The scenario is as shown in Fig. 10. Items like this need the doctors to reach the proper position and make certain gestures. Since the gesture changes are all quite simple throughout all the assessment items, we tend to make it easier for the user. What the user only needs to do is to reach the target area, and a few gray hand hints will appear as a guide. Simply a click on the hand controllers can change his gesture in the virtual world.

The appearance of the gray hand hint is also shown in Fig. 10. It will only show when the user reaches the correct area. This design still requires the user to "know" what he should do but not actually changing the gesture himself. Since spending too much time changing gestures is unnecessary for training, we tried to make the process as simple, quick, and instinctive as in the real world.

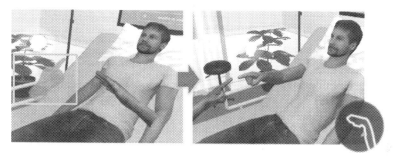

Fig. 10. The user's interaction with the virtual patient in item 7 "Limb ataxia".

4.5   The Patient Movements

Due to the need for the patient movements required during NIHSS assessment, an essential task is to adjust the model skeleton to form the body movements. By taking real photos from various directions for comparison, we tried to imitate the movements of natural human bodies as much as possible to make the virtual patient more realistic (see Fig. 11). This is particularly important in the system of this study because slight differences in the patient behavior may lead to different scoring results. For instance, an asymmetric smile may be assessed as "minor paralysis" in item 4 "facial palsy".

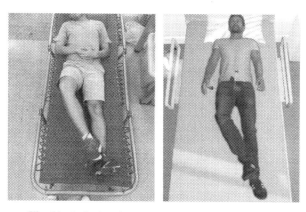

Fig. 11. Imitating the movements of a natural human.

4.6 The Scoring Screen

The scoring screen is fixed above the bed of the patient, and only one item is scored at a time (see Fig. 12). The user will be asked whether to confirm or cancel the option after clicking on a number to score the item. Once the score is confirmed, the screen will automatically display the scoring options for the following item. Therefore, if the user confirms the score, he cannot return and modify it. This design also complies with the principle of non-returning to change the score in the NIHSS guidelines. At the same time, a sound effect will notify the user of the beginning of a new item.

After all the assessment process is done, the screen will show the total use of the time as well as the correct rate of the user's assessment. The user will also get a report card as feedback to know the details of his performance in each item.

Fig. 12. The scoring screen.

5 User Study

After finishing the first prototyping, an evaluation was carried out by five experts, including two designers and three neurologists. Experts individually tested the prototype and then followed by a semi-structured interview containing questions about the value of the system and whether there were problems that needed to be improved.

5.1 Simulating Environment

The training system is programmed in Unity and presented by HTC VIVE. The hardware equipment includes a VR headset, two controllers, base stations, and a computer to run the NIHSS Stroke Assessment Training System (see Fig. 13). The user needs to wear the headset and hold the controllers. All interactions in the virtual environment are achieved through the controllers. Since most systems are designed for right-handers, a study found it more difficult for left-handed users to conduct the tasks [17]. To avoid this inequality, our system was made friendly to both left and right-handed learners by adding the same functions to both controllers.

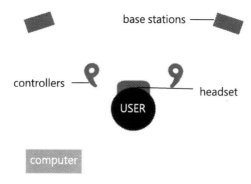

Fig. 13. The simulating environment (top view).

Since the assessment is completed mainly by the bedside, there is no need for too much space to move around. An area of about four square meters is enough to provide the space for the system. Users can use the headset wirelessly for a more comfortable and immersive experience.

5.2 Participants

Studies found that 80% of usability problems can be found within 3–5 participants, and the more addition user is less likely to find new usability problems [18, 19]. In this stage of prototyping, five experts were invited to evaluate and conduct interviews to collect their suggestions. The attending experts consist of three neurologists and two experienced ergonomics and interaction designers. The neurologists were two attending physicians and a resident from the neurology department with respectively 10, 8, and 2 years of NIHSS teaching experience.

5.3 The Evaluation of NIHSS Assessment Training System

The heuristic evaluation is often conducted by a small set of evaluators who do not have to be usability experts or the end-users to find out major usability problems in a

Fig. 14. Experts evaluating the NIHSS stroke assessment training system.

cost-efficient way [20, 21]. It can be used in the designing process with the iteration of the prototypes to keep revising the product for a better user experience [22].

After recruiting the evaluators, each of them tried the VR system individually with unlimited time to take a close look all around in the virtual environment and assess the virtual patient (see Fig. 14). The process was recorded for later review and was followed by a semi-structured interview.

5.4 The Evaluation Results

After the experts' evaluation, we actively explored the way users interact with the interface, and a few problems were found according to the ten usability heuristics [23]. In this system, the user only interacts with the virtual environment through the VR controllers. The hand controllers and their sensing buttons are shown in Fig. 15. After conducting the prototype, we found some problems that could be improved in terms of human considerations. In the modified version, we made changes in the user interface design of dialogue options and the way how users interact with it.

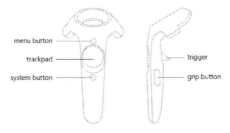

Fig. 15. The hand controllers of HTC VIVE.

The Instruction Stage. In the first prototype, the user needs to click on the dialogue icon with the trigger and use the touchpad to choose the dialogue options up and down like the operation method of the TV remote control. A translucent mask is shown to highlight the dialogue options (see Fig. 16).

Fig. 16. The original design of the instruction stage.

However, after actual operation, we found that whenever the user wants to click on the dialogue icon, he needs to shift his sight from the patient to the direction of the icon, which makes the user keep turning his head around during the training process. In addition, when shifting the dialogue options up and down, it is easy to touch other buttons accidentally because of the unfamiliarity with the buttons on the controller.

Therefore, in the modified version, we decided to let the user open the dialogue options by pressing the menu button, and a laser light will show from the user's hand for the user to align the options. Simply a click on the trigger can confirm the choice (see Fig. 17).

Fig. 17. The modified design of the instruction stage.

The rest of the interactive process also only needs the trigger, which means that during the entire training process, the number of buttons encountered by the user is reduced from 4 to 2. Users can press the menu button to open the dialogue options and use the trigger for choosing the option as well as complete the rest interactions easily. The used buttons are shown in Fig. 18. With a more straightforward interacting pattern, the users' engagement for system learning can be reduced, allowing the users to focus on the training.

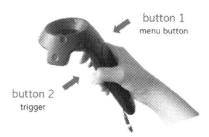

Fig. 18. The used buttons in the NIHSS Stroke Assessment Training System.

In addition, we found that the users need the dialogue options quite frequently during the assessment process, and the translucent mask also appears repeatedly, which separates the users from the virtual environment. This might lead to a negative impact on the user experience and immersion. Therefore, we redesigned the user interface of the dialogue options based on the above considerations, and made it appear directly in front of the user. In the modified version of the prototype, the changes can "minimize user memory load" and "prevent errors", which are two of the nine Nielsen & Molich's basic usability principles [24].

The Interaction Stage. There are some spatial problems found in the first prototype. For example, we placed the gray hint hands in an inappropriate position in item 3 "Visual fields". In this item, the doctor moves his fingers and asks the patient if he can figure it out to test the patient's vision in the four quadrants. The doctor's hands should be kept at a distance from the patient's face but not too close, which means the position of the gray hand hints should be modified. The scenario is shown in Fig. 19.

Fig. 19. The assessing positions in item 3 "Visual field".

The positions of the hints were modified following the experienced doctors and standardized in the system for the learners to learn from. New learners can understand and form a correct concept by learning through the VR system with a 3D environment.

6 Discussion and Conclusion

6.1 Overall User Experience

After trying the prototype, the experts suggest that the training process is very fluent. No motion sickness occurred during the assessment. Although most of the users may have little experience using VR, it wouldn't take too much time to get familiar with the hand controllers because of the system's simple operation, especially for the young generations. Moreover, it is believed that using VR as a training tool may stimulate practice motivation.

6.2 Value of the NIHSS Stroke Assessment Training System

Although there are some spatial mistakes to be modified after screening by the neurologists, the problem shows the value of conducting the NIHSS assessment process in the

3D environment. Since we created the prototype in comparison with the teaching video from which the learners learn, the learners may have similar misunderstandings with us. After being adjusted, the system can be a good training tool that breaks through the shortcomings of screen-based teaching tools, and learning in a 3D environment can help the learners form a correct concept.

Apart from conducting medical procedures in a 3D space, practicing in a safe environment with unlimited patient cases is also helpful, especially in emergency conditions with little or no fault tolerance. Another possible use mentioned by the experts is to add special cases into the system for doctors to share each other's experiences.

6.3   Solutions for the Pain Points

Some NIHSS training pain points and their solutions are shown in Table 2; both the learners and the educators benefit from the NIHSS Stroke Assessment Training System.

For the Learners. This system created a chance for them to practice before facing an actual patient. They can gain experiences to cope with the various patient conditions and refine through the actual operation simulated by the VR system.

For the Educators. The VR system is expected to release their pressure from the time-consuming process of training professional clinical staff. Moreover, the records automatically analyzed in the system can help them understand the learners' learning problems.

Table 2. The solutions of NIHSS training pain points

	Current NIHSS Training Pain Points	The solution provided by the VR system
1	The lack of practice opportunities makes learners only gain experience through clinical practice and speed up the assessment gradually	A VR simulation is provided as a practice space. Meet more patients in a short period of time to accumulate sufficient evaluation experience before clinical practice
2	Learners have no way of self-practice and improvement, so that the educators need to accompany learners for a long time to supervise their assessment process	Through the timely feedback of the system, the learners can discover their own shortcomings and improve themselves
3	Inexperienced assessors will result in slow assessments and poor accuracy, raising patients' health and safety concerns	Through realistic virtual patients and clinical environment, the clinical scene and patient performance can be shown in a safe environment for practice
4	The clinical situation cannot be completely recorded in all directions, which makes it difficult for educators to pass down their experience and for learners to learn through cases	Real patient cases can be imported according to teaching needs, and special patient cases can also be reserved for studies and discussions
5	It is difficult for the educators to standardize and quantify the learners' performance	The system automatically records and analyzes the performance within and between the learners. The educators can teach with the help of the collected data

6.4 Future Work

Since it is currently a prototype of a healthy person, in the future, we can follow the main structure of this prototype and add different patient cases to the system based on the needs of the stakeholders. By modifying the patient's performance to the specific instructions, different cases will be provided for the complete version design. Any valuable cases for teaching are welcomed to add into the system.

We will also recruit a larger scale of students for an experiment to verify the effectiveness of the training system. Although such VR systems are relatively difficult to be commercialized [25], we still expect this training system to reach more medical education institutes. In conclusion, according to the evaluation results, virtual reality is arguably suitable to be used as an NIHSS education tool. It shows the values in training based on expert evaluation and is hoped to be launched to clinical application in the very near future.

References

1. Powers, W.J., et al.: Guidelines for the early management of patients with acute ischemic stroke: 2019 update to the 2018 guidelines for the early management of acute ischemic stroke: a guideline for healthcare professionals from the American Heart Association/American Stroke Association. Stroke **50**, e344–e418 (2019)
2. Oliveira-Filho, J., Samuels, O.B.: Approach to reperfusion therapy for acute ischemic stroke. UpToDate. UpToDate, Waltham, MA (2022). Accessed 10 Feb 2022
3. Oliveira-Filho, J., Mullen, M.T.: Initial assessment and management of acute stroke. UpToDate, Waltham, MA (2021). Accessed 10 Feb 2022
4. Goldstein, L.B.: Use and utility of stroke scales and grading systems. In: Kasner, S., Dashe, J. (eds.) UpToDate. UpToDate, Waltham, MA (2021). Accessed 10 Feb 2022
5. Lyden, P., et al.: Improved reliability of the NIH stroke scale using video training NINDS TPA stroke study group. Stroke **25**, 2220–2226 (1994)
6. Chiu, S.-C., et al.: The effectiveness of interactive computer assisted instruction compared to videotaped instruction for teaching nurses to assess neurological function of stroke patients: a randomized controlled trial. Int. J. Nurs. Stud. **46**, 1548–1556 (2009)
7. Koka, A., Suppan, L., Cottet, P., Carrera, E., Stuby, L., Suppan, M.: Teaching the national institutes of health stroke scale to paramedics (E-Learning vs Video): randomized controlled trial. J. Med. Internet Res. **22**, 8 (2020)
8. Suppan, M., et al.: Asynchronous distance learning of the national institutes of health stroke scale during the COVID-19 pandemic (E-Learning vs Video): randomized controlled trial. J. Med. Internet Res. **23**, 19 (2021)
9. Okuda, Y., et al.: The utility of simulation in medical education: what is the evidence? Mount Sinai J. Med. J. Transl. Pers. Med. **76**, 330–343 (2009)
10. Pottle, J.: Virtual reality and the transformation of medical education. Future Healthcare J. **6**, 181 (2019)
11. Lerner, D., Mohr, S., Schild, J., Göring, M., Luiz, T.: An immersive multi-user virtual reality for emergency simulation training: usability study. JMIR Serious Games **8**, e18822 (2020)
12. Butt, A.L., Kardong-Edgren, S., Ellertson, A.: Using game-based virtual reality with haptics for skill acquisition. Clin. Simul. Nurs. **16**, 25–32 (2018)
13. Hsieh, M.-C., Lee, J.: Preliminary study of VR and AR applications in medical and healthcare education. J. Nurs. Health Stud. **3**, 1 (2018)

14. Pantelidis, V.S.: Reasons to use virtual reality in education and training courses and a model to determine when to use virtual reality. Themes Sci. Technol. Educ. **2**, 59–70 (2010)

15. Truong, K.N., Hayes, G.R., Abowd, G.D.: Storyboarding: an empirical determination of best practices and effective guidelines. In: Proceedings of the 6th Conference on Designing Interactive Systems, pp. 12–21 (2006)

16. Kleinsmith, A., Rivera-Gutierrez, D., Finney, G., Cendan, J., Lok, B.: Understanding empathy training with virtual patients. Comput. Hum. Behav. **52**, 151–158 (2015)

17. Kardong-Edgren, S., Breitkreuz, K., Werb, M., Foreman, S., Ellertson, A.: Evaluating the usability of a second-generation virtual reality game for refreshing sterile urinary catheterization skills. Nurse Educ. **44**, 137–141 (2019)

18. Virzi, R.A.: Refining the test phase of usability evaluation - how many subjects is enough. Hum. Factors **34**, 457–468 (1992)

19. Nielsen, J., Landauer, T.K.: A mathematical model of the finding of usability problems. In: Proceedings of the INTERACT 1993 and CHI 1993 Conference on Human Factors in Computing Systems, pp. 206–213 (1993)

20. Jeffries, R., Miller, J.R., Wharton, C., Uyeda, K.: User interface evaluation in the real world: a comparison of four techniques. In: Proceedings of the SIGCHI Conference on Human Factors in Computing Systems, pp. 119–124 (1991)

21. Nielsen, J.: Finding usability problems through heuristic evaluation. In: Proceedings of the SIGCHI Conference on Human Factors in Computing Systems, pp. 373–380 (1992)

22. Nielsen, J.: How to conduct a heuristic evaluation. Nielsen Norman Group **1**, 1–8 (1995)

23. Nielsen, J.: Ten usability heuristics (2005). Accesses 4 Mar 2010

24. Nielsen, J., Molich, R.: Heuristic evaluation of user interfaces. In: Proceedings of the SIGCHI Conference on Human Factors In Computing Systems, pp. 249–256 (1990)

25. Wang, K.-J., Shidujaman, M., Zheng, C.Y., Thakur, P.: HRIpreneur thinking: strategies towards faster innovation and commercialization of academic HRI research. In: 2019 IEEE International Conference on Advanced Robotics and its Social Impacts (ARSO), pp. 219–226. IEEE (2019)

Analysis of Unconscious Interaction Design for Smartphone Drop-Down Menu

Senyi Liu and Yongyan Guo[✉]

East China University of Science and Technology, Shanghai, China
g_gale@163.com

Abstract. Objective To analyze and explore the inner logic and application value of unconscious design in excellent interaction nowadays. Methods Large-screen cell phones bring advantages and disadvantages, and human-computer analysis for different positions of drop-down menus of smart large-screen cell phones, sliding from top-left to bottom-left for the first task, top-right to bottom-right for the second and third tasks, respectively. Through questionnaire and experimental design, the subjects' finger movement range and operating comfort in different task environments were recorded according to the operation duration, operation error rate, gesture changes and users' subjective feelings after the experiment, and then the data were analyzed by SPSS. Conclusion For right-handed users, the human-computer comfort of the first task environment is lower than that of the second task environment; for left-handed users, the human-computer comfort of the first task environment is higher than that of the second task environment, and the functions with higher priority will be placed in the upper-right to lower-right drop-down menu in the design; different functional module layouts also have different user experiences, and the unconscious behaviors of users in the third task environment also provide a basis for future related. The unconscious behavior of users in the third task environment also provides theoretical and data support for future related unconscious design of non-contact interaction; it also provides theoretical basis for the distribution of commonly used modules in drop-down menus and the design of specific module positions after drop-down.

Keywords: Unconscious design · Large-screen cell phone · Drop-down menu · User experience · Function module distribution

1 Introduction

1.1 Limitations of Operating a Large Screen Phone with One Hand

The era of large smartphone screen has come, people enjoy the enjoyment brought by the large screen at the same time, often ignore the hazards of large screen to people's hands. A more intuitive feeling is that people feel more and more difficult to use cell phones due to the mismatch between the size of the phone and the human-computer data of the hand. Xin Yizhong [1] and others in the study of the comfort range of one-handed large-screen cell phones pointed out that the thumb starts to fall (the location of the

M. Kurosu (Ed.): HCII 2022, LNCS 13304, pp. 182–193, 2022.
https://doi.org/10.1007/978-3-031-05412-9_13

asterisk in the figure) is located at the bottom right of the screen but close to the center of the screen, and the gray area is the range that the thumb can sweep to the axis of the base of the finger. In the right hand, for example, the closer the upper left corner of the screen, the less likely it is to be touched. Studies have shown that the longer you play with your phone, the more abnormal your posture is, the more "cell phone disease" will come along with it, such as tendonitis [2] (see Fig. 1).

Fig. 1. The landing point and controllable range of the thumb when operating the mobile phone with one hand, which has been redrawn by the author.

1.2   Research on the Advantages of One-Handed Drop-Down Menu Interaction

Once the iPhone x was introduced in 2017, it set off the era of smartphone "bangs screen" form of full screen, so the smartphone based on iOS12 system innovatively uses the function partition of upper left and upper right human-machine interface. In order to ensure the design flexibility and convenience of the cell phone system, you can directly wake up the function in a different area to enter the secondary function interface, and in the secondary function interface must take into account the human machine size, page layout, overall style, design specifications and other related information [3]. Therefore, Apple sets the commonly used functions in the drop-down menu secondary interface, which is considered from the user psychology perspective, ergonomics and user big data perspective. This interface is laid out with a number of commonly used functions, and for users who will use their right hand as their usual hand, the software's prompted messages have been browsed without the need to click again, so the left drop-down menu becomes a secondary point. And the core common function module is mainly in the upper right drop-down menu and in the comfort zone of the phone.

1.3   Unconscious Design in Drop-Down Menu Interaction Design Process

Freud's famous "iceberg theory" believes that the mind is divided into consciousness, preconsciousness and unconsciousness, comparing the three to a large mountain [4]. The unconscious is mainly studied from user's action, psychological and embodied cognitive aspects, such as from user's action, behavioral habits and intuitive experience; psychological emotional state and experience satisfaction; the influence of embodied cognitive sensorimotor system, human-computer-environment system [5].

Unconscious design (Without Thought) was first proposed by Naoto Fukasawa as a design that transforms unconscious behavior into something that can be perceived, touched, and met by the user's potential needs [6]. Unconscious design is the need to explore the deep, potential, and comprehensive needs of users from the user's perspective, and then the needs can be analyzed based on Maslow's hierarchy of needs theory and the Carnot model, so that the priority of user-level needs can be derived, and then the unconscious design process can be carried out. The significance of unconscious design is that a large number of unconscious behaviors in life can be found and used to form a familiar and excellent interaction experience between users and products. The current domestic research methods for unconscious design include user observation method, assessment scale method, and implicit measurement methods such as eye movement, EEG, and skin electrical response at the neuropsychological level to provide scientific basis for quantitative research of unconscious design [4]. This experiment explores the implicit logic of current excellent interaction behaviors through qualitative and quantitative methods, leading to the following work.

1.4   Related Jobs

Kiseok Sung believes that large-screen cell phones can cause accessibility problems during operation. Therefore, the user interface design of large-screen smartphones should consider a reasonable hierarchy of functions and layout [7]. Nowadays, studies on user human-computer interaction have been analyzed in the literature, and more consideration has been given to users with "digital affinity disabilities", who always encounter barriers when using digital devices [8]. For example, elderly people sometimes have difficulty using touch screen devices and should be involved in the design of interactions. [9] But even for the "digital affinity" user group, there is a latent HCI (Human-Computer Interaction) requirement, where the potential HCI can actively wake up the function or adjust the interface to help users achieve their goals, and provide adaptive services for users by recording their interaction behavior. The potential HCI can actively wake up functions or adapt the interface to help users achieve their goals, and provide adaptive services to users by recording their interaction behavior. [In this paper, based on iOS 12.0 and above, the functional module layout of the secondary interface fully considers the potential needs of users, and analyzes the difference in comfort level between module layouts and the reasons for the difference in user experience by collecting information from users, user experience and subjective evaluation. It provides reference for the interface logic and UI design of mobile devices or large touch or non-touch devices.

In recent years, research on smart large-screen cell phones and large touch or non-touch screens has received increased attention. Naoto Ageishi created a deep neural network that states that a gesture recognition system can recognize hand postures with 97.31% accuracy. [11] a Convolutional Neural Network (CNN) based gesture segmentation algorithm, solved the problem of incomplete gesture images and incorrect recognition rate in non-touch gesture recognition influenced by human face. Thus the accuracy rate of gesture recognition of non-touch hand parts are above 91% [12]. In terms of realization technology, Mr. Fan Chao, CEO of Anhui Dongchao Technology Co., Ltd. of China, believes that real-time aerial imaging can be realized through the phenomenon of negative refractive index, which uses the reconstruction of the light field to reconstruct the image of the plane equivalently in the daily air, forming an aerial plane that can be operated, the real image is composed of tens of millions of real light sources, and the user can directly touch the real image plane, so It is possible to achieve contactless screen operation, which perfectly realizes the contactless design and brings inspiration to the interaction design in the post-epidemic era [11]. Therefore, when users operate the phone with one hand or use it flat on the desktop, the interface design regarding the partitioning of functions, layout, and other forms of contactless interaction should be worth further study in the unconscious design for the screen interface that does not conform to the user's human hand size.

2   Method

Large-screen cell phones have limitations for one-handed operation. By not limiting the subjects or limiting them as little as possible, the subjects' operation duration, functional modules, reasons for clicking, and even operation error rates in different task environments were recorded, as well as subjective evaluations using Likert scales after the subjects were tested.

2.1   Subject Thumb Data Statistics

Table 1. Percentile of right thumb data of young men and women (mm)

Size	5th	50th	95th	Average value	Standard deviation
Male	56.21	62.51	69.51	62.74	5.43
Female	49.93	58.32	64.70	57.65	6.05

The thumb length was based on the straight-line distance from the midpoint of the palmar flexion line at the base of each finger to the tip point of each finger [13], and the experimenter used a vernier caliper to take the average value three times. Accordingly, the mean value in Table 1 was used as a reference.

Through literature analysis, the most comfortable cell phone screen size values in the smartphone screen development law are 4.7 inches (iPhone se), 5.4 inches (iphone12 mini) and 5.8 inches (iphone xs), in that order. Corresponding to the 5th, 50th, 95th size respectively, so the iPhone xs (screen size of 5.8 inches) was chosen for the human analysis.

2.2 User-Specific Study

With the help of questionnaires and observational measurements, we collected information on users' habits of using cell phones, their tendency to use cell phones with one or both hands, and their tendency to click on hot zones, and conducted statistics and analysis on the collected data.

Subjects and Contents of the Study. A total of 110 respondents (54 males and 56 females) aged 19 to 35 years old participated in the subjective survey. They were physically healthy, had healthy hands, normal vision and had at least 3 years of smartphone usage experience. The main members were students, social workers, etc.

The investigators mainly understand the respondents' gender, commonly used phone size, commonly used single-handed, commonly used left and right-handed, whether they are familiar with the ios system, commonly used functions, the most comfortable area for thumb operation based on actual experience, and the sorting of commonly used function choices in the drop-down menu.

Results and Analysis. A total of 110 questionnaires were collected by the end of this survey, and 110 valid questionnaires were obtained after the invalid questionnaires were eliminated by the investigators, with a valid recovery rate of 100%, which meets the relevant requirements. After the questionnaires were collected, the data were organized and the statistical results are shown in Table 2 (Fig. 2).

From the questionnaire survey, it can be seen that for the purpose of this paper to conduct qualitative research, the questionnaire results show that the most users with 5.7–6.4-inch cell phone screen is 53.64%; the most users with one-handed operation of cell phone is 63.64%; the most users with right hand is 78.18%; the most common functions are adjusting volume and screen brightness, 86.36% and 73.64% respectively. For the right-handed users, A and E are the areas with higher comfort. In spss26.0, gender and phone size were selected as independent variables and screen comfort ranking area was selected as the dependent variable, and the data analysis showed that the chi-square <0.05 indicated significant differences (Table 3).

Table 2. Basic information statistics of questionnaire survey

Description variables	Statistical Information	Percentage
sexy	male	49.09%
	female	50.91%
Common phone sizes (inches)	4.2-4.9	7.27%
	5.0-5.6	28.18%
	5.7-6.4	53.64%
	6.5及以上	10.91%
One hand or both hands when using cell phones	One hand	63.64%
	Two hands	36.36%
Whether you have used iOS 12.0 and above		50%
	no	50%
Commonly used hand is left-handed or right-handed	left	21.82%
	right	78.18%
What are the common cell phone functions	Switching flight mode	30%
	Switching network connections	64.55%
	Switching network connections	60.91%
	Adjusting screen brightness	73.64%
	Switching flashlight	57.27%
	Switching power saving mode	40.91%
	Adjusting the volume	86.36%
	Switching cameras	64.55%
	Other	5.45%
When using the phone with one hand, the red area in the screen is ranked according to the comfort of use1	A	86.80%
	E	56.80%
	C	50.00%
	D	37.60%
	B	32.00%
When using the phone with one hand, the red area in the screen is ranked according to the comfort of use2	A	82.00%
	E	59.80%
	C	52.00%
	D	36.80%
	B	35.20%
When using the phone with one hand, the red area in the screen is ranked according to the comfort of use3	A	78.40%
	C	57.60%
	E	51.60%
	B	40.80%
	D	36.60%
When using the phone with one hand, the red area in the screen is ranked according to the comfort of use4	A	72.60%
	C	54.20%
	E	51.60%
	D	50.00%
	B	33.40%

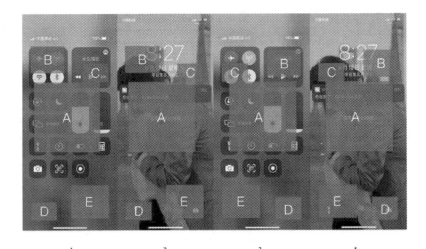

Fig. 2. Screen comfort zone 1–4 in the questionnaire

Table 3. Chi square table of SPSS cross analysis (part)

	Value	Degree of freedom	Progressive significance (Bilateral)
Pearson Cardinal	53.721[a]	5	.000
Likelihood ratio	61.570	5	.000
Number of active cases	110		

[a] The minimum expected count is 1.31. a. 5 cells (41.7%) have an expected count of less than 5.

2.3 Quantitative Analysis

The purpose of this experiment is to test the changes in task completion duration, gestures, and user comfort level of using each area when the thumb operates the phone in different areas during one-handed operation, and to verify the optimal layout area of the drop-down menu function module for one-handed phones.

Experiment. A total of 18 subjects were recruited for this experiment, including 9 males and 9 females, with an average age of 23 years old. All subjects had normal (or corrected) visual acuity, no hand disease, their dominant hand was right-handed, and all had more than 3 years of smartphone usage experience. During the investigation, the investigators were ready to answer the doubts of the subjects.

Experimental Equipment and Tasks. Experimental equipment: iPhone xs with iOS 14.5 system, screen size 5.8. Timer, vernier calipers, and laptop computer using a Macbook pro with M1 chip.

First, the length of the thumb was measured with a vernier caliper, and the straight line distance from the midpoint of the palmar flexion line at the base of the thumb to the tip point of each finger; the subjects filled in their own gender, age, height, size of their usual cell phone, whether they had used iOS 14 or above, and whether their usual hand was left or right. Subjects who were not familiar with the ios system were informed of the basic interaction and task flow as shown in Table 4.

Table 4. Experimental task details

Serial number	Task content
One	Upper right drop-down menu to select a function independently
Two	Top left drop-down menu, browse notification bar
Three	Top right drop-down menu, select five specific functions

Note: The five specific functions in Task 3 are: adjust screen brightness, switch on/off flight mode, switch on/off power saving mode, switch on/off flashlight, and open camera.

After task completion, subjects rated their comfort level with each task interaction operation, as well as subjective ratings for the three interaction tasks. Subjective ratings in task three were quantified using a Likert scale, where a score from 1 to 5 indicates increasing satisfaction, with 5 being a perfect score. The researchers recorded the click module, interaction time, interaction error rate, interaction gestures, and subjective evaluations. The lapse phenomena mainly include the inability to reach the screen at a longer distance with one hand; waking up other unrelated interfaces; and functional module click lapses.

Experimental Variables. The independent variables are two interaction tasks, and the dependent variables are interaction time; interaction error rate; interaction gesture; task one function module, reason for clicking; and subjective evaluation.

Experimental Procedure. The subjects were first introduced to the function before the experiment started, and the subjects needed to understand and adapt to the operation in advance. In order to avoid the psychological suggestion of the researcher to the subjects, the subjects were not informed of the specific purpose of the experiment during the task. Once the formal experiment began, 19 subjects were tested sequentially between 9:00 am and 4:00 pm. Subjects completed 2 (two directions) * 3 (three tasks) * 3 (three experiments) = 18 experimental tasks in sequence according to the experimental requirements. Therefore, excluding the number of mishaps, the total number of experiments for the 18 subjects was 324. The purpose of conducting three repetitions of the experiment was to reduce the error of the experimental results.

According to the experimental requirements, all volunteers operated the phone with their dominant hand only and used the appropriate technology to complete the target selection task. When the task was completed, the next trial was conducted; when a miscalculation occurred, the trial was terminated and restarted. Each set of tasks was repeated three times.

After the task was completed, the subjects were asked to make a subjective evaluation of their comfort level for each task and for the two directional drop-down menus (Table 5).

Table 5. Experimental data

subject	one	two	three
			4.15
			4.18
Average time (s)			3.78
	7.37	3.01	3.81
			4.58
Average number of errors	0.33	0.33	0.22
Operating comfort			3.83
			2.83
			3.50
			3.67
			3.28

3 Results

3.1 Average Time Spent

A total of 3 * 7 * 18 = 378 time data were obtained for this experimental task. From the time data in task 3, it can be concluded that the longest time was spent on switching the flight mode; the shortest time was spent on switching the power saving mode. This is consistent with the frequency of commonly used functions in the questionnaire and the difference in the range of clicks.

3.2 Average Error Rate

This experiment includes subjects who are familiar with the ios system and subjects who are not familiar with the ios system, so there will be frequent errors in the latter; in addition, the smaller the thumb size of the subject's hand, the greater the number of operation errors, and at the same time bring about changes in gestures.

3.3 Subjective Evaluation

According to the data, the highest ratings were obtained for adjusting the screen brightness and switching the flashlight; the lowest ratings were obtained for switching the flight mode. This is consistent with the difference in click range in the questionnaire.

In addition (right-handed) subjects were more satisfied with the user experience of sliding down the screen from the top right than from the top left; in the sliding menu, for screen brightness adjustment and switching the flashlight user comfort was the highest, followed by power saving mode and switching the photo, and finally turning on and off the flight mode; the interaction time was longer on the top right than on the top left. Misuse mostly occurs on subjects who are not familiar with iOS, and users who are more friendly to digital affinity can also complete this experimental task smoothly.

4 Discussion

From the questionnaire results and experimental data, different interaction areas and functions have significant effects on task completion time, task error rate, gestures, and users' subjective evaluations, which is consistent with expectations, indicating that drop-down menus based on the ios system take full account of the human hand size when designing the layout, as well as based on different life scenarios, commonly used functions should be recommended to be designed and laid out in areas that are more comfortable for one-handed operation. Experimental results show that right-handed users are significantly more comfortable in the middle of the screen and the right area of the screen than other areas. As in the questionnaire comfort area A, E. When designing the process framework, the hierarchical priority of functions should also be considered, considering the first level of importance (interface) - second level of importance (interface) - third level of importance (interface). As the interaction behavior and gestures become more and more complex nowadays, multi-finger operation, non-contact operation and other types of interaction methods appear. By using the technique of gravity distance method to process the hand contour and thus detect the fingertip position, the fingertip can be recognized effectively in complex backgrounds. [14] A new method of gesture recognition using a faster region convolutional neural network deep learning algorithm with five layers of neural networks can identify gesture recognition categories effectively, quickly and accurately with low computational cost. The accuracy can reach 99.2%, which is important for human-computer interaction applications. [15] In terms of design theory, the unconscious design is mainly explored, and through scientific experimental arguments, users make evaluations of behavior after tapping for unconscious design, which can help designers better grasp the information of users' unconscious behavior. [16] Based on the ios system, Apple has raised user experience to the level of product strategy. iOS interaction system is excellent in details, this paper only cuts from the drop-down menu for behavior analysis and discussion, there are still more innovative and excellent interaction experiences and scenarios worth to learn, which is also the purpose of this experimental study. Now that the HongMeng system has been released, I found that the drop-down menus based on the HongMeng system are in line with the research objectives of this paper, and based on this learning approach, more excellent interaction experiences can be tapped. Previously, Huawei also realized the new interaction method of operating some functions over the air, which not only can realize long-distance overhead operation, but also can avoid device pollution. East super technology of aerial interaction imaging technology. In addition media-free aerial imaging technology has been used in many scenarios in transportation, medical, education and home appliances, and has already achieved sales. Aerial interaction imaging technology to a certain extent turns the user's hand interaction form from two-dimensional to three-dimensional, and there must also exist the best comfortable operation area as well as sub-comfortable area for spatial interaction, so the experiment can be based on this experiment. In August 2020, General Secretary Xi Jinping experienced the "interactive aerial imaging technology" of Dongchao Technology and encouraged independent innovation to support China's "smart" manufacturing. It can be seen that there is a huge development space between human-machine intelligent interaction.

5 Conclusion

The significance of this study is to know the user's behavior habits and the area with the highest comfort level when using the phone with one hand, the best comfort area when the user clicks in unconscious behavior, and the function area clicked in unconscious behavior related to the layout of common function modules. Therefore, when setting the default module function layout, people's best comfort area under unconscious clicks should be considered, and the theoretical model of the plane should also be applied to contactless human-computer interaction, which is one of the focuses of future research. The shortcoming of the paper is that the experimental material is limited and more interaction experiences are not tried. The feasibility of more functions can be tested in the future through the design and improvement of the program. It is suggested that users should not blindly follow the trend of "big screen", but should choose a suitable screen size according to their own hand size to improve user satisfaction. [17] The user is advised not to follow the trend of "big screen" blindly, but to choose the right screen size according to their own hand size to improve user satisfaction.

References

1. Yizhong, X., Yang, L., Yan, L., Xinhui, J.: A one-handed target selection method for large-screen cell phones. J. Comput.-Aided Des. Graph. **28**(10), 1750–1756 (2016)
2. Zhu, S., Cui, L., Chen, Z., Wu, J., Shen, Z., Zhang, J.: The effect of cell phone usage and duration on the development of "cell phone disease". Health Care Med. Res. Pract. **XCX13**(05), 24–27+30 (2016)
3. Yang, L., Jiwu, X., Bo, L.: Application of human-computer interaction technology in interface design of digital media mobile. Mod. Electron. Technol. **44**(06), 155–158 (2021)
4. Cao, X., Li, M.: The application of behavioral stimulation in unconscious design to the design of household bakeware [J/OL]. Packaging Engineering, pp. 1–11, 16 September 2021. http://kns.cnki.net/kcms/detail/50.1094.TB.20210305.1604.028.html
5. He, C., Lu, C.-C.: Unconscious design in the perspective of embodied cognition. Packag. Eng. **41**(08), 80–86 (2020)
6. Limin, G., Shiying, W.: The application of the concept of "unconscious design" in product design. Packag. Eng. **39**(10), 162–166 (2018)
7. Sung, K., Cho, J., Freivalds, A.: Effects of grip span in one-handed thumb interaction with a smartphone. Proc. Hum. Factors Ergonomics Society Ann. Meet. **60**(1), 1048–1052 (2016)
8. Dong, H.: Human-computer interaction challenges and inclusive design. Design **33**(15), 7 (2020)
9. Monika, J., Helena, L., Madeleine, B.: Exploring limitations of user interface design to understanding the gap between technology and seniors. Stud. Health Technol. Inform. **281**, 931–935 (2021)
10. Alvarez, C., Zurita, G., Baloian, N.: Applying the concept of implicit HCI to a groupware environment for teaching ethics. Personal Ubiquit. Comput. 1–19 (2021)
11. Roy, D., et al.: Real-time hand-gesture recognition based on deep neural network. SHS Web Conf. **102**, 04009 (2021)
12. Liu, B.-W.: Research on human-computer interaction based on gesture recognition for Android platform. Southeast University (2019)
13. Liu, P., Fu, D.-N., Jiang, S.-Q., Chen, H., Shen, S.-C., Li, M.-W.: A survey study on hand anthropometry of young medical students in China. Human Ergonomics **23**(03), 60–66 (2017)

14. Changzheng, L., Shuang, N.: Fingertip detection during motion. Small Microcomput. Syst. **39**(03), 578–583 (2018)
15. Yu, X., Yuan, Y.: Hand gesture recognition based on faster-RCNN deep learning. J. Comput. **14**(2), 101–110 (2019)
16. Zhu, Q.: Research and application of unconscious phenomena in product design. Beijing University of Technology (2020)
17. Huang, H.-N.: Research on the factors influencing cell phone operation performance under single hand grip. Nanjing Normal University (2020)

Analysis of Changes Before, During, and After Simulated Postoperative Delirium Experience Using VR for Clinical Nurses

Jumpei Matsuura[1]([✉]), Takahiro Kunii[2], Hiroshi Noborio[3], Katsuhiko Onishi[3], and Hideo Nakamura[4]

[1] Naragakuen University, Nara, Nara, Japan
jmatsuura@nara-su.ac.jp
[2] Kashina System Co., Hikone, Shiga, Japan
kunii@tetera.jp
[3] Department of Computer Science, OECU, Neyagawa, Osaka, Japan
{nobori,kaoru,onishi}@osakac.ac.jp
[4] Department of Health-Promotion and Sports Science, OECU, Neyagawa, Osaka, Japan
h-nakamu@osakac.ac.jp

Abstract. In this study, 13 nurses with more than 10 years of experience as clinical nurses in the surgical field were given a simulated experience of postoperative delirium using VR, and the changes that occurred before, during, and after the experience were analyzed from three perspectives: subjective data, psychological data, and objective data. The results showed that the subjective data before and after the VR viewing changed in a way that was more in tune with the patient's inner world. The psychological data showed significant differences in six of the eight items, including "anger-hostility," "confusion-embarrassment," and "tension-anxiety". Objective data showed significant differences in two of the six items: "Falling ceiling" and "No change for the second time," and "Cockroaches appeared on the ceiling" and "A person wearing a protective suit appeared.

Keywords: VR · Delirium · Nursing

1 Introduction

Delirium, according to the American Psychiatric Association (DSM-V), is when the symptoms are "disturbance of consciousness, cognitive changes", "appearance of perceptual disturbances", and "fluctuates throughout the day" [1].

There are three factors that contribute to the development of delirium: preparatory factors, direct factors, and triggering factors. Preparatory factors include chronic central nervous system vulnerabilities that the patient already possesses, such as old age, dementia, and the chronic stage of cerebrovascular disease. Direct factors include drug addiction, central nervous system disease, metabolic disorders affecting the brain, and alcohol withdrawal. Triggering factors include psychological and social stress, sleep disturbances, sensory deprivation or sensory overload, and physical restraints or forced bed rest [2].

Symptoms of delirium include insects crawling on the ceiling, hallucinations of people who are not actually present, and auditory hallucinations of sounds that are not actually being heard.

As a previous study, the author created a simulated ICU using Unity, and created a video to simulate the postoperative delirium that occurs there in VR. The author conducted a study to analyze the physiological changes in sympathetic and parasympathetic nerves and the psychological changes using the mood profile test (POMS) by simulating the VR experience for nursing college students. The results showed that there were no significant differences in the sympathetic and parasympathetic changes during VR viewing, while the POMS results showed significant differences in six out of eight items. The POMS scale assesses a wide range of mood states with seven items: Anger-Hostility (AH), Confusion-Bewilderment (CB), Depression-Depression (DD), Fatigue-Alertness (FI), Tension-Anxiety (TA), Vibrancy-Vitality (VA), and Friendliness (F). FI + TAVA is the Total Mood Disturbance (TMD) score; TMD is an indicator of the degree of distress and affective disturbance.

2   Objective

The purpose of this study was to analyze the subjective, physical, and psychological changes that occur before, during, and after viewing a simulated postoperative delirium video using VR by skilled nurses with more than 10 years of experience to provide basic data for the development of a program to deepen the understanding of postoperative delirium.

3   Method

We used Unity to create a VR model of the world of postoperative delirium as experienced by patients with postoperative delirium. The duration of the video is 12 min, and the content of the VR video changes every 2 min. Oculus Quest 2 was used for VR viewing (Fig. 1).

The subjects were 13 nurses with more than 10 years of clinical experience in the surgical field. The data to be analyzed were interviews before and after the VR viewing, psychological data using POMS, and two types of data on the sympathetic and parasympathetic nerves of the autonomic nervous system during the viewing, which were compared between groups by one-way analysis of variance. The dominance level was set at 5% in both cases.

(1) A virtual reality system (Unity) was used to create a 12-min visualization of the world as seen by a patient with postoperative delirium.

The order of the images was as follows: no change, cockroaches appear, the ceiling falls, people in protective clothing appear, soldiers attack, and no change.

The data created by Unity was connected to Oculus Quest 2 (Head Mount Display (HMD)) for viewing.

(2) The data created by Unity was connected to an Oculus Quest 2 (Head Mount Display: HMD) for the participants to watch.

(3) Subjective data (questionnaire survey form) and objective data (physiological data such as autonomic nervous system) were collected and analyzed as evaluation items.

As for the subjective data and objective data, the postoperative delirium simulated experience created in Unity reproduced the postoperative state in the ICU ward, and the subjects were asked to measure their mood using the POMS (Profile of Mood States), a mood evaluation scale, before and after the simulated experience. Physiological data was collected using HeartBIT (IBM), and changes in heartbeat over time were collected. SPSS Ver.26 was used as the analysis software.

This study was conducted with the approval of the Research Ethics Review Committee of Nara Gakuen University (2-004).

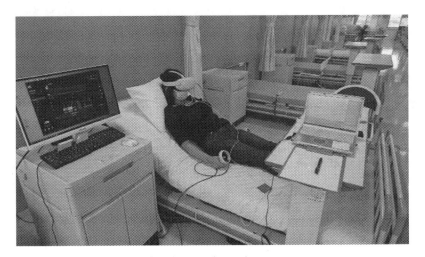

Fig. 1. Experimental scene

4   Results

The results of the interviews before and after the viewing of the VR show that before the viewing of the VR, many of the comments were thought for the convenience of the nurses, not for the patients who developed delirium. However, after watching the VR, they said, "I thought I might have delirium if I were put in that situation. I can't sleep. After watching the VR, many people said, "I don't know where I am, where I am, or what time it is, and I'm trying my best to understand my situation. I'm trying to make sense of my situation, and I have a lot of questions about how long this is going to last. I felt like I didn't know how to deal with the situation, and because I didn't know what to do, I became aggressive. My anxiety was very strong. These were some of the comments that were heard (Table 1).

Table 1. Subjective results on the image of patients with delirium

ID	Before	After
1	I'm still a little crazy. I can't control myself	It's still a mess. I'm hooked up to a tube and I want to take it out
2	I can't sleep, especially at night. He speaks unintelligible words and does not understand what we are saying	I felt like I was really nervous about something I felt like I was really nervous about something
3	Restlessness. Angry, violent, self-extraction, low level	Angry. Restless and violent. Self-extraction. Unable to communicate. Decreased level
4	Dangerous, poor, dangerous, what should I do, scary, sorry, I don't want to be in that situation myself. I feel scared	I thought that I would have delirium. I thought that if I were put in that situation, I might have delirium too. I couldn't sleep. It was different from my daily environment, and I still felt trapped and restrained. I felt like someone was watching me, and I was already scared
5	I have a big image of being confused. I don't think you know what you're confused about. Patients say a lot of things, but it's difficult to deal with them realistically, and as a nurse, I can't see them, so I can only imagine them	I knew what delirium was, but if I didn't, I think it would be quite frustrating. Especially the rhythm of the monitor sound was quite nerve-wracking. I thought it was quite nerve-wracking when I was asleep
6	There are times when I feel like I have to tell her that she can't do something because I want to treat her. I wonder what I should do there	I need to get back to where I always am. So I look for a way out. I really felt the need to see where I was. People say they see insects on the ceiling, but I think about what I would do if they fell on me, and how I would escape. When people appeared, I was scared unless they called out to me, and I didn't know what they were doing to me, so I searched for an escape route
7	I don't understand the situation I'm in at all, so I'm very anxious and scared	I lose track of where I am, or where and when I am, and I try my best to understand my situation. It's like I have a lot of questions about how long this is going to last. I felt like I didn't know how to deal with it, and because I didn't know what to do, I became aggressive. My anxiety was very strong

(*continued*)

Table 1. (*continued*)

ID	Before	After
8	After the surgery, or on the same day, or a couple of days later, all of a sudden, what they say doesn't add up, or they say, or they don't know that they have a broken bone	I was bothered by the sound of the monitor, insects appearing and disappearing on the ceiling, people in white coats appearing and disappearing, people waving their arms, etc. I was bothered by these things, and my eyes would go to them, and I felt like I couldn't calm down, and just when I thought I could rest, I would hear the sound of the monitor, so I couldn't rest at all. Just when I thought I was going to be able to rest, I would hear the sound of the monitor, so I couldn't rest at all. When I think of the delirium patients seeing the world like this, I feel like I can't calm down, and I think they would say they want to go home
9	Forgetfulness, dementia, not pressing the nurse call. Easy to lose things, deafness. Insomnia, listening back to others often. Difficulty in calculation. Forgetfulness. Nervousness, tries to do everything by himself/herself. Tends to be reserved	I'm anxious. Nervousness. Forgetfulness, inability to do calculations. I try to do everything by myself. I am anxious
10	He is anxious. He's confused. You know where you are, where you are, and the pain you're in	Let me reassure you that I'm confused. It's strange to call it sympathy. I've had a major surgery, and the anesthesia is affecting me, and the medication is affecting me, so I'll try to reassure her
11	I think it's more common among men. Those who do not express themselves well. Those who don't talk much. People who are patient	People with high anxiety, a little finicky, mostly men. Serious people, people who can't sleep. People who lack self-confidence. People who were relying on someone else
12	Often bugs are flying, and they don't add up. Self-extraction of routes due to lack of instructions, which can easily lead to incidents. Day and night are reversed	I thought after the experience that there were bugs on the ceiling. The sound of the monitor is such a loud thing. I feel like my ears are so focused on that sound that I don't pay much attention to anything else. When the soldiers came by, I felt terrified
13	I imagine that many people get delirium at night	I don't feel rested, and I can't sleep. That's the kind of person I'm talking about. It's an image of being in such a situation, whether you can talk to them or trust them

As a result of analyzing the changes in autonomic nervous system during VR viewing, significant differences were found between two of the six items: "Falling ceiling" and "No change for the second time," and "Cockroaches appearing on the ceiling" and "Person in protective clothing appearing (Fig. 2).

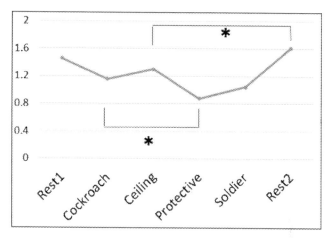

Fig. 2. Autonomic changes

As a result of analyzing the psychological data using POMS before and after the VR viewing, significant differences were found in six items: AH: Anger-Hostility, CB: Confusion-Bewilderment, TA: Tension-Anxiety, VA: Vigor-Vitality, F: Friendship, and TMD: Total Mood Score, excluding two of the eight items: DD: Depression-Depression and FI: Fatigue-Anxiety (Figs. 3, 4, 5, 6, 7, 8, 9 and 10).

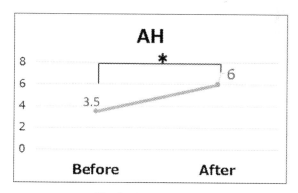

Fig. 3. Anger-Hostility

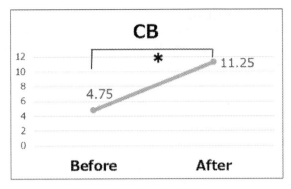

Fig. 4. Confusion-Bewilderment

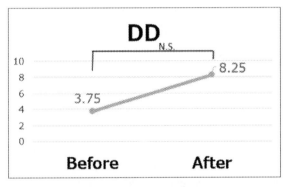

Fig. 5. Depression-Depression

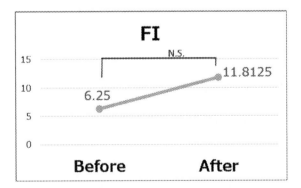

Fig. 6. Fatigue-Anxiety

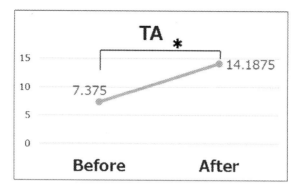

Fig. 7. Tension-Anxiety

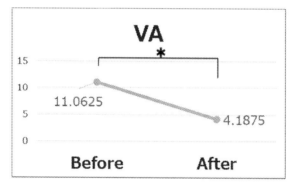

Fig. 8. Vigor-Vitality

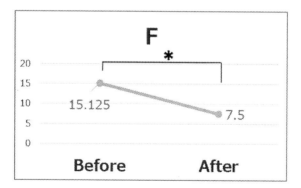

Fig. 9. Friendship

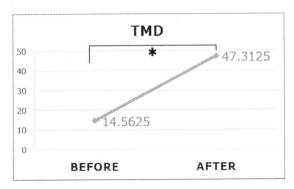

Fig. 10. Total mood score

5   Discussion

Of the domestic medical and psychological studies using VR, two studies used POMS as an evaluation index: one was an evaluation of the effects of different mood states on current pain sensitivity and autonomic nervous system activity for pain management using VR [3]. The other was the effect of autonomic activity on workers in overnight residential healing health tourism [4].

As for research in the field of nursing using VR, a VR dementia experience program that simulates the world experienced by dementia patients has been developed and reported to be effective [5]. In order to understand the way dementia patients feel and to be closer to their hearts, a study [6, 7] has been conducted to experience the world experienced by schizophrenia patients. There are few studies on postoperative delirium using VR in the world. There have been few studies of simulated postoperative delirium using VR in the world, except for a study conducted by Matsuura on seven third- and fourth-year nursing students [8] and another study conducted by Matsuura on 18 s- to fourth-year nursing students [9].

The results of the subjective data showed a clear change in the image of delirium patients before and after viewing the VR. Specifically, before viewing the VR, many people did not understand the patient's actions and behaviors. However, after watching the program, the number of comments made by the nurses increased as they realized that the patient's actions and behaviors had meaning. The nurses believe that actually experiencing the hallucinations caused by delirium through VR will lead to a better understanding of the inner life of delirium patients, and can be expected to change the way they respond to patients in the future.

In the results of the autonomic nervous system data, in the first stage of the previous study, a pilot study of VR simulated experience conducted on a total of seven male and seven female third- and fourth-year nursing university students [2], and in the second stage of the previous study, a study of VR simulated experience conducted on a total of 18 male and female second- to fourth-year nursing university students [5] No significant differences were found in all six items of the POMS. However, in the current study conducted on nurses, significant differences were found between two of the six items:

"Falling ceiling" and "No change second time," and "Cockroach appears on ceiling" and "Person in protective clothing appears.

For "falling ceiling" and "second time with no change," we speculate that "falling ceiling" may have been the result of a stress reaction due to the fear that they would be crushed, while "second time with no change" may have been the result of a stress reaction due to the fear that something would appear again.

As for the "appearance of cockroaches" and "appearance of a person in protective clothing," the "appearance of cockroaches" is one of the hallucinatory symptoms that patients with delirium often talk about. In the case of the "appearance of a per-son in a protective suit," the color of the suit was white, the same color as the nurses' white coats, so the nurses may have felt stressed because they felt that their col-leagues did not do anything even though they came to support them, and that they were not on their side even though they thought they were.

In terms of psychological data results, in a previous study conducted on nursing college students, significant differences were found in six out of a total of eight items. Two items, "Anger-Hostility" (AH) and "Vigor-Vitality" (VA), were not significantly different. In the present study of nurses, significant differences were found in six of the eight items. There were no significant differences in the two items of "depression-depression" (DD) and "fatigue-anhedonia" (FI). The other results showed that the nurses were able to imagine how the patients were feeling based on their clinical experi-ence, since they were actually involved in caring for patients with delirium, and that the two items of "depression-depression" (DD) and "fatigue-anhedonia" (FI) were not significantly different. Therefore, the two items of "depression-depression" (DD) and "fatigue-anhedonia" (FI) may not have been significantly different.

6 Conclusion

This study analyzed the subjective, physical, and psychological changes that occurred before, during, and after nurses watched a VR simulated experience of postoperative delirium. The following three points were revealed by the nurses' experience of the simulated VR delirium.

In the analysis of the subjective changes, the nurses had a vague image of the delirium patient before the VR viewing. However, after viewing the VR, the number of comments that showed a greater understanding of the inner life of the delirium patient increased.

In the analysis of the autonomic nervous system, significant differences were found in the two items, "appearance of cockroaches on the ceiling" and "appearance of a person in protective clothing," and "falling ceiling" and "no change for the second time.

In the analysis of psychological changes, significant differences were found in six of the eight items: "Anger-Hostility" (AH), "Confusion-Bewilderment" (CB), "Depression-Depression" (DD), "Fatigue-Alertness" (FI), "Tension-Anxiety" (TA), "Vitality-Vitality" (VA), "Friendship" (F), and "Total Mood State" (TMD), except for two items, "Depression-Depression" and "Fatigue-Alertness.

7 Future Works

Although this study was conducted on 13 skilled nurses, we believe that it is necessary to increase the number of subjects in the future to verify the results.

References

1. Lipowski, Z.J.: Delirium. Acute Confusional States, pp. 54–70. Oxford University Press, New York (1990)
2. American Psychiatric Association: Diagnostic and Statistical Manual of Mental Disorders DSM-5, p. 596 (2014)
3. Ryosuke, K., et al.: Evaluation of the effects of different mood states on current pain sensitivity and autonomic nervous activity for pain management using VR. J. Jpn. Soc. Welfare Eng. **23**(1), 34–41 (2021)
4. Sayaka, F., et al.: Effects on autonomic activity of workers in lodging-stay healing health tourism. J. Jpn. Soc. Med. Nurs. Educ. **26**(3), 9–12 (2018)
5. Shimogawara, T., et al.: Application of VR in nursing: fostering person-centered care through VR dementia experience. J. Jpn. Soc. Nurs. Educ. **29**, 64 (2019)
6. Wakisaki, Y., et al.: Changes in nursing students' understanding of schizophrenic patients with visual and auditory illusions in psychiatric nursing: a study from the content analysis of questionnaires after simulated experience and clinical practice. J. Jpn. Soc. Nurs. Educ. **15**, 125 (2005)
7. Wakisaki, Y., et al.: Changes in psychiatric nursing students' under-standing of Schizophrenic patients with visual and auditory illusions: a content analysis of questionnaires before and after the simulated experience. J. Jpn. Soc. Nurs. Educ. **15**, 125 (2004)
8. Matsuura, J., Kunii, T., Noborio, H., Watanabe, K., Onishi, K., Nakamura, H.: Development of a VR/HMD system for simulating several scenarios of post-operative delirium. In: Kurosu, M. (ed.) HCII 2021. LNCS, vol. 12763, pp. 582–600. Springer, Cham (2021). https://doi.org/10.1007/978-3-030-78465-2_42
9. Matsuura, J., et al.: Changes in the perception of postoperative delirium before and after a simulated experience of postoperative delirium in nursing students. In: 6th International Conference on Intelligent Informatics and Biomedical Sciences, pp. 101–106 (2021)

The User Experience of Public Health Websites: A Survey Study

Aimee Kendall Roundtree[✉] [iD]

Texas State University, San Marcos, TX 78666, USA
akr@txstate.edu

Abstract. This survey study gathered information about public health website visitors' user experience and habits. User experience (UX) information helps designers use evidence to empathize and imagine what happens when users interact with the product and encounter problems. Prior studies have covered particular public health websites for specific needs and reviewed standard features. This study extends previous work by starting with the users rather than the websites and sharing information about their use patterns. The study recruited 600 participants from Qualtrics Panels, a demographically and politically representative sample, to answer 17 closed-ended questions about their interactions with public health sites. They typically used public health websites for data gathering (average ranking 2.03) more than for decision making (2.95), policymaking (3.78), report writing (4.30), public relations (4.7), planning (5.06), or presentation preparation (5.6). Users were more likely to use the sites for data gathering and decision-making; therefore, messaging about solutions is as important as messaging about risks. Designers should look to the CDC and other popular Federal public health sites for inspiration. Future research will provide in-depth qualitative themes to explain these trends.

Keywords: User experience · Usability · Public health websites · Survey study

1 Introduction

This survey study gathered information about public health website visitors' user experience and habits. User experience (UX) includes all aspects of end-user interaction with digital products and companies. In UX design, teams rely on user feedback, attitudes, needs, and preferences to create products that provide meaningful and relevant experiences to users. UX helps designers use evidence to empathize and imagine what happens when users interact with the product and encounter problems. Studies suggest that user interface and interaction account for 45–65% of coding, 40% of the development effort, and 80% of unexpected fixes. Forbes reports that the return on investment of UX design is $100 for every $1 invested. IBM found that UX research and design improved time to market two-fold, reduced design time and cost by 75%, reduced development time by 33%, and reduced design defects and maintenance costs in half.

Prior studies have analyzed clusters of public health websites for specific needs and reviewed standard features. Studies examined 195 websites per web accessibility

M. Kurosu (Ed.): HCII 2022, LNCS 13304, pp. 205–213, 2022.
https://doi.org/10.1007/978-3-031-05412-9_15

guidelines and found that several did not meet basic requirements [1, 2]. A review of the accessibility of public health information portals found several errors with governmental sites compared to commercial news portals [3]. A quality check of 31 international aesthetic medicine society websites found that only two of the websites fulfilled the threshold score [4]. A content analysis of 32 websites to analyze public information about recommended vaccines revealed the most common risk communication approaches [5]. Another study in Alabama examined info about the opioid crisis on the websites of 230 public libraries. They conducted a content analysis and found that the sites shared news and upcoming/past events, resources to use, and collections of drug and overdose information. However, the websites did not provide info on assigned opioid-related roles, strategic representation, or internal departments [6]. Another study employed a preexisting usability scoring methodology to create recommendations for improving health center websites. They conducted heuristic evaluation and scoring of 72 websites. The websites were split into categories: accessibility, marketing, content quality, and technology. Sutter Health Design and Innovation had the highest accessibility, general usability, and content quality scores. The Mayo Clinic Center was top for marketing. The Texas Southwestern Office for Technology Development earned the top score for technology [7]. This study extends insights from these studies by providing insights from users rather than insights from the web pages themselves. This study starts with insights from multiple users rather than from numerous websites.

Prior studies have also conducted user tests on individual web pages. One study examining user tasks of a public health website asked users to evaluate a site before and after preliminary evaluation. The new website design post initial evaluation and revision the preliminary evaluation inspired showed improvements in all sections with only one scoring below 75% satisfaction. The study called for further studies on larger groups of users [8]. The State of Hawaii Child and Adolescent Mental Health Division (CAMHD) created a website to distribute EBP information to families. They tracked user stats and found that as of 2018, the website had 29,100 user visits from 150 different countries and 66 different areas in Honolulu [9]. The Pitt Public Health Dean's office tested their website by conducting five interviews with the website committee and seven focus groups with seven students, 13 alumni, seven faculty members, and 16 staff members. Findings revealed difficulty finding information, specifically contact information, a lack of updated information, a need for better communication between the school and its internal and external audiences, and more social media and mobile usability [10]. Five experts evaluated 16 public health department websites and found that the websites were usable, but many contained insufficient messaging about infection risk [11]. A study evaluated heat- and health-related government webpages in the United States. Researchers found that local government webpages had less information than government webpages. Some had little information on populations at greater risk, but all had information on actions to reduce risk. None of the websites included everything needed to help the public with heat-related health issues [12]. This study extends the prior work by starting with users and their broad use patterns rather than specific users for a particular site. It also includes more users from across the country.

Finally, prior studies in technical and professional communication also provide insights about health-related digital products. One study of social health content and activity on Facebook surveyed 455 users and found that offline social health activities do not transfer online [13]. Another analyzed four select infographics communicating Ebola risk during the outbreak that began in West Africa in 2014 using warm and cool colors, high versus low-context, and collectivism versus individualism and found that maps showed Ebola activity breaching national and international borders. However, line graphs showed increases in cases and deaths in Liberia and Sierra Leone [14]. Another analysis of 50 intergovernmental organizations (IGOs) and 20 non-governmental organizations (NGOs) found that English is the dominant language used, but sites contained inconsistencies with cyber language policies [15]. These studies confirm prior findings across a diverse set of digital products. The current study contributes by focusing on public health websites.

2 Methods

The study recruited 600 participants from Qualtrics Panels, a demographically and politically representative sample, to answer 17 closed-ended questions about their interactions with public health sites. The Texas Department of State Health Services (TDSHS) sponsored the survey. JASP, an open-source project supported by the University of Amsterdam, offered standard analysis procedures [16]. Survey questions were designed from TDSHS needs and synthesis of best practices lists for UX surveys.

The IRB approved the study protocol at Texas State University (IRB#7912).

Participants were selected were using the Qualtrics panel, a community of millions of respondents across the United States. Participants were targeted by demographics and professional profiles of audiences of interest to the DSHS, including medical workers, researchers, journalists, government workers, and others. The sample also included an oversample of Texans by request. Survey testing and administration took place in August and September 2021. The survey was anonymous. Qualtrics pays their panel participants per the amount that they agreed upon before participants entered into the survey. Participants are from all areas of the general public joining from various sources. The survey was designed to request general user demographics and information and user experience specific to TDSHS web products.

The questionnaire included general demographics, general use patterns, reasons for using public health websites, and sites featured used. Best practices in user experience survey design determined question sections and questions [17–22]. Thirteen closed-ended questions comprised these sections. The survey was validated with an iterative design using pilot testing and survey revision per test feedback. Qualtrics also offered recommendations during survey design for improved survey quality.

We used JASP for statistical analysis. JASP is an open-source project supported by the University of Amsterdam. The software offers standard analysis procedures in both their classical and Bayesian form. We calculated descriptive statistics to characterize the data. We conducted ANOVA and regression modeling to identify and measure relationships between variables. ANOVA indicated continuous outcomes based on one or more categorical predictor variables. Regression predicted continuous outcomes based on one or more continuous predictor variables.

3   Results

Most were ages 30–39 (n = 191), 18–29 (n = 163), 40–49 (n = 114), 50–59 (n = 60), or 60–69 (n = 52). The participants included approximately as many men (n = 296) as women (n = 299). Most were either white (n = 400), black (n = 105), Hispanic (n = 89), Asian (n = 32) or Native American (n = 18). Participants were permitted to declare more than one race and ethnicity. Most reported having completed high school (n = 169), bachelor's degree (n = 159), master's degree (n = 129), or associate degrees (n = 103).

Most worked in Texas (n = 179), California (n = 51), New York (n = 31), Georgia (n = 31) or Florida (n = 27). Most of the participants worked in health and medicine (n = 154), entrepreneurship and business (n = 90), banking and finance (n = 87), leisure (n = 87), education (n = 74), government (n = 30), energy (n = 27), nonprofit (n = 20), legal (n = 15), or research (n = 10) industries. Most were managers (n = 61), owners or CEOs (n = 61), teachers (n = 28), or nurses (n = 17). Most had worked in their field for 0 to 5 years (n = 206), 6 to 10 years (n = 162), 11 to 15 years (n = 99), or 16 to 20 years (n = 80).

Most reported using PCs (n = 296), Android devices (n = 221), iPhones (n = 207), MacBooks (n = 84) or iPads (n = 69) or other tables (n = 62) to access the internet for work. They reported spending fewer than an hour (n = 203), 2 to 4 h (n = 105), 5 to 7 h (n = 88), or 8 or more hours (n = 61) per week using public health websites. See Table 1.

Table 1. Demographics and use patterns.

		n	%
Age	30–39	191	31.83
	18–29	163	27.17
	40–49	114	19.00
	50–59	60	10.00
	60–69	52	8.67
	70–79	20	3.33
Gender	Men	296	49.33
	Women	299	49.83
	Other	5	0.83
Race, Ethnicity	White	400	66.67
	African American	105	17.50
	Hispanic	89	14.83
	Asian	32	5.33
	Native American	18	3.00
	Other	6	1.00

(*continued*)

Table 1. (*continued*)

		n	%
Education	High school	169	28.17
	Bachelor's	159	26.50
	Master's	129	21.50
	Associate	103	17.17
	Doctorate	29	4.83
	Other	11	1.83
Work field	Health/medicine	154	25.67
	Entrepreneur/business	90	15.00
	Banking/finance	87	14.50
	Leisure	79	13.17
	Education	74	12.33
	Government	30	5.00
	Energy	27	4.50
	Nonprofit	20	3.33
	Legal	15	2.50
	Research	10	1.67
	Other	14	2.33
Years in field	0–5 yrs.	206	34.33
	6–10 yrs.	162	27.00
	11–15 yrs.	99	16.50
	16–20 yrs.	53	8.83
	Over 21 yrs.	80	13.33
Tech used	iPhone	242	40.33
	Android phone	175	29.17
	PC/laptop	120	20.00
	Other	18	3.00
	iPad	17	2.83
	MacBook	14	2.33
	Android tablet	13	2.17
	Other	1	0.17
Use per week	<60 min	203	33.83
	1–2 h	135	22.50
	2–4 h	105	17.50
	5 to 7 h	88	14.67
	8 or more hours	61	10.17
	Other	7	1.17

When asked to rank what type of public health websites they use from one (used the most) to seven (used the least), participants rated Federal sites such as the CDC (average = 2.69) higher than the following: state sites such as state health services (average = 2.85); local sites such as county or city health departments (average = 3.14); private national sites such as WebMD (average = 3.34); international sites such as the WHO (average = 4.39); or professional organizations such as the American Public Health Association (average = 4.86). When asked to rank their purpose for using public health websites from one (used the most) to eight (used the least), they typically used public health websites for data gathering (average = 2.03) more than for decision making (average = 2.95), policymaking (average = 3.78), report writing (average = 4.30), public relations (average = 4.7), planning (average = 5.06), or presentation preparation (average = 5.6). When asked to rate the website functions they most use or need from one (used the most) to eight (used the least), they wanted the options of downloading

Table 2. Use pattern average rankings.

What public health websites do you use?	Federal	2.69
	State	2.85
	Local	3.14
	National	3.34
	International	4.39
	Organizational	4.86
	Other	6.73
For what purposes do you typically use them?	Research/data gathering	2.03
	Policymaking	3.78
	Decision-making	2.95
	Report writing	4.30
	Public relations	4.70
	Planning/proposal writing	5.06
	Presentations	5.61
	Other	7.57
What website features do you need, want?	Download spreadsheet	3.35
	Data by timeframe	3.50
	Data by location	3.70
	Data by demographics	4.15
	Links to sources	4.37
	Search tool	4.16
	General stats/data	4.96
	Other	7.81

spreadsheets from the site (average = 3.35), finding data by timeframe (average = 3.49), and finding data by location (average = 3.7) more than finding data by demographics (average = 4.15), finding links to sources (average = 4.37), using search tools (average = 4.15), or finding general statistics (average = 4.96). See Table 2.

Per ANOVA and linear regression analysis, what technology was used to visit public health websites was slightly influenced by education ($\beta = 0.17$, $t = 4.23$, $p = < .001$) and age ($\beta = 0.13$, $t = 3.44$, $p = .001$). Preferences for downloading spreadsheets ($\beta = 0.13$, $t = 3.31$, $p = .001$) and finding data by timeframe ($\beta = 0.13$, $t = 3.28$, $p = .001$) were also slightly influenced by age. Education somewhat influenced how participants spent using public health websites per week ($\beta = 0.21$, $t = 4.99$, $p = < .001$). And the use of national public health websites was also slightly inversely influenced by the number of years in the field of work ($\beta = -0.14$, $t = -3.64$, $p = < .001$). See Table 3.

Table 3. Linear regression and ANOVA.

AGE	Unstandardized Coefficients	Standardized Coefficients				ANOVA		
Model	B	Beta	Standard error	t	p-value	df	F	p-value
Technology used	0.11	0.13	0.03	3.44	0.001	25	4.53	<.001
Download spreadsheet	0.08	0.13	0.03	3.31	0.001	25	4.53	<.001
Data by timeframe	0.11	0.13	0.03	3.28	0.001	25	4.53	<.001
EDUCATION	Unstandardized Coefficients	Standardized Coefficients				ANOVA		
Model	B	Beta	Standard error	t	p-value	df	F	p-value
Technology used	0.14	0.17	0.03	4.23	<.001	25	2.72	<.001
Time spent	0.19	0.21	0.04	4.99	<.001	25	2.72	<.001
YEARS IN FIELD	Unstandardized Coefficients	Standardized Coefficients				ANOVA		
Model	B	Beta	Standard error	t	p-value	df	F	p-value
National websites	-0.11	-0.14	0.03	-3.64	<.001	25	2.36	<.001

4 Conclusion

Users included older adults, so accessibility is essential. Users were more likely to use the sites for data gathering and decision-making; therefore, messaging about solutions is as important as messaging about risks. PCs and Androids were more common than Apple products, so designers should plan accordingly. Most use the sites for 60 min or less per week to make decisions and gather information, so the design should accommodate quick visits. Designers should look to the CDC and other popular Federal public health sites for inspiration. Future research will provide in-depth qualitative themes to explain these trends.

This study extends the literature on the user experience of public health websites with new insights. First, prior studies found that public health websites share high quality, broad news, and information, particularly national and governmental websites. This study extends the work by showing that such sites are preferred to international and organizational sites, particularly for those new in their fields of work. Prior studies also found that users experienced difficulties finding information, and they desired more information. This study showed that users wanted to download spreadsheets and find information by timeframe and location. The user's age influenced these variables, younger users ranking spreadsheets higher. Finally, there might be a disparity between offline and online health behaviors, according to prior research. This study illustrates an associated detail: most users spent less than 4 h on public health websites per week. Education might influence the length of use per week; the more education, the more time spent. Public health websites might help resolve the disparity and serve all populations by using plain language, more illustrations, and appealing design.

User patterns in this study can help with site design and redesign, particularly given the relatively representative demographics of participants in this study. Minorities represented over a third of the sample. Users were inclined to use PCs and Apple products, so digital products should be prepared for ease of use on both platforms. Users spend fewer than four hours per week on the websites, so wayfinding features such as headers, breadcrumb menus, and search tools are vital. Users favored governmental and national sites, which will very likely inform their use patterns and expectations for all other public health sites. They used the sites for gathering data and making decisions, so plain language and practical implications are essential to include and highlight in the website content.

The study is limited as it does not include qualitative or open-ended data that might explain why these trends persist. The study also does not include international public health users. The trends and expectations might be different in other countries and settings. However, the work does provide user-centered feedback about their public health website preferences, needs, and expectations. Designers and public health workers can use the information to create user-centered websites and digital content. Future studies will discuss comments and qualitative feedback gathered about public health websites.

Acknowledgements. This study was funded by a Texas Department of State Health Services research contract Kallen Ledford-Treadway assisted with the literature review.

References

1. Mancini, C., Zedda, M., Barbaro, A.: Health information in Italian public health websites: moving from inaccessibility to accessibility. Health Info. Libr. J. **22**(4), 276–285 (2005)

2. Alajarmeh, N.: Evaluating the accessibility of public health websites: an exploratory cross-country study. Univ. Access Inf. Soc. **27**, 1–9 (2021)
3. Yu, S.Y.: A review of the accessibility of ACT COVID-19 information portals. Technol. Soc. **1**(64), 101467 (2021)
4. Battineni, G., Pallotta, G., Nittari, G., Chintalapudi, N., Varlaro, V., Amenta, F.: Development of quality assessment tool for websites of the international aesthetic medicine societies. Inform. Med. Unlocked **1**(23), 100559 (2021)
5. Vivion, M., Hennequin, C., Verger, P., Dubé, E.: Supporting informed decision-making about vaccination: an analysis of two official websites. Public Health **1**(178), 112–119 (2020)
6. Mehra, B., Jaber, B.S.: Opioid consumer health information literacies in Alabama's public libraries: an exploratory website content analysis. In: Roles and Responsibilities of Libraries in Increasing Consumer Health Literacy and Reducing Health Disparities. Emerald Publishing Limited, Bingley, U.K. (2020)
7. Calvano, J.D., Fundingsland, Jr. E.L., Lai, D., Silacci, S., Raja, A.S., He, S.: Applying website rankings to digital health centers in the united states to assess public engagement: website usability study. JMIR Hum. Factors **8**(1), e20721 (2021)
8. Puspitasari, I., Cahyani, D.I.: A user-centered design for redesigning e-government website in public health sector. In 2018 International Seminar on Application for Technology of Information and Communication, pp. 219–224. IEEE (2018)
9. Okamura, K.H., et al.: Insights in public health: the help your Keiki website: increasing youth and caregiver awareness of youth psychosocial mental health treatment. Hawai'i J. Med. Public Health **77**(8), 203 (2018)
10. Hughes, L.: Evaluation of University of Pittsburgh Pitt Public Health Website. Doctoral dissertation, University of Pittsburgh (2013)
11. Momenipour, A., Rojas-Murillo, S., Murphy, B., Pennathur, P., Pennathur, A.: Usability of state public health department websites for communication during a pandemic: a heuristic evaluation. Int. J. Ind. Ergon. **86**, 103216 (2021)
12. Zottarelli, L.K., Blake, S.A., Garza, M.T.: Communicating Heat-Health Information to the Public: Assessing Municipal Government Extreme Heat Event Website Content. Weather, Climate, and Society, December 2021
13. Roundtree, A.K.: Social health content and activity on Facebook: a survey study. J. Tech. Writ. Commun. **47**(3), 300–329 (2017)
14. Welhausen, C.A.: Visualizing a non-pandemic: considerations for communicating public health risks in intercultural contexts. Tech. Commun. **62**(4), 244–257 (2015)
15. Zhang, H., Wu, Y., Xie, Z.: Diversity or division: language choices on international organizations' official websites. IEEE Trans. Prof. Commun. **63**(2), 139–154 (2020)
16. JASP homepage. https://jasp-stats.org/. Accessed 18 Feb 2022
17. Qualtrics. Survey design your respondents will love. https://www.qualtrics.com/experience-management/research/how-to-make-a-survey/. Accessed 18 Feb 2022
18. MTAB. Validating a Survey: What It Means, How to do It. https://www.mtab.com/blog/validating-a-survey-what-it-means-how-to-do-it. Accessed 18 Feb 2022
19. Joyce, A.: Survey Response Biases in User Research. Nielsen Norman Group, https://www.nngroup.com/videos/survey-response-biases/. Accessed 18 Feb 2022
20. Liu, F.: Iterative Design of a Survey Question: A Case Study. https://www.nngroup.com/articles/survey-questions-iterative-design/. Accessed 18 Feb 2022
21. Gallavin, G.: 4 Tips on Great Survey Design. Digital.gov. https://digital.gov/2014/11/10/4-tips-on-great-survey-design/. Accessed 18 Feb 2022
22. Kuniavsky, M.: Observing the User Experience: A Practitioner's Guide to User Research. Elsevier, New York (2012)

Connected yet Distant: An Experimental Study into the Visual Needs of the Interpreter in Remote Simultaneous Interpreting

Muhammad Ahmed Saeed(✉) ⓘ, Eloy Rodríguez González ⓘ, Tomasz Korybski ⓘ, Elena Davitti ⓘ, and Sabine Braun ⓘ

Centre for Translation Studies, University of Surrey, Guildford GU2 7XH, UK
{m.a.saeed,e.rodriguezgonzalez}@surrey.ac.uk

Abstract Remote simultaneous interpreting (RSI) draws on Information and Communication Technologies to facilitate multilingual communication by connecting conference interpreters to in-presence, virtual or hybrid events. Early solutions for RSI involved interpreters working in interpreting booths with ISO-standardised equipment. However, in recent years, cloud-based solutions for RSI have emerged, with innovative Simultaneous Interpreting Delivery Platforms (SIDPs) at their core, enabling RSI delivery from anywhere. SIDPs recreate the interpreter's console and work environment (Braun 2019) as a bespoke software/videoconferencing platform with interpretation-focused features. Although initial evaluations of SIDPs were conducted before the Covid-19 pandemic (e.g., DG SCIC 2019), research on RSI (booth-based and software-based) remains limited. Pre-pandemic research shows that RSI is demanding in terms of information processing and mental modelling (Braun 2007; Moser-Mercer 2005), and suggests that the limited visual input available in RSI constitutes a particular problem (Mouzourakis 2006; Seeber et al. 2019). Besides, initial explorations of the cloud-based solutions suggest that there is room for improving the interfaces of widely used SIDPs (Buján and Collard 2021; DG SCIC 2019). The experimental project presented in this paper investigates two aspects of SIDPs: the design of the interpreter interface and the integration of supporting technologies. Drawing on concepts and methods from user experience research and human-computer interaction, we explore what visual information is best suited to support the interpreting process and the interpreter-machine interaction, how this information is best presented in the interface, and how automatic speech recognition can be integrated into an RSI platform to aid/augment the interpreter's source-text comprehension.

Keywords: Interpreter-machine interaction · Speech recognition · Interpreter workstation ergonomics · Remote simultaneous interpreting · Human-computer interaction (HCI) in interpreting

1 Introduction

Remote simultaneous interpreting (RSI) can be defined as an interpreting solution that is delivered by the means of ICTs and performed by an interpreter or a team of interpreters whose location is different from that of the speaker(s).

© The Author(s), under exclusive license to Springer Nature Switzerland AG 2022
M. Kurosu (Ed.): HCII 2022, LNCS 13304, pp. 214–232, 2022.
https://doi.org/10.1007/978-3-031-05412-9_16

Initial solutions for RSI involved a physical working environment for interpreters similar to traditional simultaneous interpreting, namely a soundproof booth with a console/control panel, and incoming/outgoing audio feeds enabling interpreters to listen to a speaker through headphones, while producing the interpretation into the target language in real time, spoken into a microphone for delivery to the audience. As simultaneous interpreting is cognitively demanding, interpreters normally work in pairs, taking turns (approx. every 20 mins.) and assisting each other (e.g., with terminology).

RSI solutions developed from the 2000s onwards involved interpreting booths being placed in an interpreting hub, connected to an event venue in another building, city or country (Seeber et al. 2019). More recently, however, a new generation of cloud-based simultaneous interpreting delivery platforms (SIDP) have been developed to recreate the interpreter's traditional console and work environment virtually (Braun 2019). In addition, and accelerated by the shift towards online working since the beginning of the Covid-19 pandemic, suppliers of videoconferencing platforms such as Zoom have begun to integrate features to support interpreting in online meetings. As a result of these developments, RSI has been undergoing an evolutionary process. For instance, SIDPs allow interpreters to work from home and to be physically separated from their booth partners, which can increase flexibility for both interpreters and their clients. However, the recent and rapid shift towards cloud-based RSI during the Covid-19 pandemic has also had a significant impact on interpreters' lives and working conditions and has raised many issues from different perspectives.

Research on *booth-based* RSI has found that this modality of interpreting is particularly tiring and perceived as being more stressful than traditional onsite simultaneous interpreting (Moser-Mercer 2005; Roziner and Shlesinger 2010). One of the reasons that has often been given by interpreters is the lack of a 'sense of presence' (Mouzourakis 2006). Pointing in a similar direction, a recent large-scale survey of interpreters, who at that time of the survey mostly performed *cloud-based* RSI assignments, shows that 83% of respondents consider RSI more difficult than on-site interpreting, 50% believe that their average performance is worse under RSI conditions and 67% think that working conditions are worse in RSI (Buján and Collard 2021).

Research has also shown that a more thorough analysis of interpreter's visual needs in RSI is required (Ziegler and Gigliobianco 2018). This is particularly important for the cloud-based platforms, as they involve not only remoteness but also a new technological environment, compared to a booth in a hub. However, these and other aspects of RSI are currently under-explored, and research on SIDPs from a technical and user experience perspective is sparse. Meanwhile, practice-based explorations of SIDPs have concluded that these platforms can "be used to provide interpretation services" (DG SCIC 2019), but have also highlighted that none of them are "fully ISO compliant" (AIIC 2020).

One point that emerges from both research-based and practice-based initiatives is that further investigation is needed into how interpreters can be supported in RSI. As a contribution to this, the study we present here, which comprises two PhD projects, focuses on two aspects of support, namely the optimisation of visual aids for the interpreter with a view to improving user experience (UX) and the integration of automatic speech recognition (ASR) in RSI to aid source text comprehension.

This paper specifically addresses the question of how interpreter support can be improved by increasing the 'sense of presence'. As outlined above, insufficient 'sense of presence' is one of the fundamental sources of unease for remote simultaneous interpreters. By focusing on the notions of interpreter support and presence, the broader aim of this study is to optimise the interpreters' working conditions, improve their UX and overall wellbeing.

2   Contribution of Literature

As highlighted above, bespoke SIDPs have emerged in response to the growing demand for RSI, especially since the beginning of the Covid-19 pandemic.

With the shift of RSI from booths to online platforms it is becoming ever more important to improve the platforms to suit interpreter needs and different types of interpreting assignments. Given the cognitively demanding nature of RSI (in any type of assignment) and the demonstrated links between RSI and presence, we will first review the available evidence of reported and/or observed cognitive impacts of current RSI platforms, their causes and the current knowledge of the role of presence in RSI. The final sections of this review intend to identify and examine links between the concept of presence and related concepts, as a step towards developing a novel approach to improving the interpreter's sense of presence.

2.1   Cognitive Impacts of RSI

Although empirical research on RSI has been conducted with different technological parameters (Moser-Mercer 2003; Mouzourakis 2006; Roziner and Shlesinger 2010), evidence has consistently suggested that interpreters feel uncomfortable with RSI and dissatisfied with the quality of their interpretations delivered remotely. Whilst there has been debate about the role that the interpreters' attitudes towards, and subjective perceptions of, RSI may play in (negative) self-assessments of their performance (Roziner and Shlesinger 2010), the challenges of RSI highlighted by previous research are still a cause for concern for both the interpreting community and researchers in the field.

Moser-Mercer's (2003) seminal study comparing traditional simultaneous interpreting (SI) and booth-based RSI showed that interpreters who had been provided with the same documentation, preparation time, and technical support for SI and RSI, felt physically more detached in the remote modality. The analysis of interpreting quality and post-study questionnaire responses also revealed that working remotely led to a noticeable degradation in interpreting performance over a 30-min turn, suggesting that the remote condition was more tiring (Moser-Mercer 2003). Kurz (2003), detailing the results of two UN experiments conducted during the late 1990s and early 2000s, similarly noted that, in order to maintain an acceptable performance in RSI, interpreters appeared to expend more psychological and physiological effort.

Similar findings were generated in a comparative study of traditional SI and RSI conducted by the European Parliament in 2004 (reported in Roziner and Shlesigner 2010). The study employed a similar study design to the study conducted by Moser-Mercer (2003) albeit with a larger participant group, a larger number of language pairs, and better technology. Notably, it was found that despite having superior working conditions for remote interpreting than in older experiments, supporting, for example, a better posture for the interpreter, remote interpreting had a higher burnout rate. Although no differences in physical aspects (such as physical exhaustion) and interpreting quality could be found, the authors noted that there was a clear psychological impact associated with remoteness.

Although not extensive, the existing body of research on RSI thus draws attention to the cognitive impact of remote interpreting on interpreters, and an important research question arising from these studies is how this impact can be mitigated. In the words of Mouzourakis, "it is unlikely that much progress in RI will be achieved without a more systematic understanding of the ergonomic and cognitive issues involved and, in particular, interpreter alienation or the absence of a feeling of participation in the meeting room universally observed and experienced in RI experiments" (Mouzourakis 2006, p. 56).

2.2 Causes of the Cognitive Impacts

As discussed in the previous section, feelings of stress, fatigue, and isolation are common in RSI. The feeling of isolation, in particular, has been a topic of debate within the RSI research community, where feelings of being disconnected have been noted by several researchers (Moser-Mercer 2003; Mouzourakis 2006; Roziner and Shlesigner 2010).

This feeling of isolation has also been previously documented in telephone interpreting settings (Wadensjö 1999) and is thought to increase the difficulties for the interpreter when trying to relay the speaker's message. Winteringham (2010, p. 95) contends that the "lack of closeness could place more strain on the interpreters, who may experience increased difficulty in interacting, managing speaking turns, and requesting further clarifications and may develop a sense of alienation and loss of control."

Moser-Mercer contended that interpreters working in the RSI modality seemed unable to immerse themselves in the virtual environment and suggested that the interpreters' "inability to be more closely involved with what is going on in the conference hall [...] produces a feeling of 'not being in control'" (Moser-Mercer 2003, p. 11).

Equally important, Mouzourakis (2006) highlighted that the absence of a feeling of participation is not unique to RSI but is common to most settings where tasks are performed in virtual environments. As pointed out above, this creates a strong focus for investigating the feeling of remoteness, isolation, and alienation from other perspectives. In support of this point, Ziegler and Gigliobianco (2018) also call for a more interdisciplinary approach in interpreting studies and to RSI in order to advance the design of the future workspace of interpreters.

In line with this, the remainder of this literature review will take an interdisciplinary perspective and examine innovative approaches to reducing feelings of isolation and alienation in remote work. In particular, the following sections will draw on the notions of presence and immersion, which have been developed across different fields (including technology studies, engineering, and computer sciences as well as psychology) to capture experiences of interacting and working in virtual environments.

2.3 Presence and Immersion

Before considering mitigating the feeling of isolation, it is important to describe this phenomenon in more detail. Although labels such as the feeling of remoteness or isolation can serve as an initial characterisation of it, the present study will conceptualise this phenomenon as a lack of presence.

Presence has been defined as the ability of a virtual environment to induce feelings of being present/together (Lee 2004). Franceschi et al. (2009, p. 79) describe it in their study on social presence in virtual worlds as the ability "to psychologically transport the user to an artificial environment during the experience" and further explain that "[t]his psychological transportation is known as the user's sense of presence during the virtual experience."

The concept of presence has been explored by researchers in relation to interacting with diverse types of media, including watching movies, playing games, or interacting with other people through virtual reality. In line with the concept's applicability to a wide range of subjects, there are several other definitions of presence. In addition, the concept has been subdivided into the following terms:

- "Telepresence" - being transported to a virtual space using teleoperation systems such as videoconferencing technology
- "Virtual presence" – being transported to a virtual space using virtual reality technologies such as 3D virtual worlds (Sheridan 1992).

However, to discuss how presence can be improved, it may be more helpful to consider it in general terms initially and not specifically in relation to a particular technology. For example, Lee (2004) argues that the differentiation of the concept of presence on the basis of specific technologies is meaningless as "it is a psychological construct dealing with the perceptual process of technology-generated stimuli" (Lee 2004, p. 30).

Further explaining the concept, Lee (2004, p. 32) contends that presence is "a psychological state in which the virtuality of experience is unnoticed." Arguably, this is what an interpreter may aspire to feel while performing remote interpreting. However, as discussed above, interpreters currently appear to feel unable to be connected in this way to the virtual environments (VE) in which they carry out remote interpretation. Thus, it is important to understand how this lack of presence can be overcome or mitigated/reduced.

A concept that is often considered to overlap with presence is immersion, which refers to the feeling of "existing" within a virtual world. A useful definition of immersion has been proposed by Mestre (2005, p. 1), who states that "immersion is achieved by removing as many real-world sensations as possible and substituting these with the sensations corresponding to the VE". This definition closely resembles that of presence, which has often led researchers to use presence interchangeably with immersion (Yee 2006). However, there have been countless strides to distinguish the two terms. Most notably, Slater et al. (1994) distinguish the two by characterising immersion as an objective description of the technology and presence as a subjective experience. Kalawsky (2000) also supports this by associating presence with a cognitive parameter, whilst understanding immersion as more of a physical concept, i.e., a function/ capability of the technology. Brown and Cairns (2004) classify immersion as a multi-graded construct that encompasses engagement, engrossment, and total immersion, where total immersion is similar to the concept of presence. However, the framework provided by Brown and Cairns further distinguishes the two by maintaining that immersion increases over time (i.e., time spent in a VE) whereas presence fails to have any quantifiable difference from previous stages.

The framework also suggests that attaining presence follows the same path as improving immersion, and that immersion is a necessary condition for developing a sense of presence (see also Skalski et al. 2009). Furthermore, Witmer and Singer (1998), when attempting to measure the feeling of presence, found a high correlation between immersion and presence and noted that immersion is essential for experiencing a sense of presence (Witmer and Singer 1998). A study by Gorini et al. (2011, p. 103), which investigated the role of immersion in the creation of a sense of presence, produced comparable results, and the authors contended that "the results show a significant influence of physical immersion on all the presence self-reported questionnaires, suggesting its role in increasing one of the aspects of presence".

Presence-related explorations of RSI also conclude that to improve presence, interpreter immersion needs to be improved (Braun 2019; Mouzourakis 2006; Roziner and Shlesinger 2010; Seeber et al. 2019; Ziegler and Gigliobianco 2018), but they have not yet presented systematic evidence of how this can be achieved.

2.4 Improving Immersion Through Hardware and Software

Ziegler and Gigliobianco (2018) analysed the visual input of interpreters with the aim of understanding how technological advances can be used to overcome the current limitations of RSI. The authors propose that technological enhancements such as augmented reality and immersive communication environments could offer the possibility to overcome the current lack of presence. Mouzourakis (2006) supported the same hypothesis and argued that testing alternative options for image display would be imperative to achieve a benchmark in RSI configurations. Roziner and Shlesinger (2010) specifically discussed stress and performance of interpreters during remote interpreting from the perspective of lack of presence, noting that a poor interface/display of information leads to discomfort, increased stress, and fatigue.

Other studies, conducted in the fields of psychology, computer science, and display technologies, all point towards the same direction, suggesting that an immersive viewing of information could reduce the lack of presence that is caused by remote working. One study, aimed at comparison between real-world activities and their simulated counterparts, empirically highlighted that the traditional methods of displaying information are inferior to immersive virtual environments (Blascovich et al. 2002). The authors highlighted specifically that the replication of real-world situations in virtual environments is impossible with current traditional methods of information display and that an immersive environment is required to improve the realism of the situation/scenario.

Options for adapting the mediated environment range from an increase in screen size to using curved screens and changing to augmented or virtual reality technologies (Tan et al. 2003; Ahn et al. 2014; Ziegler and Gigliobianco 2018). Some of the RSI studies suggest that improvements to the working environment and more specifically, the immersive visual display information, is key to reducing performance loss and lack of presence, such as that currently exhibited during remote interpreting (Mouzourakis 2006; Roziner and Shlesinger's 2010).

However, before moving to hardware displays, it is important to consider the software aspect of the information. As Moser-Mercer (2003), Ziegler and Gigliobianco (2018) pointed out, it is crucial that researchers analyse the visual needs of interpreters in greater detail. Findings from such research will need to be considered in both hardware and software design, as enhancing the hardware will improve the experience of the interpreter only as far as the software is ready. At the same time, a technically advanced hardware configuration of displays with a lacklustre display of information could lead to worse interpreter experiences. This is also supported by the European Parliament Interpreting Directorate test in 2001, where remote interpretation was being enabled by three large screens and eleven smaller monitors, designed in such a manner to provide a complete view of the meeting room. Despite the impressive array of displays, interpreters felt fatigued and alienated after using the setup for interpretation (Mouzourakis 2006). This might be due to a poor display of information which can negatively impact the interpreter, despite being presented through technologically advanced hardware setups.

In a more recent study, Seeber et al. (2019) analysed the performance of conference interpreters working from a hub during the 2014 FIFA World Cup and found that RSI was no longer perceived as more stressful than in-situ interpreting, previously reported by Moser-Mercer (2003). Despite this remarkable finding, the authors noted that "future studies should endeavour to identify the technical and human parameters responsible" for the lack of presence and place emphasis on "such complex human-machine interactions" to "better understand interpreters' needs in an increasingly high-tech workplace" (Seeber et al. 2019, p. 301).

Based on this review of previous research on RSI and the notions of presence and immersion, it seems that the visual information presented to the interpreter might have a key role in the overall sense of presence. Consideration of software interfaces has also become particularly pertinent since the recent rise of (software-based) simultaneous interpreting delivery platforms.

2.5 The Flow State

One further concept that is important when considering immersion through the lens of visual needs of the user is the concept of "flow." The term "state of flow" or "flow" abbreviated, was coined by Csikszentmihalyi and Csikszentmihalyi (1988) and has been described as "a mental state of operation, in which a person is fully immersed in what he or she is doing". Weibel et al. (2009, p. 2), described the characteristics of flow as "intense involvement, clarity of goals and feedback, concentrating and focusing, lack of self-consciousness, distorted sense of time, the feeling of full control over the activity and the balance between the challenge and the skills required to meet it".

According to subsequent studies conducted by Csikszentmihalyi (1990) and Klasen et al. (2012), an enhanced flow or being in the state of flow is likely to lead to better performance, as it constitutes a balance between challenge, skills, sense of control, and concentration. Csikszentmihalyi (1999) has characterised the flow state as an optimal experience, when the user feels nothing else apart from the activity they are performing.

This has led researchers to believe that the state of flow is an intense experience, and that immersion is an antecedent to flow (Brockmyer et al. 2009).

To better understand the benefits of flow state for the interpreter, it is important to understand the similarities between presence and the state of flow. The concepts of presence and flow have several similarities. For example, research has found that both presence and flow are associated with decreased frontal brain activation (e.g., Clemente et al. 2013), and that this state is maintained when attention of the user is selective (Kober and Neuper 2012; Harris et al. 2017). This situates presence at an "early stage" of total immersion and the flow state (Klasen et al. 2012). Witmer and Singer (1998) also expressed characteristics of presence which are similar to those defined by Csikszentmihalyi (1990), when describing flow. The authors mention narrow attentional focus, immersion, and involvement as the necessary conditions for presence, which coincide with the characteristics of flow.

As discussed in the previous sections, lack of presence has a major impact on the psychological wellbeing of interpreters and as highlighted in this section, there appears to be a strong link between sense of presence, immersion, and the flow state.

Although the concept of flow has not yet been applied to interpreting, it is not difficult to see how the characteristics of flow can provide a framework for analysing the interpreter's workflow, which often encompasses:

- a challenging activity-requiring skill
- high concentration on the task
- the loss of self-consciousness
- the transformation of time

Considering what is known about the interpreter's workflow in RSI (Moser-Mercer 2003; Ziegler and Gigliobianco 2018) we can assume the interpreter does enter the state of flow and is able to produce a high-quality interpretation for some time as a result of the total concentration. However, the interpreter might not be able to sustain the state of flow due to information overload, hence the degradation in performance over time found by Moser-Mercer (2003). The intention of our study is to find out more about what visual information supports the state of flow. The next sections will explore the use of less information-rich interfaces to reduce the interpreter's workflow.

2.6   Interface Design According to Flow

The state of flow has usually been associated with games (Draper 2000), as researchers have concluded that the flow state grants a positive effect to the player. However, researchers have now moved their attention to applying this concept to other areas of study, such that Johnson and Wiles (2003, p. 4) propose "that an understanding of the process, by which games generate flow, could inform the effective design of non-leisure software".

Bergman (2000) pointed out that the game design and HCI design communities had – by then - seldom commented on each other's work but that there has been growing interest in bridging these two areas over the years (Johnson 1998; Johnson and Wiles 2003). In the small body of research that has applied the concept of flow to non-leisure activities, flow has been found to have a positive impact (Lai et al. 2021; Lee 2021). This suggests that the concept of flow, if applied appropriately to work-related software, could significantly improve the psychological wellbeing of users.

To better understand how we could ease entering the flow state, it is thus, important to consider models of flow in HCI design, for example, those developed by Ghani (1995). Ghani proposed that flow is measured through constructs of enjoyment, concentration, learning and creativity, which was later found through testing to be accurate as there is an increase in perceived control (Zhang and Finneran 2005).

The characteristics of flow and guidelines for effective user interfaces (e.g., from Usability.gov 2021) suggest that a user interface should be clear and simple, and that it should provide feedback to the user. In line with this, studies from the field of User Experience often argue in favour of having less information/clutter on the screen, so as to reduce distractions for the user, gear information towards user interaction, and improve overall information clarity (e.g., Gaffar and Kouchak 2017).

Johnson and Wiles (2003) suggested that, like games, non-leisure software could benefit from having a minimal interface and that this would improve user flow. They hypothesised that "this focus on, and lack of distraction from, the major task contributes to the facilitation of flow" and that immersion is prompted when the interface is free from distractions. In a similar study investigating mobile interfaces, Johnson et al. (2020) found that 'Informativeness' and 'Functionality' were key factors for improving flow in mobile interfaces, and that a clear interface could benefit user flow significantly. Based on these studies, along with studies on presence conducted by Underwood and Schulz (1960) and Gibson (1969), it can be assumed that a clear and minimal interface could benefit user flow and presence.

A further factor that has been identified as contributing to improving immersion and flow is interactivity (Johnson et al. 2020), which can be linked to research on non-verbal, visual inputs in SI. This research suggests that non-verbal, visual inputs such as hand gestures, lip movement, and body language play an important role in comprehending the speaker's message (Rennert 2008). To further understand this phenomenon, the study reported in this paper will investigate to what extent interpreter interactivity in RSI can be improved through different speaker views. We will investigate this effect by comparing a closeup view, in which the interpreter can see only the facial expressions of the speaker, and a gesture view, in which the interpreter can see hand gestures and body language of the speaker, and more of the speaker's physical environment.

2.7   ASR as a Visual Feature

Another important aspect of interest for us is how to support the interpreter during RSI. ASR was initially discussed in the field of computer-assisted interpreting (CAI) as a supporting tool for interpreters in relation to traditional SI (Fantinuoli 2017). Research in this area has focused on the potential of ASR to assist interpreters when dealing with common problem triggers of SI such as technical terminology and numbers (Gile 2009). A pilot study using a prototype of ASR-CAI integration was designed to process ASR-generated transcripts of three English specialised speeches and to use these transcripts to identify numerals as well as automatically extracting relevant entries from a previously created terminology database. The study concluded that the use of ASR seems promising

(Fantinuoli 2017). Drawing on this research, an experimental pilot study, which used a mock-up system that transcribed, isolated and displayed the numbers of the source speech using ASR, showed that trainee interpreters who were presented with the transcript of the numbers from the original speech increased their overall accuracy on interpreting numbers from 56.5 to 86.5% (Desmet et al. 2018).

The integration of CAI, and especially ASR, in RSI has only just begun to receive attention in Interpreting Studies. For instance, Fantinuoli et al. (2022) explore the effectiveness of KUDO Interpreter Assist, a tool whose aim it is to "shorten the overall preparation time and to increase the precision of the rendition in highly specialised events" (Fantinuoli et al. 2022:1). The tool provides interpreters with a "real-time suggestion system" and the possibility of automatically creating a glossary. The ASR embedded in the "real-time suggestion system" is used to show specialised terminology and their translations, numbers (with units of measurement) and proper names. While the preliminary results presented in the paper are not based on real-life RSI conditions, the authors conclude that they "are encouraging" (Fantinuoli et al. 2022:8).

Another example of CAI and RSI integration is that of the SmartTerp project, defined by Rodriguez et al. (2021:1) as a "CAI system to support the simultaneous interpreter, especially in the RSI modality". SmartTerp also relies on ASR to extract and show entities such as terminology and numerals to the interpreters while they are interpreting.

Our approach to using ASR in RSI as a way of assisting interpreters with source speech comprehension differs from the work outlined above in that we investigate the integration of a *full* source speech transcript, generated through ASR, in an RSI user interface. One part of our experimental study currently focuses on the impact of transcript availability on interpreting quality in RSI. More specifically, we investigate the extent to which ASR can support interpreting lexically dense speeches and fast speeches, i.e., two challenging speech characteristics (Mankauskienė 2016), in an RSI context. The set-up of this experiment was preceded by discussions within the research team and, via focus groups, with professional and trainee interpreters about the design of the visual display of the ASR transcript within an RSI Interface. This is the aspect of ASR-RSI integration that we discuss in the present paper. It is in line with our broader aim to conceptualise RSI as a type of HCI, where factors such as the usability and efficacy of the machine play an essential role in the interpreters' ability to deliver high-quality interpretation and, equally important, in their wellbeing. The next section outlines the design and outcomes of the focus groups before the final section presents our initial evidence base for visual features of RSI interfaces.

3   Focus Groups

Given the current scarcity of evidence in relation to cloud-based RSI and interpreter's interface of SIDPs, we conducted two focus groups (FG) with conference interpreters to gather their feedback regarding current RSI practices, platforms, and interfaces, better understand the interpreter' needs, and collect suggestions for features of SIDP interfaces. Moreover, the involvement of interpreters in all phases of our study is also an important principle of the software design. The first phase of the study was thus centred on the current RSI platforms and how interpreters utilise them. Based on the participants' contributions to the FG, our analysis of existing platforms and review of the literature, we constructed the research methodology.

3.1 Focus Group Preparation

A total of seven participants (three professional interpreters and four trainee interpreters) were invited to participate, and the participants were split into two groups, one including the trainee interpreters, the other the professional interpreters. The small participant numbers per group facilitated moderation of the sessions, which had to take place online, and helped to avoid some participants being overshadowed by others.

The FG was designed in such a manner as to build trust with the participants and provide structure to the discussion. It included five sections: introductions and overview of RSI; pros and cons of RSI; analysis of current interfaces and participant ideas; review of research-based interface and participant reviews; wrap-up and conclusions. A total of 2.5 h was allowed for each session. Prior to the session, the participants had been instructed to have stationery available for sketching out interface designs. Otherwise, no preparation was required on the participant side. Whilst we had a detailed schedule to avoid overrunning the set length, we instructed the participants to be as vocal as possible.

As mentioned above, the FG involved a mix of trainee and professional interpreters, and because of this, an overview of RSI was given especially for the benefit of the trainee interpreters, who had little or no experience with performing RSI before the FG. Basic demographic information and information about the participants' experience was collected through an email questionnaire in the process of arranging the FGs. The 'Introduction and Overview of RSI' section in the FG was then used to corroborate the participants' experiences. Participants were invited to talk about their level of RSI experience, as far as they wished to share this with the other participants. The subsequent discussion of benefits and drawbacks of RSI was also designed in such a way that the participants could freely express their thoughts regarding RSI along with past interpreting experiences and provide recommendations regarding current RSI practices.

In addition, the team had planned a design activity to elicit the interpreters' ideas regarding RSI interface designs. To this end, a review of currently available interfaces was presented, after which participants were invited to design their own interfaces on paper and/or in Microsoft Paint to express what they require from current interfaces. As a crucial part of the FG, this activity allowed us to collect interpreters' feedback regarding desirable additions and amendments to current interfaces.

In the final part of the FG session, we demonstrated some visualisations of the interface features developed by us in line with the flow concept design principles (see Sect. 2.5), which included the following:

- Swappable video feeds, i.e., an option for an interpreter to select which feed (speaker, audience, presentation materials) to see, where and in what size;
- Hidden controls to reduce distraction from visual elements of the platform;
- Fading controls, also to reduce distraction; however, in contrast to the hidden controls, they fade out and become nearly transparent when not in use;

- Integrated chatboxes i.e., to have all chatboxes (booth chat, moderator chat, technician chat etc.) in one place, rather than each chatbox occupying a separate space on the screen.

The control and chatbox-related visual features were presented to the interpreters to gauge whether they value immediate access to meeting controls or whether they would be willing to sacrifice easy/visible access to controls in return for a less distracting and cleaner interface. The swappable video feeds were included to explore whether interpreters would want to see other camera views, and to understand which camera views have higher priority for the interpreter.

3.2 Outcomes of the Focus Groups

Whilst the FG sessions were guided and structured by our prompter questions, the participants also brought up their own points and experiences of RSI. Thus, the main themes to emerge from the FG were the participants' views towards RSI, their requirements for a healthy RSI session, insights into what should be the visual elements of an RSI platform, and features that could facilitate collaboration during an RSI event, especially between interpreters.

In terms of **overall views of RSI**, all FG participants had a positive attitude towards the use of technology for interpreting. Some participants mentioned that because of Covid-19 their use of RSI had increased significantly, and that RSI had enabled them to access interpreting assignments that were previously inaccessible. Additionally, some participants mentioned that working from home created more flexibility and that the high speed internet obviated the need to travel to the conference location.

In relation to their **requirements**, among the other items such as a non-distracting environment to focus completely on their task and on the quality of their interpretation, interpreters mentioned the technical requirements which included a good-quality headset, high speed internet (ethernet connection) and multiple screens, if possible. When talking specifically about what they use the second screen for, the participants mentioned making notes, searching through dictionaries, and running assistive tools. The interpreters also mentioned that RSI platforms lack communicative buttons for interpreters to indicate directly to the speaker that they need to increase their volume or reduce the pace at which they speak. This is particularly important in RSI, because in onsite events, although interpreters sit in a booth, there are ways of signalling their concerns to the speaker. However, remote interpreters are generally invisible to the speaker and rely on the moderator to convey those concerns.

Discussing **visual elements**, the interpreters raised the following concerns:

- Current RSI platforms lack standardisation (AIIC 2020; ISO24019) and lack visual information for the interpreter, such as good quality video of each speaker and of the conference room. Some interpreters felt that there should be a standardised set of visual information that should be available to the interpreter.
- Ideally, transcripts of the speeches and copies of presentations should be available within the RSI platform. However, our study also aims at situations where a speech script may not be available in advance. Some interpreters said they would like to be able

to download these materials separately so that they could open them (on the second screen), for example to navigate through a PowerPoint presentation independently, rather than waiting for the speaker to switch his/her slides.

- In current RSI platforms, interpreters potentially face information overload caused by visual elements that they do not use very frequently during an assignment, such as the channel settings, audio levels, and other platform-related options. Such elements may distract the interpreter and could contribute to causing fatigue and stress. This first became apparent through the enthusiasm expressed by the participants for cleaner interfaces during the design section of the FG, in which participants designed their ideal interface on paper. When shown different interfaces (minimal and maximal), participants also expressed an interest in testing the minimalist interface and its capacity to improve their focus on the speaker.

The participants also discussed a range of features that they felt would improve **collaboration with a boothmate** (i.e., an interpreter colleague with whom an assignment is shared). Some interpreters mentioned, for example, their desire to have a live notepad-style chatbox where they could exchange messages with their boothmate. Some interpreters also expressed interest in a live video feed from their boothmate as a 'nice to have' feature. In the view of some interpreters, this feature could reduce alienation and make interaction with a boothmate more efficient than typing instructions in a chatbox, while also reducing the distraction to their cognitive processing.

Among the range of research-based innovative features that we demonstrated to the FG participants, they expressed a liking towards the swappable video feeds and a cleaner interface. Some participants also said that they would like to have PowerPoint presentations available throughout the duration of a speech event. By contrast, the hidden software controls were perceived to be as cumbersome as selecting options hidden in an extensive software menu, with both potentially distracting the interpreter.

4   Informed Interfaces

Based on the findings from the focus group and the review of RSI and user experience research literature, we designed an experimental study into how various visual aspects of RSI interfaces (visual aids) can support interpreters, by increasing user experience and presence, and by assisting with source speech comprehension. In this study we test the following independent variables:

- Minimal vs maximal interface:

This variable pair consists of two distinct interface implementations seeking to examine the effect of reduction in visual information aimed at decreasing the level of interpreters' perceived lack of presence. It is hypothesised that the informed removal of specific visual information based on the concept of **flow** will lead to a potentially less distracting interface design, being referred to as **minimal** interface. This interface (layout shown in Fig. 1) primarily focuses on the view of the speaker, while the other controls are hidden in a settings ribbon.

To contrast this interface, an interface akin to the current interfaces of bespoke SIDPs – referred to as **maximal** – is also tested. In this interface users have a more information-rich visual offering, including a view of the speaker's slides/presentation, a booth chat (with another interpreter), and all functions and settings.

- Close-up view vs gesture view of speaker:

The second variable pair investigates the benefit of having a closer view of the speaker, where the interpreter can mainly see the speaker's face, offering a detailed view of their facial expressions, compared to a camera view where the interpreter can see more of the speaker including his/her body language and hand gestures.

- ASR vs no ASR:

Lastly, the study also tests the implementation of an automatic speech recognition (ASR) panel embedded within an RSI interface compared with an interface without this functionality enabled.

The remainder of this section describes the method of creating the interface and visual angle of the speaker. As we intend to test several experimental conditions, we needed an opportunity to customise the interface for each condition. This cannot be achieved with real-life SIDPs. We therefore decided to design our own 'mock-up' interfaces. Our interfaces contain the relevant visual elements created to simulate interactivity, but they are video renditions rather than fully interactive interfaces. Whilst this means that some elements which do not form part of the variables to be tested (such as the mute button, cough button, language channels etc.) are static, this approach ensures consistency, as each participant is presented with the same material.

The interfaces consist of two layers: The base layer was constructed using a vector graphics editor whereas the top layer was constructed on a video rendering software.

4.1   Base Layer Creation

The first step to design the interfaces is to create a base layer which shows a basic layout of where everything that should exist within the mock-up platform.

Minimal Prototype Base Layer. The prototype of the Minimal Interface (Fig. 1) essentially consists of a narrow meeting control ribbon situated on the left, a speaker view situated in the middle, dominating the prototype schematic, and two small areas for two other speaker images/video feeds. The minimal interface was inspired by the **flow concept** and was designed to emulate a good middle ground between the minimal interface found in non-interpreter-focused interfaces such as Zoom and the interpreter-focused interfaces of current SIDPs. The meeting control ribbon, situated to the left, contains all essential meeting and interpreter controls such as mute button, handover control, and meeting exit. However, due to the non-interactive nature of the interfaces these options will be left as inoperable and static.

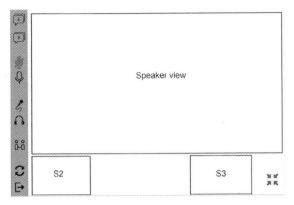

Fig. 1. Base layer (minimal interface schematic)

Maximal Prototype Base Layer. The prototype of the Maximal Interface (Fig. 2) inspired by existing RSI interfaces contains several more elements such as the presentation box on the right-hand side of the speaker view and the booth chat underneath the presentation box, which are dynamic although non operable. These additional elements were included to explore whether they prove to be useful or distracting. Simulating the look and feel of current RSI interfaces, the sound, microphone and language channel settings are displayed separately rather than being combined, along with other settings, in a single control ribbon, as is the case in the minimal interface. They were left as static and inoperable due to the non-interactive nature of the interface.

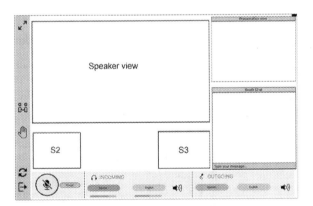

Fig. 2. Base layer (maximal interface schematic)

ASR Prototype Base Layer. The ASR prototype (Fig. 3) was also inspired by existing RSI interfaces and contains all standard elements such as views of multiple speakers, language channel settings and chat settings, which were left as inoperable due to the non-interactive nature of the interface. The only addition is a blank section for the ASR transcript, which is enabled during testing. The transcript is displayed at the bottom of the screen because that was the preferred location expressed by the participants during the focus group.

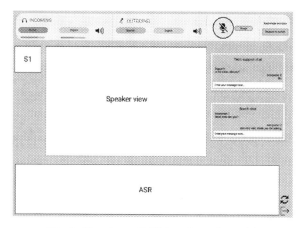

Fig. 3. Base layer (ASR interface schematic)

Top Layer Creation. Once the prototype layouts are exported from the graphics editor, these prototype schematics are imported in a video rendering software and the layouts are then populated with video recordings of the speaker, presentation slides, and animated chatbox texts. The main videos for the minimal and maximal interfaces are extracts of a recording of a real-life speech. As one of the testing variable pairs is the display of the speaker in the video frame, more specifically a close-up view and a gesture view, the (video recording of the) speech was selected with this constraint in mind. By contrast, the ASR interface contained experimental videos created specifically for our study.

To simulate a virtual boothmate in the maximal interface, text notes, which are characteristically offered by a boothmate, were created by using key terms and numbers from the real-life speech. This text was animated in the chatbox and its display time-aligned with the speech.

Lastly, the presentation slides in the maximal interface consist of several images of famous European landmarks, which were alternated throughout the presentation at various intervals. This content was chosen to simulate additional visual inputs for the interpreter. It does not contain text to facilitate control of this input variable.

5 Conclusion

This paper relates to an ongoing study of a novel and under-researched type of RSI, namely RSI using cloud-based software platforms. The context in which this study is carried out is the rapid expansion of this type of RSI since the beginning of the Covid-19 pandemic. Cloud-based RSI can be conceptualised as a complex and challenging instance of remote working and as a specific type of HCI. It requires optimisation to enable interpreters working with RSI platforms to meet their clients' needs for a high-quality interpreting service as well as improving the interpreters' user experience and supporting their wellbeing. Given the many challenges that arise in this novel type of RSI, the main goal of our study is to investigate how interpreters can be supported in RSI by employing ASR and visual aids. By placing the focus on the notions of support and presence, our study aims to optimise the performance of the interpreter and to improve their UX. As a first step towards achieving this, the present paper has investigated foundational aspects such as the cognitive impacts of the lack of sense of presence in RSI on the interpreter. We have also explored how the concept of flow, a unique concept borrowed from psychology, can be applied to the RSI workflow with a view to generating new evidence for the design of RSI interfaces. Subsequently we have presented the outcomes of two focus groups that we conducted with interpreters to elicit their views of RSI, their experiences with RSI platforms, and to test and discuss interface design ideas. This was followed by an explanation of how available evidence from the literature and the outcomes of our focus groups have informed the design of a set of interfaces and variable pairs, which we are currently testing in an experimental study. Pilot study results suggest that the impact of the flow-inspired interfaces is positive, and the overall results of the experimental study will be shared in a future publication.

References

Ahn, S., Jin, B., Kwon, S., Yun, M.: A research on curved display comparing to flat display regarding posture, tilt angle, focusing area and satisfaction. J. Ergon. Soc. Korea **33**(3), 191–202 (2014)

AIIC: Evaluation of Simultaneous Interpreting Delivery Platforms for ISO Compliance (2020). https://aiic.org/document/9506/THC. Accessed 25 Feb 2021

Bergman, E.: Information Appliances and Beyond. Morgan Kaufmann, San Francisco (2000)

Blascovich, J., Loomis, J., Beall, A., Swinth, K., Hoyt, C., Bailenson, J.: TARGET ARTICLE: immersive virtual environment technology as a methodological tool for social psychology. Psychol. Inq. **13**(2), 103–124 (2002)

Braun, S.: Interpreting in small-group bilingual videoconferences: challenges and adaptation processes. Interpreting **9**(1), 21–46 (2007)

Braun, S.: Technology and interpreting: In: O'Hagan, M. (ed.) Routledge Handbook of Translation and Technology. Routledge, London (2019)

Brockmyer, J., Fox, C., Curtiss, K., McBroom, E., Burkhart, K., Pidruzny, J.: The development of the Game Engagement Questionnaire: a measure of engagement in video game-playing. J. Exp. Soc. Psychol. **45**(4), 624–634 (2009)

Brown, E., Cairns, P.: A grounded investigation of game immersion. In: Extended Abstracts of the 2004 Conference on Human Factors and Computing Systems, CHI 2004 (2004)

Buján, M., Collard, C.: ESIT research project on remote simultaneous interpreting (2021)

Clemente, M., Rey, B., Rodríguez-Pujadas, A., Barros-Loscertales, A., Baños, R.M., Botella, C., et al.: An fMRI study to analyse neural correlates of presence during virtual reality experiences. Interact. Comp. **26**, 269–284 (2013). https://doi.org/10.1093/iwc/iwt037

Csikszentmihalyi, M., Csikszentmihalyi, I.: Optimal Experience. Cambridge University Press, Cambridge (1988)

Csikszentmihalyi, M.: Flow. The psychology of optimal experience. New York (HarperPerennial) (1990)

Csikszentmihalyi, M.: Implications of a systems perspective for the study of creativity. In: Sternberg, R.J. (ed.) Handbook of Creativity, pp. 313–335. Cambridge University Press (1999)

Desmet, B., Vandierendonck, M., Defrancq, B.: Simultaneous interpretation of numbers and the impact of technological support. In: Fantinuoli, C. (ed.) Interpreting and Technology, pp. 13–27. Language Science Press, Berlin (2018)

DG SCIC: Interpreting Platforms. Consolidated test results and analysis. European Commission's Directorate General for Interpretation (DG SCIC), 17 July 2019

Draper, S.: Analysing fun as a candidate software requirement. Pers. Technol. **3**(3), 117–122 (2000)

Fantinuoli, C.: Speech recognition in the interpreter workstation. In: Proceedings of the Translating and the Computer 39 Conference, pp. 367–377. Editions Tradulex, London (2017)

Fantinuoli, C., Marchesini, G., Landan, D., Horak, L.: KUDO Interpreter Assist: Automated Real-Time Support for Remote Interpretation (2022). http://arxiv.org/abs/2201.01800

Finneran, C., Zhang, P.: Flow in computer-mediated environments: promises and challenges. Commun. Assoc. Inf. Syst. **15**, 82–101 (2005)

Franceschi, K., Lee, R., Zanakis, S., Hinds, D.: Engaging group e-learning in virtual worlds. J. Manag. Inf. Syst. **26**(1), 73–100 (2009)

Gaffar, A., Kouchak, S.: Minimalist design: an optimized solution for intelligent interactive infotainment systems. In: 2017 Intelligent Systems Conference (IntelliSys) (2017)

Ghani, J., Deshpande, S.: Task characteristics and the experience of optimal flow in human—computer interaction. J. Psychol. **128**(4), 381–391 (1995)

Gibson, E.J.: Principles of perceptual learning and development. Appleton-Century-Crofts (1969)

Gile, D.: Basic Concepts and Models for Interpreter and Translator Training. John Benjamins, Amsterdam/Philadelphia (2009)

Gorini, A., Capideville, C., De Leo, G., Mantovani, F., Riva, G.: The Role of immersion and narrative in mediated presence: the virtual hospital experience. Cyberpsychol. Behav. Soc. Netw. **14**(3), 99–105 (2011)

Harris, D.J., Vine, S.J., Wilson, M.R.: Is flow really effortless? The complex role of effortful attention. Sport Exerc. Perform. Psychol. **6**, 103 (2017). https://doi.org/10.1037/spy0000083

Johnson, C., Bauer, B., Singh, N.: Exploring flow in the mobile interface context. J. Retail. Consum. Serv. **53**, 101744 (2020)

Johnson, D., Wiles, J.: Effective affective user interface design in games. Ergonomics **46**(13–14), 1332–1345 (2003)

Johnson, J.: Simplifying the controls of an interactive movie game. In: Proceedings of the SIGCHI Conference on Human Factors in Computing Systems, CHI 1998 (1998)

Kalawsky, R.: The validity of presence as a reliable human performance metric in immersive environments (2000)

Klasen, M., Chen, Y.-H., Mathiak, K.: Multisensory emotions: perception, combination and underlying neural processes. Rev. Neurosci. **23**(4), 381–392 (2012). https://doi.org/10.1515/revneuro-2012-0040

Kober, S., Neuper, C.: Using auditory event-related EEG potentials to assess presence in virtual reality. Int. J. Hum. Comput Stud. **70**(9), 577–587 (2012)

Kurz, I.: Physiological stress during simultaneous interpreting: a comparison of experts and novices. Interpreters' Newsl. **12**, 51–67 (2003)

Lai, C., Zhong, H., Chiu, P.: Investigating the impact of a flipped programming course using the DT-CDIO approach. Comput. Educ. **173**, 104287 (2021)

Lee, K.M.: Presence, Explicated. Communication Theory, [Online] **14**(1), 27–50 (2004). https://academic.oup.com/ct/article-abstract/14/1/27/4110793

Lee, W., Kim, Y.: Does VR tourism enhance users' experience? Sustainability **13**(2), 806 (2021)

Mankauskienė, D.: Problem trigger classification and its applications for empirical research. In: International Conference on Meaning in Translation: Illusion of Precision, MTIP2016, 11–13 May (2016)

Mestre, D.R., Vercher, J.: Immersion and Presence (2005)

Moser-Mercer, B.: Remote interpreting: assessment of human factors and performance parameters. Communicate! Summer 2003 (2003)

Moser-Mercer, B.: Remote interpreting: issues of multi-sensory integration in a multilingual task. Meta **50**(2), 727–738 (2005)

Mouzourakis, P.: Remote interpreting: a technical perspective on recent experiments. Interpreting **8**(1), 45–66 (2006)

Rennert, S.: Visual input in simultaneous interpreting. Meta **52**(1), 204–217 (2008)

Rodriguez, S., et al.: SmarTerp: a CAI system to support simultaneous interpreters in real-time. In: Proceedings of Triton 2021 (2021)

Roziner, I., Shlesinger, M.: Much Ado about something remote: stress and performance in remote interpreting. Interpreting **12**(2), 214–247 (2010)

Seeber, K.G., Keller, L., Amos, R., Hengl, S.: Expectations vs. experience: attitudes towards video remote conference interpreting. Interpreting **21**(2), 270–304 (2019)

Sheridan, T.B.: Musings on telepresence and virtual presence. Presence Teleoperators Virtual Environ. **1**(1), 120–126 (1992). https://doi.org/10.1162/pres.1992.1.1.120

Skalski, P., Tamborini, R., Glazer, E., Smith, S.: Effects of humor on presence and recall of persuasive messages. Commun. Q. **57**(2), 136–153 (2009)

Slater, M., Usoh, M., Steed, A.: Depth of presence in virtual environments. Presence Teleoperators Virtual Environ. **3**(2), 130–144 (1994). https://doi.org/10.1162/pres.1994.3.2.130

Tan, D.S., Gergle, D., Scupelli, P.G., Pausch, R.: With similar visual angles, larger displays improve performance on spatial tasks. In: Conference on Human Factors in Computing Systems, CHI 2003, pp. 217–224 (2003)

Winteringham, S.T.: The usefulness of ICTs in interpreting practice. Interpreter's Newsl. **15**, 87–99 (2010)

Underwood, B.J., Schulz, R.W.: Meaningfulness and Verbal Learning. J. B. Lippincott (1960)

Usability.gov.: User Interface Design Basics | Usability.gov. (2021). https://www.usability.gov/what-and-why/user-interface-design.html. Accessed 05 Oct 2021

Wadensjö, C.: Telephone interpreting and the synchronisation of talk in social interaction. Translator **5**(2), 247–264 (1999)

Weibel, A., Rost, K., Osterloh, M.: Pay for performance in the public sector-benefits and (hidden) costs. J. Pub. Adm. Res. Theor. **20**(2), 387–412 (2009)

Witmer, B.G., Singer, M.J.: Measuring presence in virtual environments: a presence questionnaire. Presence Teleoperators Virtual Environ. **7**(3), 225–240 (1998). https://doi.org/10.1162/105474698565686

Yee, N.: Motivations for play in online games. Cyberpsychol. Behav. **9**(6), 772–775 (2006)

Ziegler, K., Gigliobianco, S.: Present? Remote? Remotely present! New technological approaches to remote simultaneous conference interpreting. In: Fantinuoli, C. (ed.) Interpreting and Technology, pp. 119–139. Language Science Press, Berlin (2018)

Anthropomorphic Perceptions of Simple Text-Based Interfaces

Briana M. Sobel[⊠] ⓘ and Valerie K. Sims

University of Central Florida, Orlando, FL 32816, USA
brianasobel@knights.ucf.edu

Abstract. Anthropomorphism, or the perception of humanlike qualities in something that is not human, can have great influence on one's ability to interpret and predict the behavior of an object or agent, such as a computer. The objective of this study was to consider how even small differences in interface design can influence the way people understand and work with a computer interface. Specifically, whether changing the dialogue of a simple text-based interface makes it seem more humanlike, useful, and trustworthy as well as whether these perceptions are due to the interface design itself or influenced by one's inherent tendency to anthropomorphize. This was tested by having participants use a simple text search interface to look up answers to various questions. There were two versions of the interface: Anthropomorphic (e.g., used humanlike grammar and referred to itself as 'I' and 'me') and non-Anthropomorphic (e.g., simple output without sentences or reference to itself). Results showed the Anthropomorphic interface was perceived as more humanlike and inherent tendency to anthropomorphize influenced perceptions of humanlikeness, mental workload, and performance. This study showed that small changes can influence perceptions of computers, even simple ones. It also highlighted the importance of one's inherent tendency to anthropomorphize. Implications for research and design are discussed.

Keywords: Anthropomorphism · Interface design · Individual differences

1 Introduction

1.1 Background

It is commonplace for humans to find humanlike qualities in the structure and behavior of the things around them. Examples include seeing a face in the headlights and grille of a car, saying a dog is expressing a joyous smile, or believing that the office elevator is trying its hardest to make you late to an important meeting. At first glance, it may seem strange or childish to view objects in the world this way, but it can also be a powerful tool. Finding similarities between ourselves and others creates empathy and understanding. It is through this ability that humans are capable of creating strong relationships with other people, animals, objects, and even technological devices.

In the last few decades, personal computers and mobile phones have become almost ubiquitous. These devices are seen as essential tools and constant companions in everyday life. It is fascinating that people have come to readily accept and trust objects whose

M. Kurosu (Ed.): HCII 2022, LNCS 13304, pp. 233–242, 2022.
https://doi.org/10.1007/978-3-031-05412-9_17

appearance is so unnatural. These rectilinear boxes made of metal that contain unfathomable amounts of circuits and code is unlike anything experienced in the natural world. How, then, have they come to work so well with humans? The answer may lie not in the way a device looks, but the way it 'thinks.'

This present research focused specifically on views people have of computers. A key to understanding this unique human-computer relationship lies in whether the human perceives the device to be intelligent, intentional, or otherwise capable of humanlike mental capacities. Perhaps if a computer is perceived to be a fellow intelligent being instead of a black box of complex pieces, it can seem easier to understand, allowing the average user to trust it to complete a task.

1.2 Anthropomorphism

When humans perceive or attribute humanlike qualities to something that is not human, this is known as anthropomorphism [6]. Although the exact mechanisms are still unclear, anthropomorphism is hypothesized to occur when humans are interacting with something they don't understand so they apply knowledge from something they do understand: themselves and other humans [6, 12, 14]. Describing something complex like a computer in humanlike terms may make it easier to relate to.

Anthropomorphism can occur in physical features, such as seeing a human face in the windows of a house, or in mental features such as attributing emotion, intention, or cognition [3, 6, 12, 16]. Attributions of these mental features can also manifest in different ways and to different extents. For example, mindful anthropomorphism is considered the genuine *belief* that a nonhuman possesses a humanlike mind, while mindless anthropomorphism is the *behavior* of treating an entity as if it warrants a humanlike response [2, 7, 8, 11]. The extent of these beliefs and behaviors can be influenced by one's inherent tendency to anthropomorphize, a tendency that is a stable measure of individual differences [16].

When it comes to perceptions of technology, mindful and mindless anthropomorphism often do not occur simultaneously. In fact, studies show that people tend to deny that computers possess true mental capacities and yet continue to interact and respond as if they do [1–3, 6, 7, 12, 15]. Although mindful anthropomorphism is viewed as illogical, behavior does not always follow that belief, allowing technological agents to be treated as if they possess a humanlike mind.

Additionally, studies show that interactivity, particularly dialogical (i.e., back-and-forth) communication, is enough to trigger anthropomorphic tendencies [1, 2, 7, 11, 15]. One study assessing chatbots found that an agent with humanlike dialogue using informal language, having a human name, and framing interactions with 'hello' and 'goodbye' had significantly higher levels of both mindful and mindless anthropomorphism than a non-anthropomorphic interface that used formal language, had a nonhuman name, and framed interactions with the words 'start' and 'quit' [2]. Speech can also influence perceptions of personality, gender, and expertise all of which can change how a person likes and interacts with an interface [11, 12]. At the most basic level, the ability to communicate causes humans to find similarities with even the most morphologically inhuman (i.e., physically dissimilar) devices.

Another important aspect of the human-computer relationship that is heavily influenced by anthropomorphism is trust. On the one hand, anthropomorphism can cause poor trust calibration due to an increased emotional attachment to the system [4]. Undue trust allows for errors when the human operator does not monitor the system appropriately. Also, a more humanlike interface tends to have lower initial trust than a more machinelike interface but is more resilient to losses in trust after an error [5]. Since humans themselves possess the ability to learn from mistakes, an anthropomorphic interface is easier to forgive after an error than a non-anthropomorphic interface that is expected to be infallible. An understanding of how humans perceive the intelligence, reliability, and fallibility of an interface can influence the design of human-computer interfaces to promote cohesion and unity.

1.3 Current Study

The objective of this study was to consider how even small differences in interface design can influence the way people understand and work with a computer interface. Specifically, does changing the dialogue of a simple text-based interface make it seem more humanlike, useful, and trustworthy? If so, are these differences due to the interface design itself or are they influenced by one's inherent tendency to anthropomorphize?

To accomplish this, participants provided their perceptions and usability ratings for anthropomorphic or non-anthropomorphic versions of a search interface. The anthropomorphism of the interface was based solely on dialogue, with one using more humanlike language and one being more machinelike in its output. The purpose was to assess the influence of slight variations in dialogue of a simple, text-based interface on perceptions of mindful and mindless anthropomorphism, trust, and mental workload as well as performance. In turn, this study also assessed the role of inherent tendency to anthropomorphize on the perceptions of the interfaces.

2 Method

2.1 Participants

A total of 139 participants were recruited, and after removing individuals based on exclusion criteria resulted in a final sample size of $N = 128$ with an equal number in both experimental groups. Participants were undergraduate students from a large Southeastern university who were compensated with credit on a course assignment. Age ranged from 18 to 30 years ($M = 19.05$ years, $SD = 1.63$) with equal numbers of males and females.

2.2 Design

This study was a 2 (interface type: Anthropomorphic vs non-Anthropomorphic) $\times$ 2 (gender: male vs female) quasi-experimental design. Interface type was between subjects, such that participants only interacted with one interface. Participants were randomly assigned to an experimental group upon entering the lab. The inclusion criterion was age with all participants being older than 18 years. Exclusion criteria were failure to complete attention checks in the post-experiment survey or having incomplete data.

2.3   Materials

Interfaces. Two search interfaces were created for this study. Each interface was a graphic user interface (GUI) coded in Java and run directly from the computers command dialogue. They were text-based to be as simple as possible, while still being viewed as anthropomorphic or non-anthropomorphic [12, 13, 15]. The interfaces had two text boxes: the top box where participants typed questions and the bottom box where answers were displayed (see Fig. 1).

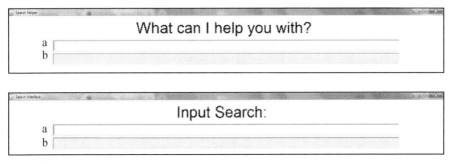

Fig. 1. Examples of the search interfaces. The top image is the Anthropomorphic interface, the bottom image is the non-Anthropomorphic interface. Box (a) is where participants typed, box (b) is where the interface displayed responses.

A list of 20 questions for participants to type into the interfaces was created to promote interaction between the user and the interface (see Table 1). Questions were chosen for their deviation from common knowledge as determined by the researcher and confirmed during pilot studies. In addition to the answer, an 'accuracy probability' was displayed, as an indicator of the likelihood that the answer given was correct. These percentages were arbitrary (a fact unknown to the participants) and determined by a random-number calculator.

Of the 20 questions in the task, the interface provided an incorrect answer for four of them. This was to create an imperfect reliability to minimize the phenomenon that machinelike interfaces tend to have higher initial levels of trust than humanlike interfaces [5]. However, research on automation shows that systems with a reliability under 70% are viewed as worse than not having automation at all [17]. Therefore, the reliability of the interfaces was set at 80% (i.e., 16/20).

All answers were identical for both interfaces, they simply differed in their form of communication. For example, when asked the question, "What is the capital of Uruguay?", the Anthropomorphic interface responded with, "It looks like there is a 67% probability of it being Montevideo" while the non-Anthropomorphic interface responded with, "67% probability of accuracy – Montevideo". The purpose was to make the non-Anthropomorphic interface appear more machinelike in its input/output dialogue while the Anthropomorphic interface would sound more like how an actual human would respond.

Table 1. List of questions input into the search interface

Question	Answer
Who directed the movie *Back to the Future*?	Robert Zemeckis
Which country was the first to ratify the United Nations in 1945?	Nicaragua
What year was the movie *The Jazz Singer* released?	1927
What country had the most camels in the 1990s?	Somalia
Who travelled to space in the Vostok 6?	Valentina Tereshkova (*interface gave incorrect answer of 'Vasily Tsibliyev'*)
Which European country was the first to allow women to vote?	Finland
What was the profession of Louis Henry Sullivan?	Architect (*interface provided incorrect answer of 'scientist'*)
What two cities are linked by the Orient Express?	Paris and Istanbul
What is the legislature of the Netherlands called?	The States General
Who wrote *The Alchemist*?	Ben Jonson
What was John Lennon's middle name?	Winston (*interface gave wrong answer of 'Harry'*)
What is the capital of Uruguay?	Montevideo
What is the highest mountain in the Andes?	Aconcagua
Which space craft travelled to Jupiter in 1972?	Pioneer 10
In which year did England abolish the death penalty for murder?	1969
What country does the airline 'Sansa' come from?	Costa Rica
Freeport International Airport is in which country?	Bahamas
What year did Frank Zappa die?	1933
From 1903 – 1958, every Pope (besides one) was named what?	Pius (*interface provided incorrect answer of 'Peter'*)
Who won Super Bowl X?	Pittsburgh Steelers

Post-Experiment Questionnaire. The final survey was completed on paper. In addition to the following scales, there were two attention checks throughout the survey that asked participants to choose a specific answer, such as "Circle the number for 'Strongly Disagree'." This was done to promote quality control of data.

Mindful Anthropomorphism Scale. This scale consisted of three items rating the interface on a scale from 1–10 across three dimensions [7]. These dimensions were 1) Human-like to Machinelike, 2) Natural to Unnatural, and 3) Lifelike to Artificial. Items were reverse-scored such that higher scores indicated that the interface was more humanlike. Scores were calculated as the average of the reverse-scores of the three items.

Mindless Anthropomorphism Scale. This scale consisted of four items rating the interface on a scale from 1–10 whether the interface was 1) likeable, 2) sociable, 3) friendly, and 4) personable [7]. Scores were calculated as the average of the four items.

Trust Scale. This scale consisted of 10 questions relating to the trustworthiness and capability of the interface [9]. Examples of items are "This program is very capable of performing its job" and "I feel very confident about the program's skills." Participants rated their agreement with the statements on a scale from 1 (Strongly Disagree) to 5 (Strongly Agree). Scores were calculated as the average of the 10 items.

'Gas Tank Questionnaire' for Mental Workload. This was a single-item assessment of mental workload [10]. Participants were given a visual of a 'gas tank' and asked, "Think about your brain as an engine. Assuming you began this study with a full tank, indicate on the fuel tank below to show how much 'gas' you have left right now." Participants drew on the 'tank' their level of current mental capacity and indicated the percentage (from 0–100) that the level corresponded to. Scores were the percentage indicated from 0–100. Since this number referred to the amount of mental capacity they had left, higher scores indicated lower required mental effort.

Individual Differences in Anthropomorphism Questionnaire (IDAQ). This scale measured individual differences in inherent tendency to anthropomorphize [16]. It consisted of 15 items rated on a scale from 0 (not at all) to 10 (very much) as to the degree that various nonhumans (technology, animals, and nature) have humanlike capabilities such as emotion, intention, or consciousness. Examples of items include "To what extent does the average robot have consciousness?" and "To what extent does the average fish have free will?" Scores were calculated as the sum of the 15 items with higher scores indicating higher inherent tendencies to anthropomorphize.

2.4 Procedure

Participants entered the lab and were seated in front of a computer with the search interface on the screen. The start protocol was explained, such that participants in the non-Anthropomorphic interface group were told to start the interface by typing 'Start' and participants in the Anthropomorphic interface group were told to start the interface by typing 'Hello'. Participants were then given a sample question to type ("Which state is the sunshine state?") to show how the interface outputs an answer. Finally, participants were informed of the end protocol such that participants in the non-Anthropomorphic interface group were told to finish by typing 'End' and participants in the Anthropomorphic interface group were told to finish by typing 'Goodbye'. Participants were then given instructions for the search task, handed a sheet of paper with the Task Questions, and were given eight minutes to ask the interface all 20 questions listed.

After the search task, the Task Questions sheets were collected by the researcher, and the participants were given a three-minute masking task of math problems. After the masking, participants were quizzed on the questions from the search task. The quiz was multiple choice and had participants choose the correct answer to each of the previously listed 20 questions. Finally, participants completed the post-experiment questionnaire and were debriefed.

3 Results

A 2 (interface: Anthropomorphic vs non-Anthropomorphic) x 2 (gender: male vs female) ANCOVA with IDAQ as a covariate was conducted to assess differences between interfaces while accounting for gender and inherent tendencies. Descriptive statistics for outcome measures are found in Table 2.

Table 2. Descriptives of all outcome measures

Measure	Anthropomorphic interface		Non-anthropomorphic interface	
	M	SD	M	SD
Mindful anthro[a]	3.50	1.95	2.60	1.31
Mindless anthro[a]	5.05	2.01	4.16	1.84
Trust[b]	2.88	0.69	2.93	.052
Mental workload[c]	78.53	18.75	80.08	18.58
Task performance[d]	12.91	2.54	12.56	3.08

Anthro = anthropomorphism. [a]Scale of 1–10. [b]Scale of 1–5. [c]Scale of 0–100. [d]Scale of 0–20.

There was a main effect of interface for mindful anthropomorphism where the Anthropomorphic interface had significantly higher ratings than the non-Anthropomorphic interface ($F(1, 123) = 10.24, p = .002$). There was a main effect of interface for mindless anthropomorphism where the Anthropomorphic interface had higher ratings than the non-Anthropomorphic interface ($F(1, 123) = 8.64, p = .004$). There was no main effect of interface for mental workload ($F(1, 123) = 0.38, p = .539$), trust ($F(1, 122) = 0.17, p = .677$), or task performance ($F(1, 123) = 0.33, p = .566$).

IDAQ scores ranged from 4 to 121 ($M = 50.55, SD = 24.60$) and were positively correlated with mindful anthropomorphism ($r = .176, p = .048$) and mindless anthropomorphism ($r = .319, p < .001$), negatively correlated with mental workload ($r = -.261, p = .003$) and task performance ($r = -.237, p = .007$), and not correlated with trust ($r = .117$, $p = .191$). Females ($M = 55.38$, $SD = 24.10$) had higher IDAQ scores than males ($M = 46.24$, $SD = 24.19$; $t(125) = 2.13$, $p = .035$). There was no significant difference in IDAQ scores between interface groups ($t(125) = .672$, $p = .503$).

The IDAQ covariate had a significant main effect for mindless anthropomorphism ($F(1, 123) = 12.99$, $p < .001$), mental workload ($F(1, 123) = 8.06$, $p = .005$), and task performance ($F(1, 123) = 6.97$, $p = .009$) with a trending effect for mindful anthropomorphism ($F(1, 123) = 3.48$, $p = .065$) such that higher tendency to anthropomorphize incurred higher ratings of mindful and mindless anthropomorphism, more mental workload, and lower performance. There was no main effect of IDAQ on trust ($F(1, 122) = 1.00$, $p = .318$).

There was no main effect of gender for mindful anthropomorphism ($F(1, 123) = 2.29$, $p = .133$), mindless anthropomorphism ($F(1, 123) = 1.92$, $p = .169$), trust ($F(1, 122) = 0.69$, $p = .409$), mental workload ($F(1, 123) = 0.05$, $p = .832$), or task performance ($F(1, 123) = 0.30$, $p = .585$).

There was no significant gender by interface interaction for mindful anthropomorphism ($F(1, 123) = 0.62$, $p = .432$), mindless anthropomorphism $F(1, 123) = .001$, $p = .970$), trust ($F(1, 122) = 1.22$, $p = .272$), mental workload ($F(1, 123) = 0.52$, $p = .472$), or task performance ($F(1, 123) = 0.15$, $p = .701$).

4 Discussion

4.1 Summary

The purpose of this study was to assess how even small differences in interface design can influence the way people understand and work with a computer interface, as well as provide insights into the various sources of anthropomorphism in a computer interface. One of these is from the features of the interface itself, as seen in the higher levels of both mindful and mindless anthropomorphism in the Anthropomorphic interface than in the non-Anthropomorphic interface. The interfaces were simplistic and identical except for small changes in dialogue, but the Anthropomorphic interface was still perceived as more humanlike. Furthermore, these ratings occurred even though participants only interacted with one interface (i.e., couldn't directly compare it to its more (or less) humanlike counterpart). However, this did not influence perceptions of trust or mental workload, nor did it influence task performance.

The second source is from the individual user, as seen in the significant correlations and effects of inherent tendency to anthropomorphize. If an individual has a higher tendency to anthropomorphize, it means they are more likely and willing to see a nonhuman as capable of human mental capacities. This tendency influenced many measures, but it was a unique influence outside of the interface cues. Higher IDAQ scores also incurred higher rates of mental workload and reduced task performance. Perhaps a greater propensity to view an interface as humanlike causes the user to place too much trust in the computer's ability. When the interface is unreliable (as in this study), this misplaced trust can cause reduced performance in the human-machine system. This finding is important for automation research, for a lack of attention (i.e., situation awareness) to automation can cause over-trust in the system. This over-trust leads to reduced performance and trust, breaking down the human-machine relationship.

4.2 Implications

These results show that even minimal changes in cues, such as slight variations in dialogue, can influence perceptions of humanlike qualities. Lifelike avatars, high-definition rendering, and realistic speech patterns may not always be required to make an interface appear intelligent. Sometimes, a simple solution is all that is needed to obtain a desired result. Therefore, when designing an interface, small changes can be made that make it seem more lifelike without requiring extensive time and cost.

Furthermore, an individual's inherent tendency to anthropomorphize has a significant influence on perceptions of a device, so some perceptions of a product will depend on the person using it. Designers must understand that they may be able to control the features of their product, but they cannot control the perceptions of their users. Creating humanlike devices will involve a full understanding of both the interface and the user.

Finally, even though the anthropomorphic interface was viewed as more social, likable, and overall humanlike, there was no significant difference in levels of trust between the two interfaces. Perhaps what designers can take from this is that trust in an interface requires more than just humanlike dialogue. Just because users like and relate to an interface does not inherently mean they trust it. A human-machine system is a team, and as important it is to like team members, they must also be trusted to do their job.

4.3 Conclusion

Overall, this study shows that anthropomorphism is an important phenomenon worth studying. It influences the way people experience the world around them, both living and nonliving. Better understanding of anthropomorphic tendencies could help interface designers understand the thought processes and behaviors of their users, as well as how to design systems that promote trust, usability, and effective interactions.

References

1. Airenti, G.: The cognitive bases of anthropomorphism: from relatedness to empathy. Int. J. Soc. Robot. **7**(1), 117–127 (2015)
2. Araujo, T.: Living up to the chatbot hype: the influence of anthropomorphism design cues and communicative agency framing on conversational agent and company perceptions. Comput. Hum. Behav. **85**, 183–189 (2018)
3. Chin, M.G., et al.: Developing an anthropomorphic tendencies scale. In: Proceedings of the Human Factors and Ergonomics Society, vol. 47, pp. 1266–1268 (2005)
4. Culley, K.E., Madhavan, P.: A note of caution regarding anthropomorphism in HCI agents. Comput. Hum. Behav. **29**(3), 577–579 (2013)
5. de Visser, E.J., et al.: Almost human: anthropomorphism increases trust resilience in cognitive agents. J. Exp. Psychol. Appl. **22**(3), 331–349 (2016)

6. Epley, N., Waytz, A., Cacioppo, J.T.: On seeing human: a three-factor theory of anthropomorphism. Psychol. Rev. **114**(4), 864–886 (2007)
7. Kim, Y., Sundar, S.S.: Anthropomorphism of computers: is it mindful or mindless? Comput. Hum. Behav. **28**(1), 241–250 (2012)
8. Lee, E.: What triggers social responses to flattering computers? Experimental tests of anthropomorphism and mindlessness explanations. Commun. Res. **37**(2), 191–214 (2010)
9. Mayer, R.C., Davis, J.H.: The effect of the performance appraisal system on trust for management: a field quasi-experiment. J. Appl. Psychol. **84**(1), 123–136 (1999)
10. Monfort, S.S., Graybeal, J.J., Harwood, A.E., McKnight, P.E., Shaw, T.H.: A single-item assessment for remaining mental resources: development and validation of the Gas Tank Questionnaire (GTQ). Theor. Issues Ergon. Sci. **19**(5), 530–553 (2018)
11. Nass, C., Lee, K.M.: Does computer/synthesized speech manifest personality? Experimental tests of recognition, similarity-attraction, and consistency-attraction. J. Exp. Psychol. Appl. **7**(3), 171–181 (2001)
12. Nass, C., Moon, Y.: Machines and mindlessness: social responses to computers. J. Soc. Issues **56**(1), 81–103 (2000)
13. Nass, C., Moon, Y., Fogg, B.J., Reeves, B., Dryer, D.C.: Can computer personalities be human personalities? Int. J. Hum Comput Stud. **43**, 223–239 (1995)
14. Nass, C., Steuer, J., Tauber, E.R.: Computers are social actors. In: Proceedings of the SIGCHI Conference on Human Factors in Computing Systems, pp. 72–78 (1994)
15. Reeves, B., Nass, C.: The media equation: how people treat computers, television, and new media like real people and places. Center for the Study of Language and Information, Chicago IL; New York, NY (1996)
16. Waytz, A., Cacioppo, J., Epley, N.: Who sees human? The stability and importance of individual differences in anthropomorphism. Perspect. Psychol. Sci. J. Assoc. Psychol. Sci. **5**(3), 219–232 (2014)
17. Wickens, C.D., Dixon, S.R.: The benefits of imperfect diagnostic automation: a synthesis of the literature. Theor. Issues Ergon. Sci. **8**(3), 201–212 (2007)

Revitalize Qiang Language and Culture by Designing Serious Games Based on Interactive Projection

Rao Xu[1] , Qin Wu[1(✉)] , Wenlu Wang[1] , Mohammad Shidujaman[2],
and Min Wei[1]

[1] Chengdu University of Information Technology, Chengdu, China
{wuqin,weimin}@cuit.edu.cn
[2] American International University - Bangladesh, Dhaka, Bangladesh
mjaman@aiub.edu

Abstract. The Qiang people is an ancient minority in western China. However, Qiang language, as the carrier of Qiang culture and spirit, is rapidly fading as less and fewer people can speak it. Despite the fact that the serious game of indigenous language has been widely discussed, there is still a dearth of research on the Qiang language and culture. This research aims to determine the efficacy of serious games based on interactive projection to encourage people's interest in Qiang language and culture. To better understand the Qiang language and cultural heritage's current state and challenges, we conducted a three-day field investigation in the Qiang village. Based on the field study's findings, we created "WhiteStone", an interactive projection device based on the heroic epic of Qiang. Our user research consists of remote verification and user testing, indicating that serious games based on projected interaction have the potential to create engrossed and interesting experiences, which can attract young people's interest in the Qiang language and culture. This paper examines the design opportunities for serious games based on interactive projection to revitalize the Qiang language and culture.

Keywords: Serious game · Indigenous language · Chinese culture · Qiang people

1 Introduction

Language is not only a means for people to communicate [3], but it is also a cultural carrier [12] and a part of national identity [11]. There are over 6,000 languages spoken throughout the world, yet 80% of them are spoken by barely 5% of the population, putting them in risk of extinction in the next century [18]. Protecting endangered indigenous languages helps to preserve human culture's "biodiversity," which is critical for civilization's inheritance and growth. Especially for indigenous languages without text, the danger of disappearing is more prominent. The Qiang people are an ancient ethnic minority living in the western

M. Kurosu (Ed.): HCII 2022, LNCS 13304, pp. 243–261, 2022.
https://doi.org/10.1007/978-3-031-05412-9_18

China with. Due to the loss of writing text, Qiang people can only pass on their language and culture orally. In recent years, the Qiang language has been on the danger of extinction, as fewer Qiang people are able to speak it. In order to help the inheritance of Qiang language and culture, many researchers have made efforts. With the development of digital technology [30], the interactive design method [6,31] has brought vitality to the development of art [7] and culture [30]. He et al. [17] designed a mobile application for learning the daily terms of the Qiang language, proving the value of digital technical support. Serious games [1] have proven to be one of the effective methods of helping indigenous language inheritance. Such as web platform [22] based on serious game and computer serious games [32]. However, it is still lacking in the design of a serious game based on interactive projections to revitalize Qiang language and culture.

Our research purpose is to explore whether the serious game based on interactive projections helps to revitalize the Qiang language and culture. Our work consists of the following three stages: (1) we conducted field research in the Qiang people's residential areas, and summarized the design principles based on the findings. (2) Inspired by the design principles derived from field research, We designed and implemented an interactive projection device based on serious games. (3) We verified the validity of the prototype through on-site user tests and remote interviews, and discussed the views of Qiang and non-Qiang people on serious games based on interactive projection.

Through verification, we found that serious games based on projected interaction have the potential to create engrossed and interesting experiences that can attract young people's interest in the Qiang language and culture. In addition, this paper provides the views of the non-Qiang people on the preservation of the Qiang language and culture, which also reveals the opportunities for the development and inheritance of the indigenous language and culture by including the non-Qiang people in the indigenous language learning.

2   Related Work

2.1   Protection of Indigenous Languages

Indigenous languages have gotten a lot of attention in recent years. Recognizing their vulnerability, The United Nations declared 2019 the International Year of Indigenous Languages [9] to highlight the severe loss of indigenous languages and the urgent need to preserve, revitalize, and promote indigenous languages. To that goal, scholars around the world make unrelenting efforts, such as recording minority languages by documentation [10,15] or dominating the immersive revitalization project in the community [2,21,27]. However, the difficulty of the task and the rapid pace of technological change have presented a significant challenge for linguists committed to recording endangered languages. The effect of community immersion projects is also limited to whether there is a solid community communication basis. With the advancement of digital information technology, researchers understood that the use of technical means [8] may open up new avenues for indigenous language protection. For example,

Evaristo Ovide et al. [19] introduced a collaborative work on Wichi language, and co-created a mobile app to learn the basics of the language. Carew et al. [5] talked about the Getting in Touch project, which is working on developing ideas for digital resources that prioritize Indigenous languages and knowledge systems. These studies have supplied knowledge and inspiration for endangered language research around the world. At the same time, a minority in the southwestern mountains of China is also facing the dangers of disappearing in indigenous languages. Qiang language [14] has been used by Qiang people for thousands of years. It is a vital conduit for Qiang culture and spirit. In order to help the inheritance of Qiang language, He et al. [17] proposed a Qiang language learning application, "the tone of Qiang", based on their own corpus, contains daily expressions in multiple scenes. Their work uses multimedia technology to digitally preserve Qiang language. In this paper, we want to explore more interesting ways to help revitalize Qiang language and culture.

2.2   Serious Games Used in Indigenous Languages and Cultures

Serious games [1] have been widely employed in education, ecology, and other sectors because they can boost knowledge acquisition and cognitive skills [28]. Some language related studies have also investigated serious games and suggest that they may be effective as educational tools [13,16]. Serious games have also been shown to have a positive impact on indigenous language and culture learning [25] since they can provide some characteristics absent in traditional teaching methods and engage learners' attention. For instance, Bykbaev et al. [22] proposed an interactive education platform based on serious games to protect the Cañari indigenous cultural heritage in Ecuador. To reintroduce indigenous rainforest sign language to the younger Penan generation, Zaman et al. [32] developed a PC-based digital Oroo' adventure game. In addition to web platforms and computer applications, VR is a research hotspot in serious games due to its immersive experience. Plecher et al. [20] and other researchers [4,26] attempted to employ virtual reality (VR) technology to revitalize indigenous languages and cultures. In contrast, in this work, we try to bring immersion by breaking away from the interaction of traditional screen media. Interactive projection allows players to move freely in the projection range [24]. Different from VR, projection interaction can be easily combined with physical entities [23,29]. These features have the potential to enhance the realistic immersion of projection interactive experience. However, there is still a lack of research on using serious games based on projection interaction to help Qiang language and culture. Our research is to explore the possibility of serious games based on projection interaction for revitalizing Qiang language and culture.

3   Needs Finding

Our objective was to obtain insight into the current situation of Qiang language transmission among the indigenous Qiang people and their perceptions of their ethnic culture, as well as to provide design concepts for developing serious games for minority languages without a written text. We designed and implemented a series of field surveys, and the research method was based on semi-structured interviews, supplemented by questionnaires.

3.1 Study Instruments

The research instruments used in this study included an interview outline and paper questionnaires.

The following topics were included in the interview outline, which was used to guide the semi-structured interviews: 1) the current state of the Qiang language heritage: the interviewees' and their families' level of mastery of the Qiang language, the main ways and methods of learning the Qiang language, etc. 2) the difficulties encountered by the Qiang people in learning the Qiang language: the possible causes of this situation, existing solutions, and effects, etc. 3) the Qiang people's ethnic and cultural identity: their level of knowledge of their traditional myths and customs, their perspectives on the current state of Qiang's cultural heritage, and their self-perception, etc.

The questionnaire consisted of three main parts: the first part was used to obtain the interviewees' background information. The second part of the questionnaire was used to understand the interviewees' current use of Qiang language and their attitudes toward Qiangic language. The third part assesses the respondents' knowledge of their own cultural content.

3.2 Participants and Procedure

A total of four researchers traveled to Li County at the end of October 2020 for a three-day field survey. Located in the southeastern Tibetan Qiang Autonomous Prefecture of Ngawa of Sichuan, Li County is one of the major Qiang communities. Participants included 21 Qiang people (Aged between 47–76, 16 males and 5 females) from 10 families. They were fluent in the Qiang language and live in three Qiang villages with a high degree of Qiang language preservation: Mukha Qiang Village, Lelie Village, and Taoping Qiang Village.

During the research, the researchers used Sichuan dialect and Mandarin to communicate with the Qiang people. We invited a local Qiang woman as our guide to introduce us to local Qiang people with special status, such as retired teachers, barefoot doctors, village cadres, etc. We conducted semi-structured interviews with some of the villagers. The interview process took between 15 and 40 min. Paper questionnaires were delivered face-to-face to a subset of participants and gathered on the spot to augment the interview content. Some respondents gave verbal response, and the researchers assisted in filling out the questionnaire. All participants took part in our research voluntarily, and the process will be recorded on audio and video. We used social media (WeChat) to keep in touch after we left Qiang village. The interview data were analyzed by summarizing and categorizing respondents' perspectives based on verbatim transcripts of the interview recordings, and then more precisely describing these categories under the headings. Several excerpts were also chosen to illustrate respondents' attitudes toward the Qiang language's heritage and ethnic perceptions. This data is used to illustrate the needs findings. The questionnaire data are primarily used to identify more appropriate story themes, but they can also be used to corroborate semi-structured interview findings.

3.3 Key Findings

After analyzing the interview data, we discovered that young people in the Qiang villages had difficulty communicating in the Qiang language on a regular basis. The absence of usage scenarios was also found to be a restriction of Qiang language heritage. There is no writable texts in the Qiang language, hence learning the language is base on memory. In addition, most Qiang teenagers lacked the motivation to learn about their culture. Older interviewees mentioned that when they told the younger generations about the Qiang people's historical hero stories, such as "The Qiang-Ge war", the youths behaved indifferently. We proposed three design principles based on these findings: 1) Involve players in serious games to attract their interest in the Qiang language and historical culture. 2) Through scenario simulation, rebuild the previous use context of the Qiang language. 3) Strengthen their awareness of national culture through nationalized content and visual design. These principles inspired us to design "WhiteStone".

4 System Design of WhiteStone

4.1 Context Design

WhiteStone is an interactive projection device based on the heroic epic of Qiang, including the Qiang language teaching session, interactive games and Qiang language testing session. These three sections are designed based on the above design principles.

Qiang Language Teaching Session: Firstly we taught players some necessary knowledge of qiang language in advance. In the pre-learning session, players can learn the pronunciation of some Qiang words that will be used in the game, so that they can play the games better. The traditional Qiang language teaching methods offer the use for reference to our learning method, such as pointing out objects and repeatedly following the pronunciation. We digitized the process and designed a set of Audible learning cards(see Fig 1). The cards are illustrated with pictures of objects correlating to the Qiang words, making it easy to visualize the meaning of the Qiang words in the mind. In addition, the cards describe the Chinese interpretation of the vocabulary, the harmonic phonetic symbols for the pronunciation, and the role of the word as a skill card in the subsequent game. Players can learn by pressing the buttons on the cards (which are set in the center of the item picture) to listen to the Qiang pronunciation of the word repeatedly. Pre-learning session as the beginning of the interactive process is

Fig. 1. (a) Audible learning cards. (b) Player press button to learn Qiang language

very necessary for the whole serious game. Considering that most players who are new to the Qiang language, it is difficult and unfamiliar and requires repeated practice to acquire. Learning the necessary skills in advance before proceeding with the game can alleviate the frustration of players due to their lack of skill level.

Interactive Games Session: We chose the story in the Qiang epic "Qiang-Ge War" as the main plot of the projection game, including two parts: "Find Rezi" and "Qiang-Ge War"(see Fig 2). In the game, the background of the story is presented in the form of an audio picture book(see Fig 3.a). We invited an Qiang elderly to tell the story in Qiang language to enrich the picture book. In order to immerse the player in the historical tradition of the Qiang people, we simulated the scenarios of adventure in caves and repelling enemy invasions with the help of projection interactive games, in which the player will play the role of the ancestral leader of the Qiang people, Ababaigou, who led the Qiang people through the difficulties.

The story of "Find Rezi" tells the story of the leader of the ancestral Qiang tribe, Aba Baigou, who led his people to migrate in search of a new home. In the "Find Rezi" game, players need to solve the puzzles according to the hints given in the game scenes. This is to emphasize the wisdom and exploration spirit of the Qiang people. To enhance the sense of immersion, we used a combination of physical and verbal gameplay, in which players pass the levels by shouting the Qiang language pronunciation and making the corresponding actions. In addition, during the field research, we also heard some interesting legends from the Qiang people: the sheep ate the scriptures with the writing, which led to the loss of the Qiang writing. When designing the levels of the game, we also added this story into the game's plot.

Fig. 2. (a) "Find Rezi" somatic interactive game. (b) "Qiang-ge War" tangible interactive game

"Qiang-Ge War" come after the Qiang people lived a stable life in Rezi, the village was invaded by the Gegi people. Ababaigou led the Qiang people, with the help of the King of Heaven, to use the white stone to repel the Geji people and defend their homeland. The "Qiang-Ge War" game recreates an exciting battle scene to demonstrate the Qiang people's bravery, unity, and power. Considering that the Qiang elders we interviewed consistently stated that the Qiang people both are valiant warriors, and we want to help strengthen this national identity in our games. In addition, during the interview, we were informed that throwing stones is one of the Qiang people's favorite childhood games. Therefore, we use the throwing action as the main game interaction method and, choose the white stone worshiped by the Qiang people as the throwing object. Players can defeat enemies by throwing white stones at the walls. (The Qiang people believe that the white stone is the incarnation of the god Aba Baigou. They put the white stone on the highest part of the roof to show respect.) Considering the safety factor, we substitute hard white stones with soft and low-elastic tennis ball props. In order to enhance the player's sense of engagement, our game allows voice input to encourage players to speak the Qiang language. For example, yelling a certain Qiang language pronunciation can assist you in gaining more points. The game characters will deploy unique powers to achieve a greater score. For instance, if the playershouts "bu per sa (the pronunciation of "Qiang flute")," the Qiang warriors will play the Qiang flute to stun and immobilize the enemy.

In addition to the integration of mythological stories and life elements in the game. The design of the visual materials integrates the cultural elements of Qiang to enhance intimacy. We attempted to depict the charm of Qiang culture by drawing on the artistic style of an important cultural relic, Qiang's Shibi Painting "Shuarile" (see Fig 3.b), paired with distinct Qiang components such as Qiang flute and Qiang towers.

Qiang Language Testing Session: Finally, in order to test the results of the Qiang language learning, we designed a game-based test session called "Qiang blockhouse messenger". In order to make the testing session lively and interesting, we used melody Qiang music and beautiful village scenery to simulate

Fig. 3. (a) Audio picture book of Qiang heroic epic. (b)Qiang's Shibi Paiting "Shuarile"

the life of the Qiang people after the battle. This helps reduce players' rejection of the testing process and allows them to use their learned Qiang language as naturally as possible.

In this session, players take on the role of ordinary villagers standing on the Qiang blockhouse and speak the corresponding Qiang language based on the pictures above the Qiang villager. The picture of the items will appear randomly as a question, and players need to say the correct Qiang language pronunciation within five seconds, otherwise the question will fail and switch to the next picture. In a test, there are 20 questions to complete. To visualize the score, the correct Qiang words will be turned into corresponding items (e.g. Yunyun shoes and Za Jiu), which will fall between two Qiang towers and pile up one by one into a sea of items. We want players to feel more accomplished when they see the words they have answered correctly.

4.2 Interactive Design

First, players use the audio cards to learn the words that will be used in the game. After the preview session, players reach the game area to start the game. The game starts with a picture book that tells the background of the story, and the player takes on the role of the Qiang leader Aba Baigou who leads his people on an adventure. The first experience is "Find Rezi", a story of solving puzzles in a cave. Players can solve puzzles by shouting out Qiang pronunciations and body movements. For example, the game's characters will follow the player's walking movements. When encountering an obstacle vine, the player needs to shout out the Qiang pronunciation of fire (mo) and make a pose to draw a bow and shoot an arrow, then the game character will shoot an arrow with fire to burn it. After solving all the puzzles, the main character arrives at his new hometown, Rezi, and the "Qiang-Ge War" comes immediately after. In order to defend the home, players pick up prop balls from the box to smash the enemies on the wall, just like the Qiang ancestors threw white stones to fight. In the game, players can show their Qiang language ability by shouting out Qiang language pronunciation to get a higher score. For instance, if the player shouts "bu per sa,"? The pronunciation of "Qiang flute", a traditional musical instrument of

Qiang.? the Qiang warriors will play the Qiang flute to stun and immobilize the enemy. Our game enables multiple players to throw and roar in unison to attack the enemy, enabling people to recognize the spirit of their Qiang ancestors and battle the attackers bravely. After a tense battle lasting 120 s, players will get their battle score. The Qiang people in the story also successfully repelled the enemy and live a peaceful and happy life again. Players can test their Qiang language learning in the game "Qiang blockhouse messenger". Players play as villagers standing on the Qiang blockhouse, according to the pictures of the objects above the Qiang villager to speak out the corresponding Qiang language pronunciation. Finally, the number of correct answers will be the score of testing session.

4.3   System Development

WhiteStone's system architecture is depicted in Fig 4.   For the audible learning

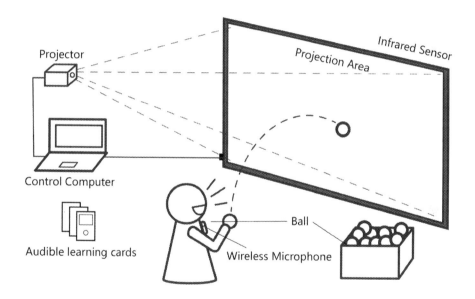

Fig. 4. System architecture of WhiteStone

cards, we record in advance through the built-in Microphone movement to preset the pronunciation of Qiang words, and then seal the cover of the card, and place the button on the painted picture position on the card. Players play audio by pressing a button to trigger.

Both two projected interactive games were developed by Unity3D. A Kinect depth camera is placed below the projection area for somatosensory input. Kinect 2.0 has a depth camera, an infrared camera, a color camera, and 25 default skeletal points. The device acquires the position of a person in a three-dimensional space through a depth camera and an infrared camera, and judges the distance relation between the corresponding positions of the skeletal points. With the help of skeletal point binding of Kinect motion sensing device, we define specific gestures in code. The specific action of the player during the game will be recognized to trigger the corresponding operation in the game. These operations are fed back to the screen of the projection area.

In addition, the recognition of the throwing position is realized by the infrared touch frame installed outside the projection area. The infrared technology touch screen is composed of infrared transmitting and receiving sensing elements installed on the outer frame of the touch screen, and an infrared detection matrix is formed on the surface of the screen. The occlusion of any object will change the infrared grid on the contact point, thus realizing the positioning of touch. The projector and the infrared touch control frame are connected with the control host through a data line; The prop tennis ball is thrown to the projection area, the position of the prop tennis ball is obtained through the infrared touch frame, and the data is transmitted to the host and fed back to the projection area.

At the same time, the wireless microphone worn by the player on the collar receives the voice audio emitted by the player and transmits it to the host for processing through Bluetooth. Speech recognition technology uses speech recognition interface based on Deep Peak2 end-to-end modeling, and makes corresponding game feedback after comparing with the established Qiang language corpus.

5   Evaluation

5.1   Study Design

To validate the potential of "WhiteStone" to motivate Qiang language learning, we conducted a user study that included both field testing and remote validation. In the remote test for the Qiang people, we focused on several research questions: (1) Is the format of a serious game based on projection interaction an appropriate way to stimulate interest in the Qiang language learning? (2) The ethnic and cultural identity of the players.

In addition, we wanted to understand the potential of "WhiteStone" in teaching the Qiang language to non-Qiang people. In our field test, we focused on (1) the effectiveness of a serious game based on projection interaction in helping indigenous language learning (2) whether the gamified learning process of the Qiang language affects the perceptions of the Qiang language, and culture among the interracial people.

Based on these questions, we hope to better understand the personal feelings that Qiang and other ethnic participants derive from our system so that we can stimulate the value of serious games based on projective interaction for the Qiang language learning.

5.2   Remote Study

Participant Due to the impact of Covid, we were unable to return to Qiang Village for field testing, we led a qualitative study with one-on-one video presentations and online interviews with Qiang people online. A total of 11 Qiang people (1 elderly, 1 middle-aged, and 9 young people) participated in the remote verification. Among them, the elderly and middle-aged people are proficient in Qiang language, only 2 young people can use Qiang language fluently, and the remaining 7 young people are in the state of understanding but not speaking, or completely incomprehensible.

Procedure and Data Collection Based on the contact information collected during field research, we conducted remote presentations and telephone interviews with nine Qiang people using social media (WeChat) as a platform. All remote validations followed the same process, with a project introduction prior to the interview, and permission to record was sought. First, a pre-interview was conducted to understand the basic information and mastery of the Qiang language and the level of knowledge of the ethnic culture of the participants. Then a remote presentation in the form of a video was given, with appropriate explanations based on the queries raised. This is followed by a core interview. Recorded interviews will be transcribed verbatim into documents and coded by the researcher for qualitative analysis.

Results (1) Is a serious game based on projection interaction an appropriate way to stimulate interest in the Qiang language learning?

The majority of respondents (n = 10) found WhiteStone to be interesting and innovative. The innovative interactive approach and the Qiang elements represented in the game were able to attract their interest. Among them, some respondents volunteered to try it for themselves after seeing the demo video. In addition, the respondents confirmed that the projection-based interactive serious game was effective in teaching simple Qiang vocabulary (n = 7), especially in engaging children's interest in learning (n = 3). However, respondents also mentioned that the corpus of games is still relatively small and needs to continue to be expanded.

(2) Players' national identity and cultural identity

Some interviewees said that they had completely forgotten the myths and legends of their own nation, and through our game, they learned about their own people's myths and legends again. This game made them start to reflect on their own attitude towards their own national culture.

Two respondents specifically mentioned that the interactive form of rock throwing evoked their childhood memories.

Proof. P3: "It reminds me of the scene when I was a kid dancing around a triangular fire pit (with a lit bonfire on top) in a potlatch, very lively." P6: "This makes me miss the days when I was a kid going around the mountains with a bunch of kids picking wild flowers, climbing, and running around."

All the interviewed Qiang people expressed positive attitudes towards the Qiang elements represented in our game, and believed that WhiteStone could make more people understand the Qiang language and culture. One of the middle-aged Qiang people expressed high encouragement and praise for our work.

Proof. P7: "I think it's great and meaningful for you young people to express Qiang culture in the form of a game for more people to understand."

5.3 Field Experiment

To investigate whether White Stone can promote effective Qiang language learning in interracial people, we conducted a controlled experimental study. We compared the memory curve of Qiang's vocabulary and pronunciation after learning the Qiang language using the ordinary learning method and using White Stone. Additionally, we interviewed participants who used White Stone to learn the Qiang language. The purpose of this study was to verify the effectiveness of White Stone in helping Qiang language learning and to gain non-Qiang people's insights into serious play based on projected interaction.

Participant. We used social media to recruit 20 undergraduates (Age between 18–22, 11 males, 9 females) from a local University. In terms of academic background, 11 students majored in computer science, while the rest majored in atmosphere, resources and environment, and communication engineering, etc. Each participant was randomly assigned to an experimental or control group on the first day, with 12 participants in the experimental group and 8 participants in the control group. The experiment takes place on a one-on-one basis for three consecutive days:

- Experimental group: Participants learn through the use of audible learning cards, and the learning content is reinforced through games.
- Control group: Participants listen to recordings of a single vocabulary in a Qiang language through their mobile phones.

Procedure. Before the experiment, we first conducted an interview to confirm with the participants whether they had learned the Qiang language and whether they knew about the Qiang culture, so as to determine the baseline ability of the participants. Among the 20 participants recruited this time, one participant in the experimental group had lived in the Qiang community for one year, and three participants had little understanding of the Qiang culture. One participant in the control group had little understanding of Qiang culture. But none of the 20 participants had studied the Qiang language and had no knowledge of the design elements involved in this experiment.

Both the experimental group and the control group were set up with two parts: the learning part and the testing part. For three consecutive days, participants were asked to complete the learning part and the testing part each day.

The Learning Part

Experimental group: The entire part is limited to be completed within 20 min, including learning Qiang language through the audible learning cards three times, playing Find Rezi once and Qiang-Ge war once. First, the participants were asked to learn the Qiang language of a single vocabulary for the first time through the audible learning cards, and the learning time of each participant was limited to 5 min. Afterward, participants were required to use the Qiang language they had learned to complete a Find Rezi, and the game time of each participant was limited to 5 min. After the first game, the participants were asked to learn the Qiang language of a single vocabulary for the second time through the audible learning cards. This time, the learning time of each participant was limited to 3 min. Finally, the participants are required to complete a Qiang-Ge war using the Qiang language they have learned, and the game time of each participant is limited to 5 min. After both games, participants were required to learn the Qiang language of a single vocabulary for the third time through the audible learning cards. This time, the learning time for each participant was limited to 2 min.

Control group: The entire part is limited to 20 min to complete. Participants were asked to learn the Qiang language by listening to the recordings of individual words repeatedly through their mobile phones without any external props. The control group experiment and the experimental group had the same learning phase process, but the participants in the control group did not participate in the interactive game but were asked to rest quietly.

The Testing Part

Both the experimental group and the control group required participants to use the Qiang language they had learned in the learning part to complete the test game-Qiang blockhouse messenger. The test game requires participants to speak the corresponding Qiang pronunciation according to the picture of the item within the specified time. Participants in the control group were presented with patterned silent cards that familiarized them with the appearance of objects corresponding to individual Qiang words before the game. Data for each test will be recorded.

With the consent of the participants, after the experiment, we conducted interviews and audio recordings of the participants in the 12 experimental groups, focusing on the participants' interactive experience in the game. Interview recordings will be transcribed verbatim and coded.

At the same time, through the data collected by the system during the test part, the three-day test scores of the experimental group and the control group were analyzed.

Results. Qiang language learning efficiency. For learning efficiency, t-tests were performed for independent samples between the control and experimental conditions ($\alpha = .05$). Invalid data from one of the controls were excluded. Overall, players could achieve scores between 0 and 200. After three days of intensive learning. Players who played the game had higher scores for correct responses

(M = 183.33, SD = 11.55) than those in the control group (M = 168.57, SD = 26.1), t(19) = −1.418, p = 0.197.

Table 1. Analysis results of testing score.

Group	Day 1	Day 2	Day 3
Experimental group (n = 12)	118.57 ± 45.98	158.57 ± 38.91	168.57 ± 26.1
Control group (n = 7)	130 ± 35.68	173.33 ± 19.23	183.33 ± 11.55
t	−0.607	−0.939	−1.418
P	0.552	0.376	0.197

Feedback on the Use of the System

Following the experiment, we conducted semi-structured interviews with the participants to collect perceptions and perceptual feedback on the use of WhiteStone from the interracial population.

Audio Cards: Nine participants thought that the audible learning cards in the pre-reading session were helpful in learning Qiang language. Reasons included being fun; being able to repeat the sounds; the physical cards being tactile; and being impressive. One player mentioned that he was impressed by the combination of the learning content and the in-game skills (A4). Some negative feedback emerged on the instability of the homebrew hardware, which could be improved by upgrading to standard hardware.

Proof. A4: "The cards incorporate the game, so the impression is a little deeper. And some text descriptions on the cards also help to remember, such as the words marked with a sure kill technique, I remember it very clearly."

Interaction and game preference: Half of the participants in the experimental group (n = 6) had experienced public projection interactivity devices in the past, e.g. in science museums, amusement parks, etc. However, 75% of the participants (n = 9) were still novel to the form of interaction in this game (physical interaction/tangible interaction/voice recognition) and indicated that the game was engaging and could hold their interest. In the interviews, we asked participants about their favorite games and why they like it. Participants' preferences for the three games were 25% (n = 3) for the "Find Rezi" tangible interactive game, 58.3% (n = 7) for the "Qiang-Ge War" tangible interactive game, and 16.7% (n = 2) for the Qiang blockhouse messenger test game. Among them, 3 participants focused more on the flow of the game and narrative, and thus were more favorable to the physical interactive games with subdivided levels and more character dialogues. The most popular game was the Qiang-Ge War, which involved throwing a prop ball, for reasons such as being challenging, more immersive with tangible objects that can be touched, physical movement that enhances engagement, and the ability to combine it with one's hobby of playing basketball. However, one female participant indicated that the throwing motion was difficult for her, so she preferred the simple test game, which was consistent with the reasons given by another participant. This reminds us of the need to adjust the difficulty of the game according to the different levels of ability of the players.

Immersion Qiang language environment creation: 8 participants felt that the game succeeded in creating an environment for the use of Qiang language due to the novel interaction, the Qiang-inspired visuals and sound effects, and the game mechanics that encouraged players to speak Qiang. In particular, The combination of projection and physical movement is considered enjoyable and immersive. The low-light environment created by the projection also helps to keep the player focused and immersed in the game. We also asked them about their perceptions of the testing game, which simulates the daily life of the Qiang people. 9 participants agreed that the gamified approach to testing made them feel more relaxed and natural. This somewhat reduced anxiety about the aptitude test.

The impression of Qiang culture: Eleven participants shared with us in the interviews what they learned about Qiang culture during the game, including Qiang distinctive items and Qiang mythology. The Qiang flute $(n = 3)$, and the legends of white stone and the sky god $(n = 7)$ were impressive elements. 10 participants expressed interest in the Qiang language and culture and wanted to learn more about it. This suggests that WhiteStone helps to spread the appeal of Qiang culture to outsiders.

6   Discussion

The findings indicate that WhiteStone has the potential to be an effective tool for conveying Qiang language and culture in a fun and interactive way. Compared with ordinary learning methods, WhiteStone achieved higher learning efficiency, albeit the difference was not significant due to insufficient samples. But participants in both the remote and field trials agreed that WhiteStone was able to attract their interest in learning about the Qiang language and culture. The Qiang people fully affirmed the significance of our work for the heritage of the Qiang language and culture.

6.1   Indigenous Language Without Written Text

This study focuses on the Qiang language, which has no written text and suffers greater obstacles in its inheritance than other languages. The paper teaching of Qiang language is inefficient, so its inheritance depends on oral transmission. In our field research, we found that the Qiang people's ability to listen is greater than their ability to speak. In other words, some Qiang people can't speak Qiang language even if they can understand what others said. One reason is the lack of a language environment. Listening to the elders speak Qiang language at home can be passive practice of Qiang listening ability, but how to improve the oral ability of young people? Since they usually use Chinese to communicate with their classmates and friends at school, they have no desire to use Qiang language. WhiteStone offers them a chance to use their Qiang language skills. We create immersion through somatosensory interaction, tangible interaction, voice input and other ways to create the use environment of Qiang language. At the same time, through the rules of the game, we limit the clearance conditions to encourage players to open more Qiang language. Our validation shows that these designs are effective. This provides ideas for the study of other endangered languages without writing.

6.2   Participation of Non-Qiang People

In this process, the non-Qiang people can also be included, through the competition mechanism to stimulate the opponent's desire to get higher scores. But we believe they are not limited to providing tension as competitors. During the remote verification, the Qiang people said, "I feel ashamed to see that other person attach so much importance to our Qiang language and culture, but we don't cherish it." We are glad to see the reflection of the Qiang people on the inheritance of their own culture caused by WhiteStone and hope that this reflection can further urge the Qiang people to take practical actions for the inheritance of their own culture. The cultural reflection of the Qiang people also brings us thinking. Is the inheritance or extinction of a language only the responsibility of ethnic minorities themselves? It is also an important part of protecting endangered languages to make people of other nationalities realize the value of minority languages and make efforts for them. The active participation of non-Qiang people may bring new vitality to the inheritance of minority languages. The inheritance and development of a national culture require the joint efforts of the ethnic minorities and other people in the language ecosphere.

6.3   Limitation and Future Work

So far we've delivered an effective serious game, WhiteStone, and evaluated it in the lab. However, due to limited conditions, we only studied the short-term effects on motivation and learning efficiency for three days in this validation, and it is unclear whether these effects are widespread over a longer period of time. Therefore, we hope to conduct field deployments to Qiang communities in the next work and conduct experiments in a longer time span to understand whether WhiteStone will motivate players to stay involved in the long term, so as to achieve long-term learning effects. In addition, due to the influence of COVID-19, we only invited non-native people to conduct field tests in this study, so the number of samples was limited. We plan to increase the sample size in the following study and invite Qiang people to participate in the game with other people. We were curious about how their experiences of competition and cooperation affected cultural consciousness. Given the diversity of potential audiences, we will also discuss topics including age at scheduled field deployments.

7   Conclusion

Revitalizing endangered indigenous languages is an important step in protecting world civilization and linguistic diversity. In particular, the Qiang language, a minority language with no written language, is in crisis as the number of people proficient in it decreases. We came up with a set of serious games called "WhiteStone" based on the design principles of field research in Qiang community. It consists of Qiang Language Teaching session, Interactive Games Session and Qiang Language testing session. To verify WhiteStone's effectiveness, we conducted a user study consist of a remote verification test and a field test to obtain insight from Qiang and non-Qiang people, respectively. Our work shows that serious games based on projective interaction have the potential to create engrossed and interesting experiences, which can attract young people's interest in learning Qiang. At the same time, the immersive game experience allows players to engage in cultural reflection as they bring their characters into the game, which helps revitalize the Qiang language and culture.

Acknowledgments. We would like to thank Xin Yang, Lingze Wu, Caiyuan Xu and Silu Liu for their help in our study operation, video recording, technical development and UI design. This project is supported by National Natural Science Foundation of China (62107007)

References

1. Alvarez, J., Djaouti, D., et al.: An introduction to serious game definitions and concepts. Serious Games Simul. Risks Manage. **11**(1), 11–15 (2011)
2. Bishop, R., Berryman, M., Ricardson, C.: Te Toi Huarewa: effective teaching and learning in total immersion Maori language educational settings. Can. J. Nativ. Educ. **26**(1), 44 (2002)
3. Bolinger, D.: Aspects of Language (1968)
4. Boulaknadel, S., Tazouti, Y., Fakhri, Y.: Towards a serious game for Amazigh language learning. In: 2019 IEEE/ACS 16th International Conference on Computer Systems and Applications (AICCSA), pp. 1–5. IEEE (2019)
5. Carew, M., Green, J., Kral, I., Nordlinger, R., Singer, R.: Getting in touch: language and digital inclusion in Australian indigenous communities. Lang. Doc. Conserv. **9**, 307–323 (2015)
6. Chen, W., Shidujaman, M., Jin, J., Ahmed, S.U.: A methodological approach to create interactive art in artificial intelligence. In: Stephanidis, C., et al. (eds.) HCII 2020. LNCS, vol. 12425, pp. 13–31. Springer, Cham (2020). https://doi.org/10.1007/978-3-030-60128-7_2
7. Chen, W., Shidujaman, M., Tang, X.: AiArt: towards artificial intelligence art. In: The 12th International Conference on Advances in Multimedia (2020)
8. Galla, C.K.: Indigenous language revitalization, promotion, and education: function of digital technology. Comput. Assist. Lang. Learn. **29**(7), 1137–1151 (2016)
9. Hasegan, T.: UN launches international year of indigenous languages 2019. IK: Other Ways of Knowing, p. 165 (2019)
10. Himmelmann, N.P.: Documentary and descriptive linguistics. De Gruyter Mouton **36**(1), 161–196 (1998). https://doi.org/10.1515/ling.1998.36.1.161

11. Hobsbawn, E.: Language, culture, and national identity. Soc. Res. **63**, 1065–1080 (1996)
12. Jiang, W.: The relationship between culture and language. ELT J. **54**(4), 328–334 (2000)
13. Johnson, W.L.: Serious use of a serious game for language learning. Front. Artif. Intell. Appl. **158**, 67 (2007)
14. LaPolla, R.J., et al.: Qiang. Universitätsbibliothek Johann Christian Senckenberg (2015)
15. Lehmann, C.: Language documentation: a program, pp. 83–98. Akademie Verlag (2014). https://doi.org/10.1524/9783050078892.83
16. Ludwig, J., Fu, D., Bardovi-Harlig, K., Stringer, D., San Mateo, C.: Serious games for second language retention. In: Interservice/Industry Training, Simulation and Education Conference (I/ITSEC), paper. No. 9164 (2009)
17. Wang, M., He, F., Chao Deng, Q.W.: The establishment and system design of the corpus based on Qiang language. In: Industrial Design Research (Sixth Series), pp. 59–65 (2018)
18. Nettle, D., Romaine, S., et al.: Vanishing voices: the extinction of the world's languages. Oxford University Press on Demand (2000)
19. Ovide, E., García-Peñalvo, F.J.: Internet technologies as a tool in indigenous education: the case of the Wichi people in "the impenetrable" area in Argentina. In: Proceedings of the 4th International Conference on Technological Ecosystems for Enhancing Multiculturality, pp. 441–445 (2016)
20. Plecher, D.A., Herber, F., Eichhorn, C., Pongratz, A., Tanson, G., Klinker, G.: HieroQuest-a serious game for learning Egyptian hieroglyphs. J. Comput. Cult. Herit. (JOCCH) **13**(4), 1–20 (2020)
21. Reyhner, J.: Indigenous language immersion schools for strong indigenous identities. Herit. Lang. J. **7**(2), 299–313 (2010)
22. Robles-Bykbaev, Y., et al.: An interactive educational platform based on data mining and serious games to contribute to preservation and learning of the cañari indigenous cultural heritage in Ecuador. In: 2018 IEEE Biennial Congress of Argentina (ARGENCON), pp. 1–6. IEEE (2018)
23. Rogers, K., et al.: PIANO: faster piano learning with interactive projection. In: Proceedings of the 9th ACM International Conference on Interactive Tabletops and Surfaces, pp. 149–158 (2014)
24. Takahashi, I., Oki, M., Bourreau, B., Kitahara, I., Suzuki, K.: FutureGym: a gymnasium with interactive floor projection for children with special needs. Int. J. Child Comput. Interact. **15**, 37–47 (2018)
25. Tanskanen, P., Arhippainen, L.: Proposing game concepts and design recommendations for minority language learning: Karelian language. In: Proceedings of the 27th Conference of Open Innovations Association, FRUCT, pp. 374–385. FRUCT Oy (2020)
26. Tazouti, Y., Boulaknadel, S., Fakhri, Y.: ImALeG: a serious game for Amazigh language learning. Int. J. Emerg. Technol. Learn. (IJET) **14**(18), 28–38 (2019)
27. Wilson, W.H., Kamana, K.: Insights from indigenous language immersion in Hawai'i (2011)
28. Wouters, P., Van der Spek, E.D., Van Oostendorp, H.: Current practices in serious game research: a review from a learning outcomes perspective. In: Games-Based Learning Advancements for Multi-Sensory Human Computer Interfaces: Techniques and Effective Practices, pp. 232–250 (2009)

29. Wu, Q., Wang, J., Wang, S., Su, T., Yu, C.: MagicPAPER: tabletop interactive projection device based on tangible interaction. In: ACM SIGGRAPH 2019 Posters, pp. 1–2 (2019)

30. Wu, Z., Ji, D., Yu, K., Zeng, X., Wu, D., Shidujaman, M.: AI creativity and the human-AI co-creation model. In: Kurosu, M. (ed.) HCII 2021. LNCS, vol. 12762, pp. 171–190. Springer, Cham (2021). https://doi.org/10.1007/978-3-030-78462-1_13

31. Yue, F., Tian, W., Shidujaman, M.: A design method of children playground based on bionic algorithm. In: Kurosu, M. (ed.) HCII 2021. LNCS, vol. 12764, pp. 173–183. Springer, Cham (2021). https://doi.org/10.1007/978-3-030-78468-3_12

32. Zaman, T., Winschiers-Theophilus, H., Yeo, A.W., Ting, L.C., Jengan, G.: Reviving an indigenous rainforest sign language: digital Oroo' adventure game. In: Proceedings of the 7th International Conference on Information and Communication Technologies and Development, pp. 1–4 (2015)

Research on Aging Design of ATM Human-Machine Interface Based on Visual Features

Jiaqi Zhang and Tianyu Huang[✉]

College of Design Art and Media, Nangjing University of Science and Technology, Nanjing 210094, China
2623746400@qq.com

Abstract. The purpose of this paper is to improve the aging suitability of ATM human-machine interface and to improve the experience of elderly users using ATM human-machine interface. The interface was tested using an eye-tracking device, and the degree of aging suitability of the interface was analyzed and evaluated using SUS system usability scale scores, eye-tracking index data and offline user interviews. It was also concluded that the ATM with top and bottom functional module layout is more suitable for elderly users. And three design strategies are proposed: first, enhance the contrast of the interface function modules to meet the visual perception of the elderly; second, ensure the rationality of the interface layout to meet the vision range of the elderly; third, improve the effectiveness of the interface information to adapt to the visual acuity of the elderly. The above design strategies can provide relevant information for policy makers and ATM suppliers to improve the acceptance of ATMs by the elderly and to improve the ageing of ATMs.

Keywords: Eye movement experiment · ATM machine · Man-machine interface · Usability · Aging design

1 Introduction

ATM (Automated Teller Machine) is a common self-service terminal, which is mainly used to solve users' needs such as inquiry, transfer, and deposit and withdrawal, and is a high-use information public facility [1]. As of 2018, according to the data released by the National Bureau of Statistics, China's population is aging significantly, with the proportion of the elderly population reaching 17.8% of the total population [2].

Along with the national policy, there is a huge and growing demand for savings and cash use by the elderly as well as bank check and cash withdrawal services [3]. With the widespread acceptance of ATMs in society, the frequency of using ATMs by the elderly is increasing year by year, and the various problems encountered by the elderly in operating ATMs are increasingly drawing the attention of Chinese society [4]. The many barriers to the use of ATMs by the elderly have caused them to lose confidence and be reluctant to use ATMs [5]. Moreover, about 80% of external information for humans

M. Kurosu (Ed.): HCII 2022, LNCS 13304, pp. 262–274, 2022.
https://doi.org/10.1007/978-3-031-05412-9_19

is received through visual channels, which are the most important interaction channels. Therefore, by analyzing the visual characteristics of the elderly, we can find out the key problems of elderly users when actually operating ATMs, optimize the layout of the ATM human-machine interface, and improve the experience and trust of the elderly, which is essential for studying the aging-friendly design of ATM human-machine interface.

2 Analysis of the Visual Characteristics and Needs of the Elderly

2.1 Visual Characteristics of the Elderly

Please note that the first paragraph of a section or subsection is not indented. The first paragraphs that follows a table, figure, equation etc. does not have an indent, either. Subsequent paragraphs, however, are indented.

Reduced Visual Perception. Visual perceptivity represents the ability to visually perceive a range of stimuli. Compared with young people, the visual perception of the elderly decreases significantly, the visual threshold increases, and the perception of less intense visual stimuli is not clear. Specifically, this is reflected in the hardening of the lens, the gradual transformation of the eye into an optical system with a fixed focal point, the insignificant perception of changes in light intensity, the decrease in bright and dark vision, the adjustment time for moving vision from light to dark in the elderly being about three times that of the young, the difficulty in adapting to frequent bright and dark changes in bright and dark environments, and the speed of adaptation becoming significantly slower with age [6]. The reduced visual perception will cause a decrease in the contrast between light and dark and color discrimination of objects observed by the elderly, which will hinder visual search.

Narrower Field of View. Visual field range is the spatial scale of what the human eye observes in a state of concentration, and can also be described as the range of visual information at the receiving interface. Studies have shown that the age-related decreases in visual field capacity are evident in older adults after the age of 60 [7], and the visual field range gradually increases with age, and this also leads to a relative decrease in the observation distance and stereo vision in older adults. More importantly, in the process of visual search, the elderly are limited by the visual field, which to a certain extent affects the efficiency of interface target search and reading [8], and has a strong correlation with the rationality of the functional module layout of the human-machine interface.

Decreased Visual Acuity. Visual acuity is the ability of the eye to discriminate fine details of objects and depends mostly on the self-regulation ability of the eye. It refers to the ability of a person to quickly find the desired target among a lot of information in a certain environment and the ability to continue to maintain target-locked attention after searching for the target information. However, with aging, one's orbital fat gradually decreases, the eye gradually retracts backward into the orbit [9], and visual acuity will consequently decrease to less than one-half of the average normal level [10]. Moreover, the effect of visual acuity on processing speed and working memory aging is 34% and 12.6%, respectively [11], and the decrease of visual acuity in the elderly will affect the visual information processing ability and the speed of visual effective information extraction in the elderly. Therefore, the decrease of visual acuity in the elderly should be fully considered among the information effectiveness aspects of the human-machine interface of ATMs.

2.2 Analysis of the Needs of the Elderly

According to the study, the savings rate and cash usage rate of Chinese elderly people are huge, and the most frequently handled banking services are cash access service and amount inquiry service respectively [12]. The needs of elderly people when using ATMs were obtained in the form of questionnaires and offline interviews, and the needs were summarized according to both physiological and psychological aspects, matching visual features analysis and collation, as shown in Table 1 below. Among the two types of banking services frequently handled by elderly people, the physiological needs are mainly focused on sight search and information recognition needs, and the psychological needs are mainly focused on safety and pleasure. Therefore, in the study of ATM human-machine interface for aging, the human-machine interaction interface for the services involved in cash withdrawal and access will be carried out to conduct an eye-tracking test experiment on the layout of ATM functional modules based on the visual characteristics of the elderly, with the aim of providing quantitative reference for the aging-friendly design of ATM human-machine interface by taking the layout of functional modules as the entry point.

Table 1. Analysis of the needs of the elderly.

Handling business/Requirements	Cash access service	Amount inquiry service
Psychological needs	Security needs Pleasure needs	Pleasure needs
Matching visual features	Field of view Visual perception Visual sensitivity	Visual sensitivity Visual perception

3 Study on the Effect of Functional Module Layout on Ageing of Human-Machine Interface of ATM Machine with Visual Perception Orientation

3.1 Research Purpose

This experiment will analyze the eye-movement data of two ATM machine function module layout types (left-right layout and top-bottom layout) based on the visual characteristics of the elderly, aiming to investigate the effect of ATM machine human-machine interface function module layout types on the operation efficiency of the elderly.

3.2   Experimental Design

Participants. This study focused on an elderly population, so a total of nine subjects were recruited for this experiment, aged 65–77 years, with normal color vision, right-handedness, and normal naked or corrected vision; all subjects had varying degrees of experience with computers and ATMs, with equal proportions of males and females, and with education levels of high school and above; the experimental site is shown in Fig. 1.

Fig. 1.   The test site

Laboratory Equipment. The test apparatus used a desktop gaze tracking system consisting of a 482.6 mm (19 inch) Apple computer with a sampling frequency of 60 Hz and a test viewing distance of approximately 64 cm, with binocular acquisition mode and the remaining parameters set by system default. The device can effectively collect the data changes of the subject's eye trajectory, first gaze point, and gaze time, which can meet the analysis needs of this experiment.

Selection and Determination of Experimental Materials. Due to the product characteristics of ATMs themselves and the use of Toby's eye-tracking equipment, it is difficult to obtain 100% accurate control of ATM variables during experimental operations. According to S. Guan and Fan Yu's study [13], it is feasible to test the visual behavioral characteristics of users using a prototype human-machine interface of a unified brand of public self-service terminal. Therefore, two real ATM HMI pictures (A1 and A2) from the same bank were used as experimental materials in the research experiment to explore the effect of the layout of functional modules on the efficiency of elderly users using ATMs. After extensive market research and analysis, it was shown that the layout types of the HMI function modules of the two different ATMs were representative, as shown in Fig. 2.

Experimental Task. The experiment was divided into two main parts. (1) the Tobbi eye-movement test apparatus and software were adjusted to introduce subjects to the main purpose of this experiment and the experimental task: withdrawing money from a bank ATM machine and performing visual search of the functional modules of the ATM machine; (2) subjects operated two human-machine interfaces A1 and A2 on the

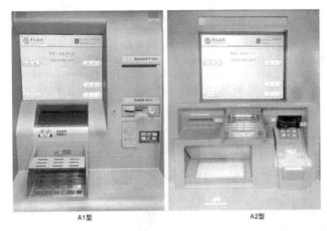

Fig. 2. Two different interface layout ATM machine man-machine interface

ATM machine according to the normal withdrawal steps, each human-machine interface corresponding to a particular step, and each picture AOI area of interest on 1 AOI area of interest. The experiment was divided into a practice group and a formal experiment group. After the formal experiment, the experimental subjects were interviewed and filled in the SUS system usability scale, and the experimenter recorded the whole experimental process, and no discussion of the experimental content was allowed during the experiment. The operation steps and the corresponding AOI interest areas are shown in Table 2, and the specific flow of the experiment is shown in Fig. 3.

Table 2. Analysis of the needs of the elderly.

Task steps	Cash access service
S1 find the card slot to insert the bank card	AOI1 card slot
S2 find the password button	AOI2 password button
S3 finds the withdrawal button	AOI3 screen withdrawal button
S4 finds the deposit and withdrawal port	AOI4 deposit and withdrawal port
S5 finds the eject button	AOI5 screen card eject button
S6 find the receipt exit	AOI1 receipt export

Experimental Variables and Evaluation Indicators. Independent variable: two ATMs functional module layout types (left-right layout, top-down layout), referred to by A1 type and A2 type.

Dependent variable: ATM human-machine interface suitability (visual perception comfort, field of view range reasonableness, and visual acuity adaptation).

Experimental indicators: system usability scale score, reaction time, first gaze point time, gaze point sequence, and observation time length.

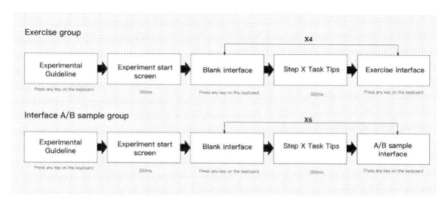

Fig. 3. Operation steps of eye movement experiment design

Control variables: color, interface content.

(The specific data reflecting the indicators of the experiment are as follows [14]: (1) SUS System Usability Scale score, which contains 10 declarative sentences, of which the odd numbered sentences are subjective positive emotional expressions the even numbered sentences are subjective negative emotional expressions [4]. (2) First gaze point time, which indicates the time it takes for the subject's sight to reach a specific target functional module for the first time, reflects the time and difficulty for the elderly to enter the field of view of the functional module of the ATM human-machine interface, and is one of the indicators of visual perceptual comfort of the interface. It is also one of the important indicators to measure whether the ATM interface layout meets the vision of the elderly. (3) Gaze point order, which indicates the transition of gaze points between the interest areas divided by each functional module of the ATM, and is also one of the important indicators to measure whether the ATM interface layout meets the vision of the elderly. (4) Total gaze time, which indicates the time the subject stays in a certain functional module area, reflecting the extraction of the difficulty of extracting the information displayed and conveyed by that functional module [15]. The longer the average total gaze time, the more difficult it is for subjects to extract information from each AOI. All data processing was performed using spss for statistics and processing (Fig. 4).

3.3 Results

Visual Perception Analysis of the Interface. Combining the test results using the SUS usability scale and the interview results. Regarding the layout of functional modules, there were significant differences in the visual perception of elderly users between different types of functional module layouts ($p = 0.00 < 0.01$). Type A1 had poor usability and the overall visual comfort of the human-machine interface was not strong, while type A2 had higher usability. Combined with the analysis of the interview after the subjects completed the operation task, the functional module layout of the A2 type ATM was more in line with the daily withdrawal process of the elderly, and the functional division

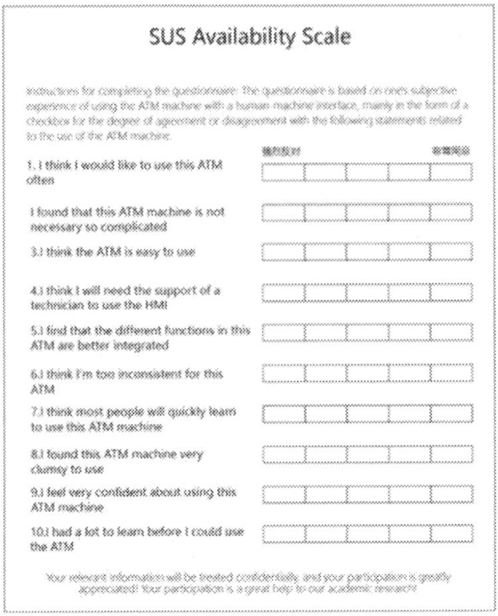
SUS Availability Scale

1. I think I would like to use this ATM often

I found that this ATM machine is not necessary so complicated

3.I think the ATM is easy to use

4.I think I will need the support of a technician to use the HMI

5.I find that the different functions in this ATM are better integrated

6.I think I'm too inconsistent for this ATM

7.I think most people will quickly learn to use this ATM machine

8.I found this ATM machine very clumsy to use

9.I feel very confident about using this ATM machine

10.I had a lot to learn before I could use the ATM

Fig. 4. SUS system availability scale

of the operation module and display module was more reasonable. Compared with Type A2, the usability test results of Type A were not satisfactory. The reasons for the poor visual perception of the elderly are. (1) Functional modules with similar brightness and contrast are arranged together, resulting in hesitation and frequent Mistake operation due to diminished visual perception during operation, resulting in weakened confidence and reduced visual comfort. (2) Loose distribution of functional modules for operation, frequent changes in light and darkness during operation, and easy visual fatigue for the elderly. (3) The password key module with high frequency of use is located far away, and there is no emphasis type sign to indicate its location, so the elderly cannot perceive its location immediately. The usability test results are shown in Table 3, and the non-repetitive one-way ANOVA for different models of ATMs is shown in Table 4.

Table 3. Usability test results (X ± S)

Task steps	Cash access service
A1	44.44 ± 6.32
A2	63.17 ± 4.00*

Interface View Range Analysis. The results of the first gaze time of each module when elderly users used A1 and A2 HMIs are shown in Table 5, in which the first gaze time of the card slot module and the password tray module in the two interfaces had significant

Table 4. Non-repeated single-factor analysis of variance for different types of ATMs

Source of difference	SS	df	MS	F	P-value	F crit
Inter-group	1577.35	1.00	1577.35	50.10	0.00	4.49
Intra-group	503.72	16.00	31.48			
Total	2081.07	17.00				

differences, while the first gaze time of other functional modules did not have significant differences (PAOI1 $= 0.00 < 0.01$, PAOI2 $= 0.00 < 0.01$, P > 0.05). (0.05) This ocular data reflected that the functional layout of A1 HMI was unreasonable compared with A2 HMI, and there were obvious problems in the location layout of card slot module and password disk module, which led to the prolonged time for elderly users to visually search for the corresponding targets. According to the characteristics of the visual field range of the elderly, the eye-movement data and interview results were analyzed: the first gaze point of the card slot module and password tray module of the A2 model is shorter, and the reduction of the visual field range changes with age, with more reduction of the upward visual field and less reduction of the downward visual field [16]. Therefore, the functional modules on the right and lower part of the HMI will enter the field of view of the elderly more quickly, while the functional modules on the left and upper part of the HMI will enter the field of view of the elderly more slowly. The loosely distributed A1-type HMI layout is unreasonable, and the integrated and ordered compact A2-type interface layout is more suitable for the viewpoint of the elderly.

The order of concerns is shown in Fig. 5 and Fig. 6. Combined with the interview results, it can be found that: firstly, most of the elderly people's first line of sight is focused on the area below the center, and secondly, they jump to the display and operation modules on the HMI from top to bottom. The comparison of sequence diagrams shows that the distance from the first line of sight to the operation module is longer in type A1 than in type A2; the trend of jumping sweeping eventually forms a "Z" type sweeping result, which indicates that the function module layout of this type of ATM is unreasonable and the visual tracking path is too long, which increases the search and operation time of the elderly. In contrast, in the A2-type interface layout, the search process among the function modules is more smooth and natural, and the path distance between the gaze points is even, indicating that the up-and-down layout method of the A2-type ATM display function modules and operation function modules is more suitable for the sight range of the elderly.

Interface Visual Acuity Analysis. The results of comparing the total gaze duration between the A1 and A2 models are shown in Table 6. The difference in gaze duration between the two groups of subjects was significant in the card slot and access portal functional modules, while the difference in total gaze duration in the other functional modules was not significant (PAOI1 $= 0.01 < 0.05$, PAOI4 $= 0.03 < 0.05$, p > 0.05). The difficulty of extracting information from the card slot and access portal functional modules in the A1 and A2 models was different for older users in the search process.

Table 5. Comparison of the first view point time for each AOI of the two ATMs (X ± S) Unit/s

	AOI1	AOI2	AOI3	AOI4	AOI5	AOI6
A1	3.64 (±0.62)	6.66 (±0.99)	12.50 (±2.81)	6.21 (±1.48)	14.28 (±3.43)	7.80 (±1.04)
A2	1.92 (±0.67)	3.34 (±0.82)	10.60 (±2.70)	4.06 (±1.16)	11.83 (±2.04)	6.33 (±1.24)
Significance (P)	0.00**	0.00**	0.19	0.72	0.10	0.72

Fig. 5. A1 Point-of-attention sequence   **Fig. 6.** A2 Point-of-attention sequence

The difficulty of extracting information was different, and there was some difficulty in extracting information from card slots and access points in the A1 model; the difficulty of extracting information from each functional module of the human-machine interface was lower in the A2 model. The analysis was conducted by combining the eye-movement data and interview results with the characteristics of the elderly with declining vision. In the process of observing the A1 model interface, most users said that the prompt text of the functional modules on the interface was too small and took longer to recognize. Compared with Type A2, it is more difficult for elderly users to obtain the corresponding information in the card slot and access module of Type A1 HMI function module, and the cognitive learning time is longer. The reasons for this are divided into the following points. First, the information in the A1 type card slot is mainly text-based and has less text. As the elderly people's vision decreases, the text information will increase the time for the elderly people to gaze at the information and the time to complete the task becomes longer. Secondly, the prompt information of A2 type access portal function module and the prompt information of password button function module are too close to each other, causing visual interference, and elderly users cannot quickly understand the meaning of the function module. Again, the prompt message of the card slot and the appearance of the access portal are very weak. As the visual sensitivity of the elderly decreases, the visual search process will subconsciously focus on the overall shape of the target for preliminary functional judgment before focusing on the prompt information next to the target [17], while the weak indicative appearance of the functional module and the vague information conveyed will increase the cognitive cost of the elderly users, thus increasing the total gaze time of the functional module.

Table 6. Comparison of the average gaze time length of each AOI of the two ATM machines (X ± S) Unit/s

	AOI1	AOI2	AO3	AOI4	AOI5	AOI6
A1	3.35 (±0.68)	2.71 (±0.56)	5.32 (±1.06)	5.08 (±0.89)	5.08 (±0.89)	2.87 (±0.63)
A2	2.41 (±0.59)	2.63(±0.68)	5.05(±1.04)	3.94 (±1.04)	1.04 (±1.04)	2.78 (±0.52)
Significance (P)	0.01**	0.78	0.61	0.03*	0.90	0.56

4   The Design Strategy and Method of ATM Human-Machine Interface Suitable for Aging

When designing specific aging ATM human-machine interfaces, designers should pay attention to the visual characteristics of the elderly. Based on the above research and analysis of the three visual characteristics of elderly people's visual perception, visual field and visual acuity on ATM HMI, the following three strategies for adaptive aging design of ATMs are proposed.

4.1   Adjust the Contrast of Interface Function Modules to Meet the Visual Perception of the Elderly

In the aging-friendly design of ATM human-machine interface, in order to meet the visual perception of the elderly and improve the usability of ATM human-machine interface, designers should focus on adjusting the contrast of interface function modules. First, unify and integrate the hardware operation function module and display function module of the ATM HMI, adjust the brightness contrast between the display module and the operation module, and reduce the frequency of light and dark adaptation conversion during the operation of the elderly. Secondly, strengthen the identification of high-frequency operation function modules such as cash withdrawal port, expand the shape gap and color brightness of different operation function modules, and reduce the problem of frequent wrong operations. Finally, apply multi-channel interaction technology to achieve accurate recognition of the operation intention of elderly users in terms of visual, voice feedback, somatosensory and other auxiliary interaction technologies, and enhance the operation contrast of the interface guidance module to provide effective feedback and help for guiding elderly users in visual search and operation to meet the visual experience of elderly users.

4.2 Ensure that the Interface is Well Laid Out to Meet the Range of Vision of the Elderly

Interface layout refers to the size, spacing and position settings of each functional module of the human-machine interface. A reasonable interface layout meets the characteristics of elderly people's sight range, and the appearance structure of functional modules will enhance the comfortable viewing experience of elderly users and improve the efficiency of elderly users' operation of the ATM interface. In the specific design, on the one hand, designers should set the commonly used and important function columns in the areas that elderly users habitually look at, especially the areas that users most often focus on are the center and bottom areas of the ATM interface. On the other hand, in order to adapt to the sight range of elderly users and ensure the efficiency of use, each function module of the ATM should follow the principle of grid-based design and standardize its position to avoid arranging important function modules in the bottom left or top right corner of the ATM human-machine interface to improve the rationality of the interface layout in order to adapt to the sight range of elderly users.

4.3 Improve the Effectiveness of Interface Information to Accommodate the Visual Acuity of the Elderly

The analysis of the eye-movement experimental data shows that, based on the reduced visual acuity of the elderly, the effectiveness of text-based hints is lower than that of icon-based hints, and the differentiated appearance of important functional modules will assist in the communication of information. Therefore, in order to improve the effectiveness of ATM human-machine interface design, first of all, the design of ATM functional module icons should follow the relevant principles: (1) the meaning of icons is clear and easy to understand, so that the elderly can accurately identify and avoid misunderstanding; (2) the icons are anthropomorphic, in line with the mental model of the elderly; (3) the icon configuration is eye-catching and clear, and as far as possible, the use of facial closed outline icon style. (4) text-based information on the interface will increase the cognitive time and load of elderly users [18], so the icon design of functional modules should be easy to understand and reduce the attention of elderly users to text or reduce the aid of unnecessary text information. Through the above design strategies for the visual sensitivity of the elderly to improve the effectiveness of the ATM interface information, adapt to the characteristics of the reduced visual sensitivity of the elderly, improve the ageing of the human-machine interface, and enhance the experience of elderly users.

5   Conclusion

Previous studies on the human-machine interface of ATMs have been conducted mainly for adults and have used the ATM screen interface as the experimental prototype [19], while relatively little research has been conducted on the aging-appropriate interaction of the physical functional module layout of the overall human-machine interface of ATMs. In this study, we extracted three visual characteristics of the elderly and their needs for using ATMs, and used a typical ATM human-machine interface as the prototype for the design study, and used an eye-movement instrument for experimental testing. In the specific design of ATM human-machine interface for aging, considering the visual characteristics of elderly users, we propose to enhance the contrast of interface function modules to meet the visual perception of the elderly, ensure the rationality of interface layout to meet the visual field of the elderly, and improve the effectiveness of interface information to adapt to the visual acuity of the elderly as the three points of ATM human-machine interface for aging. The design strategy can provide policy makers and ATM providers with information on how to improve the acceptance of ATMs by the elderly and improve the aging appropriateness of ATMs.

However, this study has major limitations. Due to the constraints of time, research equipment and our own data analysis capability, we did not conduct an in-depth study on the human-machine interface of ATMs, and we did not conduct an in-depth study on the size and color of the functional modules of the human-machine interface of ATMs, etc. We hope to expand our research from these aspects in the future.

References

1. Ying, W., et al.: Research on public product design based on the characteristics of rural elderly people's life style. Decoration **58**(6), 136–137 (2015)
2. Yi, H.: Analysis of the current situation of population aging in China. Chin. Gerontol. **32**(21), 4853–4855 (2012)
3. Xu, S.: Analysis of the demand for senior financial services of commercial banks in the context of population aging. Mod. Econ. Inf. **02** (2016)
4. Lv, F.: Research on the universal design of ATM machine interface based on eye tracking. Zhejiang University of Technology (2017)
5. E M.S.: Research on digital interface interaction design of senior products based on visual characteristics. Nanjing University of Technology (2015)
6. Cui, Z., Chen, Y., Hao, L.: A review of the research dynamics of healthy light environment in human living space based on the visual characteristics of the elderly. J. Lighting Eng. **27**(05), 21–26+86 (2016)
7. Yue, W.: Research on interface interaction design based on the cognitive characteristics of the elderly. Nanjing University of Science and Technology (2018)
8. Shao, K.: Research on ATM interface design under the perception of the elderly. Jiangnan University (2010)
9. Guo, F., Shi, C., Chen, P., Zhu, L.: Research on effective visual field testing for elderly drivers. Hum. Ergon. **25**(01), 52–59 (2019)
10. E M.S.: Research on digital interface interaction design of elderly products based on visual characteristics. Nanjing University of Science and Technology (2015)

11. Shoji, T., Mine, I., Kumagai, T., et al.: Age-dependent changes in visual sensitivity induced by moving fixation points in adduction and abduction using imo perimetry. Sci. Rep. **10**, 21175 (2020)
12. Wang, Y.F.: A study on the establishment of a human factors database architecture for the elderly: a product design for the convenience of the elderly. Tongji University, Shanghai (2009)
13. Guan, S., Yu, F.: Research on human-machine interface design of vending machine based on eye-tracking. Packag. Eng. **40**(08), 230–236 (2019)
14. Liu, Q., Xue, C., Falk, H.: Evaluation of interface usability based on eye-tracking technology. J. Southeast Univ. **40**(2), 331–334 (2010)
15. Peng, H.M., Shen, J.L.: Comparison of the role of visual acuity and contrast sensitivity in processing speed and working memory aging. In: Abstracts of the 10th National Psychology Conference. Chinese Psychological Society (2005). 47
16. Yu, X., Lv, S., Wu, J., Miyamoto, S.: A study on the impact of aging on dynamic visual field. Comput. Appl. Res. **30**(09), 2684–2688 (2013)
17. Dan, D.: Research on age-appropriate design of interface interaction based on visual selective attention. Nanjing University of Science and Technology (2017)
18. Chen, Z.: Application of cognitive psychology in UI interface design. Packag. Eng. **38**(16), 30–33 (2017)
19. Wang, Y., Lu, F.Q.: Usability testing of ATM machine interface based on eye-movement data. Hum. Ergon. **23**(01), 48–54 (2017)

Persuasive Design and Behavioral Change

Mapping Behavior Change Wheel Techniques to Digital Behavior Change Interventions: Review

Farhat-ul-Ain, Olga Popovitš, and Vladimir Tomberg$^{(\boxtimes)}$

Tallinn University, Tallinn, Estonia
vtomberg@tlu.ee

Abstract. Aims: Digital health interventions (DHIs) use different strategies to deliver behavior change techniques (BCTs). There is a lack of understanding on how BCTs can be strategized in DHIs to optimize users' experience and effectiveness of the intervention. This review aimed to explore how behavior change techniques are strategized/operationalized in DHIs de-facto. **Method:** Thirty-five studies were included in the review. Data related to behavior change strategies were extracted and coded using the taxonomy of behavior change techniques. **Results:** Overall, 125 strategies were extracted from studies and coded into 33 BCTs. Most of the studies were focused on physical activity and healthy food consumption. 'Prompts and cues' (17/35 studies), 'social support (unspecified technique)' (15/35 studies), 'goal setting (behavior technique)' (11/35 studies), and 'self-monitoring of behavior' (10/35 studies) were the most frequently used behavior change techniques. 'Prompts and cues' was mostly strategized by sending reminders via text messages/email, mobile applications, or other digital systems. 'Social support' such as encouragement or counseling was strategized by online support groups using social networking websites, text-message platforms, and counselors' phone calls. 'Goal setting (behavior technique)' was strategized via in-app calculators to set goals, build-in app features, and digital coach/virtual agents. 'Self-monitoring of behavior' was mainly strategized by transferring data in the mobile application (by users) and activity trackers. **Conclusion:** It is important to consider theories/frameworks of behavior change while selecting, strategizing, and reporting BCTs to produce effective and sustainable results. Furthermore, innovative ways of strategizing various BCTs are needed to be implemented in DHI.

Keywords: Digital health interventions · Behavior change · Behavior change techniques

1 Introduction

1.1 Problem Statement

Digital health interventions (DHIs) for behavior change, e.g., smoking cessation, improving adherence, or dietary habits, have been more prominent within the last decade [1]. The goal of digital behavior change interventions (DBCIs) is to achieve sustainable change in targeted health outcomes and improve user engagement through a positive user experience [2, 3]. Behavior Change Techniques (BCTs) are observable, replicable, and irreducible components of an intervention designed to change behaviors. DHIs are usually complex in terms of BCTs (e.g., use of multiple BCTs) or features of the technology (e.g., interactive features, ease of use, timely accessible information, personalization, privacy). Various methods have been employed in DHIs to deliver specific BCTs. E.g., wearables, smartphones applications, exergaming, and social media were used to deliver self-monitoring techniques for improving physical activity [4].

Moller et al. [5] identified some potential issues about the operationalization of BCTs. First, the studies lack an appropriate description of BCTs in terms of theory and how exactly BCTs were strategized/offered in the interventions [6–8]. For example, studies reported only methods of delivery such as text-message interventions without mentioning the BCTs specifically used. Thus, that challenges to identify, implement, and replicate the active behavior change components. Second, BCTs are strategized inconsistently with the theory. For example, a theoretical construct *'autonomy and support'* derived from self-determination theory can be strategized by giving choices to the participants. However, these choices were given inconsistently with the theory, e.g., giving too many choices or meaningless options. Third, a minimal number of BCTs have been implemented in mobile applications. E.g., less than seven BCTs on average are being implemented in apps for physical activity [9, 10]. This suggests a lack of guidance from the theory in DHI, limiting the efficacy of interventions. Thus, greater precision is needed in the operationalization and specification of BCTs to improve the potential of DHI. However, there is a lack of understanding of how BCTs could and should be strategized in digital technology. The current study aimed to conduct a literature review to understand how BCTs are typically operationalized/strategized in DHI.

1.2 Research Question

What strategies are mostly used in the existing DBCI studies to deliver the specific behavior change techniques in the digital interventions?

1.3 The Behavior Change Wheel

Studies describe active components of behavior change interventions with different labels, e.g., daily record keeping can be used as an alternative to self-monitoring [11]. Further, different frameworks, such as IDEAS [13], suggest incorporating theory into intervention design. The UK Medical Research Council [14] calls for improved methods of specifying and reporting intervention content to address the problems related to lack of consistency and consensus. Recently, Michie et al. [14] developed a behavior change framework known as the Behavior Change Wheel (BCW, see Fig. 1), which aids in the intervention design process and characterizes interventions that enable their outcomes to be linked with mechanisms of action. The behavior change wheel integrates nineteen theories of behavior change and offers a step-by-step process of designing interventions. Stage 1 of BCW (see Fig. 1) helps to understand the problem and identify the need for change based on the Com-B model (inner layer: Capability, Opportunity, and Motivation). The second stage identifies what types of intervention functions (middle layer:

broad categories of means by which an intervention can change behavior) and policy categories (outer layer) are likely to bring the desired change. The last stage is related to identifying the specific behavior change technique with the help of taxonomy of behavior change and how this should be implemented (i.e., strategies/operationalization of BCTs).

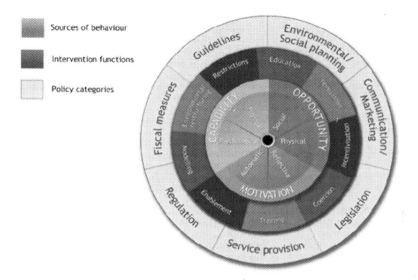

Fig. 1. Behavior Change Wheel (BCW)

The authors created a taxonomy of the behavior change techniques [16], which combined 93 BCTs (grouped into 16 categories) to establish common vocabulary and definitions of behavior change techniques. These BCTs are also categorized as more frequently and less frequently used techniques for each intervention function. This structured approach enabled precision in the intervention design, implementation, and evaluation. The taxonomy of BCTs has several benefits [16]. First, it allows designing intervention by selecting BCTs from a comprehensive list and reporting details as required by the definition of specific BCTs mentioned in the taxonomy. Second, it promotes replication of interventions strategies and labeling strategies by appropriate BCTs. Lastly, it provides reliable methods of extracting intervention strategy/content from studies and accurately labeling them. This study aimed to extract information regarding various strategies used for behavior change and to label them using behavior change taxonomy [16]. This should help in the understanding of various strategies used to deliver specific behavior change techniques.

2   Related Works

In the previous reviews [16–19], researchers evaluated BCTs delivered in commercial applications empirical studies designed for some specific targeted outcomes, e.g., sedentary behavior, alcohol consumption reduction, weight reduction. The authors synthesized the results to reflect the absence/presence of the BCTs in application or studies. For example, Morrissey et al. [16] coded commercial smartphone applications for improving medication adherence using the Behavior Change Technique Taxonomy (v1). Only 12 out of 93 possible techniques were utilized across apps. Approximately 96% of the apps included *'action planning'* and *'prompts & cues'*. Approximately 37% of studies used *'self-monitoring and feedback on behavior'*. Simeon et al. [17] coded 71 studies that used social media interventions to promote health via behavior change in adults. However, the top 5 BCTs delivered in the maximum intensity were *'social support (unspecified)'*, *'self-monitoring of behavior'*, *'information about health consequences'*, and *'credible sources'* were identified to give instructions on how to perform a behavior. Lyons et al. [18] coded behavior changes techniques implemented in commercially available electronic activity monitors. The most used techniques were *'review of goal behavior'*, *'social support'*, *'social comparison'*, *'prompts/cues'*, *'rewards'*, and *'focus on the past success'*. Dunn et al. [19] reviewed apps that have been designed to reduce the sedentary periods. The results showed that in free and paid apps, the BCTs used were only 10 out of 93, with a mean of 2.42 range (0–6) per app. The most commonly used BCTs were *'prompts/cues'*, *'information about health consequences'*, and *'self-monitoring behavior'* (n = 17). Three additional BCTs, *'graded tasks'*, *'focus on past successes'*, and *'behavior substitution'*, were coded from the four free apps. Schoeppe [20] identified 6 BCTs per app to improve diet, physical activity, and sedentary behaviors in children & adolescents, i.e., *'providing instructions'*, *'general encouragement'*, *'contingent rewards'*, and *'feedback on performance'* were the most commonly used BCTs. These literature reviews highlighted that some techniques are more frequently used in the studies than others in digital interventions.

3   Methods

Electronic databases (ACM, MEDLINE, PubMed) were searched using key terms related to digital technology/digital interventions and health behavior change intervention. Studies were included if: any form of digital technology was included (e.g., mobile applications, websites, text messages, etc.) and focused on at least one health behavior (e.g., reducing alcohol consumption, improving adherence, quality of life, etc.). Only studies from the last fifteen years were included in the current review. All types of studies (experimental, non-experimental, design, and prototype) were included. Information regarding implemented strategies was extracted and coded using the BCW taxonomy for all the included studies. Then, the authors reviewed the included studies and coded strategies.

4   Results

Thirty-five studies were included in the current review. Information related to BCTs, mode of delivery, and targeted conditions were extracted. One hundred twenty-five strategies were extracted from 35 studies and labeled using the Taxonomy of behavior change (V1). All strategies were labeled with the most appropriate BCTs. However, in some cases, an adequate description of the strategy was not mentioned, which was labeled as *'not enough information to code'*. Moreover, some studies utilized interventions that cannot be coded as BCTs were labeled as '*No BCT present*'. The included studies ranged from the year 2013-to 2021.

4.1   Targeted Domains for Health Behavior Change

The examined studies targeted multiple health behaviors for change (see Fig. 2). Most of the studies were focused on physical activity/reduction in sedentary health behaviors (12/35), followed by health food consumption (9/35), e.g., healthy diet, healthy food purchase, and general health behaviors (9/35), e.g., sunscreen use, sleeping patterns, stress reduction, sexual behaviors. In addition, six studies focused on managing diseases (e.g., reduced colorectal cancer risk, cardiac rehabilitation, hypertension, medication adherence) and reducing drug use (smoking cessation, alcohol consumption reduction).

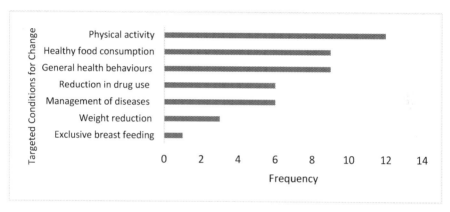

Fig. 2. Frequency of targeted outcomes for behavior change in the included studies

4.2   Modes of Delivery

Various digital modes are used to deliver the BCTs. Figure 3 shows that mobile applications have been prominently used mode of delivery (2013–2021). However, text messages/email/website, virtual agents, online video coaches declined after 2015. Use of social networks (e.g., Facebook, social media platforms), online systems (e.g., canteen system), messaging platforms (e.g., WhatsApp, WeChat), and wearables (e.g., pedometers) increased after 2016.

4.3   Utilization of BCTs

The taxonomy of behavior change techniques grouped 93 techniques into 16 groups. Only a few techniques were used from all intervention groups (Table 1), except the social support and social comparison groups. Moreover, approximately 75% of techniques were utilized from '*comparison of behaviors*', '*comparison of the outcome*', '*natural consequences*', and '*goals and planning*'. Less than 50% of the techniques are

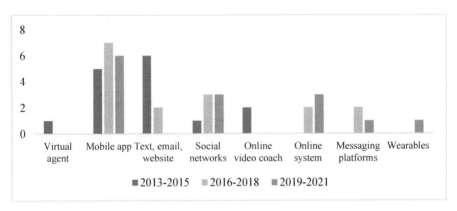

Fig. 3. Various modes to deliver digital interventions

used from other BCT groups, i.e., '*regulation*', '*self-belief*', '*identity*', '*feedback and monitoring*', '*repetition and substitution*', '*associations*' and '*reward and threat*'. None of the techniques were selected from '*antecedents*', '*covert learning*', and '*scheduled consequences*'.

Table 1. Frequency of Included intervention in the studies for each BCT Group

BCT groups	Included techniques in studies	Total techniques in the group
Social support	3	3
Comparison of behaviour	3	3
Comparison of outcomes	2	3
Covert learning	0	3
Shaping knowledge	2	4
Regulation	1	4
Self-belief	1	4
Identity	2	5
Natural consequences	4	6
Antecedents	0	6
Feedback and monitoring	2	7
Repetition and substitution	1	7
Associations	1	8
Goal and planning	6	9
Scheduled consequences	0	10
Reward and threat	3	11
Total	32	93

Only 32 out of 93 techniques were utilized in the included studies. Figure 4 represents the most and least frequently used BCTs in the included studies. The most frequently used BCTs are *'prompts and cues'* (17/35 studies), 'social support *(unspecified)'* (15/35 studies), *'goal setting (behavior)'* (11/35 studies), and *'self-monitoring of behavior'* (10/35 studies). Another important category, i.e., no BCT present, was coded in almost 12 studies (reflects that the strategy has been used for behavior change but cannot be given any code). All other techniques were included in one to six studies.

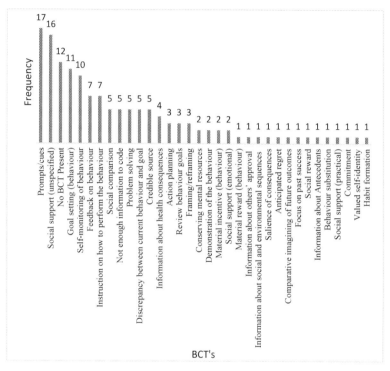

Fig. 4. Frequency of BCTs used in studies

4.4 Strategizing BCTs in Digital Interventions

Table 2 represents how BCTs were strategized/operationalized in digital interventions. All the strategies mentioned in the included studies were labeled using Taxonomy of behavior change techniques and summarized in Table 2.

Table 2. Strategies for various BCTs used in studies

BCTs & strategies	Target conditions
Goal and planning	
Goal setting (behavior) [21–31] - Goal setting using in-app calculators, personalized goal setting, predetermined goals, and tweak suggestions - Negotiating goals and developing plans using a virtual agent or digital health coach	Physical activity, Healthy food consumption, Weight reduction, General health behaviors
Review behavioral goals [24, 28, 30, 32] - Users report their goals on assigned activities using the in-app team features. The digital coach provides the feedback or through telephone sessions	Physical activity, Healthy food consumption, General health behaviors
Problem solving [27, 28, 33, 34] - In-app interactive tools, tailored textual/auditory messages were used to suggest problem-solving strategies - Telephone sessions with the coach to identify barriers and solutions - Apps helped to monitor habits/ triggers and methods to overcome habits	Healthy food consumption, Reduction in drug use, General health behaviors
Discrepancy between current behavior & goal [21, 30, 31] - Avatar-based dialogue to make the person aware of the discrepancy - Mobile applications visually showed the current state of the goal and selected goals	Healthy food consumption, Reduction in drug use, Physical activity
Action planning [33, 35] - Users created their action plan using the build-in app menu 'action plan.' - Mobile applications suggested action plans	Healthy food consumption, Physical activity
Commitment [29] - Participants were asked to change behavior by pledging social media	Weight reduction
Feedback and Monitoring	
Feedback on Behavior [23, 25, 27, 29, 32, 36, 37] - Feedback using visual/graphical display (bar chart, graphs, pie chart) via mobile applications and online systems - Personalized online feedback sessions delivered by health coaches	Healthy food consumption, General health behaviors, Weight reduction,

(continued)

Table 2. (*continued*)

BCTs & strategies	Target conditions
Self-monitoring of behavior [23, 25, 26, 28–30, 34, 38–40] - User transfer data related to health goals in mobile applications - Self-monitoring using wearables and build in-app tracking devices	Physical activity, Healthy food consumption, General health behaviors, Weight reduction, Management of diseases
Associations	
Prompts and cues [21–23, 25, 27, 29, 31, 34, 37, 38, 41–47] - Sending reminders/prompts to perform health-related activities through mobile applications, calendar-based systems, email/text messages (WhatsApp), prompting questions, and daily challenges - Personalized reminders based on selected time/day by the users	Reduction in drug use, Physical activity, Healthy food consumption, General health behaviors, Weight reduction
Social support	
Social support (unspecified) [24, 28–30, 32–35, 38, 39, 42, 48–52] - Support and encouragement through apps, text messages, testimonials, WhatsApp groups, and online community forums - Phone calls for counseling by clinicians and counselors - Clinicians or users were posting on Facebook or a team-based app	Healthy food consumption, Reduction in drug use, Physical activity, Weight reduction, General health behaviors
Social support (practical) [47] - Nutritionists' posts provide answers in real-time using we chat	Healthy food consumption
Social support (emotional) [28, 37] - Emotional support was provided by sending encouraging texts/calls to the users by the therapists	General health behaviors, Management of diseases
Comparison of behavior	
Social comparison [37, 40, 43, 53] - Users were asked to post achieved goals on Facebook or in the mobile app (e.g., Bulletin board)	Reduction in drug use, Physical activity, Weight reduction, General health behaviors
Information on other's approval [31] - Subjective roles correction in the form of gamified quiz	Reduction in drug use

(*continued*)

Table 2. (*continued*)

BCTs & strategies	Target conditions
Demonstration of behavior [31] - Animated stories were used to demonstrate behaviors	Reduction in drug use
Rewards & threats	
Material rewards [53] - Water bottle and a healthy cookbook on number of footsteps and likes on Facebook was given; however, this is not the digital mode of delivery	Management of diseases
Social reward [51] - A positive feedback message through a mobile application was sent	Physical activity in type II diabetic patients
Material Incentive [43, 54] - Participants were informed that they could get free nicotine replacement therapy from NHS smoking services - Money incentives were also provided for attending the session. However, none of the studies utilized any digital form	Reduction in drug use
Self-belief	
Focus on past success [43] - A message was sent via the app after a period of successful attempts (both intentional and non-intentional)	Reduction in drug use
Comparison of outcomes	
Credible source [32, 34, 42, 44, 47] - Lectures by experts in WeChat - Personalized help was provided by experts (phone calls, email, and mobile app)	Management of diseases, Physical activity, Reduction in drug use, Healthy food Consumption
Comparative imagining of future outcomes [43] - Positive stories from peers about life after smoking cessation and a prompt to consider future outcomes	Reduction in drug use
Repetition and substitution	
Habit formation [33] Monthly follow-up moments are created to encourage respondents to revisit the app (non-digital)	Healthy food consumption

(*continued*)

Table 2. (*continued*)

BCTs & strategies	Target conditions
Behavioral substitution [27] - Application suggesting context-specific replacement of behavior through a mobile application (e.g., where do it sit tool to suggest replacement of sitting behavior)	General health behaviors
Natural consequences	
Information on health consequences [31, 33–35, 47] - Information on health risk behaviors was sent via mobile applications (text), WeChat, and animated stories	Physical activity, Healthy food consumption, Reduction in drug use
Information on social and environmental consequences [31] - Presented a gamified quiz showing the consequence of drug use	Reduction in drug use
Salience of consequence [31] - Feedback on incorrect responses targeted correcting students' expectations about the drug's effect	Reduction in drug use
Anticipated regret [31] - Feedback on wrong answered responses targeted to increase awareness about the patient regret students may experience from drug use	Reduction in drug use
Regulation	
Conserving mental resources [33, 47] - Information on nutritional properties of oils, a list of fruits and vegetables, and recipes were uploaded in the mobile app	Healthy food consumption
Shaping Knowledge	
Instructions on how to perform a behavior [27, 30, 31, 34, 41, 43] - Animated stories and Text messages were sent to help users to learn behaviors - Mobile applications were used to teach various behaviors, e.g., Instructions on type and duration of exercise, estimating food portion, etc.	Physical activity, Healthy food consumption, Reduction in drug use, General health behaviors
Information on antecedents [27] - The mobile app provided information on behavior/emotional antecedents	General health behaviors

(*continued*)

Table 2. (*continued*)

BCTs & strategies	Target conditions
Identity	
Valued self-identity [31] - Story-telling exercise was suggested to produce self-statements of the life they want	Reduction in drug use
Framing [31, 43, 54] - Gamified quiz score to change expectations, altering beliefs using mobile applications and SNS	Reduction in drug use

4.5 Commonly Used BCT Groups

The 93 BCTs were combined into 16 groups. Figure 5 represents the frequency of different BCT groups used in studies. The most used group across studies were '*goals and planning*', '*social support*', '*feedback and monitoring*', and 'associations. However, some of the studies also coded as '*No group,*' i.e., either enough description was not available to code the strategy or the given description cannot be coded as strategy according to BCT taxonomy. '*Goals and planning*' is the most frequently used group, and it is often combined with all other groups except '*comparison of behavior*', '*reward and threat*', and '*social support*'. *Social support* is the second most frequently used group with all other groups except for '*comparison of behavior*', '*identity*', and 'self-belief'. '*Associations*' group is used with all other groups except for '*natural consequences*. '*Feedback and monitoring*' is used with most techniques except for '*shaping knowledge*', '*reward and threat*', '*regulation*', and '*identity*'.

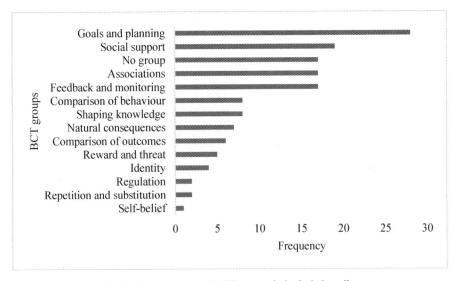

Fig. 5. Frequently used BCT groups in included studies

5 Discussion

The review aimed to explore how various BCTs were strategized in DHIs. 125 strategies were coded from 35 studies using behavior change taxonomy [15]. 33 behavior change techniques from taxonomy of 93 techniques were utilized in the included studies. The results indicated that the most frequently used techniques were *'prompts and cues'*, *'social support (unspecified technique)'*, *'goal setting (behavior technique)'*, and *'self-monitoring of behavior'* (almost present in 10–17 studies). Previous reviews [16–19] also found these techniques most frequently used. However, some techniques used frequently in other literature reviews were not highlighted in the current review. For example, Lyons [18] found *'social comparison'* and *'focus on the past success'* as the most used techniques. Similarly, Dunn [19] also found *'information about health consequences'* as the frequently used technique. Furthermore, the present study has not explored the link between various BCTs and intervention functions of BC. It is worth mentioning that *'Goal setting (behavior technique)'* and *'self-monitoring of behavior'* are the most frequently used techniques for different intervention functions such as enablement, education, training, incentivization/coercion. Similarly, *'social support (unspecified technique)'* is the most frequently used technique for enablement, and *'prompts and cues'* are mentioned as the most frequently used technique for education. Further studies need to specify the procedure of selecting BCTs to establish these links in more detail.

'Prompts and cues' was the most frequently used technique in the included studies. Sending reminders and notifications were the common strategies for *'Prompts and cues'* (Table 2). *'Prompts and cues'* are the stimuli designed to prompt action/reaction on specific behaviors from the users, also known as "Triggers" [55], in the form of SMS reminders/Push notifications/alerts. *'Prompts and cues'* help to learn and elicit new behaviors through forming new routines. SMS are the excellent feasible source of electric reminders [56]; similarly, Push notifications allows the delivery of personalized alters and timely updates through mobile application [36, 48]. In-depth personalization features can also be added to digital triggers; however, triggers could be a source of alert fatigue, habituation, or ignorance of triggers [55]. It is also essential to consider that only this technique from the 'associations" group has been used. Future studies are needed to explore new methods of strategizing other techniques from this group and in combination with other techniques.

'Social support (unspecified technique)' is the second most used technique defined as arranging social support (e.g., family, peers, or staff) related to behavior. The current review explored that encouragement and counselling were delivered through various social networks, phone, text messages, etc. (Table 2). Social support is one of the important factors for promoting behavior change [57]. The increased use of social media and messaging platforms have fostered a novel way of providing health-based interventions due to features such as, e.g., identity representation, peer grouping, and web-based social networking [58]. Various other modes of delivering social support such as via bulletin boards, or synchronous chat rooms, interactions in web-enabled interventions were also used in previous studies. Online support systems can also deliver techniques such as "social comparison". In the current review, few studies used social media to encourage comparison and competition using bulletin boards, encouraging to post achieved goals on Facebook [27, 42].

Self-regulation is one of the critical mechanisms in behavior change. It can be improved through various techniques such as goal setting, self-monitoring of behavior, reviewing progress feedback on behavior, problem-solving, etc. [59]. *'Goal Setting (behavior technique)'* and *'self-monitoring'* were also prominent in the included studies. Various strategies have been employed to deliver goal setting, such as in-app calculators, personalized goal setting, and predetermined goals in mobile applications. However, digital interventions lack incorporating 'action planning' techniques (included only in three studies). Therefore, incorporating action planning features, i.e., detailed planning on the performance of the behavior, can improve intervention design and effectiveness. New technologies enable users to use modern self-monitoring methods, e.g., self-tracking devices, wearable devices, in-app sensors are now commonly used ways of monitoring ones' behavior. Hennessy et al. [59] concluded that intervention components, such as self-monitoring, feedback, and goal setting, were successful, but their efficacy varied across health behaviors and populations. *'Goals and planning'* is the most frequently used group in the included studies, and different strategies from *'goals and planning'* and *'feedback and monitoring'* were used in the included studies. It is important to note that goals and planning' were not used with other 'Reward and threat' and "Social Support". Goal setting along with rewards and support can help to improve intervention results.

Three studies delivered techniques using non-digital modes such as *'material rewards'* by giving cookbooks/water bottles and *'material incentives'* using monetary incentives [53]. Rewards are commonly used techniques in interventions for behavior change (improve motivation). They are classified into two major categories, i.e., tangible rewards (e.g., material/ financial reward) and non-tangible rewards (e.g., congratulatory messages). However, using tangible rewards (monetary/material rewards) within digital interventions for behavior change is relatively new. For example, Ahn [60] explored the effect of the points-based reward system in gamification on children's physical activity. After successfully achieving the goals, children earned the points, and points can be used to buy more tricks for their virtual dogs. However, the results were not significant. Similarly, Mitchell [61] aimed to increase health knowledge rewarded users with loyalty points that can be redeemed for other consumables. Loyalty points can be earned through downloading the app, sharing with friends, and completing short education health quizzes. Therefore, new innovative strategies are needed to explore to deliver tangible rewards.

The focus of the current review was to explore behavioral change techniques that were strategized/implemented in digital interventions rather than the overall efficacy of the intervention techniques. However, only twenty-two studies reported the overall effectiveness of the intervention, out of which 14 studies suggested effective results. Few studies suggested improvement in the targeted outcomes but were not statistically significant, and effects declined over after some time [22, 48]. *'Social comparison'*, *'material reward & incentive)'*, *'information about health consequences'*, *'habit formation'*, *'social support (unspecified technique, emotional technique)'*, *'problem-solving'*, *'action planning'*, *'conserving mental resources'*, *instruction on how to perform the behavior'*, *'prompts/cues'*, *self-monitoring of behavior'*, *'goal setting (behavior technique)'*, *'Review behavior goals'*, *'Feedback on behavior'*, *'social, reward'*, *'framing/reframing'*, *'credible source'*, *and 'discrepancy between current behavior and goal'* produced effective results. It should be noticed that most of these techniques were used only in a few studies in a combination of other techniques *and, in some cases, also produced non-effective results.* Two important categories emerged from the current review, i.e., 'no BCT present', for strategies that cannot be coded into any specific category, e.g., educational material delivered via text and video. In addition, limited information presented in the studies about the intervention's descriptions resulted in another code, i.e., 'not enough information to code' for strategies, e.g., "goal setting, exercise scheduling and overcoming barriers". Lastly, limited information was given on the exact content of the intervention, i.e., what exactly is sent in a text message as prompts and cues?' Therefore, it is important to consider theories/frameworks of behavior change while selecting, strategizing, and reporting BCTs to produce effective and sustainable results. Furthermore, innovative ways of strategizing various BCTs are needed to be implemented in DHI.

Acknowledgment. This work was supported by the Tallinn University Research Fund grant TF4920.

References

1. Webb, J., et al.: Preliminary outcomes of a digital therapeutic intervention for smoking cessation in adult smokers: randomized controlled trial. JMIR Ment. Health 7(10), e22833 (2020). https://doi.org/10.2196/22833
2. Perski, O., Blandford, A., West, R., Michie, S.: Conceptualising engagement with digital behaviour change interventions: a systematic review using principles from critical interpretive synthesis. Transl. Behav. Med. 7(2), 254–267 (2016). https://doi.org/10.1007/s13142-016-0453-1
3. Cole-Lewis, H., Ezeanochie, N., Turgiss, J.: Understanding health behavior technology engagement: pathway to measuring digital behavior change interventions. JMIR Formative Res. 3(4), e14052 (2019). https://doi.org/10.2196/14052
4. Fulton, E., Kwah, K., Wild, S., Brown, K.: Lost in translation: transforming behaviour change techniques into engaging digital content and design for the StopApp. Healthcare 6(3), 75 (2018). https://doi.org/10.3390/healthcare6030075
5. Moller, A.C., et al.: Applying and advancing behavior change theories and techniques in the context of a digital health revolution: proposals for more effectively realizing untapped potential. J. Behav. Med. 40(1), 85–98 (2017). https://doi.org/10.1007/s10865-016-9818-7
6. Michie, S., Fixsen, D., Grimshaw, J.M., Eccles, M.P.: Specifying and reporting complex behaviour change interventions: the need for a scientific method. Implement. Sci. 4(1), 40 (2009). https://doi.org/10.1186/1748-5908-4-40
7. Zhang, S., Hamburger, E., Kahanda, S., Lyttle, M., Williams, R., Jaser, S.S.: Engagement with a text-messaging intervention improves adherence in adolescents with type 1 diabetes: brief report. Diab. Technol. Ther. 20, 386–389 (2018). https://doi.org/10.1089/dia.2018.0015
8. Markowitz, J.T., et al.: Text messaging intervention for teens and young adults with diabetes. J. Diab. Sci. Technol. 8, 1029–1034 (2014). https://doi.org/10.1177/1932296814540130
9. Conroy, D.E., Yang, C.-H., Maher, J.P.: Behavior change techniques in top-ranked mobile apps for physical activity. Am. J. Prev. Med. 46, 649–652 (2014). https://doi.org/10.1016/j.amepre.2014.01.010

10. Ch, Y., Jp, M., De, C.: Implementation of behavior change techniques in mobile applications for physical activity. Am. J. Prev. Med. **48**, 452–455 (2015). https://doi.org/10.1016/J.AMEPRE.2014.10.010

11. Michie, S., Johnston, M., Francis, J., Hardeman, W., Eccles, M.: From theory to intervention: mapping theoretically derived behavioural determinants to behaviour change techniques. Appl. Psychol. **57**, 660–680 (2008). https://doi.org/10.1111/J.1464-0597.2008.00341.X

12. Mummah, S.A., Robinson, T.N., King, A.C., Gardner, C.D., Sutton, S.: IDEAS (integrate, design, assess, and share): a framework and toolkit of strategies for the development of more effective digital interventions to change health behavior. J. Med. Internet Res. **18**(12), e317 (2016). https://doi.org/10.2196/jmir.5927

13. Skivington, K., et al.: A new framework for developing and evaluating complex interventions: update of Medical Research Council guidance. BMJ **374**, n2061 (2021). https://doi.org/10.1136/bmj.n2061

14. Michie, S., Atkins, L., West, R.: The behaviour change wheel: a guide to designing interventions. https://books.google.ee/books/about/The_behaiour_change_wheel_a_guide_to_de.html?id=1TGIrgEACAAJ&redir_esc=y. Accessed 03 May 2021

15. Michie, S., et al.: The behavior change technique taxonomy (v1) of 93 hierarchically clustered techniques: building an international consensus for the reporting of behavior change interventions. Ann. Behav. Med. **46**, 81–95 (2013). https://doi.org/10.1007/S12160-013-9486-6

16. Morrissey, E.C., Corbett, T.K., Walsh, J.C., Molloy, G.J.: Behavior change techniques in apps for medication adherence: a content analysis. Am. J. Prev. Med. **50**, e143–e146 (2016). https://doi.org/10.1016/J.AMEPRE.2015.09.034

17. Simeon, R., et al.: Behavior change techniques included in reports of social media interventions for promoting health behaviors in adults: content analysis within a systematic review. J. Med. Internet Res. **22**(6), e16002 (2020). https://doi.org/10.2196/16002

18. Lyons, E.J., Lewis, Z.H., Mayrsohn, B.G., Rowland, J.L.: Behavior change techniques implemented in electronic lifestyle activity monitors: a systematic content analysis. J. Med. Internet Res. **16**, e192 (2014). https://doi.org/10.2196/JMIR.3469

19. Dunn, E.E., Gainforth, H.L., Robertson-Wilson, J.E.: Behavior change techniques in mobile applications for sedentary behavior. Digit. Health **4**, 2055207618785798 (2018). https://doi.org/10.1177/2055207618785798

20. Schoeppe, S., et al.: Apps to improve diet, physical activity and sedentary behaviour in children and adolescents: a review of quality, features and behaviour change techniques. Int. J. Behav. Nutr. Phys. Act. **14**, 1–10 (2017). https://doi.org/10.1186/S12966-017-0538-3/TABLES/2

21. Lisetti, C., Amini, R., Yasavur, U., Rishe, N.: I can help you change! An empathic virtual agent delivers behavior change health interventions. ACM Trans. Manage. Inf. Syst. **4**(4), 1–28 (2013). https://doi.org/10.1145/2544103

22. Damen, I., van den Heuvel, R., Brankaert, R., Vos, S.: Advancing digital behavior change interventions by exploring a calendar-based suggestion system; advancing digital behavior change interventions by exploring a calendar-based suggestion system. In: European Conference on Cognitive Ergonomics 2021 (2021). https://doi.org/10.1145/3452853

23. Goodman, S., Morrongiello, B., Meckling, K.: A randomized, controlled trial evaluating the efficacy of an online intervention targeting vitamin D intake, knowledge and status among young adults. Int. J. Behav. Nutr. Phys. Act. **13**(1), 116 (2016). https://doi.org/10.1186/s12966-016-0443-1

24. Hartzler, A.L., et al.: Acceptability of a team-based mobile health (mHealth) application for lifestyle self-management in individuals with chronic illnesses. In: Annual International Conference of the IEEE Engineering in Medicine and Biology Society, pp. 3277–3281. IEEE Engineering in Medicine and Biology Society (2016). https://doi.org/10.1109/EMBC.2016.7591428

25. Bonn, S.E., Löf, M., Östenson, C.-G., Trolle Lagerros, Y.: App-technology to improve lifestyle behaviors among working adults - the Health Integrator study, a randomized controlled trial. BMC Pub. Health **19**, 273 (2019). https://doi.org/10.1186/s12889-019-6595-6

26. Recio-Rodríguez, J.I., et al.: Combined use of smartphone and smartband technology in the improvement of lifestyles in the adult population over 65 years: study protocol for a randomized clinical trial (EVIDENT-Age study). BMC Geriatr. **19**(1), 19 (2019). https://doi.org/10.1186/s12877-019-1037-y

27. Buman, M.P., et al.: BeWell24: development and process evaluation of a smartphone "app" to improve sleep, sedentary, and active behaviors in US Veterans with increased metabolic risk. Transl. Behav. Med. **6**(3), 438–448 (2015). https://doi.org/10.1007/s13142-015-0359-3

28. An, L.C., et al.: A randomized trial of an avatar-hosted multiple behavior change intervention for young adult smokers. JNCI Monogr. **2013**(47), 209–215 (2013). https://doi.org/10.1093/jncimonographs/lgt021

29. Patrick, K., et al.: Design and implementation of a randomized controlled social and mobile weight loss trial for young adults (project SMART). Contemp. Clin. Trials **37**, 10–18 (2014). https://doi.org/10.1016/j.cct.2013.11.001

30. Pellegrini, C.A., et al.: Design and protocol of a randomized multiple behavior change trial: make better choices 2 (MBC2). Contemp. Clin. Trials **41**, 85–92 (2015). https://doi.org/10.1016/j.cct.2015.01.009

31. Vasiliou, V.S., Byrne, M., et al.: Reducing Drug-use Harms among Higher Education Students: X Contextual-Behaviour Change Digital Intervention Development Using the Behaviour Change Wheel (2020). https://doi.org/10.21203/rs.3.rs-86503/v1

32. Bell, D.L., et al.: Computer-assisted motivational interviewing intervention to facilitate teen pregnancy prevention and fitness behavior changes: a randomized trial for young men. J. Adolesc. Health **62**, S72–S80 (2018). https://doi.org/10.1016/j.jadohealth.2017.06.015

33. Elbert, S.P., Dijkstra, A., Oenema, A.: A mobile phone app intervention targeting fruit and vegetable consumption: the efficacy of textual and auditory tailored health information tested in a randomized controlled trial. J. Med. Internet Res. **18**, e147 (2016). https://doi.org/10.2196/jmir.5056

34. Garrison, K.A., et al.: Craving to quit: a randomized controlled trial of smartphone app-based mindfulness training for smoking cessation. Nicotine Tob. Res. **22**, 324–331 (2020). https://doi.org/10.1093/ntr/nty126

35. Recio-Rodríguez, J.I., et al.: Combined use of smartphone and smartband technology in the improvement of lifestyles in the adult population over 65 years: study protocol for a randomized clinical trial (EVIDENT-Age study). BMC Geriatr. **19**, 19 (2019). https://doi.org/10.1186/s12877-019-1037-y

36. Stacey, F., et al.: A cluster randomized controlled trial evaluating the impact of tailored feedback on the purchase of healthier foods from primary school online canteens. Nutrients **13**(7), 2405 (2021). https://doi.org/10.3390/nu13072405

37. Burner, E., et al.: Design and patient characteristics of the randomized controlled trial TExT-MED + FANS a test of mHealth augmented social support added to a patient-focused text-messaging intervention for emergency department patients with poorly controlled diabetes. Contemp. Clin. Trials **80**, 1–8 (2019). https://doi.org/10.1016/j.cct.2019.03.003

38. Forman, D.E., LaFond, K., Panch, T., Allsup, K., Manning, K., Sattelmair, J.: Utility and efficacy of a smartphone application to enhance the learning and behavior goals of traditional cardiac rehabilitation: a feasibility study. J. Cardiopulm. Rehabil. Prev. **34**, 327–334 (2014). https://doi.org/10.1097/HCR.0000000000000058

39. Hebden, L., Cook, A., van der Ploeg, H.P., King, L., Bauman, A., Allman-Farinelli, M.: A mobile health intervention for weight management among young adults: a pilot randomised controlled trial. J. Hum. Nutr. Diet. Official J. Br. Diet. Assoc. **27**, 322–332 (2014). https://doi.org/10.1111/jhn.12155

40. Lee, M.-K., Lee, D.Y., Ahn, H.-Y., Park, C.-Y.: A novel user utility score for diabetes management using tailored mobile coaching: secondary analysis of a randomized controlled trial. JMIR Mhealth Uhealth **9**, e17573 (2021). https://doi.org/10.2196/17573

41. Szabó, C., Ócsai, H., Csabai, M., Kemény, L.: A randomised trial to demonstrate the effectiveness of electronic messages on sun protection behaviours. J. Photochem. Photobiol. B Biol. **149**, 257–264 (2015). https://doi.org/10.1016/j.jphotobiol.2015.06.006

42. Chiang, N., Guo, M., Amico, K.R., Atkins, L., Lester, R.T.: Interactive two-way mHealth interventions for improving medication adherence: an evaluation using the behaviour change wheel framework. JMIR Mhealth Uhealth **6**(4), e87 (2018) https://mhealth.jmir.org/2018/4/e87. 6, e9187 (2018). https://doi.org/10.2196/MHEALTH.9187

43. Fulton, E., Brown, K., Kwah, K., Wild, S.: StopApp: using the behaviour change wheel to develop an app to increase uptake and attendance at NHS stop smoking services. Healthcare **4**(2), 31 (2016). https://doi.org/10.3390/healthcare4020031

44. Mackenzie, K., Goyder, E., Eves, F.: Acceptability and feasibility of a low-cost, theory-based and co-produced intervention to reduce workplace sitting time in desk-based university employees. BMC Pub. Health **15**, 1294 (2015). https://doi.org/10.1186/s12889-015-2635-z

45. Blake, H., Suggs, L.S., Coman, E., Aguirre, L., Batt, M.E.: Active8! technology-based intervention to promote physical activity in hospital employees. Am. J. Health Prom. AJHP **31**, 109–118 (2017). https://doi.org/10.4278/ajhp.140415-QUAN-143

46. Schmidtke, K.A., et al.: An exploratory randomised controlled trial evaluating text prompts in Lebanon to encourage health-seeking behaviour for hypertension. Int. J. Clin. Pract. **75**, e13669 (2021). https://doi.org/10.1111/ijcp.13669

47. Zhu, R., Xu, X., Zhao, Y., Sharma, M., Shi, Z.: Decreasing the use of edible oils in China using WeChat and theories of behavior change: study protocol for a randomized controlled trial. Trials **19**(1), 631 (2018). https://doi.org/10.1186/s13063-018-3015-7

48. Inauen, J., et al.: Using smartphone-based support groups to promote healthy eating in daily life: a randomised trial. Appl. Psychol. Health Well Being **9**, 303–323 (2017). https://doi.org/10.1111/APHW.12093

49. Looyestyn, J., Kernot, J., Boshoff, K., Maher, C.: A Web-based, social networking beginners' running intervention for adults aged 18 to 50 years delivered via a facebook group: randomized controlled trial. J. Med. Internet Res. **20**, e67 (2018). https://doi.org/10.2196/jmir.7862

50. Ramsey, R.R., et al.: A systematic evaluation of asthma management apps examining behavior change techniques. J. Allergy Clin. Immunol. Pract. **7**(8), 2583–2591 (2019). https://doi.org/10.1016/j.jaip.2019.03.041

51. Bonn, S.E., et al.: App-technology to increase physical activity among patients with diabetes type 2 - the DiaCert-study, a randomized controlled trial. BMC Pub. Health **18**, 119 (2018). https://doi.org/10.1186/s12889-018-5026-4

52. Oeldorf-Hirsch, A., High, A.C., Christensen, J.L.: Count your calories and share them: health benefits of sharing mHealth information on social networking sites. Health Commun. **34**, 1130–1140 (2019). https://doi.org/10.1080/10410236.2018.1465791

53. Key, K.V., Adegboyega, A., Bush, H., Aleshire, M.E., Contreras, O.A., Hatcher, J.: #CRCFREE: using social media to reduce colorectal cancer risk in rural adults. Am. J. Health Behav. **44**, 353–363 (2020). https://doi.org/10.5993/AJHB.44.3.8

54. Namkoong, K., Nah, S., Record, R.A., van Stee, S.K.: Communication, reasoning, and planned behaviors: unveiling the effect of interactive communication in an anti-smoking social media campaign. Health Commun. **32**, 41–50 (2017). https://doi.org/10.1080/10410236.2015.1099501

55. Muench, F., Baumel, A.: More than a text message: dismantling digital triggers to curate behavior change in patient-centered health interventions. J. Med. Internet Res. **19**(5), e147 (2017). https://www.jmir.org/2017/5/e147. 19, e7463 (2017). https://doi.org/10.2196/JMIR.7463

56. Hernández-Reyes, A., Molina-Recio, G., Molina-Luque, R., Romero-Saldaña, M., Cámara-Martos, F., Moreno-Rojas, R.: Effectiveness of PUSH notifications from a mobile app for improving the body composition of overweight or obese women: a protocol of a three-Armed randomized controlled trial. BMC Med. Inform. Decis. Mak. **20**, 1–10 (2020). https://doi.org/10.1186/S12911-020-1058-7/FIGURES/4

57. Greaney, M.L., Puleo, E., Sprunck-Harrild, K., Haines, J., Houghton, S.C., Emmons, K.M.: Social support for changing multiple behaviors: factors associated with seeking support and the impact of offered support. Health Educ. Behav. **45**, 198–206 (2018). https://doi.org/10.1177/1090198117712333

58. Elaheebocus, S.M.R.A., Weal, M., Morrison, L., Yardley, L.: Peer-based social media features in behavior change interventions: systematic review. J. Med. Internet Res. **20**(2), e20 (2018). https://www.jmir.org/2018/2/e20. 20, e8342 (2018). https://doi.org/10.2196/JMIR.8342

59. Hennessy, E.A., Johnson, B.T., Acabchuk, R.L., McCloskey, K., Stewart-James, J.: Self-regulation mechanisms in health behaviour change: a systematic meta-review of meta-analyses, 2006–2017. Health Psychol. Rev. **14**, 6 (2020). https://doi.org/10.1080/17437199.2019.1679654

60. Ahn, S.J. (Grace), Johnsen, K., Ball, C.: Points-based reward systems in gamification impact children's physical activity strategies and psychological needs. Health Educ. Behav. **46**, 417–425 (2019). https://doi.org/10.1177/1090198118818241

61. Mitchell, M., et al.: Uptake of an incentive-based mHealth app: process evaluation of the carrot rewards app. JMIR Mhealth Uhealth **5**(5), e70 (2017). https://mhealth.jmir.org/2017/5/e70. 5, e7323 (2017). https://doi.org/10.2196/MHEALTH.7323

Usability Testing of a Gratitude Application for Promoting Mental Well-Being

Felwah Alqahtani[1,2](✉) ⓘ, Alaa Alslaity[1] ⓘ, and Rita Orji[1] ⓘ

[1] Dalhousie University, Halifax, NS, Canada
{Felwah.alqahtani,Alaa.alslaity,Rita.orji}@dal.ca
[2] King Khalid University, Abha, Saudi Arabia

Abstract. Despite the increasing number of mental health applications (apps), the perceived usability of these apps from the viewpoint of end users has rarely been studied. App usability can impact users' acceptance and engagement with a self-guided mobile health intervention. This study aims to evaluate the usability of a gratitude application called *Be Grateful* from the perspective of end-users to identify existing design, functionality, and usability issues and elicit users' views and experiences with the app. We designed the app and conducted usability testing, a combination of interview and questionnaire study of 14 participants who have experienced mental health issues based on self-diagnosis. Participants used *Be Grateful* app for ten days, completed the System Usability Scale (SUS) validated measure of system usability, and were interviewed at the end of the study. We found that the end-user appreciated the simplicity, straightforwardness of the app and provided positive feedback about the layout. Participants also gave the system high scores on the SUS usability measure (mean = 83.93). Results indicated that the *Be Grateful* app is usable and will be more likely to be adopted and used by users. Participants were generally excited about the app and eager to use it. This paper reports the lessons learned from the design and evaluation of the app's usability. We discuss design implications for future work in the area of designing interactive mobile apps for health and wellness, with a focus on mental health interventions.

Keywords: Persuasive technology · Usability testing · Mental health · Mobile applications · Apps · Design implications

1 Introduction

Usability, users' satisfaction, and engagement are paramount to the success of any interactive software application (app). If the users find the app easy to use, useful, and engaging, they are more likely to use it, which will, in turn, lead to the app achieving its design goals. Therefore, app developers should consider these factors throughout the development process. The techniques used to evaluate a product to assure users' satisfaction are known as usability testing. This testing gives early feedback on how real users will interact with the system, which helps avoid changes in advanced stages of the system development. Usability testing also supports user-centric design by revealing

© The Author(s), under exclusive license to Springer Nature Switzerland AG 2022
M. Kurosu (Ed.): HCII 2022, LNCS 13304, pp. 296–312, 2022.
https://doi.org/10.1007/978-3-031-05412-9_21

users' expectations, which, in turn, assists in selecting the most appropriate and best-performing designs and features. Thus, usability testing is seen as a mandatory practice in developing software systems [25]. The importance of usability testing is shared among several domains. Wichansky [38] stated, *"Industry experience indicates that usability testing is alive and well in computer, software, communications, consumer products, and media development"*. Besides, there is almost a consensus that usability testing is the best method for investigating systems' usability [17]. Previous studies recommended that usability testing should be done carefully and be documented completely [23, 24]. Despite the exponential increase in the number of mobile health (mHealth) apps, only a few studies have reported and published usability testing results.

This work aims to test the usability of *Be Grateful* app, a persuasive intervention app developed to promote users to be mentally and emotionally healthy by affirming the goodness or positive things in their lives. We conducted usability testing to identify existing design, functionality, and usability issues and elicit users' views and experiences. Fourteen participants were involved in the study. All participants have experienced mental health issues based on self-diagnosis. Participants were asked to use *Be Grateful* app for ten days and complete the System Usability Scale (SUS), a validated measure of system usability [27]. We used a questionnaire method because it is the most predominant method in mobile health (mHealth) apps [22]. However, questionnaires provide an overall usability evaluation but do not define the specific problems to be addressed. Therefore, in addition to the SUS, we also used a qualitative method because it is more helpful in identifying the exact issues [22]. Particularly, after using the app and completing the questionnaire, participants were interviewed at the end of the study. Finally, a thematic analysis was done to analyze users' responses to the interview.

Based on the usability testing results, we found that the end-user appreciated the simplicity, straightforwardness of the app and provided positive feedback about the layout. Participants also gave the system high scores on the SUS usability measure (mean = 83.93). Results indicated the *Be Grateful* app is usable and will be more likely to be adopted and used by the users. Participants were generally excited about the app and eager to use it. This paper reports the lessons learned from the design and evaluation of the usability of the app. We discuss design implications for future work in the area of designing interactive mobile apps for health and wellness, with a focus on mental health interventions.

2 Background

This section presents an overview of mental health intervention and usability testing.

2.1 Mental Health Interventions

Mental health and emotional well-being research in human-computer interaction (HCI) is rapidly growing. There are various types of interventions designed to prompt mental health and emotional well-being. First, some mental health apps are designed to predict users' mental health issues. For example, Canzian and Musolesi [14] designed a mental health app to predict users' depressive moods by collecting mobility patterns of 28 users and their depressive moods. The results showed a significant correlation between the changes in mobility metrics and the variations in users' depressive moods.

Other mental health apps are designed to improve users' awareness and understanding of their mental health issues by collecting their personal data. For example, Bardram et al. [9] designed an app that allows users with bipolar disorder to track their mood and other factors called "MONARCA" app. They conducted a study to assess the effectiveness of MONARCA app compared with paper-based forms. The results showed that the app was easy to use, and useful and increased adherence compared with paper-based forms.

Moreover, some mental health apps are designed based on Cognitive Behavioral Therapy (CBT) to promote positive change in mental welling. For example, Bakker et al. [8] conducted an evaluation study to improve mental health using a mobile app called MoodMission, which was built based on CBT for mood and anxiety issues. The results showed that the MoodMission app helps to improve well-being, the ability to cope, and self-efficacy for people who experienced moderate depression or anxiety.

Finally, some other mental health apps are designed based on positive psychology activities that aim to improve mental well-being, cultivate positive feelings, behaviors, or cognitions such as practicing optimistic thinking, expressing gratitude, and practicing kindness. For example, Coelhoso et al. [15] conducted a study to evaluate the effectiveness of an app developed to promote stress management and well-being among working women compared with a control app. They found that the group who used the wellbeing app presented a significant increase in work-related well-being and a reduction in overall stress. Many studies investigated the impact of positive psychology interventions on different aspects of mental well-being, such as happiness, engagement, positive emotions, and others [33, 35]. Moreover, two meta-analyses reviews show the possible effect of positive psychology interventions on promoting mental wellbeing [10, 36]. However, White et al. [37] conducted a meta-analysis and showed that the impact of positive psychology interventions on well-being is overestimated. Nevertheless, among all three meta-analysis studies, gratitude interventions are perceived as one of the most effective positive psychology interventions. In addition, a recent meta-analysis of gratitude interventions showed the effect of gratitude interventions to promote mental wellbeing [16]. Consequently, we designed *Be Grateful* app based on gratitude interventions.

2.2 Usability Testing

Usability testing is "*any technique in which users interact systematically with a product or system under controlled conditions to perform a goal-oriented task in an applied scenario, and some behavioral data are collected*" [38]. It was first introduced in the late 1980s, but it became popular in the late 1990s [13]38. Since the advent of usability engineering, usability testing has become a common and widely used method for evaluating users' acceptance and perception of systems or products. Moreover, it has been widely recognized by researchers and practitioners as a fundamental method to evaluate products and systems. Usability testing mainly aims to assist developers in delivering usable, appreciated, and engaging products that are more likely to be accepted and used by the target audience. Researchers identified the main goal of usability testing as "…

to identify and rectify usability deficiencies existing in computer-based and electronic equipment and their accompanying support materials prior to release" [31].

Usability is one of the key factors in the successful implementation of mobile health (mHealth) apps, as it is for other apps. There are several methods for conducting usability testing of mHealth apps. According to a review by Maramba et al. [22], six major usability testing approaches are followed in mHealth literature: questionnaires, task completion, 'Think-Aloud', interviews, heuristic testing, and focus groups. The study also found that the majority of the studies use one or two methods of testing, and questionnaires are the most commonly used usability testing methods in health-related studies [22]. Thus, we used a combination of usability testing methods, namely, the System Usability Scale and semi-structured interviews to evaluate the usability of *Be Grateful* app.

3   Gratitude Intervention Design and Development

The *Be Grateful* is an app-based gratitude intervention that promotes users to be mentally/emotionally healthy by affirming the goodness or good things in an individual's life. The app design was informed by three studies.

First Study: We conducted a systematic review of 103 apps from app stores and identified various persuasive features employed in their design. We used some keywords such as "mental health," "mood," "emotions," "stress", "anxiety," and "depression" during the search on the App Store and Google Play. We also used various combinations of the keywords joined using the conjunctions "OR" and "AND". The initial search returned 437 apps. After filtering these apps and excluding nonrelated apps, a total of 103 apps were included in our analysis based on the selection criteria. Two researchers independently downloaded and reviewed the 103 apps to identify persuasive features using the Persuasive Systems Design (PSD) model and Behavior Change Techniques (BCTs). The researchers then met to agree on the initial codes. Any discrepancies between the two researchers were resolved by involving a third researcher to mediate and ensure an agreement is reached. The systematic review of 103 apps shows that self-monitoring, personalization, reminder, rewards, and normative influence emerged as the top five most frequently implemented persuasive features in mental health apps [1].

Second Study: Building on the findings from the first study, we conducted six focus groups with 32 participants to uncover more insight regarding mental health app features. All participants have experienced mental health issues such as stress, low mood, negative thought, worry, fear, and anxiety based on self-diagnosis. The focus-group sessions were designed to unfold over three stages: 1) we asked participants about their experiences with mental health issues to explore the ways they manage symptoms and overcome their issues; 2) we gathered participants' viewpoints regarding two existing mental health apps (Happify app and the Self-Help Anxiety Management app[1]) to understand their opinions, preferences, ideas, experiences, and needs; and 3) we then asked participants to engage in a design session where they each sketched a design for their

---

[1] https://apps.apple.com/us/app/happify-for-stress-worry/id730601963. https://apps.apple.com/ca/app/self-help-for-anxiety-management/id666767947.

ideal mental health and wellbeing mobile app [5]. The findings show that the following features are important for users of mental health apps: personalization, customization, self-monitoring, contact for help, social support and providing encouragement, praise, relaxation exercises, and audio, trusted information, suggestions, distraction tools, lock features, and privacy policy [5].

Third Study: We implemented the common features that emerged from the first and second studies in persuasive app prototypes promoting mental health. Then we conducted a large-scale study of 561 participants who have experienced mental health issues such as stress, low mood, negative thought, worry, fear, and anxiety based on self-diagnosis to evaluate the perceived persuasiveness of the implemented feature. The perceived persuasiveness of a persuasive feature or a system is an estimation of its ability to promote the desired behavior [26]. The results show that Self-Monitoring, Reminders, Social Support, and Suggestions were perceived as the most effective persuasive features [2]. Consequently, the *Be Grateful* app includes all these four persuasive strategies.

3.1 Implementation

Based on the three studies mentioned above, we designed and developed the *Be Grateful* app using Flutter as a development platform. Flutter is an open-source, multi-platform mobile SDK that can be used to build an app on both iOS and Android, using a single codebase, and uses "Dart" as the programming language. *Be Grateful* is a mobile mental health app specifically designed based on gratitude intervention to enhance users' mental wellbeing. *Be Grateful* app encourages users to express what they are grateful for daily. It mainly involves the following features: Entering gratitude, self-monitoring, and visualization of the feeling, social community in the app, reminder notification, and suggestion notification. Figure 1 shows screenshots of the *Be Grateful* app. The app

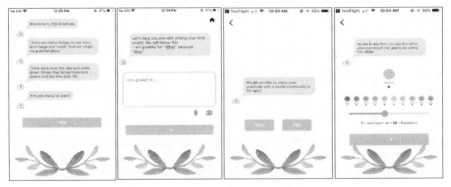

(a): Introduce user to gratitude

(b): Allow users to enter their gratitude

(c): Ask user if they would like to share their gratitude

(d): Ask users to rate their feelings

Fig. 1. Interfaces of the Be Grateful app

works as follows: First, it introduces users to gratitude interventions by explaining what they need to do (Fig. 1 (a)). Then it guides users to write down what they are grateful for and allows them to take a picture/attached it with their gratitude (Fig. 1(b)). The app then asks users if they would like to share their gratitude in the social community in the app (Fig. 1 (c)) and asks them to rate their mood after expressing gratitude using the faces slider rating (Fig. 1 (d)).

The *Be Grateful* app also contains the following screens: a journal screen showing users gratitude entries and pictures users attach or capture (Fig. 2), a mood summary screen enabling users to see their feeling pattern as column chart weekly and monthly (Fig. 3), and social community screen allowing users to see their shared gratitude and read others gratitude and like them (Fig. 4). In addition, *Be Grateful* reminds users of their previous gratitude by showing them an affirmation of their exact gratitude or a positive quote related to their gratitude (Fig. 5). For example: if users were grateful for having a family on one day, the app shows a quote about the family on the morning of the next day (the default of the affirmation is 7 am, but the user can change it). If the user's gratitude does not match the positive quote database, the app shows what users were grateful for from the previous day. The app also reminds them to enter their gratitude (Fig. 6) and encourages users to perform some acts of kindness by showing them as a daily notification (Fig. 7).

Fig. 2. The journal showing users gratitude entries

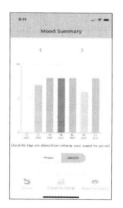

Fig. 3. Mood summary showing users feelings over time

Fig. 4. Social community of the app

Fig. 5. Affirmation notification

Fig. 6. Encouraging to enter gratitude

Fig. 7. Suggesting doing act of kindness

4 Methodology

4.1 Study Design

We employed a mixed-method design (qualitative and quantitative data). The goal of using such a design is to increase the depth of evaluation and to improve the reliability and validity of our results [19]. Specifically, we evaluated the usability of *Be Grateful* app using a qualitative interview along with a quantitative study. Qualitative interviews allow for a more comprehensive understanding of participants' experience and encourage participants to think about ways to improve usability, identify usability issues and obtain further information about what participants like and dislike about the app. Before the interview, we presented the System Usability Scale (SUS) scale that has been used widely for usability testing in eHealth studies [22] and is found to be a reliable and valid tool for evaluating the usability of mobile apps [20]. It consists of a 10-item questionnaire with a 5-point Likert-type scale ranging from 1 = strongly disagree to 5 = strongly agree.

We recruited 14 participants (age range of most of our participants [93%] was 18–34 years; eight males and six females) who have experienced mental health issues such as stress, low mood, negative thought and mood, and so on based on self-diagnosis. A total of 4 participants have used a mental health app to promote their mental health, and the most mental health issue that participants had experienced was stress. Table 1 shows participants' demographics for the study.

During the interview, we asked participants about their overall views of the app, what they liked, disliked, their opinion of each feature and if there is any usability issue they faced, and how we can improve the usability of the app. This study has been approved by the research ethics board at Dalhousie University.

Table 1. Participants' demographic information

Total participants = 14	
Gender	Females (43%), Males (57%),
Age	18–24 (50%), 25–34 (43%), 35–44 (7%)
Education	Bachelor's degree (71%), Master's degree (21%), High School or equivalent (7%)
Mental health issue	Stress (23%), worry (17%), negative feelings (13%), negative thoughts (19%), low moods (15%), fear (8%), and anxiety (6%)

4.2 Data Collection and Analysis

The study evolved through three phases: First, we obtained participant consent and demographics before using the app. Second, participants who signed the consent form were given the *Be Grateful* app. These users were asked to use the app for ten days. During these ten days, we asked participants to express their gratitude daily using the app. At the end of the 10th day, we asked participants to fill out the SUS scale. Finally, we met the participants for an online interview. The interviews were audio-recorded and transcribed for coding.

The data collected through the online interviews were analyzed using thematic analysis. The thematic analysis allows us to analyze the data in a systematic manner to uncover patterns in the text while considering the context of what participants said, which helps to inform our interpretation of the data more accurately. A thematic analysis was undertaken as outlined by Braun and Clarke [19]: (1) becoming familiar with the data, (2) generating initial codes, (3) searching for themes, (4) defining themes, (5) iteratively reviewing themes, and (6) writing up the results.

Specifically, two researchers individually coded sample transcripts by reading and re-reading the sample transcripts (iteratively) to identify codes using open coding. The two researchers then met to compare the initial codes, which were expanded, developed, and modified as new codes emerged. Any discrepancies between the two researchers were resolved through discussion. The initial codes were used to code the remaining transcripts, and they were extended as necessary. For creating the themes, the two researchers systematically refined the themes by going back and forth between the data and the coding framework. We provide quotes as specific examples from each theme within the results section. To preserve participants' privacy and anonymize the responses, we identify participants by anonymized IDs (e.g., P1, P2, etc.). We also used descriptive statistics to summarize the quantitative data from the SUS.

5 Results

5.1 Quantitative Results

Overall, SUS scores and item means were reported to provide a complete view of the usability of the gratitude app. The score was calculated using the method described in

[11]. The mean SUS score was 83.93, which indicates that the usability of the app was above average [11], and the app has higher usability than 73% of all products tested [32].

5.2 Qualitative Results

After setting the initial codes, revisiting them, and updating when required, our thematic analysis resulted in defining three themes: functionality of gratitude app, the user interface of gratitude app, and design of gratitude app. The following subsections define each one of these themes and provide sample quotes as examples.

Functionality of the Gratitude App. This theme reflected how the participants appreciated the simple and straightforward functionality of the gratitude app. Based on our analysis, all participants highlighted simplicity and ease of use as one of the desirable characteristics of the gratitude app that they liked.

For example, *"It's **really simple. So, this is the beauty of the app**, I like it. It is very simple and easy to use"* [P1].

Moreover, participants mentioned that process of entering gratitude in the app is straightforward and does not require too much effort to be used or understood.

For example, *"It is very simple. You don't have to think a lot or what you need to do. **So, it is something very straightforward**. You just open the app and it's right there to write what you're grateful for and it gives you a template. So, **I love that because I didn't have to worry about like, okay, this is another task that I need to think about, and to put a lot of energy into that** because I already have a lot of other stress and things in my life. So that's why I liked it"* [P3].

User Interface of the Gratitude App. This theme reflects users' opinions about the overall appearance of the app design. Most participants liked the well-structured and visually appealing UI of the app.

For example, *"I really enjoyed using the app because the look of the app was really interesting to me and I **love the green aesthetic of the app and the design overall**"* [P10].

*"I really like how it looks. **It's very visually pleasing. It's a calming theme. The color scheme is really nice.** Everything laid out very well"* [P2].

Design of the Gratitude App. This theme reflects the most common issues and points mentioned by participants regarding the usability of the app liked features and requested features to improve the usability of the app. It is worth noting that the gratitude app consists of five features: general design of gratitude intervention, self-monitoring and visualization of the feeling, social community in the app, reminder notification, and suggestion notification. In the following subsections, we provide users' feedback regarding the design of each feature.

General Design of Gratitude Intervention. Entering what participants are grateful for each day helped most participants improve their mood by helping them remember and reflect on good things that happened to them throughout the day. However, 4 out of 14 participants felt that writing gratitude each day is not for them because they felt that expressing gratitude is a personal feeling and is not for recording in an app. Below are some sample comments from participants.

"For somebody like me who is not used to logging their own gratitude using an app. So, **it may not be an everyday thing for me***"* [P5].

"It might not be something I would use myself. I wouldn't be that much willing to have an app close to me. So, **like expressing gratitude, these are sort of somewhat personal feelings or expressions that I would keep to myself** *"* [P2].

Participants liked attaching a picture with their gratitude and felt this made the journaling gratitude more personal for them. Few participants liked the affirmation that reminds participants of their previous gratitude entry by showing them a positive quote related to their gratitude or their exact gratitude. Below are some sample related comments from participants.

"I like the feature that allows me **to add a photo to my gratitude***. So, it gives more sense of personality for me"* [P1].

"It's good to have something to **remind you about good things that have happened to you***"* [P10].

However, most of the participants were confused regarding using "affirmation" as the title for the notification, and they did not know what it means. Thus, some participants requested that we change the title to be more understandable for the general population.

For example, "I had **some confusion regarding what's the meaning of affirmation***"* [P6].

"It's confusing when you look at affirmation… *Break it down to something that can be understood by the general people"* [P4].

Moreover, two participants requested including gamification techniques to increase users' engagement in the app.

For example, *"If maybe there are certain things in the app that can keep me engaged, maybe something that like* **introducing things around gamification and the app that can probably nudge people each day to do something for a reward"** [P5].

Self-monitoring and Visualizing Feelings. Most participants appreciated using the faces slider rating to rate their feelings. They highlighted that using faces slider rating made it easy to rate their feeling after expressing gratitude. Below are some sample related comments from participants.

"I like the monitoring most; I like the faces slider because it was easy to understand and to tell how I was feeling because of the colors and also the numbers and the faces. I think it was pretty easy" [P3].

Some participants requested to track their feeling before expressing gratitude and after to see how their feelings change.

For example, *"I would like to suggest that the app asks me my mood first, like, you know, ask me to rate my mood from 1 to 10"* [P6].

"It would be nice to have a pre mood's assessment" [P7].

For visualizing the feelings, even though some participants liked the visualizing section because it helped them see how their feelings improved over the ten days, most participants requested some improvement in the visualization to be more usable. Participants were confused regarding the month view and week view and preferred showing the whole month in one screen for the month view instead of tapping to see the rest of the days.

For example, *"For the month view in the visualization, you can compress the chart to show the entire days of the month in one screen"* [P5].

Participants also requested that we show the name of the month on the top of the visualization. So, when users move from month to month, they do not need to look at the x-axis to know which month they were in. They also requested to show the faces instead of a number in the graph because they might forget what the number means.

For example, *"You know when you have the front and the back arrow so you can move from one month to the other month. I think it's good to have the months that you are dealing with as a title there"* [P5].

"I suggested that you use the faces in the graph, just to give another option of what the numbers mean" [P3].

Some participants mentioned that using a bar chart for visualizing feelings would not be effective. Instead, they prefer using another visualization such as calendar visualization and showing what participants were grateful for by clicking on the faces in the calendar.

For example," *You may keep the analytics screen as a Month view only, showing a calendar of an entire month and an emoji on each day depending on the mood of the user"* [P6].

Social Community in the App. Based on our thematic analysis, most participants appreciated the social community feature because it encouraged them to share their gratitude and made them think more about good things in their lives which they took for granted while reading what others are grateful for.

For example, *"**In the community feature**, I got an opportunity to think of others and what they are grateful for which **made me think more about the good things in my life**" [P6].*

*"I like the fact that it's **showing me what people share that they were grateful for. I know when I read that, sometimes I take for granted and I see that people are grateful for it**" [P13].*

Another feature that the participants appreciate is the anonymity of the social community.

For example, *"The thing I like very much is that **there is no way to know who likes your gratitude on social community**" [P1].*

However, one participant felt that seeing how many likes they got added a cognitive load in their mind. Also, few participants felt that gratitude is something personal, so they hesitated or did not prefer to share it with the social community in the app. As a result, they appreciated how the app gave them an option to share their gratitude in the app.

For example, *"I found that **sharing in social community added a cognitive load in my mind** because I started to measure my gratitude by the number of likes that I would get" [P10].*

*"For somebody like me. **I just didn't feel like posting my gratitude out there**. I mean, I liked it, but I see that **something personal in a way**" [P14].*

For example, *"There are other things which are **personal to me that I did not share with the community**" [P4].*

Moreover, participants suggested some improvements in the social community, such as the ability to interact with other users, inviting people to the social community, and adding more reactions.

For example, *"There **should be a way of interacting aside from just liking in social community**" [P11].*

*". Now, you have only heart reaction in the social community, but **you can add more reaction such as a flower or a green leaf or a smile**" [P10].*

Reminder Notification. On our app, we have a reminder to remind users to enter their gratitude, and this reminder includes encouragement statements to motivate users to enter their gratitude. Most participants liked how the app encourages and reminds them at the same time to enter their gratitude. However, they requested that the app keep reminding them to enter their gratitude if they missed it before the end of the day.

For example: *"if I have not logged by 7 pm, for example, **there should be a different or another notification that would tell me to log**" [P5].*

Suggestion Notification. The app notifies users with some suggestions that randomly suggest performing some act of kindness. Some participants liked the variety and the content of the suggestion and how they were easy to do. Other participants requested some improvement by personalizing the suggestions and receiving the suggestion based on the user's mood or when they wanted.

For example, *"There were some **useful notifications**. **I remember the one, which encourages me to do some act of kindness using a motivation quote. I really like this suggestion"** [P2].

*"You can improve the app by **providing personalized recommendations**, like for example, using what I type in and also what the others typed similar to what I've typed to give a personalized recommendation"* [P4].

6 Discussion

Evidence-based interventions, such as mHealth apps to promote mental wellbeing, are important to enhance the quality of life. Although mHealth offers a promising way to deliver the interventions, there are still high levels of drop-outs/attrition for this form of intervention [6, 30]. One potential reason for abandoning mental health apps is poor usability, particularly when the app is designed based on a self-help way [4].

In this study, we conducted usability testing of a mental health app called *Be Grateful* that aims to promote mental wellbeing by focusing on good and positive things in people's lives by expressing gratitude. *Be Grateful* app designed using persuasive design strategies to improve user experience. This study aimed to identify usability concerns and improve the current design of the *Be Grateful* app. Moreover, perceived usability data were obtained from end-users to evaluate preferences and perceptions of the app.

6.1 Principal Findings and Design Implications

Overall, participants gave the *Be Grateful* app high scores on validated usability scales. They also provided many positive comments on the app design. We found that users perceived an easy-to-use interface and straightforward functionality as the most important usability features in the app. We also found that the clear and visually appealing design of the user interface was integral to the level of usability. The findings of this study are consistent with previous research, which found that ease of use and simplicity of the app were the most important characteristics of mental health apps that were highlighted by users [3]. Moreover, a visual appeal was among the most important features of a mental health app that participants considered in previous studies [5, 28]. **Therefore, if the mental health app is difficult to use, users may cease to use the app even if it is useful. Users do not like using an app that may add to their stress.**

Most participants liked practicing gratitude and the way the app reminded them of their previous gratitude. They also felt that their mental well-being improved. However, some people think recording their gratitude in the app makes it no longer personal or private. This concern probably has to do with privacy issues, especially for privacy-conscious people. Although we provided social features that allow users to share their daily gratitude if they would like to, it seems that some users still don't feel free to share it with the app. This probably has to do with the sensitive nature of mental health-related topics. **Hence, designers of mHealth apps, especially those focused on mental-health-related issues, should pay serious attention to ensuring and assuring users of their privacy. They should also use social features with great caution as they may trigger some sense of insecurity and lack of privacy even when it's optional**. This is probably because most commercially available mental health apps designers cannot be trusted with respect to the way they handle users' data and information. Research has shown they often do not have a clear privacy policy, and even when they do, they do not keep to it [29].

One of the features in the app design was to leverage self-monitoring of mood after expressing gratitude as a way to show participants their mood over the days of practicing gratitude. Even though participants reported that the mood monitoring scale and associated graphical feedback increased self-awareness of how their mood improved over time in relation to practicing gratitude which is also consistent with prior research in which the use of self-monitoring of mood increased self-awareness of users, **the design of the graphical feedback should be clear and provide information that makes it easy to understand.** In addition, although self-monitoring has been successfully deployed in various mHealth apps, individuals' responses to self-monitoring vary [12]. Thus, **self-monitoring needs to be personalized and individualized to improve users' adherence.**

In regard to social and community features, participants appreciated the app for giving them an option to share their gratitude in the social community. Also, our findings show that allowing people the opportunity to read what others are grateful for increases their awareness of the good things in their lives, which inevitably makes them happy and grateful. Previous research found that there is significant evidence that sharing positive experiences is associated with increased daily positive emotion and subject wellbeing [18], life satisfaction and happiness [21], and resilience [7]. Hence, sharing gratitude is a good way to share happiness. **We, therefore, suggest that app designers provide an opportunity to view other people's gratitude.** However, as mentioned above, some users have concerns about sharing their gratitude, which is probably due to privacy issues and the possibility of sharing gratitude to threaten privacy. **Therefore, designers should plan to preserve privacy while inculcating sharing features. For instance, designers could give users control over the app features and functionality by** Giving users agency in the app to decide what they want or not**; designers may also implement mechanisms that let users anonymize their identity or use nicknames.** Nevertheless, social activities do not come without negative impacts. Using social features such as (likes and comments) may introduce some negative comparisons and cause mental stress to the users. **Hence, designing social-related features should be done with caution.**

One of the recommendations that participants also suggested is to include rewards to motivate users and increase their engagement. Although only a few mental health apps employed rewards in their design [3], users with mental health issues might benefit from rewards to motivate them to keep using the app. Moreover, according to Orji et al. [26], performing health behaviors is often difficult because of a lack of immediate tangible benefits. Offering intermediate rewards such as points may help to engage the users while they await the intrinsic reward. **Therefore, designers of mental health apps could employ rewards to motivate users and enhance their engagement in the app.**

Although participants liked the variety of the suggestions and how they were easy to do, few participants recommended personalizing the suggestions and showing them based on users' moods. This is consistent with previous research, which found that lack of personalization might impact the system's overall usability [3]. **Therefore, we recommend designers to model the app's users and personalize some of the app's functionality accordingly. Personalization can enhance the overall usability and ensure a personalized experience for each user.**

Improving the usability of persuasive strategies is crucial to the effectiveness of gratitude apps, as other mHealth apps. The more usable an app is, the more likely an individual keeps using the intervention. Indeed, higher engagement through logins and repeated use is associated with better participant health outcomes [34].

7   Conclusion

This study aims to evaluate the usability of Be Grateful, an app-based gratitude intervention, from the perspective of end-users to identify existing design, functionality, and usability issues and elicit their views and experiences with the app. We evaluated the app using a quantitative (using the SUS scale), and a qualitative study, which is conducted with 14 participants who have experienced mental health issues based on self-diagnosis. The SUS results show that the app was successful. Also, the qualitative study revealed that participants appreciated the simplicity of the app and provided positive feedback about the layout as well as other app functions. Usability data from this study broadly supported the use of Be Grateful App for promoting mental wellbeing, with particularly positive feedback received from the end-user. Based on the results, we provide design implications for future work in the area of designing an interactive mobile application for health and wellness, with a focus on mental health interventions.

Acknowledgements. This research was undertaken, in part, thanks to funding from the Canada Research Chairs Program. We acknowledge the support of the Natural Sciences and Engineering Research Council of Canada (NSERC) through the Discovery Grant.

References

1. Alqahtani, F., Al Khalifah, G., Oyebode, O., Orji, R.: Apps for mental health: an evaluation of behavior change strategies and recommendations for future development. Front. Artif. Intell. **2**, 30 (2019). https://doi.org/10.3389/frai.2019.00030
2. Alqahtani, F., Meier, S., Orji, R.: Personality-based approach for tailoring persuasive mental health applications. User Model. User-Adapt. Interact. (2021). https://doi.org/10.1007/s11257-021-09289-5
3. Alqahtani, F., Orji, R.: Insights from user reviews to improve mental health apps. Health Inform. J. (2020). https://doi.org/10.1177/1460458219896492
4. Alqahtani, F., Orji, R.: Usability issues in mental health applications. In: ACM UMAP 2019 Adjunct - Adjunct Publication of the 27th Conference on User Modeling, Adaptation and Personalization, pp. 343–348 (2019)

5. Alqahtani, F., Winn, A., Orji, R.: Co-designing a mobile app to improve mental health and well-being: focus group study. JMIR Form. Res. **5**(2), e18172 (2021). https://doi.org/10.2196/18172

6. Arean, P.A., et al.: The use and effectiveness of mobile apps for depression: results from a fully remote clinical trial. J. Med. Internet Res. **18**(12), e330 (2016). https://doi.org/10.2196/jmir.6482

7. Arewasikporn, A., Sturgeon, J.A., Zautra, A.J.: Sharing positive experiences boosts resilient thinking: everyday benefits of social connection and positive emotion in a community sample. Am. J. Community Psychol. **63**(1–2), 110–121 (2019). https://doi.org/10.1002/ajcp.12279

8. Bakker, D., Rickard, N.: Engagement in mobile phone app for self-monitoring of emotional wellbeing predicts changes in mental health: MoodPrism. J. Affect. Disord. **227**(2018), 432–442 (2018). https://doi.org/10.1016/j.jad.2017.11.016

9. Bardram, J.E., Frost, M., Szántó, K., Faurholt-Jepsen, M., Vinberg, M., Kessing, L.V.: Designing mobile health technology for bipolar disorder: a field trial of the MONARCA system. In: Conference on Human Factors in Computing Systems - Proceedings, pp. 2627–2636 (2013)

10. Bolier, L., Haverman, M., Westerhof, G.J., Riper, H., Smit, F., Bohlmeijer, E.: Positive psychology interventions: a meta-analysis of randomized controlled studies. BMC Public Health **13**(1), 1–20 (2013). https://doi.org/10.1186/1471-2458-13-119

11. Brooke, J.: SUS: a "quick and dirty" usability scale. In: Usability Evaluation in Industry, pp. 189–194. Taylor & Francis (1996)

12. Burke, L.E., Swigart, V., Turk, M.W., Derro, N., Ewing, L.J.: Experiences of self-monitoring: successes and struggles during treatment for weight loss. Qual. Health Res. **19**(6), 815–828 (2009). https://doi.org/10.1177/1049732309335395

13. Butler, K.A.: Usability engineering turns 10. Interactions **3**(1), 58–75 (1996). https://doi.org/10.1145/223500.223513

14. Canzian, L., Musolesi, M.: Trajectories of depression: unobtrusive monitoring of depressive states by means of smartphone mobility traces analysis. In: UbiComp 2015 - Proceedings of the 2015 ACM International Joint Conference on Pervasive and Ubiquitous Computing, pp. 1293–1304, September 2015

15. Coelhoso, C.C., et al.: A new mental health mobile app for well-being and stress reduction in working women: randomized controlled trial. J. Med. Internet Res. **21**(11), e14269 (2019). https://doi.org/10.2196/14269

16. Davis, D.E., et al.: Thankful for the little things: a meta-analysis of gratitude interventions. J. Counsel. Psychol. **63**(1), 20–31 (2016). https://doi.org/10.1037/cou0000107

17. Desurvire, H., Kondziela, J., Atwood, M.E.: What is gained and lost when using methods other than empirical testing, vol. 125 (1992)

18. Gable, S.L., Impett, E.A., Reis, H.T., Asher, E.R.: What do you do when things go right? The intrapersonal and interpersonal benefits of sharing positive events. J. Pers. Soc. Psychol. **87**(2), 228–245 (2004). https://doi.org/10.1037/0022-3514.87.2.228

19. Green, C.A., Duan, N., Gibbons, R.D., Hoagwood, K.E., Palinkas, L.A., Wisdom, J.P.: Approaches to mixed methods dissemination and implementation research: methods, strengths, caveats, and opportunities. Adm. Policy Ment. Health **42**(5), 508–523 (2014). https://doi.org/10.1007/s10488-014-0552-6

20. Kortum, P.T., Bangor, A.: Usability ratings for everyday products measured with the system usability scale. Int. J. Hum.-Comput. Interact. **29**(2), 67–76 (2013). https://doi.org/10.1080/10447318.2012.681221

21. Lambert, N.M., et al.: A boost of positive affect: the perks of sharing positive experiences. J. Soc. Pers. Relationsh. **30**(1), 24–43 (2013). https://doi.org/10.1177/0265407512449400

22. Maramba, I., Chatterjee, A., Newman, C.: Methods of usability testing in the development of eHealth applications: a scoping review. Int. J. Med. Inform. **126**, 95–104 (2019)

23. Molich, R., Ede, M.R., Kaasgaard, K., Karyukin, B.: Comparative usability evaluation. Behav. Inf. Technol. **23**(1), 65–74 (2004). https://doi.org/10.1080/0144929032000173951

24. Molieh, R., et al.: Comparative evaluation of usability tests. In: Conference on Human Factors in Computing Systems - Proceedings, pp. 83–84 (1999)

25. Nielsen, J.: Usability engineering (1994)

26. Orji, R., Reilly, D., Oyibo, K., Orji, F.A.: Deconstructing persuasiveness of strategies in behaviour change systems using the ARCS model of motivation (2018). https://doi.org/10.1080/0144929X.2018.1520302

27. Peres, S.C., Pham, T., Phillips, R.: Validation of the system usability scale (SUS): SUS in the wild. In: Proceedings of the Human Factors and Ergonomics Society, pp. 192–196 (2013)

28. Peters, D., Deady, M., Glozier, N., Harvey, S., Calvo, R.A.: Worker preferences for a mental health app within male-dominated industries: participatory study. J. Med. Internet Res. **20**(4), e30 (2018). https://doi.org/10.2196/mental.8999

29. Price, M., Sawyer, T., Harris, M., Skalka, C.: Usability evaluation of a mobile monitoring system to assess symptoms after a traumatic injury: a mixed-methods study. JMIR Mental Health **3**(1), e3 (2016). https://doi.org/10.2196/mental.5023

30. Roepke, A.M., Jaffee, S.R., Riffle, O.M., McGonigal, J., Broome, R., Maxwell, B.: Randomized controlled trial of SuperBetter, a smartphone-based/internet-based self-help tool to reduce depressive symptoms. Games Health J. **4**(3), 235–246 (2015). https://doi.org/10.1089/g4h.2014.0046

31. Rubin, J., Chisnell, D.: Handbook of usability testing: how to plan, design, and conduct effective tests. J. Am. Soc. Inf. Sci. **47**(3), 258–259 (1996). https://doi.org/10.1002/(sici)1097-4571(199603)47:3<258::aid-asi18>3.3.co;2-l

32. Lewis, J.R., Sauro, J.: Quantifying the User Experience: Practical Statistics for User Research (2013)

33. Seligman, M.E.P., Steen, T.A., Park, N., Peterson, C.: Positive psychology progress: empirical validation of interventions. Am. Psycholo. **60**(5), 410–421 (2005). https://doi.org/10.1037/0003-066X.60.5.410

34. Senf, K., Liau, A.K.: The effects of positive interventions on happiness and depressive symptoms, with an examination of personality as a moderator. J. Happiness Stud. **14**(2), 591–612 (2013). https://doi.org/10.1007/s10902-012-9344-4

35. Sheldon, K.M., Lyubomirsky, S.: How to increase and sustain positive emotion: the effects of expressing gratitude and visualizing best possible selves. J. Posit. Psychol. **1**(2), 73–82 (2006). https://doi.org/10.1080/17439760500510676

36. Sin, N.L., Lyubomirsky, S.: Enhancing well-being and alleviating depressive symptoms with positive psychology interventions: a practice-friendly meta-analysis. J. Clin. Psychol. **65**(5), 467–487 (2009). https://doi.org/10.1002/jclp.20593

37. White, C.A., Uttl, B., Holder, M.D.: Meta-analyses of positive psychology interventions: the effects are much smaller than previously reported. PLoS ONE **14**(5), e0216588 (2019). https://doi.org/10.1371/journal.pone.0216588

38. Wichansky, A.M.: Usability testing in 2000 and beyond. Ergonomics **43**(7), 998–1006 (2000). https://doi.org/10.1080/001401300409170

Persuasive Mobile NOW Interactions

Rosaline Barendregt[1,2(✉)] and Barbara Wasson[1,2]

[1] Centre for the Science of Learning and Technology,
University of Bergen, Bergen, Norway
{rosaline.barendregt,barbara.wasson}@uib.no
[2] Department of Information Science and Media Studies,
University of Bergen, Bergen, Norway

Abstract. This paper addresses the challenge of increasing adherence to
self-report questionnaires by introducing a mobile communication technique called NOW Interactions. NOW Interactions persuades people to
provide bits of information in a moment, at the right time, with minimal interruption of their current activity, and makes it easier for users
to respond than to dismiss an information request, without opening an
application. NOW Interactions is based on principles from interaction
design, microinteractions, and persuasive design. Timely and smooth
interactions are ensured by taking into account the process that users
go through when providing information. We illustrate NOW Interactions in a functional prototype that aims to reinforce the quality and
reliability in e-healthcare solutions by innovating the methods used to
gather information through self-report questionnaires. Results from a
pilot study confirm the need for innovation of self-report questionnaires,
indicate potential for NOW Interactions, and suggest the need for further
research on NOW Interactions to test interplay with sensors, authoring
tools, and integration in health applications.

Keywords: NOW interactions · Mobile communication · Persuasive
interactions

1 Introduction

Modern technology plays a great role in the ongoing shift from a closed, clinician-
driven health care system, towards a collaborative environment where patients
are actively involved in their own treatment. Over the last years, dozens of
traditional treatments have been transformed into digital interventions, allowing
people to access therapy and treatment on their mobile phones, at any time.
This allows therapists to treat more patients simultaneously, while using less
resources, increasing efficiency [3,6].

Self-report questionnaires, which are increasingly delivered through mobile
applications, are one of the most used assessment tools in clinical psychology,
in practice and in research settings [9]. They are widely used in combination
with traditional face-to-face therapy as well as Internet Delivered Psychological
Treatment (IDPT) and form the basis for Experience Sampling Methods (ESM).

M. Kurosu (Ed.): HCII 2022, LNCS 13304, pp. 313–326, 2022.
https://doi.org/10.1007/978-3-031-05412-9_22

Self-report questionnaires gather information, for instance, on the well-being of patients, and are of great value to researchers and practitioners alike, as they are designed to get a specific piece of information that is necessary to assess the situation of the patient and to decide the next step in a treatment plan.

When self-report questionnaires are delivered online, they are usually provided in the same reliable format that has been proven to function offline. However, there are a number of open questions that arise when inquiring through online self-report questionnaires as compared to the classical format. This research focuses on ways of increasing adherence through NOW Interactions; in fact, there is a significant correlation between the time spent on IDPT and clinical effects [5,10,17], and high response rates in ESM give a more complete picture of the studied phenomena [30].

From a design perspective, adherence is negatively affected by 1) questions being asked retrospectively, 2) long questionnaires, and 3) sub-optimal designs for mobile interfaces. First, asking information retrospectively requires extra effort from patients, which may result in a feeling of exhaustion and may make the collected data prone to low validity. Second, many questions in a single questionnaire can negatively impact completion rate, for instance, by not having enough time or concentration at hand. Third, online questionnaires are often similarly constructed as their paper-pencil twins, and do not take advantage of new presentation and interaction formats available on mobile interfaces, giving a better user experience.

NOW Interactions is based on principles from interaction design [11], microinteractions [12], and persuasive design [7]. In the e-health use case, they aim to help people accomplish the task of providing information through self-report questionnaires. Timely and smooth interactions are ensured by dividing complex information requests into sequences of small steps presented as microinteractions. The user interface is designed to function as a means to facilitate motivation by sending effective triggers that cater to the ability of the user, by being timed to a fitting moment, and by allowing information to be provided instantly without opening an app. This makes it easier, or just as easy, to provide the information as it is to dismiss the request, see Fig. 1 for an example of NOW Interactions.

2   Background and Related Work

2.1   Self Report Questionnaires

Self-report techniques are used to let respondents report on their own behaviour, feelings, or intentions without interference [20]. These techniques are used in many different fields and situations, for example to measure public opinion, carry-out research studies, assess psychological health and other medical issues, and to support behavioural studies. Advantages of using self-report include low development costs and the possibility to reach a large sample group with relatively little effort. The main disadvantage to using self-report might be the possibility of providing invalid answers, as the answers given by respondents cannot be fact-checked but are taken for granted at face-value [9].

Fig. 1. An example of NOW Interactions containing a question about activation (l) and valence (r), in Norwegian.

In clinical psychology, standardised self-report questionnaires are one of the most used assessment tools in practice and in research settings [9]. Respondents are asked to read questions and select their response. The questions in standardised self-report questionnaires are most often retrospective; they for instance ask the respondent how often something has occurred over the last two weeks. In clinical psychology, such questionnaires are widely used in combination with traditional face-to-face therapy as well as Internet Delivered Psychological Treatment (IDPT). The questionnaires are used to gather information, for example, on the well-being of patients, and are of great value to researchers and practitioners, as they are designed to get a specific piece of information that is necessary to assess the situation of the patient and to decide the next step in a treatment plan.

Self-report is also the base for the Experience Sampling Method (ESM) and Ecological Momentary Assessment (EMA), where people are asked to self-report in real time on subjective experiences from their lives. These techniques have been applied in numerous clinical studies in order to, for example, evaluate indicators of substance abuse or to gain better insight in social Interaction or mental health. The collected data from such studies helps to advance both science and practice.

2.2 Adherence and Response Rate

Adherence is seen as a very important factor in clinical psychology. There is a significant correlation between the time spent on IDPT and clinical effects [5,10,17]. Thus, finding methods to uphold communication with participants and to increase adherence could contribute to the health of participants.

Similarly, response rate in ESM (also 'compliance rate' in medical literature) is seen as very important. The response rate describes the number of answered notifications divided by total amount of notifications sent in the sample. A high response rate gives a more complete picture of the studied phenomena [30]. Literature suggests several methods to increase response rates including incentives, providing feedback [15,28], and incorporating gamification elements [13,14,19,31]. There is an expressed need to investigate how creative input methods on mobiles can help to reduce participant burden and increase response rates [30].

2.3 Responding to Questionnaires

Questionnaires are traditionally considered a communication process between the questionnaire initiator and the respondent [11,16]. This is important to keep in mind when constructing appropriate questions and integrating questionnaire logic, but also a reason to consider how design can facilitate this communication.

Responding to questionnaires is also seen as an iterative process where each question represents an iteration that includes several steps of complex information processing [2,29]. The first step in this process is understanding the question, the second step includes the retrieval of information from memory, the third step involves a judgement process related to answering truthful or not, and the fourth step is to match the fabricated answer to the provided response options [21], see Table 1.

At any point during this process there is a chance the respondent stops answering. Insight into this process can be valuable for understanding how and where design can support this communication process, and thus maximise the chance of the respondent fulfilling the questionnaire. Table 1 shows how the steps in the cognitive process connect with design factors that could influence these steps.

Table 1. A simplified version of the steps in the cognitive process of responding to questionnaires

	Step 1	Step 2	Step 3	Step 4
Cognitive process	Understanding the question	Retrieval of information from memory	Judgement process related to answering truthfully	Matching the generated answer to the provided response options
Design factors	Question clarity, Question length, typeface/font, colour, contrast	Timing of triggers	Influenced by step 1 and 2 + the content of the Question	Answer options clarity

2.4 Questionnaires on Mobile Phones

Usually, the respondent receives a notification on their phone with a suggestion to answer the questionnaire; the respondent taps the notification, which opens the self-report questionnaire in a browser window or an app where the respondent answers the questions and hopefully fulfils the whole questionnaire.

When self-report questionnaires are delivered online, they are usually provided in the same reliable format that has been proven to function offline. Validated paper-based questionnaires are often used as the basis for self-report questionnaires, they have proven to measure what they aim to measure, which benefits researchers and clinicians as it makes it easier to compare the collected data to prior research.

Unfortunately, the questions are often asked retrospectively. This requires extra effort from respondents, which may result in a feeling of exhaustion and may make the collected data prone to low validity. Step 2 and 3 from Table 1 might be in jeopardy here.

Second, many questions in a single questionnaire can negatively impact completion rate, for instance, by not having enough time or concentration at hand. Mobile users are likely to be interrupted at any time due to the nature of the device, so this is something to take into account.

Questionnaires that are originally developed for the paper medium do not take advantage of new presentation and interaction formats available for mobile interfaces. Long, complex questions may even be directly unsuitable to present to mobile users, as readers are known to have more difficulties to comprehend digital text [8]. Also, questions that include many answer options may become problematic due to space issues on small screens. Related to this, it should be considered that when the medium on which one presents self-report questionnaires has (great) influence on the results of the questionnaire, it becomes part of the methodology. Researchers might need to rethink their idea of standardised validated self-report questionnaires, update them to a new standard, and make them mobile compatible and thereby more user-friendly.

Thus, from a design perspective, adherence and response rates are negatively affected by 1) questions being asked retrospectively, 2) long questionnaires, and 3) sub-optimal designs for mobile interfaces.

2.5 Questionnaire Redesigns

Research has been carried out about questionnaire design and how they can be optimised for mobile use [4,7]. Literature suggests survey designers should optimise the lay-out of their questionnaires for mobile phone use. Suggestions include simplifying questions to include suitable answer input types for mobile [4].

There have also been solutions introduced that use the unlocking mechanism of the phone to collect answers to a simple question; this is called 'unlock journaling' [34].

NOW Interactions goes beyond this and aims to improve the whole interaction by maximising the amount of information collected while having as few interactions as possible, thus taking as little as possible energy and time from the respondents.

3 NOW Interactions

NOW Interactions facilitates a communication that benefits both respondents and questionnaire initiators. The user interface of NOW Interactions is designed to persuade people to provide bits of information in a moment, at the right time, with minimal interruption of their current activity. This makes it easier for users to respond than to dismiss an information request, without even needing to open an application. The overarching idea is to maximise the amount of information collected, while having as few and as small interactions as possible; thus taking as little as possible energy and time from respondents. This reduces participant burden and increases adherence, which is the ultimate goal.

3.1 Design Foundation

The overarching principle of NOW Interactions, is based on behaviour theory [12]. By making the task (answering a question) as low effort as possible, the chance of the respondent actually performing the task increases. According to the theory of persuasive design, when performing an action, such as providing health related information by answering questions, people need motivation, ability, and triggers; if one of these is missing, the action will likely not be performed [12]. The theory also shows an interplay between motivation and ability; to perform a difficult task, one needs higher motivation than to perform a simple task that takes little effort. NOW Interactions embodies this concept by employing the user interface to facilitate motivation and cater to ability, with good timing, to have effective triggers. This concept also aligns with equity theory, which suggests that people are more likely to provide input if the cost/benefit ratio is in their favour [1]. NOW Interactions reduce the time and energy people need to use on responding to a question or questionnaire, thus increases the chance that the task will be performed.

Interaction design focuses on designing interactive products to support people in their everyday and working lives [24] and helps people achieve their goals in the best way possible. Questionnaires can be seen as two-folded, on one side, questionnaire initiators really want answers to their questions, yet they depend on respondents to take the effort to answer. By focusing on respondents and the whole process respondents go through when answering questionnaires, designers can better adjust to their needs. NOW Interactions connects the steps within the cognitive process of answering questionnaires to motivate design choices. Table 2 is an updated version of Table 1 with NOW Interactions design choices.

Mobile self-reporting implies the context situation where respondents are likely to be interrupted, either by other notifications on their phone, or real-life happenings. NOW Interactions anticipates this situation by presenting questions as microinteractions. Microinteractions are interactions that focus around a single use case, such as answering a single question, and making this use case as pleasant and convenient as possible [27]. Dividing complex tasks into smaller sub-tasks, makes it easier for the respondent to stay concentrated on each individual task, as well as to pick up where they left off when they get interrupted. This makes the task at hand more manageable and less overwhelming.

Mobile notifications have been shown to play a key role in getting users attention [23]. NOW Interactions shifts the use of such notifications from being used as reminders towards being the interaction itself. The question functions as a reminder, which can be answered straight away, without extra steps, taps, or waiting time such as needing to open an app. This is makes NOW Interactions timely and very suitable for in situ self-report questionnaires, as it reduces the time between the reading of the question and the provision of the answer.

Table 2. A simplified version of the steps in the cognitive process of responding to questionnaires related to the design of NOW Interactions

	Step 1	Step 2	Step 3	Step 4
Cognitive process	Understanding the question	Retrieval of information from memory	Judgement process related to answering truthfully	Matching the generated answer to the provided response options
Design factors	Question clarity, Question length, typeface/font, colour, contrast	Timing of triggers	Influenced by step 1 and 2 + the content of the Question	Answer options clarity
NOW	Phrase questions to fit notification	Timely triggers, phrasing questions to be answered right NOW		Fitting answer options to notification, icon use

3.2 Interaction Model

A single NOW Interaction relies on one notification, which includes both a question and the accompanying answer possibilities. After an answer has been chosen, the notification disappears.

This single NOW Interaction is envisioned to be part of a larger model that relies on different data sources to make a substantiated decision on whether or not a NOW Interaction is required; and if so, when it should happen and what it should contain. Different sources feed data to a User Profile; this could include sensor data, mobile phone use data, data from wearables, background information, user interactions, and direct input from the user, etc.

The user profile allows NOW Interactions to adapt in real-time to the personal and current situation of the user. A decision process, based on an analysis of the user profile, determines the details of the NOW Interaction. This way, it is ensured that the interactions are adapted and personalised to the needs of the user. For example, no requests will be sent while the user is sleeping or at the gym, and the questions depend on which health data should be provided.

NOW Interactions collect data throughout the day in moments that fit the user, by sending short inquiries. This releases people from having to answer many questions at once and the information that they need to provide is still fresh in their memory. The collected data feeds back into the user profile, which decides the next step; this could be, for example, another NOW Interaction, an in-app questionnaire, a guided exercise, or nothing (in the case that all information for this moment has been collected).

4   Prototype

To evaluate the potential of NOW Interactions to improve information collection from self-report questionnaires, to test the feasibility of this method, as well as gauge user acceptance, a functioning prototype was designed and developed and eventually tested in a small pilot study.

4.1   Prototype Development

The prototype was developed in two phases. The first phase included idea development by carrying out desk research and semi-structured interviews with two patients that had gone through an IDPT to improve their mental health and a psychologist specialised in working with IDPTs. The focus of these interviews included mapping how patients use IDPTs and what type of elements they believe could help them adhere to such programs. The results of these interviews included suggestions about how IDTPs and patients can benefit from redesign. Both patient interviews revealed that a low-threshold way to stay in touch with the programme was missing. This resulted in the idea of NOW Interactions and an accompanying non-functional digital prototype. Figure 2 shows an example from one of the first digital designs.

Fig. 2. One of the first digital designs for NOW Interactions

In the second phase, over several iterations, the non-functional prototype was remodelled to a functional prototype. During this process, there were many sessions where designers and software developers came together to discuss the progress of finding the best approach. This was a challenging process as there were no off the shelve solutions available, so the technology to run NOW Interactions needed to be built from scratch; this went not without snags. Androids were chosen for the prototype due to the possibility for interactive push notifications, however, limitations of the platform and the required functionality resulted into concessions, both from the development team and the design team. An example is that Android's notification platform is not very flexible with the design space for notifications, i.e., there are limits to how much space is available to fit both questions and answer options. Figure 3 shows how the available space eventually was utilised for an individual NOW Interaction. Note that the focus of this prototype was not to test different layouts of these notifications, but rather test the interaction.

The result of this phase was a working prototype that sends two predefined NOW Interactions three times a day, to collect information, without connecting it to a user profile. The first NOW Interaction in the pair is set to be send at a certain time, while the second NOW Interaction launches after the answer to the first notification has been received by the server.

Before testing the prototype in the pilot study, it was pretested on a simulator and ten Android devices with different screen sizes and settings; this revealed some issues such as when dark mode was enabled on the device.

Fig. 3. The design space for Android notifications & how it was utilised for NOW Interactions

4.2 Area of Application

To make a prototype with meaningful content, we decided to make use of an adapted version of the Swedish short self-report measure of core affect [32,33], often used in psychological evaluations. Core affect presents how we are feeling and comprises a combination of two dimensions: valence (pleasant to unpleasant) and activation (deactivated to activated) [22,26].

Traditionally, core affect has been measured by using a number of self-report rating scales with adjective end-points [25]. The Swedish short self-report measure of core affect demonstrated that it is possible to greatly reduce the number of scales necessary to get an accurate measurement of core affect. They also showed there is no significant difference between different answering scales [32]. For this prototype we decided to use one valence and one activation question for each pair of NOW Interactions. Three times a day, at dedicated times, a notification was sent with a question directed to measure activation, see Fig. 1 (left). After an answer has been selected, the notification disappears, and the second question is prompted, this time directed to measure valence, see Fig. 1 (right). The three question sets comprise different questions, but uses the same response format as the other sets, as seen in Table 3.

Table 3. The timing and content for the NOW Interactions in the pilot study

	10.00	15.00	21.00
Question 1	Activation question 1	Activation question 2	Activation question 3
Norwegian	*Hvordan føler du deg nå, mer Avslappet eller Aktiv?*	*Hvordan føler du deg nå, mer Søvnig eller Opplagt?*	*Hvordan føler du deg nå, mer Slapp eller Energisk?*
Question 2	Valence question 1	Valence question 2	Valence question 3
Norwegian	*Føler du deg nå mer Lei deg eller Glad?*	*Føler du deg nåmer Nedstemt eller Opprømt?*	*Føler du deg nåmer Frustrert eller Fornøyd?*

4.3 Pilot Study

The pilot consisted of three parts: 1) a workshop including a focus group discussion, a demonstration, and a user test with the aim to reveal any complications with the chosen icons or problems with the concept, 2) a hands on test of the prototype over two days, and 3) a follow-up interview and a TWEETS evaluation [18] to reveal any hidden issues that may have occurred during the hands on test and to add final thoughts.

Two high school classes with twelve students of approximately 18 years of age agreed to participate in the first part of the study. They were asked to design icon sets to fit the questions as shown in Fig. 1, and to perform a user test on each other, where they would scope for mindset around the idea of answering questions this way.

As a preparation for the second part of the pilot study, it was explained to the students that this tool is meant to keep track of how people that may experience difficulties in their lives are feeling, and that this may or may not apply to them personally. It was also explained that the app would anonymously collect their answers together with a time stamp, but that this data would not be used to do any psychological modelling and only be used to improve the performance of the app.

Due to lack of Android mobile phones amongst the students, only three students were able to test the NOW Interactions on their own phone and participate in the hands-on testing of the prototype and the interviews. Restrictions due to Covid-19 greatly limited the access to find and follow up students. (To compensate for the possible lack of finding technical errors, we set up an additional informal user-test with five participants during an academical workshop, which revealed only a few minor technical problems.)

Table 4 shows an overview of the categories of collected data, note that in some cases individuals have provided several answers in the same category.

Table 4. An overview of the type of collected data during the pilot study

	Participants	Responses	Type of data
Icon design	21	11	Icon suggestions, opinion about icon use
User test	21	11	Judgement about icons, opinion about such notifications, opinion about suitability for mobile use, estimation of ease of use
NOW test	3	27 (total)	Data entries as answers to NOW interactions including timestamp
Semi-structured interview	3	3	Opinion about answering such notifications, feedback about technical issues, other possible use-cases, time used, opinion on icon, opinion on answering two questions after each other, opinion about interruptibility
TWEETS	3	3	Opinion expressed through 9 questions about engagement with app

4.4 Lessons Learned

The user test gave some answers that address the aims of this pilot study. The prototype with the NOW Interactions worked and seemed suitable for collecting information. It was possible to employ NOW Interactions for use in a health domain, and the user test showed the users were curious about the future possibilities of NOW Interactions.

From the data that we collected from the students through NOW Interactions, we noticed that the time between sending the notification and the answer was reduced from the second set of questions on. This made us wonder if they took the time to actually read the questions. In the follow up interview, the participants confirmed that they did not realise that the three question sets during the day asked different questions, though with similar icons.

All participants were positive about not having to open an application, but still being able to have a meaningful interaction. They believed that this would greatly increase the chance of them answering questions. Two participants mentioned that they did not feel that the NOW Interactions were interrupting in their activities at hand, even though they received two questions in a sequence.

5   Discussion

Based on the feedback from the students in the pilot study, NOW Interactions seem worthy of investigation, however, there are still many aspects that need further thought, design, development, and research.

We managed to ensure smooth interactions by dividing complex information into sequences of small steps, and present them to the users as microinteractions. However, even though the technique is working, and seems promising, the actual design and layout of NOW Interactions still needs more work. We need to find out why the test participants did not read the questions and find solutions to make sure that in future versions, they will. Different layouts need to be tested, as well as alternative response formats. We also have to research if personalising icons to individual user preferences can be can be beneficial.

There are also technical limitations to solve. At the moment, NOW Interactions is only available for Android devices, as IOS does not support this technique. Even though the Android mobile platform allows for this type of communication, it is not a widely used feature, and will require careful planning, as not to be abused. An overflow of such notification questions would probably be overwhelming for users.

Although this small test group did not seem to find these interactions intrusive, we have to do extensive research about how people that are not feeling well will receive this technology. Possibly, receiving notifications related to one's illness could influence this perspective, as it handles about personal medical data. This is also a technological challenge, as to how sensitive data is handled.

NOW Interactions aim to not just rethink the design of self-report questionnaires, but to rethink the whole interaction. Related to this should be considered that when the medium on which one presents self-report questionnaires has (great) influence on the results of the questionnaire, it becomes part of the methodology. Researchers might need to rethink their idea of standardised validated self-report questionnaires, update them to a new standard, and make them mobile compatible.

Once the new designs are ready, a next step for research on NOW Interactions is to test them over a longer period of time, possibly in combination with an IDPT- or medical tracking app such as menstrual cycle tracking, water intake measurement, or headache diaries. It is also necessary to test how the notification questions themselves should be improved to fit the users own preferences and needs, toggling the use of colours, different icons, and different lay-outs.

Furthermore, we have an aim to test the interplay between NOW Interactions, wearable devices, and activity data. Activity data could be used to time the notifications, as well as to design a meaningful time frame in which interactions should be completed.

Even though the results of this pilot-study seems promising, there are still many dots to connect and steps to take in furthering the research, and making NOW Interactions ready for use.

6 Conclusion

In this paper we have argued that it is time to take advantage of the presentation and interaction features mobile technology has to offer.

On a more general, but very important note, this requires a discussion between clinicians and technicians about how standardised self-report questionnaires can be updated while keeping their great, established value, but also making use of the possibilities of modern technology and the needs of respondents.

References

1. Adams, J.S.: Towards an understanding of inequity. Psychol. Sci. Public Interest **67**(5), 422 (1963)
2. Aday, L.A., Cornelius, L.J.: Designing and Conducting Health Surveys: A Comprehensive Guide. Wiley, Hoboken (2006)
3. Andersson, G., Cuijpers, P.: Internet-based and other computerized psychological treatments for adult depression: a meta-analysis. Cogn. Behav. Ther. **38**(4), 196–205 (2009)
4. Antoun, C., Katz, J., Argueta, J., Wang, L.: Design heuristics for effective smartphone questionnaires. Soc. Sci. Comput. Rev. **36**(5), 557–574 (2018)
5. Baumeister, H., Reichler, L., Munzinger, M., Lin, J.: The impact of guidance on internet-based mental health interventions-a systematic review. Internet Interv. **1**(4), 205–215 (2014)
6. Carlbring, P., Andersson, G., Cuijpers, P., Riper, H., Hedman-Lagerlöf, E.: Internet-based vs. face-to-face cognitive behavior therapy for psychiatric and somatic disorders: an updated systematic review and meta-analysis. Cogn. Behav. Ther. **47**(1), 1–18 (2018)
7. Couper, M.P., Peterson, G.J.: Why do web surveys take longer on smartphones? Soc. Sci. Comput. Rev. **35**(3), 357–377 (2017)
8. Delgado, P., Vargas, C., Ackerman, R., Salmerón, L.: Don't throw away your printed books: a meta-analysis on the effects of reading media on reading comprehension. Educ. Res. Rev. **25**, 23–38 (2018)
9. Demetriou, C., Ozer, B., Essau, C.: Self-report questionnaires. In: Cautin, R.L., Lilienfeld, S.O. (eds.) The Encyclopedia of Clinical Psychology, 1st edn. Wiley, Hoboken (2015)
10. Farrer, L.M., Griffiths, K.M., Christensen, H., Mackinnon, A.J., Batterham, P.J.: Predictors of adherence and outcome in internet-based cognitive behavior therapy delivered in a telephone counseling setting. Cogn. Ther. Res. **38**(3), 358–367 (2014)
11. Foddy, W., Foddy, W.H.: Constructing Questions for Interviews and Questionnaires: Theory and Practice in Social Research. Cambridge University Press, Cambridge (1994)
12. Fogg, B.J.: A behavior model for persuasive design, pp. 1–7 (2009)
13. Hall, L., Hume, C., Tazzyman, S.: Five degrees of happiness: effective smiley face Likert scales for evaluating with children. In: Proceedings of the the 15th International Conference on Interaction Design and Children, pp. 311–321 (2016)
14. Harms, J., Biegler, S., Wimmer, C., Kappel, K., Grechenig, T.: Gamification of online surveys: design process, case study, and evaluation. In: Abascal, J., Barbosa, S., Fetter, M., Gross, T., Palanque, P., Winckler, M. (eds.) INTERACT 2015. LNCS, vol. 9296, pp. 219–236. Springer, Cham (2015). https://doi.org/10.1007/978-3-319-22701-6_16

15. Hsieh, G., Li, I., Dey, A., Forlizzi, J., Hudson, S.E.: Using visualizations to increase compliance in experience sampling. In: Proceedings of the 10th International Conference on Ubiquitous Computing, pp. 164–167 (2008)
16. Hunt, S.D., Sparkman, R.D., Jr., Wilcox, J.B.: The pretest in survey research: issues and preliminary findings. J. Mark. Res. 19(2), 269–273 (1982)
17. Karyotaki, E., et al.: Do guided internet-based interventions result in clinically relevant changes for patients with depression? An individual participant data meta-analysis. Clin. Psychol. Rev. 63, 80–92 (2018)
18. Kelders, S.M., Kip, H.: Development and initial validation of a scale to measure engagement with eHealth technologies. In: Extended Abstracts of the 2019 CHI Conference on Human Factors in Computing Systems, pp. 1–6 (2019)
19. Keusch, F., Zhang, C.: A review of issues in gamified surveys. Soc. Sci. Comput. Rev. 35(2), 147–166 (2017)
20. Lavrakas, P.J.: Encyclopedia of Survey Research Methods. Sage Publications, Thousand Oaks (2008)
21. Lietz, P.: Research into questionnaire design: a summary of the literature. Int. J. Mark. Res. 52(2), 249–272 (2010)
22. Linnenbrink, E.A.: The role of affect in student learning: a multi-dimensional approach to considering the interaction of affect, motivation, and engagement. In: Emotion in Education, pp. 107–124. Elsevier (2007)
23. Pielot, M., Church, K., De Oliveira, R.: An in-situ study of mobile phone notifications. In: Proceedings of the 16th International Conference on Human-Computer Interaction with Mobile Devices & Services, pp. 233–242 (2014)
24. Preece, J., Sharp, H., Rogers, Y.: Interaction Design: Beyond Human-Computer Interaction. Wiley, Hoboken (2015)
25. Russell, J.A.: A circumplex model of affect. J. Pers. Soc. Psychol. 39(6), 1161 (1980)
26. Russell, J.A.: Core affect and the psychological construction of emotion. Psychol. Rev. 110(1), 145 (2003)
27. Saffer, D.: Microinteractions: Designing with Details. O'Reilly Media Inc., Newton (2013)
28. Stone, A.A., Kessler, R.C., Haythomthwatte, J.A.: Measuring daily events and experiences: decisions for the researcher. J. Pers. 59(3), 575–607 (1991)
29. Tourangeau, R., Rips, L.J., Rasinski, K.: The Psychology of Survey Response (2000)
30. Van Berkel, N., Ferreira, D., Kostakos, V.: The experience sampling method on mobile devices. ACM Comput. Surv. (CSUR) 50(6), 1–40 (2017)
31. Van Berkel, N., Goncalves, J., Hosio, S., Kostakos, V.: Gamification of mobile experience sampling improves data quality and quantity. In: Proceedings of the ACM on Interactive, Mobile, Wearable and Ubiquitous Technologies, vol. 1, no. 3, pp. 1–21 (2017)
32. Västfjäll, D., Friman, M., Gärling, T., Kleiner, M.: The measurement of core affect: a Swedish self-report measure derived from the affect circumplex. Scand. J. Psychol. 43(1), 19–31 (2002)
33. Västfjäll, D., Gärling, T.: Validation of a Swedish short self-report measure of core affect. Scand. J. Psychol. 48(3), 233–238 (2007)
34. Zhang, X., Pina, L.R., Fogarty, J.: Examining unlock journaling with diaries and reminders for in situ self-report in health and wellness. In: Proceedings of the 2016 CHI Conference on Human Factors in Computing Systems, pp. 5658–5664 (2016)

Breathing Cushion: Keep Changing Posture for Reducing the Effects of Sedentary Behavior During Working Times

Hao Chen[1] [ID] and Chenwei Chiang[2]([✉]) [ID]

[1] National Taipei University of Technology, 10608 Taipei, Taiwan
[2] National Taipei University of Business, 100025 Taipei, Taiwan
chenwei@ntub.edu.tw

Abstract. Along with technological progress and era advances, People always spend a great deal of time on sedentary behavior. The sitting time in the office addresses almost more than 50% of working hours for the office workers. It also generates a significant negative influence on human health. When you have a long sitting hour and maintain the same and single posture for a long time, it would bring up the spine and some other joints with a single angle of burden and cause low back pain. The influence will be relieved through keeping change the sitting posture while seated.

The study submits the concept of a Breathing Cushion to promote the user to change the sitting posture more frequently through aggressively changing the cushion's shape and further relieving the danger to the health caused by sitting for long hours. We made the operational prototype and invited ten participants to be tested and observe the interaction between the participants and the Breathing Cushion, and through the semi-structural interview to study the feasibility of the concept.

According to the analysis of experimental outcome, 18.6% of changing the sitting posture is related to the change of Breathing Cushion. The participant changed him 13.2 times sitting posture per hour on average. The test result indicates that such a concept is surely pushing the user to change their seating posture more frequently. We also observed quite a few interesting phenomena during the experiment, which can also help us improve the experience of the sitting posture of the Breathing Cushion. We expect to establish a more solid basis for Breathing Cushion and develop the different applications at various layers.

Keywords: Creativity · Human-Robot Interaction · User experience (UX) · Sedentary behavior · Posture induction

1 Introduction

Along with era advances, people's living style has been closely related to sitting long hours. People always spend a great amount of time on sedentary behavior [1, 2]. The feature of the working pattern for the office worker has been challenged initially. The sitting time in the office addresses almost more than 50% of working hours [3]. It also generates a significant negative influence on human health [4]. To maintain the same posture for long would easily cause some burden on the spine and some other joints with a single angle of burden [5]. Besides, the static working posture may cause muscle fatigue even faster than in dynamic working condition [6]; in the meantime, the seating posture in static even require a longer recovery time for the muscle than in dynamic seating posture [6]. Even so, the body posture for the long hours sitting group is generally restricted by the surface of the chair, the back of the chair, and the table as the external restriction, and additionally, sometimes they need to focus on doing the job during the office hour, or it is easy for these people to forget or to deliberately ignore the thought that they are supposed to change the sitting posture continuously.

We submit the Breathing Cushion: the pad to constantly change the shade; the purpose is to help the workers change their seating posture with balance even more frequently. The Breathing Cushion consists of nine independent inflatable areas. To control the electric magnetic valve in Arduino to proceed to inflatable and leaking respectively, and then to change the shape accordingly. We invite ten participants (5 men and 5 women) to participate in the experiment. We want to study by taking the simulation testing method: (1) how the user will interact with the Breathing Cushion during daily office hours? (2) How the Breathing Cushion would influence the user to change their posture? (3) How does the user think of a Breathing Cushion?

During the experiment, the participants can freely execute the work on the computer without any restriction and do their best to keep focusing on the content of the work by using the computer has no limit. The participants decide the content of the mission based on their demand, and during the period of the experiment, they can freely change any posture and get up to take a break with no limitation. The final result of the Research indicates the Breathing Cushion can frequently push the user to change the sitting postures constantly. We also gain some feedback through such Research, which helps us improve the seating posture experience with the Breathing Cushion. The contribution of this study is shown as follows:

- Go to propose and execute the Breathing Cushion; such a Breathing Cushion can aggressively change the shape to promote the user to change the seating posture.
- We understand how the cushion interacted with the user through the Research, how it influenced the user's sitting posture, and how aggressively the user will accept the cushion.
- To submit the potential conceptual advantages, the negative influence, and the subsequential direction of the improvement based on the result of the experiment.

2   Background and Related Work

2.1   Sedentary Behavior

Sedentary behavior refers to an energy expenditure ≤ 1.5 METs while sitting or reclining under the waking condition [7]. Back to early 2003 and 2004, it's an investigation indicates that the average long hours sitting daily is around 7.3 to 9.3 h for all the ages section [1]. In a proportion point of view, 51–68% of the time, while the adult is waking, sits for a long hour [2]. The long hours sitting behavior is so close to the human beings daily living, and many of the Research also testified the long hour sitting behavior does bear a huge potential dangerous factor, as John P Buckley et al. indicate that the long hours sitting would significantly increase the human being to suffer diabetes and cardiovascular disease, cancer or die prematurely [4]. To the office worker, such a risk can not be overlooked. Due to the pattern and the mode of the office work, the daily accumulated long hour sitting becomes astonishing, and the huge possibilities increase the mortality rate or the risk of being myocardial cell metabolic derangements [3]. Cormac G Ryan et al. apply the wearable physical activity monitoring systems and objectively quantifies the long hour sitting workers in Glasgow Caledonian University, and the finding is the daily sitting time on the average accounts for 66% of the working hours in a working day, and barely interrupt their long hour sitting within 30 min [8].

2.2   Posture Changes

In the last 20 years, the study for the sitting posture has been changed from the suggestion to maintain the optimal single posture turned out to be the point of view to add the dynamic. The change of sitting posture has been getting important along the way. Bendix's study indicates that a long time sitting has something to do with the fixed posture, and keeping the same posture during the working hour bears more hazardous than sitting there for long [9]. Lueder also mentions the same conclusion: fixed posture easily leads to negatively affect our health, comfort, and effectiveness at work [10]. Besides, you may learn from Reenalda et al.'s study the ordinary person's oxygen saturation is greater than 95%, but when it is reduced down below 50%, the hip would be pressed, and changing the seated posture will distract the pressure for the pelvis, the hip will acquire a temporary relief due to the change of sitting posture, also change oxygen saturation by increasing 2.2% on the average [11]. Such a result indicates that the change of posture will have a positive impact and help the body especially for sitting for a long hour.

2.3   Sitting Posture Induction

For the reduction of the worker who maintains the fixed positions, in the long run, the person comes from Dutch - Studio RAAAF (Rietveld-Architecture-Art-Affordances) and Barbara Visser form an experimental office named "The End of Sitting" [12]. In the space with no existing of a single chair, but many large chunks of the polygon instead, to help the people in seated, a reclining or lying position; one of each position only provide the temporary comfortableness, the purpose is to push the workers frequently change the working posture. Jeong ki Hong et al. proposed role-playing in the pattern of the flower, providing the current condition related to the posture through the exercise, voice, and color changes [13]. Joongi Shin et al. designs a moving computer monitor with extremely slow speed, with a very minimal degree of interference to the user's posture [14, 15]. Such a concept has been adopted and applied to the user interface in virtual reality [16]. Besides, Bokyung Lee et al. apply a table that can automatically change the height of the table to influence the users working posture. The Research participants three kinds of time change points; its purpose is to diminish the disturbance end uncomfortableness when the height of the table is changed [17].

2.4 Cushion Application

Congcong Ma et al. believes the smart cushion can improve the condition of long-hour sitting behavior along with the technology development, and it is supposed to be introduced to daily living, including the participants' sitting posture activity data, and even to identify the indication of the current feeling status [18]. For the purpose to directly understand to proceed the pressure to the hip of the long hours setting group, sitting posture, and the dynamic, Guanqing Liang et al. applied the Sparse Pressure Sensor into the cushion for the purpose to receive and the collect the data of the pressure, and further to identify the sitting posture [19]. On the other hand, Xipei Ren et al. applies the music game combined with a pressure sensor cushion; the purpose is to encourage disabled seniors to aggressively change the various sitting posture through the method of interaction [20]. Kazuyuki Fujita et al. proposed to aggressively lean the seat to push the user to change the posture. The purpose is to control the incline of the chair to break out the condition of being sitting for a long hour [21]. Shiotani et al.'s Research: to have a group of healthy participants stay seated for an hour and observe the hip with autonomous and involuntary movement. During the Research, the idea of the structure of pressure reduction cushion is supposed to be adjusted along with sitting variety of sitting posture and further to propose the dynamic pressure reduction auxiliary cushion [22].

3   Breathing Cushion

We propose the Breathing Cushion based on the above background: the cushion would aggressively change the shape to push the user with more frequency to change to the sitting posture. Our core thinking is that when the workers focus on doing the job and forget to change the setting posture, it will help the workers be more frequent balance the change of seating posture and further relieve the hazardous to our health.

3.1 System Design

The cushion and the long hours sitting group bear the most direct interactive relationship; compared with the chair, the cushion is portable and can be used in multiple scenarios and economical, which can be more directly involved in user's daily living. If the user can take advantage of the feature, the cushion can directly respond to the users sitting posture dynamic; it can also influence the long hours sitting group and change the pressure the pelvis suffers. It's the media with connection in a high degree with long hours sitting group. The cushion can then be installed onto the regular office chair and provide the experience of complete essential sitting posture remaining for the user [21]. To summarize what we mentioned above, we believe a Breathing Cushion is most appropriate with the interaction of a long hour sitting group. The user experience is very important; Breathing Cushion needs to have sufficient fluency during the change of exercising, the additional mechanical quiver, abnormal speed changes are not allowed, Simultaneously it has to be easy to manipulate, and also the support to sustain the weight of the human body and sufficient comfortableness. We refer to Shiotani et al.'s depressurization motion assistance system [22] and Kazuyuki Fujita et al.'s TiltChair [21], we understand the advantage of the air inflatable bear. We are talking about whether the comfortableness and support to the hip dynamic [20] or the support and the formability are quite high [23, 24]. Therefore we select the air inflatable type as the concept of Breathing Cushion.

3.2 Implementation

To allow Breathing Cushions to fit all kinds of office chairs, we refer to a wide variety of office cushions (Purple Double Seat Cushion, Tempur-Pedic Seat Cushion, Xtreme Comforts Large Seat Cushion). Finally, we decided the dimension is W450 * D450 mm. About the height of the cushion, Roman Peter Kuster et al. has a study related to a dynamic sitting posture and working chair which indicates among the working posture, if there is excessive translation to user's head, chest, and pelvis, it will easily distract the worker during the operation [25]. Stopper further influences the willingness to use the product. Nevertheless, Kazuyuki Fujita et al. in Research explored the relationship between comfortableness and three types of cushion inclination angles. The Research for the user indicates that smaller than 15° have almost no negative influence; the angle greater than 30° seems disturbing to the seating poster [21]. So based on it, we adjust the highest inclined angle at 15° for the cushion; after the calculation by using the formula, the highest thickness that the Breathing Cushion can reach is 120 mm. Considering the variety of user and sitting posture, the possibility to explore some other sitting posture in the future, The Breathing Cushion was made up of nine individual non-connected cube airbags (when it is fully inflated 120 * 120 * 120 mm, PVC), one of each bag has an open allows the air go outside, in three by three square array (Fig. 1).

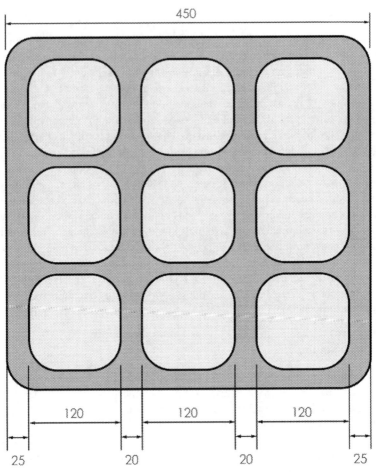

Fig. 1. The Breathing Cushion dimension. The 20 mm gap between the airbag is for the arrangement of silicon hose to carry the air going through. (unit: mm)

The Breathing Cushion inflates through the mini pump (CJAP37, MABUCHI MOTOR); the pump is connected to a metaled air shunt with two ways and eight exits to lead the air to nine airbags, respectively, through the silicone hose (inside diameter: 1/8 in.). The exit of one of each airbag is connected with a three-way Solenoid Valve (SC0726G, Skoocom) by using Arduino Nano as the switch of controlling the electric magnetic valve of the microcontroller board (Fig. 2).

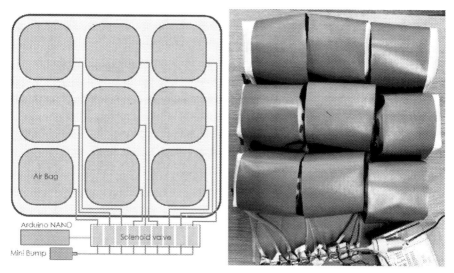

Fig. 2. The mechanical arrangement (left) and interior photo (right) for the prototype of the Breathing Cushion.

The Breathing Cushion controls the change of cushion shape through the permutation and combination for one of each inflation and the leakage. We use the mini pump (CJAP37, MABUCHI MOTOR) with 2.0 LPM of airflow; the volume of an airbag is 1.728 * 106 mm^3/s. Although the standard full inflated airbag reaches a height up to 120 mm, once the effect of the user's body weight and movement of body posture applies, it will possibly lead the airbag to swell horizontally; we gain the parameter when the user with the body weight 40 to 75 kg and sitting on the cushion, the actual height raised is between 86 to 108 mm through the repeated tests. The Breathing Cushion was designed to always inflate three airbags simultaneously for one of each time change. After the calculation, every time the cushion starts to change the shape, one of each airbag will rise at the speed of 0.62 ± 0.07 mm/s (under the condition, the user's body weight is between 40 to 75 kg). In other words, it takes two minutes and 36 s for a cushion to be fully inflated from empty; such a result is very close to some outcome of the experiment Research done by Kazuyuki Fujita et al.: the participant barely sense the change to the cushion under the speed of 5°/min, and the degree the mission to interfere is minimum, too [21].

3.3 Working Process

We analyze the sitting posture for most of the users through the collection done by somebody else. At first, we refer to the Global Posture Study from the office furniture manufacturing company - Steelcase Inc. Furthermore, for gaining further information about the posture during the work, they found nine postures none of the current chairs can fully support among more than 2,000 people's sitting posture in global six continents [26]. Guanqing Liang et al. took the cushion as the input device of interaction, adapted four basic sitting postures, including lean on the left, lean on the right, lean on forward, and being erected [19]. Joongi Shin et al. categorized posture frequently appear when using the computer for the purpose of calibrating the sitting posture into lean on forward, lead on backward, not to face the front and the head tilt [14]. Besides, in the study of Dimitris Papanikolaou et al., The preliminary collection of the day presents five different body characteristics of sitting posture: sit straight, lean left, lean right, lean forward, lean backward, but the findings at sequential experiment indicate lean back-left or lean back-right are also required to be considered when these are also frequently seen posture [27]. We consider it is experimental for the influence of the basic sitting posture; we take seven basic sitting postures from Dimitris Papanikolaou et al., the posture of the sit straight is also divided into two types – fully inflated (high) and completely leakage (low), so the cushion will be presenting in eight various types as Fig. 3 showed.

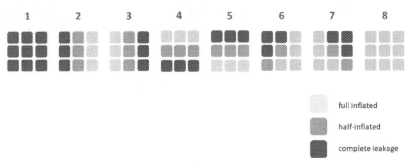

Fig. 3. The top in the picture is the user's heading while sitting; the color array from dark to light is in a sequence representing a full inflated airbag, half-inflated, complete leakage. The numbers 1 to 8 corresponding to the sitting posture in sequence are: sit straight (high), lean right, lean left, lean forward, lean backward, lean back-right, lean back-left, sit straight (low).

We also consider the user in the working hour can more evenly change the posture, but to lean on the certain side for a long hour, we arrange all these postures in a sequence of marked numbers and take a turn to proceed with the change in cycle. The user begins with no. 1 and starts inflating the air and slowly changes until the condition of total leakage. Three airbags are simultaneously inflated once there is a change, and do some estimations based on the early mentioned raising speed; the airbag becomes completely empty from fully inflated takes 2 min and 36 s. The sitting posture was divided into "change stage" and "remain stage" when cushion change and two of these stages takes four minutes in total, the cushion proceeds the cycle change in 30 min, the detail change is shown in Fig. 4:

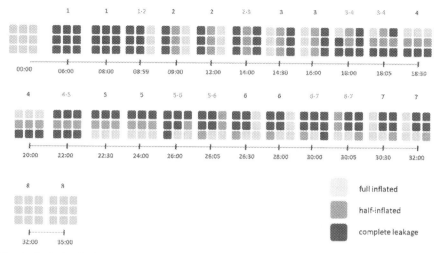

Fig. 4. In the beginning, the cushion will be activated for inflation; the experiment will be started in five minutes; the participant starts with a fully inflated cushion with various changes along the way until complete leakage, then accomplish the experiment.

4   User Study

To understand how Breathing Cushions influence a user's posture and the user's feedback, we produce an operational cushion prototype for proceeding with a simulation experiment. Through the experiment, we want to know:

- How does the user interact with the Breathing Cushion during daily office hours?
- How would the Breathing Cushion influence the user to change their posture?
- How does the user think of a Breathing Cushion?

4.1   Methods

We invited the participants to come to the research room at our school to proceed with the simulation experiment. During the experiment, the participants will sit on the Breathing Cushion for doing 30 min of office mission. The ongoing period could be too short and hardly can present fatigue and some other effects in the long run, but it is sufficient to observe the interaction mode between participants and the Breathing Cushion and the user's feedback, and also it is compliant with the purpose of the experiment at the very beginning.

For proceeding with the simulation of daily working scenarios, we allow the participant to take their notebook computer in the experiment and also agree that they can do their regular content of the assignment. Still, recreational activities - playing the game watching video is prohibited. The participant will be told before the test begin that once they sit on the Breathing Cushion in the office, they can freely get up and adjust their posture, and everything needs to be kept naturally and feel comfortable. The full video record will be taken during the experiment, including the participant's all posture changes. The participant needs to fill up a simple questionnaire before the experiment and after the experiment. And also to proceed with the semi-structural interview. There are three parts for the questionnaire including the participant's basic information, the aggressive using condition of Breathing Cushion, and how they feel about the Breathing Cushion (the score in the questionnaire is divided into five different grades, number one is Strongly Disagree and number five is Strongly Agree). The content of the semi-structural interview will proceed for particularly the aggressive description for the Breathing Cushion, the ordinary sitting posture that people get used to, the willingness to use the cushion for a long run, and also the suggestion to the cushion.

The experiment is proceeded based on the government announcement regarding the COVID-19 epidemic prevention guideline. All participants are in good physical condition, and the last two weeks, not been involved with any contagious people. The mask wore during the experimental period, all the devices were disinfected with alcohol before and after the experiment, and kept the good ventilation during the experiment.

4.2 Participants

We invited ten participants to participate in the experiment, including the student in graduate school and office workers (five male, five female); the participant is on the average of 28 years old (SD = 5.31). All the participants were informed about taking the notebook computer with them and will proceed with the ordinary daily assignment, and did not provide any additional information for the study. Besides, we need to make sure all the tests have a body weight between 40 to 75 kg. According to their self-assessment,

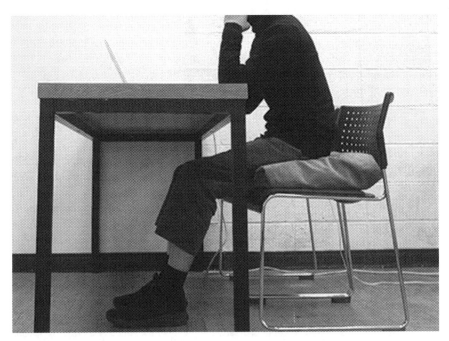

Fig. 5. The participant sits on the Breathing Cushion during working hours in the office.

70% of the participants spend more than six hours daily on the chair, and they all indicate that most of the time, they are seated for using the computer or doing office work. By the end of the experiment, we paid the participants with the reward of a beverage that costs NT dollars 65 (Fig. 5).

4.3 Procedure

1. We already informed participants before we sent our invitation:
   - The official experiment takes 30 min; the participant can use a notebook computer and proceed with the ordinary office work. Therefore, we ask the participants to prepare their computers when they are coming.
   - During the experimental period, non-office work - playing the game, watching the video, and eating is prohibited.
   - Try not to wear any coat during the experiment for the convenience of taking this shot and record sitting posture.
   - The whole process will be recorded, including voice and the video, all the data for academic Research only; the research team will comply with research ethics and never disclose the personal information to the general public to secure the stealthiness of data.
2. When the participant arrives, the notebook computer and some other device they're going to use will be properly set up at the office desk. In the meantime, the workers of the experiment will activate the switch and fully inflate the cushion in advance.
3. The participant sits on the ordinary chair to fill up the basic information on the questionnaire and sign up for the agreement.
4. The participants can move the chair with a Breathing Cushion to the location where they felt comfortable and was told feel natural and comfortable then sit on the cushion and do the job, and they can freely get up any time to adjust the posture and all the reaction and the interaction without any limits.
5. The participant is at the cushion and does the ordinary job assignment; the experiment takes 30 min in total and to be recorded all the way through.
6. When the experiment is accomplished, the participant goes back to the ordinary chair to accomplish the other copy of the questionnaire after the experiment and then proceed to semi-structural interview meetings (Fig. 6).

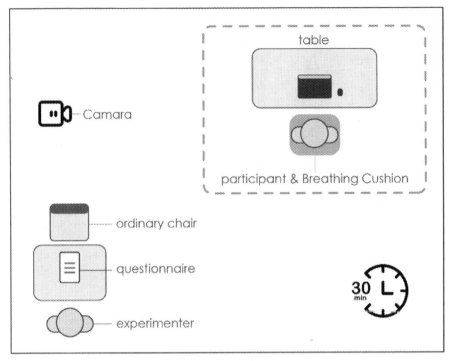

Fig. 6. The location of the experiment is in the research room of the school. The entire arrangement is shown in the picture.

5   Results

All the participants with their notebook computer and required tools based on our observation and the feedback from the participant, the office work in the computer including programming, 3D painting model, making the report, the script edition, and the reply the message. From an overall point of view, the participant and the Breathing Cushion with apparent and frequent interaction.

5.1   Posture Changing

To acquire a further understanding of how participants react to Breathing Cushions, we take one of each participant's change of sitting posture to mark the timeline (Fig. 7). As long as the aggressive action of getting up, stretching, and gesture adjustment are observed, they will all be marked in the timeline. We separate the male and female for subsequential the difference comparison.

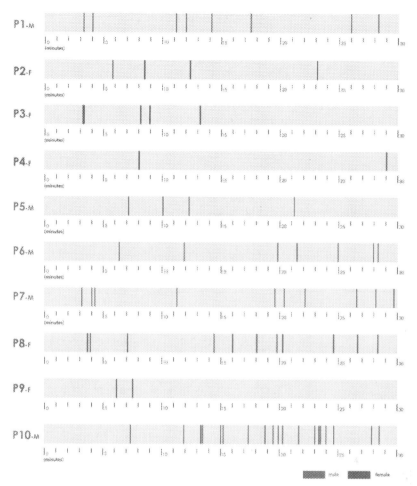

Fig. 7. The general illustration of the timeline of participant's change of sitting posture, one of each line marked on the timeline represents one group with sitting posture change.

First, for the differences of the influence made to the participant to compare the subject of "change stage" and "remain stage," this will help us understand how the Breathing Cushion influences the user's sitting posture. We integrate all the participants' timelines of the change of sitting posture and overlap and compare the change of Breathing Cushion's timeline. Figure 8 indicates that 80.6% of the posture change events overlap with the timeline for the process of Breathing Cushion shape change, 19.4% is the proportion for participants to change the posture, but the cushion remains the shape. For the total number of the events of change the sitting posture, the participant changed the sitting posture 6.6 times on average in a half of an hour (SD = 5.32); in other words, 13.2 times of sitting posture change per hour on the average.

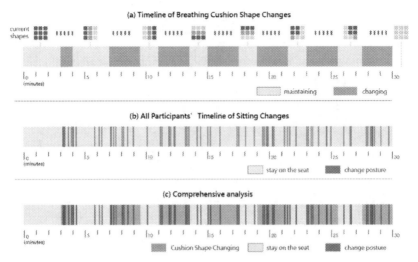

Fig. 8. (a) The timeline of Breathing Cushion at "change stage" and "remain stage," (b) the integration of timeline for the change of sitting posture for all the participants (c) the comparison of overlap.

Besides, we found something is interesting while comparing the difference between genders. Although both genders were very close to the proportion to be influenced to the sitting posture at "change stage" and "remain stage" (79% for male, 79.5% for female) when the calculation is only for the times to change the sitting posture, you may find that the total times of sitting posture change for a female is much less than male, not even half of times the male bear. In this period of 30 min, the male changes the sitting posture 9.6 times (SD = 5.68), 3.6 times for the female (SD = 2.97).

5.2 Sitting Experience

After the experiment, we asked about the using condition while the cushion changes in the aggressive assessment questionnaire. To consider the overall aspect of view, almost none of the participants believe they will not be influenced by the Breathing Cushion (M: 1.8, SD: 0.63) regardless of positive or negative. Except for one participant (P3), all the participants express that they want to adjust the sitting posture when the cushion continuously changes the shape (M: 4.1, SD: 1.29). They also try to change the sitting posture as much as to be compliant with the current shape of the cushion (M: 4.3, SD: 1.25). Such a result is similar to the conclusion observed directly in the previous experiments. Under the background like this, we submit a question: when the participant sits on the cushion, what stage of cushion change intends the participant to change the sitting posture? When the participant realizes the cushion is about to change the shape, they immediately pay attention to following the cushion to change the posture or change the posture because they can not stand for the current shape of the cushion? The conclusion of the questionnaire indicates that more participants belong to the first one, but two participants (P2, P6) say they will keep focusing on changing the posture along with the cushion changing the shape (M: 3.9, SD: 1.37).

About the participant's aggressive feeling to the Breathing Cushion, In the questionnaire, we ask some questions including interesting, to stimulate the curiosity, irritating, influence the attention, and the influence to the work efficiency on an aggressive point of view. In the aspect of being interesting and curiosity is stimulated, the result tends to be affirmative (M: 3.6, SD: 1.35). These could be related to the comfortableness of the cushion and that effect on the work efficiency. Most of the participants indicate in the questionnaire the shape change Breathing Cushion is irritating and annoying (M: 3.5, SD: 0.97), it will influence attention when doing the job (M: 3.9, SD: 1.60). Even so, two participants (P1, P7) believe their focus and intention will not be influenced by the Breathing Cushion at all.

5.3 Qualitative Feedback

We proceed to a semi-structural interview with the participant right after the experiment. Initially, we questioned them about how they felt about the cushion; many participants (P1, P5, P7, P9, P10) mentioned that at the beginning they tried sitting on the cushion they felt irritating, and they were not used to it but gradually when they focus on the work they do, the acceptance is improved and gradually get used to it. But there are few participants (P4, P8) who just cannot get used to the change of the cushion from the beginning to the end. P4 indicates, "I feel sore to my waist and the neck from the beginning to the end, and I need to use my belly and the feet during the whole process and push hard; it made me very uncomfortable." And P8 said, "I don't feel too good. What I'm feeling is it pushed me away. Later on, I would directly move my hip to the air-free area, Unconsciously try to be away from the air-inflated area, I think it probably wants me to get up and take a break?". The time the participant feel the most uncomfortable, many participants (P8, P9, P10) feel lean to the right at the beginning is the moment feel uncomfortable, but some people also feel bad to lean left (P6) or to lean forward (P7) is the moment they feel that extremely uncomfortable.

Besides, we also asked the participant whether they would continuously change their posture in the office under the normal situation. The interesting thing is, six of them feedback: "We will change the way we sit once we start to work in the office until the mission is over." All the participants are female (P2, P3, P4, P8, P9), but one is male (P10). Such a condition allows us to pay attention to the posture change that may have some differences between the genders; in the meantime, this corresponds to what we observed at an early stage of the experiment. The rest of the feedback "we do have the habit of changing the way we sit ordinarily," among these people (P1, P5, P6, P7) they mentioned respectively "this cushion reminds me to change the posture, and it is a change with the balance and the rhyme, it allows me not to feel sore for maintaining some improper seating posture for too long" (P6, P7), and "sit on the cushion would give me the feeling not to move but maintaining the posture because what I feel is it will help me to change the posture, so I don't need to move my body." (P1, P5).

The question is whether these participants will continually use the Breathing Cushion; some of the participants provide positive answers (P3, P5, P6, P7). But in the negative reply when we ask them the reason including "I probably need to spend money to buy a new table or the chair to fit the cushion" (P8), "It's very annoying for continuously moving" (P9), "Does it have some influence to my health condition to the pelvis and the spine?" (P10).

Finally, we investigate whether the participants have some additional Suggestions to design or the heading to thc improvement For the Breathing Cushion. Two participants (P3, P9) mention that they expect to have a massage and the thermal function, P7 say all that friction force is too low, and it's easy for the person to become slippery and can hardly stay on the cushion, so he suggests the sheet material for the cushion may consider to increase the friction force or to add some sort of support at the front of the cushion. P9 submits the idea that if it is available of APP, it will help the user meet adjustment till the end goal and the frequency, and it may improve the user willingness to use it in the long run. P2 feedback that sometimes the degree of incline and the strength of the action seem to be way too far, the person who has an injury at the waist may have trouble using it for additional damage. P8 has some doubts about the noise the cushion created: the noise is too loud when the cushion suddenly leaks the air; such a noise even bears a higher interfere degree than the shape change of it to me.

5.4 Discussion

The analysis for the outcome of the experiment shows that the frequency for the user to change the sitting posture has a significant relationship with a Breathing Cushion. We also acquire some feedback which is helpful for us to improve the Breathing Cushion experience of sitting posture.

At first, at the point of timeline for the change of sitting posture, we discovered 80.6% of the event of sitting posture change has something to do with the Breathing Cushion. And 13.2 times of sitting posture change on the average per hour vs. 7.8 ± 5.2 times of sitting posture change on the average per hour from the study of Jasper Reenalda et al. has a significant gap [11]. The outcome is very similar to the feedback from the participant in the questionnaire: except to one participant, almost no participant would feel the Breathing Cushion would not influence them, and also because the cushion will continuously change the shape, the participant well keep thinking about adjusting the seating posture to fit the current shape of the cushion. Such a discovery will help us to understand how Breathing Cushion influences the user to change the posture, and such a concept will become the foundation for subsequential development.

Besides, we also found a phenomenon worth noticing in the experiment: The differences in changing the sitting posture between male and female participants. From the point of average times for one of each participant's times to changing the sitting posture, the times for the female is not even reach 50% times for the male; this is perhaps related to their original working habits. We also asked about the sitting posture in the office during the ordinary working day in the semi-structural interview meeting. All the female participants mentioned that when they fully focus on doing the job in the office, they barely change any sitting posture until the mission is accomplished or the break time arrives, but male participants are almost in the opposite situation. It allows us to notice that all the participants in the study of Jasper Reenalda et al. are male [11], and there is no discussion mentioning the differences in sitting posture change between females and males. It requires more research samples and time; then, it can take further study to find out the differences. We also suggest for subsequential study, especially to the subject of changing sitting posture and the related field need to include differences between the genders.

We understand the same height of the cushion, angle, shape, and frequency can hardly fit one of each person through the questionnaires and the interview. Some participants feel most uncomfortable when they lean to the right, but the other person feels most uncomfortable when they lean left or lean forward. Each participant has a different reaction and points at a timeline when coping with the change of Breathing Cushion. Such an outcome of the experiment, plus the early mention of gender difference, allows us to disclose the P9 participant submits "to take APP to control the Breathing Cushion with potential to change the frequency and the angle." The user can reach the maximum performance of the cushion if they can make some arrangements based on the user habit and the demand. It is perhaps the essential factor if the Breathing Cushion needs to be practically used in daily living.

The negative influence of Breathing Cushion includes the noise generated during inflation, the sudden and ongoing shape change, the incline to cause the sore waist, and the uncomfortableness caused by the cushion itself. Although many participants mentioned that all these issues would distract the working concentration and diminish the working efficiency; strictly speaking, the core of the concept for Breathing Cushion is to prevent the user from immersing in such a comfortable but unbalanced sitting posture. The shape change caused temporary uncomfortableness, then pushed the user to be more frequently to change the current sitting posture and to relieve the hazardous caused by long hours sitting. Of course, the concept will conflict with the expectation of an ordinary cushion, but it is also obvious that is the goal we need to overcome and take the step further to get over with.

6   Conclusion and Future Work

The study presents the Breathing Cushion and expects to apply the feature of constantly changing to the cushion's shape to increase the user's frequency to change the sitting posture to diminish caused damage to health. We execute this simulation test through the physical prototype to explore the interaction model, the potential user experience, and the heading of design improvements. All this preliminary exploration and the study are beneficial to subsequential development and some other application with that concept.

In the future, we will take the concept of Breathing Cushion as the foundation and combine to user feedback of this experiment to develop more applications in various layers. It includes adding the pressure transmitter to enable the cushion and the user to develop more different interactions. And change pattern can be extended to the back of the chair or even the entire chair. We go deeper into the research to the number of the area or the category of sitting posture. And to establish an even more stable basis with the concept and to carry out aggressive sitting posture to reduce the damage caused to the human body. Besides, such a device is also possible to be applied to some other territories, the pressure transmission to assist seniors in changing the sitting posture to reduce the chance to suffer decubitus or to help the person with the wheelchair get up through the inflated shape change. In the past few years, smart house living and the human-computer interaction prosperously developed in many different subjects, simultaneously promoting the new generation of non-language, physical, and embedded experiments. We anticipate that we can bring up more discussion and improvement in the human-computer interaction territory along with further development and innovative concept.

References

1. Matthews, C., et al.: Amount of time spent in sedentary behaviors in the United States, 2003–2004. Am. J. Epidemiol. **167**, 875–881 (2008)
2. Healy, G., et al.: Objectively-measured sedentary time, physical activity and metabolic risk: the AusDiab study (2021)
3. Parry, S., Straker, L.: The contribution of office work to sedentary behavior associated risk. BMC Public Health **13**, 296 (2013)
4. Buckley, J., et al.: The sedentary office: an expert statement on the growing case for change towards better health and productivity. Br. J. Sports Med. **49**, 1357–1362 (2015)
5. Van Dieen, J., Looze, M., Hermans, V.: Effects of dynamic office chairs on trunk kinematics, trunk extensor EMG and spinal shrinkage. Ergonomics **44**, 739–750 (2001)
6. Carter, J., Banister, E.: Musculoskeletal problems in VDT work: a review. Ergonomics **37**, 1623–1648 (1994)
7. Network, S., Ridgers, N.: Letter to the editor: standardized use of the terms "sedentary" and "sedentary behaviours" (2012)
8. Ryan, C., Grant, P., Dall, P., Granat, M.: Sitting patterns at work: objective measurement of adherence to current recommendations. Ergonomics **54**(6), 531–538 (2011)
9. Bendix, T.O.M., Poulsen, V., Klausen, K., Jensen, C.: What does a backrest actually do to the lumbar spine? Ergonomics **39**, 533–542 (1996)
10. Lueder, R.: Ergonomics of seated movement. A review of the scientific literature. Humanics ergosystems, Encino (2004)
11. Reenalda, J., Geffen, P., Nederhand, M., Jannink, M., Ijzerman, M., Rietman, J.: Analysis of healthy sitting behavior: interface pressure distribution and subcutaneous tissue oxygenation. J. Rehabil. Res. Dev. **46**, 577–586 (2009)
12. Rietveld, E.: Situating the embodied mind in a landscape of standing affordances for living without chairs: materializing a philosophical worldview. Sports Med. **46**(7), 927–932 (2016). https://doi.org/10.1007/s40279-016-0520-2
13. Hong, J.-K., Song, S., Cho, J., Bianchi, A.: Better posture awareness through flower-shaped ambient avatar. In: Proceedings of the Ninth International Conference on Tangible, Embedded, and Embodied Interaction - TEI 2014, pp. 337–340 (2015)
14. Shin, J., Choi, W., Lee, U., Saakes, D.: Actuating a monitor for posture changes. In: Extended Abstracts of the 2018 CHI Conference on Human Factors in Computing Systems, pp. 1–6 (2018)
15. Shin, J.-G., et al.: Slow robots for unobtrusive posture correction. In: Proceedings of the 2019 CHI Conference on Human Factors in Computing Systems - CHI 2019, pp. 1–10 (2019)
16. Shin, J.G., Kim, D., So, C., Saakes, D.: Body follows eye: unobtrusive posture manipulation through a dynamic content position in virtual reality, pp. 1–14 (2020)
17. Lee, L.B., Wu, S., Reyes, M.J., Saakes, D.: The effects of interruption timings on autonomous height-adjustable desks that respond to task changes, pp. 1–10 (2019)
18. Ma, C., Li, W., Gravina, R., Du, J., Li, Q., Fortino, G.: Smart cushion-based activity recognition: prompting users to maintain a healthy seated posture. IEEE Syst. Man Cybern. Mag. **6**, 6–14 (2020)

19. Liang, G., Cao, J., Liu, X., Han, X.: Cushionware: a practical sitting posture-based interaction system. In: Conference on Human Factors in Computing Systems - Proceedings (2014)
20. Ren, X., Visser, V., Lu, Y., Brankaert, R., Offermans, S., Nagtzaam, H.: FLOW pillow: exploring sitting experience towards active ageing. In: Proceedings of the 18th International Conference on Human-Computer Interaction with Mobile Devices and Services Adjunct, Florence, Italy, pp. 706–713. Association for Computing Machinery (2016)
21. Fujita, K., Suzuki, A., Takashima, K., Ikematsu, K., Kitamura, Y.: TiltChair: manipulative posture guidance by actively inclining the seat of an office chair, pp. 1–14 (2021)
22. Shiotani, K., Sakamoto, Y., Chugo, D., Yokota, S., Hashimoto, H.: A depressurization motion analysis and its assistance for pressure sore prevention of a seated patient on a wheelchair, pp. 1510–1515 (2014)
23. Ghosal, R., Rana, B., Kapur, I., Parnami, A.: Rapid prototyping of pneumatically actuated inflatable structures. In: The Adjunct Publication of the 32nd Annual ACM Symposium on User Interface Software and Technology, New Orleans, LA, USA, pp. 78–80. Association for Computing Machinery (2019)
24. Sato, H., et al.: Soft yet strong inflatable structures for a foldable and portable mobility. In: Extended Abstracts of the 2020 CHI Conference on Human Factors in Computing Systems, Honolulu, HI, USA, pp. 1–4. Association for Computing Machinery (2020)
25. Kuster, R., Bauer, C., Gossweiler, L., Baumgartner, D.: Active sitting with backrest support: is it feasible? Ergonomics **61**, 1–33 (2018)
26. Steelcase Inc.: Global Posture Study (2015). http://www.steelcase.com/en/products/category/seating/task/gesture/pages/global-posture-study.aspx
27. Papanikolaou, D., Brush, A.J., Roseway, A.: BodyPods: designing posture sensing chairs for capturing and sharing implicit interactions. In: TEI 2015 - Proceedings of the 9th International Conference on Tangible, Embedded, and Embodied Interaction, pp. 375–382 (2015)

User Feedback Design in AI-Driven Mood Tracker Mobile Apps

Hsi Yuan Chu and Yvette Shen[(✉)]

The Ohio State University, Columbus, OH, USA
{chu.617,shen.1049}@osu.edu

Abstract. AI-driven civilian healthcare systems can offer personalized mental health care to more people. When users provide feedback to the system, they can influence the results of the AI models and improve their user experiences over time. In this study, we investigate feedback designs in mood tracker apps and identify feedback implementation opportunities through the lens of user experience and user interface design. We reviewed the feedback designs on popular mood tracker apps and discovered that the feedback mechanisms were not regularly implemented in all stages of tracking moods. To explore feedback design opportunities in line with user actions, user mindsets, and user emotions, a journey map was developed to visualize the interaction with a mood tracker app from the user perspective. Based on the journey map, a mood tracker app prototype was created for the purpose of user testing. The preliminary user testing results validated some feedback design recommendations that highlight the human-centered design approach of crafting user experiences that leverage AI.

Keywords: Feedback design · User interface design · User experience design · Mood tracking · AI-driven health apps

1 Introduction

The development of technology enables new methods of mental health care and mental health analysis. Technological innovations help people connect with mental health professionals, receive diagnoses, manage or mitigate symptoms, track health parameters, and monitor treatments. Technology-enabled mental health support can have the benefit of making the mental health resources more accessible to more people, providing consistent and objective assistance, and empowering consumers to have a more active role in their own well-being [1, 2]. Among the substantial number of mental health-related mobile apps, one popular function is mood tracking. Mood tracking is a positive psychology strategy to help individuals actively manage their mental health. It involves recording a person's mood at set time intervals and then identifying patterns in how their mood changes [3]. It has been suggested as a method to help healthy individuals to stay in healthy emotional states and assist people who suffer from mental diseases such as anxiety and bipolar disorder to better manage their health conditions [3, 4].

© The Author(s), under exclusive license to Springer Nature Switzerland AG 2022
M. Kurosu (Ed.): HCII 2022, LNCS 13304, pp. 346–358, 2022.
https://doi.org/10.1007/978-3-031-05412-9_24

Mood and emotion are subjective experiences. Consequently, most mood tracker apps rely on users to self-report their mood and related data. These apps include the basic functions of asking the users to log their mood and what contributes to it. When users share their emotions with the app, their responses are recorded and charted to show patterns over time. In a recent study on features and user reviews of different mood tracker apps [5], participants identified that the most desirable feature was the ability to personalize mood options and data results. Personalized information and messaging are effective motivations to help individuals make desired behavioral changes [6]. The emergence of artificial intelligence (AI) and machine learning can add a unique value to the user experience by creating more personalized mood tracking experience. Features to provide personalized mood data analysis and early interventions while monitoring users' mental health are examples of where the AI approach has more advantages. For AI-driven products, user feedback and control are also critical for improving the outputs of the underlying AI model and the user experience [7]. Therefore, giving users various opportunities to offer their feedback enables them to play a direct role in their interaction experience. A balanced user control may influence the results of the AI model so that the model can better serve the users with continuously improved algorithms.

In this paper, we investigate feedback designs in mood tracker apps and identify feedback implementation opportunities through the lens of user experience and user interface design. Feedback mechanisms designed from the users' perspective can potentially draw and maintain user engagement with the tool for personal and sustainable mental health support. Based on the five-stage model of personal informatics [8] we describe the design space of feedback implementation opportunities and how they could be applied to each stage of user interactions. We highlight the human-centered design approach of crafting user experiences that leverage AI, by making feedback design recommendations based on the preliminary results of user testing on a mood tracker app prototype.

2 Related Work

2.1 Implicit and Explicit Feedback

User feedback refers to any form of user reaction to a product or service that conveys information about users' preferences. The feedback is an essential communication channel between the users and the product and is the foundation for a personalized user experience [9]. AI system uses specific algorithms to analyze and interpret user inputs and data autonomously in order to provide predictions and insights as outputs. For users, providing feedback can help improve the AI algorithm and personalize the content.

User feedbacks include implicit and explicit information about the user's interest or preference for items [9–11]. Implicit feedback refers to the user actions received by the system regardless user's desire to influence the AI system [12]. It usually happens as part of regular product usages, such as the time duration users spent on the app, or the buttons they pressed in the app. Explicit feedback refers to the proactive actions performed by the user to provide commentary on the system output [9]. The number of times a video is played by the user is an example of implicit feedback. When users rate a video with a thumb up or thumb down button, it is an example of explicit feedback. Sometimes feedback may contain both implicit and explicit signals simultaneously. For example, a video added to the playlist is both a way to perform tasks of using the app (implicit) and directly provide signals to the system for better-personalized content (explicit). However, in such dual feedback, it is not always clear how users' actions match with their true intent. For example, although someone adds a video to a playlist, it does not necessarily always mean the user desires to watch more of the same type of content. It is important to consider the context of both signals and how they should be used for user experience enhancement.

The technology of AI highly relies on leveraging user feedback to build trust and connection with users, provide personalized content, and improve the overall user experience [7]. But not all feedback on an AI-driven mobile app is connected to the AI model. Some feedback mechanisms are available for customizing user settings and preference display. Some are used to collect suggestions and ideas for future improvement of the general usage of the app. In this paper, we only focus on feedback designs that have the potential of influencing the AI model.

2.2   User Interface and Experience Design Theories

Because user feedback is an indispensable part of most AI systems, how and when to incorporate a feedback can have a profound impact on the AI technology and the understanding of the user. On the topic of balancing the information that AI needs to know and the information users are willing to provide, little study is done through the lens of user interface (UI) and user experience (UX) design. One literature contribution is the People + AI Guidebook developed by Google [7]. The "Feedback and Control" chapter of the guidebook discussed some guidelines when designing feedback systems. The guidelines include keeping the data collection process transparent and adjustable for users, balancing control and automation, and communicating value- and time-to-impact to users.

Many theories and principles rooted in cognitive psychology, behavioral science, and graphic design are useful resources when designing feedback systems for AI. We categorized some key theories into three focus areas: user attention, user interactions, and user decisions.

User Attention. *Attentional bias* refers to how people's perception is affected by selective factors in their attention [13]. Understanding the attentional bias helps designers to consider using additional values or visual stimuli for items that are more in line with users' specific concerns and interests.

Visual anchors are design elements that are used to guide users' eyes on the screen [14]. These design elements are tangible visual marks such as lines, shapes, and textures which carry energy and tensions based on orientation, position, and proximity to each other. The design elements are also controlled by visual channels of size, color, position, shape, and tilt, which can create contrast and emphasis that influence the perceived hierarchy of information. The interplay of the energy and tension creates directional forces in a composition that guides viewers' visual flow and attention.

In psychology, *sensory adaptation* refers to change in responsiveness to constant stimulus over time [15]. Users tend to gradually tune out stimuli they are repeatedly exposed to. Therefore, if users are expected to take notice and take actions, the elements that induce that action need to appear fresh and different.

User Interactions. *Fritts law* states that the longer the distance and the smaller the target's size, the longer it takes for users to interact with [16]. Size and distance from the desired interactions should be considered when designing the UI element with which the user interacts.

The principle of least effort means that users are more likely to act when the effort is small [17]. The least effort can be applied to the amount of thought, time, energy, or finger taps. When a design is intuitive and has a simple state of flow, it provides cognitive ease to the user.

The *endowment effect* refers to how users value something more if they feel it is theirs [18]. When designing user experience, if the product has been proven to be of personal value to users, it will enhance the prospects of user retention.

User Decisions. *Hick's Law* describes the time it takes for a person to make a decision: the more stimuli or more options users face, the harder it is for them to decide. Therefore, reducing complexity and simplifying the decision-making process for users can enhance the user experience [19, 20].

Nudge theory proposes positive reinforcement and indirect suggestions as ways to influence the behavior and decision-making of people [21]. By implementing the right "nudges" which are subtle and easy for a person to decline, designers can influence users' decision-making process in predictable and seamless ways.

Framing effects are when people's responses are influenced by the way information is presented to them. When all other things are equal, users have been consistently found to change their preference in the choice between a sure and a risky outcome when the prospects are framed in terms of gains or losses [22]. Therefore, framing questions the right way improves data accuracy and reliability.

2.3   UI Design of the Feedback Component

We identified feedback interface design patterns by reviewing collections of user flows and interface components on dribble.com, pageflows.com, and uxarchive.com. Feedback related interface design can appear in the following forms: *picklist* – users can choose one option from a pre-selected list; *multi-select* – users can select more than one option for their answers; *rating scale* – it can be a Likert scale (five or seven-point scale) or binary ratings such as thumbs up or down; *Open text* - the question format asks users to provide comments and opinions, or details on the reason behind any individual number rating. Based on the content and the context of how and where the system asks for the feedback, the purpose of different feedback collection methods include: evaluating system recommendations, improving product user experiences, and communicating with other users.

3   Research Approaches

This study takes a two-step approach to investigate the connections between feedback designs and user experiences with AI-driven mood tracker apps. The first step is to review feedback designs on available mood tracker apps and identify design patterns and missing opportunities. The second step is to use a user-centered design approach of creating a mood tracker app prototype to assess potential areas and methods of feedback integration. The design of the prototype was based on user interactions visualized by a user journey map. Among different touchpoints from the journey map, we intend to identify users' thinking and feeling, what resources, information, or confirmation may be anticipated from the feedback system.

3.1   Case Studies Reviews

Existing Mood Tracker Apps. Our initial search of existing mood tracker apps in the Apple App Store and Google Play Store is generated from the searching keywords of "mood" or "emotions" or "feelings" AND "track" or "journal" or "diary". The next-step selection is based on the following criteria: 1) the app is in the English language, 2) the app has more than 1k reviews, 3) mood tracking is the main function of the app, and the record is self-reported, 4) the app includes explicit feedback mechanisms, 5) the app provides personalized data results, predictions and/or suggestions of improvements in the free version. We identified six mood tracker apps based on these criteria at the time of the research.

Both authors downloaded the chosen apps, tested the apps, and extracted the feedback designs included in the overall in-app user experience. We focused on feedback designs that allow users to rate or comment or select the output from the system's suggestions while using the app. Therefore, push notifications were excluded from this study. Because personalized care is one of the key features of AI-driven mood tracker apps, the five-stage model of personal informatics [8] is used to examine the integration of feedback designs. The five stages and their corresponding mood tracker app content are: *Preparation*: background introductions and activities before data collection begins; *Collection*: when users input their mood-related data into the system; *Integration*: data display and data connections based on user input; *Reflection*: the summarized display of user data that allows users aware of their mood status in a short or long term; *Action*: activities triggered by users' newfound understanding of themselves [5, 8].

Feedback Implementation Results. From the six mood tracker apps, two of them are mainly based on chatbot platforms to interact with the users and collect the user data. The other four rely on selections or scales to interact with the users and gather information. Table 1 shows the comparisons of feedback implementations and their interface visual representations on the six tested apps.

Table 1. Feedback design comparisons

	Preparation stage	Collection stage	Integration stage	Reflection stage	Action stage
MindDoc	Picklist (*personal information*)	N/A	N/A	Rating scale (*insightfulness*)	Like button
Reflectly	N/A	N/A	N/A	N/A	Yes/no (*Accept daily challenge*)
Sanvello	Multi-select (*User goals*)	N/A	N/A	N/A	N/A
Woebot*	N/A	Multi-select/Thumbs up/dn, Like button	N/A	Thumbs up/dn, Like button	Thumbs up/dn, Like button, Open textbox
Wysa*	Multi-select (*User goals*)	Open text-box	N/A	Thumbs up/dn, emoticon	Open textbox (User type in their feelings)
Sayana	Multi-select (*User goals*)	N/A	N/A	Yes/no question (*do you find this helpful?*)	Yes/no question (*do you find this helpful?*)

* Chatbot-based interaction

In general, feedback mechanisms are not fully implemented in all tested apps. Most apps include implicit feedback in the beginning (preparation stage) and the end (action stage) of the user interaction. In the other stages of mood tracking, the feedback design is limited to binary ratings such as a thumbs up/like button, or a shared button which could indicate the user's likeness of the content. The selection buttons include the following scenarios: selecting different content, selecting different qualitative evaluations, or selecting Yes or No for a given task. Very few feedback areas allow customized input data from users. The ones that do, user input data are not validated by the system. For example, users may type random letters responding to a question, and the system will still reply with a generic statement. None of the mood tracker apps frame their feedback requests in terms of specific user needs. The benefits and suggestions are also framed around pre-determined lists provided by the app rather than customized responses. The reason behind the generic approach could relate to issues of technology, privacy, ethics, and regulation [23]. We do not have sufficient data to show whether the implemented feedback systems are aligned with AI model improvement with these Apps.

3.2 User Journey Analysis

To understand the essence of the entire experience from the user's perspective, design researchers use journey maps to shed light on users' mindset and envision the experience from the user's standpoint. A journey map is a visualization that illustrates the sequence users go through, over time, as they encounter the various facets of connecting to the product [24]. It is used, in this study, to hypothesize how a mood tracker app is used and consider feedback design opportunities during the user interaction process.

Because most commercial mood tracker apps are designed for the general population, the user persona [25] in this designed scenario is a healthy college student. This student wants to use a mood tracker app to help monitor her mood over time, and learn how external factors may affect her mental wellness. The app functions are based on the six popular mood tracker apps we tested in the first stage of this study. We used the journey map to plot the insight of user actions, user mindsets, and user emotions while going through the steps of interacting with the app. These insights provide the opportunity to understand how feedback design may optimize the user experience. The journey phases are also structured from the five-stage model of personal informatics. With each phase, we document anticipated features from a mood tracker app, anticipated actions taken by the user, and the user's mindsets mapped to the actions. By plotting out all the steps the user goes through and achieve her goal, the visual artifact helps us to discover opportunities for implementing feedback designs for an improved user experience. These opportunities can turn journey maps from design artifacts that visualize a journey into an action plan for introducing changes that create a better user experience for end-users.

There are feedback opportunities in every stage of mood tracking as indicated in Fig. 1. Knowing users' precise intent from the very beginning and using feedback to improve the AI model can be helpful to create a positive feeling of personal care and support. It also helps to remove the need for users to do extra work along the process. Therefore, slightly decrease the cost of action and the opportunities to be distracted from the user's side. Users would also be more willing to provide accurate information when they know how it might benefit them directly. The impact scope of this benefit needs to communicate to users in a transparent way at different stages. Other contextual considerations with the goal of not overburdening users' limited faculties include chunking of the information, timing and framing of the messages.

Fig. 1. Journey map of a healthy college student using a mood-tracker app.

4   Prototype Design and Usability Testing

A mood tracker app prototype was developed based on the user journey map to help test concepts, validate ideas, and understand users' expectations one step further. The main design goal of the prototype is to include more seamless feedback opportunities which are "authentic and personal" in order to establish trust between the user and the data tracking system. The preparation stage is designed to include minimal steps but with a clear message to encourage user interactions by leveraging their personal gains. After an iterative prototyping process, we discovered that more feedback opportunities could be incorporated by integrating the collection and action stages. For example, at the end of one data collection activity, a question will appear in response to the current user input (Fig. 2). It emphasizes a personalized recommendation, and it also explains to the users why such recommendations are made. If the collection and action stages are separated, like how they are operated on most of the tested apps, then the feedback is only seen at the end of the action stage (Fig. 3).

Fig. 2. More feedback opportunities can be included when we integrate the collection and action stage.

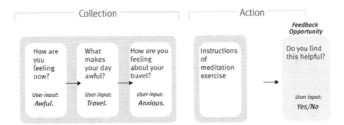

Fig. 3. There is only one feedback opportunity when the collection and action stages are separated.

The questions to prompt user input are framed to emphasize user benefits, and the tone of voice focuses on a tailored, personal appeal. We created two versions of the reflection screen to compare how interface designs of data summary might influence user retention. One design relies on multiple graphs and pictograms to summarize user data, which is similar to what we see from the tested mood tracker apps (Fig. 2-A). The other design uses one simple graph and mainly tells the users their data story from a first-person witness point of view (Fig. 2-B) (Fig. 4).

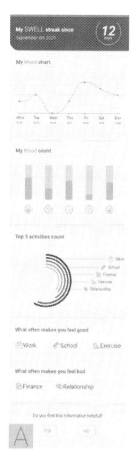

Fig. 4. Each participant is shown both designs of the reflection screen and is asked which version they prefer.

User testing was conducted with the observational method and an online question-naire. The moderated testing sessions were performed remotely using screen-sharing software Zoom. Participants were asked to click through the app prototype and per-formed several tasks facilitated by the design researcher. As the participant performed these tasks, the facilitator observed the participant's behavior and listened for feedback. The questionnaire provides additional information related to users' overall impression of the app, the sense of trust, and users' inclination of providing data and feedback.

We tested the prototype with seven users [26]. The overall impression of the app prototype is positive. All participants identified "friendly" and "easy-to-use" to describe their overall experiences. All participants identified "relevant", "sincere", or "friendly" to describe the questions they were asked from the prototype. The concern about integrating collection and action stages is that the user may feel the entire process being too long and inquisitive. But participants were able to reach the end of the interaction without feeling overwhelmed or discomfort. Five participants said that they would provide accurate information to the app. The reason of why two users selected "probably not" to provide accurate information to the app was because that they "need to learn more about the app" before making the decision.

The preference between the two summary screens was split evenly among the participants. The ones who preferred screen A liked how the visual methods helped them to see trends more clearly and invited them to pay more attention. The ones who chose screen B thought that the text was easy to interpret at a quick glance. Both screens share the same levels of efficacy to motivate the participants to continue using the app.

5   Conclusions

AI-driven civilian healthcare systems can offer personalized mental health care to more people. When users provide feedback to the system, they can influence the results of the AI models and improve their user experiences over time. We reviewed the feedback designs on six popular mood tracker apps and discovered that the feedback mechanisms were not regularly implemented in all stages of tracking moods. Feedback gathering mostly occurred at the beginning (preparation stage) and the end (action stage) of user interactions. Most feedback interface designs were limited to multi-select and binary ratings. To investigate feedback design opportunities in line with user actions, user mindsets, and user emotions, we used a journey map to visualize the interaction with a mobile app from the user perspective. The journey map demonstrated that the user experience could be improved by including more sources of feedback. Based on the journey map user experience, we designed a mood tracker app and tested the prototype with observational method and a questionnaire. Participants responded positively to the overall usability and the interactive experience. The additional feedback-related touchpoints had no negative impact on the user experience when the questions reflected personal benefits clearly.

Personalized care and support are expected from an AI-driven healthcare system. Knowing the precise intent from the user can lead to a more efficient process that addresses user's needs. However, the current available mood tracker apps all rely on generic content to provide advice and suggestions to help users build better mental health for themselves. Presenting users with corresponding feedback opportunities can have the potential of training a personalized AI model and offering relevant output that effectively fulfill users' needs. The system needs to build trust with the user before collecting data from them, and it needs to explain clearly of why the data is needed and how it is used. Qualitative data collection has been missing from almost all feedback designs in existing mood tracker apps. Chatbot platforms mainly use selection buttons with pre-filled messages to collect user input. The few examples of where personal and authentic feedback are allowed, user input data is not validated and the reaction to such data is still limited to a blanket response. There are great opportunities in feedback collection of identifying key ideas, themes, and patterns through unstructured data that can bring new levels of insight and help users with their individual mental health concerns.

For AI-driven products, there is an essential balance between automation and user control [7]. The level of control users have over the AI can also influence their willingness to provide valuable feedback. The tradeoffs of collecting or not collecting different feedback data need to be discussed with all stakeholders, such as engineers and business executives, in addition to the general users. The next step of this study will focus on identifying the balance of the automation and control threshold and testing different design stimuli that facilitate feedback interactions between the users and the AI system.

References

1. Donker, T., Petrie, K., Proudfoot, J., Clarke, J., Birch, M.R., Christensen, H.: Smartphones for smarter delivery of mental health programs: a systematic review. J. Med. Internet Res. **15**(11), e247 (2013)
2. NIH National Institute of Mental Health, Technology and the Future of Mental Health Treatment. https://www.nimh.nih.gov/health/topics/technology-and-the-future-of-mental-health-treatment/index.shtml. Accessed 20 Jan 2022
3. Malh, G.S., Hamilton, A., Morris, G., Mannie, Z., Das, P., Outhred, T.: The promise of digital mood tracking technologies: are we heading on the right track? Evid. Based Ment. Health **20**(4), 102–107 (2017)
4. Nicholas, J., Larsen, M.E., Proudfoot, J., Christensen, H.: Mobile apps for bipolar disorder: a systematic review of features and content quality. J. Med. Internet Res. **17**(8), e198 (2015)
5. Caldeira, C., Chen, Y., Chan, L., Pham, V., Chen, Y., Zheng, K.: Mobile apps for mood tracking: an analysis of features and user reviews. In: AMIA Annual Symposium Proceedings, AMIA Symposium, pp.495–504 (2017)
6. Kreuter, M., Farrell, D., Olevitch, L., Brennan, L., Rimer, B.K.: Tailoring Health Messages: Customizing Communication with Computer Technology, 1st edn. Routledge, New York (2000)
7. Google PAIR, People + AI Guidebook. https://pair.withgoogle.com/chapter/feedback-controls/. Accessed 20 Jan 2022
8. Li, I., Dey, A., Forlizzi, J.: A stage-based model of personal informatics systems. In: Proceedings of the 28th International Conference on Human Factors in Computing Systems, SIGCHI, pp. 557–566 (2010)
9. Jawaheer, G., Szomszor, M., Kostkova, P.: Comparison of implicit and explicit feedback from an online music recommendation service. In: 1st International Workshop on Information Heterogeneity and Fusion in Recommender Systems (HetRec 2010), pp.47–51. Association for Computing Machinery, New York (2010)
10. White, R., Jose, J., Ruthven, I.: Comparing explicit and implicit feedback techniques for web retrieval: TREC-10 interactive track report. In: Proceedings of the Tenth Text Retrieval Conference (TREC-10), Gaithersburg, Maryland (2001)
11. Jannach, D., Zanker, M., Felfernig, A., Friedrich, G.: Recommender Systems: An Introduction. Cambridge University Press, Cambridge (2010)
12. Szaszko, M.: UX design for implicit and explicit feedback in an AI product. https://becominghuman.ai/ux-design-for-implicit-and-explicit-feedback-in-an-ai-product-9497dce737ea. Accessed 25 Jan 2022
13. Baron, J.: Thinking and Deciding, p. 187. Cambridge University Press, Cambridge (2008)
14. Wesslen, R., Santhanam, S., Karduni, A., Cho, I., Shaikh, S., Dou, W.: Investigating effects of visual anchors on decision-making about misinformation. Comput. Graph. Forum **38**(3), 161–171 (2019)
15. Webster, M.A.: Evolving concepts of sensory adaptation. F1000 Biol. Rep. **4** (2012)
16. Fitts, P.M.: The information capacity of the human motor system in controlling the amplitude of movement. J. Exp. Psychol. **47**(6), 381–391 (1954)

17. Mann, T.: Library Research Models: A Guide to Classification, pp. 91–101. Oxford University Press, Oxford (1993)

18. Morewedge, C.K., Giblin, C.E.: Explanations of the endowment effect: an integrative review. Trends Cogn. Sci. **19**(6), 339–348 (2015)

19. Hick, W.E.: On the rate of gain of information. Q. J. Exp. Psychol. **4**(1), 11–26 (1952)

20. Proctor, R.W., Schneider, D.W.: Hick's law for choice reaction time: a review. Q. J. Exp. Psychol. **71**(6), 1281–1299 (2018)

21. Thaler, R.H., Sunstein, C.R.: Nudge: Improving Decisions About Health, Wealth, and Happiness. Penguin Publishing Group, New York (2009)

22. Hartmann, J., De Angeli, A., Sutcliffe, A.: Framing the user experience: information biases on website quality judgement. In: Proceedings of the SIGCHI Conference on Human Factors in Computing Systems, pp. 855–864. Association for Computing Machinery, New York (2008)

23. Bauer, M., et al.: Smartphones in mental health: a critical review of background issues, current status and future concerns. Int. J. Bipolar Disord. **8**(1), 1–19 (2020). https://doi.org/10.1186/s40345-019-0164-x

24. Gibbons, S.: Journey Mapping 101. Nielsen Norman Group. https://www.nngroup.com/articles/journey-mapping-101/. Accessed 26 Jan 2022

25. Pruitt, J., Grudin, J.: Personas: practice and theory. In: Proceedings of the 2003 Conference on Designing for User Experiences, DUX 2003, pp. 1–15. Association for Computing Machinery, New York (2003)

26. Nielsen, J.: Why you only need to test with 5 users. Nielsen Norman Group. https://www.nngroup.com/articles/why-you-only-need-to-test-with-5-users/. Accessed 1 Feb 2022

Keep on Running! An Analysis of Running Tracking Application Features and Their Potential Impact on Recreational Runner's Intrinsic Motivation

Dorothea Gute, Stephan Schlögl[(✉)] [ID], and Aleksander Groth

Department of Management, Communication and IT,
MCI – The Entrepreneurial University, Innsbruck, Austria
stephan.schloegl@mci.edu
https://www.mci.edu

Abstract. Physical activity is known to help improve and maintain one's health. In particular, recreational running has become increasingly popular in recent years. Yet, lack of motivation often interferes with people's routines and thus may prohibit regular uptake. This is where running tracking applications are frequently used to overcome one's weaker self and offer support. While technology artifacts, such as sport watches or running applications, usually count as extrinsic drivers, they can also impact one's intrinsic motivation levels. The aim of this study was thus to investigate upon the motivational impact of distinct features found within applications specifically used for running. Focusing on the 22 most famous running applications, a semi-structured, problem-centered interview study with $n = 15$ recreational runners showed that intrinsic motivation is stimulated from diverting runners, aiding them in their goal setting, decreasing their efforts, improving and sharing their run performance, allowing them to receive acknowledgements, as well as providing them with guidance, information, and an overall variety in their training routines.

Keywords: Running apps · Recreational runners · Intrinsic motivation · Laddering

1 Introduction

Physical activity has various benefits on humans' health which is continuously outlined by the World Health Organization (WHO)[1] as well as health professionals all around the world. Backed by a consequently increased health awareness, running has become a particularly popular recreational activity in our modern society. It requires little expertise and may be exercised in a variety of different

---

[1] Online: https://www.who.int/news-room/fact-sheets/detail/physical-activity [accessed: October 10th, 2021].

M. Kurosu (Ed.): HCII 2022, LNCS 13304, pp. 359–373, 2022.
https://doi.org/10.1007/978-3-031-05412-9_25

environments [28]. Yet, while regular engagement in running activities may boost one's overall health status, lack of time, motivation or enthusiasm are often cited as significant adversaries [3]. Recreational runners in particular have to bring in and sustain a high level of intrinsic motivation in order to keep them going [39].

Motivated people seem to be energized, while a lack of motivation is often described as 'missing the drive' or lacking inspiration to carry out an action [25]. Moreover, research has shown that intrinsic as opposed to extrinsic motivation leads to *"greater interest, greater effort, better performance, a more positive emotional tone, higher instances of flow, higher self-esteem, better adjustment, [and] greater satisfaction"* [23, p. 6]. This can be explained by the observation that intrinsically motivated individuals take action because they find it enjoyable and interesting, whereas extrinsically motivated people do so because of an outcome said action will have – one, which is usually not connected to the action itself [25]. With respect to practicing sports, intrinsically motivated people exercise because they derive pleasure and amusement from this activity, while extrinsically motivated athletes rather engage in sports to receive tangible advantages such as objects (e.g., prices), social acknowledgment, or to prevent punishment [37].

Applications for tracking runs, usually connected to different types of wearables (e.g., smartwatches), are widely used to help fight runners' lack of motivation and consequently, to a certain extend, aim to trigger behavioural change in people. Yet, in order for these applications to have a lasting effect they *"need to create enduring new habits, turning external motivations into internal ones"* [22, p. 1]. Inspired by this endeavor, the aim of this work was to investigate, how well the most popular of these running applications live up to this challenge of affecting a runners' motivation. In other words, we were investigating:

> *Which running tracking application features impact on recreational runners' intrinsic motivation, and how?*

Our report starts with a discussion of the relevant theoretical framework for the respective investigation in Sect. 2. Then, Sect. 3 describes our methodological approach including our sampling strategy. Section 4 summarizes and discusses the gained results, before Sect. 5 concludes and provides some directions for further research.

2   Theoretical Framework and Related Work

Intrinsic motivation is critical for sustaining physical activity due to it being perceived as enjoyable [27]. Further, it has been found that being extrinsically motivated, e.g. to win an award or a competition, decreases one's intrinsic motivation, for one perceives the action as controlling rather than enjoyable [6,7]. Moreover, when individuals engage in an activity which has been extrinsically motivated, they endure it less than when this external motivator is removed [23]. However, when these extrinsic rewards are not dependent on the activity or a specific achievement, their influence and consequently their controlling effect decreases. It may thus be argued, that intrinsic and extrinsic motivation are not additive [9].

2.1   Self Determination Theory

Deci & Ryan [10] suggest that intrinsic motivation becomes effective when an activity is experienced as being self-determined, and at the same time improbable or inhibited, when said activity is experienced as being controlled externally. To this end, Self Determination Theory (SDT) assumes that humans are inherently active, motivated, knowledge desiring and keen on being successful. One's social environments can endorse a person's self-determined nature, but at the same time also impede it. According to SDT, humans generally strive to feel *competent, autonomous*, and *related to others* and that social contexts can influence one's fulfillment of these needs positively as well as negatively [9,26]. While competence and autonomy have the strongest influence on intrinsic motivation, relatedness is less influential, yet still supportive (ibid.).

Vallerand distinguishes between three types of intrinsic motivation, where *"intrinsic motivation to know can be defined as engaging in an activity for the pleasure and satisfaction one experiences while learning, exploring, or trying to understand something new* [34, p. 280]. In the context of sports, an example for this type of motivation would be a basketball player who enjoys learning new offensive moves [35]. Deriving pleasure from exceeding one's own accomplishments or creating something, on the other hand, is considered *"intrinsic motivation to accomplish things"*. Lastly, taking action to experience enjoyable sensations is known as *"intrinsic motivation to experience stimulation"* (ibid.).

2.2   Hierarchical Model of Intrinsic Motivation

Enhancing SDT, the Hierarchical Model of Intrinsic Motivation (HMIM) distinguishes three hierarchical levels of motivation, i.e., the *global, contextual,* and *situational* level. Motivation at the global level understands humans to generally act according to one inherent form of motivation, disregarding the context or situation they find themselves in [34]. For example, an athlete who is intrinsically motivated towards sports behaves the same way towards their education, work, friends and leisure time [29]. On the other hand, adapting one's motivation towards a certain context is considered being motivated at the context level [34]. That is, a person being amotivated (i.e., not motivated) towards sports can simultaneously be intrinsically motivated towards their occupation [29]. Finally, situational motivation is experienced while undertaking an action. For instance, an athlete can be intrinsically motivated to study a difficult type of movement, so as to fulfill an individual need for competence [29].

Furthermore, perceived *competence, autonomy* and *relatedness* mediates the influence of social factors on these three levels. A stable social network (e.g., one's parents) that supports one's need for autonomy, may be considered a global factor, whereas the support of a trainer may be considered a contextual factor, and a positive performance review for a distinct training unit a situational factor [29].

Another rule of HMIM assumes that hierarchically higher forms of motivation influence the lower levels, which signifies a so-called *top-down effects*. Consequently, contextual motivation impacts situational motivation stronger than global motivation does and global motivation influences situational motivation [34]. In other words, a person who has high levels of intrinsic motivation on a global level will most likely possess the same type of motivation in several contexts, e.g., sports, and accordingly in specific sport situations, e.g., a particular exercise during training [29].

On the other hand, motivational changes are taken into consideration by suggesting that motivation at one level can have a *bottom-up effect* at the next higher level (ibid.). That is, intrinsic motivation at a contextual level (i.e., motivation for doing sport) can be increased during an athlete's individual training by providing him/her with a scope of action, performance feedback and a pleasant atmosphere (situational level).

Concludingly, HMIM assumes that motivation causes important consequences concerning *affect*, *cognition*, and *behavior*, leading to higher levels of creativity and learning, increased interest, positive emotions, and greater task persistence [34]. Figure 1 summarizes the different hierarchy levels of HMIM and their interrelations.

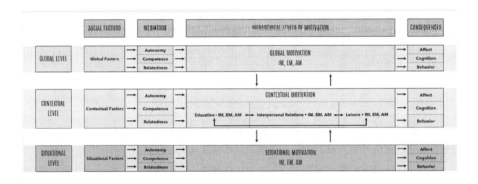

Fig. 1. Hierarchical model of intrinsic motivation adapted from Vallerand & Lalande [36, p. 46]

2.3 Goal Setting

Individual goals guide actions, particularly in athletics [12]. Difficult and specific goals are given more attention, exertion, and perseverance and therefor have a higher probability of being achieved [18]. As a result, a sense of commitment and determination to overcome or plan around potential obstacles [12] is created. Achievement Goal Theory (AGT) defines achievement behavior as *"behavior in which the goal is to develop or demonstrate - to self or to others - high ability, or to avoid demonstrating low ability"* [21, p. 328]. Respective goals may be *ego-oriented* or *task-oriented*, where the former focuses on the performance results (e.g., in the sense of a competition or social comparison) and the latter on learning and task completion (ibid.). Performance-oriented people aim to demonstrate their skills to others by competing with them, which may result in disappointment, frustration, and loss of motivation, and generally have a negative effect on one's perceived competence [11,12]. Task-oriented people, on the other hand, orient towards individual standards, and are thus less afraid of failure, which leads to a higher level of perceived competence. In a sports context, task-orientation is further associated with increased joy, intrinsic interest, and willingness for endeavor. Transferred to motivation, this means that focusing on one's tasks, i.e., the activity itself, rather than on comparing oneself to others, fosters intrinsic motivation [12]. And although McAuley & Tammen found that winning can increase intrinsic motivation, one's perceived level of competence contributes even stronger [19].

Furthermore, Ryan & Deci (2000b) state that self-reporting one's achievements increases intrinsic motivation [26] and receiving feedback contributes to one's feeling of competence [32]; although when said feedback is perceived as pressuring or controlling, it may undermine intrinsic motivation [31].

2.4   Flow

The concept of *flow* describes an optimal state of motivation, representing a prototype of intrinsic motivation [29]. Csikszentmihalyi aimed to understand an optimal experience and found that a flow effect is achieved as *"a state of concentration so focused that it amounts to absolute absorption in an activity"* [5, p. 1]. In a sports context, flow states occur when athletes are neither concerned about rational reasons against an activity, e.g., time that must be invested, nor about reasons in favor of engaging in that activity, like increased health [29]. Participation is rather encouraged by the activity itself and in doing so leading to a feeling of enjoyment [5]. Flow requires *a clear set of goals* and a balance between perceived challenges and perceived skills, as well as clear and immediate feedback; goals help direct one's behavior by conveying attention. The focus lies on the balance of challenge and skill requirements, for when the former are too demanding, one becomes too concerned about failure. When challenges are not perceived at all, one loses interest. Immediate feedback advises on ones' progress and possible adjustment of actions resulting in empowerment [4].

The four most important characteristics of flow include: (1) concentration on the task at hand, (2) merging of action and awareness, (3) having a sense of control over the activity, and (4) transformation of time [29]. Csikszentmihalyi argues that, when experiencing flow, one concentrates strongly on the given task and is able to suppress unpleasant facets of their life. The action itself merges with one's awareness and functions almost automatically. Being in control during the activity, means precisely exercising control and, therefore, providing a decrease in stress during demanding situations. Also, time seems to pass differently from how it normally does when experiencing flow. Most commonly, sequences of the action are perceived as if time would stand still, however, the experience itself is perceived as if time was passing remarkably fast [5]. While flow is known to enable peak performances, research has shown that it can also have negative effects, such as risk taking or underestimating.

2.5 Running Applications

Smartphone-based applications that track physical activities such as running, usually consist of four components [1]:

1. a logger which measures and stores exercise related data,
2. a virtual personal trainer that adds an analysis functionality and provides visual and audible performance feedback,
3. gaming and entertainment functions, and
4. community and social sharing features.

They allow for individual use (e.g., goal setting) and support social interaction (e.g., sharing and feedback). Thus, these applications aim to induce both intrinsic as well as extrinsic motivation by either engaging users in taking action *"due to feelings of pleasantness and satisfaction inherent in the activity [...] [or by receiving] recognition or approval from others (or the app itself)"* [14, p. 1428]. Investigating the potential for behavioural change based on the SDT, Villalobos-Zúñiga & Cherubini [38] found that certain application features, depending on their perceived level of external control, can either positively or negatively influence intrinsic motivation (e.g., reminders, activity feedback, motivational messages, rewards, etc.). With a particular focus on running, Bauer & Kriglstein [2] further suggest that the music and audio feedback, different types of visualization, as well as an app's competition and comparison feature helps foster athlete's motivation.

Our goal was to investigate whether those suggestions are still valid and how the different features are perceived by a specific target group; i.e., recreational runners.

3 Methodology

Building upon the work of Bauer & Kriglstein [2], we focused on the 22 top running tracking applications currently available for iOS and Android OS, and analyzed their features via $n = 15$ guided, semi-structured, problem-centered interviews. Our sampling approach used a screening questionnaire to identify participants with low intrinsic motivation towards running. We then used Kuckartz [16] structuring content analysis approach and a slight adaptation of Gutman's laddering technique [13] to explore interviewees' inherent attitudes as to how various application features may impact on their intrinsic motivation to run.

3.1 App Selection

Bauer & Kriglstein [2] analyze *"the top free running tracking applications on the market with their functionalities to identify which motivation strategies are supported by these applications in 2013"* [p. 2]. They chose to include three feature elements which they thought would motivate runners, i.e., *music and audio feedback*, *visualization*, as well as *competition and comparison with others*. As Fig. 2 shows, the authors' analysis consisted of seven steps.

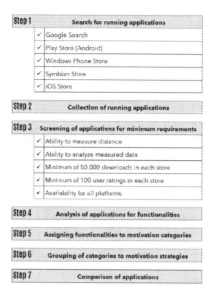

Fig. 2. Analysis of motivation strategies in running tracking applications adapted from Bauer & Kriglstein [2, p. 2]

First, a search for running applications on Google and in the different app stores (i.e., Play Store, Windows Phone Store, Symbian Store, iOS Store) had been conducted. After collecting these applications, they screened them for five minimum requirements (i.e., ability to measure distance, ability to analyze measured data, a minimum of *50K* downloads in each store, a minimum of *100* users ratings in each store, and availability for all platforms). Subsequently, the apps' functionalities were tested, assigned to different motivation categories, grouped into respective strategies and eventually compared.

Our approach followed the same example, yet as 8 years have past since Bauer & Kriglstein's work, we integrated some additional limitations. That is, based on statistics by Appfigures & VentureBeat,[2] Google's Play store was the app store with the most available apps in the first quarter of 2021 (3.482.452 applications), followed by Apple's iOS store (2.226.823 applications). Consequently, we decided to focus on these two app stores in combination with a Google search for *"Free running tracking applications"*, and to exclude the Windows phone store due to its minor size (only 669.000 available apps)[3] as well as the Symbian store, as Nokia terminated its development and support in January 2014.[4]

---

[2] Online: https://www.statista.com/statistics/276623/number-of-apps-available-in-leading-app-stores/ [accessed: January 13th, 2021].

[3] Online: https://www.statista.com/statistics/276623/number-of-apps-available-in-leading-app-stores/ [accessed: January 13th, 2021].

[4] Online: http://www.allaboutsymbian.com/news/item/18502_New_Symbian_and_Meego_applicat.php/ [accessed: January 13th, 2021].

Furthermore, we observed that Apple's iOS store does not disclose the number of downloads or reviews per application, but rather the number of zero-to-five-star ratings and their average. Since research has shown that online zero-to-five-star ratings tend to be predominantly positive and additionally rather unreliable in terms of indicating the success of a product [17], we focused solely on Google's play store to check for an app's download and review requirements, presuming that the most popular applications would be available and similarly well-known (i.e., downloaded and reviewed) in Apple's iOS store. Thus, eventually we considered apps that had at least *50K+* downloads and *100+* reviews on Google's Play store, and were also available on iOS. As this resulted in a selection of 36 running tracking apps we increased the number of minimum downloads to *500K+* so that we ended up with 22 running tracking apps for our analysis. Figure 3 shows all apps which were considered in the first round and where we defined the cut-off.   All of the 22 selected running tracking applications were installed on an iPhone SE. User profiles were created and after some test runs we started with our feature analysis.

3.2   Feature Analysis

In order to investigate the contribution of different application features to intrinsic motivation, we focused on a target population of recreational runners who show little intrinsic motivation. We used the Intrinsic Motivation Inventory (IMI) [20], which is grounded in Self Determination Theory [24] as a screening instrument. The inventory consists of seven Likert-type subscales, considering one's *interest/enjoyment, perceived choice, effort, value/usefulness, pressure/tension, perceived choice* and *relatedness*, last of which is used as a measure of relevance for interpersonal interactions.

We were able to recruit $n = 15$ participants fitting this sample frame (9 female, AVG age $=$ 24) with whom we conducted semi-structured, problem-centered interviews, using an adaptation of Gutman's laddering technique [13]. According to Schultze & Avital such a laddering technique *encourages the interviewee to elaborate on the meaning of his/her personal constructs by narratively forging links between them [...] which is achieved by asking how and why questions"* [30, p.9].

Interviewees were asked to talk about different app functions and the consequences they would attach to using them. This technique was repeated until interviewees arrived at a point where they had clearly explained their feelings towards a certain functionality of a feature and its use. Additionally, interviewees were asked to suggest features they believed running tracking applications could integrate to motivate them.

All interviews were recorded, transcribed and subsequently analyzed using Kuckartz's [16] structuring content analysis. Main categories were based on the features linked to Bauer and Krieglstein's framework. Sub-codes were created based on interviewees' perceptions regarding the feature's motivational impact. A second round of analysis assured coding reliability.

Top Running Tracking Applications 2021	Requirements			
	Google Play Store	Apple Store	Downloads	Reviews
1. Adidas Runtastic	✓	✓	50,000,000+	1,141,486
2. Nike Run Club	✓	✓	10,000,000+	1,010,123
3. Pacer	✓	✓		803,500
4. Strava	✓	✓		689,272
5. Runkeeper	✓	✓		577,444
6. Map My Run	✓	✓	5,000,000+	342,569
7. Sports Tracker	✓	✓		223,880
8. Relive: Run, Ride, Hike & more	✓	✓		227,563
9. Gstep: Pedometer, Step Counter, Running Tracker	✓	✓		135,630
10. Running Distance Tracker +	✓	✓		130,705
11 Polar Beat: Running & Fitness	✓	✓	1,000,000+	49,175
12. Decathlon Coach - Sports Tracking & Training	✓	✓		38,895
13. Yodo - Cash for walking & running	✓	✓		38,567
14. One You Couch to 5K	✓	✓		34,712
15. Runtopia: GPS Tracker for Run, Walk, Fitness, Bike	✓	✓		34,674
16. Zombies, Run!	✓	✓		23,660
17. Start to Run. Running for Beginners	✓	✓		19,434
18. Pumatrac	✓	✓		17,728
19 JomRun – Let's Run	✓	✓	500,000+	8,283
20. Charity Miles	✓	✓		7,395
21. Running Trainer: Run Tracker & 5K Running App	✓	✓		4,087
22. 5K to 10K	✓	✓		4,031
23. Teamfit - Running, Biking, Bodyweight Training	✓	✓	100,000+	3,673
24. Half Marathon Training Coach	✓	✓		1,451
25. U4FIT - GPS Track Run Walk	✓	✓		1,276
26. The Run Experience: Running Coach & Home Workouts	✓	✓		959
27. RunGPS Trainer Lite	✓	✓		510
28 eRoutes GPS running & walking	✓	✓		489
29. Walkmeter GPS Pedometer - Walking, Running, Hiking	✓	✓		287
30. RunMotion Coach - Running Training & Tips	✓	✓		226
31. 42Race Running & Fitness Club	✓	✓	50,000+	2,870
32. Run With Hal: Running, Marathon Training Plans App	✓	✓		861
33. Run for Weight Loss by MevoFit	✓	✓		326
34. Runnin'City - Running with GPS & Audioguide	✓	✓		258
35. RunGo App	✓	✓		241
36. Runmeter GPS - Running, Cycling, Walking, Jogging	✓	✓		213

Fig. 3. Top running tracking applications in 2021

4   Discussion of Results

Results show that running tracking application features do contribute to recreational runners' intrinsic motivation by (1) diverting them, (2) aiding their goal setting, (3) decreasing their efforts, (4) improving and (5) sharing their performance, (6) giving them acknowledgement as well as providing them with (7) guidance, (8) information, and (9) a greater variety in training options. Figure 4 shows that, depending on runners' perceptions, these features help satisfy needs,

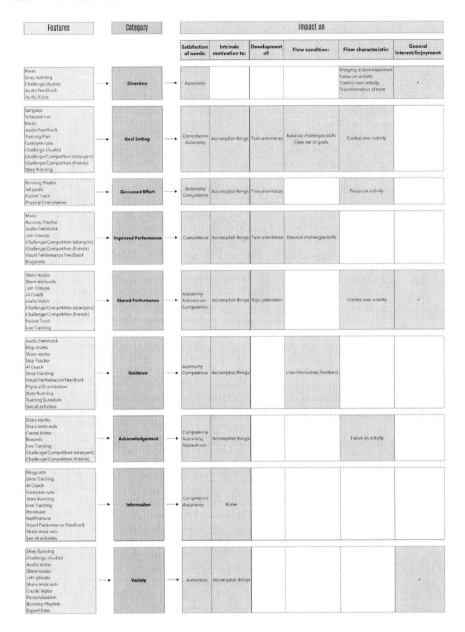

Fig. 4. Categorisation of features and their impact

they impact on motivation, they help achieve flow-like experiences, or generally trigger interest or enjoyment.

For example, runners' intrinsic motivation seems to benefit from features which increase their felt autonomy and perceived competence, such as those which help to individually schedule (and thus not postponed) runs, or those which log individual achievements and thus provide information on runners' change in competence. Features that particularly aid in improving peoples' running performance (e.g., audio feedback by the app, listening to a running playlist that fits their pace, etc.) further boost this perceived competence improvement.

Furthermore, being acknowledged by others (i.e., virtually being cheered on) for achievements or acknowledging oneself, by sharing a run, helps create a certain level of relatedness and consequently encourages runners to keep working on their set goals (cf. [10]). To this end, interviewees also found that sharing one's performance and comparing oneself to others can have significant positive effects on their intrinsic motivation (cf. [33]). Competing may even initiate a certain ego-orientation, which according to Elbe & Schüler encourages athletes [12]. Loosing such a comparison, however, can easily diminish the feeling about one's competence and thus hamper motivation [11].

Interestingly, the setting of external goals, e.g., the completion of a challenge or public competition set to a specific distance, date or time frame, was often perceived as controlling and thus interfering with runners' desire for autonomy. So were features which would provide continuous (i.e., too much) guidance and feedback.

Also, a permanent push towards exceeding one's running abilities was criticized, as one interviewee puts it: *"Maybe I do not want to run any faster at that moment but have actually just found a great pace where I do not get a stitch or anything else and have a good rhythm"*.

Some features, such as clearly set goals or (motivating) running playlists, were found to decrease runners' efforts and thus to increase the likelihood for them to convert their intention into a concrete action, i.e., start their run. Hence, being guided through, e.g., hearing audio feedback, hearing a story or being able to map routes was considered empowering and helpful in preparing runs: *"[W]hen I see the route and it is eight kilometers, for example. Well, eight kilometers is not really eight kilometers. There is altitude in it, there are traffic lights [...] For example, you could make five kilometers in the same duration as the eight kilometers. Then I could know how to best combine duration and distance"*.

Interviewees also found that features which would foster task-orientation (cf. [12]), such as the use of a training plan, would encourage them to take action, or at least think about it, which might also increase one's intrinsic motivation to accomplish things (cf. [34]).

The opposite effect was described by interviewees when using the pocket track feature, since here they want a conscious decision and therefore to keep autonomy over the beginning of a training. As one interviewee states, pressing the start button and seeing the countdown is like crossing a psychological barrier: *"Yes, it is important because then I know: It [the run] starts now"*. The physical examination feature, however, was described as effort increasing, as interviewees felt it would delay their run and consequently hamper their intention.

In terms of features providing visual guidance and feedback after the run, interviewees agreed on their empowering effect, allowing them to see and potentially disseminate their achievements. Although, some participants would like to hide certain performance values, such as pace or distance, as they feel it would pressure them into performing better.

Interviewees further found that through many of the offered features (e.g., receiving information in the form of blog posts in an application or general visual feedback of their performance) they would learn something new about themselves and their bodies, which increases the intrinsic motivation to know about and better understand personal health (cf. [34]); even more so, when they are able to apply this understanding to future runs and thus see an increase in their individual competences.

We further found that certain features (e.g., features focusing on individual progress rather than external praise) may change the type of motivation, turning extrinsically motivated runners into more intrinsically motivated ones. Other features (e.g., rewards) trigger the opposite, since interviewees see them as tangible acknowledgements of their achievements. To this end, the possibility of donating through their runs has been perceived as particularly valuable by some interviewees, as it would allow them to easily help others. As such a reward is usually not depending on a specific goal, it is also not perceived as controlling and therefore does not hamper one's intrinsic motivation (cf. [25]).

A variety of features, however, seem to polarize, e.g., story running, creating a video of a run, hearing an actual challenge, or setting the type of voice for the audio feedback. While these features were described as interesting, encouraging, enjoyable and helpful in providing training variety, by some participants, others identified them as unauthentic, unnecessary or annoying. And even if they would be curious about them they would soon lose interest. For example, regarding the type of audio feedback voice one interviewee stated: *"it always seems a bit fake [...] [y]ou can already hear the laughter in their voice although they are not laughing"*. To this end, it was also pointed out that certain voice types may even be disrupting. Others, however, stated that the audio feedback would motivate and help them focus on the running activity. This direct influence on one's motivation may further trigger the transfer from a situational to a contextual level of intrinsic motivation, where runners' episodic running experiences can change their intrinsic motivation towards running in general [34].

Finally, we found that those features which allow for (1) an appropriate balance between perceived challenges and existing skills (e.g., use of a training plan, or listening to a playlist based on one's pace), (2) a clear goal setting, and (3) immediate feedback, can help runners reach a flow-like experience [4], and therefore may move them towards an optimal state of motivation. This particularly includes features which would help them concentrate on the act of running while at the same time providing them with a sense of control over and awareness for the activity; e.g., features that divert from nearing exhaustion, such as listening to a story or challenge to complete.

5   Conclusion and Future Outlook

Summarizing, our investigation has shown that certain features of running track-ing applications, e.g.: *using specific running playlists, hearing audio feedback, stories and challenges, setting goals, using training plans, competing against strangers and friends, live tracking or sharing one's workout*, can contribute to recreational runners' intrinsic motivation. Depending on runners' perceptions, these features may have beneficial or detrimental effects. First, they satisfy needs of autonomy, competence and relatedness, which according to Deci & Ryan [8] strongly impact on intrinsic motivation. Second, they let runners know about and accomplish goals, which can help transfer situational and contextual levels of motivation into general motivation to run [34]. Third, they trigger task- and ego-orientation, leading to competitiveness which can have both positive (i.e., when winning) [19] or negative (i.e., when losing) [11] effects on intrinsic motiva-tion. Finally, their use may trigger flow-like states through offering control over the activity as well as providing clear and immediate feedback which is in line with peoples' distinct abilities [29].

Our analysis focused on recreational runners possessing low levels of intrinsic motivation towards the sport. Hence, results may not generalize to other athlete groups. And also older runners may have very different perceptions concern-ing the use and potential benefits of running tracking applications used by our analysis (note: the average age of our interviewees was 24).

Future work should thus aim to close this gap and evaluate the extent to which the above presented insights also apply to other target populations. Fur-thermore, we recommend expanding upon these findings and focus on features which help create more individual running experiences. Janssen et al., for exam-ple, developed an online tool to support users in finding a running tracking application that best fits their individual needs [15]. More such research, which aims to increase the chance of running tracking applications being capable of creating long lasting habits for runners, may eventually ensure that we reach the level of regular physical activity the WHO recommends.

References

1. Ahtinen, A., Isomursu, M., Huhtala, Y., Kaasinen, J., Salminen, J., Häkkilä, J.: Tracking outdoor sports – user experience perspective. In: Aarts, E., et al. (eds.) AmI 2008. LNCS, vol. 5355, pp. 192–209. Springer, Heidelberg (2008). https://doi.org/10.1007/978-3-540-89617-3_13
2. Bauer, C., Kriglstein, S.: Analysis of motivation strategies in running tracking applications. In: Proceedings of the 13th International Conference on Advances in Mobile Computing and Multimedia, pp. 73–79 (2015)
3. Burgess, E., Hassmén, P., Pumpa, K.L.: Determinants of adherence to lifestyle intervention in adults with obesity: a systematic review. Clin. Obes. **7**(3), 123–135 (2017)
4. Csikszentmihalyi, M., Abuhamdeh, S., Nakamura, J., Andrew, J., Dweck, C.: Handbook of Competence and Motivation, pp. 598–608. Guilford Publications, New York (2005)

372   D. Gute et al.

5. Csikszentmihalyi, M., Csikzentmihaly, M.: Flow: The Psychology of Optimal Experience, vol. 1990. Harper & Row, New York (1990)
6. Deci, E.L., Betley, G., Kahle, J., Abrams, L., Porac, J.: When trying to win: competition and intrinsic motivation. Pers. Soc. Psychol. Bull. **7**(1), 79–83 (1981)
7. Deci, E.L., Koestner, R., Ryan, R.M.: A meta-analytic review of experiments examining the effects of extrinsic rewards on intrinsic motivation. Psychol. Bull. **125**(6), 627 (1999)
8. Deci, E.L., Ryan, R.M.: The "what" and "why" of goal pursuits: human needs and the self-determination of behavior. Psychol. Inq. **11**(4), 227–268 (2000)
9. Deci, E.L., Ryan, R.M.: Facilitating optimal motivation and psychological well-being across life's domains. Can. Psychol. **49**(1), 14 (2008)
10. Deci, E.L., Ryan, R.M.: Intrinsic Motivation and Self-determination in Human Behavior. Springer, Cham (2013). https://doi.org/10.1007/978-1-4899-2271-7
11. Duda, J., Hall, H.: Achievement goal theory in sport: recent extensions and future directions. In: Handbook of Sport Psychology, vol. 2, pp. 417–443 (2001)
12. Elbe, A.-M., Schüler, J.: Motivation und Ziele im Kontext Sport und Bewegung. In: Schüler, J., Wegner, M., Plessner, H. (eds.) Sportpsychologie, pp. 141–164. Springer, Heidelberg (2020). https://doi.org/10.1007/978-3-662-56802-6_7
13. Gutman, J.: A means-end chain model based on consumer categorization processes. J. Mark. **46**(2), 60–72 (1982)
14. Hosseinpour, M., Terlutter, R.: Your personal motivator is with you: a systematic review of mobile phone applications aiming at increasing physical activity. Sports Med. **49**(9), 1425–1447 (2019)
15. Janssen, M., Lallemand, C., Hoes, K., Vos, S.: Which app to choose? An online tool that supports the decision-making process of recreational runners to choose an app. In: Proceedings of the 6th International Conference on Design4Health Amsterdam 2020 (2020)
16. Kuckartz, U.: Qualitative Inhaltsanalyse. Methoden, Praxis, Computerunterstützung. Grundlagentexte Methoden, Beltz Juventa (2014). https://books.google.at/books?id=j0ZMnwEACAAJ
17. de Langhe, B., Fernbach, P.M., Lichtenstein, D.R.: Navigating by the stars: investigating the actual and perceived validity of online user ratings. J. Consum. Res. **42**, 817–833 (2016)
18. Locke, E.A., Latham, G.P.: A Theory of Goal Setting & Task Performance. Prentice-Hall, Inc., Hoboken (1990)
19. McAuley, E., Tammen, V.V.: The effects of subjective and objective competitive outcomes on intrinsic motivation. J. Sport Exerc. Psychol. **11**(1), 84–93 (1989)
20. Monteiro, V., Mata, L., Peixoto, F.: Intrinsic motivation inventory: psychometric properties in the context of first language and mathematics learning. Psicologia: Reflexão e Crítica **28**(3), 434–443 (2015)
21. Nicholls, J.G.: Achievement motivation: conceptions of ability, subjective experience, task choice, and performance. Psychol. Rev. **91**(3), 328 (1984)
22. Patel, M.S., Asch, D.A., Volpp, K.G.: Wearable devices as facilitators, not drivers, of health behavior change. JAMA **313**(5), 459–460 (2015)
23. Pelletier, L.G., Fortier, M.S., Vallerand, R.J., Briere, N.M.: Associations among perceived autonomy support, forms of self-regulation, and persistence: a prospective study. Motiv. Emot. **25**(4), 279–306 (2001)
24. Ryan, R.M.: Control and information in the intrapersonal sphere: an extension of cognitive evaluation theory. J. Pers. Soc. Psychol. **43**(3), 450 (1982)
25. Ryan, R.M., Deci, E.L.: Intrinsic and extrinsic motivations: classic definitions and new directions. Contemp. Educ. Psychol. **25**(1), 54–67 (2000)

26. Ryan, R.M., Deci, E.L.: Self-determination theory and the facilitation of intrinsic motivation, social development, and well-being. Am. Psychol. **55**(1), 68 (2000)

27. Ryan, R., Frederick, C., Lepes, D., Rubio, N., Kennon, M.: Intrinsic motivation and exercise adherence. Int. J. Sport Psychol. **28**(4), 335–354 (1997)

28. Scheerder, J., Breedveld, K., Borgers, J.: Running Across Europe: The Rise and Size of One of the Largest Sport Markets. Springer, Cham (2015). https://doi.org/10.1057/9781137446374

29. Schüler, J.: Intrinsische Motivation im Kontext Sport und Bewegung. In: Schüler, J., Wegner, M., Plessner, H. (eds.) Sportpsychologie, pp. 165–183. Springer, Heidelberg (2020). https://doi.org/10.1007/978-3-662-56802-6_8

30. Schultze, U., Avital, M.: Designing interviews to generate rich data for information systems research. Inf. Organ. **21**(1), 1–16 (2011)

31. Smith, R.E., Sarason, I.G.: Social anxiety and the evaluation of negative interpersonal feedback. J. Consult. Clin. Psychol. **43**(3), 429 (1975)

32. Suh, A., Wagner, C., Liu, L.: The effects of game dynamics on user engagement in gamified systems. In: 2015 48th Hawaii International Conference on System Sciences, pp. 672–681. IEEE (2015)

33. Tauer, J.M., Harackiewicz, J.M.: The effects of cooperation and competition on intrinsic motivation and performance. J. Pers. Soc. Psychol. **86**(6), 849–861 (2004)

34. Vallerand, R.J.: Toward a hierarchical model of intrinsic and extrinsic motivation. Adv. Exp. Soc. Psychol. **29**, 271–360 (1997)

35. Vallerand, R.J.: Intrinsic and extrinsic motivation in sport and physical activity: a review and a look at the future. In: Handbook of Sport Psychology, pp. 59–83 (2012)

36. Vallerand, R.J., Lalande, D.R.: The MPIC model: the perspective of the hierarchical model of intrinsic and extrinsic motivation. Psychol. Inq. **22**(1), 45–51 (2011)

37. Vallerand, R.J., Losier, G.F.: An integrative analysis of intrinsic and extrinsic motivation in sport. J. Appl. Sport Psychol. **11**(1), 142–169 (1999)

38. Villalobos-Zúñiga, G., Cherubini, M.: Apps that motivate: a taxonomy of app features based on self-determination theory. Int. J. Hum. Comput Stud. **140**, 102449 (2020)

39. Wijnalda, G., Pauws, S., Vignoli, F., Stuckenschmidt, H.: A personalized music system for motivation in sport performance. IEEE Pervasive Comput. **4**(3), 26–32 (2005)

SleepyCloud: Examining the Effect of Odor Cue on Reducing Bedtime Procrastination

Pei-Yi Kuo[1(✉)], Nien-Hsin Wu[1], and Yi-Ci Jhuang[2]

[1] Institute of Service Science, National Tsing Hua University, Hsinchu, Taiwan
{pykuo,nelly.wu}@iss.nthu.edu.tw
[2] Institute of Systems Neuroscience, National Tsing Hua University, Hsinchu, Taiwan
yicijhuang@gapp.nthu.edu.tw

Abstract. Bedtime procrastination refers to delaying bedtime without external reasons. It has become serious among the younger generation due to smartphone popularity, leading to several physical and mental disorders. Odor cue has the potential to reduce bedtime procrastination, as prior research has demonstrated its effectiveness in conveying information and triggering desired emotion and behaviors. However, limited research investigates the effect of odor on bedtime regulation outside of clinical settings. We designed and implemented *SleepyCloud*, a device aiming to deliver odor cue one hour before people's scheduled bedtime. Our study examines the effectiveness of odor cue on reducing students' bedtime procrastination using *SleepyCloud*. Our results suggested that the odor cue was helpful on reducing bedtime procrastination for those who procrastinated due to leisure activities, and that the odor cue also helped regulate sleep. We provide implications for future investigation on this topic.

Keywords: Procrastination · Bedtime procrastination · Odor · Odor cue · Smell · Sensory cue · Field study

1 Introduction

Bedtime procrastination (BP) is a form of self-regulation failure that involves needlessly and voluntarily delaying going to bed, and it is one of the leading causes for insufficient sleep, which could negatively influence one's performance and health [28]. Recent research has found that the sleep deficit among students is associated with poor declarative and procedural learning. Previous research also indicates that insufficient sleep results in several physical disorders, such as obesity, diabetes, hypertension, cardiovascular disease, and memory impairment [2, 28, 43, 45]. It is also found that BP is related to the depressive symptoms of college students [4, 15]. Due to the popularity of new media, more and more people suffer from BP, especially the younger generation. According to prior study, the U.S. adolescents were approximately 17% more likely to have sleep deficit compared to the last decade, and this is associated with the increase in new media screen time, especially the use of social media [45].

To our best knowledge, research on sleep health mostly explores sleep problems of people who suffer from disorders like insomnia and sleep apnea in clinical context. The

M. Kurosu (Ed.): HCII 2022, LNCS 13304, pp. 374–388, 2022.
https://doi.org/10.1007/978-3-031-05412-9_26

short sleep issue among the general population is understudied. It is not until the recent years that sleep researchers attempt to explore BP [4, 27, 28, 34, 46, 48]. These efforts involve strengthening one's motivation to attain the scheduled bedtime, but the effects of these interventions on one's bedtime is insignificant [1, 20, 29, 32, 46]. Still, some of the existing research and consumer sleep technologies seek to regulate sleep with sensory cues, such as haptic smart alarm, smart light bulb, and sound interventions [13, 16, 35, 36, 40–42]. However, their effects still remain unclear, and the application of odor cue, which is potential in reducing BP, is still left to be explored. Research has shown that odor cue is effective in conveying information, triggering desired behavior and emotion, and inducing sleep [10, 11, 17, 19, 31]. Building on these gaps and empirical findings, our study aims to examine how odor cue helps people reduce bedtime procrastination.

2   Related Work

2.1   Bedtime Procrastination (BP): Causes, Consequences, Interventions

Bedtime procrastination (BP) refers to "going to bed later than intended, without external reasons for doing so" [27]. The sleep deficit of bedtime procrastinators is usually not from diagnosed sleep disorders or shift work, but from their self-regulation failure [28]. According to prior research, there are three major causes for BP, including deliberate procrastination, mindless procrastination, and strategic delay [34]. These three types of causes for BP do not exist independently - they could happen in sequence. For instance, people may have started procrastinating deliberately but ended up losing track of time.

Research has shown that BP can cause several negative influences on people's daily life as well as physical and mental well-being. It can lead to decreasing academic and workplace performance [5, 6]. It is also associated with the risk of obesity, diabetes, hypertension, cardiovascular disease, and memory impairment [2, 28, 43, 45] as well as the increased likelihood of depression [2, 4]. According to prior research, the U.S. adolescents are more likely to report less than seven hours of sleep per night compared to the last decade, and this is related to the increase in new media screen time [45]. Common activities before bed for the student population engaging in new media include playing mobile games, watching video with online-streaming platforms, and using social media, and these activities are related to their delayed bedtime and shortened sleep duration [14, 25, 37, 39].

The intervention for reducing BP is still understudied. Existing studies focus more on special groups of people (e.g., shift workers and the elderly) [46], but there are still some intervention studies conducted for improving sleep sufficiency of the general population by fostering better sleep hygiene practices with different strategies [1, 20, 29, 32, 46].

2.2   Sensory Interventions for Better and More Regular Sleep

A stream of existing HCI research and consumer sleep technologies adopt the multimodal sensory approach to explore the effects of different sensory cues on facilitating regular sleep (including avoiding BP, inducing sleep, and improving wake-up experience). For the visual cue, previous studies explore the effect of delivering bedtime reminder via push notifications on desktop and mobile devices. Mobile notifications are found to be effective in reminding people of their bedtime, and the ideal time of delivering notification is 30 min to 1 h before bedtime [7]. Dynamic indoor lighting simulating the nature is suggested to be helpful in shortening sleep latency [44]. Audio cue is found to be effective on inducing sleep [3, 21]. Research also indicates that personalized alarm sound selected based on user's information (e.g., gender, occupation, and current weather) could create a pleasant wake-up experience [47]. As for the haptic cue, previous researchers explore the effect of haptic smart alarm delivered with the vibration of wristband. The patterns of vibration need to be constantly changed to maintain its effect [26]. These interventions demonstrate how different sensory cues are used to facilitate regular sleep. Among these sensory modalities, none utilizes odor cue so far, despite of the effectiveness of aromatherapy on inducing sleep and improving one's sleep quality [19].

2.3 Effect of Odor on People's Behavior and Perception

The sense of smell is connected to our limbic system, which deals with our emotions [9, 10]. Prior research has discovered that by applying the right mapping between certain scent and emotion, odor cue could trigger the desired emotion and behavior [10, 11, 17, 30]. For instance, it has been found that the smell of rose is effective in stimulating the emotion of calm and safer driving behavior [10]. Odor cue is also effective in conveying information. Recent HCI research has been exploring the effect of olfactory notification in different contexts, such as in-car notification and workplace messaging [10–12, 30, 31]. Odor cue can positively influence the recall of information with the same accuracy level as visual and auditory cues [17, 22]. Prior research also revealed that people's reaction time to odor cue is the same as to visual ones [31], and it requires lower cognitive load than other kinds of sensory stimulus [23, 24].

3   Methods

3.1 Study Design and Procedure

We conducted a 3-week field study to explore the effect of odor cue on bedtime procrastination (Fig. 1). A scent-delivery device called *SleepyCloud* and an app were developed to deliver odor cue as well as collect sleeping data in the study. A total of five participants were recruited. Participants were asked to report their scheduled bedtime and fill out a brief sleep diary on a daily basis. The scheduled bedtime data was meant to measure how much participants procrastinate their bedtime each day by subtracting the actual bedtime with it. This measurement was used by prior bedtime procrastination studies to have a quantified, objective, and easily comparable result [7, 28, 46]. As for the sleep dairy, it is commonly adopted by studies on regulating sleep and bedtime procrastination to capture how participants' sleeping behavior develop during the study [28, 33, 34, 46].

The Baseline Week (First Week of the Study). Participants were instructed to input their scheduled bedtime in the app at 9 p.m. daily through a push notification (Fig. 1). One hour before and upon their scheduled bedtime, the app prompts them to answer

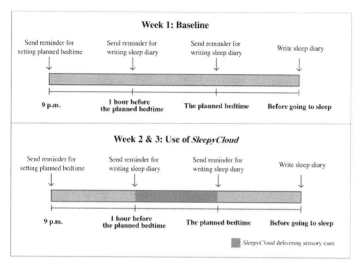

Fig. 1. Overview of study procedure: baseline week (*top*) and experiment weeks (*down*)

questions in a brief sleep diary, asking for their actual bedtime, awareness to any smell, and the level of perceived relaxation. Participants are reminded to wear the activity tracker we provided (used to track participants wake-up time) upon completing the sleep diary.

The Experiment Weeks (Second and Third Weeks of the Study). Participants performed the same procedure as the first week, while *SleepyCloud* was introduced and deployed in participants' home during the experiment weeks. *SleepyCloud* is designed to start functioning one hour before people's scheduled bedtime to remind participants to go to bed and induce their sleep, and it stops functioning at their scheduled bedtime (Fig. 1). We set *SleepyCloud* to start functioning one hour prior to the scheduled bedtime, as our pilot study results suggested that it usually takes one hour from "preparing to go to bed" to "actually going to bed". *SleepyCloud* emits the scent of lavender intermittently. For every five minutes, it emits the scent that lasts one minute to avoid habituation effect [30]. Lavender is chosen as it has been shown to be effective in inducing sleep and elicit the emotion of relaxation [19]. Based on prior odor-related work in HCI, our scent was made with essential oil diluted with water [30], and the oil is from a certified off-shelf product. *SleepyCloud* was placed near where participants normally stay before bedtime to ensure they can sense the smell. It is noteworthy that participants were not informed by the flavor of odor, or how *SleepyCloud* functions prior to study participation to prevent participants from having any preconceived perception toward it. This information was revealed to participants at the end of the post-study interview.

3.2 Recruitment and Participant Characteristics

Since BP is more serious among the younger generation [45], we recruited college students as participants for our study over social media channel. Our inclusion criteria are people who: (1) procrastinate their bedtime, (2) have no sleeping or mental disorder,

(3) do not have the habit of using scent product or have allergic reaction to any scent, (4) do not share bedroom with others, and (5) are Android phone users with Android 7 or higher version. We assess these criteria during the recruitment phase using an online pre-screening questionnaire. Participants' level of bedtime procrastination was also measured using the Bedtime Procrastination Scale (BPS) through this pre-screening survey. BPS asks one's frequency of having trouble going to sleep on time and delaying bedtime. One's level of bedtime procrastination was determined following these scores (low: below 2.332, moderate: between 2.332 and 3.668, high: above 3.668) [18].

Among a pool of 47 respondents who did the pre-screening survey, five of them were selected as our participants as they met all the criteria above, and were willing to engage in a three-week field study. There were two males and three females, and their age range between 20 and 22 years old (mean = 21.3, SD = 0.89) (Table 1). Participants' bedtimes range between 1 a.m. and 3 a.m. Their levels of bedtime procrastination are either at the moderate or high level according to the Bedtime Procrastination Scale. All of them indicated they need to go to bed earlier. The study has obtained approval from the University Institutional Review Board - all participants were consented to participate in the study.

Table 1. Overview of participant characteristics.

Participant ID	Age	Gender	Grade	Usual bedtime	BPS*	Residence
P1	22	Female	Graduate student (1st year)	2–3 a.m.	3.89 (high)	Rental place
P2	20	Male	College student (3rd year)	1–2 a.m.	3.67 (high)	Rental place
P3	22	Female	Graduate student (1st year)	2–3 a.m.	3.67 (moderate)	Rental place
P4	21	Female	College student (4th year)	2–3 a.m.	2.78 (moderate)	Rental place
P5	22	Male	Graduate student (1st year)	12–1 a.m.	3.78 (high)	Dorm

*BPS: Bedtime Procrastination Scale

3.3   Data Analysis

Quantitative Data (Sleeping Behavior Data from the App and the Activity Tracker). The scheduled bedtime and actual bedtime data were collected on a daily basis with the app. To measure bedtime procrastination, we calculated the bedtime discrepancy score by subtracting actual bedtime from the scheduled bedtime. Higher score suggests higher level of bedtime procrastination. As to the sleep duration data, it was collected through activity tracker, which estimates one's sleep duration through a combination of the wearer's movement and heart-rate patterns. The level of relaxation before bed was measured using a 5-point Likert scale in the sleep diary to see whether the smell of lavender is effective in eliciting the desired emotion (relaxation), as suggested in existing research [10, 11, 17, 19, 30]. We also asked participants two questions in the sleep diary to assess whether the smell of lavender was indeed delivered to participants. We conducted all statistical analysis on these behavioral data using RStudio.

Qualitative Data (Post-Study Interviews). We conducted one-hour post-study interviews with all five participants, resulting in a total of 5 h and 48 min of audio recorded data. Our interview protocol contains seven aspects of questions: (1) pre-experiment sleeping behavior/habits, (2) reactions to setting up scheduled bedtime and answering questions in sleep diary daily during the baseline week, (3) perception and reactions to the odor cue from *SleepyCloud* during experiment weeks, (4) sleeping behavior and habits during the experiment weeks, (5) overview of sleeping data from participants, (6) suggestions regarding *SleepyCloud*, and (7) experience of study participation. All interviews were manually transcribed. We conducted inductive open coding [38] to identify emerging themes in each of the seven aspects of questions.

4 Design

4.1 Design and Implementation of *SleepyCloud*

The appearance of *SleepyCloud* was made to look like a cloud, which is a common metaphor for a good night of sleep (Fig. 2, left). The water atomization module of *Seeed Studio* along with the Arduino Nano board are used for delivering the odor cue, which produces the ultrasonic mist when the ultrasonic transducer plate is moistened (Fig. 2, right). In order to avoid odor habituation, the module is programmed to produce the mist for one minute every five minutes. When receiving participants' daily scheduled bedtimes at 9 p.m. daily, we remotely schedule *SleepyCloud* to turn on one hour before their scheduled bedtime, and then turn it off.

4.2 The Mobile App

We built a mobile app to collect participants' scheduled bedtime and sleep diary data. Participants' scheduled bedtime and sleep diary data were captured and stored in real-time. We sent participants customized push notification at designated times every day to remind them to submit their scheduled bedtime at 9 p.m. and their responses to the sleep diary right before their scheduled bedtime.

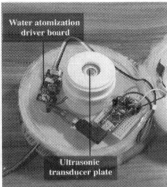

Fig. 2. Deployment of *SleepyCloud* in participant homes (*left*) and the inner composition of *SleepyCloud* (*right*).

5 Results

5.1 Participants' Pre-bedtime Activities and Procrastination Behavior

Our interview data revealed that there were two types of BP behaviors mentioned by our participants. Figure 3 illustrates each participant's behaviors between the time they arrived home and their bedtime. Two participants (P1 & P2) indicated they procrastinated their bedtime due to studying, while the other three participants (P3, P4, P5) procrastinated due to their leisure activities using smartphone. Note that P1 and P2 also used their smartphone to conduct leisure activities before sleep, yet they specifically pointed out studying as the cause leading to BP instead of leisure activity. Moreover, a common behavioral pattern shared among P3, P4, and P5 was that they only had leisure activities after arriving home, and did not study. These participants used smartphone to watch videos on YouTube, read online novels, and chat with friends for 30 to 60 min before their bedtime. They also mentioned the last thing they did with their smartphone before bed was to set up an alarm for the next day.

Based on the differences in BP behavior we observed among our participants, we analyzed the data for participants who procrastinated due to studying (P1 & P2) and those who procrastinated due to leisure activities (P3, P4, P5) separately in the following to have a better understanding of the effect of *SleepyCloud* under different user scenarios.

During the first week of the experiment (baseline week), participants were not exposed to *SleepyCloud*, and did not know what this device looks like. Our data suggested that the actual bedtime of all participants was generally later than their scheduled bedtime, which showed the sign of BP. Besides, participant responses to the daily sleep diary indicated that they did not perceive any smell in their environment prior to sleep. This question was asked to ensure there was no odor in participants' living space before we deployed *SleepyCloud* during the experiment weeks.

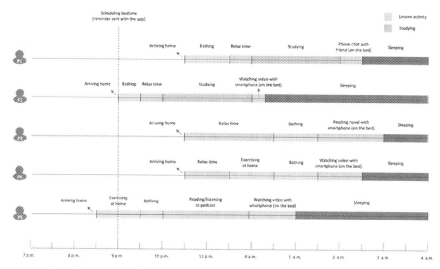

Fig. 3. Overview of each participant's general schedule after arriving home.

5.2 Effects of Odor Cue on Participants' Bedtime During Experiment Weeks (Weeks 2 & 3)

As we noticed P1 and P2 procrastinated their bedtime with different reasons than the remaining three participants (P3, P4, P5), we reviewed and analyzed their data separately. The bedtime is measured with the actual bedtime data participants reported in the sleep diary collected via the app (Fig. 4, right). According to the data, the average bedtime of participants in each week ranged from 0:26 a.m. to 3:20 a.m.

Results of the Paired Sample T-test showed that there was no significant difference between the average bedtimes of weeks 1 and 2 ($M_{Week\ 1} = 1564.29$, $M_{Week\ 2} = 1555.9$, $t(20) = -0.54$, $p = 0.3$), but the average bedtime of week 3 was significantly earlier than those of week 1 ($M_{Week\ 1} = 1564.29$, $M_{Week\ 3} = 1516.67$, $t(20) = -3.05$, $p < 0.05$) and week 2 ($M_{Week\ 2} = 1555.9$, $M_{Week\ 3} = 1516.67$, $t(20) = -2.13$, $p < 0.05$) for participants 3, 4 and 5. As for participants 1 and 2, there were no statistically significant differences for the average bedtimes among the three weeks.

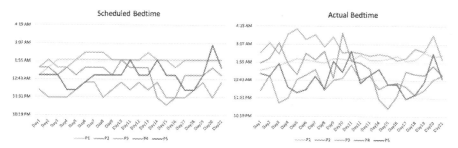

Fig. 4. The scheduled bedtime (*left*) and the actual bedtime (*right*) of each participant across three weeks.

According to participants' self-reported scheduled bedtime data, most participants (P2, P3, P4, P5) adjusted their scheduled bedtime daily, and only one participant (P1) scheduled the bedtime at a fixed time after adjusting it during the first few days (Fig. 4, left). Participants' scheduled bedtime ranged from 11:30 p.m. to 2:30 a.m.

We also examined whether there was a significant change in participants' scheduled bedtime. Prior literature indicates one could set the bedtime to a later time over time to make the scheduled bedtime easier to be accomplished [46], and we made sure our data was not affected by this factor. The results of the Paired Sample T-test indicated that participants' scheduled bedtime did not significantly become later over time.

5.3   Effects of Odor Cue on Participants' Bedtime Procrastination During Experiment Weeks (Weeks 2 & 3)

BP was measured with bedtime discrepancy score, which was calculated by subtracting one's actual bedtime to scheduled bedtime. Higher score suggests higher level of BP. Participants' weekly average bedtime discrepancy scores range from -29.43 min to 85 min (negative value indicates that participants went to bed ahead of their scheduled time).

Similarly, as we noticed P1 and P2 procrastinated their bedtime with different reasons than the remaining three participants (P3, P4, P5), we analyzed their data separately here. The data of P1 and P2 suggested that there was a slight increase in their bedtime discrepancy scores over the 3 weeks, yet these were not statistically significant (Fig. 5). On the other hand, the bedtime discrepancy scores of P3, P4, and P5 dropped over three weeks. Specifically, the result of Paired Sample t-test showed that the discrepancy score of week 2 was significantly lower than that of week 1 ($M_{Week\ 1} = 45.71, M_{Week\ 2} = 22.57$, $t\ (20) = -2.37, p < 0.05$), and the score of week 3 was also significantly lower than that of week 1 ($M_{Week\ 1} = 45.71, M_{Week\ 3} = 5.24, t\ (20) = -5.26, p < 0.05$). As to weeks 2 and 3, there was no significant difference between the two weeks for participants 3, 4, and 5.

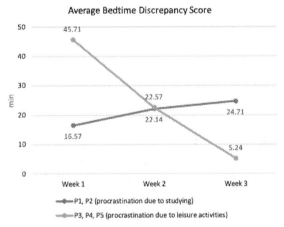

Fig. 5. Weekly average bedtime discrepancy scores of participants with different causes of BP.

Similar to the quantitative data, our interview results suggested that the bedtime of two participants (P1 & P2) was not influenced by the odor cue from *SleepyCloud*. Participants 1 and 2 specifically mentioned they failed to go to bed at their scheduled bedtimes due to unfinished study tasks (*"It seems that (my bedtime) had nothing to do with SleepyCloud because I still thought I have to get my work done before sleep. – P1"*; *"Though the scent was there during the 2nd and 3rd week, I started to have more assignments and projects to work on. I studied late during this period, so I still went to bed 0.5 to 1 h later than my scheduled bedtime. – P2"*).

As for P3, P4, and P5, they reported they were "urged" to go to bed by the smell cue, and that they went to bed earlier during the experiment weeks (weeks 2 and 3). Two participants (P3 and P5) mentioned that the odor cue reminded them of their bedtime when they sensed the smell from *SleepyCloud*. For example, P5 stated that he found the odor cue as an effective reminder, and the odor also made him feel sleepy before bed (*"… it (the scent) reminded me it's time for sleep. I think the odor also made me feel sleepy, and this might influence the time I spent on smartphone before sleep. – P5"*). Additionally, P3 and P4 also mentioned self-checking if they need to hurry things up to get to sleep on time when noticing *SleepyCloud* was functioning (*"… After I learned about its pattern (turned on 1 h before the scheduled bedtime), I felt like it pushed me to go to bed. I would try to finish taking a shower and preparing myself for going to bed before it started functioning. – P3"*). P4 also reported she stopped using her phone when noticing *SleepyCloud* was *not* functioning (*"I put it (SleepyCloud) beside my bed. I usually went to bed after it functioned for half an hour or so. Then if I noticed it stopped functioning, I put down my smartphone and went to sleep. – P4"*).

5.4 Participants' Perception of *SleepyCloud* and Its Odor Cue

All participants reported perceiving different levels of intensity of odor throughout the experiment weeks. Both our quantitative and qualitative data suggested that the difference in the perceived intensity of odor did not have statistically significant influence on our participants. The Pearson's correlation coefficient results showed that the perceived intensity of smell had no statistically significant strong correlation to participants' level of relaxation, bedtime discrepancy score, and bedtime. In the interviews, all participants reflected that the difference in the perceived intensity of smell did not matter much to them.

Moreover, participants observed how *SleepyCloud* functioned during the study (they were not told how *SleepyCloud* would function prior to study participation). The interview data showed that all participants were able to recognize the function of *SleepyCloud*, and sensed the odor from it (*"I think it was like if I scheduled my bedtime to 2 a.m., it would start functioning at 1 a.m.… the smell would be delivered intermittently. – P3"*).

6 Discussion

6.1 Odor Cue as Useful Behavioral Reminder for Bedtime Procrastination

Statistically significant results were observed in the bedtime discrepancy scores of three participants (P3, P4, P5). Bedtime discrepancy score serves as the indicator of BP in our study – the lower the sore, the lower the level of BP is. The bedtime discrepancy scores of P3, P4, and P5 decreased during the experiment weeks (week 2 lower than week 1, week 3 lower than week 1), showing the usefulness of the odor cue delivered by *SleepyCloud*. We also conducted additional analysis to ensure participants did not adjust their bedtime deliberately to make their scheduled bedtime easier to accomplish. Besides, P3 and P4 indicated they checked if they should hurry things up to meet the sleep goal when noticing *SleepyCloud* was functioning. P5 mentioned being affected by the smell, making him feel sleepy.

Although the odor cue did not influence the bedtime discrepancy scores of P1 and P2, they both mentioned being able to sense the odor delivered intermittently from *SleepyCloud*. They delayed bedtime due to studying instead of self-regulation failure. P2 also indicated the odor made him feel relaxed, made it easier for him to fall asleep, and there was smaller variance in his sleep durations during the experiment weeks. This corresponds to the findings of existing research that odor cue is effective in improving the sleep of shift workers who have irregular sleep schedules [19].

To make the odor cue more explicit in the scenario of BP due to studying, there are three potential solutions. First, it might be helpful to include another sensory cue (e.g., visual or audio) beside odor cue to catch participants' attention more proactively. As prior research emits the odor and visual cues separately when assessing people's reaction time to these cues [31], future research is needed to examine whether this stays true when both cues are delivered simultaneously. Second, the timing of odor emitting can be adjusted to 9 p.m. when participants are prompted to input their scheduled bedtime, or right after bathing, depending on the amount of studying tasks to be completed. Third, add a secondary odor (another flavor of odor) and use behavioral mapping [31] to give people another cue to finish their study tasks on time.

6.2 Awareness to Pre-bedtime Activities Could Boost Intervention Outcomes

Figure 3 illustrating participants' general schedule after arriving home contains important and useful information as we tease out details of the cause of BP for each participant. We relied on post-study interviews to collect this contextual information, and did cross-comparison with their quantitative sleeping behavior data to see if there existed any logical flaws. An interesting pattern emerged from our data set – we realize those who procrastinated due to studying tend to bath first after arriving home, and have brief break time with some leisure activities right after bathing and studying, respectively (P1, P2). Those who procrastinated due to leisure activities tend to conduct leisure activities both before and after bathing, and the leisure activities performed after bathing were usually with their smartphones and on the bed (P3, P4, P5). We recommend future researchers to collect participants' typical daily schedule, especially activities performed between the time they arrive home and their bedtime prior to the beginning of study through pre-screening surveys. Adding this step to study design could also help participants build awareness toward their arrangement of time and activities beforehand.

6.3 Bedtime Procrastination Caused by Study Versus Leisure Activities

Among the participants in our study, the smartphone use activity of P3, P4, and P5 linked to two types of procrastination identified in existing research. First, participants related their smartphone use before bed as "bad" habit. Existing research refers this as "deliberate procrastination", which describes one's desire of conducting entertaining and leisure activities as short-term rewards for the entire day [27, 34]. This was seen as a way of dealing the self-regulation dilemma between immediate impulses (engage in leisure activity) and long-term intentions (go to bed on time) [8]. Second, participants' inability of controlling time spent on smartphone is referred as "mindless procrastination", meaning losing track of time due to immersive activities before bed [34].

Our quantitative data suggested that P1 and P2 did not go to bed earlier during the experiment weeks, and that P3, P4, and P5 went to bed earlier during experiment weeks (statistically significant). However, we are unable to claim that the odor cue failed to reduce procrastination due to unfinished study tasks (P1, P2). In fact, P2 indicated the odor made him feel relaxed before bedtime and helped him sleep better. As existing research does not discuss how study tasks influence BP, and most work targets at particular groups of people such as shift workers [28, 34, 46], more research is needed to further examine how study tasks relate to BP in addition to sleep duration.

7 Limitations, Conclusion, and Future Work

In this study, we present the effects of the odor cue from *SleepyCloud* on reducing BP. Our results showed that the odor cue was useful for reducing BP of those who procrastinated bedtime due to leisure activities, and the odor cue was helpful in inducing and regulating one's sleep regardless of their procrastination reasons. Different from the BP interventions in previous research seeking to improve people's self-regulation before bed by strengthening their motivation in attaining long-term sleep goal [1, 20, 29, 32, 46], the odor cue deals with people's self-regulation failure by improving their awareness toward time and their behaviors.

Our study has two primary limitations. First, our study will benefit from a larger sample size to help generalize our findings to a larger student population. Second, we plan to automate the timer function of *SleepyCloud* in future prototype iteration to reduce manual operation. As part of the future work, we plan to improve the intervention with *SleepyCloud* by further investigating how study tasks influence one's BP, and how the odor cue can help reduce BP of those who procrastinate due to studying.

Acknowledgement. We thank our study participants for their participation and feedback as well as the anonymous reviewers for their helpful comments. This work was supported by the Ministry of Science and Technology in Taiwan (MOST grant 109-2221-E-007-063-MY3).

References

1. Brown, F., Buboltz, W., Soper, B.: Relationship of sleep hygiene awareness, sleep hygiene practices, and sleep quality in university students. Behav. Med. **28**, 33–38 (2002). https://doi.org/10.1080/08964280209596396

2. Buxton, O.M., Marcelli, E.: Short and long sleep are positively associated with obesity, diabetes, hypertension, and cardiovascular disease among adults in the United States. Soc. Sci. Med. **71**(5), 1027–1036 (2010). https://doi.org/10.1016/j.socscimed.2010.05.041
3. Chen, C.-K., et al.: Sedative music facilitates deep sleep in young adults. J. Altern. Complement. Med. **20** (2013). https://doi.org/10.1089/acm.2012.0050
4. Chung, S.J., An, H., Suh, A.: What do people do before going to bed? A study of bedtime procrastination using time use surveys. Sleep **43**, 4 (2020). https://doi.org/10.1093/sleep/zsz267
5. Connor, J., et al.: Driver sleepiness and risk of serious injury to car occupants: population based case control study. BMJ (Clin. Res. ed.) **324**, 1125 (2002)
6. Curcio, G., Ferrara, M., De Gennaro, L.: Sleep loss, learning capacity and academic performance. Sleep Med. Rev. **10**(5), 323–337 (2006). https://doi.org/10.1016/j.smrv.2005.11.001
7. Daskalova, N., et al.: Informing design of suggestion and self-monitoring tools through participatory experience prototypes (2014)
8. de Witt Huberts, J., Evers, C., de Ridder, D.: "Because I Am Worth It" a theoretical framework and empirical review of a justification-based account of self-regulation failure. Personal. Soc. Psychol. Rev. off. J. Soc. Personal. Soc. Psychol. **18** (2013). https://doi.org/10.1177/1088868313507533
9. Delplanque, S., Coppin, G., Sander, D.: Odor and Emotion. In: Buettner, A. (ed.) Springer Handbook of Odor. SH, pp. 101–102. Springer, Cham (2017). https://doi.org/10.1007/978-3-319-26932-0_40
10. Dmitrenko, D., et al.: CARoma therapy: pleasant scents promote safer driving, better mood, and improved well-being in angry drivers. In: Proceedings of the 2020 CHI Conference on Human Factors in Computing Systems, pp. 1–13. Association for Computing Machinery (2020)
11. Dmitrenko, D., Maggioni, E., Obrist, M.: Towards a framework for validating the matching between notifications and scents in olfactory in-car interaction (2019)
12. Dobbelstein, D., Herrdum, S., Rukzio, E.: inScent: a wearable olfactory display as an amplification for mobile notifications (2017)
13. Fitbit. https://www.fitbit.com/global/tw/home
14. Galland, B.C., de Wilde, T., Taylor, R.W., Smith, C.: Sleep and pre-bedtime activities in New Zealand adolescents: differences by ethnicity. Sleep Health **6**(1), 23–31 (2020). https://doi.org/10.1016/j.sleh.2019.09.002
15. Guo, J., et al.: The impact of bedtime procrastination on depression symptoms in Chinese medical students. Sleep Breath. **24**(3), 1247–1255 (2020). https://doi.org/10.1007/s11325-020-02079-0
16. Hello: Meet Sense. https://www.kickstarter.com/projects/hello/sense-know-more-sleep-better
17. Herz, R.: Odor-associative learning and emotion: effects on perception and behavior. Chem. Senses **30**(Suppl. 1), i250–i251 (2005). https://doi.org/10.1093/chemse/bjh209
18. Herzog-Krzywoszanska, R., Krzywoszanski, L.: Bedtime procrastination, sleep-related behaviors, and demographic factors in an online survey on a polish sample. Front. Neurosci. **13**, 963 (2019). https://doi.org/10.3389/fnins.2019.00963
19. Hwang, E., Shin, S.: The effects of aromatherapy on sleep improvement: a systematic literature review and meta-analysis. J. Altern. Complement. Med. **21** (2015). https://doi.org/10.1089/acm.2014.0113
20. Irish, L., Kline, C., Gunn, H., Buysse, D., Hall, M.: The role of sleep hygiene in promoting public health: a review of empirical evidence. Sleep Med. Rev. **22** (2014). https://doi.org/10.1016/j.smrv.2014.10.001

21. Iwaki, T., Tanaka, H., Hori, T.: The effects of preferred familiar music on falling asleep. J. Music Ther. **40**, 15–26 (2003). https://doi.org/10.1093/jmt/40.1.15

22. Kay, M., et al.: Lullaby: a capture & access system for understanding the sleep environment (2012)

23. Keller, A.: Attention and olfactory consciousness. Front. Psychol. **2**, 380 (2011). https://doi.org/10.3389/fpsyg.2011.00380

24. Keller, A.: The evolutionary function of conscious information processing is revealed by its task-dependency in the olfactory system. Front. Psychol. **5**, 62 (2014). https://doi.org/10.3389/fpsyg.2014.00062

25. Kolhar, M., Kazi, R.N.A.N., Alameen, A.: Effect of social media use on learning, social interactions, and sleep duration among university students. Saudi J. Biol. Sci. **28** (2021). https://doi.org/10.1016/j.sjbs.2021.01.010

26. Korres, G., Jensen, C., Park, W., Bartsch, C., Eid, M.: A vibrotactile alarm system for pleasant awakening. IEEE Trans. Haptics, 1 (2018). https://doi.org/10.1109/TOH.2018.2804952

27. Kroese, F.M., De Ridder, D.T.D., Evers, C., Adriaanse, M.A.: Bedtime procrastination: introducing a new area of procrastination. Front. Psychol. **5**, 611 (2014). https://doi.org/10.3389/fpsyg.2014.00611

28. Kroese, F.M., Nauts, S., Kamphorst, B.A., Anderson, J.H., de Ridder, D.T.D.: Bedtime Procrastination: A Behavioral Perspective on Sleep Insufficiency. In: Sirois, F.M., Pychyl, T.A. (eds.) Procrastination, Health, and Well-Being, Chapter 5, pp. 93–119. Academic Press, San Diego (2016)

29. Loft, M.H., Cameron, L.D.: Using mental imagery to deliver self-regulation techniques to improve sleep behaviors. Ann. Behav. Med. **46**(3), 260–272 (2013). https://doi.org/10.1007/s12160-013-9503-9

30. Maggioni, E., Cobden, R., Dmitrenko, D., Hornbæk, K., Obrist, M.: SMELL SPACE: mapping out the olfactory design space for novel interactions. ACM Trans. Comput. Hum. Interact. **27**(5), Article no. 36 (2020). https://doi.org/10.1145/3402449

31. Maggioni, E., Cobden, R., Dmitrenko, D., Obrist, M.: Smell-O-Message: integration of olfactory notifications into a messaging application to improve users' performance. In: Proceedings of the 20th ACM International Conference on Multimodal Interaction, Boulder, CO, USA, pp. 45–54. Association for Computing Machinery (2018). https://doi.org/10.1145/3242969.3242975

32. Mairs, L., Mullan, B.: Self-monitoring vs. implementation intentions: a comparison of behaviour change techniques to improve sleep hygiene and sleep outcomes in students. Int. J. Behav. Med. **22**(5), 635–644 (2015). https://doi.org/10.1007/s12529-015-9467-1

33. Min, J.-K., et al.: Toss 'N' turn: Smartphone as sleep and sleep quality detector. In: Conference on Human Factors in Computing Systems – Proceedings (2014). https://doi.org/10.1145/2556288.2557220

34. Nauts, S., Kamphorst, B., Stut, W., Ridder, D., Anderson, J.: The explanations people give for going to bed late: a qualitative study of the varieties of bedtime procrastination. Behav. Sleep Med. **17**, 1 (2018). https://doi.org/10.1080/15402002.2018.1491850

35. Philips Hue. https://labs.meethue.com

36. Phillips Wake-Up Light. https://www.usa.philips.com/c-p/HF3520_60/smartsleep

37. Rodgers, S., Maloney, B., Ploderer, B., Brereton, M.: Managing stress, sleep and technologies: an exploratory study of Australian university students (2016)

38. Saldaña, J.: The Coding Manual for Qualitative Researchers. Sage, New York (2021)

39. Sampasa-Kanyinga, H., Hamilton, H.A., Chaput, J.P.: Use of social media is associated with short sleep duration in a dose-response manner in students aged 11 to 20 years. Acta Paediatr. **107**(4), 694–700 (2018). https://doi.org/10.1111/apa.14210

40. Sleep as Android. https://sleep.urbandroid.org

41. Sleep Cycle. https://www.sleepcycle.com
42. SleepBot. https://mysleepbot.com
43. Spiegel, K., Leproult, R., Van Cauter, E.: Impact of sleep debt on metabolic and endocrine function. Lancet **354**(9188), 1435–1439 (1999). https://doi.org/10.1016/s0140-6736(99)013 76-8
44. Stefani, O., et al.: Changing color and intensity of LED lighting across the day impacts on circadian melatonin rhythms and sleep in healthy men. J. Pineal Res. **70** (2020). https://doi.org/10.1111/jpi.12714
45. Twenge, J.M., Krizan, Z., Hisler, G.: Decreases in self-reported sleep duration among U.S. adolescents 2009–2015 and association with new media screen time. Sleep Med. **39**, 47–53 (2017). https://doi.org/10.1016/j.sleep.2017.08.013
46. Valshtein, T.J., Oettingen, G., Gollwitzer, P.: Using mental contrasting with implementation intentions to reduce bedtime procrastination: two randomised trials. Psychol. Health **35**, 275–301 (2019)
47. Wang, J., et al.: Mobile crowdsourcing based context-aware smart alarm sound for smart living. Pervasive Mob. Comput. **55**, 32–44 (2019). https://doi.org/10.1016/j.pmcj.2019.02.003
48. Zhang, M., Anise, W.: Effects of smartphone addiction on sleep quality among Chinese university students: the mediating role of self-regulation and bedtime procrastination. Addict. Behav. **111**, 106552 (2020). https://doi.org/10.1016/j.addbeh.2020.106552

Case Study of Intelligent Fitness Product Interaction Design Based on Service System

Yihe Liu and Yongyan Guo[✉]

Institute of Art Design and Media, East China University of Science and Technology,
No. 130 Meilong Road, Xuhui Dstrict, Shanghai 200237, China
g_gale@163.com

Abstract. Background and Purpose: In recent years, people pay more and more attention to physical health. As the epidemic continues to affect people's life and bring certain restrictions to people's travel, home fitness has become a new trend. Since there is no trainer to participate in home fitness in real time, the standardization, consistency and standard of movements need to be corrected and adjusted for bodybuilders. How to enhance the service experience of bodybuilders in the exercise process of mobile apps? After analyzing the advantages and disadvantages of intelligent fitness products at the present stage, and finding the development direction of intelligent fitness products in the future is the part of this paper. By improving the intelligent fitness product service system to improve users' fitness experience, aiming at the comparative experience of several fitness apps and discovering problems, the problems and innovation points to be explored at the current stage of fitness APP are explored through user research, and the problems are put into the user journey map to compare the improved APP. To ensure the standardization, consistency and standardization of users' movements in the process of fitness, and to provide users with various and more perfect home fitness experience and improve the service system of fitness APP.

Methods: Users' behavioral process and experience changes were studied by using the user journey map method, and users' evaluation in the experience of fitness was analyzed by Using KANO model. The user journey map can accurately locate the state changes of users in the service system, and find out the positioning of intelligent fitness products through psychological state, behavior, contact points and other parts. KANO model can more carefully analyze the functional attributes and user satisfaction of each intelligent fitness product. Through user demand classification and importance analysis, it is found that by comparing the similarities and differences between the two attributes of intelligent fitness products, it can find the attributes that need to be improved and innovative at the present stage. Through two methods to find out the intelligent fitness products service system needs to be improved and the needs of users.

Results: According to the user evaluation of a series of intelligent fitness products, users pay special attention to the effectiveness, accuracy, standard movement and the effect of their own fitness. Fitness effectiveness has focused on fitness in the process of interactive, accuracy is mainly aimed at the user action and power whether standard, consistent, to ensure the safety of users fitness effect and fitness, how to through the establishment of intelligent fitness service system is to establish the accuracy of the connection between the product and user interaction process and an important point of perfect service system. Establishing a more perfect user feedback system can improve the quality of service and enhance user fitness experience. Through the investigation of users with different fitness needs, the main problem reflected in the user experience flow chart is how to find the most accurate fitness mode for users, and how to reduce the application time of users to fitness APP to reduce the time cost of fitness standards. Finally, user demand analysis of KANO model and user service process analysis of user journey map are combined to find user demand points and innovation points in the process of fitness service. Not only should we consider the user's physical strength and attention consumption during the exercise process, but also help users relieve fatigue and establish good fitness habits after the exercise.

Conclusion: At present, online fitness has been able to meet the basic needs of users in the fitness process. How to improve the quality of users' online fitness, increase user engagement, ensure the safety, quality and user experience of the fitness process, and establish a more perfect intelligent fitness service system are the innovation points to be explored in the future intelligent fitness. Through the analysis of user fitness process by KANO model and user journey map, it is found that intelligent fitness products lack interaction with users at the present stage, the problem of mismatching with users' fitness environment in the process of use, and the lack of consistency of users' actions and forces. In the future, intelligent fitness products should focus on the establishment of a perfect fitness service system, through virtual reality technology, big data and other new technologies to accurately explore user touch points, improve user fitness experience. It provides some reference for the development of intelligent fitness field.

Keywords: User journey map · The KANO model · Customer satisfaction · Interaction process · Intelligent fitness service system

1 Introduction

This thesis mainly focuses on the current development status of interaction design of smart fitness products, through the KANO model and user journey diagram, three smart fitness product APPs are selected for comparison and analysis, comparing their effects on users' fitness experience at the data level, and analyzing whether the product is suitable for the direction of smart fitness development. Whether the smart fitness products combined with virtual reality technology, Internet and Internet of Things are the right development direction for users' fitness experience, the three smart fitness product APPs are analyzed separately using the four attributes of excitement, expectation, basic and non-differentiation attributes in the KANO model, and the results obtained are plotted into scatter diagrams and tables for comparison, and the scatter diagrams and tables are compared with the generalized user journey diagram. The results are compared with the results of the generalized user journey diagram to study the basic attributes of smart fitness products and the attributes that need to be added or deleted in the future. Smart fitness products are essential products for home fitness users, and the demand is increasing. How to design smart fitness products to better fit users' personal attributes, fitness habits, and increase smart attributes is the development direction of smart fitness products at this stage.

2   Smart Fitness Products APP Status

Fitness products have gradually accelerated in this year, and tend to be more humanized, intelligent, gamified and service-oriented. Fitness products began to gradually get rid of the stage of people to adapt to the product, began to be designed for people, the function of intelligent fitness products gradually increased, but also to adapt to people and add some emotional design. The interaction means of smart fitness products are also more diversified, there is interactivity and encouragement mechanism, for example, when doing the movement of bench press, smart fitness products can analyze the current group and training program according to the number of bench press sets and dumbbell weight is reasonable, the user in the process of fitness, smart fitness products can give judgment for the current fitness methods and movements, can be displayed on the screen or through the form of voice Tell the user that there are errors in the action and give correction. The existence of intelligent fitness equipment is also the result of the development of scientific and technological means, perceptual engineering, ergonomics and other disciplines, giving a certain degree of emotion to the machinery, giving users a comfortable product service experience, continuous research in the four directions of personalization, intelligence, gamification and service, so that the in-depth development of fitness products, the combination of research results in the four directions together, so that fitness products are not only a product, but also a part of life It is a part of life.

The interaction design in smart fitness products can improve user experience, product diversity and product intelligence, not only to achieve fitness effects, but also to allow users to get some encouragement in the process of fitness, view their own physical condition and modify their training plans in time. The interaction of a small button on the product can also have a colorful user experience effect, for example, when the user presses the button, an energy ring appears around the button, and when the energy ring is full, fitness training begins, and a full energy ring means that the user's energy is the highest at the beginning of training. The product and the user are one and the same, their own physical strength and the product is a certain correlation.

In order to make fitness equipment into a part of life, a North American sports company invented a fitness "magic mirror" - "mirror", this intelligent fitness products can be fitness function Show in the mirror, and when not working out to ensure that the daily use of the product function, the user does not use the product, it is a flat full body mirror, when the user opens the product and use, the internal fitness tutorials and fitness data can be displayed on the mirror. This product has hundreds of built-in fitness tutorials, users can choose courses according to their preferences and physical condition, follow the movements of the product "coach" fitness training. In the training process, the "coach" will continue to encourage users by communicating with them to stimulate the desire to exercise and improve the exercise effect. In order to let users get user experience in fitness and training results after fitness, this product will have real-time personalized feedback, evaluation and analysis of the exercise process, such as the movement specification, and then feedback to the user.

2.1 Personalization Brings Higher Popularity to Fitness Products

At this stage there are some very serious problems are the lack of service level in traditional gyms, aging fitness equipment, distance, fitness time, etc. and these problems are still affecting the efficiency of people's fitness, but the humanized and personalized customized services covered in smart fitness products can subtly solve these problems. Research shows that gyms and smart fitness products are more attractive to the younger generation than gyms, as users can turn on their fitness equipment at home when they want to work out, learn the classes in the fitness system and follow the exercises, which is very convenient compared to gyms that need to consider the workout time, the number of people and the fitness equipment. We analyze the advantages of personalization based on the features included in smart fitness products at this stage. With more and more diverse ways of interaction design, the effect of interaction design is colorful, and users can also adjust the color of interaction, button size, function module, sound recognition, etc. according to their own preferences, allowing users to set the interaction APP belonging to the user's personal preferences can make the fun of fitness enhanced.

Personalization in smart fitness products is not set entirely according to personal choice, in the process of user use, will be based on the user's fitness habits, fitness plans and fitness standards adaptive user, in order to ensure that the user's fitness effect, each fitness before the user selects the button, can help the user to establish a reasonable fitness plan and fitness time. Personalized settings can also be set by way of the cell phone APP, through the simplicity of the APP, the fitness process required to show the value on the APP, the user can easily observe the data in the phone. Personalization in the main application of intelligent fitness products are: (1) wearing a measurement bracelet on the user's bracelet to analyze the user's health data, real-time detection of heart rate, blood pressure and other values in the fitness process, and after the end of the fitness will be the data changes in the curve on the screen. (2) Provide users with "cloud village", each user of fitness products can show their fitness tips and fitness plans and fitness results in the "cloud village" after fitness, so that users can encourage each other, share with each other, and become each other's teachers and coaches. The users can encourage each other, share with each other, become each other's teachers and coaches, and become each other's teachers while relying on smart fitness equipment. (3) In the device and APP can set a certain fitness plan, according to the fitness plan, the product system will consider how to change the fitness plan into fitness games, through the form of gamification so that fitness is no longer a boring and tedious group change and physical change.

2.2 Intelligent is the Development Direction of Fitness Product Interaction

The interaction we are talking about now is not only a simple click function between the user and the product, user view and various identification devices, but also includes some new means of interaction, such as gesture commands, brain-computer interaction, etc. The user can directly replace the training items in the fitness process through the change of gestures, and brain-computer interaction is not yet commonly put into use, but in the design of some fitness products, brain-computer Although brain-computer interaction is not yet commonly used, but in the design of some fitness products, brain-computer interaction has been added to the future interaction design trends. The future trend of interaction design is to make products smarter, more convenient and more concise, and to increase virtual reality technology in fitness products.

Keep sports APP in the movement detection function is the embodiment of intelligent fitness APP. When we open the running, walking, cycling and other sports mode, the user will automatically pause the movement count in the APP after stopping the movement, and when the user moves again, the APP counter will automatically open. This intelligent counter facilitates the user to pause the count without operating the APP interface when the exercise is paused, which not only provides convenient and fast exercise counting function, but also provides good user experience.

The functions of KeepAPP are listed and analyzed on the KANO model diagram, and these basic functions are sorted and categorized according to the user needs obtained from the research, and the linear ranking of user satisfaction of KeepAPP functions is analyzed. Through the KANO model, the functions of the APP are classified according to user needs and expectations into: (1) essential attributes; (2) desired attributes; (3) charming attributes; and (4) undifferentiated attributes.Charm attribute: unexpected by users, user satisfaction will not decrease if this requirement is not provided, but when this requirement is provided, user satisfaction will be greatly increased.

Desired attribute: when this requirement is provided, user satisfaction will be increased, when this requirement is not provided, user satisfaction will be decreased.

Essential attributes: when optimizing this requirement, user satisfaction does not increase, and when not providing this requirement, user satisfaction decreases significantly.

Non-differentiating factor: user satisfaction does not change when this requirement is provided or not provided, and users simply do not care.

Reverse attribute: users do not have this demand at all, and user satisfaction will be decreased after providing it.

The KANO questionnaire consists of two questions for each quality attribute, positive and negative, to measure the user's response in the face of the presence or absence of a quality attribute, respectively (Fig. 1).

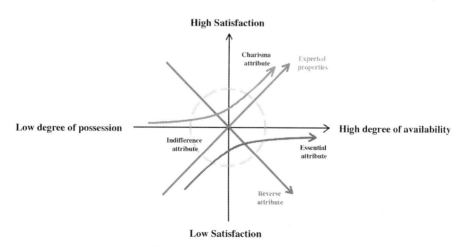

Fig. 1. The basic content and curve of Kano model

2.3   Keep Fitness App Has Developed in the Field of Smart Fitness

In the discussion of Kano attribute attribution, we analyze all the functions, categorize and compare them according to user needs and user evaluation, and calculate the Better-Worse coefficient by the percentage for the function attribute categorization, which indicates that a function can increase the degree of satisfaction or eliminate the influence of very dislike. When the Better percentage is higher and the Worse coefficient is lower, it means that the charm coefficient of this function is higher, and vice versa is a necessary attribute. the higher or lower Better-Worse coefficient does not represent the good or bad of this function, but can only judge the state that this function is needed now, not needed now, needed in the future, and not needed in the future, and choose the right function according to the current situation. It is the intelligent fitness APP that is needed (Figs. 2, 3).

function1	Regular training
function2	community
function3	course
function4	mall
function5	Live courses
function6	Intelligent training
function7	Customized personalized program

Fig. 2. Function list and description. Taking Keep Fitness App as a case, we will list the more commonly used and needed functions and put them in the following figure for comparison. A total of 7 functions are included.

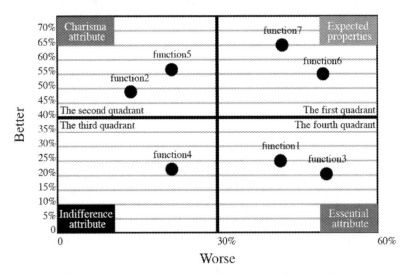

Fig. 3. Table of Better-Worse coefficient values for 7 functions

The first quadrant indicates that the value of the better coefficient is high and the absolute value of the worse coefficient is also high. The attributes that fall into this quadrant are called expectation attributes, which means that if the product provides this feature, user satisfaction will increase, and when it does not provide this feature, user satisfaction will decrease, which is a competitive attribute of quality, and every effort should be made to meet the expectation-type needs of users. Provide additional services or product features that users like, so that their products and services are better and different from competitors, leading users to strengthen the good impression of this product.

The second quadrant indicates: the case where the value of the better coefficient is high and the absolute value of the worse coefficient is low. The attributes that fall into this quadrant are called charm attributes, which means that user satisfaction will not be reduced if this feature is not provided, but when this feature is provided, user satisfaction and loyalty will be greatly enhanced.

The third quadrant indicates that the value of the better coefficient is low, and the absolute value of the worse coefficient is also low. The attributes that fall into this quadrant are called non-differential attributes, i.e., whether these features are provided or not, user satisfaction will not change, and these feature points are features that users do not care about.

The fourth quadrant indicates that the value of the better coefficient is low and the absolute value of the worst coefficient is high. The attributes that fall into this quadrant are called essential attributes, which means that when the product provides this function, user satisfaction will not be increased, and when this function is not provided, user satisfaction will be significantly reduced; it means that the functions that fall into this quadrant are the most basic functions, and these requirements are things that users think we are obligated to do.

After analyzing through the table, function 1 and function 3 are essential attributes, which means that regular training and training courses are what users will often use when they use the APP, and these two functions can meet their daily fitness needs; function 2 and function 5 are charming attributes, community and live courses are the features that users feel are the highlights of this APP, and in the process of using it, users can share their daily training results in the community In the process of use, users can share their daily training results in the community, and also exchange fitness tips with other users. Function 6 and Function 7 are desired functions, users hope their APP can have personalization and smart training function, which can be personalized by the way they are used to APP function arrangement and module emission. Smart training function is not yet fully open function, it needs a lot of training mode import and course import to produce a certain intelligent recognition function to achieve smart training. If companies can start from the desired function, develop the training methods expected by users and provide certain APP personalization mode, it may win more users and win in the competition. Function 4 is the mall purchase, most APPs in consideration of the main functions can be achieved, as with other types of APPs, smart fitness APPs need to ensure the necessary attributes to promote their charming features, while developing the desired attributes of the function, in order to ensure that the premise of the user needs to constantly update the iteration of new products, so that smart fitness APPs truly intelligent (Fig. 4).

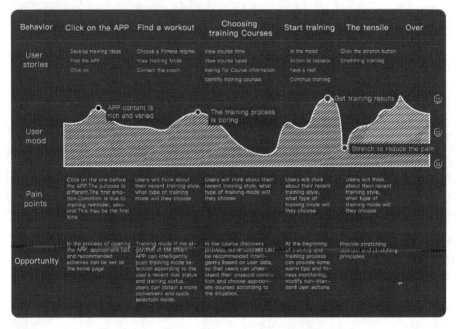

Fig. 4. Keep Fitness APP user journey diagram analysis

In the process of users using KeepAPP, we selected the most typical user profile, users who have used this APP for a period of time and have a better understanding of the iterative process of APP and the way to use APP. can be explored, together with the product features out of the point and user stories. From this chart, it can be extracted that the intelligence of smart fitness APP is a very high demand function at this stage.

3   Gamification Elements Can Enrich the Fitness Experience

First of all, the principle of gamification design is human-centered, providing a user experience with certain fun through setting game rules, and allowing users to have more participation and presence in the fitness process through the guidance of games. Although gamification is an effective way to improve user stickiness and user pleasure in Internet products nowadays, it is necessary to set the game play reasonably if the game elements can positively influence the user experience of the construction products. Secondly, in the process of fitness there will inevitably be safety problems, such as muscle strains, cramps, overtraining, bruises, etc. In order to ensure that users can understand and learn the correct exercise methods in the process of training, to avoid the strenuous exercise and dumbbell exercise in the process of fitness to cause harm to the body, you can set some interesting fitness games before training, especially for fitness beginners, the use of interesting The fitness game quickly and effectively allows users to establish the correct fitness ideas and methods. Lastly, a gamified stretching game can be used to make users who neglect stretching after workouts due to physical exertion realize the importance of stretching and the correct way to stretch. In the whole construction process, users get data through the gamification program of APP, and these data are transformed into "results" after the user's fitness, and even reward mechanism, so that users can feel the beauty of fitness games in the boring fitness.

4 Establish a Reasonable Fitness APP Service System

The large-scale use of an APP product will inevitably lead to various "problems" encountered by users in the process of use, which require adjustment and refinement at the level of UI interaction, product features, product flow, etc. UI interaction is the most effective way to improve the user experience of APP products, with stunning visual effects, simple functions The stunning visual effect, simple function and function sorting, humanized and emotional interaction form can provide better interaction experience for the product. Product functional features are the key point to reflect the basic and additional attributes of the product, and set up relevant product functions for specific user needs. For example, AI smart TV sets a camera at the top to correct fitness posture in the process of fitness, or let the fitness coach teach online through video call, and collect all the fitness data into the phone for analysis to get the output of fitness effect. Establishing a reasonable fitness system will not only improve the efficiency of the user in the fitness process, but also ensure that the user's fitness methods and approaches are reasonable, effective and long-lasting.

5 The Development of Fitness Products and Services System

Fitness needs stage training and long-term adherence to form a certain effect, in order to promote the improvement of fitness product quality, user fitness more humane, intelligent and lightweight, need to establish and improve the fitness service system to provide users with quality fitness services. The current stage of intelligent fitness product services lack of systematic exercise process, the user in the process of using these products and did not get feedback, such as the most simple exercise after the consumption of calories feedback can bring the user certain results. The service system is not just after-sales service and product use service, but to provide users with the entire service system, fitness products are only the starting point and anchor point of the user experience, through this product can allow users to obtain a complete service system and the related added value brought by the service system.

For example, the service system of mint health, users in the process of using the mint health APP, through the user initiative to upload daily recipes, their own weight, height, age and other data, this APP can give you feedback on the maximum daily calorie intake, if the user's eating habits have disadvantages, then you can buy fitness food to adjust and improve eating habits, the process of buying fitness food. This mint health can also provide body fat scale to measure body fat and muscle rate, after users use the product in stages, the APP through the data of the body fat scale intelligent projection of the user's current fitness effect is effective, fitness method is correct, and according to the results of the measurement to give a reasonable fitness plan and diet with, if the user has doubts about the APP intelligent projection of the data, fitness plan and diet with, it If the user has doubts about the APP intelligent data, fitness plan and diet, he can get the help of fitness coach and nutritionist through manual consultation, and make the fitness plan and nutrition match with the user's own condition (Fig. 5).

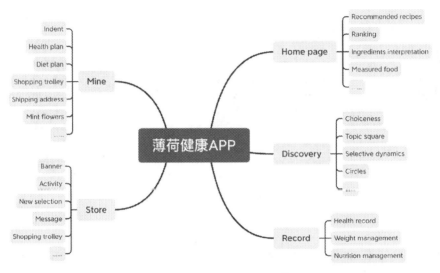

Fig. 5. Mint Health APP system diagram

6   Summary

Intelligent fitness is one of the future development directions of fitness products, the main problem of such APP products is that the product use scenario is still not rich enough, the user experience of the product needs to be more concise and clear, the measurement accuracy is still not high. At this stage, products need to be more adapted to the crowd, rather than people to adapt to the product, intelligence is to help the crowd to improve the user experience, increase the functional characteristics of the product and simplify the use of the process, rather than become a burden on the product. The addition of new forms of product experience such as virtual reality technology, meta-universe and intelligent tracking can bring greater potential and good user experience for fitness APP.

Appendix: The Existence of Smart Fitness App Products

Xiaomi Sports app can be perfectly integrated with Xiaomi devices to provide powerful recording and monitoring functions. It records all-day activities, detects daily sleep, and can also be used with Xiaomi bracelet and other smart wearable devices. Build Xiaomi complete ecology, multi-device, multi-functional perfect integration, to provide users with intelligent technology life.

References

1. Wu, Y.: Intelligent health management service design based on user experience. Design **19**, 83–85 (2021)
2. Zhang, Z., Cao, Y., Wang, J.: Research on intelligent fitness product design based on gamification. Ind. Des. **08**, 73–74 (2021)
3. FITURE Magic Mirror: Home exercise demand spurt Smart fitness mirror into the "new top stream". Consumer Daily (B03), 14 October 2021
4. Zeng, S.: Research on the Interaction Design of Fitness Training App Based on User Experience. Jiangnan University (2021)
5. Yan, Z., Zhang, Y.: Research on fitness-oriented physical interaction behavior design. Design **05**, 134–136 (2017)
6. Qiao, Q.: Design and Research of Interactive Home Gym. Dalian University of Technology (2017)
7. Li, Y., Liu, H., Zhu, L.: An optimal design method for user experience of APP for the elderly based on Kano model and joint analysis. Packag. Eng. **42**(02), 77–85 (2021)
8. Farrokhi, A., Farahbakhsh, R., Rezazadeh, J., Minerva, R.: Application of Internet of Things and artificial intelligence for smart fitness: a survey. Comput. Netw. **189**, 107859 (2021). prepublish
9. Park, S.Y., Lee, J.H.: An explorative study on development direction of a mobile fitness app game associated with smart fitness wear. J. Dig. Contents Soc. **19**(7), 1225–1235 (2018)
10. Xu, J., Zhang, X., Zhou, M., You, I.: A high-security and smart interaction system based on hand gesture recognition for Internet of Things. Secur. Commun. Netw. **2018** (2018)

TidyHome: A Persuasive App for Supporting Victims and Survivors of Domestic Violence

Joseph Orji[✉] [iD], Amelia Hernandez[iD], Biebelemabo Selema, and Rita Orji[iD]

Dalhousie University, Halifax, NS B3H1W5, Canada
{joseph.orji,amelia.hernandez,bselema,rita.orji}@dal.ca

Abstract. Domestic violence is a prevalent issue affecting women worldwide. This issue has been intensified by the COVID-19 pandemic. While several measures have been attempted to address domestic violence, the use of technology has been shown to provide support for victims when planning for their safety. In this paper, we designed a persuasive mobile app, called TidyHome, targeted at women ages 15–49 years who are victims or survivors of domestic or intimate partner violence. The app addresses the issue of domestic violence with the aim of promoting safety behavior and safety consciousness in victims and survivors of domestic violence. To achieve this, we followed a user-centered design approach. Specifically, we obtained user preferences by conducting focus group sessions to gather ideas and opinions on features to be implemented in the app. We then designed low-fidelity prototypes (LFP) illustrating various features of TidyHome based on our findings from the focus group. Thereafter, we conducted a user study evaluating the LFP and assessing the perceived persuasiveness of the features illustrated in the LFP. Based on the results obtained from the LFP evaluation, we designed high-fidelity prototypes (HFP) reflecting only the features perceived as significantly persuasive. Finally, we conducted an evaluation of the HFP assessing its usability, and refined the HFP based on qualitative feedback after thematic analysis. Our results indicate that 8 features of the app were considered persuasive and very relevant for supporting female victims of domestic violence (Knowledge-Box, Panic Button, Third Ear, Meditime, Daily Companion, Diary, Encourage, and Self-Discovery). Likewise, the results display that the TidyHome app shows effective usability and user experience.

Keywords: Domestic violence · Victim · Survivor · Safety · Augmented reality · Persuasive app

1 Introduction

Domestic violence is a prevalent issue affecting women worldwide. This issue has been intensified by the COVID-19 pandemic. Domestic violence (DV) refers to patterns of behavior (not limited to stalking, physical, sexual, and emotional violence) used by one person to gain power and control over another person with whom they have or previously had an intimate relationship [2, 7, 24]. While anyone can experience domestic violence irrespective of their age, race, socio-economic status or gender, women are

© The Author(s), under exclusive license to Springer Nature Switzerland AG 2022
M. Kurosu (Ed.): HCII 2022, LNCS 13304, pp. 400–415, 2022.
https://doi.org/10.1007/978-3-031-05412-9_28

greatly impacted in Canada. The United Nations records that 1 in 3 women worldwide experience physical or sexual violence, mainly from an intimate partner [26]. Also, data across Canada shows that seven out of ten people who experience domestic violence are women or girls with Indigenous women being three times more likely to experience domestic violence than non-Indigenous women [2].

This number has also drastically increased in Canada and around the world with the occurrence of the COVID-19 pandemic [23]. Several governments worldwide including Canada implemented a stay-at-home policy as part of the public health interventions to reduce the spread of the virus [23]. While this was shown to be effective at protecting public health, this led to a surge in the occurrence of domestic violence [23]. Hence, there is a need to find ways to tackle the occurrence of domestic violence and support victims.

The widely recommended intervention to address domestic violence is the safety planning [12, 21]. This involves developing a plan that can assist with the victim's mental and physical safety in a case of domestic violence and help reduce the risk of future harm [21]. Due to the complexity of safety planning, the use of technology could play a role in making the process easier for victims and survivors.

In this paper we designed a safety app, called TidyHome as a technology intervention for promoting safety behavior and safety consciousness in both survivors and victims of domestic violence or intimate partner violence using a user-centered design approach. The application is targeted towards women ages 15–49 years who are victims or survivors of domestic or intimate partner violence. The age group was chosen as the target audience because statistics shows that 243 million women around the world within the target age range have been significantly subjected to domestic violence [23, 26]. Although the words victims and survivors have been used interchangeably, this paper makes firm distinctions to both words for design purposes. In this paper, a victim refers to a person who is currently living in the same domestic sphere with their abuser whereas a survivor is a person who was once a victim of domestic violence in the past but no longer lives in the same domestic sphere as their abuser. The objective of the app is to:

- Regain and promote the user's feeling of safety at home and other environments
- Promote users' safety awareness of their surroundings
- Develop safety consciousness after trauma
- Build users' confidence and self-esteem to encourage them to leave a violent situation
- Develop user's knowledge on actions that can be taken to ensure their safety

To achieve our goal, we employed the user-centered design (UCD) approach [25] to app design and evaluation, as described in the following five stages:

1. We obtained user preferences by conducting two focus groups with participants who had varying levels of interaction with our target audience. The objective of the sessions was to understand users' willingness to use the safety app and the features they would like to see implemented in a safety app that targets victims and survivors of domestic violence. The interview method allowed us to gather ideas and opinions from the participants and streamline features implemented in the app.

2. We designed low-fidelity prototypes (LFP) showing our selected features based on the qualitative feedback and suggestions received during the focus groups.
3. We conducted a user survey to evaluate the perceived persuasiveness of the features in the LFP design. The perceived persuasiveness [3] measures each feature's perceived effectiveness in promoting safety for victims and survivors of domestic violence.
4. We designed high-fidelity prototypes (HFP) implementing the features perceived as persuasive based on the results of the LFP evaluation.
5. We conducted another user survey to evaluate the usability of HFP design and thereafter implemented design feedback received.

2 Related Work

Technological solution is one that has proved helpful in the aspect of domestic and intimate partner violence. As part of a literature review, we identified some applications that provide technology solutions for victims or survivors of domestic violence. A summary of all safety related technology interventions as shown in Table 1 [1, 5, 8, 9, 11, 13, 17, 19, 20, 22, 27, 28].

Table 1. Summary of existing software applications for victims of domestic violence

App name	System objective	Software platform
Abhaya	By a single click in the app, the victim's location is sent to registered contacts message with location coordinates [27]	Android
A safety decision app	Provides educational resources to assist men identify abuse in their relationships and get access to additional help and resources specific to men [8]	All smart phones
Bonitaa	Provides resources and support that assist victims with their mental and physical health as well as provide legislative information in the event of rape [9]	Android
Evo	Provides a platform for victim to create a safety plan and keep relevant information regarding their safety [17]	All smart phones
FEMME	Sends an alert to local authorities via SMS to a contact saved on the app [11]	Android

(continued)

Table 1. (*continued*)

App name	System objective	Software platform
Fightback	The app assists the victim by sending a call for help alert to victim's contacts through email or SMS [13]	Android
MyPlan	Provides a safety and educational platform for college students and young women to prevent intimate partner violence during dating [5]	Web-based and all smart phones
Rakhsa	By pressing a button, the app can send a location of the user to emergency contacts and send an SMS alert when there is no internet connectivity [19]	Android
Safetipin	Notifies user of safe environments ranked by a scale of safety scores assigned to neighborhoods [20]	Android
Suraksha	Sends instant location and a SOS message to local authorities and saved emergency contacts [1]	GSM
Smart	Predicts unsafe situations to the user by observing facial expressions [28]	Image processing, GSM
Security SafeRing	Sends a safety alert and victim's last location to emergency contact [13]	GPS
Sunny	Provides an educational module on domestic violence to victims and provides information to federal authorities to contact if help is needed [22]	All smart phones

3   Method

Our goal is to develop a user-centered app that targets domestic violence on women. To achieve this goal, first, we ran a focus group to learn from users' thoughts and needs. We used the feedback obtained from the focus group to design a low fidelity prototype (LFP). Second, we ran a study to evaluate the perceived persuasiveness of the LPF. Afterwards, we used the results from the second study to turn the LPF into a high-fidelity prototype (HFP). Finally, we ran a third study to evaluate and later improve the HFP.

3.1 Study 1: Focus Group

To design a user-centered app, we were interested in learning what our target audience wanted to see in an app targeting domestic violence in women; therefore, we ran a focus group. Focus groups are a great approach to discover what users want from a system, their preferences and needs [4]. We leveraged the potential of the focus group to determine what participants thought would be useful to have in an app as a victim or survivor of domestic violence. Hence, we recruited 8 participants within the ages 20 to 35, which we divided into two groups of four participants each one FG1 (n = 4) and FG2 (n = 4). Each session lasted 60 min and included the participants, a moderator, and two assistant moderators. The moderator described different features, asked questions, and facilitated the conversation between the participants. The assistant-moderators took notes, took track of the time, and recorded the session. The focus group was divided into two main parts:

- Introduction: The moderator introduced the purpose of the study and collected demographic information from the participants. Likewise, the moderator made sure that all the participants agreed to record the session.
- Discussion: The moderator described 10 different features that have the purpose of helping female victims and survivors of domestic violence obtained from the literature. The moderator described the features one by one, and asked the two following questions: (1) would you use this feature if you were a victim? Why or why not? (2) Would you use this feature if you were a survivor? Why or why not? At the end of the interview, the moderator asked for general recommendations for an app targeting domestic violence in women.

Data Analysis and Results. In order to analyze the results, we transcribed the two focus group recordings into text. Afterwards, we used the text from the recordings and the notes we took to carry out a thematic analysis. The thematic analysis helped us to identify common themes from all the participants' input to later inform the design of the app's low fidelity prototype LFP.

Through the whole session participants shared their thoughts and views on different features. From the different contributions, we uncovered 6 themes. (1) Privacy concerns, (2) requesting emergency help, (3) emotions and wellbeing, (4) connecting with people, (5) cognitive load, (6) secondary effects. The themes helped us to make sure that the needs of the target users were satisfied. The preferred features of the participants from the focus groups are the following:

1. Panic button: 75% of the participants mentioned interest in a feature that allows them to press a button, and the system will automatically contact the authorities to send help. "If something happening over here, I think I will use the panic button when I am in distress." (P1)

2. Daily companion: 50% of the participants mentioned interest in a feature to connect with a hotline, a counsellor, or chatbot for having someone to talk to and receive support. The first half of the participants think that a chatbot (SallyDBot) could encourage them to speak about their problems without being judged. However, the other 50% of the participants mentioned that they are more interested in connecting with humans and not chatbots because they lack the human touch. "Yeah, I think I would use it because I would prefer to speak to the bot more than speaking to someone personally." (P4)

3. Self-Discovery: 75% of the participants mentioned they would be interested in a feature in the form of questionnaire that would assess where a user is in their DV journey and their mindset towards DV. The responses to the questionnaire will help the app to personalize the content to the user's needs. "I will use the feature because the questionnaire would help me even better understand what I'm going through." (P2)

4. Diary: 62% of the participants mentioned interest in a feature to log their daily thoughts such as mood, feelings, and activities. From participants' feedback, we decided to include a functionality to track their mood through what the user writes in their diary and use machine learning ML for performing sentiment analysis. "I think that it is really good idea journaling and mood tracking, and especially when you can see over years or months how you've been doing, that will be really helpful and also for managing emotions or managing the situation." (P3)

5. Knowledge-Box: 50% of the participants mentioned interest in a feature that would provide personalized materials and resources to help them through their journey based on the results from the Self-Discovery feature. Participants mentioned that they are interested in resources such as videos or short articles. "Getting those types of articles to read, encouraging articles to read, at least it will put a smile on yourself or your face, at least for the day or for the time." (P2)

6. Third ear: 50% of the participants mentioned interest in a feature that listens and analyses the sound in the environment. If any distress sound is detected, the app contacts the authorities automatically. Nonetheless, participants expressed privacy concerns related to this feature. Participants don't want the feature to listen to all the sounds in their environment. Additionally, participants are concerned about false positives that could cause an undesired call to the emergency service. Thus, we decided to add an option to enable and disable the third ear feature, so that users can decide when to activate the feature. Likewise, we included the possibility for the users to record their own emergency code, so that the system will recognize that specific word or sound and only then call the emergency service. "I think it can recall lots of false positives and that will be a lot of privacy and security issues attached, so, I would not want someone to be listening all the time because then that will not be something I'm comfortable with." (P3)

7. Disguise feature: 37% of the participants were interested in a feature to help them hide the app from their abusers. The participants that were not interested in this feature, mentioned that having two different passwords added cognitive load and made the feature hard to use specially in dangerous situations when their abusers are nearby. This feedback made us redesign the feature for the LFP. Instead of having two passwords, we created a safe mode in which the user can enter the following PIN "0000", and it will unlock an app for home organization instead of a domestic violence app. Here is a sample comment: "From your description, it sounding sounds very complicated and if it's something I'm supposed to reach easily." (P2)

8. Encouragement: 37% of the participants mentioned interest in a feature that gives them encouragement phrases to improve their mood. "This situation being a very sensitive situation, it can be very depressing. So checking your phone and creating that type of message, it will be very, very encouraging." (P2)

9. Trust finder: 25% of the participants mentioned interest in a feature to locate other victims or survivors (people using the app) in their area, so that they can connect with and discuss their challenges and journey. However, participants also showed many privacy concerns. Their main worry is that their abusers could join the app and they would be able to locate them. This would represent a potential danger to the victim or survivor. Therefore, from the feedback, we decided to remove this feature to make it safer. "I suggest disabling the feature of finding people nearby or in the location. It should only be a social platform where people from different places connect irrespective of their location, otherwise if the abuser figure it out it could be troublesome." (P1)

10. Meditime: 12% of the participants mentioned interest in a feature that uses Augmented Reality (AR) to give the user an opportunity to virtually practice domestic violence scenarios that could happen in real life and survival skills. Likewise, it could also help survivors to overcome the shock of their past experiences, or offer a guided meditation using AR. However, participants were concerned of the secondary effects of this feature, as it could trigger bad memories and increase the trauma. Hence, we decided to transform the feature into an AR meditation feature to promote wellbeing. "I won't want to use that because it would mean imagining or listening to traumatic memories that affect my psychological state or my mental health." (P2)

3.2   Study 2: Low-Fidelity Prototype and Evaluation

The findings of the focus group (FG) session enabled us fine tune the proposed features, make some adjustment based on feedbacks from the FG, then design Low Fidelity Prototypes (LFP) using Balsamiq tool [16] to illustrate the 11 features. Using the LFP, we conducted a user study of 14 people to assess the perceived persuasiveness of the features. Figure 1 shows the LFP for Knowledge-Box, Third Ear, and Panic button features.

Fig. 1. Low fidelity prototype illustrating learn (knowledge-box), third ear feature and panic button feature.

With an online Survey, we evaluated the Low Fidelity Prototype (LFP). We presented detailed description of what the prototype does, and a link to the Balsamiq platform were users can interact with the LFP. For each of the features, we presented to the participants an image illustrating the feature, a brief description of the feature followed by questions that assesses the perceived persuasiveness of the feature. Adapted from [3], the questions were based on Validated scale which is often used in many persuasive computing research as seen in [14, 15]. The questions were measured on a 5-point Likert scale ranging from 1 – Strongly disagree to 5-Strongly Agree. We personalized the questions to each feature and asked the participant how persuasive the feature was to them. Example, the Knowledge-Box feature had the following questions:

- This feature would motivate me to take action for my safety and wellbeing.
- This feature would improve my habits to take action for my safety and wellbeing
- This feature would influence my action towards safety and wellbeing.
- The Diary feature had the following sets of perceived persuasive questions:
- This feature would motivate me to change my current behavior of dealing with overwhelming emotions.
- This feature would improve my habits of dealing with overwhelming emotions.
- This feature would influence me to deal with overwhelming emotions.

In addition, we also asked demographic questions and open-ended questions to enable the participants give us qualitative data. We got a total of 14 responses but removed 3 due to incomplete responses, we targeted audience between the age of 18 and 45 who may have experienced or been in close contact with someone who has experienced domestic violence. The demographic information revealed that 50% of our participants were between the ages of 18–25, 35.7% between the ages of 26–35, while 14.3% were between 36–45 years old. We had 57.1% male participants and 42.9% female participants, amongst the participants were 71.4% singles and 28.6% married.

Data Analysis and Results. For analysis, we computed the average score of response gotten for each feature, and then with a One Sample t-test, we were able to determine the persuasiveness of each feature with respect to the neutral score 3 (from a 5-point Likert scale). The result of the one sample t-test showed that 9 out of the 11 features were perceived to be significantly persuasive by the participants. As shown in Fig. 2.

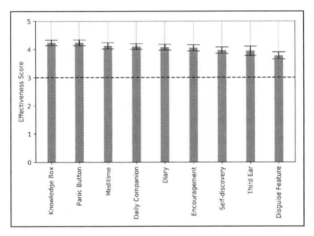

Fig. 2. A bar chart showing the effectiveness of the features on a scale 1 to 5 and 3 as the neutral point.

Knowledge-Box (mean = 4.24, SD = 0.47) and Panic Button (Mean = 4.24, SD = 0.51) were perceived most effective features followed by Meditime (Mean = 4.13, SD = 0.52) and "Daily Companion" (Mean = 4.10, SD = 0.48). However, "Disguise feature" was perceived as the least effective (Mean = 3.77, SD = 0.56). The other features' ("Diary features", "Third ear", "Self-Discovery", TrustFinder and "Encourage") were in the middle.

In Summary, these 9 features are perceived to be significantly effective: Knowledge-Box, Panic Button, Meditime, Daily Companion, Diary, Encouragement, Self-discovery, Third ear, and Disguise feature, see Fig. 2. We used these features in designing the high-fidelity prototype (HFP).

Thematic Analysis of Qualitative Feedback of LFP. As part of the low fidelity prototype evaluation, we conducted a thematic analysis on the feedback and suggestions to find patterns and themes from participants' responses. Table 2 exhibits sample comments from participants copied verbatim, 6 themes were uncovered: improvement in safety; personal improvement, self-esteem, and wellbeing; motivated to use the app; motivated to seek help, social integration; and suggestion.

Table 2. Resulting themes of the LFP thematic analysis.

Improvement in safety: Users' affirmation to the app's ability to improve their safety in domestic violent environment. "I think this combined with the third ear would be a very good safety system in place for users of the app to easily access help, but that of course depends on if the help is gotten or not. How effective the service is" (P11)
Personal improvement, self-esteem and well-being: Users' affirmed the app's ability to help them improve their self-esteem and wellbeing. "This would function as a typical diary/journal and thus would be helpful in dealing with my emotions" (P5)
Motivated to use the app: Users' affirmation to their tendency to use the app. "Being greeted with a simple message of encouragement can be a positive reinforcement. It might make the end user feel more inclined to open the app each day." (P5)
Motivated to seek help: Users' affirmed the app's ability to motivate them seek for help instead of suffering in silence. "Having the option to message instead of talking on the phone can make people who are usually shy feel more comfortable" (P8)
Social integration: Users' affirmed the app's ability to help users interact with people in a similar violent situation. "This is a great way to share experiences and learn from one another's journey "(P1)
Suggestions: Recommendations from participants. "This seems useful, but I am unsure how much a user in distress want to be looking at tutorial videos will. Probably such short tutorial videos can be added as a suggestion to view on completion of Self-Discovery feature. A suggestion like "You should check out what Mr. XYZ from Harvard has to say about anger issues. Would you like to watch a 2 min video?" (P12)

3.3 Study 3: High-Fidelity Prototype and Evaluation

Based on the results obtained from the LFP evaluation in Study 2, we created a high-fidelity prototype (HFP) illustrating the 9 features that were perceived as persuasive and effective in promoting safety for female victims and survivors of domestic violence. Moreover, we used the qualitative feedback and suggestions provided by the participants to improve the usability of TidyHome. Study 3 provided us with the knowledge to make sure that TidyHome is usable and acceptable to users.

The HFP was designed using the Proto.io prototyping tool [18]. Thereafter, we conducted a user study with 21 participants to evaluate the usability of our app. Our participants consisted of both male and female between ages 18–49 who followed the study from the interview stage to the usability testing of the system. Table 3 shows the demographic information of participants.

The online survey consists of three parts: demographic questions, overall system usability question, and feature based usability questions. Participants were asked to interact with the HFP using a link to the prototype included in the survey and thereafter respond to the survey. Likewise, the survey included a link to a short video explaining how to interact with the prototype using Proto.io to make it easier for the participants

Table 3. Demographic information of participants.

Total participants = 21	
Age	18–24 (40%), 26–35(48%), 36–45 (12%)
Gender	Male (48%), Female (53%)
Marital status	Single (68%), Married (32%)
Education level	High School Diploma (4%), Bachelor's (48%), Master's (48%)

to explore the app. The usability questions in the survey evaluated the features and the overall system to explore the following:

- Ease of use and overall user experience.
- Determine whether users were able to complete tasks successfully and independently.
- Assessed the users' performance and mental state (willingness or frustration) as they try to navigate the app.
- Evaluate the willingness to use the app based on the aesthetics (e.g., color, graphics, layout, etc.)

Throughout the survey, participants were asked to justify their responses via qualitative comments and provide recommendations as necessary. Figure 3 illustrates the HFP of Panic Button, Third Ear, and Daily Companion features.

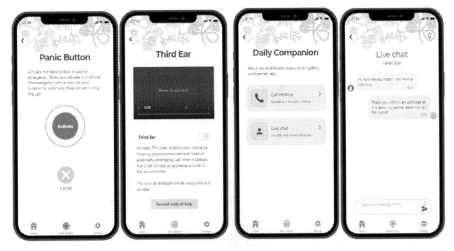

Fig. 3. High fidelity prototype illustrating panic button, third ear, and daily companion features.

Usability Evaluation of the HFP. From the quantitative analysis of Study 3, our findings show that 80% of the participants liked the aesthetics of the app, while 100% found the app to be easy to use as well as being able to use the app independently and correctly.

In terms of the overall user experience, 80% of the participants had good experience navigating the app based on their feedback of not running into difficulties while using the app. From the qualitative responses of Study 3, we performed a qualitative analysis to uncover themes related to the usability of the TidyHome app. Table 4 shows the resulting themes of the HFP thematic analysis.

Table 4. Themes, Description and Sample comments from high-fidelity prototype evaluation.

Ease of use: Users expressed how easy it's to use the app independently and correctly. 'It was straightforward to use it."(P8)
Good aesthetics: Users highlighted their overall satisfaction with app's aesthetics: colors, graphics, and layout. "The aesthetics of the app is pleasant to the eye and nothing too flashy (which I like)." (P7)
Good user experience and navigation: Users expressed positive overall experience, ease of navigation and satisfaction with the app. "It was easy to find information in the application n and navigate the system" "The application seems simple enough for me to understand and use it daily" (P10)
Theme customization: Users highlighted the need for customizable features that they can control. "The app design is clean and it looks good. I'd like to have an option to select themes. I hate pink (P1)
Simplicity and Learnability: Users highlighted that the app is simple and with a very low learning curve for first time users. "The interface is simple to use with just a few minutes without prior knowledge, it is simple to adjust to the application and navigate through" (P4)
Suggestions and Recommendations: Users provided some suggestion for improving the app. "There should be a suggestion, after writing a dairy journal" "The guide to local domestic violence laws can be added in this section too" (P1)

The following list presents the refinements we included in the HFP based on the feedback of Study 3. The improvements are organized by theme.

- Theme customization: We included an option to Change theme color for allowing users to personalize their system and make it compatible with their taste.
- Simplicity and learnability: (1) we added more detail to the descriptions of some of the features of the app. This would allow users to understand the purpose of the features and provide guidance on how to use them. (2) We added examples of codes of help for the Third Ear feature, so that the user can have guidance to record their own.
- Suggestions and Recommendations: (1) we included a link to appropriate resources after writing a diary journal according to the resulting emotions from the sentiment analysis. This with the objective of helping users to handle those emotions. (2) We added the names of organizations that are working to prevent and solve the problem of domestic violence to create trust in the content of the app. As a note, we used resources that these organizations have available on their websites to build the content of the app. (3) we included the option to access the contents to local domestic violence laws.

4 Discussion

In this paper, we designed a user-centered persuasive mobile app called TidyHome to help victims of domestic violence to achieve several goals: seek help, access help, and discover if they are in an unhealthy relationship - as some victims of domestic violence have gotten used to it that they think it is normal. We first analyzed the thoughts and needs of victims of domestic violence with which we designed the TidyHome app. We conducted a focus group to understand how much these features can address the need of domestic violent victims, the outcome of the focus group helped us fine-tune the features and come up with a low fidelity prototype. A previous study has shown that user-centered designs, that gets users involved, often result in more effective and acceptable apps [10]. Table 5 shows the features in TidyHome and the persuasive strategies behind them.

Table 5. Core features of TidyHome and persuasive strategies.

Features	Description	Persuasive strategies
Daily companion	This feature provides an opportunity to get personalized and confidential help via specialized hotline and a live chat with trained domestic violence advocates	Expertise, authority
Diary	With this feature, the user is able to log their daily thoughts such as mood, feelings, and activities. From the text that the user types, the app automatically performs a sentiment analysis using Machine Learning (ML) to identify the predominant emotions of the user and provides them with appropriate resources to handle those emotions	Self-monitoring
Self-discovery	This feature assesses where the user is in their DV journey and their mindset towards DV through a questionnaire. The responses to the questionnaire help the app to personalize the content to the user's needs	Personalization
Knowledge-box	This feature provides the user with personalized learning resources on domestic violence topics. The resources are based on their situation and their stage in the domestic violence journey	Personalization, expertise

(*continued*)

Table 5. (*continued*)

Features	Description	Persuasive strategies
Meditime	This feature aims at distracting the user from the present violent environment, so they can meditate and have some peace. This feature provides a virtual meditation space for users with the use of augmented reality (AR). Users can transport themselves to a preferred location and practice meditation with the goal of improving their wellbeing	Tunneling
Third ear	This is a utility feature in the app that enables the user set up a pre-recorded distress sound in the case of an emergency. If the sound is detected, the user's emergency contact and emergency authorities are notified. This feature is aimed at giving the user the confidence that they are not alone and they can get help automatically	Reduction, personalization
Panic button	A second utility feature in the app that gives the user an opportunity to alert their emergency contact and relevant authorities of a dangerous situation by pressing the button	Reduction
Encourage	This feature gives daily words of encouragement from authoritative sources according to the user's mood to help them improve their self-esteem as victim or survivor of DV. It also reminds the user not to give-up on the quest to overcome DV	Authority, reminders

5   Conclusion

This paper presents the design of TidyHome, a persuasive app for supporting female victims and survivors of domestic violence as women are the most affected group by Domestic Violence after COVID-19 outbreak. We applied the user-centered design (UCD) approach by running three user studies. First, we conducted a focus group (FG) to learn from the users' need and thoughts. Based on the findings of the FG, we designed a Low-Fidelity Prototype and conducted a second study to evaluate the perceived persuasiveness of the features. The results indicated that 9 features were considered as persuasive (Knowledge-Box, Panic Button, Third Ear, Meditime, Daily Companion, Diary, Encourage, and Self-Discovery). Later, we designed a High-Fidelity Prototype that includes those features and conducted a third study to evaluate the usability of those features and the app in general. The results showed that TidyHome is easy to use, useful, easy to navigate, and has good aesthetics. Finally, we refined the HFP using the qualitative comments from the participants to enhance the usability and user experience of TidyHome.

As future work, we plan to deploy the app and conduct a long-term study with a large sample of female victims and survivors of Domestic Violence.

References

1. Bhardwaj, N., Aggarwal, N.: Design and development of "Suraksha"-a women safety device. Int. J. Inf. Comput. Technol. **4**(8), 787–792 (2014)
2. Domestic violence | Ontario.ca. https://www.ontario.ca/page/domestic-violence. Accessed 14 Sept 2021
3. Drozd, F., Lehto, T., Oinas-Kukkonen, H.: Exploring perceived persuasiveness of a behavior change support system: a structural model. In: Bang, M., Ragnemalm, E.L. (eds.) PERSUA-SIVE 2012. LNCS, vol. 7284, pp. 157–168. Springer, Heidelberg (2012). https://doi.org/10.1007/978-3-642-31037-9_14
4. Focus Groups in UX Research: Article by Jakob Nielsen. https://www.nngroup.com/articles/focus-groups/. Accessed 14 Sept 2021
5. Glass, N., et al.: A safety app to respond to dating violence for college women and their friends: the MyPlan study randomized controlled trial protocol. BMC Public Health **15**(1), 1–13 (2015). https://doi.org/10.1186/S12889-015-2191-6
6. Google Forms: Free Online Surveys for Personal Use. https://www.google.ca/forms/about/. Accessed 14 Sept 2021
7. Ilesanmi, O., et al.: Domestic violence amid the COVID-19 lockdown: a threat to individual safety. Glob. Biosecur. **3**(1), (2020). https://doi.org/10.31646/GBIO.94
8. Lindsay, M., et al.: Survivor feedback on a safety decision aid smartphone application for college-age women in abusive relationships **31**(4), 368–388 (2013). https://doi.org/10.1080/15228835.2013.861784
9. Mahmud, S.R., et al.: BONITAA: a smart approach to support the female rape victims. In: 5th IEEE Region 10 Humanitarian Technology Conference 2017, R10-HTC 2017, January 2018, pp. 730–733, February 2018. https://doi.org/10.1109/R10-HTC.2017.8289061
10. McDermott, M.J., Garofalo, J.: When advocacy for domestic violence victims backfires: types and sources of victim disempowerment **10**(11), 1245–1266 (2016). https://doi.org/10.1177/1077801204268999
11. Monisha, D.G., et al.: Women safety device and application-FEMME. Indian J. Sci. Technol. **9**(10) (2016). https://doi.org/10.17485/ijst/2016/v9i10/88898
12. Murray, C.E., et al.: Domestic violence service providers' perceptions of safety planning: a focus group study. J. Fam. Violence **30**(3), 381–392 (2015). https://doi.org/10.1007/s10896-015-9674-1
13. Nazrul Islam, M., et al.: SafeBand: a wearable device for the safety of women in Bangladesh. In: Proceedings of the 16th International Conference on Advances in Mobile Computing and Multimedia, 18 (2018). https://doi.org/10.1145/3282353
14. Orji, R., et al.: Personalizing persuasive strategies in gameful systems to gamification user types. In: Proceedings of the 2018 CHI Conference on Human Factors in Computing Systems (2018). https://doi.org/10.1145/3173574
15. Orji, R., et al.: Towards personality-driven persuasive health games and gamified systems. In: Proceedings of the 2017 CHI Conference on Human Factors in Computing Systems (2017). https://doi.org/10.1145/3025453
16. PersuasiveComputing | Balsamiq Cloud. https://balsamiq.cloud/sfhlyp4/p1er11u/rC12B. Accessed 14 Sept 2021
17. PLEIS-NB • Public Legal Education and Information Service of New Brunswick. http://www.legal-info-legale.nb.ca/en/index.php?mact=News,cntnt01,detail,0&cntnt01articleid=433&cntnt01origid=24&cntnt01returnid=252. Accessed 14 Sept 2021

18. Proto.io - Prototyping for all. https://proto.io/. Accessed 15 Sept 2021
19. Raksha - Women Safety Alert 1.0 Free Download. https://raksha-women-safety-alert.soft112. com/. Accessed 14 Sept 2021
20. Safetipin | Safetipin, Creating Safe Public Spaces for Women. https://safetipin.com/. Accessed 14 Sept 2021
21. Safety Planning | RAINN. https://www.rainn.org/articles/safety-planning. Accessed 14 Sept 2021
22. Sunny app | 1800RESPECT. https://www.1800respect.org.au/sunny. Accessed 14 Sept 2021
23. Violence against women and girls: the shadow pandemic | UN Women – Headquarters. https://www.unwomen.org/en/news/stories/2020/4/statement-ed-phumzile-violence-aga inst-women-during-pandemic?gclid=CjwKCAjwgviIBhBkEiwA10D2jwZRAPq9ceNc0JW nl18DDgVTvG5OvSEoBVn5eF-B1Pei-bGeSZ7p3RoCJ9UQAvD_BwE. Accessed 14 Sept 2021
24. Walker, L.E.: Psychology and domestic violence around the world. Am. Psychol. **54**(1), 21–29 (1999). https://doi.org/10.1037/0003-066X.54.1.21
25. What is User Centered Design? | Interaction Design Foundation (IxDF). https://www.intera ction-design.org/literature/topics/user-centered-design. Accessed 14 Sept 2021
26. What we do: Ending violence against women | UN Women – Headquarters. https://www.unw omen.org/en/what-we-do/ending-violence-against-women. Accessed 14 Sept 2021
27. Yarrabothu, R.S., Thota, B.: Abhaya: An Android App for the safety of women. In: 12th IEEE International Conference Electronics, Energy, Environment, Communication, Computer, Control: (E3-C3), INDICON 2015 (2016). https://doi.org/10.1109/INDICON.2015. 7443652
28. An Intelligent Security System for Violence against Women in Public Places 65

Towards an Architectural Concept for a Wearable Recommendation System to Support Workplace Productivity and Well-Being

Henning Richter(ID), Michael Fellmann(✉)(ID), Fabienne Lambusch(ID),
and Maik Kranzusch

University of Rostock, 18051 Rostock, Germany
{henning.richter,michael.fellmann,fabienne.lambusch,
maik.kranzusch}@uni-rostock.de

Abstract. Modern information technology has a high potential to assist people in their daily life via assistance systems. However, such systems surprisingly still lack appropriate solutions tackling the challenges of modern work-life. By now, work aspects such as productivity have been considered mainly separately from other aspects such as one's health and fitness level. Regarding the latter, wearable technologies (like smartwatches or fitness trackers) are commonly used to gather sensor data (such as GPS, heart rate, etc.) and provide supportive recommendations. To support employees in promoting balance between different aspects of their work-life such as productivity and well-being, these features should be more integrated than this is the case in existing systems. To this end, we present an architectural concept for a wearable recommendation system designed to provide personal recommendations with the ultimate goal of supporting workplace productivity and well-being. In addition, our architectural concept also covers the aspect of user feedback to allow for improvements regarding the relevance of recommendations. We derived our conceptual architecture from related work, by considering the characteristics of the technology to be integrated and motivational scenarios describing the intended use of the system. With our architecture, we hope to inspire future efforts towards wearable recommender systems that integrate productivity and well-being.

Keywords: Wearables · Smartwatches · Recommendation system ·
Architectural concept · Workplace productivity · Wellbeing · Work-life-balance

1 Introduction and Motivation

In the past decades, working conditions and requirements have changed for many employees. Overall, more knowledge-intense and complex tasks emerged accompanied by higher workloads. Many employees have to deal with a higher degree of flexibility in their daily work [1, 2]. In turn, those employees are required to provide advanced skills in self-management, i.e., in managing their resources such as time, attention, focus, motivation, health, and other aspects. This also challenges employees to balance their work and private life, as those boundaries increasingly tend to vanish [2, 3], especially when working from home. Hence, employees may even suffer from health issues caused by those circumstances, which, in turn, results in a possible loss of human capital for organizations [4].

Furthermore, the COVID-19 pandemic has intensified those existing issues and even caused new ones. For instance, Fröböse and Wallmann-Sperlich [5] reported that young Germans have become "world champions" in daily sitting with an average of 10.5 h per day, mostly due to their work. The average for the overall German population was estimated at 8.5 h of sitting per day, which is also significantly high and dangerous for maintaining a healthy lifestyle. Additionally, Nesher Shoshan and Wehrt [6] believe that virtual meetings (whose number and relevance has drastically increased due to the COVID-19 pandemic) are significantly more exhausting to people than conventional meetings (which were usually common before).

These issues indicate an urgent demand for interventions, measures, and compensations to sustain long-term productivity, health, and well-being. However, providing interventions is challenging. *First*, due to the lack of awareness that interventions in the form of recommendations are necessary at all. In this regard, Fröböse and Wallmann-Sperlich [5] discovered a remarkable gap between the people who are actually living in a healthy way (which are just approximately 1 out of 9) and those who are just perceiving themselves this way (which are approximately 61% out of all). This indicates that many people would require and benefit from a healthier and more balanced way of life while not even being aware of that. *Second*, many effects and interrelations must be considered to provide relevant recommendations. For example, according to Abdel Hadi et al. [7], doing sport can mediate negative effects from work, such as exhaustion. Unfortunately, they also discovered that work-related rumination actually inhibits such recovery activities by decreasing the motivation to become physically active. This effect is even amplified for highly intrinsically motivated employees who experience less job-detachment than extrinsically or unmotivated employees. Thus, simply providing recommendations for increased motivation or productivity and at the same time providing suggestions for increased physical activity might not lead to the desired effect. *Third*, even if it is possible to generate relevant recommendations, there is still a gap between knowing and acting. Just being aware of problematic circumstances and relevant solutions regarding productivity and health does not necessarily lead to actual better behavior in response. This is even amplified by habits that could interfere with or inhibit behavior change.

In the light of these challenges, advanced systems are required that (i) can raise people's awareness for potential productivity and/or health and well-being issues, (ii) provide relevant recommendations, and (iii) nudge the user to follow the recommendations or to provide feedback to the system usable for tailoring the recommendations to the user's needs.

These requirements inevitably lead to complex systems that track the user's context via sensors, generate relevant recommendations, and adapt to user feedback. Since only a few systems up to now exist and building such systems is challenging due to the high complexity of the components and their relations, we have developed a generic architecture for such systems. It could serve as a blueprint for building such systems.

The remainder of the paper is structured as follows. Section 2 provides a brief overview of background literature and related work. This is followed by motivational scenarios in Sect. 3 that demonstrate how a visionary wearable recommendation system optimizing workplace productivity and well-being could be applied. Afterwards, we derive our conceptual architecture in Sect. 4. Finally, we conclude our work and provide an outlook on our ongoing developments in Sect. 5.

2 Background and Related Work

In this section, we briefly introduce the fields of the quantified self, smart wearables, and smartwatches. We look at those fields as our anticipated system has to observe its users and their behavior through sensors. This is usually discussed in the field of the quantified self, where wearables are used to sense important physiological data of an individual, making them worthwhile to explore. Furthermore, this section introduces some related work containing architectures or frameworks with a scope similar to our vision of a wearable recommendation system.

2.1 Quantified Self

The term *quantified self* does not originate from the scientific community. According to a team of authors around Gary Wolf [8], its core idea is all about "self-knowledge through numbers". That is, gaining more comprehension and understanding about oneself by measuring and interpreting some values in numbers (e.g., steps per day, heartbeats, etc.). Swan [9] provides a more precise and well-defined definition to extend this approach. It states that *quantified self* is an umbrella term for the practice of tracking any kind of biological, physical, behavioral, or environmental data about itself. Moreover, individuals may be highly intrinsically motivated in gathering such data and changing their behavior accordingly. In contrast to this definition, we believe that the individual does not have to track its data manually to satisfy the core idea by Gary Wolf et al. [8]. Instead, we assume that it is just enough that an individual's data is tracked (e.g., by a technical device) with that individual's consent. By the data and information gathered this way, individuals should be supported in achieving their personal objectives. To understand what such tracked data can be, Augemberg [10] and Swan [9] provide an overview categorized and summarized with examples in Table 1.

However, from our perspective, this overview lacks considering physiological data, as it is not covered by any other category yet. Further, physiological data is already measured by many devices [11] and is key to compute derivative factors like happiness, energy, or stress. Hence, we added it to Table 1. For this work, we mainly focus on such quantified self data that can be captured with wearable devices.

Table 1. Overview for categories of quantified self data and examples by Augemberg [10] and Swan [9] with the extension of physiological data

Data type	Examples
Physical activities	Miles, steps, calories, repetitions, sets, metabolic equivalents
Diet	Calories consumed, carbs, fat, protein, specific ingredients, glycemic index, satiety, portions, supplement doses, tastiness, cost, location
Psychological states and traits	Mood, happiness, irritation, emotions, anxiety, self-esteem, depression, confidence
Mental and cognitive states and traits	IQ, alertness, focus, selective/sustained/divided attention, reaction, memory, verbal fluency, patience, creativity, reasoning, psychomotor vigilance
Environmental variables	Location, architecture, weather, noise, (environmental) pollution, clutter, light, season
Situational variables	Context, situation, gratification of the situation, time of day, day of the week
Social variables	Influence, trust, charisma, karma, current role/status in the group or the social network
Physiological data	*Heart rate (variability), blood pressure, skin temperature, skin conductance, respiratory rate*

2.2 Smart Wearables and Smartwatches as Building Blocks for Wearable Recommender Systems

Smart wearables are portable, computationally sufficient, and compact devices that are body-worn and useful for everyday tasks [12]. The most commonly used smart wearable is the smartwatch, as it combines many features that are desired by customers (e.g., paying via NFC, making calls). Further, it can be equipped with several sensors like accelerometers, gyroscopes, microphones, optical sensors, contact sensors, ambient light sensors, or GPS [11]. For instance, this enables them to track physiological data, physical activities, environmental and situational variables. Additionally, a smartwatch can receive further information by connecting to the internet via eSIM, WIFI, or a smartphone via Bluetooth. In the light of wearable recommendation systems, these capabilities enable smartwatches to be part of a larger system. Such a system may have the following characteristics:

1. It integrates with various data sources, such as smartwatch data and other sensors.
2. It has a modular and decentralized structure where all components can be developed and adapted independently.
3. It is based on the idea of sourcing out computational expensive tasks to components with larger computational capacities to save energy on devices with small batteries.

Regarding the first point (integration of various data), smartwatches are highly limited in terms of user dialogue/input capabilities due to their relatively small screen sizes [11, 14, 15]. So it seems inevitable to complement data from smartwatches with data from other devices or even self-assessments that are filled in on, e.g., personal computers. Furthermore, many findings indicate that smartwatches suffer from hard signal noises and data quality regarding their sensors, especially when active movement by the user is involved [11, 15]. Thus, having the possibility to consider sensor data by a variety of additional (and more reliable) sources would be a considerable advantage of a wearable recommendation system.

Regarding the second point (decentralized, modular architecture), Lutze and Waldhör [14] point out that decentralized software architectures are most appropriate for smartwatch apps. In this way, companion apps installed on a paired smartphone can be used for more complex user interactions like changing settings or exploring comprehensive data sets via data visualizations.

Regarding the third aspect (outsourcing of computationally expensive tasks), the smartphone can perform computational-intense tasks required for the smartwatch app, which, in turn, reduces power consumption on the smartwatch. This is highly relevant since battery capacity usually is scarce on smartwatches. According to El-Gayar et al. [13], the device's battery capacity is key to the continued use of smartwatches alongside appeal (e.g., via styling) and dialogue support.

2.3 Related Work: Architectures of Existing Research-Oriented Systems

The architecture of wearable and mobile recommendation systems that support workplace productivity and foster well-being is still an underresearched topic. However, we could identify some contributions that lead in a similar direction.

Niknejad et al. [16] introduce *PRISM* (passive real-time information for sensing mental health) and its architecture. The system gathers data from different sources (e.g., a smartwatch and a PC). Moreover, data acquisition is separated from data storage and processing. In addition, access to the system is enabled via a web application frontend where the results can be shown to users.

Roy et al. [17] introduce a framework for health monitoring and recommendation services. They distinguish between five separate blocks: hardware, software, information unit, recommendation unit, and analytics unit. They also aim for a server/cloud (inside the information unit) that communicates (independently from the wearable devices) with the recommendation and analytics unit to create recommendations.

Next, D'Aloia et al. [18] introduce *Cicero*, a middleware that can be used to develop persuasive mobile applications. Its key idea is detecting and considering different situations, contexts, and scenarios. Therefore, it considers different factors such as location, motion, environment, time, and social activities.

Soares Teles et al. [19], propose a computational architecture for context-sensitive mobile applications that requests the users to give information/feedback on their mental states. In addition, web services are used to transfer data from the system to consultative professionals (e.g., medical doctors). Those professionals can also provide remote interventions to their patients/users through this connection.

Further, Banos et al. [20] introduce *Mining Minds*, a framework for personalized health and wellness support. They distinguish between four layers: the data curation layer (DCL), information curation layer (ICL), service curation layer (SCL), and a supporting layer (SL). The DCL aims at processing and persisting data from variously different sources. That data is furtherly used by the ICL, which detects contexts and information for the users. Next, that information is used by the SCL to generate intelligent recommendations. For all of those three layers, the SL provides the possibility to link third-party applications which, in turn, can access the data, information, and recommendation services.

Lastly, Li and Guo [21] introduce *Wiki-Health*, a big data service platform for collecting, storing, tagging, retrieving, searching, and analyzing personal health sensor data from various sources and data types (e.g., structured, unstructured, etc.). Its architecture consists of three layers: the application layer, query & analysis layer, and a data storage layer. For the data storage layer, they consider using different types of storage and databases, depending on the actual data one is dealing with. Further, Wiki-Health has a mobile app that can track several activities, provide alerts or detections, consider the feedback given by the users, and present data visualizations.

To conclude, these contributions exhibit valuable features that can inform our architecture. However, they all are still lacking in presenting a compact and generic conceptual architecture that can be used to develop a wearable recommendation system. Out of all the inspirations we could gather from those sources, we mainly adopt the need for a decentralized system architecture (i.e., sourcing out some functionalities such as the generation of recommendations to a server). Furthermore, we also cover the aspect of considering various sensor data from various sources for computing relevant context and situation-sensitive recommendations.

3 Motivational Scenarios for Wearable Recommender Systems

As a first step towards developing a wearable recommendation system, some motivational scenarios are described below. Requirements for a system can be derived from the assumed usage behavior of the fictitious persons involved in the scenarios. This should provide orientation as to which requirements are relevant and in which contexts a recommendation system could be used.

3.1 Scenario 1: Self-management Assistance System for Managers, Freelancers, and Knowledge Workers

Karl (48) is a self-employed management consultant and family man. Karl has built up a base of satisfied regular clients, some of whom he has been assisting for many years. Unfortunately, his workload is difficult to predict because clients can spontaneously come forward with smaller assignments. Of course, he does not want to turn down these clients – especially since he knows many of them well personally. In this respect, Karl needs to manage his limited time well. On this Friday, his smartwatch wakes him up at 6:00 am, an hour earlier than normal. This is because the wearable recommender has recognized that there will be a lot of traffic on the roads on Friday evening. He now uses the system consistently after the first signs of burnout and a sick leave last year. So he had better start interviewing clients at 8 o'clock to return in time before the traffic jams start. At the same time, the system knows that Karl has enjoyed an excellent quality of sleep the nights before and has abstained from coffee late in the evening (which he did after receiving a brief, system-generated feedback), so getting up early is not a problem. The system seldom gives recommendations during the working day, as it is aware of the "customer contact" type diary entries and knows that disruptions are undesirable here. However, since Karl has scheduled four interview appointments seamlessly and, contrary to a warning from the system, one after the other, even over the lunch break, the system unobtrusively intervenes with vibration. It suggests that the next appointment be made while standing or during a walk. This is because the system wants to prevent Karl's back complaints, which he had ticked off in the list of common complaints when filling out the system's last weekly questionnaire on his state of health. Karl then suggests to his client that the conversation take place during a short walk through the nearby city park. The client happily agrees and immediately suggests inviting Karl to his favorite café near the lake in the park.

After a fulfilling working day, Karl drives home early without traffic jams. He arrived home at 3:30 pm and immediately started to evaluate the interviews and the documents he had been given from his clients. Unfortunately, it turns out that some important data was not mentioned in the interview, and he has to do some more research. Still completely absorbed in his work, the assistance system calls again at 5 pm. It informs him that Karl's planned time budget for this client has been exhausted. At the same time, it suggests that he should now play with the children or cook for his family. Alternatively, he could now get a birthday present for his mother, as her birthday is next Wednesday, but Monday and Tuesday are already planned with appointments all day. Karl decides to prepare dinner and set the table together with his children. He will write an email to the client and ask him to send the missing data instead of doing further research himself. He plans to get the gift on Saturday when he goes shopping.

Karl's wife returns from work at 6 pm. She is delighted to see that dinner has already been prepared and surprises Karl with a planned visit to the theatre that evening – after all, the children are now old enough to look after each other. Since Karl has not burned enough calories and exercised enough today, the assistance system suggests taking the tram for one stop and then walking the rest of the way to the theatre. They enjoy the warm summer evening, and Karl can now really switch off because he has achieved all his professional and private goals thanks to the coaching provided by his wearable recommender system.

Fundamental Requirements for the Wearable Recommender System
Provision of Information

- Display of messages
- Triggering of vibration
- Triggering of an alarm clock

Data collection

- Recording of sleep quality
- Activity level recording
- Recording of steps taken (pedometer)
- Recording of calories burned

3.2   Scenario 2: Assistance System to Support Person-Centered Services

Anna (26) completed her studies in social education two years ago and now works at a family counseling center. In addition, she has been doing a part-time doctorate as an external doctoral candidate at the University of Rostock in service management for social institutions since she graduated. As part of her professional work, she looks after several clients in the same town.

It is Tuesday morning, at 8 o'clock. Anna has an appointment in the city center at 9 am today. Still, her wearable recommender system notifies her of road closure and the associated traffic jam, so Anna chooses the indicated tram connection as an alternative just in time. Anna has a meeting with her most difficult client today, notorious for his choleric temper. After Anna has already had several heated discussions with the client, she is now, on the advice of her colleagues, using a new conversation technique that has a de-escalating effect. She has downloaded the instructions for this into her recommender system. Shortly before the appointment, she is shown the essential rules of conduct again, as she has noted in her calendar that she wants to use this conversation technique for the appointment. Surprisingly, the appointment was very pleasant and constructive, so Anna succeeded. Her wearable recommender system confirms the subjectively good feeling. Her pulse was only elevated at the beginning and then just above the resting pulse during the entire conversation.

Anna wants to go back right now, as there are no more appointments planned for today. However, one of her colleagues seems to have noticed that a client's signature is still missing. As Anna passes the client with the missing signature on her way to the tram, the wearable recommender suggests she visits the client for the signature. Anna succeeds and sends a scan of the document to her colleague. Her colleague is delighted and promises to take over the next on-call duty for her at the weekend.

When Anna arrives home, she immediately sets about completing the minutes of her appointment today. While she is briefly researching a spelling on the web – after all, she wants to edit everything correctly – she accidentally becomes aware of an old school friend's birthday via a social network site. She just wants to write him a few lines, but it turns out that he is also online now, so a conversation develops in which memories of the old school days are revoked. When Anna has already forgotten time and space, the wearable recommender system intervenes with the message that Anna's time budget for social media has been exhausted this month. At the same time, the system offers to open the document of her dissertation, as the time target she had set herself for this month has not yet been reached. When her school friend wants to start a new topic of conversation, Anna suggests continuing the conversation another time.

After dinner, Anna sits down at her desk and begins to analyze the data material she has collected during work for her doctorate. That evening she wants to transcribe two longer interviews. After 11 pm, the wearable recommender system calls with praise late in the evening. Anna is very hard-working – she has done enough work for today. Would she like to take a short walk around the block and then go to sleep? The background of this message is that the system has noticed a deterioration in her sleep quality in recent weeks. Anna has always worked on her doctorate in a disciplined manner in the evenings. Also, the ambient light sensor has determined that there is too little light in the room, which leads to increased absorption of the bluish light from the computer monitor, which, according to recent scientific findings, also has an unfavorable effect on sleep. In addition, the pulse has already dropped to the level of absolute relaxation, which suggests a rather less concentrated and thus ineffective work. Anna likes the idea of her wearable recommender system suggesting a walk. Since there is a full moon today and the beautifully landscaped gardens of the neighbors with their rose beds also look nice at night, she decides to leave the flat once more and take a short walk around her housing estate. As the last message of the day, she sees praise from the wearable recommender system for climbing the stairs to her attic flat several times today.

Fundamental Requirements for the Wearable Recommender System
Provision of Information

- Display of messages
- Triggering of vibration

Data acquisition

- Recording of the pulse
- Reading GPS data
- Sleep quality recording
- Activity level recording
- Recording of calorie consumption
- Recording of stairs climbed

4 Architectural Concept

Based on (i) the background literature with different types of data to sense and the features and limitations of wearable devices (especially smartwatches), (ii) the related work with architectures or frameworks of systems aiming for a similar scope, and (iii) the exemplary motivational scenarios, we derived our conceptual architecture (cf. Fig. 1).

It consists of three main areas with an additional fourth comprising a single component. **Area 1** (cf. upper left in Fig. 1) comprises the devices belonging to the end-user. **Area 2** (cf. bottom left in Fig. 1) comprises all potentially additional sources for sensor data. **Area 3** (cf. bottom right in Fig. 1) comprises all components placed on a cloud-like server-side. **Area 4** (cf. upper right in Fig. 1) comprises the general capability of accessing information and manipulating important settings via HTTP using a common browser. We assigned descriptive labels in the form of verbs ("sense", "display", and "interact") to those areas, except for the server-side. Whereas the server-side serves for

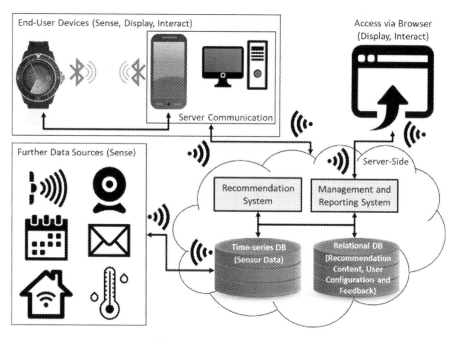

Fig. 1. The architectural concept

storing data and processing it (e.g., creating recommendations and reports), the components of the remaining three areas fulfill the tasks of either sensing data, displaying it, or interacting with it. They are the interface to the recommendation system itself. In the following, we describe further details of our architecture.

4.1   Area 1: End-User Devices for Sensing, Displaying, and Interacting

In this area, our architecture contains multiple end-user devices. Regarding end-user devices, we distinguish between their capability of communicating with the server on their own or not. As a usual smartwatch does not have this capability, it requires a connection via Bluetooth to a smartphone which can contact the server via WIFI or LTE/5G (especially for Apple devices, as their smartwatch apps cannot run without a companion app installed on the paired iPhone). Moreover, smartwatches can be used to capture tracking data via their sensors. Once this data has been sent to the server, it can be analyzed and considered to create recommendations. Additionally, smartphones or PCs could also be used to sense relevant data (e.g., by logging the activities – such as running software, detecting keystroke or mouse clicks when in use). As the end-users are working with these devices, tools for displaying the recommendations created for them and manipulating their individual user preferences or settings could be deployed on those devices.

4.2   Area 2: Further Data Sources for Sensing

This area of our architecture contains several exemplary data sources communicating with the time-series database located on the server-side. Thereby, we intend to emphasize the flexible adaptability of our architecture. The key idea is that any reasonably further sensor besides the actual end-user devices can add data. Hence, the recommendation system does not have to rely only on the sensors of end-user devices (which may be limited in covering contextual situations). Instead, it can take those further sensors of any kind also into consideration. For instance, a sensor for the oxygen content in a room could provide insights on whether the worker should open a window. Further, a calendar integration could ensure that no recommendations are provided in unsuitable situations like important business meetings.

4.3   Area 3: The Server-Side

On the server-side, our architecture contains two different databases and systems. The time-series database is key for storing sensor data. It provides special features that are more beneficial for such data than those from a relational database, as it is built around timestamps, which are crucial to detect contextual and situational information. Any sensor data that the recommendation system should consider (i.e., the data sensed by the end-user devices and any further sensors) has to be added to that time-series database. In contrast, the relational database covers all the data that is required besides the sensor data (e.g., the pool or content of recommendations, user feedback to the recommendations given, user preferences, and other settings).

The recommendation system generates recommendations based on both sensor data from the time-series database and relevant additional data from the relational database. Furthermore, the management and reporting system provides additional features. Firstly, it analyzes and processes the data stored in both databases. For instance, it could provide the end-users with visually appealing graphs or diagrams on their data over time. Secondly, it manages all the settings that the end-users want to tune. For instance, the user could select special recommendations that are either highly desired or completely undesired. In turn, such tuning could be considered by the separate recommendation system.

4.4   Area 4: Access via Web Browser for Displaying and Interacting

To provide an easy presentation and manipulation of information, the system should be accessible via web browser. In this way, dashboards that visualize important data generated by the reporting system can be displayed to the user. Due to advanced possibilities for data visualization on large screens of personal computers, users can leverage this component of the architecture, e.g., for reflecting on and "playing" with their data that could support self-reflection. In addition, web-based access could also be used for an easy system configuration of the recommendation system showing all parameters on a single screen.

4.5 Overall Characteristics of the Architecture

Overall, the loose coupling of all components is the key advantage of our presented architecture (cf. Fig. 1). By that, each component can focus on its key competencies and be developed and maintained independently without risking losing any functionalities of the other components. For instance, developers could easily add further sensors to the system without being forced to update the software on the end-user devices.

In addition, the functionalities of tracking data and displaying/interacting with it could be divided into two separate applications on end-user devices. For example, a smartwatch could run two separate apps: one for capturing sensor data and another for displaying recommendations received from the server. If one of the apps stops working or crashes, the other could still be running. In this way, the principle of loose coupling and modularity could also be applied to end-user devices since their sensors are added to the system as if they were further, additional data sources.

Moreover, separating the recommendation system from the end-user devices, sensors, and databases allows tuning or replacing recommendation techniques or algorithms without the system losing its other functionalities (e.g., sensing data and displaying recommendations).

Finally, sourcing out the main computational activities like generating recommendations or storing and maintaining data to a server-side saves valuable energy consumption and battery life for all end-user devices, especially smartwatches.

5 Conclusion and Outlook

In this paper, we have introduced our conceptual architecture for wearable recommendation systems that may assist individuals in their workplace productivity and well-being. Firstly, we have motivated this topic by summarizing recent major challenges many employees face. Afterwards, we briefly introduced the relevant background knowledge for such systems in the field of the quantified self, wearables, and related works with a similar focus. Next, we have sharpened the demand for a wearable recommendation system by introducing illustrative motivational scenarios. In those scenarios, a visionary wearable recommendation system guides its users and helps navigate the complexities and tackle ordinary working days' challenges. Finally, we have introduced our conceptual architecture, which addresses many issues we derived from the background literature, related work, and motivational scenarios.

In our ongoing work, we are currently developing an instantiation of our architectural concept. In this way, we will be able to validate our presented architecture empirically as part of our future work. For our prototype, we currently use Android Studio to develop the smartwatch app running on WearOS and the companion app installed on the smartphone running on Android. Furthermore, we use an InfluxDB as our time-series database that runs on a server that also hosts the simple script implementing the rule-based recommender system written in PHP. This PHP system gathers the data from the InfluxDB, generates a corresponding recommendation and sends it to the user's smartphone, which, in turn, sends it to the smartwatch displaying the recommendation to the user. Further, the user can give simple feedback on the recommendation received. Additionally, the feedback could be enriched on the server-side with the stored data in the databases.

Thereby, the feedback quality could be increased in future approaches involving, e.g., automated learning of decision trees. Also, the smartwatch can track physiological data and transmit it to the InfluxDB via the paired smartphone.

Moreover, we can already consider data from multiple sources. We recently explored the possibilities of using additional data, e.g., in the form of data provided by a webcam that extracts user characteristics such as pulse or pose, or data provided by a desktop activity tracking tool. Using these data sources is possible using InfluxDB and simple communication over HTTP. Setting up a separate relational database still remains an open task.

All in all, we are quite satisfied with our architectural concept. It gives us the flexibility and modularity needed to design and implement complex systems that generate context-sensitive recommendations for mobile and wearable devices.

References

1. Biletta, I., et al.: Working Conditions and Sustainable Work. An Analysis Using the Job Quality Framework. Publications Office of the European Union, Luxembourg (2021)
2. Green, F.: It's been a hard day's night: the concentration and intensification of work in late twentieth-century Britain. Br. J. Ind. Relat. **39**, 53–80 (2001). https://doi.org/10.1111/1467-8543.00189
3. Barber, L.K., Jenkins, J.S.: Creating technological boundaries to protect bedtime: examining work-home boundary management, psychological detachment and sleep. Stress. Health **30**, 259–264 (2014). https://doi.org/10.1002/smi.2536
4. James, S.L., Abate, D., et al.: Global, regional, and national incidence, prevalence, and years lived with disability for 354 diseases and injuries for 195 countries and territories, 1990–2017: a systematic analysis for the Global Burden of Disease Study 2017. Lancet **392**, 1789–1858 (2018). https://doi.org/10.1016/S0140-6736(18)32279-7
5. Froböse, I., Wallmann-Sperlich, B.: Der DKV-Report 2021. Wie gesund lebt Deutschland? (2021). https://www.ergo.com/de/Newsroom/Reports-Studien/DKV-Report
6. Nesher Shoshan, H., Wehrt, W.: Understanding "Zoom fatigue": a mixed-method approach. Appl. Psychol. (2021). https://doi.org/10.1111/apps.12360
7. Abdel Hadi, S., Mojzisch, A., Krumm, S., Häusser, J.A.: Day-level relationships between work, physical activity, and well-being: testing the physical activity-mediated demand-control (pamDC) model. Work Stress, 1–22 (2021). https://doi.org/10.1080/02678373.2021.2002971
8. Quantified Self: Homepage - Quantified Self (2021). https://quantifiedself.com/
9. Swan, M.: The quantified self: fundamental disruption in big data science and biological discovery. Big Data **1**, 85–99 (2013). https://doi.org/10.1089/big.2012.0002
10. Augemberg, K.: Building that perfect quantified self app: notes to developers, Part 1. The Measured Me Blog, 9995-10 (2012)
11. Reeder, B., David, A.: Health at hand: a systematic review of smart watch uses for health and wellness. J. Biomed. Inform. **63**, 269–276 (2016). https://doi.org/10.1016/j.jbi.2016.09.001
12. Yoon, H., Park, S.-H., Lee, K.-T.: Lightful user interaction on smart wearables. Pers. Ubiquit. Comput. **20**(6), 973–984 (2016). https://doi.org/10.1007/s00779-016-0959-z
13. El-Gayar, O., Elnoshokaty, A., Behrens, A.: Understanding design features for continued use of wearables devices. In: AMCIS 2021 Proceedings (2021)
14. Lutze, R., Waldhör, K.: The application architecture of smartwatch apps-analysis, principles of design and organization. Informatik 2016 (2016)

15. Niknejad, N., Ismail, W.B., Mardani, A., Liao, H., Ghani, I.: A comprehensive overview of smart wearables: the state of the art literature, recent advances, and future challenges. Eng. Appl. Artif. Intell. **90**, 103529 (2020). https://doi.org/10.1016/j.engappai.2020.103529
16. Kamdar, M.R., Wu, M.J.: PRISM: a data-driven platform for monitoring mental health. In: Biocomputing 2016. World Scientific (2015). https://doi.org/10.1142/9789814749411_0031
17. Roy, S.N., Srivastava, S.K., Gururajan, R.: Integrating wearable devices and recommendation system: towards a next generation healthcare service delivery. J. Inf. Technol. Theory Appl. **19**, 2 (2018)
18. D'Aloia, A., Lelli, M., Lee, D., Helal, S., Bellavista, P.: Cicero: middleware for developing persuasive mobile applications. In: Meschtscherjakov, A., De Ruyter, B., Fuchsberger, V., Murer, M., Tscheligi, M. (eds.) PERSUASIVE 2016. LNCS, vol. 9638, pp. 137–149. Springer, Cham (2016). https://doi.org/10.1007/978-3-319-31510-2_12
19. Soares Teles, A., et al.: Enriching mental health mobile assessment and intervention with situation awareness. Sensors **17**, 127 (2017). https://doi.org/10.3390/s17010127
20. Banos, O., et al.: Mining minds: an innovative framework for personalized health and wellness support. In: Proceedings of the 9th International Conference on Pervasive Computing Technologies for Healthcare. ICST (2015). https://doi.org/10.4108/icst.pervasivehealth.2015.259083
21. Li, Y., Guo, Y.: Wiki-health: from quantified self to self-understanding. Future Gener. Comput. Syst. **56**, 333–359 (2016). https://doi.org/10.1016/j.future.2015.08.008

The Influence of Interaction Design on Relation Making: A Scoping Review

Petra Salaric[✉], Emilene Zitkus, and Rebecca Cain

School of Design and Creative Arts, Loughborough University, Loughborough L11 3TU, UK
p.salaric@lboro.ac.uk

Abstract. Dating applications and dating sites are designed interventions that can change behaviour and influence user wellbeing. However, research from the design perspective around relation-making interventions is still scarce. This paper presents findings of a scoping review that aimed to collect current published knowledge on the influence of online communication on user behaviour, to understand its implications for relation-making. The study gathered findings from across disciplines to provide a holistic understanding of the various influences that online environment and interactions can have on user behaviour. Keyword combinations were run through five databases with a priori criteria and produced 1651 results published from the date range of 2016 to 2020. From the results, 717 abstracts were screened, and 82 papers were selected for full screening, out of which 46 were included for thematic analysis. The findings of the review show how interaction design and the online environment can influence user behaviour and thus impact how users form relationships. This scoping review is an initial study to provide an overview in a currently under-researched area. Its contribution is in presenting the needs and opportunities for future research and summarises the practical implications for interaction design that nurtures relationships.

Keywords: Online communication · Romantic relationships · User experience

1 Introduction

Today, there are more than 1500 dating applications that allow people to connect with a single swipe [1]. Dating platforms are replacing the traditional forms of meeting one's partner, such as through friends, family, work, or church [2–6]. However, there is a concern about the behaviours encouraged and created through these digital forms of interactions in relation to user wellbeing. In recent times, there have been reports of antisocial behaviour such as bullying, harassment, and racism experienced in the online environment [7–9]. The features of online environments have, furthermore, enabled creation of new forms of behaviour that are becoming a common feature of an online experience, yet are abusive and can cause distress [8, 11–13]. Haynes [10] describes some of these behaviours as following: *slow fading* – in which someone becomes less and less available for the other; *breadcrumbing* – receiving little and random attention; *haunting* – stalking with the help of social media; *catfishing* – purposefully misrepresenting oneself when communicating with others; and *ghosting* – the act of sudden disappearance of a potential partner. Since the development of dating sites and applications (apps), research has found an increase in depression and lowering of one's self-image, especially with extended usage [14–17]. Experts worry about the long-term effect of usage of dating applications and sites, even more as they change the entry to relationships and disable users' ability to practice the interactions that are required for long-term relationships, such as practicing intimacy, vulnerability, conflict or reconciliation [18–22].

Finkel and colleagues [23] stated that dating interventions are capable of changing user behaviour. As it is not clear what causes changes in behaviour and to what extent the design of the digital interaction influences behaviour, which is an imperative to explore. So far, there is a lack of published studies on the impacts of the design of computer-mediated communication (CMC) on relationship outcomes, nor specifically on relationship initiation. With the great usage of online communication and dating platforms [6], there is a need for a more focused analysis of the user experience and specifically the design features and their impact on behaviour and well-being [24]. Figure 1 visualises some of these elements that were identified through previous exploratory studies with the aim to understand the experience of users within online platforms and the influence of interaction design on behaviour.

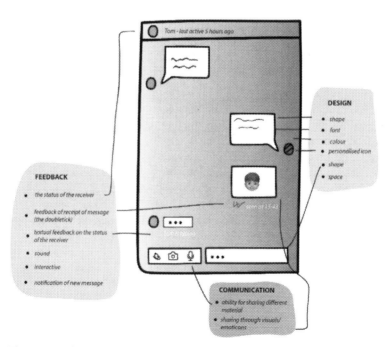

Fig. 1. The aspects of interaction design (feedback, communication, and design features) that are aimed to be investigated to understand the influence on behaviour (authors visual)

To address the gap in knowledge, this scoping review aims to provide an overview of current knowledge on the influence of design features of online communication on human behaviour, and further translate these behaviours to relationship initiation in the online environment. These findings will not only help in understanding the role that design plays in relationship making but also how design can positively influence the wellbeing of users. Relationships greatly influence one's health and overall wellbeing. There is a clear connection of one's stable relationships with disease recovery, disease development, longevity of life, and overall happiness [23, 25–29]. Therefore, understanding the way dating applications are constructed is not only important for the romantic outcome of users but also to their overall health and wellbeing.

2 Method

A scoping review, also known as 'mapping' [30–32], is a rigorous and transparent method for mapping areas of research on a broad topic, and represents the findings based on the terms of nature, specific features, and characteristics of primary data [33]. Scoping reviews aim to rapidly map key aspects on a broader topic, especially in the areas that have not been reviewed before [32–36] or on which there is little evidence, such as in emerging areas [31, 35, 36]. For this reason, using a scoping review in the area of online communication technologies, with its rapid development, was considered appropriate [30, 33, 37].

This study followed five stages, drawing upon Joanna Briggs Institute guidance [32], and a framework originally developed by Arksey and O'Malley [33] with the recommendations from Levac, Colquhoun and O'Brien [31]: 1. Identifying the research question, 2. Identifying relevant studies, 3. Study selection, 4. Charting the data, 5. Collating, summarizing, and reporting results. The study did not conduct the sixth and optional stage – *consultation* or *the interview with experts* - due to the time limitation.

This scoping study was conducted by the first researcher and aimed to answer the following research question:

How do elements of the design of computer-mediated communication (CMC) influence behaviour? in order to understand how these elements could influence the relationship initiation.

Twelve keyword combinations were created out of four different categories – society, behaviour, language, marketing, and design. These categories were formed based on the findings from a previous unpublished literature review and the findings from an autoethnographic study conducted from the perspective of the first author [38] that aimed to encompass elements that influence user's behaviour in the online environment. General keywords that were used for developing the keyword combinations were following: *online communication, intimacy, online dating, romantic relationships, interface design, user experience.*

The purpose of the keyword combinations were to explore two elements:

1) to what extent do the **external elements, (that of the user such** as society, culture, or marketing) influence the behaviour of the user and how?
2) to what extent, and how do **the internal elements of online communication** (construction and interactions elements) influence the behaviour of the user?

The databases were used to gather a perspective from a range of areas that could provide an understanding on the behaviour in online communication, beyond just the design elements (Table 1). The databases and the keyword combinations were discussed among researchers, colleagues, and with the academic librarian prior to the execution.

Table 1. Databases and selection criteria.

Category	Database	Reasoning
General search	Web of Science Scopus	*Provision of peer reviewed articles*
Psychology	PsychInfo	*Information on psychology or influence of elements of CMC on behaviour and wellbeing*
Wider search	Google Scholar	*When believed more data required and for a wider search*
Computing	ACM	*For retrieving articles strong in HCI and CMC*

In order to include relevant papers and exclude those that did not answer the research question, inclusion and exclusion criteria was used [33] and implemented from the start of the research as presented in the Table 2.

Table 2. Inclusion criteria.

Criteria	Reasoning
Year limitation	Year 2016 was chosen as the starting point as it was believed to provide sufficient and relevant recent finding. Furthermore, it was found that only from 2015 has the usage of smartphones started to become steady [39, 40]. Since the study was conducted in the year of 2021, the year of 2020 was chosen as the final year of inclusion as not all databases allowed inclusion of months within the search, and thus the year 2020 allowed a closed circle of papers
Sorting	By relevance (where possible)
Language	English
Type	Full peer reviewed and fully published; Where possible, journal articles only as it was believed to provide stricter and rigorous data than in other forms

Papers that met the inclusion criteria were those that referred to the following:

1. Papers that discussed *behaviour in the online environment influenced by the experience of interaction or features*
2. Papers that discussed *elements of design of the online environment that can have an influence on behaviour*

Post hoc Exclusion. The search resulted in many papers on the topic of privacy. While certain issues of privacy could be dealt with design and can influence a behaviour, these papers were excluded from the screening as it was believed to be a topic of a great breadth that includes elements that are not relevant to the researched topic (e.g. company policies or privacy rights).Furthermore, a decision was made to screen only the first fifty results of the papers on Google scholar. As discussed by Stevinson and Lawlor [41], further screening of the papers sorted by relevance does not necessarily mean bringing more relevant information and can lose time of the study.

Post hoc Inclusion. As many papers included for thematic analysis have used scoping or literature review as a method, the inclusion year criteria was stretched to include the papers (total of 12) that was believed answered the posed research questions.

Inclusion of Other Material. As the reasoning for conducting the scoping review is to provide a comprehensive overview of the researched area [30, 31, 33, 42, 43] rather than to provide a 'critically appraised or synthesised answer to a particular question' [34, p. 3], personal knowledge of certain sources or specialists was included, especially as it was believed that the results in stage two were lacking in certain areas [ibid]. The included material were books, and research papers from two researchers who specialise in topics relevant to the study – language and HCI. Even though the materials have not followed the same criteria aside from being written in English, they were included as they were believed to provide relevant information to the topic that were not caught in the search.

The selected papers for full screening were recorded and charted in a form of a Microsoft excel spreadsheet [33, 37, 44] by noting the author(s), year of publication, study populations, aims of the study, methodology, important results.

3   Findings

The scoping review collected a total of 1651 papers, out of which 717 abstracts were screened, 81 papers were fully screened, and a total of 46 papers were taken for a thematic analysis (Fig. 2). The findings from papers were then clustered, coded and analysed by hand to be further summarised and reported. Greater number of papers (12) originated from the ACM proceedings, and the most used journal was Computers in Human behaviour (5). Interestingly yet not surprisingly due to the topic of behaviour, the greater category aside from HCI and CMC came from (10). Only one paper originated from a design journal, thus showing the lack of published research from the design perspective in this area.

While the aim was to explore only the influence of the features of CMC on user behaviour, it was found that the behaviour of the user in the online environment cannot be taken alone but is mutually dependent on (1) one's experience in the online environment, (2) the interaction they make with others, and the (3) context the user comes from. To maximise the usefulness of the findings for use by interaction designers, they are structured into three categories – 1) the influence of the environment, 2) the influence of interaction design, 3) and the influence of the user identity on the behaviour and communication with others.

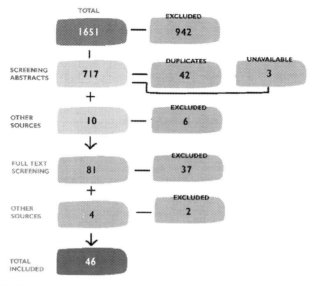

Fig. 2. Prisma diagram of the conducted scoping review (own visual, 2021)

3.1 The Influence of the Designed Environment on Behaviour and Interaction

When designing for online communication it is important to think about the environment where communication takes place as it can create an impact on the further engagement user makes with others. These are elements such as the background colour, layout, graphical elements, chat bubbles, and type choice (Table 3).

Table 3. Elements of the online environment on behaviour and interaction.

Category	Findings	References
Layout	**Early perception.** One of the most influential factors in early perception; users first focus on hedonic qualities (graphical and visual elements), and only then practical	[45–47]
	Engagement. The *appeal of the elements* (colour, light, and texture information) and *geometry of the elements* (posture, shape, and movement) are important as they influence the aesthetics, that was further connected to trustworthiness, performance, and evaluation of content. It also dictates further engagement and positive involvement if the content is found to be aesthetically pleasing. The engagement of users was also found to be influenced by warmth of the background	[45–48]
Design Elements	**Curvature typeface.** Round typefaces are associated with smooth and soft, thus it can create a comfortable feeling and trustworthiness (Fig. 3) **Colour.** Coloured chat bubbles were found to be intuitive and unobtrusive (Fig. 3) and can support conveying of emotions	[49, 50]

3.2 The Influence of the Interaction Design on Behaviour and Interactions with Others

The features of online communication can influence behaviour in the ways users behave towards others, how they perceive others, and how they portray themselves [38]. Table 4 shows how the way interaction and communication is designed influences behaviour, communication and interaction with others.

Table 4. Influence of interaction design and design features on behaviour and interaction with others.

Category	Findings	References
Self-representation	**Selective self-presentation**. People can present and create their ideal selves online, which is not possible in face-to-face communication (FtF)	[51]
Selective usage	**Different mediums for different purpose.** Features of interaction can create selected usage, such as Snapchat was reported to be used for flirting because the content disappears	[52, 53]
Colour	**Emotions.** Colour has a systematic effect on the emotional state of the person viewing the colour; it was found that brighter and more saturated colours were matched to joy expressions, and pleasant and happy atmosphere was associated with bright and lively colours	[54]
	Trust. Colour, being one of the elements of visual design, was found to influence trust in users. However, a choice of colour should be contextual, and if the colour is perceived 'appropriate', it could support engagement in a user	[55, 56]
Lack of non-verbal features	**Miscommunication.** Bringing any element of non-verbal communication was shown to support communication by clarifying the message or emphasizing, and by bringing understanding, validation, and care to the conversational partners. The inclusion of voice notes was found to help in conveying tone and emotions, and illustration (like emoji) were found to work better than other visual symbols as they are similar to real-life-non-verbal behaviour. Supporting messages with added visuals (such as a combination of text with a sticker) can produce an intimate experience rather than only text based or sticker based response (Fig. 3)	[57–61]
	Social presence. The elements that resemble ftf communication (rich modality cues, video profiles, reality stickers and similar) contribute to the feeling of social presence. Social presence, the feeling of presence of the conversational partner when using a communicational medium, was found to alleviate fear and distrust and increase one's willingness to meet in real life. The experience of bonding with another person was found to be primarily achieved in the in-person interaction, followed by video, audio, and lastly instant messaging	[62, 63]

(continued)

Table 4. (*continued*)

Category	Findings	References
	Support. Receiving support in-person or over the phone was experienced with high oxytocin production, while instant messaging as to those who have not received support	[64]
Feedback design	**Processing information.** People are found to more easily process visual information that is supported with sonification as it reduces visual clutter and is supportive in conveying information and meaning to the user **Anxiety.** The feeling of the 'response pressure', where the person is aware that their activity (such as 'seen' or 'delivered' like in Messenger or the double blue tick in Whatsapp) (as shown in Fig. 3) or their status (online/offline) can bring them to feel that they are required to answer and react immediately	[50, 65]
Communication design	**Asynchronous communication.** Online communication is asynchronous and thus is not related to a sense of connection. It can be less engaging than Ftf communication which is instantaneous and facilitated with non-verbal features. Therefore, Skype and video chatting in general was favoured in long-term relationships, but also in the initiation phase. Skype and video was found to facilitate a healthy amount of disclosure as in-person, and was specifically good for sensitive topics. Furthermore, inclusion of the history of the chat was found to influence user engagement as it resembles the synchronicity of Ftf communication. Similarly, text messaging can often seem like a never-ending conversation and can therefore bring to a feeling of connected presence	[59, 61, 66–69]
Design of interaction	**Anthropomorphism.** People apply the same behaviour towards computers as they do to humans. Therefore, including elements of anthropomorphism (such as the Microsoft Words Clippy; or with the personalised sticker that resembles the identity of the user) can increase trust resilience	[70]
	Human presence. Creating the feeling of human presence increases engagement. In a study no difference was found in interaction of a user with a human or a machine due to the enhancement of non-verbal features. The feeling of human presence can also be created by sharing information through the UI (the change of environment and colour, or a status change)	[71, 72]
	Arousal. The arousal a design creates can influence the experience and further interaction. Unlike the initial belief that high-arousal design could bring higher irritation in the future, it was found that the low-arousal designs decrease liking in the long-run	[73]
	Customisation. The ability to customise one's expression and communication with selected conversational partners was found to reinforce intimacy. Customisation can be individualised, shared, or have a customisable ecosystem, such as that of Facebook Messenger (as shown in Fig. 3)	[69]

(*continued*)

Table 4. (*continued*)

Category	Findings	References
Negative behaviours	**Lower wellbeing**. Online communication has allowed creation of a number of negative behaviours. Ghosting can cause physical pain by activating the pain network in the brain, even in the early stages of relationships like partner selection and initiation of interaction. Aside from lowering of one's self esteem and negatively influencing one's wellbeing, ghosting can have a long term effect - distrust in others, depression and panic attack	[53, 74]
	Sanctioning. Online communication allows different forms of sanctioning. Sanctioning can be performed as *invisible* (where the other person is often unaware that they have been sanctioned, such as unfollowing the user, but the other one may still be following them), or it can be *visible* (directly blocking or unfriending). Sanctioning is often conducted without direct confrontation, and the other person is often left unaware of what they have done to deserve such action	[13, 53]

3.3   The Influence of the User Identity on Interaction and Behaviour

Culture and norms guide beliefs which in turn guides the behaviour on platforms and in the online environment [52]. It is important to consider the visible and the invisible cultural characteristics to increase acceptance of the services, but also to avoid miscommunication in the online environment. If the design is not in alliance with the cultural background of the users it can result in rejection [75] (Table 5).

Table 5. Culture and identity and its influence on behaviour.

Category	Findings	References
Culture and colour	Colour influences satisfaction, trust, and perception. However, colour also holds meaning depending on the country – e.g. red is happiness for east Asian countries, while for western countries it signifies alertness. Readability of the content was also found to depend on cultural background, among the experience, motivation, and the optical properties of the eye	[46, 76–78]
Culture and interaction	The way the elements are used, processed or interpreted is based on one's cultural context and the exposure to its visual expression. A great influence on one's behaviour is whether the person originates from a collectivistic or individualistic background – such as in use of selfies. In UK, it was found that selfie usage is more connected to showing of the 'ideal self", while in China, which is more collectivistic, it serves as an 'online avatar', or a digital representation of the self. Culture was also found to influence the perception of others' behaviour. This was researched through the lens of content sharing - a shared content can be experienced as excessive or intense and to be 'getting into our one's own space', depending on the culture and norms	[53, 79]

(*continued*)

Table 5. (*continued*)

Category	Findings	References
Culture and Language	Gender that is ascribed to objects through one's language was found to control the qualities that are ascribed to these same objects – a bridge in Germany is of feminine gender and is thus described as elegant, beautiful, fragile or slender, while in Spain, being of male gender, is correlated to big, long, strong and sturdy	[80–82]
Online culture	The existing online culture directs behaviours in the online environment. Language used in the online world is continuously changing and exists within its own realm. Users often use abbreviations, they interchange capital letters and spaces, with different font usage, thickness, italics etc., and these elements hold meaning when sharing information. Furthermore, the present ghosting culture is taken as a normal and prominent behaviour to be experienced when interacting online. Its existence impacts how one behaves or interacts with others, such as in what information one shares, or how one will guard themselves to prevent it from happening to them	[13, 80, 83, 84]

3.4 Implications for Relationship Initiation

Considering the influence of design on trust and engagement is important, especially when designing for interactions that aim to achieve a relationship among users. In dating apps particularly, encountering miscommunication in the initiation phase could more quickly result in dissolution as there was no commitment yet formed.

Moreover, the online environment with its strong visual affordances, gaming and haptic interactions (such as swiping) can enhance treatment of others like objects rather than people, resulting in emotional distancing and superficial interactions [13, 85].

It is therefore believed that enabling and enhancing the non-verbal elements in online communication is beneficial for a steady formation and healthy intimacy formation [67]. Furthermore, enabling video was shown to be a good supporter in disclosure without excess, and for vulnerable topics [67]. Furthermore, customisation can reinforce intimacy, and history of the chat can support engagement. Finally, colour coding such as with chat bubbles and providing a good set of emojis can allow better communication and avoid miscommunication.

4 Discussion

This scoping review has shown that the design of interaction can influence how users experience the online environment, how they behave, and how they interact with others.

The scoping review highlights the influence of design in dealing with two major issues of the online environment – (dis)trust and (dis)engagement. The study shows that the inclusion of non-verbal features, either through direct access (such as a video call) or through visual symbols (GIF, emoji, emoticon, meme) brings a feeling of social

3.1. The influence of the designed environment on behaviour and interaction

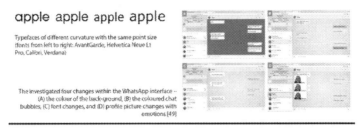

apple apple apple apple

Typefaces of different curvature with the same point size (fonts from left to right: AvantGarde, Helvetica Neue Lt Pro, Calibri, Verdana)

The investigated four changes within the WhatsApp interface – (A) the colour of the back-ground, (B) the coloured chat bubbles, (C) font changes, and (D) profile picture changes with emotions [49]

3.2. The influence of the interaction design on behaviour and interactions with others

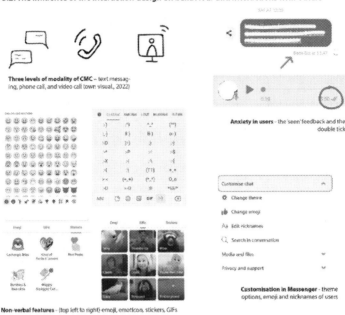

Three levels of modality of CMC – text messaging, phone call, and video call (own visual, 2022)

Anxiety in users - the 'seen' feedback and the double tick

Customisation in Messenger - theme options, emoji and nicknames of users

Non-verbal features - (top left to right) emoji, emoticon, stickers, GIFs

Fig. 3. Examples of visuals and influences discussed in findings.

presence, and enables the users to better express themselves which helps in avoiding miscommunication and provides better understanding and trust [57–64, 86]. It was also shown that enhancing the feeling of social presence, either with non-verbal features or through other elements of design information (such as including the location of the user or their activity status) [72] was correlated to the users willingness to meet in real life [62]. Finally, the study highlights the importance of the layout and the environment, as they are the first interactions user makes with the design and can set the experience and direct further engagement (or disengagement) [45–48].

The scoping review also showed the importance of understanding the other aspects besides the design - the cultural background of the users. Having the understanding of users language [82, 84] and culture [53], how different cultures experience colour [76,

79] or knowing their visual literacy and whether they come from an individualistic or collectivistic context [79] provides designers with the tools to create successful interactions and to avoid miscommunication of users.

However, personal devices cannot be seen merely as tools, but as mediators and even influencers to one's communication and relationships with others [38]. The way that the communication within our personal devices is constructed is important for the today's 'always online' culture [87] with the smartphone usage only increasing by year [39]. Furthermore, search for a partner is increasingly made through the internet and dating sites [6], therefore, the way these platforms operate also influences how we initiate and what are the grounds we build new relationships on.

The design industry and design research are still lacking in understanding of how the designed interactions influence relationship formation and what that means for the long term wellbeing, both of the individuals and the couple. This scoping review thus provides the starting point in understanding the influence design elements can make on the important elements of online communication for relationship formation – trust and disengagement. The study also posits questions over the aspects that are still missing and are important to be answered and therefore creating implications for further research.

Limitations. While some researchers state the importance of two or more researchers to review the papers to ensure an objective perspective on picking and inclusion and exclusion of papers [31], others are not as strict on this matter [33]. However, it is important to acknowledge that this study was conducted by the first author due to pragmatic reasons and time limitations, and therefore, a single view and judgement may influence the results. Furthermore, better preparation would have contributed in conducting the study by including more relevant results, such as a priori screening trial to have an understanding of the time required for conducting the study.

Further Recommendations. More research is needed from the design perspective to understand the influence of CMC and online environment on relationship formation and wellbeing of users. This could include analysing experiences over different platforms. As was found, people use different platforms for different purposes, however, it is not known whether the design of these platforms influences these preferences. Furthermore, while it is found that language can influence understanding of objects and surroundings, it is not yet understood whether language used in the design of the platforms can influence interactions and relationships.

5   Conclusion

This scoping review provides an overview of the influence of interaction design and online environment on user behaviour and relationship formation. The paper shows the importance of including non-verbal features – such as video possibilities, voice, different types of emojis, and gifs, to allow easier expression and customisation of communication to allow truthful expression, but also to ensure that certain obstacles in the online environment such as trust and disengagement are alleviated. The scoping review is one of the first in the area of design for relation making and contributes to an overview of the influence of interaction design on wellbeing. Therefore it provides a foundation for future studies, which consequently will have practical implications for the design of online interaction to ensure wellbeing of users.

Acknowledgments. The researcher wishes to thank the school librarian, Barbara Whetnall, for providing support and training to conduct this study.

References

1. Lin, M.: "Online Dating Industry Breakdown | Toptal," Toptal. https://www.toptal.com/fin ance/business-model-consultants/online-dating-industry. Accessed 06 Jan 2021
2. Bargh, J.A., McKenna, K.Y.A., Fitzsimons, G.M.: Can you see the real me? Activation and expression of the 'true self' on the internet. J. Soc. Issues **58**(1), 33–48 (2002). https://doi.org/10.1111/1540-4560.00247
3. Bargh, J.A., McKenna, K.Y.A.: The Internet and social life. Annu. Rev. Psychol. **55**, 573–590 (2004). https://doi.org/10.1146/annurev.psych.55.090902.141922
4. Cacioppo, J.T., Cacioppo, S., Gonzaga, G.C., Ogburn, E.L., Vanderweele, T.J.: Marital satisfaction and break-ups differ across on-line and off-line meeting venues. Proc. Natl. Acad. Sci. U. S. A. **110**(25), 10135–10140 (2013). https://doi.org/10.1073/pnas.1222447110
5. Jiang, L.C., Bazarova, N.N., Hancock, J.T.: The disclosure-intimacy link in computer-mediated communication: an attributional extension of the hyperpersonal model. Hum. Commun. Res. **37**(1), 58–77 (2011). https://doi.org/10.1111/j.1468-2958.2010.01393.x
6. Rosenfeld, M.J., Thomas, R.J., Hausen, S.: Disintermediating your friends: how online dating in the United States displaces other ways of meeting. Proc. Natl. Acad. Sci. U. S. A. **116**(36), 17753–17758 (2019). https://doi.org/10.1073/pnas.1908630116
7. Anderson, M., Vogels, E.A., Turner, A.: "Online Dating: The Virtues and Downsides," Pew Research Center, 06 February 2020. https://www.pewresearch.org/internet/2020/02/06/the-virtues-and-downsides-of-online-dating/. Accessed 06 Jan 2021
8. Lauckner, C., et al.: 'Catfishing', cyberbullying, and coercion: an exploration of the risks associated with dating app use among rural sexual minority males. J. Gay Lesbian Ment. Health **23**(3), 289–306 (2019). https://doi.org/10.1080/19359705.2019.1587729
9. Thompson, L.: 'I can be your tinder nightmare': Harassment and misogyny in the online sexual marketplace. Fem. Psychol. **28**(1), 69–89 (2018). https://doi.org/10.1177/095935351 7720226
10. Haynes, G.: Cushioning, breadcrumbing or benching: the language of modern dating. The Guardian, 08 May 2017. https://www.theguardian.com/lifeandstyle/2017/may/08/cushio ning-breadcrumbing-benching-language-modern-dating. Accessed 25 Nov 2021
11. Navarro, R., Larrañaga, E., Yubero, S., Víllora, B.: Psychological correlates of ghosting and breadcrumbing experiences: a preliminary study among adults. Int. J. Environ. Res. Public Health **17**(3), 1116 (2020). https://doi.org/10.3390/ijerph17031116
12. Stoicescu, M.: The globalized online dating culture: reframing the dating process through online dating. J. Comp. Res. Anthropol. Sociol. **10**(1), 21–32 (2019). http://compaso.eu. Accessed 06 Oct 2021
13. Timmermans, E., Hermans, A.-M., Opree, S.J.: Gone with the wind: exploring mobile daters' ghosting experiences. J. Soc. Personal Relationships **38**(2), 783–801 (2020). https://doi.org/10.1177/0265407520970287
14. Her, Y.C., Timmermans, E.: Tinder blue, mental flu? Exploring the associations between Tinder use and well-being. Inf. Commun. Soc. (2020). https://doi.org/10.1080/1369118X.2020.1764606

15. Hobbs, M., Owen, S., Gerber, L.: Liquid love? Dating apps, sex, relationships and the digital transformation of intimacy. J. Sociol. **53**(2), 271–284 (2017). https://doi.org/10.1177/144078 3316662718

16. Holtzhausen, N., Fitzgerald, K., Thakur, I., Ashley, J., Rolfe, M., Pit, S.W.: Swipe-based dating applications use and its association with mental health outcomes: a cross-sectional study. BMC Psychol. **8**(1), 22 (2020). https://doi.org/10.1186/s40359-020-0373-1

17. Strubel, J., Petrie, T.A.: Love me Tinder: body image and psychosocial functioning among men and women. Body Image **21**, 34–38 (2017). https://doi.org/10.1016/j.bodyim.2017.02.006

18. Lovink, G.: Sad by Design: On Platform Nihilism (2019)

19. Singer, J.A.: Narrative identity in a digital age: what are the human risks? Psychol. Inq. **31**(3), 224–228 (2020). https://doi.org/10.1080/1047840X.2020.1820217

20. Sprecher, S., Wenzel, A., Harvey, J.: Handbook of Relationship Initiation (2008)

21. Turkle, S.: Alone Together: Why We Expect More from Technology and Less from Each Other. Basic Books, New York (2012)

22. Turkle, S.: Reclaiming Conversation: The power of Talk in a Digital Age. Penguin Books, New York (2016)

23. Finkel, E.J., Eastwick, P.W., Karney, B.R., Reis, H.T., Sprecher, S.: Online dating: a critical analysis from the perspective of psychological science. Psychol. Sci. Publ. Interest **13**(1), 3–66 (2012). https://doi.org/10.1177/1529100612436522

24. Blabst, N., Diefenbach, S.: WhatsApp and wellbeing: a study on WhatsApp usage, communication quality and stress (2017). https://doi.org/10.14236/ewic/HCI2017.85

25. Pinker, S.: The Village Effect: Why Face-to-Face Contact Matters. Atlantic Books, London (2014)

26. van Lankveld, J., Jacobs, N., Thewissen, V., Dewitte, M., Verboon, P.: The associations of intimacy and sexuality in daily life: temporal dynamics and gender effects within romantic relationships. J. Soc. Pers. Relat. **35**(4), 557–576 (2018). https://doi.org/10.1177/026540751 7743076

27. Waldinger, R.J., Schulz, M.S.: What's love got to do with it? Social functioning, perceived health, and daily happiness in married octogenarians. Psychol. Aging **25**(2), 422–431 (2010). https://doi.org/10.1037/a0019087

28. Waring, E.M.: Measurement of intimacy: conceptual and methodological issues of studying close relationships. Psychol. Med. **15**(1), 9–14 (1985). https://doi.org/10.1017/S00332917 00020882

29. Wilson, C., Oswald, A.: How does marriage affect physical and psychological health? A survey of the longitudinal evidence. IZA Discuss. Pap. **1619** (2005)

30. Davis, K., Drey, N., Gould, D.: What are scoping studies? A review of the nursing literature. Int. J. Nurs. Stud. **46**(10), 1386–1400 (2009). https://doi.org/10.1016/j.ijnurstu.2009.02.010

31. Levac, D., Colquhoun, H., O'Brien, K.K.: Scoping studies: advancing the methodology. Implement. Sci. **5**, 69 (2010). https://doi.org/10.1186/1748-5908-5-69

32. Peters, M.D.J., Godfrey, C.M., Khalil, H., McInerney, P., Parker, D., Soares, C.B.: Guidance for conducting systematic scoping reviews. Int. J. Evid. Based Healthc. **13**(3), 141–146 (2015). https://doi.org/10.1097/XEB.0000000000000050

33. Arksey, H., O'Malley, L.: Scoping studies: towards a methodological framework. Int. J. Soc. Res. Methodol. **8**(1), 19–32 (2005). https://doi.org/10.1080/1364557032000119616

34. Mays, N., Roberts, E., Popay, J.: Synthesising research evidence. In: Allen, P., Black, N., Clarke, A., Fulop, N., Anderson, S. (eds.) Studying the Organisation and Delivery of Health Services: Research Methods (2001)

35. Munn, Z., Peters, M.D.J., Stern, C., Tufanaru, C., McArthur, A., Aromataris, E.: Systematic review or scoping review? Guidance for authors when choosing between a systematic or scoping review approach. BMC Med. Res. Methodol. **18**(1), 1–7 (2018). https://doi.org/10. 1186/s12874-018-0611-x

36. Tricco, A.C., et al.: A scoping review on the conduct and reporting of scoping reviews. BMC Med. Res. Methodol. **16**(15), 1 (2016). https://doi.org/10.1186/s12874-016-0116-4

37. Higgins, J.P.T., et al.: Cochrane Handbook for Systematic Reviews of Interventions, 2nd edn. Wiley, Chichester (2019)

38. Salaric, P., Cain, R., Zitkus, E., Visch, V.: Tinder and heartbeats: wellbeing in the use of dating applications (2021)

39. O'Dea, S.: Smartphone users 2026 | Statista, statista, June 2021. https://www.statista.com/statistics/330695/number-of-smartphone-users-worldwide/. Accessed 07 Dec 2021

40. O'Dea, S.: Number of smartphone users worldwide from 2016 to 2021. Statista, 10 December 2020. https://www.statista.com/statistics/330695/number-of-smartphone-users-worldwide/. Accessed 16 Feb 2021

41. Stevinson, C., Lawlor, D.A.: Searching multiple databases for systematic reviews: added value or diminishing returns? Complement. Ther. Med. **12**(4), 228–232 (2004). https://doi.org/10.1016/J.CTIM.2004.09.003

42. Peters, M., et al.: Updated methodological guidance for the conduct of scoping reviews. JBL Evid. Synth. **18**(10), 2219–2226 (2020). https://doi.org/10.11124/JBIES-20-00167

43. Tricco, A., Oboirien, K., Lotfi, T., Sambunjak, D.: Scoping reviews: what they are and how you can do them | Cochrane Training. Cochrane Training. https://training.cochrane.org/resource/scoping-reviews-what-they-are-and-how-you-can-do-them. Accessed 30 Sep 2021

44. Pham, M.T., Rajić, A., Greig, J.D., Sargeant, J.M., Papadopoulos, A., McEwen, S.A.: A scoping review of scoping reviews: advancing the approach and enhancing the consistency. Res. Synth. Methods **5**(4), 371–385 (2014). https://doi.org/10.1002/jrsm.1123

45. Gronier, G.: Measuring the first impression: testing the validity of the 5 second test. J. Usability Stud. **12**(1), 8–25 (2016)

46. Hawlitschek, F., Jansen, L.E., Lux, E., Teubner, T., Weinhardt, C.: Colors and trust: the influence of user interface design on trust and reciprocity. Proc. Annu. Hawaii Int. Conf. Syst. Sci. **2016**, 590–599 (2016). https://doi.org/10.1109/HICSS.2016.80

47. Norman, D.: Emotional Design: Why We Love (Or Hate) Everyday Things Onals Marketing Wisdom Kart ikeya Kompella Editor. Basic Books (2003)

48. Uribe, S., Álvarez, F., Menéndez, J.M.: User's web page aesthetics opinion: a matter of low-level image descriptors based on MPEG-7. ACM Trans. Web **11**(1), 5 (2017). https://doi.org/10.1145/3019595

49. Wang, L., Yu, Y., Li, O.: The typeface curvature effect: The role of typeface curvature in increasing preference toward hedonic products. Psychol. Mark. **37**(8), 1118–1137 (2020). https://doi.org/10.1002/MAR.21287

50. Poguntke, R., Mantz, T., Hassib, M., Schmidt, A., Schneegass, S.: Smile to me: investigating emotions and their representation in text-based messaging in the wild. Proc. Mensch Comput. **2019**, 373–385 (2019). https://doi.org/10.1145/3340764.3340795

51. Wotipka, C.D., High, A.C.: An idealized self or the real me? Predicting attraction to online dating profiles using selective self-presentation and warranting. Commun. Monogr. **83**(3), 281–302 (2016). https://doi.org/10.1080/03637751.2016.1198041

52. Attrill-Smith, A., Fullwood, C., Keep, M., Kuss, D.J., Weeks, C.D., Subrahmanyam, K.: Adolescent and emerging adult perception and participation in problematic and risky online behavior. In: Attrill-Smith, A., Fullwood, C., Keep, M., Kuss, D.J., Weeks, C.D., Subrahmanyam, K. (eds.) The Oxford Handbook of Cyberpsychology, pp. 75–97. Oxford University Press (2019). https://doi.org/10.1093/oxfordhb/9780198812746.013.6

53. Rashidi, Y., Kapadia, A., Nippert-Eng, C., Su, N.M.: It's easier than causing confrontation: sanctioning strategies to maintain social norms and privacy on social media. Proc. ACM Hum. Comput. Interact. **1**(23), 1–25 (2020). https://doi.org/10.1145/3392827

54. Wilms, L., Oberfeld, D.: Color and emotion: effects of hue, saturation, and brightness. Psychol. Res. **82**(5), 896–914 (2017). https://doi.org/10.1007/s00426-017-0880-8

55. Kim, J., Moon, J.Y.: Designing towards emotional usability in customer interfaces—trustworthiness of cyber-banking system interfaces. Interact. Comput. **10**(1), 1–29 (1998). https://doi.org/10.1016/S0953-5438(97)00037-4

56. Wu, W.-Y., Lee, C.-L., Fu, C.-S., Wang, H.-C.: How can online store layout design and atmosphere influence consumer shopping intention on a website? Int. J. Retail Distrib. Manag. **42**(1), 4–24 (2014). https://doi.org/10.1108/IJRDM-01-2013-0035

57. Derks, D., Fischer, A.H., Bos, A.E.R.: The role of emotion in computer-mediated communication: a review. Comput. Human Behav. **24**(3), 766–785 (2008). https://doi.org/10.1016/j.chb.2007.04.004

58. Coyle, M.A., Carmichael, C.L.: Perceived responsiveness in text messaging: the role of emoji use. Comput. Human Behav. **99**, 181–189 (2019). https://doi.org/10.1016/j.chb.2019.05.023

59. Hertlein, K.M., Chan, D.: The rationale behind texting, videoconferencing, and mobile phones in couple relationships. Marriage Fam. Rev. **56**(8), 739–763 (2020). https://doi.org/10.1080/01494929.2020.1737624

60. Wang, S.S.: More than words? The effect of line character sticker use on intimacy in the mobile communication environment. Soc. Sci. Comput. Rev. **34**(4), 456–478 (2016). https://doi.org/10.1177/0894439315590209

61. Hampton, A.J., Rawlings, J., Treger, S., Sprecher, S.: Channels of computer-mediated communication and satisfaction in long-distance relationships. Interpersona **11**(2), 171–187 (2017). https://doi.org/10.5964/ijpr.v11i2.273

62. Jung, S., Roh, S., Yang, H., Biocca, F.: Location and modality effects in online dating: rich modality profile and location-based information cues increase social presence, while moderating the impact of uncertainty reduction strategy. Cyberpsychol. Behav. Soc. Netw. **20**(9), 553–560 (2017). https://doi.org/10.1089/cyber.2017.0027

63. Sherman, L.E., Michikyan, M., Greenfield, P.M.: The effects of text, audio, video, and in-person communication on bonding between friends. Cyberpsychology **7**(2) (2013). https://doi.org/10.5817/CP2013-2-3

64. Seltzer, L.J., Prososki, A.R., Ziegler, T.E., Pollak, S.D.: Instant messages vs. speech: hormones and why we still need to hear each other. Evol. Hum. Behav. **33**(1), 42–45 (2012). https://doi.org/10.1016/J.EVOLHUMBEHAV.2011.05.004

65. Rönnberg, N.: Musical sonification supports visual discrimination of color intensity. Behav. Inf. Technol. **38**(10), 1028–1037 (2019). https://doi.org/10.1080/0144929X.2019.1657952

66. Hrastinski, S.: Asynchronous and synchronous e-learning. Educ. Q. **31**(4), 51–55 (2008). https://er.educause.edu/-/media/files/article-downloads/eqm0848.pdf. Accessed 25 Nov 2021

67. Jenner, B.M., Myers, K.C.: Intimacy, rapport, and exceptional disclosure: a comparison of in-person and mediated interview contexts. Int. J. Soc. Res. Methodol. **22**(2), 165–177 (2019). https://doi.org/10.1080/13645579.2018.1512694

68. Shyam Sundar, S., Bellur, S., Oh, J., Jia, H., Kim, H.-S.: Theoretical importance of contingency in human-computer interaction: effects of message interactivity on user engagement. Commun. Res. **43**(5), 595–625 (2016). https://doi.org/10.1177/0093650214534962

69. Griggio, C.F., Mcgrenere, J., Mackay, W.E.: Customizations and expression breakdowns in ecosystems of communication apps. Proc. ACM Hum. Comput. Interact. **3**(CSCW), 26 (2019). https://doi.org/10.1145/3359128

70. De Visser, E., et al.: Almost human: anthropomorphism increases trust resilience in cognitive agents. J. Exp. Psychol. Appl. **22**(3), 331 (2016). https://doi.org/10.1037/xap0000092

71. Hoorn, J.F., Konijn, E.A., Pontier, M.A.: Dating a synthetic character is like dating a man. Int. J. Soc. Robot. **11**(2), 235–253 (2018). https://doi.org/10.1007/s12369-018-0496-1

72. Niemantsverdriet, K., Van Essen, H., Pakanen, M.: Designing for awareness in interactions with shared systems: the DASS framework. ACM Trans. Comput. Interact **26**(6), 41 (2019). https://doi.org/10.1145/3338845

73. Buechel, E.C., Townsend, C.: Buying beauty for the long run: (Mis)predicting liking of product aesthetics. J. Consum. Res. **45**, 275–296 (2018). https://doi.org/10.1093/jcr/ucy002

74. Nolan, M.P.: Learning to circumvent the limitations of the written-self: the rhetorical benefits of poetic fragmentation and internet 'catfishing. Pers. Stud. **1**(1) (2015). https://doi.org/10.3316/informit.967696119864418

75. Kyriakoullis, L., Zaphiris, P.: Culture and HCI: a review of recent cultural studies in HCI and social networks. Univ. Access Inf. Soc. **15**(4), 629–642 (2015). https://doi.org/10.1007/s10209-015-0445-9

76. Cheng, C., Wang, H.Y., Sigerson, L., Chau, C.L.: Do the socially rich get richer? A nuanced perspective on social network site use and online social capital accrual. Psychol. Bull. **145**(7), 734–764 (2019). https://doi.org/10.1037/bul0000198

77. Cheng, F.F., Wu, C.S., Leiner, B.: The influence of user interface design on consumer perceptions: a cross-cultural comparison. Comput. Human Behav. **101**(181), 394–401 (2019). https://doi.org/10.1016/j.chb.2018.08.015

78. Pušnik, N., Možina, K., Podlesek, A.: Effect of typeface, letter case and position on recognition of short words presented on-screen. Behav. Inf. Technol. **35**(6), 442–451 (2016). https://doi.org/10.1080/0144929X.2016.1158318

79. Ma, J.W., Yang, Y., Wilson, J.A.J.: A window to the ideal self: a study of UK Twitter and Chinese Sina Weibo selfie-takers and the implications for marketers. J. Bus. Res. **74**, 139–142 (2017). https://doi.org/10.1016/J.JBUSRES.2016.10.025

80. Boroditsky, L.: How does our language shape the way we think? Edge (2009)

81. Boroditsky, L., Schmidt, L.A., Phillips, W.: Sex, syntax and semantics. In: Gentner, D., Goldin-Meadow, S. (eds.) Language in Mind: Advances in the Study of Language and Thought, pp. 61–78. MIT Press, Cambridge (2003)

82. Vlad Oprea, S., Magdy, W.: The effect of sociocultural variables on sarcasm communication online. Proc. ACM Hum. Comput. Interact. CSCW1 **4**, 29 (2020). https://doi.org/10.1145/3392834

83. Khairutdinov, R.R., Gabdulbarovna Mukhametzyanova, F., Gaysina, A.R.: Socio-psychological characteristics of the subject use of slang and abbreviations in English-speaking social networks. Turk. Online J. Des. Art Commun. (2017). https://doi.org/10.7456/1070ASE/090

84. Thibodeau, P.H., Boroditsky, L.: Natural language metaphors covertly influence reasoning. PLoS ONE **8**(1), e52961 (2013). https://doi.org/10.1371/journal.pone.0052961

85. Lefebvre, L.E.: Ghosting as a relationship dissolution strategy in the technological age. In: Punyanunt-Carter, N.M., Wrench, J.S. (eds.) The Impact of Social Media in Modern Romantic Relationships, pp. 219–235. Lexington Books, Maryland (2017)

86. Short, J., Williams, E., Christie, B.: The Social Psychology of Telecommunications. Wiley, Toronto (1976)

87. Cecchinato, M.E., Cox, A.L., Bird, J.: "Always on(line)? user experience of smartwatches and their role within multi-device ecologies. In: CHI Conference on Human Factors in Computing Systems, pp. 3557–3568 (2017). https://doi.org/10.1145/3025453.3025538

Keep Moving! A Systematic Review of App-Based Behavior Change Techniques and Visualizations for Promoting Everyday Physical Activity

Tom Ulmer[(✉)] [iD] and Matthias Baldauf [iD]

OST – Eastern Switzerland University of Applied Sciences, Institute for Information and Process Management, Rosenbergstrasse 59, 9001 St. Gallen, Switzerland
{tom.ulmer,matthias.baldauf}@ost.ch

Abstract. Health apps are supposed to support fighting sedentary lifestyles and, consequently, a variety of chronic diseases. For promoting physical activity in a sustained manner, these apps and corresponding research draw upon a variety of behavior change techniques and visualizations. To provide a structured overview of recent approaches and identify research gaps, we conducted a systematic literature review of empirical research works on app-based approaches for promoting everyday physical activity. In the 42 relevant studies identified, we thoroughly analyzed the applied behavior change techniques and in-app visualization types. We found a recent emphasis on feedback and monitoring as well as goal setting techniques, while the application of others such as informing about health consequences or shaping the user's knowledge are applied only in rare cases. The range of visualization types is limited. Traditional charts and gamified illustrations turned out to be predominant. However, empirical research on alternative approaches such as innovative chart visualizations is scarce.

Keywords: Mobile health · Behavior change · Literature review

1 Introduction

Insufficient physical activity (PA) is a well-known risk factor for a widening variety of chronic diseases, including cardiovascular disease, obesity, diabetes mellitus and others. The global prevalence of insufficient PA is about 28%, for high-income countries even 37% [19]. Among adolescents globally more than 80% of students aged 11–17 years were insufficiently physically active (according to recent PA guidelines [20]). It is a global priority to encourage people engaging in PA and reduce the burden of non-communicable disease.

M. Kurosu (Ed.): HCII 2022, LNCS 13304, pp. 447–461, 2022.
https://doi.org/10.1007/978-3-031-05412-9_31

The usage of mobile health apps on smartphones seems to be a promising approach to tackle this challenge. Health apps (HA) can inform the users about the importance of PA and its health relations, track their movements easily using built-in and external sensors and compare the numbers with international health recommendations to stay on track. Despite the increasing numbers of HA in the app stores, though, it seems that there is just modest evidence about their effectiveness and efficacy in improving health behaviors or health outcomes [32, 40, 49].

Providing knowledge alone to let people reflect upon and make beneficial decisions based on rationale is often not working. This information-centered approach can be supplemented with behavior change techniques (BCTs) or the concept of nudging to support users to improve their PA. Nudging is a form of choice architecture, that helps to change people's behavior in a predictable way to their advantage. The design of the choice environment in which the information is presented can also influence the outcome [56].

While several related prior works aimed at overviewing the large number of nudging theories, studies, and applications in the health domain, a systematic review of digital behavior change interventions for promoting PA from an HCI perspective is missing. For example, Forberger et al. [17] gave an overview of the scope of interventions using choice architecture techniques to promote physical activity with a focus on prompts at public locations. Laiou et al. [31] systematically appraised the evidence on nudging interventions with an emphasis on healthy diet interventions. Bondaronek et al. [4] reviewed nudging mechanisms for PA of popular publicly available PA apps within an overall quality evaluation.

In contrast, in our work we aim to survey and critically reflect on the existing body of scientific knowledge on smartphone and wearable-based behavior change interventions targeting PA from an HCI perspective. We set focus on everyday life PA such as walking and jogging due to its low-threshold integration without specific equipment and its location independence. We conducted a thorough systematic literature review to identify respective BCTs and HCI-related insights.

The contribution of our work consists of an overview of studies with focus on digital health intervention on PA and the included BCTs as well as the implemented visualization types. Based on these findings we draw conclusions and identify possible future research on mobile interventions based on BCTs for promoting everyday PA.

2 Method

In the following, we describe the process of our systematic review in detail. Figure 1 provides an overview of the study selection process.

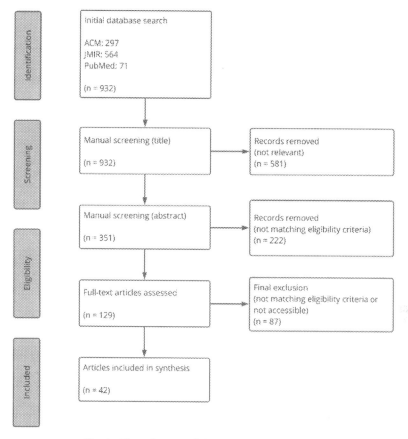

Fig. 1. Flow diagram of the study selection process

2.1 Data Sources and Search Strategy

Since relevant research is published in both computer science- and medicine-related conferences and journals, our scientific sources consulted include the online literature databases of ACM, PubMed, and JMIR Publications. As search term (within the title, abstract, and keywords) we used

- *physical activity*
- AND *smartphone/mobile phone/mobile health/mHealth/app/apps/mobile app*
- AND *behavior change/behaviour change/behavioral change/behavioural change/nudging/nudge*

For each literature database, the syntax of this pseudo search term was adapted to the database's specific requirements. Further search parameters that were manually applied through respective search settings were restrictions regarding the publication year (2017–2021) and the publication language (English).

2.2 Data Cleansing and Screening

The three result lists were exported and compiled into one spreadsheet for collaborative processing. For each of the 932 entries, the spreadsheet contained the publication's title, abstract, keywords, author(s), and year. Further information included the publication venue, type (conference/journal), publisher, ISBN and DOI. As expected, we did not identify any duplicates (checked by the publications' DOIs), since publications were searched and retrieved from three different publishers' databases.

During the subsequent screening process, two researchers applied an extensive set of eligibility criteria to further specify the list of relevant publications. We explicitly focused on peer-reviewed primary studies that (1) used a smartphone app in an intervention to promote PA or reduce sedentary behavior (SB), (2) included one or more BCTs, and (3) regarding the design, we included empirical studies, like randomized controlled trials (RCT), cross-sectional and longitudinal observational studies, pre- and post-design studies and experimental field trials.

The accepted units of measurements for the PA related outcomes were steps, active time, time in moderate to vigorous physical activity (MVPA), gait speed, burned calories, climbed stairs or floors, traveled distance, and METs (Metabolic Equivalent of Task).

2.3 Inclusion Criteria of Studies

- Interventions to promote measurable everyday PA (walking, running, climbing stairs or floors, etc.).
- Interventions using smartphones, smartwatches, smart bands, other types of activity trackers, or wireless transmitters (like BT-beacons).
- Target groups for the study include healthy populations of adolescents, adults, and older adults.
- The intervention must include any form of BCT to promote PA or reduce SB.
- The effectiveness of the intervention must be measured/discussed.

2.4 Exclusion Criteria of Studies

We excluded non-experimental study designs such as case studies, conceptual papers, literature reviews or theoretical views, opinion papers and studies reporting prevalence or trend data.

- We excluded interventions based on activities that require additional equipment like treadmills, steppers, mountain climbers, bicycles etc.
- We excluded interventions relying on additional monitoring equipment like chest straps, ECGs, smart shoes, IoT devices etc.
- Activities that require specific locations (swimming etc.) or strength exercises (bodyweight exercises, weightlifting etc.) were also an exclusion criterion.
- We excluded sick populations, patients during treatments and women during pregnancy as well as kids up to 12 years.
- Combined interventions like PA with sleep, nutrition, or mental aspects (like mood or stress) were excluded as well.

2.5   Data Analysis

After the screening process, 42 studies were considered relevant for our review and included for in-detail analysis. Figure 2 shows the number of publications for the five years considered. Relevant research per year increased from 6 publications in 2017 to 12 publications in 2021. The works include a broad range of empirical studies, e.g., with sample sizes ranging from 6 [7] to 6 million participants [1] and study durations between one week [43] and five years [1].

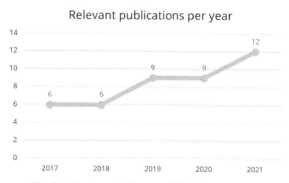

Fig. 2.   Number of relevant publications per year.

In a thorough analysis of these studies, we identified BCTs and visualization types. BCTs were coded according to the Behavior Change Techniques Taxonomy 1 (BCTTv1, [39]). If BCTs were related to other frameworks or taxonomies (e.g., CALO-RE, [38]) or did not match the naming convention of our selected taxonomy, we translated the behavior intervention to the best matching replacement. BCTs which did not directly target PA were omitted. Visualization categories were created in an inductive coding approach.

3   Results

This section presents the results of our analysis of the included publications. We report on the different BCTs and visualization techniques applied.

3.1   Behavior Change Techniques

Table 1 shows in detail BCTTv1 (sub)categories [39] addressed by the publications reviewed. Figure 3 depicts the numbers of applications of respective BCTs in the reviewed research studies on everyday PA interventions. Each study combined several different BCTs. The number of BCTs per intervention ranged from 2 to 11, while on average 5 to 6 different BCTs were combined in one intervention.

Table 1. BCT (sub)categories (Michie et al. ref) addressed by the publications reviewed

BCT (sub)category	Publications
1 Goals and planning	
1.1 Goal setting (behavior)	[2, 3, 5, 7–10, 12–14, 16, 18, 22–30, 33, 34, 36, 37, 41, 43–47, 50–52, 55, 58]
1.2 Problem solving	[12, 36, 46, 50]
1.4 Action Planning	[12, 23, 28, 36, 44, 50, 52, 55]
1.5 Review behavior goal(s)	[14, 36, 50]
1.6 Discrepancy between current behavior and goal	[2, 36, 51]
1.9 Commitment	[7, 36]
2 Feedback and monitoring	
2.1 Monitoring behavior by others without feedback	[1, 3, 21, 22, 29, 57]
2.2 Feedback on behavior	[1, 2, 5, 8–10, 12, 13, 16, 22, 23, 25, 27, 30, 33, 36, 37, 41, 42, 44, 48, 51, 58]
2.3 Self-monitoring behavior	[1–3, 5, 7–10, 12–16, 18, 21–30, 33, 34, 36, 37, 41–48, 50, 51, 55, 57, 58]
3 Social support	
3.1 Social support (unspecified)	[5, 13, 14, 21–24, 29, 37, 47, 50]
3.2 Social support (practical)	[16, 25, 26, 33, 43, 45, 46, 52, 57]
3.3 Social support (emotional)	[16, 25, 26, 33, 43, 45, 46, 52, 57]
4 Shaping knowledge	
4.1 Instruction on how to per-form a behavior	[5, 12, 14, 22, 26, 29, 46, 51, 55]
6 Comparison of behavior	
6.2 Social comparison	[1, 3, 13, 16, 23, 24, 33, 37, 43–46]
7 Associations	
7.1 Prompts/cues	[7, 9, 13, 25–28, 30, 33, 36, 37, 44, 46, 48, 55, 57]
10 Reward and threat	
10.1 Material incentive (behavior)	[15, 22, 30, 34, 41, 44]
10.2 Material reward (behavior)	[9, 27, 44]
10.3 Non-specific reward	[3, 10, 13, 33, 34, 37, 43, 46, 47, 57]
12 Antecedents	
12.5 Adding objects to the environment	[7, 33, 47]
13 Identity	
13.1 Identification of self as role model	[16, 22–24, 37, 45, 46, 52]

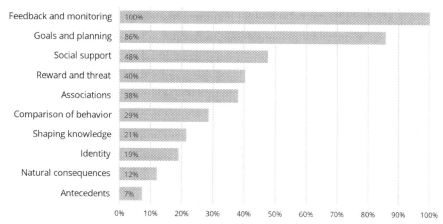

Fig. 3. The relative usage of BCT techniques in empirical studies on apps for increasing everyday PA shows an emphasis on "goals and planning" and "feedback and monitoring" techniques. Each study combined several different BCTs.

We found a clear emphasis on the two strategies "feedback and monitoring" and "goals and planning". "Feedback and monitoring" techniques were used in each of the 42 studies reviewed. Almost every mHealth intervention provides self-monitoring for the users' behavior, e.g., via app or smartwatch. In many cases monitoring is also performed by others with feedback (by staff or buddies) or without feedback [3, 21]. "Goals and planning" features were found in 36 studies (86%). Goals related to physical activity and condition include both predefined or individual goals stated by the app (i.e., determined by the app provider) or self-set goals. These goals explicitly address the user's behavior change, e.g., by targeting a specific number of steps or time amount of MVPA. In contrast, gamified approaches make use of game-related goals, thus, indirectly initiating the user's behavior change.

The third-ranked technique "social support" was only applied by 20 of the 42 studies (48%). Typical examples include encouragements by team members or buddies via in-app communication or by sending virtual approval, like high fives or virtual gifts such as digital flowers to support the user in achieving his or her activity goals. Besides these solely digital features, further "social support" implementations bridge the digital and the analog world, e.g., by enabling to organize running groups within the app [24]. 17 studies (40%) applied the "reward and threat" technique: They featured either incentives (before the PA as a prospect) or rewards (after the PA). We found both implementations of analog material rewards, e.g., money and vouchers, and digital ones, e.g., virtual badges and trophies.

16 of the studies reviewed (38%) made use of "associations", i.e., prompts and cues nudging users to perform everyday PA. In most cases, this is accomplished through context-sensitive push notifications. E.g., due to the device's current location or the current time of day, the user is reminded of pending PA ("*You haven't yet been active for 30 min today!*") and prompted to perform PA ("*Take 2000 steps in the next 20 min!*").

While popular in various sports tracking apps, the "comparisons of behavior" technique turned out to be less investigated in HA studies on everyday PA. Only 12 of the 42 publications (29%) included typical social comparison features such as leader boards or notifications on buddies' recent PA. 9 publications (21%) included "shaping knowledge" features by investigating advise, training, or explanations on how support behavior change regarding everyday physical activity. Some of the examples include instructions on how to correctly perform heart rate measurements, hints on suitable running equipment, or suggestions regarding fitness exercises. Such information was provided through different channels, e.g., through notifications, text messages, or via telephone-based lifestyle coaching.

In the group "identity" the BCT "identification of self as role model" was implemented in 8 studies (19%), e.g., when group members were encouraged to be the team captain and to support group interaction and encouragement [16].

"Natural consequences" of sufficient PA (or SB, on the contrary) were communicated within 5 research works (12%). This includes information about health consequences such as being less/more susceptible to diseases or live longer/shorter due to specific behaviors.

A few studies made use of "antecedents" by adding (virtual) objects to the environment. This approach was in use for some GPS-based gamified interventions to motivate users to reach a specific location, where the objects can be discovered or collected [7, 47].

3.2 Visualization Types

Besides the actual usage of existing BCTs, we were further interested in how relevant information was visualized for the user. Table 2 presents the different visualization types identified in our literature body in conjunction with the respective literature sources.

Figure 4 depicts the relative usage of different visualization types in recent research on health apps for promoting everyday PA. Graphs turned out to be the most frequently used visualization type in our review. In 23 publications (55%), bar, line, and ring charts were applied to either present key metrics of the user's (or buddies') physical activities over recent days or weeks or to indicate active time (MVPA). Only 2 publications (5%) showed respective data by numbers only.

Table 2. Different visualization types identified in the literature body.

Visualization type	Publications
Graphs	[2, 3, 10, 12, 15, 16, 21, 22, 27, 28, 30, 33, 36, 37, 41–43, 45, 50, 51, 55, 57, 58]
Numbers only	[8, 9]
Gamified	[3, 7, 13, 16, 23, 33, 37, 43, 47, 57]
Activity feed (timeline)	[1, 7, 10, 13]
Tables/rankings	[13, 21–24, 33, 37]

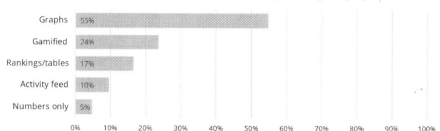

Fig. 4. The relative usage of visualization types in empirical studies on apps for promoting everyday PA: traditional graphs and gamified illustrations are predominant.

Beyond graph-style and numbers-only representations of PA performance data, we found 10 gamified visualizations (24%) in a broad range of implementations. Typical examples are virtual trophies and badges for specific achievements. Advanced concepts include collecting virtual playing cards which can be traded with other users or chasing virtual objects anchored at real-world locations.

7 of the 42 research works (17%) used rankings to directly compare the user's PA performance with those of his or her buddies or competitive teams. Variations include the performance metrics (e.g., steps, time spent, points achieved) as well as the compared group (within a specified team of buddies or global). Finally, only 4 studies (10%) investigated app prototypes with activity feeds. These social media-like news streams either show a scrollable list of the users' own or the buddies' activities.

In 8 publications (19%) we did not find any information on the visualization type applied in the respective study.

4   Discussion

In the following, we reflect on the results of our literature review. We discuss the usage of BCTs and visualization types in recent research on interventions to promote everyday PA, particularly regarding their efficiency.

4.1   Behavior Change Techniques

The most common BCTs used in interventions are goal setting (behavior), feedback on behavior and self-monitoring of behavior. The combination of those three BCTs within one intervention study was also the most common (e.g., [2, 8, 58]). However, some promising goal setting BCTs like problem solving [12, 50] or reviewing behavior goals (and adapting behavior change strategies) [14, 36, 50] were only found in a few interventions and seem to be used rarely in most modern PA promoting health apps and digital health interventions.

Social support in different variations seem to be promising BCTs to promote PA [16, 21, 22, 26, 43]. Several studies focused on examining the effects of peer groups or teams which tried to reach a common PA goal. Physical contact (instead of online contacts) or proximity of location [45] as well as higher frequency of communication [21] seem to be supporting factors. Exposing data about the PA to the public also significantly increased the effort and changed behavior compared to self-monitoring [3].

Monetary incentives and rewards [15, 27, 30] and virtual rewards (e.g., trophies or badges) [10, 37] seem to be an acceptable strategy to trigger behavior change. It motivates users to reach artificial daily step goals, whereby most users cease their PA efforts after the incentivized goals are reached [27, 34]. However, incentives and rewards can also have negative effects in the long-term on intrinsic motivation of the participants, as shown by [9].

It is common to deliver prompts, feedback and reports relative to goal achievements (e.g., a percentage of the step goal) or at specific times (e.g., [9]). However, some studies implement just-in-time-adaptive-interventions (JITAI), which are a promising alternative approach to deliver nudges and provide BCTs within the most appropriate context and when the user would be receptive to it [28, 41, 48].

Some BCTs are incorporated via push notification to either prompt behavior, inform about reached goals or provide information like health facts. However, studies show that there is an attrition effect if the message frequency is too high, or there is already a high emergence of other notifications (e.g., from social media like Facebook, Instagram, Snapchat, and others). This effect is also apparent if there is too much repetition content-wise or just because of lack of interest [51].

The most common BCTs used in interventions are goal setting (behavior), feedback on behavior and self-monitoring of behavior. The combination of those 3 BCTs within one intervention study was also the most common (e.g., [2, 8, 58]). Regarding the combination of different BCTs, it seems noteworthy that a higher number of BCTs used in interventions does not necessarily provide better results or stronger effects. There were studies with only a few BCTs (e.g., [15, 28, 58]) with significant effects on PA and studies with higher numbers of used BCTs without significant effects on PA (e.g., [46]).

4.2 Visualization Types

Our analysis showed a strong emphasis on graphs for visualizing performance and key metrics in health apps on everyday PA. In most cases, very basic traditional chart types such as bar, line, and ring charts are used; in most cases in combination with static performance goals. While most users probably are familiar with these traditional chart types and thus this decision is reasonable from a usability perspective, we see potential for future research in specialized chart visualizations considering adaptive goals.

(Self-)Moderated or adaptive activity goals seem to be more accepted and motivating than static goals (e.g., [58]). Especially the widespread 10,000 steps goal, which orig-inated in marketing, has been described by some authors as detrimental to motivation. However, it is frequently used in our research body [3, 8, 34, 58]. To follow current health recommendations and support motivation, time-based qualitative activity goals or intensity goals (MVPA) should be considered, as pointed out in some of the studies (e.g., [18, 29, 46, 50]).

A related visualization approach is *Movilio* [54], which applies a combination of bar charts for visualizing a continuous floating 7-day activity goal. Users can shift the visualized period forth and back to see how the activities of different intensities influence the PA necessary to achieve the desired health benefits. The app calculates the effort still required to reach the goal depending on the past activities. However, this novel visualization approach is not empirically validated so far.

Despite various attempts to keep users engaged, e.g., through gamified visualizations, the drop-off of PA tracking is a general problem seen in many studies, especially with longer duration. For example [34] with its big sample of 140,000 participants shows a drop to 54% after one month and only 9% of all participants remaining after 6 months of tracking. Several other studies report on drop-off rates between 30% and 50% [12, 25, 37, 49].

Finally, alternative visualization types beyond charts seem under-explored for promoting everyday PA through mobile apps. While we found some examples of creative visualizations such as avatars or a blooming garden in prior work (e.g., [11, 35, 53]), no comparable visualization approaches were found in our body of literature.

4.3 Limitations

Through our systematic literature review, we aimed at providing an overview of recent research efforts on promoting everyday PA through health apps. In consequence, we limited our search to articles published within the past five years. We queried three major scientific databases from both the computer science and medicine domain. Still, additional publisher databases and search engines for scientific articles might provide further relevant research works. During the coding process of the documents, we captured BCTs that were explicitly described by the authors. In cases, where the descriptions might have lacked relevant details, a respective BCT could have been missed.

5 Conclusion and Outlook

In this review we gave an overview of recent empirical studies with mobile health interventions to promote PA based on BCTs. Our findings show that there is an emphasis on feedback and monitoring as well as goal setting techniques, while the application of other techniques such as informing about health consequences or shaping the user's knowledge are applied only in rare cases. The range of visualization types that is used to communicate performance metrics and goals is limited. Traditional charts and gamified illustrations turned out to be predominant while custom alternative approaches are scarce.

Due to heterogeneity of study and intervention types, target populations and BCT implementations there is no clear evidence about consistent patterns of superior strategies or better performing combinations of BCTs. Interaction and interdependency of multicomponent interventions remain unclear.

None of the studies made a specific evaluation of BCT usage or quantified BCT-related app features (e.g., how frequently or how long specific app features are activated or recalled). Only one study evaluated efficacy of single BCTs and combinations [50] and concluded that different combinations of BCTs may be effective to promote PA and reduce SB. Future work could focus more on comparison of single BCTs and combinations thereof to provide evidence for BCTs with more potential and those with less. The effects of interventions did not increase with higher number of implemented BCTs. Interventions could therefore benefit from less complex implementations of a few effective BCTs to promote PA.

References

1. Althoff, T., Jindal, P., Leskovec, J.: Online actions with offline impact: how online social networks influence online and offline user behavior. In: Proceedings of the Tenth ACM International Conference on Web Search and Data Mining, pp. 537–546 (2017)
2. Alqahtani, D., Jay, C., Vigo, M.: The effect of goal moderation on the achievement and satisfaction of physical activity goals. Proc. ACM Interact. Mob. Wearab. Ubiquit. Technol. 4(4), 1–18 (2020)
3. Altmeyer, M., Lessel, P., Sander, T., Krüger, A.: Extending a gamified mobile app with a public display to encourage walking. In: Proceedings of the 22nd International Academic Mindtrek Conference, pp. 20–29 (2018)
4. Bondaronek, P., Alkhaldi, G., Slee, A., Hamilton, F.L., Murray, E.: Quality of publicly available physical activity apps: review and content analysis. JMIR Mhealth Uhealth 6(3), e9069 (2018)
5. Brickwood, K.J., Ahuja, K.D., Watson, G., O'Brien, J.A., Williams, A.D.: Effects of activity tracker use with health professional support or telephone counseling on maintenance of physical activity and health outcomes in older adults: randomized controlled trial. JMIR Mhealth Uhealth 9(1), e18686 (2021)
6. Brooke, J.: SUS-A quick and dirty usability scale. Usab. Eval. Indust. 189(194), 4–7 (1996)
7. Cambo, S.A., Avrahami, D., Lee, M.L.: BreakSense: combining physiological and location sensing to promote mobility during work-breaks. In: Proceedings of the 2017 CHI Conference on Human Factors in Computing Systems, pp. 3595–3607 (2017)
8. Cauchard, J.R., Frey, J., Zahrt, O., Johnson, K., Crum, A., Landay, J.A.: The positive impact of push vs pull progress feedback: a 6-week activity tracking study in the wild. Proc. ACM Interact. Mob. Wearab. Ubiquit. Technol. 3(3), 1–23 (2019)
9. Cherubini, M., Villalobos-Zuniga, G., Boldi, M.O., Bonazzi, R.: The unexpected downside of paying or sending messages to people to make them walk: comparing tangible rewards and motivational messages to improve physical activity. ACM Trans. Comput. Hum. Interact. 27(2), 1–44 (2020)
10. Ciravegna, F., Gao, J., Ireson, N., Copeland, R., Walsh, J., Lanfranchi, V.: Active 10: brisk walking to support regular physical activity. In: Proceedings of the 13th EAI International Conference on Pervasive Computing Technologies for Healthcare, pp. 11–20 (2019)
11. Consolvo, S., et al.: Activity sensing in the wild: a field trial of ubifit garden. In: Proceedings of the SIGCHI Conference on Human Factors in Computing Systems, pp. 1797–1806 (2008)
12. Damschroder, L.J., et al.: Effect of adding telephone-based brief coaching to an mhealth app (Stay Strong) for promoting physical activity among veterans: randomized controlled trial. J. Med. Internet Res. 22(8), e19216 (2020)
13. Edney, S., et al.: User engagement and attrition in an app-based physical activity intervention: secondary analysis of a randomized controlled trial. J. Med. Internet Res. 21(11), e14645 (2019)
14. Ellingson, L.D., et al.: Evaluating motivational interviewing and habit formation to enhance the effect of activity trackers on healthy adults' activity levels: randomized intervention. JMIR Mhealth Uhealth 7(2), e10988 (2019)
15. Elliott, M., Eck, F., Khmelev, E., Derlyatka, A., Fomenko, O.: Physical activity behavior change driven by engagement with an incentive-based app: evaluating the impact of Sweatcoin. JMIR Mhealth Uhealth 7(7), e12445 (2019)

16. Esakia, A., McCrickard, D.S., Harden, S., Horning, M.: FitAware: mediating group fitness strategies with smartwatch glanceable feedback. In: Proceedings of the 12th EAI International Conference on Pervasive Computing Technologies for Healthcare, pp. 98–107 (2018)

17. Forberger, S., Reisch, L., Kampfmann, T., Zeeb, H.: Nudging to move: a scoping review of the use of choice architecture interventions to promote physical activity in the general population. Int. J. Behav. Nutr. Phys. Act. 16(1), 77 (2019)

18. Gaudet, J., Gallant, F., Bélanger, M.: A bit of fit: minimalist intervention in adolescents based on a physical activity tracker. JMIR Mhealth Uhealth 5(7), e7647 (2017)

19. Guthold, R., Stevens, G.A., Riley, L.M., Bull, F.C.: Worldwide trends in insufficient physical activity from 2001 to 2016: a pooled analysis of 358 population-based surveys with 1·9 million participants. Lancet Glob. Health 6(10), e1077–e1086 (2018)

20. Guthold, R., Stevens, G.A., Riley, L.M., Bull, F.C.: Global trends in in-sufficient physical activity among adolescents: a pooled analysis of 298 population-based surveys with 1·6 million participants. Lancet Child Adolesc. Health 4(1), 23–35 (2020)

21. Hamamatsu, Y., Ide, H., Kakinuma, M., Furui, Y.: Maintaining physical activity level through team-based walking with a mobile health intervention: cross-sectional observational study. JMIR Mhealth Uhealth 8(7), e16159 (2020)

22. Hamaya, R., et al.: Effects of an mHealth app (Kencom) with integrated functions for healthy lifestyles on physical activity levels and cardiovascular risk biomarkers: observational study of 12,602 users. J. Med. Internet Res. 23(4), e21622 (2021)

23. Haque, M.S., Kangas, M., Jämsä, T.: A persuasive mHealth behavioral change intervention for promoting physical activity in the workplace: feasibility randomized controlled trial. JMIR Format. Res. 4(5), e15083 (2020)

24. Hollander, J.B., Folta, S.C., Graves, E.M., Allen, J.D., Situ, M.: A fitness app for monitoring walking behavior and perception (Runkeeper): mixed methods pilot study. JMIR Format. Res. 5(3), e22571 (2021)

25. Jang, I.Y., et al.: Impact of a wearable device-based walking programs in rural older adults on physical activity and health outcomes: cohort study. JMIR Mhealth Uhealth 6(11), e11335 (2018)

26. Joseph, R.P., Ainsworth, B.E., Hollingshead, K., Todd, M., Keller, C.: Results of a culturally tailored smartphone-delivered physical activity intervention among midlife African American women: feasibility trial. JMIR Mhealth Uhealth 9(4), e27383 (2021)

27. Jung, G., Oh, J., Jung, Y., Sun, J., Kong, H.K., Lee, U.: "Good Enough!": flexible goal achievement with margin-based outcome evaluation. In: Proceedings of the 2021 CHI Conference on Human Factors in Computing Systems, pp. 1–15 (2021)

28. Klasnja, P., et al.: Efficacy of contextually tailored suggestions for physical activity: a micro-randomized optimization trial of HeartSteps. Ann. Behav. Med. 53(6), 573–582 (2019)

29. Koorts, H., et al.: Translatability of a wearable technology intervention to increase adolescent physical activity: mixed methods implementation evaluation. J. Med. Internet Res. 22(8), e13573 (2020)

30. Künzler, F., Mishra, V., Kramer, J.N., Kotz, D., Fleisch, E., Kowatsch, T.: Exploring the state-of-receptivity for mhealth interventions. Proc. ACM Interact. Mob. Wearab. Ubiquit. Technol. 3(4), 1–27 (2019)

31. Laiou, E., et al.: Nudge interventions to promote healthy diets and physical activity. Food Policy 102, 102103 (2021)

32. Lee, A.M., et al.: Efficacy and effectiveness of mobile health technologies for facilitating physical activity in adolescents: scoping review. JMIR Mhealth Uhealth 7(2), e11847 (2019)

33. Leinonen, A.M., et al.: Feasibility of gamified mobile service aimed at physical activation in young men: population-based randomized controlled study (MOPO). JMIR Mhealth Uhealth 5(10), e6675 (2017)

34. Lim, B.Y., Kay, J., Liu, W.: How does a nation walk? Interpreting large-scale step count activity with weekly streak patterns. Proc. ACM Interact. Mob. Wearab. Ubiquit. Technol. **3**(2), 1–46 (2019)

35. Lin, J.J., Mamykina, L., Lindtner, S., Delajoux, G., Strub, H.B.: Fish'n'Steps: encouraging physical activity with an interactive computer game. In: Dourish, P., Friday, A. (eds.) UbiComp 2006. LNCS, vol. 4206, pp. 261–278. Springer, Heidelberg (2006). https://doi.org/10.1007/11853565_16

36. Lyons, E.J., Swartz, M.C., Lewis, Z.H., Martinez, E., Jennings, K.: Feasibility and acceptability of a wearable technology physical activity intervention with telephone counseling for mid-aged and older adults: a randomized controlled pilot trial. JMIR Mhealth Uhealth **5**(3), e6967 (2017)

37. Mamede, A., Noordzij, G., Jongerling, J., Snijders, M., Schop-Etman, A., Denktas, S.: Combining web-based gamification and physical nudges with an app (MoveMore) to promote walking breaks and reduce sedentary behavior of office workers: field study. J. Med. Internet Res. **23**(4), e19875 (2021)

38. Michie, S., Ashford, S., Sniehotta, F.F., Dombrowski, S.U., Bishop, A., French, D.P.: A refined taxonomy of behaviour change techniques to help people change their physical activity and healthy eating behaviours: the CALO-RE taxonomy. Psychology health **26**(11), 1479–1498 (2011)

39. Michie, S., et al.: The behavior change technique taxonomy (v1) of 93 hierarchically clustered techniques: building an international consensus for the reporting of behavior change interventions. Ann. Behav. Med. **46**(1), 81–95 (2013)

40. Milne-Ives, M., Lam, C., Cock, C.D., Velthoven, M.H.V., Meinert, E.: Mobile apps for health behavior change in physical activity, diet, drug and alcohol use, and mental health: Systematic review. JMIR mHealth uHealth **8**(3), e17046 (2020)

41. Mishra, V., Künzler, F., Kramer, J.N., Fleisch, E., Kowatsch, T., Kotz, D.: Detecting receptivity for mHealth interventions in the natural environment. Proc. ACM Interact. Mob. Wearab. Ubiquit. Technol. **5**(2), 1–24 (2021)

42. Miyake, A., Takahashi, M., Hashimoto, R., Nakatani, M.: StepUp forecast: predicting future to promote walking. In: Proceedings of the 23rd International Conference on Mobile Human-Computer Interaction, pp. 1–12 (2021)

43. Morrison, A., Bakayov, V.: Stickers for steps: a study of an activity tracking system with face-to-face social engagement. In: Proceedings of the ACM on Human-Computer Interaction, 1 (CSCW), pp. 1–10 (2017)

44. Piao, M., Ryu, H., Lee, H., Kim, J.: Use of the healthy lifestyle coaching chatbot app to promote stair-climbing habits among office workers: exploratory randomized controlled trial. JMIR Mhealth Uhealth **8**(5), e15085 (2020)

45. Ren, X., Yu, B., Lu, Y., Brombacher, A.: Exploring cooperative fitness tracking to encourage physical activity among office workers. In: Proceedings of the ACM on Human-Computer Interaction, 2 (CSCW), pp. 1–20 (2018)

46. Ridgers, N.D., et al.: Effect of commercial wearables and digital behaviour change resources on the physical activity of adolescents attending schools in socio-economically disadvantaged areas: the RAW-PA cluster-randomised controlled trial. Int. J. Behav. Nutr. Phys. Act. **18**(1), 1–11 (2021)

47. Santos, L.H.D.O., et al.: Promoting phyousical activity in Japanese older adults using a social pervasive game: randomized controlled trial. JMIR Ser. Games **9**(1), e16458 (2021)

48. Saponaro, M., Vemuri, A., Dominick, G., Decker, K.: Contextualization and individualization for just-in-time adaptive interventions to reduce sedentary behavior. In: Proceedings of the Conference on Health, Inference, and Learning, pp. 246–256 (2021)

49. Schoeppe, S., et al.: Efficacy of interventions that use apps to improve diet, physical activity and sedentary behaviour: a systematic review. Int. J. Behav. Nutr. Phys. Act. **13**(1) (2016)

50. Schroé, H., et al.: Which behaviour change techniques are effective to promote physical activity and reduce sedentary behaviour in adults: a factorial randomized trial of an e-and m-health intervention. Int. J. Behav. Nutr. Phys. Act. **17**(1), 1–16 (2020)
51. Simons, D., De Bourdeaudhuij, I., Clarys, P., De Cocker, K., Vandelanotte, C., Deforche, B. (2018)
52. Simoski, B., Klein, M.C., Van Halteren, A.T., Bal, H.: User acceptance of real-life personalized coaching in social fitness apps. In: Proceedings of the 13th EAI International Conference on Pervasive Computing Technologies for Healthcare, pp. 198–207 (2019)
53. Turchaninova, A., Khatri, A., Uyanik, I., Pavlidis, I.: Role model in human physical activity. In: Proceedings of the conference on Wireless Health, pp. 1–6 (2015)
54. Ulmer, T., Maier, E., Reimer, U.:The myth of 10,000 steps: a new approach to smartphone-based health apps for supporting physical activity. In: HEALTHINF, pp. 641–647 (2020)
55. Wang, Y., König, L.M., Reiterer, H.: A smartphone app to support sedentary behavior change by visualizing personal mobility patterns and action planning (SedVis): development and pilot study. JMIR Format. Res. **5**(1), e15369 (2021)
56. Weinmann, M., Schneider, C., Vom Brocke, J.: Digital nudging. Bus. Inf. Syst. Eng. **58**(6), 433–436 (2016)
57. Zhao, Z., Arya, A., Orji, R., Chan, G.: Effects of a personalized fitness recommender system using gamification and continuous player modeling: system design and long-term validation study. JMIR Ser. Games **8**(4), e19968 (2020)
58. Zhou, M., et al.: Evaluating machine learning–based automated personalized daily step goals delivered through a mobile phone app: randomized controlled trial. JMIR Mhealth Uhealth **6**(1), e9117 (2018)

Shopping in the Dark

Effects of Platform Choice on Dark Pattern Recognition

Christof van Nimwegen[✉] and Jesse de Wit

Faculty of Science, Department of Information and Computing Sciences, Utrecht University,
Princetonlaan 5, 3584 CC Utrecht, The Netherlands
c.vannimwegen@uu.nl, j.dewit@students.uu.nl

Abstract. Dark patterns are user interfaces designed to trick users into doing things they might not otherwise do. Human psychological insights are carefully exploited by designers to craft these patterns. This study investigates the relation between dark pattern recognition and platform choice. An experiment was designed in which 54 participants performed a shopping task. In the website different dark pattern types were implemented, such as "Sneak into Basket", "Toying with emotions" and "Trick Questions". Results showed that mobile users are twice as likely to fall for one of the patterns. In addition, a significant correlation was found between falling for that same dark pattern and the age of users. The older the user, the more chance of falling for that pattern. Lastly it showed that the higher the website's "honesty" is rated, the higher the "navigability" is rated.

Keywords: Dark patterns · Design ethics · Deceptive interfaces · Mobile devices · Online trust

1 Introduction

Over the past decades information technology and the internet have become indispensable to modern society. It is embedded in cars, smartphones and our homes. Many pillars of society have gained benefit from the rise of information technology and the internet in some form or another. However, the internet also induced less desirable practices such as phishing and unethical hacking: the act of attempting to access computer systems without authorization [8]. As modern life takes place online more than ever before, organizations are exploiting human psychology and using it to their advantage. By adding misleading or deceptive interfaces to their websites they hope to gain benefit (e.g., personal information) from users. These types of design choices are called "dark patterns". With the rise of smartphones that navigate the web, specific dark patterns targeted at mobile users have been created, for example the illusion of a hair on the screen, see in Fig. 1. The expectation is that users will (try to) remove the hair by swiping the screen, and thus involuntarily visit the website it links to. Another extreme example is shown in Fig. 2: an airline making it purposely hard to NOT buy travel insurance ("Don't insure me" is hidden in the alphabetical country list).

© The Author(s), under exclusive license to Springer Nature Switzerland AG 2022
M. Kurosu (Ed.): HCII 2022, LNCS 13304, pp. 462–475, 2022.
https://doi.org/10.1007/978-3-031-05412-9_32

Fig. 1. Mobile dark pattern: illusion of a hair on the screen

Fig. 2. Air travel web site making it purposely hard to NOT to buy travel insurance ("Don't insure me" is in country list)

One of the first articles that was published about dark patterns was on "A List Apart" by Harry Brignull, who coined the term a year earlier in 2010 [2]. In this article he introduces dark patterns by comparing honest and deceptive applications of human psychological insights. He states that A/B-tests that include dark patterns test very well, simply because users get tricked into doing something.

2   Related Work

2.1   User Interface and the User Experience

A growing number of studies have investigated User Interface (UI) and User Experience (UX) design [1, 13]. In a study set out to clarify User Experience [13] argue that the human-computer interaction process (e.g., buying something online) needs to be visual, empathic and emotionally driven to be successful or meaningful to the user. The perceived quality of the experience may decline if the interaction process fails to manifest these features. This could happen unintentionally when a designer has not enough knowledge of the mentioned features. However, sometimes practitioners create deceptive interactions intentionally, causing users to perform involuntary actions.

2.2   User Interface Stakeholder Values vs. User Values

The actions mentioned in the previous section benefit the business, while the same actions hinder or take advantage of users. Amazon for example makes it extremely difficult for users to delete their account. First, users must reach a page that is intentionally difficult to find. Second, when users finally manage to reach this page, it is impossible for them to delete the account themselves. The user has no choice but to chat with an employee to delete the account. It is assumed that Amazon strategically designed this as a retention strategy to discourage the user from going through with account deletion. Another big player, Facebook, prompts users to review and manage their data sharing settings, but whenever users click "Accept and continue", the setting is automatically turned on and Facebook can show users ads based on data from third parties. In the same way, Google requires users to actively look for advertisement personalization settings. [10] refer to this kind of interaction design as "asshole design" because the interaction purpose can be perceived as unethical or manipulative.

2.3 Persuasive Technology

Designers of interaction technology design strategically so that their designs result in predefined user behavior. In the context of interaction design, [9] views persuasive technology as "designing for behavior as something we cause to occur and/or preventing a target behavior from happening". In other words, interaction designers have the ability and the responsibility to induce behavioral change in a positive or negative manner. Persuasive technology is known for the potential benefit it can have on the lives of individual users as well as society. Mobile smoking cessation applications are examples of how persuasive technology can be used for self-improvement. In parallel with the aforementioned claim the possibility of ethical persuasion and defined a set of guidelines so practitioners can apply these in an ethical manner. By following these guidelines designers use persuasive technology to enhance the usability of applications instead of decreasing it. However, [9] warns that persuasive technology is a controversial topic and that there should be awareness of its negative applications.

2.4 Dark Patterns

UX designer consultant Harry Brignull coined the term dark patterns and introduced a set of 12 different types of dark patterns, which he published on his website [2]. Meanwhile several (online) newspapers have published articles where they address the issue of dark patterns in interaction design [3, 4, 15]. This gives reason to assume that many UI and UX practitioners are familiar with manipulative or deceptive design practices. A study by [5] showed that student UX designers valued stakeholder-focused outcomes over human values in their decision making, even when their initial design activity was user-focused. An extensive study investigated the presence of dark patterns on shopping websites [14]. A total of 11,000 websites were crawled, 1254 websites contained dark patterns and 1,818 instances of dark patterns were found. Another study [8] in which the researchers scraped twitter for the hashtag "#darkpatterns" found that practitioners are using social media to generate awareness about dark patterns. Twitter users most frequently used the hashtag to publicly shame companies for using dark patterns.

Dark Pattern Strategies. A study by [12] focused on identifying, categorizing and evaluating various types of dark patterns. They argue that there are five main types of dark pattern strategies. Table 1 shows an overview of the types and subtypes. The subtypes contain 9 of 12 patterns from Brignull's initial list.

Table 1. Dark pattern strategy types [12].

Type	Description	Subtypes
Nagging	Redirection of expected functionality that persists beyond one or more interactions.	-
Obstruction	Attempting to hide, disguise, or delay the divulging of information that is relevant to the user.	Roach Motel (Bignull), Price Comparison Prevention (Brignull) and Intermediate Currency
Sneaking	Making a process more difficult than it needs to be, with the intent of dissuading certain action(s).	Forced Continuity (Brignull), Hidden Costs (Brignull), Sneak into Basket (Brignull) and Bait and Switch (Brignull)
Interface Interference	Manipulation of the user interface that privileges certain actions over others.	Hidden Information, Preselection, Aesthetic Manipulation, Toying with Emotion, False Hierarchy, Disguised Ad (Brignull) and Trick Questions (Brignull).
Forced Action	Requiring the user to perform a certain action to access (or continue to access) certain functionality.	Social Pyramid, Gamification and Privacy Zuckering (Brignull)

Nagging. Nagging is a redirection of expected functionality. They include interruptions such as pop-ups or other distractions within the interface that interfere with the user's focus. An example is Fig. 3 in which Google prompts and encourages the user to enable its location services, but when the 'Don't show this again' checkbox is checked, the 'Disagree' option is greyed out. A pre-selection favoring Google is made, but not by the user, who must invest effort to choose what he might want ('Disagree').

Fig. 3. Nagging: 'Don't show again' is selected, 'Disagree' is greyed out

Fig. 4. Twitter using Interface Interference: Automatic opt-in after email notification update.

Obstruction. Whenever a user's task flow is intentionally interrupted while trying to accomplish a given task, one speaks of Obstruction. Within this primary category, various subcategories exist. They are Brignull's Roach Motel, which is defined as making a situation easy to get into, but hard to get out of (e.g., Amazon makes it easy to create an account but extremely difficult to delete them). Another subtype is Brignull's Price Comparison Prevention, which makes it hard for users to compare prices of products. The final subtype of Obstruction is Intermediate Currency. This subtype tries to make users spend money on virtual currency (e.g., in-app purchases within mobile games). The pattern distorts the view of the user's value spent, making the user spent their virtual currency differently than they would have if it was real money.

Sneaking. Sneaking is defined as attempting to hide, delay or disguise information that is relevant to the user. Often, this pattern is used to make users perform actions they may object to if they had knowledge of it. Within Sneaking, four subtypes exist. First, Brignull's Forced Continuity makes users pay for services after their initial service has expired. Second, Brignull's Hidden Costs pattern fails to inform users about costs in a reasonable time span, i.e. hidden tax or shipping. Third, Brignull's Sneak into Basket pattern secretly adds items into the user's basket. Fourth, Brignull's Bait and Switch pattern suggests a certain action will happen, only for users to find out that a different action happens. A common situation includes the manipulation of muscle memory. For example, the mobile game "Two Dots" repositions a button to buy more moves to the position previously used to continue to the next level.

Interface Interference. This occurs when interfaces privilege certain specific actions over others. A subtype of Interface Interferences is "Hidden Information" (actions that are relevant to the user but are not made visible or accessible). There is also "Preselection" (when an unfavorable option to the user is preselected), e.g., when Twitter updated e-mail notifications in 2018, they automatically opted all their users into the service (Fig. 4). Another subtype is Toying with emotion, where emotions are evoked with language, color, style or any other element to persuade users into certain actions, see as Fig. 5. The first option reads 'Keep me in the loop' and the second option 'No thanks, happy to be the last to know'. The former is associated with positive emotion, while the latter is rather negative. The user is manipulated to stay subscribed.

Fig. 5. Fragment of screen of Dutch bank "bunq", manipulating emotions of users.

Other instantiations of Interface interference are Aesthetic Manipulation and Brignull's Disguised Ad. The latter is used to make users think an advertisement is a game. When users click to interact with the 'game', they get sent to a different page. A last instantiation of Interface interference is Brignull's "Trick Questions", used to confuse with double negatives, confusing wording or other types of language manipulation.

Forced Action. These patterns feature in situations where users are required to perform an action in order to proceed. A well-known example is found in Windows 10; when a system update is made available, there is no option for users to shut the computer down without updating. Three subtypes of Forced Action were identified [12]; Social Pyramid, Gamification and Brignull's Privacy Zuckering. The Social Pyramid pattern requires users to recruit other users to the application or service in order to gain advantage on the platform. Gamification is used where platform specific benefits can be earned through repeated (sometimes unwanted) use of the service. Lastly, Privacy Zuckering refers to being tricked into sharing more information about themselves than they want.

2.5   Research Question

As mentioned in the introduction, there are dark patterns that are created specifically for mobile devices. This ties in with the significant number of mobile dark patterns found in the UXP2 dark pattern corpus. Therefore, this gives reason to investigate which platform performs better in terms of dark pattern recognition. Although studies have recognized that dark patterns are used widely in practice, research has yet to investigate the effects of them in a controlled setting. This project aims to fill this gap by performing an experiment where dark patterns are presented to participants in an online shopping environment, where distinction between desktop and mobile users is made. This research project consequently aims to answer the following research question:

What are the differences in dark pattern recognition between desktop and mobile users in an online shopping environment?

3   Method

3.1   Experimental Design

An online between-subjects experiment was designed. Participants are assigned to one of two groups in almost equal numbers: a group that carries out tasks on a desktop computer and a group that carries out that same task on a mobile phone. Also the possible relation between the age of participants and dark pattern recognition will be analyzed.

3.2   Variables

The dependent variable of this study is "Platform": **desktop or mobile** (see Table 2). A choice had to be made concerning *which* dark patterns to implement. As the first dependent variables we chose the recognition of "**Sneak into Basket/Toying with emotion**" dark pattern. These are actually *two* subtypes, falling under *two different* main dark pattern types: "Sneaking" and "Interface" interference (see Table 1). However, we treat the score as 1 score, the labels are combined here. The reason is that the way we implemented it here (see Fig. 6) applies to both; something is "sneaked into the basket" *using* "toying with emotion". The second dark pattern is "**Sneak into Basket**" recognition. Scores on these both variables are binary; their values can be "clicked" or "not clicked" and "checked" or "unchecked", respectively. Furthermore, dependent variables 3 and 4 are "**Perceived honesty**" and "**Perceived navigability**" of the website. This will be scored after completing the task with the website. Finally, "Age" variable is collected as a continuous variable.

Table 2. Experimental design and the variables of this study.

	Independent Variable = Platform	
	Desktop	Mobile
	Group A	Group B
	28 participants	26 participants
Dependent Variable 1	Sneak into Basket recognition	
Dependent Variable 2	Trick Questions recognition	
Dependent Variable 3	Perceived honesty	
Dependent Variable 4	Perceived navigability	
Covariate	Age	

3.3 Material

A shopping website was constructed for both platforms, the Dark patterns were implemented as follows:

Dependent Variable 1: "Sneak into Basket/toying with emotions"

On the cart page, the "Sneak into Basket" pattern is implemented using two buttons. "*Checkout as gift*" is easily recognized because of its shape and color. However, the text "*No thanks I don't like pretty gifts*" is also clickable, but this is not very clear (Fig. 6). Users tend to click the default option when presented with a choice. Designers of dark patterns happily use this tendency to their advantage. Once participants clicked the 'Checkout as gift' button, a 5 Euro gift wrap was added ("sneaked") to their shopping cart. In addition, the suggestive language applied can be seen as the "Toying with Emotion" pattern. The clickable text, in grey was "*No thanks, I don't like pretty gifts*". The goal of this specific design choice is to make participants feel as if they are missing out (toyed emotion) on something. In this case, a gift wrap.

Fig. 6. Dark pattern "Sneak into Basket/Toying with emotions": Gift wrap is added on the checkout page after clicking 'Checkout as gift'. The other option (not buy gift wrap) is chosen when clicking grey text *"No thanks, I don't like pretty gifts"* (both marked in red). (Color figure online)

Dependent Variable 2: "Trick Questions"

The second dark pattern strategy that was implemented was "Trick Questions" (Fig. 7). The form on the checkout page has a checkbox that includes a double negative in order to mislead participants. When the checkbox is left checked, the user opts-in for potentially unwanted e-mails. When it is left unchecked, the user opts-out. In this case, it is in the user's best interest to uncheck the checkbox.

Fig. 7. "Trick Questions": Double negative implemented on the checkout page.

Technical Implementation

Both versions of the website were hosted on the Utrecht University server. HTML5, CSS3, JavaScript and the Bootstrap framework6 were used to create the website. The preliminary questionnaire on the informed consent page and the concluding questionnaire at the end used Google Forms and implemented by wrapping Google's code snippet in an iframe element. The mobile website (the exact same content and functioning) was created using Bootstrap's grid system. Screenshots can be found in Fig. 8, the center screenshot shows the "Sneak into Basket/Toying with Emotion" pattern.

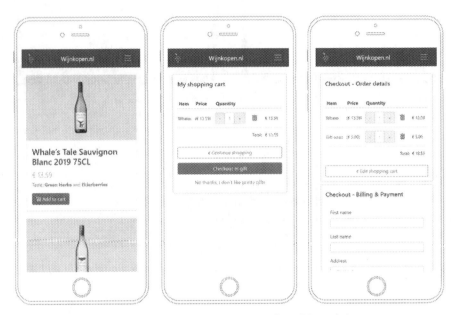

Fig. 8. Screenshots of the mobile version of the website.

3.4 Hypotheses

Based on the research question and literature the following hypothesis will be tested:

H0: Desktop users are equally likely to recognize dark patterns as mobile users
H1: Desktop users are not equally likely to recognize dark patterns as mobile users

3.5 Participants and Procedure

Participants were recruited through Facebook, LinkedIn and Whatsapp, after which they were randomly assigned to the desktop or mobile condition. The sample consisted of 54 participants (N = 54) aged 15–76 years old. The experiment had three phases.

Preparatory Phase
Here participants were shown an introductory page explaining the procedure of the experiment and participants signed the informed consent and entered their age and platform (mobile or desktop). The nature of the task implies that participants should not click the 'Checkout as gift' button and should instead click the 'No thanks, I don't like pretty gifts' button, since the purchase for evening on couch. The task instruction was:

"Wijnkopen.nl is a company that sells wine to consumers. You decide to buy wine for a nice evening on the couch".

Experiment Phase

Participants were sent to the regular or mobile version of the website where participants performed the given task. When participants were finished adding or removing products, clicking the 'View cart' button would lead them to the cart page. From here (Fig. 6) they had two options. Here dependent variable 1, the Sneak into Basket/Toying with Emotion patterns was implemented. The first option was to click '*Checkout as gift*' (Fig. 6). The second option was the gray '*No thanks, I don't like pretty gifts*' text-button. Once participants clicked one of the two buttons, they were sent to the checkout page (Fig. 7). Here, participants were presented with an overview of their basket and a checkout form. On this page, dependent variable 2, the "Trick Questions" dark pattern is implemented as a checkbox label that reads:

"Do not uncheck this if you wish to be contacted via email about product updates, upgrades, special offers and pricing".

What is being tested is whether implemented dark patterns were recognized or not and analyze this per platform. In the task, *two actions* from the user (scores on a variable) are related to this. Correct recognition of the dark patterns is demonstrated when:

- the participant chose '*No thanks, I don't like pretty gifts*' (score on variable 1)
- the participant *unchecked* the confusing sentence

Concluding Phase

Whenever participants finished the main experiment, they were sent to fill out a final short questionnaire. Participants were asked to rate the honesty and navigability of the website on a scale ranging from 1 to 5. After rating the website, the participants were asked to close the browser window in order to complete the experiment.

4   Results

Data analysis was performed using IBM SPSS version 25. Of the 54 participants 28 used the desktop version, 26 used the mobile version.

4.1   Dark Pattern Recognition

Various statistical tests were performed in order to test the hypothesis. Of the two dark patterns we investigated whether participants "fell" for the pattern or not. The dependent variable "Sneak into Basket recognition/Toying with emotions" is scored observing whether or not participants clicked the button. The dependent variable "Trick Questions" is scored observing whether or not participants left the checkbox checked. Chi-Square tests were performed as well as Spearman rank-order tests.

Sneak into Basket/Toying with Emotions

A chi-square test was performed to examine scores on recognition of the "Sneak into Basket/Toying with emotions" pattern. The mobile users fell for this more often and yielded a higher percentage than the desktop condition (84.6% vs. 42.9%). This difference was significant, $\chi2$ (1, N = 54) = 10.081, p = .001. Desktop users are *more likely* than mobile users to correctly recognize and not fall for the "Sneak into Basket/Toying with emotions dark pattern". Results of a Spearman rank-order correlation indicated that there was a significant *negative* association between age of users and "Sneak into Basket/Toying with emotions" recognition, (rs(54) = −.352, p = .009). Younger users are *more likely* to click the button and thus *less likely* to recognize the Sneak into Basket/Toying with emotions dark pattern. Figure 9 shows the scatterplot of age and whether or not participants clicked the Sneak into Basket dark pattern.

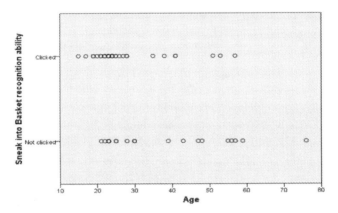

Fig. 9. Scatterplot of 'Age' and 'Sneak into Basket recognition'.

Trick Questions Recognition

A chi-square test was performed to examine the relation between platform and "Trick Questions" recognition. Although the mobile condition yielded a higher percentage than the desktop condition (42.3% vs. 28.6%), the difference between these variables was *not significant*, χ^2 (1, N = 54) = 1.115, P = .291. Mobile users were equally likely as desktop users to recognize the "Trick Questions" dark pattern by 'unchecking' that checkbox. Results of the Spearman rank-order correlation indicated that there was *no significant association* between age and "Trick Questions" recognition, (rs(54) = .181, P = .190). Figure 10 shows the scatterplot of age and whether or not participants unchecked the checkbox that contained the "Trick Questions" dark pattern.

4.2   Perceived Honesty and Navigability

After the task, participants rated the website on perceived honesty and navigability using 1–5 Likert scales. The variables are ordinal, therefore a Spearman rank-order correlation test was used. There was a significant positive association between perceived honesty and perceived navigability, (rs(48) = .345, p = .016). The higher perceived honesty was rated, the higher perceived navigability was rated, see Fig. 10.

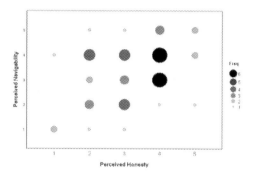

Fig. 10. Fluctuation plot of 'Perceived honesty' and 'Perceived navigability'.

5   Discussion and Conclusion

The results show that for the first studied dark pattern "Sneak into Basket/Toying with emotions" there was a significant difference between the two platforms. The number of mobile platform users fell for this pattern about twice as often as desktop users. A potential reason for this could be the setting: mobile users might not take the time to look at every single element on a webpage in detail, while desktop users may take more time to do so. Positioning, and size of buttons could also be reason why mobile users were more likely to fall for the pattern: mobile button positioning was vertical, whereas desktop button positioning was horizontal, and the buttons are smaller, scrutinizing requires more effort. This result is in line with the alternative hypothesis, stating that desktop and mobile users are *not* equally likely to recognize dark patterns in an online shopping environment. When looking at the age of the participants in relation to falling for the "Sneak into Basket/Toying with emotions" pattern, a significant correlation was found. It showed that the younger users, the more the fell for this pattern. An explanation for this could be that older users are more careful when spending money regardless of whether they are shopping offline or online. This might lead them to be more careful and precise over the whole range of actions when shopping online. In contrast, younger users are likely to be more familiar with technology, which could result in them being less careful while shopping online. Recognition of the second studied dark pattern "Trick Questions" did not differ significantly between platforms, although the same trend is visible; mobile users seem to fall for this more often. Also the age of the participants in relation to falling for the "Trick Questions" was analyzed, but also no significant correlation was found.

With respect to the perceived honesty and navigability of the website, there is a significant correlation indicating that a user's perceived honesty of this online shopping environment has a relation with the user's perceived navigability of the same environment, in both platforms.

These results of this study should be interpreted with some caution as the sample size (N = 54) of the study is limited. Also the age distribution among participants was suboptimal, there were not as many elderly participants as desired. Regarding ecological validity, there is of course the fact that participants did not experience any negative outcomes (such as losing money or sharing personal information unwillingly) when they fell for one of the dark patterns. The results of this study could have been different if *real* negative consequences were tied to dark pattern recognition failure. Lastly, the number of dark pattern types that were evaluated was limited to two. This is only a small portion of the total number of identified dark pattern types, in future research it is recommended that more subjects, and more/other dark patterns.

Resuming, this research aimed to identify the differences in dark pattern recognition between desktop and mobile users in an online shopping environment. Based on a quantitative analysis of dark pattern recognition in response to platform, it can be concluded that, to some extent, mobile users are more likely to fall for at least certain dark patterns in online shopping environments. The results indicate that age also plays a role in the dark pattern identification process, but this should be taken with caution due to the limited number of older participants.

It is important that this knowledge is spread, so that internet users can eventually make better informed decisions when they encounter dark patterns 'in the wild'. When looking at this study from a broader perspective, the outcomes of this research are part of a wake up call that is heard more and more these days.

References

1. Benyon, D.R.: Designing Interactive Systems: A Comprehensive Guide to HCI, UX and Interaction Design (No. 1). Pearson, Harlow (2014)
2. Brignull, H.: Dark Patterns (2010). https://www.darkpatterns.org/. Accessed 07 May 2020
3. Brignull, H.: Dark Patterns: Deception vs. Honesty in UI Design (2011). http://alistapart.com/article/dark-patterns-deception-vs.-honesty-in-ui-design. Accessed 01 May 2020
4. Brignull, H.: Dark Patterns: inside the interfaces designed to trick you (2013). http://www.theverge.com/2013/8/29/4640308/dark-patterns-inside-the-interfaces-designed-to-trick-you
5. Chivukula, S.S., Brier, J., Gray, C.M.: Dark intentions or persuasion? UX designers' activation of stakeholder and user values. In: Companion: Proceedings of the 2018 Designing Interactive Systems Conference (DIS 2018), pp. 87–91 (2018)
6. Chivukula, S.S., Watkins, C.R., Manocha, R., Chen, J., Gray, C.M.: Dimensions of UX Practice that Shape Ethical Awareness. In: Proceedings of the 2020 CHI Conference on Human Factors in Computing Systems, pp. 1–13 (2020)
7. Dhamija, R., Tygar, J.D., Hearst, M.: Why phishing works. In: Proceedings of the Sigchi Conference on Human Factors in Computing Systems, pp. 581–590 (2006)

8. Fansher, M., Chivukula, S.S., Gray, C.M.: #Darkpatterns: UX practitioner conversations about ethical design. In: Proceedings of the Conference on Human Factors in Computing Systems 1–6 April 2018 (2018). https://doi.org/10.1145/3170427.3188553

9. Fogg, B.: Computers as persuasive social actors. Persuas. Technol. 89–120 (2003)

10. Forbrukerrådet. Deceived by Design (2018). https://fil.forbrukerradet.no/wp-content/uploads/2018/06/2018-06-27-deceived-by-design-final.pdf

11. Friedman, B., Kahn Jr., P.H., Borning, A.: Value Sensitive Design: Theory and Methods. Technical Report (2002)

12. Gray, C.M., Kou, Y., Battles, B., Hoggatt, J., Toombs, A.L.: The dark (patterns) side of UX design. In: Proceedings of the Conference on Human Factors in Computing Systems, pp. 1–14 (2018)

13. Hassenzahl, M., Tractinsky, N.: User experience - a research agenda. Behav. Inf. Technol. 25(2), 91–97 (2006)

14. Mathur, A., et al.: Dark patterns at scale: findings from a crawl of 11K shopping websites. In: Proceedings of the ACM on Human-Computer Interaction, 3 (CSCW), pp. 1–32 (2019)

15. McKay, T.: Senators Introduce Bill to Stop 'Dark Patterns' Huge Platforms Use to Trick Users (2019). https://gizmodo.com/senators-introduce-bill-to-stop-dark-patterns-huge-plat-1833929276. Accessed 07 May 2020

16. Mirnig, A.G., Tscheligi, M.: (Don't) Join the Dark Side: An Initial Analysis and Classification of Regular, Anti-, and Dark Patterns. In: Proceedings of the 9th International Conference on Pervasive Patterns and Applications, pp. 65–71 (2017)

Interacting with Chatbots and Virtual Agents

Defining Requirements for the Development of Useful and Usable Chatbots: An Analysis of Quality Attributes from Academy and Industry

Malu Mafra[1]([✉]) [ID], Kennedy Nunes[1] [ID], Adailton Castro[1] [ID],
Adriana Lopes[2,3] [ID], Ana Carolina Oran[3] [ID], Geraldo Braz Junior[1] [ID],
João Almeida[1] [ID], Anselmo Paiva[1] [ID], Aristofanes Silva[1] [ID], Simara Rocha[1] [ID],
Davi Viana[1] [ID], Aurea Melo[4] [ID], Raimundo Barreto[3] [ID], and Luis Rivero[1] [ID]

[1] PPGCC, Universidade Federal do Maranhão, São Luis, Brazil
{malu.gabriele,kennedy.anderson,adailton.castro}@discente.ufma.br,
{geraldo.braz,joao.dallyson,anselmo.paiva,ac.silva,simara.rocha,
davi.viana,luis.rivero}@ufma.br
[2] Instituto de Pesquisas Eldorado, Manaus, Brazil
adriana.damian@eldorado.org.br
[3] Universidade Federal do Amazonas, Manaus, Brazil
{ana.oran,rbarreto}@icomp.ufam.edu.br
[4] Universidade Estadual do Amazonas, Manaus, Brazil
asmelo@uea.edu.br

Abstract. Chatbots are conversational interfaces that enable human-like dialogue and can be designed in a textual chat format or a graphical interface with voice and embedding options. In the last year, there has been a significant growth in the emergence of chatbots in the market and this popularization has attracted the efforts of researchers to this area. Despite the existence of techniques to evaluate these tools, there is an urgent need to propose solutions that also support the chatbot design process. Currently, there is no knowledge of a specific list of requirements capable of supporting development teams in the process of designing these tools. In view of this, this directed study proposes a literature review aiming at deepening the knowledge about these tools and identifying important quality attributes in academic and industry sources. As a result, this directed study presents a list composed of 82 requirements related to Usefulness, Ease of Use and Presence to aid the design of these tools. These requirements presented in this study are useful to guide developers in the process of building quality chatbots, making this task less challenging and for researchers who aim to propose technologies that contribute to the development of better and better chatbots.

Keywords: Chatbots · Requirements · Literature review · Quality assurance

M. Kurosu (Ed.): HCII 2022, LNCS 13304, pp. 479–493, 2022.
https://doi.org/10.1007/978-3-031-05412-9_33

1   Introduction

Conversational interfaces are tools that enable the establishment of dialogues that resemble human conversation [13]. There are several types of conversational interfaces, such as text-based chatbots, voice chatbots and voice assistants [29]. Intelligent Personal Assistants or Voice Assistants are designed with Artificial Intelligence voice recognition and require a device to work (e.g. Amazon's Alexa tool with an Echo Dot and Apple's Siri with the iOS operating system)[4]. On the other hand, Chatbots, also known as bots or conversational agents, are conversational interfaces in chat format, which, in addition to text messages, can integrate voice and animation that portray humanity [21]. They can also be developed with integration of Artificial Intelligence (AI) or just based on pre-established rules and keywords [8]. Due to their simplicity and easy access, the popularity of chatbots has increased, exploring user centered design processes for their development [10,18].

With the technological evolution of conversational agents, these systems are being created and modeled in several ways [30], such as: rule-based [25], artificial intelligence [8], with open domain [24] or closed domain [15], with or without voice incorporation [16]. Consequently, software development teams face difficulties regarding the design and evaluation process of these systems in order to obtain a product that meets quality standards. Also, the evaluation of these systems can be complex, since part of the evaluation process is performed based on human judgment [24]; and it is difficult to apply a single evaluation scale for all types of chatbots due to the diversity of characteristics that change from one conversational agent to another [21].

As the popularity of chatbots grows, researchers and practitioners are working to propose technologies able to support their evaluation. For instance, Sedoc et al. [24] proposed the ChatEval Framework, a paid platform in which developers submit their chatbots to a two-step evaluation process. Kuligowska [11], in turn, presented a means of evaluation for embedded commercial chatbots, by extracting attributes from the literature and subsequently comparing the chatbots with the identified attributes. Furthermore, Sugisaki and Bleiker [26] focused on the usability of chatbots, proposing an inspection checklist based on Nielsen's heuristics to support their evaluation.

Although there are evaluation approaches applicable to chatbots, there is a need to support the design of these systems as well. By supporting the initial definition steps of a chatbot, software development teams can benefit from understanding minimum requirements that make a chatbot appealing and easy to use by end-users, increasing their acceptance rate in the market [22]. Therefore, in this paper, we support the design process of chatbots by providing an initial list of requirements that could improve their quality from the point of view of end-users. This list was proposed based on a literature review and an analysis of industry suggestions. This list of requirements can be used by software engineers, developers and researchers who want to understand more about chatbots and how to improve their quality before their implementation, or evaluate if they meet quality criteria.

The remainder of this paper is organized as follows. In Sect. 2, we present an overview of conversational agents and chatbots, while discussing work related with this research. In Sect. 3, we present our research methodology. Section 4 presents our results with a list of requirements for the design of chatbots. Finally, our conclusions and future work are described in Sect. 5.

2   Background

2.1   Chatbots and Current Status

Conversational Agents or Chatbots are computer systems that can interact with human beings through an interface, which can be textual, voice or both. The goal of this systems is to behave as if a human was behind the conversation to improve the comunication with users [13]. These systems must have three main characteristics [23]: Comprehension, allowing textual or oral input to be analyzed using natural language processing tools; Competence, having access to an external knowledge base and storing context information to respond to user's requests; and Presence, allowing the feeling of having an entity, generating the feeling of trust. The first known conversational agent was ELIZA. This tool was developed in 1960 by MIT professor Joseph Weizenbaum, with the purpose of simulating being a virtual psychologist [31]. ELIZA used a strategy of reformulating snippets of sentences captured from users, making it appear that she had a vast vocabulary. This attempt to look like a real human being, also known as the Turing Test, consolidated ELIZA as the mother of all chatbots.

Over the decades, these tools have evolved in a way that they are being developed integrating Artificial Intelligence and using Natural Language Processing. Though these technologies, the dialogue can be perceived as similar to a real conversation and the system can also gain the ability to learn during conversations. There are also chatbots developed in a simpler way, only based on pre-established rules and keywords [8]. Chatbots with Artificial Intelligence can also be classified into: a) Open domain chatbots [24], which are capable of chatting on various topics; and closed domain chatbots [15], which have the ability to discuss a specific topic.

With regards to the use of chatbots in Brazil, the number of active chatbots has increased [1]. Also 65% of these tools are aimed at customer service in various business areas [19], but it is also possible to find chatbots aimed at education, health and leisure [6].

With regards to development, there are several known platforms. For instance, the Rasa AI tool [3] is an open source platform for chatbot development, based on Natural Language Processing and Machine Learning. This platform is commonly used in the research community, despite not offering cloud infrastructure (scalability, managed hosting, others). On the other hand, it provides common principles of open source software such as (self-hosting, adaptability, data control, others). The platform has two main components, RASA NLU for natural language processing and RASA Core for machine learning. Both can be used separately [6]. Another platform to build chatbots is DialogFlow. This platform is from Google and allows developing conversational interfaces for applications and devices with natural language processing. It is possible to combine programming languages and libraries, such as Android, iOS, Webkit HTML5, JavaScript, Node.js, and Python with this chatbot platform [6]. The tool uses concepts for creating intentions, entities, contexts and agents [17].

Considering that there is a growing interest in the development of chatbots in Brazil, the authors of this paper investigated how to support the development of high quality chatbots. In the following subsection, we present works related to our research.

2.2   Related Work

This section presents an overview of studies published in recent years related to quality attributes and evaluation methods of chatbots. In recent years, chatbot researchers have been striving to develop measurement technologies that focus on user satisfaction. For instance, Sedoc et al. [24] carried out a study that resulted in a platform for evaluating chatbots, ChatEVAL. In this platform, researchers submit their tools for a paid assessment, which is performed in two stages: a human assessment and an automatic assessment. The human assessment is performed by a chatbot specialist. On the other hand, the automatic assessment is performed to identify defects and weaknesses, calculating metrics related to lexical diversity (distinct-n), mean cosine similarity between embedded responses and the actually generated responses, mean BLEU-2 score, and response perplexity, as measured by the probability of the model predicting the correct response. After the evaluation process, the generated report is made available.

In another work, Kuligowska [11] presented a study on commercial chatbots in the Polish language, aimed at serving end consumers. The study identified quality attributes in the literature and evaluated the quality components of 6 chatbots, such as the look of the tool, way of implementation on the website, voice synthesis unit, integrated knowledge base (with general and specialized information), presentation of additional knowledge and functionality, conversation, professional skills and context sensitivity, personality traits, customization options, emergency responses in unexpected situations, possibility of user rating of the chatbot and website. This evaluation process was conducted by assigning scores according to the Likert scale from 1 (very bad) to 5 (very good) to the components of the chatbots and then the simple average of the evaluated points was calculated, giving, according to the researcher, an overview of the quality of the 6 chatbots. After the study, the lack of usability metrics to guide and evaluate chatbot projects motivated Langevin et al. [13] to pursue alternatives to improve the quality of chatbots. As a result, the researchers used Nielsen's Usability Heuristics [20] in their work to propose a set of 12 new usability heuristics for chatbots. The study was carried out in four stages: (1) the first stage was the development of a set of new heuristics based on Nielsen's heristics for the design of chatbot interfaces using results from literature reviews; (2) the second stage consisted of presenting the developed heuristics to nine experts in chatbot design and heuristic evaluation, in order to collect their feedback; (3) the third step was the application of the new heuristics in two interfaces, Amazon's echo dot with Alexa and an online chatbot, comparing the new heuristics with Nielsen's heuristics to observe their effectiveness in identifying usability problems with chatbots; (4) the fourth phase took place after the appropriate iterations of the new heuristics, aiming to improve their performance in online chatbots. After carrying out these phases, tests and evaluations were carried out with designers and experts showing that adapting Nielsen's heuristics for evaluating chatbots is an effective method, useful to highlight issues related to dialogue content, interaction design, help and guidance, human characteristics and data privacy [13].

In another study, Sugisaki and Bleiker et al. [26] analyzed the rules proposed by Nielsen in several scientific works and proposed a Checklist. In their paper, Nielsen's heuristics were detailed in 53 verification items useful for evaluating conversational interfaces. The proposed checklist was submitted to an evaluation by 15 professionals, who analyzed each item and answered a questionnaire about the relevance of each one of them, and about how efficient, pleasant, convenient and effective the checklist was. The results indicated that 80% of the checklist items were considered relevant, but some verification items were highlighted by the reviewers as very technical and difficult to understand.

Finally, the study by Borsci et al. [2] is also similar. The researchers proposed a technique for evaluating chatbots with artificial intelligence, Bot-Check. This scale with 42 verification items, although not completely inspired by Nielsen's Heuristics like the other works cited, used heuristics in combination with several attributes from literature review. The attributes for this study were taken from the work of Radziwill and Benton [21] who identifies important characteristics for quality chatbots. This list of attributes was validated in an online survey of chatbot designers and end users to find out if they were kept or dropped from the list. Subsequently, the Bot-Check scale was validated with 141 participants to identify its relevance. The results indicated that the proposed scale can be used by designers as a tool to ensure quality in the design of chatbots before testing with end users.

Despite proposing relevant techniques for evaluating chatbots, important attributes that the Industry could provide were not considered in the creation of the verification items of these techniques. If used carefully, gray literature can provide valuable sources of information for researchers, as it can benefit Software Engineering research, as it is able to fill gaps that the formal review does not fill [7]. Furthermore, to the best of our knowledge, requirements for the design of chatbots were not specified in a research paper. Despite that the analyzed evaluation checklists contain verification items that can be written in the form of requirements, most of the items we found presented quality attributes but not their translation in the form of requirements, which is important to understand the needs of users before designing and implementing chatbots.

Considering the above, there is a need to identify generic chatbot requirements that can be useful in the design of these systems. Also, these requirements could be identified in gray literature, so relevant information shared by software companies/practitioners is considered and validated during the development of requirements or evaluation checklists. In the following section, we present the steps for identifying the list of requirements for chatbots considering research papers and gray literature.

3   Research Methodology

During our research, we followed a methodology that focused on the discovery of essential quality attributes for chatbots, both in academy and industry, so that they could be later translated into requirements. To this end, we carried out a literature review to discover quality attributes for chatbots. Figure 1 shows the applied methodology in this research, which is explained below.

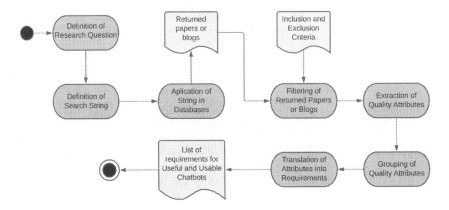

Fig. 1. Methodology followed in this research for the definition of requirements usable and useful chatbots

In the first step, to guide this review, we defined the following Research Question: "What quality attributes are necessary in the development of chatbots?". Then, we developed a search strings to be applied in the main scientific databases: ACM Digital Library, IEEE, SCOPUS and Science Direct. The search string was as follows: (("attribute" OR "feature" OR "characteristic" OR "aspect") AND ("bot" OR "conversational agent" OR "chatbot" OR "conversational user interface"). We applied a set of inclusion (IC) and exclusion (EC) criteria to filter the returned papers based on this search string:

- IC1 - The work addresses quality attributes for chatbots.
- EC1 - The work is not in English.
- EC2 - The work is not a scientific paper.

- EC3 - The work is not available for download.
- EC4 - The work is duplicated.
- EC5 - The work does not address quality attributes for chatbots.

Papers containing and describing quality attributes in the field of Human-Computer Interaction related to Ease of Use, Usefulness and Presence were selected [28,32]. Also, papers that used other names to report these attributes were considered, but the definitions or descriptions of the attributes were related to the ones previously identified.

After this process, three papers were selected, containing evaluation techniques for chatbots and important attributes. We highlight that this was not a systematic literature review not a systematic mapping study, as it was the first step to identify an initial set of papers in which quality attributes were listed, so that they could be used as input for a systematic mapping study in the future, supporting the identification of search terms and related papers.

Complementary to this initial literature review, to identify quality attributes for chatbots in Industry, the same search strings were used, returning blogs, magazines and other sources that could contain attributes in the context of chatbots. All selected Industry sources were specifically focused on the chatbot subject. Basically, they were recognized blogs and magazines with specific content from chatbots produced by experienced practitioners on the subject. As a result of this review, three more sources were selected.

After identifying the set of sources containing quality attributes, we listed the identified attributes within each source and grouped them if two or more sources referred to the same quality attribute. After that, the best (i.e. the most clear and detailed) definition was selected as prime definition for the quality attribute, yielding a list of single attributes. For example, four sources referred to the same attribute: The system must, from the beginning, make clear its ability not to frustrate the user [2]; The system must provide the user with information about its functionality [9]; The system must be able to tell the user what it can and cannot do [12]; and The system should introduce itself to the user and list the services it can provide [5]. These attributes were considered a group and the last definition used as main description of the attribute as it was more clear and understandable by the researchers.

After combining related quality attributes, yielding a unique list, these attributes were considered as basis for the development of requirements, following the structure proposed by Leite et al. [14]. In their paper, the authors proposed a structure for defining requirements, which can be useful for software engineers in the development process. For instance, the quality attribute "In the case of misunderstandings, does the CUI expresses clearly what type of clarification is needed by the human partner?" was transformed into "The chatbot must, in case of misunderstandings, clearly express the kind of clarification it expects from the user".

In the following section, we indicate which sources we identified that contained quality attributes for both academy and industry, as well as their transformation into a set of requirements that could be useful for designing usable and useful chatbots.

4 Results and Discussion

After the execution of the methodology, 6 sources were selected: three research papers [2, 9, 26]; and three blogs/magazines LANDBOT [12], CHATBOTSLIFE [5] and TAKE [27]. Using these sources, we identified a total of 82 requirements. Table 1 indicates each of the identified requirements along with the sources in which the quality attributes that originated the requirements were found.

Table 1. Identified requirements for chatbots found in literature from academy and industry.

Cat.	Chatbots Requirements	[26]	[2]	[9]	[12]	[5]	[27]
U01	The chatbot should always make it clear whose turn it is in the conversation	X					
U02	The chatbot must clearly indicate when it is processing a response	X					
U03	The chatbot must clearly recognize, understand, accept or reject the purpose or intent of the user	X					
U04	The chatbot must make it clear to the user who said what in the chat history	X					
U05	The chatbot must store relevant information to maintain the context of the user conversation	X	X				
U06	The chatbot must be able to report details about any previous arrangement (e.g. scheduled task, alarm settings)	X					
U07	The chatbot must be proactive during the conversation, offering tips and explanations	X		X			
U08	The chatbot must be able to give correct answers	X		X			
U09	The chatbot must have the look, personality and identity that suits its skill and role	X					
U10	The chatbot must use vocabulary appropriate to the user's knowledge	X	X				
U12	The chatbot must be able to cooperate with the user to solve his problem and reach his objective	X	X				
U13	The chatbot must allow the user to decide when the conversation starts	X					
U14	The chatbot must allow the user to decide when the conversation ends	X					
U15	The chatbot must give the user control to determine the pace of the conversation, and in case of interruption, maintain the preservation of the conversation	X					
U16	The chatbot must allow the user to determine the subject of the conversation	X					

(continued)

Table 1. (*continued*)

Cat.	Chatbots Requirements	[26]	[2]	[9]	[12]	[5]	[27]
U17	The chatbot should make it easy for the user to access and manage the preferences used to personalize the conversation	X					
U18	The chatbot should allow for a fluid, natural and engaging conversation	X	X				
U19	The chatbot must, in case of user doubt, explain the format of the answer he expects	X					
U20	The chatbot must offer the user the list of options or examples available in case of decision making	X					
U21	The chatbot must provide a summary of the transaction prior to confirmation	X					
U22	The chatbot must allow the use of shortcuts for advanced users	X					
U23	The chatbot should effectively use autocompletion and autocorrection to speed up entry and reduce misunderstandings	X					
U24	The chatbot should make it possible to alternate the use of buttons and other GUI elements with text input for selections and choices	X					
U25	The chatbot must allow the user to transfer the chatbot conversation to an attendant at any time	X					
U26	The chatbot must allow the user to receive the log with the record of the conversation	X					
U27	The chatbot must ask for confirmation before taking potentially irreversible actions (e.g. permanent deletion of data)	X					
U29	The chatbot must follow the conventions, guidelines and best practices of the environment in which it is integrated	X					
U30	The chatbot must follow the established conversational conventions of other chatbots (same hotkeys, for example)	X					
U33	The chatbot must be able to maintain user privacy		X				
U34	The chatbot must meet the user's needs regardless of age, health conditions and well-being		X				
U35	The chatbot should be considered pleasant and engaging to use		X				
U37	The chatbot must work according to what it proposes to do or surpassing the user's expectations			X			
P01	The chatbot must understand synonyms and variations within your domain	X					
P02	The chatbot must be able to understand various language styles	X	X				
P03	The chatbot must understand the user's response and handle it in case of excess or lack of information	X					

(*continued*)

Table 1. (*continued*)

Cat.	Chatbots Requirements	[26]	[2]	[9]	[12]	[5]	[27]
P04	The chatbot should, if possible, utilize knowledge about the user (e.g. preferences) from previous conversations with the chatbot and its environment	X		X			
P05	The chatbot must ensure that the length of sentences is adequate	X	X				
P06	The chatbot must ensure that sentences are relevant to the user's context and purpose	X	X				
P07	The chatbot must be able to handle unfocused requests and small talk	X		X			
P08	The chatbot must communicate properly, pleasantly and politely	X					
P09	The chatbot must be able to respond gracefully if the user is not polite	X					
P10	The chatbot must follow at least a minimal conversational structure, with greetings and self-identification, without forcing the user to follow this structure	X					
P11	The chatbot must be able to handle common typos, spelling mistakes and grammatical challenges (e.g. incorrect punctuation, letter switching)	X					
P12	The chatbot must be able to establish consensus in case of ambiguous and unclear statements from users	X	X				
P13	The chatbot must, in case of misunderstandings, clearly express the kind of clarification it expects from the user	X					
P14	The chatbot should offer tips to help the user understand it (e.g. offer alternatives, ask simple clarifying questions)	X					
P16	The chatbot should provide context-sensitive help on request	X					
P17	The chatbot must be able to provide the appropriate amount of information about itself (for example, its identity, skills, competencies and responsibilities)	X					
P18	The chatbot must be able to provide information on how to interact more efficiently with it (e.g. shortcuts, abbreviations)	X					
P19	The chatbot must be able to handle clarifying questions about its features in the middle of the task/topic	X					
P20	The chatbot must be able to resume the conversation after dealing with a clarifying question	X					
P21	The chatbot must, in case of using a specific style of language (emoji, dialects, regionalisms), use it in its utterances and understand the user's sentences	X					
P22	The chatbot must use specific vocabulary about the domain subject consistently and correctly	X					

(*continued*)

Table 1. (*continued*)

Cat.	Chatbots Requirements	[26]	[2]	[9]	[12]	[5]	[27]
P23	The chatbot must ensure that your sentences are spelled and grammatically correct and consistent	X					
P24	The chatbot must be able to recognize the user's intent and guide him towards his goals		X				
P25	The chatbot must be able to handle unexpected situations		X	X			
P26	The chatbot must understand the meaning of negative statements			X			
P27	The chatbot must be able to ask intelligent questions to engage the user			X			
P28	The chatbot must be able to finish the conversation gracefully			X			
P29	The chatbot must be able to convey a sense of good humor			X			
E01	The chatbot must make it clear how the user can initiate the conversation		X				
E02	The chatbot must be in a visible and easily accessible location		X				
E03	The chatbot must provide interactive elements in the interface to attract the user's attention			X			
E04	The chatbot must present its description in the interface and the main menu			X			
E05	The chatbot must have an avatar (graphical representation)				X		
P30	The chatbot must have persona (hobbies and other human characteristics)				X		
P31	The chatbot must have personality				X	X	
P32	The chatbot should appreciate short answers				X		
P33	The chatbot must be able to suggest responses to the user				X		
P34	The chatbot must respond in active voice				X		
P35	The chatbot should avoid asking the user too many questions						X
P36	The chatbot must choose to use neutral language for inclusion.						X
U38	The chatbot must have the option of evaluating satisfaction at the end of the service						X
U39	Chatbot should avoid asking users for more than two personal data						X
U40	The chatbot must indicate your service availability						X
U41	The chatbot must explain the reason in case of request for personal data						X

(*continued*)

Table 1. (*continued*)

Cat.	Chatbots Requirements	[26]	[2]	[9]	[12]	[5]	[27]
U11	The chatbot must be able to learn about user preferences and use them in conversation	X				X	
U28	The chatbot should allow the user to easily revert or interrupt the execution of their command	X			X		
U31	The chatbot must, from the beginning, make its ability clear so as not to frustrate the user		X	X	X	X	
U32	The chatbot must be able to use its resources to guide the user to his goal		X			X	
U36	The chatbot must adjust the response time so that the conversation is natural		X				X
P15	The chatbot should make it easier for the user to correct misunderstandings	X			X		

In Table 1, the identified requirements were categorized according to the aspect they focus on: (U) Usefulness, (E) Ease of Use and (P) Presence. According to Weng et al. [32], Ease of Use refers to the perceived ease of using the chatbot from the users' point of view. Usefulness refers to the degree of usefulness of the chatbot to perform tasks subjectively perceived by users [32]. Finally, Presence, according to Toader et al. [28] represents the feeling that the user is interacting with a person. Note that we also ordered the requirements considering if: (a) they were only considered in academic sources; (b) they were only considered in industry sources; and (c) they were considered in both academy and industry sources. The goal was to verify to what extent, both academy and industry agree to which requirements should be implemented in the development process of a chatbot.

When analyzing Table 1, one can see that the requirements range from basic capabilities of a chatbot, such as positioning the chatbot on the screen and maintaining a dialogue with correct and adequate information; to more complex capabilities, such as presenting personality, good humor, recognizing users' intentions and keeping the conversation interesting, engaging the user. When analyzing the list of requirements proposed in Table 1, 50% (41) of the requirements are related to Chatbot Usefulness, 6% (5) are related to Ease of Use and 44% (36) are related to Presence. In addition, 78% (64) of the requirements are found in research papers, 15% (12) are found only in industry sources, and 7% (6) are found by both. These results suggest that there is a need to identify other industry sources and assess the extent to which attributes found in research papers are adopted by the industry and how they affect the experience of end users of chatbots. Nevertheless, this initial list with 82 requirements can already help development teams that intend to build their conversational agents, as they can select which requirements are more appropriate to the design of their chatbots.

5   Conclusions and Future Work

Conversational agents are software used to simulate a dialogue as if they were a human being. These tools are increasingly popular and are useful in various contexts, such as education, public service and leisure. In this paper, we identified quality attributes related to these tools while defining requirements relevant for their development.

We identified a total of 82 requirements related to usefulness, ease of use and presence for the design of chatbots. This list of requirements can be used by chatbot designers and developers willing to improve the quality of these systems, meeting attributes that will ensure a final product that satisfies users. It can also be used by HCI researchers who aim to propose solutions that support the design, development and evaluation of chatbots; and by any consultant or specialist in chatbots as support material to propose improvements in existing chatbots.

As future work, this research aims to evaluate the requirements presented in real development contexts from the point of view of practitioners and end users, analyzing their impact and providing a more complete set of specific requirements for chatbots. We also aim to contribute with the development of technologies for the design and evaluation of conversational agents. These technologies will be proposed after a more in-depth literature review than the one presented in this paper. With this research, we intend to support both academy and industry in the design, evaluation and evolution of chatbots' development.

References

1. de Andrade, G.G., Silva, G.R.S., Júnior, F.C.M.D., Santos, G.A., de Mendonça, F.L.L., de Sousa Júnior, R.T.: Evatalk: a chatbot system for the Brazilian Government Virtual School. In: Proceedings of the 22nd International Conference on Enterprise Information Systems (ICEIS 2020) (2020)
2. Borsci, S., et al.: The chatbot usability scale: the design and pilot of a usability scale for interaction with AI-based conversational agents. Personal Ubiquit. Comput. **26**(1), 95–119 (2022)
3. Braun, D., Mendez, A.H., Matthes, F., Langen, M.: Evaluating natural language understanding services for conversational question answering systems. In: Proceedings of the 18th Annual SIGdial Meeting on Discourse and Dialogue, pp. 174–185 (2017)
4. Brill, T.M., Munoz, L., Miller, R.J.: Siri, Alexa, and other digital assistants: a study of customer satisfaction with artificial intelligence applications. J. Market. Manag. **35**(15–16), 1401–1436 (2019)
5. ChatbotsLife. 9 tips to write the perfect chatbot script (2021). https://chatbotslife.com/9-tips-to-write-the-perfect-chatbot-script-bcb2695a5d0d
6. Correa, J., Viana, D., Teles, A.: Desenvolvendo chatbots com o dialogflow. Sociedade Brasileira de Computação (2021)
7. Garousi, Vahid, Felderer, Michael, Mäntylä, Mika V.., Rainer, Austen: Benefitting from the grey literature in software engineering research. In: Contemporary Empirical Methods in Software Engineering, pp. 385–413. Springer, Cham (2020). https://doi.org/10.1007/978-3-030-32489-6_14

8. Gomes, B.R., Jacob Jr, A.F.L., Pinto, I.d.J.P., Colcher, S.: Ágata: um chatbot para difusão de práticas para educação ambiental. In: Anais Estendidos do XXVI Simpósio Brasileiro de Sistemas Multimídia e Web, pp. 85–89. SBC (2020)
9. Jain, M., Kumar, P., Kota, R., Patel, S.N.: Evaluating and informing the design of chatbots. In: Proceedings of the 2018 Designing Interactive Systems Conference, pp. 895–906 (2018)
10. Kim, M., Seo, B.G., Park, D.H.: Development process for user needs-based chatbot: focusing on design thinking methodology. J. Intell. Inf. Syst. 25(3), 221–238 (2019)
11. Kuligowska, K.: Commercial chatbot: performance evaluation, usability metrics and quality standards of embodied conversational agents. Profess. Center Bus. Res. 2 (2015)
12. Landbot. Chatbot checklist for new makers (2021). https://landbot.io/blog/chatbot-checklist. Accessed 05 Feb 2022
13. Langevin, R., Lordon, R.J., Avrahami, T., Cowan, B.R., Hirsch, T., Hsieh, G.: Heuristic evaluation of conversational agents. In: Proceedings of the 2021 CHI Conference on Human Factors in Computing Systems, pp. 1–15 (2021)
14. Leite, J.C., Zhao, L., Kopcznńska, S., Supakkul, S., Chung, L.: Report from the 6th international workshop on requirements patterns (REPA'16). ACM SIGSOFT Softw. Eng. Notes 42(1), 32–33 (2017)
15. Lokman, A.S., Ameedeen, M.A.: Modern chatbot systems: a technical review. In: Arai, K., Bhatia, R., Kapoor, S. (eds.) FTC 2018. AISC, vol. 881, pp. 1012–1023. Springer, Cham (2019). https://doi.org/10.1007/978-3-030-02683-7_75
16. Magalhães, L.F.G.R.A.d.: Natureza morfológica dos chatbots. Ph.D. thesis, Universidade Católica Portuguesa (2018)
17. Maldonado, J.A.V., Cuadra, J.A.G.: Natural language interface to database using the dialogflow voice recognition and text conversion API. In: 2019 8th International Conference On Software Process Improvement (CIMPS), pp. 1–10. IEEE (2019)
18. Miner, A.S., Laranjo, L., Kocaballi, A.B.: Chatbots in the fight against the covid-19 pandemic. NPJ Dig. Med. 3(1), 1–4 (2020)
19. MobileTime. Panorama mobiletime - mapa do ecossistema brasileiro de bots 2021 (2021)
20. Nielsen, J.: Ten usability heuristics (2005)
21. Radziwill, N.M., Benton, M.C.: Evaluating quality of chatbots and intelligent conversational agents. arXiv preprint arXiv:1704.04579 (2017)
22. Ruggiano, N., Brown, E.L., Roberts, L., Suarez, C.V.F., Luo, Y., Hao, Z., Hristidis, V., et al.: Chatbots to support people with dementia and their caregivers: systematic review of functions and quality. J. Med. Internet Res. 23(6), e25006 (2021)
23. Sansonnet, J.-P., Leray, D., Martin, J.-C.: Architecture of a framework for generic assisting conversational agents. In: Gratch, J., Young, M., Aylett, R., Ballin, D., Olivier, P. (eds.) IVA 2006. LNCS (LNAI), vol. 4133, pp. 145–156. Springer, Heidelberg (2006). https://doi.org/10.1007/11821830_12
24. Sedoc, J., Ippolito, D., Kirubarajan, A., Thirani, J., Ungar, L., Callison-Burch, C.: Chateval: a tool for chatbot evaluation. In: Proceedings of the 2019 Conference of the North American Chapter of the Association for Computational Linguistics (Demonstrations), pp. 60–65 (2019)
25. Silva, K.K.C., Tierno, R.O., Branchine, S.M., Vilaça, D.S.S., Oliveira, F.H.M.: Desenvolvimento de ferramenta de chatbot como soluçao para a comunicaçao do ifb. In: Anais Estendidos do XVII Simpósio Brasileiro de Sistemas de Informação, pp. 185–188. SBC (2021)

26. Sugisaki, K., Bleiker, A.: Usability guidelines and evaluation criteria for conversational user interfaces: a heuristic and linguistic approach. In: Proceedings of the Conference on Mensch und Computer, pp. 309–319 (2020)

27. Take. Chatbot de qualidade: quais são as boas práticas para o contato inteligente (2020). https://www.take.net/blog/. Accessed 05 Feb 2022

28. Toader, D.C., et al.: The effect of social presence and chatbot errors on trust. Sustainability **12**(1), 256 (2020)

29. Van Pinxteren, M.M., Pluymaekers, M., Lemmink, J.G.: Human-like communication in conversational agents: a literature review and research agenda. J. Serv. Manag. (2020)

30. Venkatesh, A., et al.: On evaluating and comparing conversational agents. arXiv preprint arXiv:1801.03625 vol. 4, pp. 60–68 (2018)

31. Weizenbaum, J.: Eliza-a computer program for the study of natural language communication between man and machine. Commun. ACM **9**(1), 36–45 (1966)

32. Weng, F., Yang, R.J., Ho, H.J., Su, H.M.: A tam-based study of the attitude towards use intention of multimedia among school teachers. Appl. Syst. Innov. **1**(3), 36 (2018)

Exploring the Opinions of Experts in Conversational Design: A Study on Users' Mental Models of Voice Assistants

Isabela Motta[✉] and Manuela Quaresma

LEUI | Laboratory of Ergodesign and Usability of Interfaces – Department of Arts and Design, Pontifical Catholic University of Rio de Janeiro, Rio de Janeiro, Brazil
isabelacanellas@tecgraf.puc-rio.br

Abstract. Voice Assistants (VAs) are growing in popularity, but some barriers to these systems' usage and adoption still prevail. Such obstacles may be related to users' mental models, which are unaligned with VAs' actual capabilities. Considering the influence of design aspects on users' perceptions, VA designers have a significant role in designing solutions that improve users' mental models and the quality of interactions. Thus, this study aimed to explore the opinions of professionals experienced in conversational design concerning users' mental models of VAs. Specifically, we aimed to identify the experts' opinions on 1) causes for users' misperceptions of VAs and 2) potential solutions to deal with the issue. To this end, we conducted a three-round questionnaire-based Delphi study with developers and researchers of conversational interfaces. The results showed that design aspects such as VAs' high humanness and the lack of transparency influence users' mental models. Nevertheless, removing VAs' humanness and excessively displaying information about VAs might not be an immediate solution. In turn, designers should assess the context and task domains in which the VA will be used to guide design decisions. Finally, developing teams should have a correct and homogeneous understanding of VAs and possess the necessary knowledge, skills, and tools to employ solutions properly.

Keywords: Voice Assistants · Mental models · Conversational design

1 Introduction

Voice Assistants (VAs) are artificial intelligence (AI)-powered virtual assistants that can perform a range of tasks in a system, which users interact through a voice interface that may be supported by a visual display [1]. As exemplified by Amazon's Alexa, which was able to perform over 70.000 skills in the USA by 2020 [2], available features are rapidly growing in number, ranging from tasks such as weather forecast to home automation. Forecasting indicates that VAs are expected to reach 8.4 billion units by 2024 [3] and that the voice recognition technology market will be worth 30 billion U.S. dollars by 2026 [4].

Despite the projections suggesting growth in VA usage, studies indicate that barriers to the adoption of these systems still prevail. In the first place, surveys have shown that

© The Author(s), under exclusive license to Springer Nature Switzerland AG 2022
M. Kurosu (Ed.): HCII 2022, LNCS 13304, pp. 494–514, 2022.
https://doi.org/10.1007/978-3-031-05412-9_34

users consider VAs as not relevant or not very useful [5], and such perceptions of low usefulness have been reported to negatively impact VA adoption [6]. Additionally, both market and scientific publications have shown that users frequently report facing errors throughout interactions [7, 8], and such technical issues have been related to low satisfaction measures [9]. To recover from failures, users apply strategies that might hamper the interaction's naturality, such as repeating requests, adjusting a command's structure, wording, or information amounts, changing pronunciation, and speaking louder [10, 11]. Finally, users' attitudes towards voice interaction affect VA usage [12]. Particularly, studies have indicated that users are concerned about the privacy of their data, creating negative attitudes towards VAs [6, 13].

While there still exist technological restraints that might partially account for the issues above, the interaction's quality might be influenced by users' mental models of VAs: a type of conceptual model that represents how the system works [14], comprising a set of expectations about its components, functioning, and proper usage [15]. Although these models are essential and dictate performance levels [16], the literature indicates that users' mental models of VAs do not match these systems' actual capabilities, displaying an overall low understanding of VAs' functioning and unrealistic expectations for system features, intelligence, and conversational capabilities [17, 18]. Such misperceptions might be relevant to the before mentioned adoption and usage barriers. For example, in a previous study, we showed that users do not utilize some tasks due to the unawareness of their availability [19], which could account for the belief that VAs have low usefulness. The possible unawareness of available features might also lead to errors since some failures may be caused by requests to perform activities out of the VAs' scope. Moreover, users' difficulty in recovering from failures might be related to their low comprehension of error sources, influential for users' error-handling strategies [11, 20–22]. Likewise, negative attitudes towards VAs and privacy concerns might be caused by the lack of understanding of VAs' functioning, as users are unaware of privacy controls and privacy-related information [23–25].

Considering the issues presented above, aligning users' mental models of VAs with these systems' actual capabilities is paramount for VA adoption, and such a task is highly dependent on the work of VAs' designers. As explained by Norman [14], the designer – based on their own conceptualizations of the product – designs a product's physical structure (e.g., format, materials, affordances, etc.). Since designers and users usually cannot communicate, users are left to rely on such a physical structure (i.e., the system image) to develop their mental models, making design aspects vital to accurate perceptions. Therefore, improving design characteristics that constitute VAs' system image be essential to align users' models. However, to aid such work, VA designers must be aware of the causes affecting users' mental models and assess appropriate solutions to deal with misperceptions.

Hence, this study aimed to explore the opinions of professionals experienced in conversational design concerning users' mental models of VAs. Specifically, we aimed to identify the experts' opinions on 1) causes for users' misperceptions of VAs and 2) potential solutions to deal with the issue. To support the investigation, we conducted a three-round questionnaire-based Delphi study with such professionals. Our main contribution is a set of recommendations to aid conversational designers in aligning users' mental models of VAs and improving interactions.

2   Method

To achieve this study's objective, we conducted a questionnaire-based Delphi study with professionals experienced in conversational design. The Delphi method aims to provide a procedure for a group of people knowledgeable on a subject to reach a consensus of opinions on a topic of interest [26, 27]. Therefore, the Delphi method involves different rounds of anonymized, remote data collection, usually employing questionnaires as tools.

2.1   Participants and Recruitment

In this study, we recruited professionals with experience in researching or developing conversational interfaces since participants must be involved in the matter being studied and have information and knowledge to share [28]. We conducted an unsystematic search on LinkedIn, ResearchGate, and Google Scholar to identify developers with work experience and researchers who had publications in the field of conversational interfaces. We also recruited participants through indications. Hence, we had a combination of snowball sampling and purposive sampling.

The area of conversational interfaces is a relatively new field of work, making it challenging to find professionals who have been working exclusively on projects of this kind for longer periods. Therefore, we did not impose minimum time spam in work experience since even professionals entering the field could contribute. We also considered developers of conversational interfaces other than VAs (e.g., chatbots, voice bots) as such systems share enough similarities with VAs to cause analogs issues on users' perceptions. Finally, we searched for participants from different backgrounds since VA development requires varied profiles of professionals.

After the selection, we invited eligible participants, recruiting the professionals over September and November 2021. Table 1 shows the sample's characteristics.

Table 1.   Participants' profile. (n = 22)

Characteristic	Categories	Number
Years of work experience	Less than a year	2
	Between 1 and 2 years	6
	Between 2 and 3 years	7
	Between 3 and 5 years	3
	For longer than 5 years	4
Field of graduation	Computer science	8
	Communication studies	2
	Information systems	3

(*continued*)

Table 1. (*continued*)

Characteristic	Categories	Number
	Artificial Intelligence	1
	Painting	1
	Design	1
	Informatics	1
	Pharmacy	1
	Marketing	1
	Electronic engineering	1
	Cognitive Science/Psychology	1
Job position	Researcher	13
	Developer	7
	Design lead	1
	Designer	1
	CTO	1
	UX Designer	1
	Professor	4

2.2 Study's Format, Procedure, Materials, and Analysis

The study was structured as a questionnaire in three rounds [27]: 1) initial exploration, 2) identification of consensuses and disagreements, and 3) review and final considerations. Overall, the first round asked participants to freely express their opinions on the mental model matter. Then, we categorized and synthesized the professionals' responses, developing statements to reflect the group's opinions. In the second round, the same participants were asked to rate their agreement level with each statement. In the final round, we exposed the second round's results to the participants, highlighting the group's accordance with which statement. We detail each round below.

Round One. Once the professionals agreed to participate, we sent the link to the first questionnaire and a free and informed consent term. In total, 22 out of the 90 invited professionals agreed to participate and answered the first round.

The first questionnaire was created with the Google Forms platform. Following literature recommendations [28], the questionnaire started with overall instructions about the study's first phase. Then, it presented the issue to be discussed: users' mental models of VAs. The passage exposed a definition of mental models to align all participants' understanding of the concept and presented the issue of users' unaligned mental models of VAs. Thereafter, we posed two open-ended questions:

1. In your opinion, what are the **causes** that lead users to form mental models that are unaligned with Voice Assistants' real capabilities? Please, state at least three causes and, for each one, explain why it is relevant.
2. In your opinion, what **solutions** could solve the issue of users' incorrect mental models of Voice Assistants? Please, present at least three solutions and, for each one, explain why it is appropriate.

Finally, we provided an open field for optional comments and asked questions about social-demographic data.

Round One's Analysis: We conducted a five-step thematic analysis using an affinity diagram [29], following literature suggestions [28] (Table 2):

Table 2. Steps followed in round one's analysis.

Step	Description
1	We transposed all the participants' responses into two tables (one for each question). Since we asked the participants to provide at least three topics for each question, we separated each topic into different cells
2	For each topic, we identified its general theme and attributed a representative code
3	After coding each topic, we reviewed all of the codes to identify similarities among them, and, from this process, we created categories
4	We pasted all responses to a digital board, placing them according to the major categories and, then, elaborated the affinity diagram using a bottom-up approach to find emerging topics and similar contents among the responses
5	From the emerging topics identified in the previous step, we created the statements for round two. These phrases were validated and refined through expert review

Round Two. In the second round, we sent the second questionnaire's link along with instructions and a 15-day deadline through email to all participants. A total of 18 participants completed the second questionnaire.

The second questionnaire –created on the Eval&Go platform – aimed to enable participants to judge the group's opinions provided on the first round. Firstly, the questionnaire presented instructions for the second round, and participants could revisit the study's problematization. Then, we presented the statements summarizing the group's responses to the first round and asked the professionals to provide their agreement level with each phrase on a 7-point Likert scale. We also provided open fields for optional comments. The questionnaire presented 35 statements, divided into two parts: 16 statements representing the causes that lead to misalignments in users' mental models of VAs and 19 phrases describing solutions to deal with the issue.

Round Two's Analysis: The second questionnaire required both quantitative and qualitative analysis due to the nature of the data collected. As for determining consensuses, since we had participants answer a 7-point Likert scale for this study, we adhered to Fish and Busby's [26] recommendation of using the Interquartile Range (IQR). Nevertheless, as indicated by Giannarou and Zervas [30], many studies have used a combination of the IQR with supplementary metrics. Thus, after tabulating the data, we used the software Excel to calculate the sample's: 1) mean, 2) median, 3) IQR, and 4) percentages of agreement, neutrality, and disagreement. The latter represented the percentage of respondents who tended to agree, disagree, or stay neutral towards a statement. To determine the statements that have reached a consensus among the group, we established two criteria:

1) An IQR of 1 or lower [26]
2) A percentage of agreement, neutrality, or disagreement of 75% or higher. We determined the threshold of 75% since the literature has pointed that 70% to 80% thresholds are common for indicating consensus in Delphi studies [30].

We determined that statements that met both criteria have reached a strong consensus among the group. However, we also considered that statements that met only one of the criteria had reached a mild consensus.

As for the qualitative data analysis, we performed a top-down thematic analysis. We transposed the responses to a digital board according to their corresponding statements and we identified similarities to determine emerging topics of interest.

Round Three. Finally, the last round reported the second round's results, providing fields for optional comments. The round gave the experts the opportunity to review their judgments after viewing the group's opinion and conved the feeling of closure [28]. However, only 5 participants filled the form, and only 2 left comments.

3   Results

In this section, we will present round's one and two results (round three will not be addressed due to its low response rate). In each subsection, we show the categories derived from round one's results, alongside the summarizing statements. For statements that reached a strong consensus (highlighted in green) or mild consensus (highlighted in orange), we also display the metrics reflecting round two's results.

3.1   Causes for Issues in Users' Mental Models

From the 68 responses provided for round one's first question, we identified twelve categories of factors mentioned by the participants to influence users' mental models, from which 16 statements were created. Overall, five phrases led to a strong consensus, four led to a mild consensus, and seven did not provoke any consensus.

Category 1 - Users' Limited Understanding of Technology. The category comprised responses that highlighted the influence of low comprehension of the technology on users' mental models. A theme observed in this category was that people who face hardships dealing with technology in general, specifically AI-powered systems, are not used to VAs and may have trouble interacting. Some participants specifically mentioned users' lack of understanding of VAs' speech recognition limits and awareness of a social context. Likewise, the professionals also mentioned that such a lack of knowledge leads to frustrating user-VA interactions. Table 3 shows that the statement representing this category only reached a mild consensus.

Table 3. Group's evaluation of the statement for category 1.

Statement	Mean	Med	IQR	%A	%N	%D
Users do not know the Voice Assistants and the Artificial Intelligence technical limitations and require the Assistant to perform tasks and recognize commands beyond its capabilities	6,17	6,5	1,75	94%	6%	0%

Category 2 - Users' Previous Experiences with Voice Interfaces. Only one professional mentioned this category. We rephrased their comment and, as exposed in Table 4, the affirmation was a consensus among the group. One professional posed that such a phrase would only be true for real-life interfaces, not mediatic representations.

Table 4. Group's evaluation of the statement for category 2.

Statement	Mean	Med	IQR	%A	%N	%D
Bad previous experiences with other voice interfaces create negative expectations for the Voice Assistants on users	6,22	6	1	100%	0%	0%

Category 3 - Users' Learning Practices. Mentioned by three participants, the category revolved around users' lack of dedication and interest in learning about the VA before purchasing or starting using it. One participant also mentioned that such a lack of interest in learning might originate from users' perceptions of low usefulness for VAs. From this category, we created one statement: "*Users do not look for information about the Voice Assistant before buying it, especially for tasks that are deemed unnecessary.*" The group did not reach a consensus for this statement in round two, and two participants opposed the phrase by arguing that it would not make sense to read about skills considered unnecessary, and not reading manuals is standard user behavior for any product. Both professionals also considered that the statement unfairly blames users for issues with VAs rather than the product's design.

Category 4 - Users' Privacy Concerns. In summary, two professionals argued that users are afraid to interact due to concerns about how the VA will manage their data or that others could hear their interactions, impeding them from constructing a solid mental model. To represent this category, we developed one statement: *"Privacy concerns hinder users from interacting with the Assistants for long enough to construct correct mental models."* Nevertheless, despite a slight tendency to disagree with the statement (median = 3), the group's opinions were split, not reaching any level of consensus. Three experts commented that, while people with strong privacy concerns simply avoid using VAs, such concerns are not significant for how users interact.

Category 5 - Users' Expectations for Human-Like Conversations. Cited by six professionals, the category exposed how the use of speech in VAs leads users to expect sophisticated and natural conversations. Generally, the responses mentioned that: 1) people are used to talking to other humans; 2) users have high expectations for VAs' conversational capabilities since they compare VAs and humans; or 3) VAs' actual conversational capabilities do not match those of humans, causing frustration. As displayed in Table 5, this category's statement led the group to accord strongly.

Table 5. Group's evaluation of the statement for category 5.

Statement	Mean	Med	IQR	%A	%N	%D
Users construct their mental models of conversations through human interactions, but Voice Assistants have lower conversational skills, letting down expectations and causing frustration	6,11	6	1	89%	11%	0%

Category 6 - VAs' Anthropomorphic Features. VAs' anthropomorphic features were mentioned as an impacting factor by eight participants. The professionals argued that anthropomorphism might lead users to believe that VAs are more capable than reality, suggesting human-level skills. The participants also included a set of humanizing characteristics: voice, name, gender, metaphors, and humorist prompts. We combined both topics into a statement (Table 6), which caused a strong consensus.

Table 6. Group's evaluation of the statement for category 6.

Statement	Mean	Med	IQR	%A	%N	%D
Characteristics that induce anthropomorphism (e.g., voice, name, gender, metaphors, humor) cause users to expect Voice Assistants would be as capable as a human	5,61	6	1	89%	6%	6%

Category 7 – VAs' Transparency. Four topics emerged from this category. Firstly, we identified comments arguing that VAs generally present little information about their functioning and utilization, such as available features, ways of usage, command processing, decision-making, and error-recovery mechanisms. Furthermore, some professionals pointed out that VAs do not explain their limitations for specific tasks or actions to users, lacking clarifications on the differences between actions and their requirements. Another matter explained by one participant was the lack of transparency in VAs' updates since VAs do not notify nor explain updates to users. For this category's last topic, some experts argued that VAs do not present instructions during initial interactions, affecting users' understanding and expectations.

This category's synthesis resulted in four statements (Table 7), among which two led the group to mildly accord and two did not provoke any consensus. These phrases were: *"Voice Assistants do not tell users when they update, nor explain the updates in their skills."* and *"Voice Assistants do not present initial instructions to users, leaving them without knowing what to expect from the product."* The group left comments that revolved around the need to present some pieces of information with questionable relevance for users. "Updates in skills" and "processing of commands" were cited as examples of unimportant information. Moreover, one expert argued that providing detailed information could jeopardize the experience and complicate the VA.

Table 7. Group's evaluation of the statement for category 7.

Statement	Mean	Med	IQR	%A	%N	%D
Voice Assistants do not explain to users about their skills, how they should be utilized, how they process commands, how they make decisions, or how to recover from failures	5,72	6	2	89%	6%	6%
Voice Assistants do not explain their limitations for certain actions, such as recognizing the conversational context	5,61	6	2	83%	6%	11%

Category 8 – VAs' High Complexity. This category encompassed a single response. We rewrote the comment to create a statement representing this category (Table 8), which was the only affirmation that caused a consensus of disagreement on the group. That is, it was unanimous that a high level of complexity in VAs does not lead to issues in users' understandings. Through comments, one professional highlighted that VAs are not complex nor require too much cognitive load. However, another participant argued that VAs complexity could be an issue for novice users.

Table 8. Group's evaluation of the statement for category 8.

Statement	Mean	Med	IQR	%A	%N	%D
Voice Assistants are too complex and demand too much of the users' cognition	2,67	2	1	11%	11%	78%

Category 9 – Differences Between VAs. Only one answer fell into this category. By rephrasing the response, we created one statement: *"Voice Assistants from different brands have different skills, leading to the belief that an Assistant might have the same skills as the others."* The group did not accord with the affirmation in round two, and only one professional commented that the brand distinction is clear, but the similarity in VAs' humanization might be more nuanced.

Category 10 – Unrealistic Marketing. This category, mentioned by eight participants, comprised two emerging topics. The first topic reflects that VAs' developing companies do not present enough content to explain how conversational interfaces and AI works. This theme resulted in the phrase: *"Brands present little institutional content about the Assistants and Artificial Intelligence, leading users to buy the product without being aware of its capabilities."* In round two, however, the cause was not unanimously agreed upon. On this phrase, one professional explained that users might receive VAs as gifts and, thus, have no previous awareness of their functioning.

The second emerging topic was the unrealistic nature of VAs' marketing. The professionals argued that companies usually advertise the system by choosing simple and flawless use cases. Such marketing also tends to overplay the VAs' intelligence and capacity. The resulting statement (Table 9) provoked a mild consensus on the group.

Table 9. Group's evaluation of the statement for category 10.

Statement	Mean	Med	IQR	%A	%N	%D
Marketing raises users' expectations by exaggerating the Voice Assistant's social skills and intelligence, showing use cases that are too simple and fluid	5,78	6	1,75	78%	17%	6%

Category 11 – Influences from Science Fiction. Overall, the responses of five participants reported that science-fiction media picture AI systems as highly intelligent and capable of features that current VAs do not match, influencing users' expectations. The experts strongly accorded with this category's resulting statement (Table 10).

Table 10. Group's evaluation of the statement for category 11.

Statement	Mean	Med	IQR	%A	%N	%D
In Science Fiction, systems powered with Artificial Intelligence are pictured as futuristic, intelligent, sensitive, talkative, and capable, creating unaligned perceptions about current Assistants	6,22	6,5	1	89%	11%	0%

Category 12 – Lack of User Research. Finally, the last impacting factor for users' models was the lack of user research conducted by developers. Only one participant approached this theme, arguing that user research is paramount for user experience. We rewrote the response as a phrase: *"Developers conduct little research about user experience, which is paramount to creating conversational flows."* Nonetheless, the phrase was the closest to neutrality (median = 4,5), dividing the group. In their comments, two participants reported that conversational design is a new area, still lacking tools or skilled professionals to deal with user experience appropriately.

3.2 Solutions to Deal with Misalignments in Users' Mental Models

The group provided 59 answers to round one's second question, resulting in twelve categories of potential solutions to be applied to VAs, synthetized in 19 statements. In total, eight affirmations caused a strong consensus, eight caused a mild consensus, and only three did not led to any consensus.

Category 13 – Changes in Users' Behavior. Seven professionals provided comments suggesting that users should change their behavior to align their mental models. Some participants argued that users should look for information on VAs to improve the interactions' quality. The summarizing phrase of this emerging theme (*"users should inform themselves better about the Assistants before utilizing them; e.g., read official and unofficial content about the product"*) did not lead the group to any consensus.

Additionally, two professionals suggested that users should be trained on how to interact with VAs. This proposal resulted in the first statement in Table 11, which with the participants collectively tended to stay neutral (median = 4). Four participants argued that users usually do not read manuals or instructions and that such a solution could diminish the naturality of user-VA interactions. Rather, information should be provided subtly throughout interactions. Moreover, one expert mentioned another theme, arguing that, similar to other technology, people will learn how to use VAs over time, not requiring any interventions. This solution reached a mild consensus of disagreements, an expected result since the group acknowledged many impactful factors for issues in users' perceptions, which might require actions to be dealt with.

Table 11. Group's evaluation of the statement for category 13.

Statement	Mean	Med	IQR	%A	%N	%D
Users should receive training on how to use Voice Assistants, including supported language patterns	4,00	4	1	33%	44%	22%
No solution should be applied to Voice Assistants since users will naturally learn how to interact	2,72	2,5	1,75	17%	6%	78%

Category 14 – Increase VAs' Transparency. The first theme that emerged from responses in this category was the need for explicit explanations from the VA about how it functions and how broad its scope is. Likewise, some professionals proposed that these explanations should be embedded throughout interactions to guide the users to a more solid understanding of the system. The category was synthesized into two phrases (Table 12), but despite being the most mentioned category in round one, both affirmations only reached a mild consensus. Such a tendency may be due to the group's concern that presenting too much information for users (e.g., tips) could make interactions slow and boring, as commented by a professional in round two.

Table 12. Group's evaluation of the statement for category 14.

Statement	Mean	Med	IQR	%A	%N	%D
Voice Assistants should provide examples and explanations about their skills' scope and action execution, decision making, and learning processes	6,06	6,5	2	94%	6%	0%
Voice Assistants should present usage tips throughout interactions, including mechanisms to clarify the conversation context	6,00	6,5	1,75	89%	6%	6%

Category 15 - Highlight User-VA Collaboration. The two responses in this category argued that VAs could learn from users, improving the VA generally and aligning it with the users' preferences. A phrase was developed (*"the Voice Assistant should clarify the importance of the collaboration between user and system, allowing users to teach content to the Assistant."*), but no consensus was reached.

Category 16 – Improve Error-Handling Mechanisms. This category resulted in two themes that proposed different channels to present error-handling mechanisms. One participant proposed creating an independent interface for users to review failures and understand the problems' sources and out-of-scope commands. Oppositely, other professionals argued that error-recovery strategies should be embedded in interactions. The prior solution provoked a mild consensus, while the latter was strongly agreed upon by the group (Table 13). Comments on this category explained that users would not utilize an error-visualization platform and, as previously exposed in category 13, such proposal places the responsibility of change on users rather than the VA.

Table 13. Group's evaluation of the statement for category 16.

Statement	Mean	Med	IQR	%A	%N	%D
There should be a platform that shows failed past interactions to help users understand the reasons for errors and the system's scope	5,50	5,5	2	78%	17%	6%
Developers should create error recovery mechanisms (ex: inform what was misunderstood and how to reformulate the command)	6,44	7	1	94%	6%	0%

Category 17 – Mitigate VAs' Anthropomorphism. We identified two solutions in this category's comments, which were transformed into statements: 1) remove or diminish features such as voice, name, gender, and metaphors to mitigate anthropomorphism, and 2) clarify to users that the VA is not a human (Table 14). Interestingly, although VAs' anthropomorphism was unanimously considered a strong cause for users' misperceptions, removing humanizing characteristics divided the group, not even reaching a mild consensus (statement: *"Developers should avoid characteristics that humanize the Voice Assistant; e.g., name, gender, natural voice, metaphors"*). Whereas some experts argued that human-like VAs are more approachable, and it might be too late to abolish anthropomorphism, others argued that highly humanized VAs might not be beneficial or safe for some tasks.

Table 14. Group's evaluation of the statement for category 17.

Statement	Mean	Med	IQR	%A	%N	%D
Voice Assistants should make it clear for users that they are talking to a machine and not a human	5,56	6,5	2	78%	11%	11%

Category 18 - Offer Supplementary Content and Tutorials. A group of experts suggested that users' initial interactions should be supported by tutorials and instructions to aid users' learning. Similarly, two participants argued that developers and companies should offer content explaining how the technology works – specifically AI. From these themes, two phrases were created (Table 15). In round two's comments, some participants expressed concerns about presenting too much information to users.

Table 15. Group's evaluation of the statement for category 18.

Statement	Mean	Med	IQR	%A	%N	%D
Voice Assistants should present initial instructions, tutorials, and information about new supported actions and new ways to formulate commands	6,00	6,5	1	83%	6%	11%
Manufacturers and professionals from the Artificial Intelligence field should offer information about such technology to the population in an accessible manner (e.g., institutional material)	5,72	6	2	78%	17%	6%

Category 19 – Handle Privacy Concerns. In this category, the participants argued that privacy concerns might hamper other solutions, being necessary to clarify how users' data are handled. The resulting statement (Table 16) led to a mild consensus.

Table 16. Group's evaluation of the statement for category 19.

Statement	Mean	Med	IQR	%A	%N	%D
The Voice Assistant should explain to users about the privacy of their data to help them decide which tasks to perform	5,67	6	2	78%	17%	6%

Category 20 - Change Marketing Strategies. In line with the findings of the previous section, showing that VAs' marketing is considered unrealistic, the professionals reported that VAs' advertisements should present to these system's true capacities. Table 17 shows this category's phrase, which provoked a strong consensus.

Table 17. Group's evaluation of the statement for category 20.

Statement	Mean	Med	IQR	%A	%N	%D
Marketing on Voice Assistants should stick to these systems' actual capabilities, presenting common and realistic use cases	6,28	6	1	100%	0%	0%

Category 21 – Improve the Developers' Skills. This category derived from a professionals' comment who explained that properly designing the conversational flow is key to improving VAs, but conversational designers are not always aware of technical limitations. The group strongly accorded with the proposal (Table 18), and one expert extended the recommendation for developers of error-handling mechanisms.

Table 18. Group's evaluation of the statement for category 21.

Statement	Mean	Med	IQR	%A	%N	%D
Developers of conversational flows should receive training on the Assistans' technical limitations so they can produce appropriate flows	6,11	7	1	83%	11%	6%

Category 22 – Conduct Research and Understand Usage Contexts.

Six experts answered that developers should understand the users and their contexts when designing solutions. Such comprehension included users' objectives, characteristics, interactional behavior, and mental models. Expressly, some experts also indicated the need to research human-human communication practices to adapt user-VA interactions. For each of these topics, a statement was created (Table 19), and the group strongly agreed upon both solutions. On round two's comments, however, a participant mentioned that VAs already count on qualified professionals from the linguistics or natural language processing (NLP) fields to study human communication. Another participant also argued that command-based interactions might be beneficial in some cases.

Table 19. Group's evaluation of the statement for category 22.

Statement	Mean	Med	IQR	%A	%N	%D
Developers should understand users (e.g., profiles, goals, contexts, behavior, semantics, mental models) to create solutions that address their needs and context	6,33	7	1	94%	6%	0%
Developers should research mechanisms in human conversations and adapt them to interactions with Voice Assistants	6,11	6	1	94%	6%	0%

Category 23 – Apply Best Practices.

Applying best practices of usability and conversational design was another category focused on the developers' work. Although this category's resulting phrase (Table 20) led to a strong consensus, it was commented that due to VAs' novelty, it might be necessary to evaluate the existing best practices' suitability to VAs' scenario. If necessary, new best practices should be created.

Table 20. Group's evaluation of the statement for category 23.

Statement	Mean	Med	IQR	%A	%N	%D
Developers should always apply best practices of usability and voice interaction when designing Voice Assistants	6,28	7	1	89%	11%	0%

Category 24 – Improve Speech Recognition. Finally, three participants suggested that improving speech recognition would aid users in improving their mental models. Responses from this category seemed to propose dealing with users' misperceptions by improving the VA to meet their expectations. The synthesis of this category (Table 21) was unanimously accorded by the group.

Table 21. Group's evaluation of the statement for category 24.

Statement	Mean	Med	IQR	%A	%N	%D
Developers should improve speech recognition technology (e.g., synonyms, intents, words in other languages, accents, localization, and different voice types and users)	6,11	6,5	1	89%	0%	11%

4 Discussion

This paper aimed to explore the opinions of professionals experienced in conversational design concerning users' mental models of VAs. This section discusses the results of both Delphi's rounds in light of the literature.

In the first place, the most controversial subject was the influence of VAs' anthropomorphic characteristics on users' perceptions and how to manage such features. Similar to literature findings [17, 18, 24], the participants pointed to names, natural voices, metaphors, gender, and a humoristic conversational style as aspects that induce humanness. There was a general agreement that VAs' humanness leads users to expect human-level skills, including conversational capabilities. As a consequence, the experts reported that users frequently hoped to interact with VAs in a human-like manner, applying conversational styles that are not supported by the interface.

Despite the professionals' general agreement on the influence of VAs' humanness on users' misperceptions, the group was divided on the adequacy of removing these features. On the one hand, some professionals argued that humanizing the VAs makes interactions more natural for users. They indicated that the aspect contributes to VAs' image and popularity, which reinforce literature findings showing that VAs' humanness is related to user satisfaction [9] and is a driver for adoption [31, 32]. On the other hand, experts who disagreed with humanizing VAs argued that more straightforward interactions might lead to fewer errors and support task performance. Such opinions echo literature suggestions to reduce VAs' humanness [18].

VA transparency levels was another broadly discussed theme caused friction of opinions. In the first round, several transparency-related factors were linked to users' misunderstandings about VAs. Notably, various participants reported that the system fails to present relevant information for users' mental models, including available features, ways of usage, technical functioning (i.e., command processing and decision making), and initial instructions to support learning, explanations on error sources and recovery paths, and clarifications on system updates.

Nonetheless, the second round's results suggest that while transparency is a general issue to users' perceptions, the group could not agree on what information specifically is relevant for users' mental models. Concerning the causes, the professionals did not reach a strong consensus on any transparency-related statements, and some expert argued that information such as "limitations for certain actions", "command processing", and "updates in skills" are not relevant. Likewise, while the group could strongly agree on the relevance of initial instructions and error-handling mechanisms, other solutions were not unanimous (e.g., embedding usage tips in interactions, training users, presenting examples and explanations on VAs' scope, and creating an error-visualization platform). In line with previous studies [21, 33], the group expressed concerns that interactions could become slow, unnatural, tedious, or that users would not want to consult supplementary content. Therefore, the professionals' divergent opinions on what to present to users were probably driven by uncertainty on which information is truly relevant and the threshold between too little or excessive content.

According to the results, to determine appropriate levels of humanness and transparency, it is essential to consider the users' context. The group reached a strong consensus that designers should understand users (i.e., profiles, goals, contexts, behavior, semantics, etc.) and tailor solutions to address their needs, rather than expecting users to change their behavior spontaneously. The professionals mentioned that attributing issues in users' mental models to their lack of interest in learning about VAs puts the blame on users. Echoing literature on interaction design [34], some experts judged such a view inappropriate since the product and its developers are to blame for any misperceptions. Solutions such as offering users supplementary content and training were also considered a shift in responsibility.

Considering the proposition above, it might also be necessary to account for contextual factors such as the VAs' operational domain and task types, users' characteristics, and other cultural factors. VA tasks have been shown to differ in usability and complexity [19], and thus information amounts to be presented may be established according to task complexity. Complex tasks might require more transparency and explicability than simple activities (e.g., investment skills *versus* music players). Moreover, users' characteristics such as age, technical background, and experience with VAs might dictate humanness and transparency levels. For example, children might attribute more value to humanized agents [32] when compared to adults, and novice users might need more guidance to interact than experienced users [35]. Additionally, as unanimously accorded by the group, cultural factors such as of science fiction media might be relevant for users' mental models and should be considered.

To correctly evaluate and apply adequate solutions, the developing team's qualification was considered paramount by the experts. The professionals mentioned that developers should possess the necessary knowledge and skills to design interactions. Applying usability and voice interaction best practices were considered essential, and the professionals strongly agreed that researching human linguistic practices and adapting interactions is an adequate solution to deal with users' misperceptions.

However, literature reports put doubt on whether such standards are being met in the industry. Souza and Quaresma [36] reviewed market reports and observed that a significant share of UX Designers has no graduate degree in Design or related areas and are often self-taught. Similarly, agile methods – frequently used in the technology industry – have been demonstrated to only partially support important User-Centered Design (UCD) guidelines, which are frequently deferred in favor of deadlines [37].

Another challenge mentioned by some professionals was related to VAs' novelty, which could require unexplored skills to design interactions. As a participant proposed, it might be necessary to assess the suitability of existing best practices and make adaptations when needed. Such a tendency may also apply to development and evaluations tools, as indicated by studies showing that tools initially developed to assess graphic interfaces are not suitable for evaluating voice interactions [38]. Furthermore, VAs' novelty might be challenging for developers to understand the technology's functioning and limitations. The participants' previously mentioned difficulty in determining which information to display for users might indicate this hypothesis, which is strengthened by the group's consensus on the need to train designers of conversational flows on VAs' technical aspects.

Finally, conversational agents such as VAs are complex systems, usually put together by large development teams who might possess incongruent mental models. The results of this study, which gathered varied professionals, reinforce this possibility. In the second round, the group accorded and tended to have more assertive evaluations for solutions than for causes of users' misperceptions (i.e., more extreme mean and median values), reaching a strong consensus for only five causes. Moreover, although the solutions on which the group strongly accorded are valuable, we did not identify a strong cause-solution parallelism. That is, among the eight solution-type statements reaching strong accordance, none seem to directly tackle the five cause-type phrases that also led to a strong consensus. Consistently, aside from the need for error-handling mechanisms, all solutions leading to strong consensus seemed to suggest generic actions, such as improving speech recognition technologies, applying usability best practices, and improving the developers' skills.

The lower accordance on influential issues, the lack of cause-solution parallelism, and the solutions' generic nature reinforce the possibility that a diverse group of professionals might have had divergent views. Such variations in the VA developers' views could bring both benefit and harm. On the one hand, the professionals' views should be carefully assembled so the team can accord on which issues to address and how to solve them. As Ackoff (1974 apud [39]) argues, designers should be more attentive in selecting the wrong problem rather than the wrong solution to the right problem, but this study's group had a lower tendency in agreeing on the causes to users' misperceptions than to paths to solutions. At the same time, incongruent points of view may result in identifying a higher number of trouble sources and numerous proposals to solve them, as observed in the first round. As discussed, such proposals are highly valuable for designing VAs' that induce correct mental models on users.

5   Conclusion

Voice Assistants (VAs) bring several benefits to users and are increasingly popular, but some barriers to these systems' usage and adoption still prevail. Such obstacles may be related to users' mental models, which are unaligned with these systems' actual capabilities. Considering the influence of design aspects on users' perceptions, VA designers have a significant role in designing solutions that improve users' mental models and the quality of interactions. Thus, this study aimed to explore the opinions of professionals experienced in conversational design concerning users' mental models of VAs. To this end, we conducted a three-round questionnaire-based Delphi study with developers and researchers of conversational interfaces.

This study's findings can be translated into a few recommendations for VA design. Firstly, developers should consider VAs' usage context when designing solutions, including users' profile, interests, and goals, VAs' usage domains and task characteristics. Secondly, developers should adequate VAs' levels of humanness and transparency based on the usage context, granting that these features will not hamper the interaction's usability or create obstacles for task performance. In addition, developers must possess the required skills to design VAs and search for new knowledge and adapt development and evaluation tools when needed. These professionals should also search for information to adequately understand VAs' functioning and limitations. Finally, new methodologies and processes might be beneficial to VA development, aiding the teams' communication and supporting a more homogeneous understanding of the VAs' project at hand. Such a solution might lead to the better identification of issues and problem solving, possibly inducing improvements in the system image.

This study had a few limitations. We only conducted three rounds, and we did not allow the participants to review their quantitative evaluations of the statements. Adding subsequent questionnaires until more statements reached a consensus could have strengthened the study's findings, but such an attempt might have failed considering the low response rate in round three. Moreover, we could have added different question types in the second round (e.g., ranking, scoring), although such a design could make the questionnaire too long, endangering the response rate.

Acknowledgements. This study was financed in part by FAPERJ and the Coordenação de Aperfeiçoamento de Pessoal de Nível Superior - Brasil (CAPES) - Finance Code 001.

References

1. West, M., Kraut, R., Han Ei, C.: I'd blush if I could (2019). https://unesdoc.unesco.org/ark:/48223/pf0000367416.page=1. Accessed 29 Apr 2019
2. Statista. Total number of Amazon Alexa skills in selected countries as of January 2020 (2020). https://www.statista.com/statistics/917900/selected-countries-amazon-alexa-skill-count/. Accessed 2 Nov 2021
3. Vailshery, L.S.: Number of digital voice assistants in use worldwide from 2019 to 2024 (in billions) (2021). https://www.statista.com/statistics/973815/worldwide-digital-voice-assistant-in-use/. Accessed 2 Jan 2022

4. Vailshery, L.S.: Voice technology - Statistics & Facts (2022). https://www.statista.com/top ics/6760/voice-technology/#dossierKeyfigures. Accessed 2 Jan 2022

5. Robart, A.: Looking Ahead to the Voice Era (2017). https://www.comscore.com/Insights/Pre sentations-and-Whitepapers/2017/Looking-Ahead-to-the-Voice-Era. Accessed 29 Apr 2019

6. McLean, G., Osei-Frimpong, K.: Hey Alexa … examine the variables influencing the use of artificial intelligent in-home voice assistants. Comput. Human Behav. **99**, 28–37 (2019). https://doi.org/10.1016/j.chb.2019.05.009

7. White-Smith, H., Cunha, S., Koray, E., Keating, P.: Technology Tracker - Q1 2019 (2019). https://www.ipsos.com/sites/default/files/ct/publication/documents/2019-03/ techtracker_report_q12019_final_1.pdf. Accessed 29 Apr 2019

8. Maués, M.P.: Marcela Pedroso Maués Um olhar sobre os assistentes virtuais personificados e a voz como interface. Pontifical Catholic University of Rio de Janeiro (2019)

9. Purington, A., Taft, J.G., Sannon, S., et al.: "Alexa is my new BFF": Social roles, user satis-faction, and personification of the Amazon Echo. Conf. Hum. Factors Comput. Syst. – Proc. Part F **1276**, 2853–2859 (2017). https://doi.org/10.1145/3027063.3053246

10. Beneteau, E., Richards, O.K., Zhang, M., et al.: Communication breakdowns between families and Alexa. In: Proceedings of the 2019 CHI Conference on Human Factors in Computing Systems, pp. 1–13. Association for Computing Machinery, New York (2019)

11. Porcheron, M., Fischer, J.E., Reeves, S., Sharples, S.: Voice interfaces in everyday life. In: Proceedings of the 2018 CHI Conference on Human Factors in Computing Systems, pp. 1–12. ACM, New York (2018)

12. Moriuchi, E.: Okay, Google!: An empirical study on voice assistants on consumer engagement and loyalty. Psychol. Mark. **36**, 489–501 (2019). https://doi.org/10.1002/mar.21192

13. Burbach, L., Halbach, P., Plettenberg, N., et al.: "Hey, Siri", "Ok, Google", "Alexa". Acceptance-relevant factors of virtual voice-assistants. In: 2019 IEEE International Profes-sional Communication Conference (ProComm), pp. 101–111. IEEE (2019)

14. Norman, D.: The Design of Everyday Things, Revised an. Basic books, New York (2013)

15. Moreno, A., Mossio, M.: Cognition. In: Biological Autonomy. HPTLS, vol. 12, pp. 167–193. Springer, Dordrecht (2015). https://doi.org/10.1007/978-94-017-9837-2_7

16. Wilson, J.R., Rutherford, A.: Mental models: theory and application in human factors. Hum. Factors **31**, 617–634 (1989). https://doi.org/10.1177/001872088903100601

17. Cho, M., Lee, S., Lee, K.-P.: Once a kind friend is now a thing. In: Proceedings of the 2019 on Designing Interactive Systems Conference, pp. 1557–1569. ACM, New York (2019)

18. Luger, E., Sellen, A.: "Like Having a Really Bad PA": the gulf between user expectation and experience of conversational agents. In: Proceedings of the 2016 CHI Conference on Human Factors in Computing Systems, pp. 5286–5297. Association for Computing Machinery, New York (2016)

19. Motta, I., Quaresma, M.: Understanding task differences to leverage the usability and adoption of voice assistants (VAs). In: Soares, M.M., Rosenzweig, E., Marcus, A. (eds.) HCII 2021. LNCS, vol. 12781, pp. 483–502. Springer, Cham (2021). https://doi.org/10.1007/978-3-030-78227-6_35

20. Myers, C., Furqan, A., Nebolsky, J., et al.: Patterns for how users overcome obstacles in voice user interfaces, pp. 1–7. In: Conference on Human Factors in Computing Systems - Proceedings (2018)

21. Motta, I., Quaresma, M.: Users' error recovery strategies in the interaction with voice assis-tants (VAs). In: Black, N.L., Neumann, W.P., Noy, I. (eds.) IEA 2021. LNNS, vol. 223, pp. 658–666. Springer, Cham (2022). https://doi.org/10.1007/978-3-030-74614-8_82

22. Kim, J., Jeong, M., Lee, S.C.: "Why did this voice agent not understand me?" In: Proceedings of the 11th International Conference on Automotive User Interfaces and Interactive Vehicular Applications: Adjunct Proceedings, pp. 146–150. ACM, New York (2019)

23. Ammari, T., Kaye, J., Tsai, J.Y., Bentley, F.: Music, search, and IoT: how people (really) use voice assistants. ACM Trans. Comput. Interact. (2019). https://doi.org/10.1145/3311956
24. Cowan, B.R., Pantidi, N., Coyle, D., et al.: "What can i help you with?" In: Proceedings of the 19th International Conference on Human-Computer Interaction with Mobile Devices and Services, pp. 1–12. ACM, New York (2017)
25. Javed, Y., Sethi, S., Jadoun, A.: Alexa's voice recording behavior. In: Proceedings of the 14th International Conference on Availability, Reliability and Security, pp. 1–10. ACM, New York (2019)
26. Fish, L.S., Busby, D.M.: The Delphi method. In: Sprenkle, D.H., Piercy, F.P. (eds.) Research Methods in Family Therapy, 2nd edn, pp. 238–253. Guilford Publications (2005)
27. Linstone, H., Turrof, M.: The Delphi Method: Techniques and Applications. Addison-Wesley (1975)
28. Delbecq, A.L., Van de Ven, A.H., Gustafson, D.H.: Group Techniques for Program Planning: A Guide to Nominal Group and Delphi Processes. Scott, Foresman and Company, Glenview (1975)
29. Barnum, C.: Usability Testing Essentials. Ready, Set... Elsevier, Burlington (2011)
30. Giannarou, L., Zervas, E.: Using Delphi technique to build consensus in practice. Int. J. Bus. Sci. Appl. Manag. 9, 65–82 (2014)
31. Balasuriya, S.S., Sitbon, L., Bayor, A.A., et al.: Use of voice activated interfaces by people with intellectual disability. In: Proceedings of the 30th Australian Conference on Computer-Human Interaction, pp. 102–112. ACM, New York (2018)
32. Garg, R., Sengupta, S.: He is just like me. Proc. ACM Interact. Mobile Wearab. Ubiquit. Technol. 4, 1–24 (2020). https://doi.org/10.1145/3381002
33. Kirschthaler, P., Porcheron, M., Fischer, J.E.: What can i say?: Effects of discoverability in VUIs on task performance and user experience. In: ACM International Conference Proceeding Series (2020)
34. Hackos, J.T., Redish, J.: User and Task Analysis for Interface Design. Wiley, Toronto (1998)
35. Chen, M.-L., Wang, H.-C.: How personal experience and technical knowledge affect using conversational agents. In: Proceedings of the 23rd International Conference on Intelligent User Interfaces Companion, pp. 1–2. ACM, New York (2018)
36. Souza, B., Quaresma, M.: O perfil do UX designer: um panorama da visão do mercado de trabalho. In: Blucher Design Proceedings, p. 6121. Editora Blucher, São Paulo (2019). https://doi.org/10.5151/ped2018-7.1_AIC_03
37. Da Costa Brito, L., Quaresma, M.M.R.: O design centrado no usuário nas metodologias ágeis. In: Blucher Design Proceedings, pp. 125–139. Editora Blucher, São Paulo (2019)
38. Zwakman, D.S., Pal, D., Arpnikanondt, C.: Usability evaluation of artificial intelligence-based voice assistants: the case of Amazon Alexa. SN Comput. Sci. 2(1), 1–16 (2021). https://doi.org/10.1007/s42979-020-00424-4
39. Moraes, A.: Algumas estratégias para a implementação da pesquisa em design considerando sua importância para a consolidação do ensino de design. Número Especial, Estud em Des Maio (1997)

"I Am Scared of Viruses, Too" - Studying the Impact of Self-disclosure in Chatbots for Health-Related Applications

Caterina Neef[1,2]([⊠]) [ID], Vanessa Mai[2] [ID], and Anja Richert[1,2] [ID]

[1] Cologne Cobots Lab, TH Köln - University of Applied Sciences, Cologne, Germany
[2] Faculty of Process Engineering, Energy and Mechanical Systems,
TH Köln - University of Applied Sciences, Cologne, Germany
{caterina.neef,vanessa.mai,anja.richert}@th-koeln.de

Abstract. Chatbots are gaining popularity in the healthcare sector, as they provide easy access to information while supporting both users and medical personnel. While some users might be reluctant to talk to a chatbot about their personal health, as this is a sensitive subject area, different factors can contribute to more successful interactions between chatbots and humans - such as self-disclosure. Previous studies within human-machine-interaction have shown that self-disclosure from a chatbot or conversational agent leads to better relationship and rapport building in the interaction. In this work, we investigated if this also holds true for chatbots in health-related applications - e.g., the chatbot uttering "I am scared of viruses, too". We conducted two studies with two different chatbots and specific use cases, one health assessment chatbot and one health information chatbot. For both use cases, we compared the non self-disclosing version with the self-disclosing version of each chatbot. Overall, both studies show that the integration of self-disclosure into the conversation between chatbots and humans in the context of health-related applications has a positive effect on the rapport building between chatbot and human. We also found that there is a difference in the effect of the introduced self-disclosure depending on the specific context in which the chatbot is used.

Keywords: Chatbot · Conversational AI · Health care · Self-disclosure · Rapport

1 Motivation

Chatbots are increasingly prevalent in many fields, including the healthcare sector, as they provide time- and location-independent access to information. They have been used to assist with patient intake [25], to educate users about mental health and self-care [30], and have been shown to reduce depression when used as psychotherapy support [9]. Additionally, they are an important tool to combat shortages in health care workers, thereby supporting both medical professionals and those making use of health care services [26]. While some users

© The Author(s), under exclusive license to Springer Nature Switzerland AG 2022
M. Kurosu (Ed.): HCII 2022, LNCS 13304, pp. 515–530, 2022.
https://doi.org/10.1007/978-3-031-05412-9_35

might be reluctant to talk to a chatbot about their personal health, as this is a sensitive subject area [24], there are different factors that can contribute to more successful interactions between chatbots and humans - often mimicked after human-human interactions.

One of these factors is self-disclosure: One interaction partner discloses information about themselves, which in turn can make the other interaction partner more comfortable to open up, also [1]. The use of self-disclosure can lead to rapport and a close bond between the interaction partners [2]. This is particularly helpful in healthcare, where questionnaires are used to capture patients' own perceptions of their well-being, and it is therefore important that they provide honest information about their health. Transferring these findings into the interaction between humans and chatbots or conversational agents in different fields has shown that self-disclosure from a chatbot or conversational agent leads to relationship-enhancing and rapport-like aspects such as social attraction [15] and perceived intimacy and enjoyment [20].

In this work, we investigated if this also holds true for chatbots in health-related applications - e.g., the chatbot uttering "I am scared of viruses, too". We conducted two quantitative studies with two different chatbots and specific use cases, in which we compared the non self-disclosing (NSDC) version with the self-disclosing (SDC) version of each chatbot. In study A, users interacted with a chatbot that asked them questions about their mental and physical health - a health assessment chatbot. In study B, users interacted with a chatbot to inquire information about preventive medical examinations and checkups - a health information chatbot. Subsequently, users participated in a survey we conducted to investigate the effect of the chatbot's self-disclosure on the reported self-disclosure of their human interaction partner and its influence on the rapport between chatbot and human.

2   Related Work

Rapport Building in Human-Machine-Interaction (HMI). As is evident by the literature presented in the following, human-chatbot interaction entails several challenges. One of these challenges is to establish rapport and have a conversation on a trust level. Rapport represents a harmonious relationship in human-machine interaction characterized by ease, synchronicity, and connectedness [10,13] and can be established through nonverbal, paraverbal, and verbal influence factors. One factor, that can strengthen rapport in a human-human interaction, is self-disclosure [2]. Self-disclosure is a process in which a person reveals personal or sensitive information to others [14]. This effect has also been transferred to human-chatbot interaction.

Reciprocal self-disclosure in particular is seen as an influencing factor of rapport [4,33]. There have been studies in human-machine interaction that point to this correlation. However, these studies have not explicitly measured rapport, but have found a relationship between rapport and similar constructs that also indicate a good relationship, namely social attraction [15,23], co-presence [15, 32], and attachment [20].

Health Care Chatbots. Chatbots are also increasingly finding their way into many different areas of the healthcare sector [18]. Whether the chatbot is informing the user about health-related topics, conducting a health screening, or supporting with therapy, it is important for users to be truthful about their statements. Additionally, in order to ensure long-term engagement with the chatbot, its acceptance among users is vital. Studies have proposed and found different factors which influence both honesty and self-disclosure, as well as user acceptance towards chatbots:

Fan et al. [8] analyzed which factors in medical chatbots can contribute to improving their acceptance and engagement, in the context of using the chatbot to self-diagnose in real-world scenarios. They cite accurate, informative and understandable diagnoses and information, as well as trustworthiness and ease-of-use as significant implications for chatbot design. Van der Lee et al. [31] argue that self-disclosure is an important factor for mental health chatbots, as it can lead to feelings of relief [7].

Self-disclosure in (Health Care) Chatbots. Several healthcare studies point out the effects of self-disclosure in chatbot-human interaction: Self-disclosure has an influence on the relational, emotional and psychological level [12] and helps in building an emotional connection with the chatbot [31]. Moreover, self-disclosure in text-based human-machine interactions increases trust, closeness, and sympathy with regard to the system [29]. Further studies show that a chatbot design with pronounced self-disclosure has a positive effect on participants' self-disclosure [27]. In the context of chatbot-coaching, a research study [22] has also proven that the usage of self-disclosure of a chatbot dealing with exam anxiety has a positive effect on rapport building with the user.

As chatbots do not have the inherent ability to judge humans on their own, studies have shown that in the context of health-screening interviews, participants were less afraid to self-disclose when they believed they were talking to a computer, compared to a human [21]. Additionally, the convenience and anonymity of chatbots can also make it easier for users to self-disclose to them [28].

Research Question and Hypotheses. Many studies in the context of self-disclosure chatbots have focused on mental health and therapy support [16,19, 20,31]. In this work, we focus on conversations to assess and inform a user in regards to their health. Thus, our studies examine the impact of a chatbot's self-disclosure on a user's perceived rapport regarding an assessment of their physical and mental health (study A) and informing them about preventive medical check-ups (study B). This leads our research question: "What impact does a self-disclosing chatbot have on the self-disclosure and rapport regarding the user's physical, mental and informational health status?" Our first hypothesis is that the self-disclosure of the chatbot leads to an increase of self-disclosure of the human interaction partner. The second hypothesis is that the self-disclosure of the chatbot leads to increased rapport between chatbot and human.

3   Methods

In both studies, the conversational artificial intelligence (AI) framework Rasa (Rasa Technologies Inc, San Francisco, USA), along with the user interface (UI) of Rasa X, were used to develop and test the chatbots. Users interacted with the chatbot through text-based natural language, i.e., written word, on the Rasa X UI. When the conversation ended, the chatbot sent the user a link for an online survey. Both studies (A and B) were carried out in the same investigation period, independent of each other. Each study was first conducted with chatbot version 1 (NSDC), then 2 (SDC). Each chatbot interacted with different user groups (participants talked to either version 1 or 2).

3.1   Study A: Health Assessment Chatbot

Use Case and Conversation Structure. Study A had 62 participants. Chatbots A1 (non self-disclosure, n = 31) and A2 (self-disclosure, n = 31) interacted with users in five parts, namely greeting, self-explanation and small-talk (a), pain (b), sleep (c), mental health (d), and the end of the conversation (e). The model of the conversation design is shown in Fig. 1.

The chatbot starts with a greeting and explains its purpose and the goal of the conversation, namely assessing the health of the user. The chatbot then makes small talk about different activities like walking or biking and the preference for coffee or tea. The conversation then transitions to the health topic, where the user can choose to talk about pain, sleep, or mental health via clicking the corresponding button, or choose to end the conversation, also via clicking a button. The health questions are based on official patient reported outcome measures (PROMs) [5], which are questionnaires used to assess a patient's own perception of their well-being. Three to four questions are asked in each of the three health paths. These questions are either taken directly from different PROMs or adapted from them to fit this use case [3,6,11,17].

Each health path starts with general questions and moves to increasingly specific questions. If the chatbot detects a health issue, it asks the user to elaborate to elicit more self-disclosure from the user. If the chatbot does not understand the user's reply, it sends the fallback message "Sorry, I have not learned that yet", and the user is again offered the selection of buttons to choose either a health path or end the conversation. An example conversation and the introduction of chatbot's self-disclosure into the responses is shown in Table 1.

The non self-disclosure (NSDC) chatbot merely answers the user that being outside and exercising is healthy, while the self-disclosure (SDC) chatbot includes an additional statement from its own point of view, stating that it also likes to explore. In this study, the chatbot's self-disclosure was only implemented

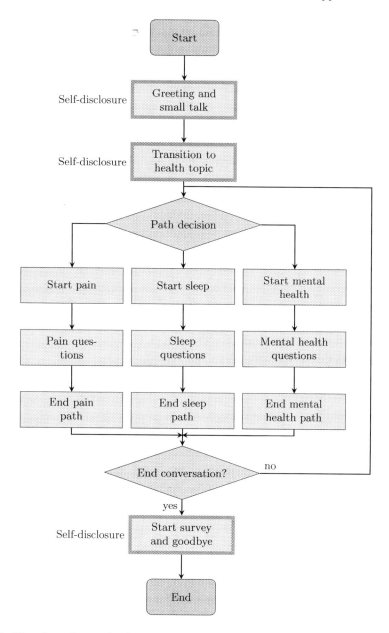

Fig. 1. Flowchart for study A, in which user's were asked about their mental and physical (pain and sleep) health. After the user successfully completed one path, they were able to choose another topic to talk to the chatbot about, or end the conversation.

Table 1. Example questions and answers of each chatbot in study A are shown.

Non self-disclosing (NSDC) chatbot	Self-disclosing (SDC) chatbot
Chatbot: Have you been out in the fresh air today?	Chatbot: Have you been out in the fresh air today?
User: Yes!	User: Yes!
Chatbot: That's good, fresh air and exercise keeps you fit and healthy.	Chatbot: That's good, fresh air and exercise keeps you fit and healthy. I like to roll around and explore the area.

into the greeting, small-talk and transition parts of the conversation to retain the seriousness and accuracy of the health assessment. Once one health path is completed, the user has the option to choose another health path, or to end the conversation. If the user chooses to end the conversation, the chatbot sends a link for the online survey and says goodbye. Self-disclosure of the chatbot is implemented here as well.

Online Survey and Data Analysis. In study A, users were sent a link to a survey created with the QuestionPro tool (QuestionPro Ltd., Berlin, Germany) with questions concerning self-disclosure and rapport. At the beginning of the survey, socio-demographic data (age and gender) of the users were enquired. Then, the ten questions listed in Table 3 were asked. The aim of the survey questions was to investigate the users' self-disclosure (SD) and rapport (R) in regards to the chatbot, in addition to general conversational (C) questions.

To determine the effect of the chatbot's self-disclosure on the self-disclosure of the users, they were asked if they were honest with the chatbot (SD-A1), if they were comfortable answering honestly (SD-A2), if they found it easy to open up to the chatbot (SD-A3), and if the chatbot motivated them to be honest (SD-A4).

To investigate the impact of the chatbot's self-disclosure in regards to rapport, the user was asked if they would have given the same answers to a close friend (R-A5). This question was chosen based on the assumption that giving the same answer to the chatbot is a sign of rapport building. Additionally, the users were asked if they were able to create some sort of bond with the chatbot (R-A6) and if they felt that their personal information was in good hands with the chatbot (R-A7), both signs of trust and rapport [29,31].

Finally, in order to assess the general impression of the user's conversation with the chatbot, they were asked if they felt interrogated (C-A8), if they sometimes understated their statements (C-A9), and if they felt the chatbot was responsive enough to their needs (C-A10).

To answer the questions a 6-point Likert scale was used, ranging from "applies completely" (corresponding to the value "6" for numerical representation and analysis) to "does not apply at all" (corresponding to "1"), and all options were fully verbalized in the survey. A quantitative analysis was chosen, including an analysis of the statistical significance of the responses for each question. The results are shown and described in Sect. 4.1.

3.2   Study B: Health Information Chatbot

Use Case and Conversation Structure. Study B had 52 participants who interacted with chatbots B1 (non self-disclosure, n = 31) and B2 (self-disclosure, n = 21). The conversation was structured into greeting and introduction (a), the main part where the user was able to choose between one or several of the following topics: medical checkups, eye checkups, dental checkups, vaccinations or none of the above (b), and the end of the conversation (c). The chosen health topics are the most common preventive medical check-ups. The option 'none of the above' is implemented in case the user does not have specific, but rather general, questions about health check-ups.

The process of the conversation is similar to the process for study A, shown in Fig. 1, but with different health paths. Again, the chatbot starts with a greeting and an explanation of its purpose. The user can then choose one of the health topics. When one topic is completed, the user can start another topic or end the conversation. As this is a more informational chatbot, which does not use questions derived or adapted from specific health questionnaires, self-disclosure was introduced into all parts of the conversation for this use case, including the health questions. Examples of the questions and replies of the chatbot, with and without self-disclosure, are shown in Table 2. Again, once the user decides to end the conversation, the chatbot also sends a link to an online survey and says goodbye.

Online Survey and Data Analysis. In study B, users were sent a link to an online survey created with the SoSciSurvey tool (SoSciSurvey Ltd., Munich, Germany) with questions concerning self-disclosure and rapport. At the beginning of the survey, socio-demographic date (age range and gender) of the users were enquired. Then, the ten questions listed in Table 4 were asked. The aim here was also to investigate the users' self-disclosure (SD) and rapport (R) in regards to the chatbot, in addition to general conversational (C) questions.

Regarding self-disclosure, the users were asked if they answered honestly (SD-B1), if they opened up about sensitives issues (SD-B2), if they found it easy to talk about medical topics (SD-B3) and if they were talkative with the chatbot (SD-B4).

To investigate the rapport between chatbot and user, the users were asked if they felt the chatbot liked them (R-B5), if they felt they built a relationship with the chatbot (R-B6), and if they would use the chatbot again (R-B7).

In order to verify that the implementation of self-disclosure into the SD chatbot was successful, the users were asked if the chatbot talked a lot about itself (C-B8). Finally, to determine the general conversational nature of the users, they were asked if they are talkative with strangers (C-B9) and if they generally find it easy to talk about medical topics (C-B10).

Table 2. Example questions and answers of each chatbot in study B are shown.

Non self-disclosing (NSDC) chatbot	Self-disclosing (SDC) chatbot
So you are interested in vaccinations. Which vaccination will you get?	So you are interested in vaccinations. I am also regularly protected against viruses with an antivirus program. So I can protect myself, but also all the data of others. Which vaccination will you get?
What thoughts do you have when you think about the upcoming appointment? Are they rather positive or rather negative?	Your appointment is coming up soon. I'm always very nervous because I don't know what I'm in for, but I am also happy when I can be optimized by examining the sources of my errors. What thoughts do you have when you think about the upcoming appointment? Are they rather positive or rather negative?

All questions again had the same six answer options, ranging from "applies completely" (corresponding to the value "6" for numerical representation and analysis) to "does not apply at all" (corresponding to "1"), and all options were fully verbalized in the survey. A quantitative analysis was chosen, including an analysis of the statistical significance of the responses for each question. The results are shown and described in Sect. 4.2.

4   Results

4.1   Study A: Health Assessment Chatbot

The results for study A (mental and physical health) are shown in Table 3. 31 users with an average age of 24.97 years, of whom 29 % were female and 71 % were male, had a conversation with the non self-disclosure (NSDC) chatbot. 31 users, with an average age of 29.68 years, of whom 35 % were female and 65 % were male, talked to the self-disclosure chatbot (SDC). The mean (M) and standard deviation (s) for the possible values of 1 (does not apply at all) to 6 (applies completely) for each chatbot (NSDC and SDC) as well as the statistical significance (p) are shown.

There is only a small and insignificant difference in honesty (M = 4.94 and 5.13) and comfortableness in answering honestly (M = 4.16 and 4.06) between the NSDC and SDC. While also not statistically significant, the difference in how easy users found it to open up is slightly larger (M = 4.26 and 4.58) and in favor of the SDC. In regards to the motivational role the chatbot played in revealing the users' honest opinion, the SDC was significantly more successful (M = 3.52 and 4.13, p = .03).

Table 3. The results of study A, in which a non self-disclosing chatbot (NSDC) and self-disclosing chatbot (SDC) are compared in an assessment of the physical and mental health of the respondents. SD represents the questions asked about self-disclosure, R about rapport and C are general conversational questions. The results show that with the exception of SD-A2, the SDC leads to slightly more self-disclosure and more rapport.

		NSDC (N = 31)		SDC (N = 31)		
	Average age	24.97		29.68		
	Gender (M, F)	22, 9		20, 11		
		Mean	s	Mean	s	p
SD-A1	Were you honest with the chatbot?	4.94	1	**5.13**	0.81	.4
SD-A2	Were you comfortable answering honestly?	**4.16**	1.42	4.06	1.44	.79
SD-A3	Did you find it easy to open up to the chatbot?	4.26	1.44	**4.58**	1.23	.35
SD-A4	Did the chatbot motivate you to reveal your honest opinion?	3.52	1	**4.13**	1.15	.03
R-A5	Would you have given the same answers to a close friend?	3.52	1.55	**4.13**	1.54	.12
R-A6	Were you able to create some sort of bond with the chatbot through the course of the chat?	2.84	1.27	**3.35**	1.36	.13
R-A7	Did you feel like your personal information was in good hands with the chatbot?	3.84	1.13	**4.1**	1.4	.43
C-A8	Did you feel interrogated by the high frequency of the questions?	3.16	1.51	**2.61**	0.86	.03
C-A9	Did you sometimes understate your statements to avoid further inquiry?	3.13	1.5	**2.77**	1.36	.33
C-A10	Did you feel that the chatbot was sufficiently responsive to your needs?	3.45	1.18	3.45	1.36	1

Investigating rapport, the users that talked to the SDC were more likely to have given the same answers to a close friend (M = 3.52 and 4.13), and were more able to create a bond with the chatbot (M = 2.84 and 3.35). Additionally, the SDC users were only slightly more inclined to feel that their personal information was in good hands with the chatbot (M = 3.84 and 4.1).

The SDC chatbot led to users feeling significantly less interrogated by the chatbot (M = 3.16 and 2.61, p = .03), and its users were less likely to understate their statements to avoid further inquiry (M = 3.13 and 2.77). In terms of the chatbot being sufficiently responsive to the users' needs, there was no difference (M = 3.45) for both chatbots. The results are discussed in Sect. 5.

4.2   Study B: Health Information Chatbot

The results for study B are shown in Table 4. 31 users with a median age range of 20–29 years, of whom 32 % were female, 65 % male and 3 % diverse, had a conversation with the non self-disclosure chatbot (NSDC). 21 users, with a median age range of 20–29 years, of whom 38 % were female and 62 % were male, talked to the self-disclosure chatbot (SDC). The mean (M) and standard deviation (s) for the possible values of 1 (does not apply at all) to 6 (applies completely) for each chatbot (NSDC and SDC) as well as the statistical significance (p) are shown.

There is only a small and insignificant difference in honesty (M = 5.16 and 5.29) and whether or not users opened about sensitive issues (M = 4.32 and 4.19) between the NSDC and SDC. While also not statistically significant, the difference in how easy users found it to talk to the chatbot about medical topics is slightly larger (M = 4.42 and 4.71) and in favor of the SDC. In terms of how talkative users were with the chatbot, there is barely any difference between the two chatbots (M = 4.32 and 4.33).

Regarding rapport, the differences are more pronounced and more significant: The SDC users were more inclined to feel that the chatbot liked them (M = 3.94 and 4.86, p = .01), that they were able to build a relationship with the chatbot (M = 2.81 and 3.52, p = .07), and that they would use it again (M = 3.74 and 4.57, p = .02).

The self-disclosure of the SDC was successfully implemented ("The chatbot talked a lot about itself.", M = 2.42 and 5.29, p = <0.001). The conversational nature of the users was found to be similar in terms of talkativeness with strangers (M = 3.81 and 3.76) and how easy they generally found it to talk about medical topics (M = 4.13 and 4.05). The results are discussed in the following.

5   Discussion

Reciprocal Self-disclosure and Rapport. The results of the survey questions regarding self-disclosure and rapport described in Sects. 4.1 and 4.2 are visualized in Fig. 2. It is important to note that the answers to each individual question for study A and B can not be compared directly, as different survey questions were used for each study.

Overall, Fig. 2 shows that the implementation of self-disclosure into the chatbot has no or only a small visible positive impact on the reported self-disclosure of the users. The only statistically significant difference is seen in question SD-A4 in study A ("Did the chatbot motivate you to reveal your honest opinion?"). Interesting is, however, that while users of the self-disclosure chatbot indicated to be more motivated by the chatbot to be honest, the reported honesty for this chatbot is only slightly higher than for the non self-disclosure chatbot. To investigate this further, a qualitative analysis of the conversation histories for both chatbots should be conducted in the future.

Table 4. The results of study B, in which a non self-disclosing chatbot (NSDC) and self-disclosing chatbot (SDC) are compared in conversation about preventive medical exams and vaccinations with the respondents. The results show that with the exception of SD-A2, the SDC leads to slightly more self-disclosure and more rapport.

		NSDC (N = 31)		SDC (N = 21)		
	Median age range	20–29		20–29		
	Gender (M, F, D)	20, 10, 1		13, 8		
		Mean	s	Mean	s	p
SD-B1	Did you answer honestly?	5.16	0.9	**5.29**	0.9	.63
SD-B2	Did you open up about sensitive issues?	**4.32**	1.22	4.19	0.98	.68
SD-B3	Did you find it easy to talk to the chatbot about medical topics?	4.42	1.18	**4.71**	1.15	.37
SD-B4	Were you talkative with the chatbot?	4.32	1.14	**4.33**	0.97	.97
R-B5	Did you feel the chatbot liked you?	3.94	1.46	**4.86**	0.91	.01
R-B6	Did you feel like you could build a relationship with the chatbot?	2.81	1.28	**3.52**	1.47	.07
R-B7	I would use the chatbot again.	3.74	1.34	**4.57**	1.03	.02
C-B8	The chatbot talked a lot about itself.	2.42	1.23	**5.29**	0.72	<0.001
C-B9	Are you talkative with strangers?	3.81	1.4	3.76	0.83	.9
C-B10	Do you generally find it easy to talk about medical topics?	4.13	1.2	4.05	0.97	.8

The first hypothesis ("self-disclosure of the chatbot leads to an increase of self-disclosure of the human interaction partner") regarding reciprocal self-disclosure can therefore not yet be confirmed. A limitation of this study is that we conducted only one conversation and subsequent survey with each user. To further study reciprocal self-disclosure between chatbot and human, studies need to be conducted in the future where the user interacts with the chatbot more than once and over longer periods of time.

While the self-disclosure behavior of users is only slightly more evident with the self-disclosing chatbot, the difference in rapport is more pronounced in both studies. Especially for study B, the rapport values for the self-disclosing chatbot are significantly higher than for the non self-disclosing chatbot. This confirms the results of previous studies, which found that the introduction of self-disclosure into human-chatbot-interaction is an important factor in building rapport between both parties [10,15,20]. The second hypothesis ("self-disclosure of the chatbot leads to increased rapport between chatbot and human") can therefore be confirmed. Additionally, the results in Sect. 4 show that the chatbots used in both studies have a good acceptance overall, indicating a promising future for chatbots in health-related applications.

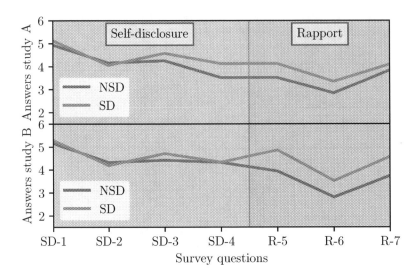

Fig. 2. The results for the questions regarding self-disclosure and rapport are visualized for both study A and B, revealing a larger impact of the chatbot's self-disclosure on the rapport between chatbot and user than on the user's self-disclosure.

The Context-Dependent Impact of Self-disclosure. The analysis of the impact of a self-disclosing chatbot in two different application fields in the health care domain not only provides more evidence to link self-disclosure to rapport in human-chatbot-interaction, but also indicates that this impact might be context-dependent. Figure 3 displays the calculated differences of means of the non self-disclosing (NSDC) and the self-disclosing chatbot (SDC) for both studies, to visualize how big the impact of the introduction of self-disclosure into the chatbot is (difference = mean$_{SDC}$ - mean$_{NSDC}$).

Again, it is important to note that the answers to each individual question for study A and B can not be compared directly, as different survey questions were used for each study. However, the visualization in Fig. 3 shows the more pronounced differences, particularly in the context of rapport for study B. A possible explanation for this finding is the differences in the use cases for each study. While study A used a chatbot that performed a health assessment, in part using questions from validated health assessment questionnaires, study B had a more informative character in the context of preventive medical check-ups. Additionally, because of this difference in goals, the self-disclosure was only implemented into the greeting, small talk, transition and end of conversation in study A. For study B, however, self-disclosure was integrated into all parts of the conversation process. A derived research question from this discovery is whether the amount of self-disclosure and the goal of the conversation (assessing vs. informing) plays a role in reciprocal self-disclosure and thus rapport building between human and chatbot.

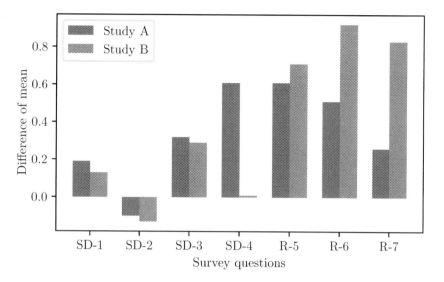

Fig. 3. The difference of the calculated means between the non self-disclosing and self-disclosing chatbot for both study A and B are shown, indicating a larger impact of the introduction of self-disclosure for study B.

6 Conclusion

We conducted two different studies to investigate the impact of self-disclosure in chatbots for health-related applications. Both studies show that the integration of self-disclosure into the conversation between chatbots and humans in the context of health-related applications has a small positive effect on the self-disclosure of the human, but a significant positive effect on the rapport between human and chatbot. Additionally, we raised the question whether the amount of self-disclosure and the goal of the conversation plays a role, which needs to be examined further.

For future investigations regarding this topic, the chatbots will be optimized and extended in terms of what they understand and the variety of answers they can give. The conversation histories will be analyzed, and varying amounts of self-disclosure and longer interaction periods will also be studied. In particular, a qualitative investigation of the conversation histories is necessary in order to determine, for example, to what extent self-disclosure statements of the test subjects are reflected in the chat processes. Additionally, the chatbots will be integrated into a social robot to compare the effect of self-disclosure in interactions with humans with both chatbots and social robots.

Acknowledgements. We would like to thank Marcel Germer, Sebastian Hell, Leon Hommel, Martin Junge, Marvin Kindermann, Andrea Linden, Christina Löcker, Johannes Sittel and Tim Wittig for their invaluable contributions to the studies described in this paper.

References

1. Altman, I.: Reciprocity of interpersonal exchange. J. Theory Soc. Behav. **3**(2), 249–261 (1973). https://doi.org/10.1111/j.1468-5914.1973.tb00325.x
2. Altman, I., Taylor, D.A.: Social Penetration: The Development of Interpersonal Relationships. Rinehart & Winston, Holt (1973)
3. Amtmann, D., et al.: Development of a promis item bank to measure pain interference. Pain **150**(1), 173–182 (2010). https://doi.org/10.1016/j.pain.2010.04.025
4. Argyle, M.: The biological basis of rapport. Psychol. Inq. **1**(4), 297–300 (1990). https://doi.org/10.1207/s15327965pli0104_3
5. Black, N.: Patient reported outcome measures could help transform healthcare. BMJ **346**, f167 (2013). https://doi.org/10.1136/bmj.f167
6. Cella, D.: PROMIS Health Organization Measuring Quality of Life in Neurological Disorders: Final Report of the Neuro-QoL Study (2018)
7. Choi, Y.H., Bazarova, N.N.: Self-disclosure characteristics and motivations in social media: extending the functional model to multiple social network sites. Hum. Commun. Res. **41**(4), 480–500 (2015). https://doi.org/10.1111/hcre.12053
8. Fan, X., Chao, D., Zhang, Z., Wang, D., Li, X., Tian, F.: Utilization of self-diagnosis health chatbots in real-world settings: case study. J. Med. Internet Res. **23**(1), e19928 (2021). https://doi.org/10.2196/19928
9. Fitzpatrick, K.K., Darcy, A., Vierhile, M.: Delivering cognitive behavior therapy to young adults with symptoms of depression and anxiety using a fully automated conversational agent (Woebot): a randomized controlled trial. JMIR Mental Health **4**(2), e7785 (2017)
10. Gratch, J., Wang, N., Gerten, J., Fast, E., Duffy, R.: Creating rapport with virtual agents. In: Pelachaud, C., Martin, J.-C., André, E., Chollet, G., Karpouzis, K., Pelé, D. (eds.) IVA 2007. LNCS (LNAI), vol. 4722, pp. 125–138. Springer, Heidelberg (2007). https://doi.org/10.1007/978-3-540-74997-4_12
11. Hanmer, J., Jensen, R.E., Rothrock, N.: A reporting checklist for HealthMeasures' patient-reported outcomes: ASCQ-Me, Neuro-QoL, NIH Toolbox, and PROMIS. J. Patient-Rep. Outcomes **4**(1), 1–7 (2020). https://doi.org/10.1186/s41687-020-0176-4
12. Ho, A., Hancock, J., Miner, A.S.: Psychological, relational, and emotional effects of self-disclosure after conversations with a chatbot. J. Commun. **68**(4), 712–733 (2018). https://doi.org/10.1093/joc/jqy026
13. Huang, L., Morency, L.-P., Gratch, J.: Virtual rapport 2.0. In: Vilhjálmsson, H.H., Kopp, S., Marsella, S., Thórisson, K.R. (eds.) IVA 2011. LNCS (LNAI), vol. 6895, pp. 68–79. Springer, Heidelberg (2011). https://doi.org/10.1007/978-3-642-23974-8_8
14. Ignatius, E., Kokkonen, M.: Factors contributing to verbal self-disclosure. Nordic Psychol. **59**(4), 362–391 (2007). https://doi.org/10.1027/1901-2276.59.4.362
15. Kang, S.H., Gratch, J.: People like virtual counselors that highly-disclose about themselves. Annu. Rev. Cyberther. Telemed. **2011**, 143–148 (2011). https://doi.org/10.3233/978-1-60750-766-6-143
16. Kawasaki, M., Yamashita, N., Lee, Y.C., Nohara, K.: Assessing users' mental status from their journaling behavior through chatbots. In: Proceedings of the 20th ACM International Conference on Intelligent Virtual Agents, no. 32, pp. 1–8. Association for Computing Machinery, New York (2020)

17. Keller, S.D., Yang, M., Treadwell, M.J., Werner, E.M., Hassell, K.L.: Patient reports of health outcome for adults living with sickle cell disease: development and testing of the ASCQ-Me item banks. Health Qual. Life Outcomes **12**(1), 125 (2014). https://doi.org/10.1186/s12955-014-0125-0

18. Laranjo, L., et al.: Conversational agents in healthcare: a systematic review. J. Am. Med. Inf. Assoc. **25**(9), 1248–1258 (2018)

19. Lee, Y.C., Yamashita, N., Huang, Y.: Designing a chatbot as a mediator for promoting deep self-disclosure to a real mental health professional. Proc. ACM Hum. Comput. Interact. **4**(CSCW1), 1–27 (2020). https://doi.org/10.1145/3392836

20. Lee, Y.C., Yamashita, N., Huang, Y., Fu, W.: "I hear you, i feel you": encouraging deep self-disclosure through a chatbot. In: Proceedings of the 2020 CHI Conference on Human Factors in Computing Systems (CHI 2020), pp. 1–12. Association for Computing Machinery, New York (2020). https://doi.org/10.1145/3313831.3376175

21. Lucas, G.M., Gratch, J., King, A., Morency, L.P.: It's only a computer: virtual humans increase willingness to disclose. Comput. Hum. Behav. **37**, 94–100 (2014). https://doi.org/10.1016/j.chb.2014.04.043

22. Mai, V., Wolff, A., Richert, A., Preusser, I.: Accompanying reflection processes by an AI-based StudiCoachBot: a study on rapport building in human-machine coaching using self disclosure. In: Stephanidis, C., et al.: (eds.) HCII 2021. LNCS, vol. 13096, pp. 439–457. Springer, Cham (2021). https://doi.org/10.1007/978-3-030-90328-2_29

23. Moon, Y.: Intimate exchanges: using computers to elicit self-disclosure from consumers. J. Consum. Res. **26**(4), 323–339 (2000). https://doi.org/10.1086/209566

24. Nadarzynski, T., Miles, O., Cowie, A., Ridge, D.: Acceptability of artificial intelligence (AI)-led chatbot services in healthcare: a mixed-methods study. Digit. Health **5**, 2055207619871808 (2019). https://doi.org/10.1177/2055207619871808

25. Ni, L., Lu, C., Liu, N., Liu, J.: MANDY: towards a smart primary care chatbot application. In: Chen, J., Theeramunkong, T., Supnithi, T., Tang, X. (eds.) KSS 2017. CCIS, vol. 780, pp. 38–52. Springer, Singapore (2017). https://doi.org/10.1007/978-981-10-6989-5_4

26. Palanica, A., Flaschner, P., Thommandram, A., Li, M., Fossat, Y.: Physicians' perceptions of chatbots in health care: cross-sectional web-based survey. J. Med. Internet Res. **21**(4), e12887 (2019). https://doi.org/10.2196/12887

27. Ravichander, A., Black, A.W.: An empirical study of self-disclosure in spoken dialogue systems. In: Proceedings of the 19th Annual SIGdial Meeting on Discourse and Dialogue, pp. 253–263. Association for Computational Linguistics, Melbourne (2018). https://doi.org/10.18653/v1/W18-5030

28. Skjuve, M., Brandtzæg, P.B.: Chatbots as a New User Interface for Providing Health Information to Young People (2018)

29. van Uffelen, L., van Waterschoot, J., Theune, M.: Show me yours if i show you mine: self-disclosure in conversational agents. In: Proceedings Robo-Identity 2021. Association for Computing Machinery (ACM) (2021)

30. Vaidyam, A.N., Wisniewski, H., Halamka, J.D., Kashavan, M.S., Torous, J.B.: Chatbots and conversational agents in mental health: a review of the psychiatric landscape. Canadian J. Psychiatry **64**(7), 456–464 (2019). https://doi.org/10.1177/0706743719828977

31. van der Lee, C., Croes, E., de Wit, J., Antheunis, M.: Digital Confessions: Exploring the Role of Chatbots in Self-Disclosure (2019)

32. von der Pütten, A.M., Hoffmann, L., Klatt, J., Krämer, N.C.: Quid pro quo? Recip-
    rocal self-disclosure and communicative accomodation towards a virtual inter-
    viewer. In: Vilhjálmsson, H.H., Kopp, S., Marsella, S., Thórisson, K.R. (eds.) IVA
    2011. LNCS (LNAI), vol. 6895, pp. 183–194. Springer, Heidelberg (2011). https://
    doi.org/10.1007/978-3-642-23974-8_20
33. Zhao, R., Papangelis, A., Cassell, J.: Towards a dyadic computational model of rap-
    port management for human-virtual agent interaction. In: Bickmore, T., Marsella,
    S., Sidner, C. (eds.) IVA 2014. LNCS (LNAI), vol. 8637, pp. 514–527. Springer,
    Cham (2014). https://doi.org/10.1007/978-3-319-09767-1_62

Don't Throw It Over the Fence! Toward Effective Handover from Conversational Agents to Service Employees

Mathis Poser[(✉)] [iD], Talissa Hackbarth[iD], and Eva A. C. Bittner[iD]

Universität Hamburg, Hamburg, Germany
{mathis.poser,eva.bittner}@uni-hamburg.de,
9hackbar@informatik.uni-hamburg.de

Abstract. Contemporary conversational agents (CAs) are capable of reliably answering repetitive low-complexity requests in online customer service, but regularly breakdown when dealing with high content or semantic complexity. The resulting service failures have a detrimental impact on customers' satisfaction and their willingness to use CAs in the future. By aiming to avert CA breakdown in service encounters with a hybrid service recovery strategy via handover UI, we address a knowledge gap in service literature. As automated recovery strategies via conversation repair do not invariably prevent CA breakdown, real-time handover of customer interaction from CA to service employee (SE) is increasingly applied and investigated. This hybrid service recovery strategy places high demands on SEs, as they must keep waiting times short and avoid repetition of questions to customers after handover. Considering SEs limited cognitive capacities for information processing, we present a handover user interface (UI) with relevant information to support SEs after handover. Following a Design Science Research approach, we define design principles for the handover UI, based on meta-requirements derived from kernel theories and expert interviews. By evaluating the design principles via prototype instantiation, we show that the information types and their presentation in the handover UI keep cognitive efforts for SEs at a manageable level and help them initiate customer interaction quickly.

Keywords: Handover · Hybrid service recovery · Conversational agent · Customer service

1 Introduction

Digitalization in all areas of life creates expectations concerning the ubiquitous accessibility and availability of information in general and of digital services in particular. To meet these changing demands, service companies in various industries (e.g., e-commerce, finance, IT) have increasingly automated online customer service (OCS) encounters with self-service solutions [1, 2]. With the objective of improving efficiency, personalization, and quality of these automated customer-facing interactions, companies are steadily deploying conversational agents (CAs), such as chatbots [3]. Powered

© The Author(s), under exclusive license to Springer Nature Switzerland AG 2022
M. Kurosu (Ed.): HCII 2022, LNCS 13304, pp. 531–545, 2022.
https://doi.org/10.1007/978-3-031-05412-9_36

by recent developments in machine learning (ML), CAs are capable of autonomously interacting with users via natural language in a human-like fashion [4–6]. This allows intuitive and engaging service interactions with customers in a large number of simultaneous encounters [7]. At present, CAs are capable of reliably answering repetitive, predictable, low-complexity requests from customers [8]. However, requests with high content or semantic complexity exceed the bounded capabilities of CAs and lead to conversation breakdowns or loops [9, 10]. As such service failures result in unanswered customer matters [11], value might get deconstructed and customer satisfaction could be jeopardized [12, 13].

To avoid CA failure, so far, automated repair strategies have been investigated to minimize conversation breakdowns [14, 15]. However, this form of service recovery does not work when repeated repair attempts have failed. Therefore, real-time handover of the preceding customer interaction from CA to service employee (SE) is increasingly applied and studied as a promising fallback mechanism [14, 16–18]. This hybrid service recovery strategy places high demands on SEs, as they must keep waiting times short and avoid repetition of questions to customers after handover. Hence, to ensure the efficiency and effectiveness of service delivery after CA failure, a handover solution is required that supports SEs to seamlessly and effortlessly continue request processing [19, 20]. However, handover as a service recovery strategy is so far under researched, needs of SEs in hybrid work settings have been given little consideration, and the required interplay of CA and SE in socio-technical systems of companies' customer service is not yet well developed [2, 14, 21]. To address these knowledge gaps, we develop a requirements-based user interface (UI) to support SEs after handover, so service delivery can continue efficiently after CA failure. Accordingly, we address the following research questions (RQs): *RQ1: How should a handover UI be designed from the perspective of SEs for instant request processing after handover? RQ2: What effect does the use of the handover UI have on SEs' behavior toward and perception of the UI?*

To answer these research questions, we present the second design cycle of a larger Design Science Research (DSR) project. With the aim of allowing seamless continuation of chat-based service encounters after CA failure by SEs, we derive prescriptive design knowledge via theoretical insights and expert interviews. The instantiation of a prototype serves to evaluate the efficiency of a UI that allows to adopt a hybrid service recovery strategy for CAs. The remaining paper structure unfolds as follows. First, we present the conceptual background by elaborating on trends in OCS and hybrid service delivery. Next, we describe our research approach, outline the derivation of the design knowledge and demonstrate its instantiation in a web-based prototype with UI. Subsequently, we present the results of a mixed-method evaluation. We close with a discussion of obtained insights and provide an outlook for future research.

2   Conceptual Background

2.1   Online Customer Service and Service Failure

Spurred by digitization, organizations' delivery of intangible services directed toward objects or people has been fundamentally transformed [22, 23]. Based on technology-driven service innovations, self-service solutions have emerged that allow efficient service production via online channels enabling high service quality and customer satisfaction [1, 24]. The investigation of various self-service technologies has proven their capability to rapidly, conveniently, and cost-effectively deliver service to customers [25]. To capitalize on technical progress and elevate customer experience, the role of technology that is based on artificial intelligence (AI) has increasingly been explored and investigated in recent years [21, 26, 27]. As such, AI-based CAs have been studied and deployed in research and practice as they meet current customer demands for personalized, bidirectional, and chat-based service encounters [28, 29]. CAs are defined as intelligent software systems that communicate with users via spoken or textual natural language [4, 5]. To create and improve personalized service experiences with a human-like touch, previous research has investigated interaction-related as well as technical aspects of CAs (e.g., response time, appearance) [30–33]. However, despite their potential and technical advances, CAs are still prone to fail [13]. To identify the underlying reasons, previous research has initiated the investigation of different types of conversation breakdowns and derived distinct automated repair strategies [14, 16, 34]. If these strategies do not hinder CA breakdown in service encounters, service failures occur which causes customer dissatisfaction and compromises the benefits of CAs.

In literature, service failures are defined as the incapacity of service providers to deliver desired outcomes or processes [11]. As these failures are ubiquitous and insights in relation to their implication for AI-based service delivery are scarce [35], research effort has been devoted to generate insights on the effects of AI-based failures (e.g., effect on perceived humanness, service satisfaction) [36, 37]. In addition, initial research has explored the effectiveness of service recovery strategies. So far, strategies with informative explanations or immediate assistance have been examined to avert the negative impact of service failures on customers' satisfaction [38, 39]. As strategies with immediate assistance are more promising due to their likelihood for recovery success and short waiting times for customers, handovers to SEs are increasingly investigated [14, 40]. Until now, however, there is a lack of knowledge on how to implement this particular service recovery strategy.

2.2   Hybrid Service Delivery

The integration and adoption of AI in organizations requires fundamental modifications of service systems, processes, and interactions between customer, AI, and SE [41–44]. As a result, hybrid service delivery settings are emerging that transform the service encounter [2]. In this regard, [45] distinguishes between three AI-based encounters: AI takes over the interaction and co-creation with the customer in (**1**) **AI-performed** encounters. (**2**) **AI-supported** refers to the assistance of the SE by an AI application during the interaction invisible to customers, whereas in (**3**) **AI-augmented** AI is visibly involved to assist the encounter with the customer. These innovative forms of customer interactions allow the exploitation of respective strengths of AI and SEs in terms of specific requirements during service delivery. **AI-supported** and **AI-augmented** encounters are suitable to answer complex customer requests. As AI is, inter alia, capable to quickly sift through large amounts of information to identify and suggest suitable solutions, human limited information processing capacity can be compensated [46]. Complementarily, humans can contextualize presented suggestions by the AI. In addition, emotional needs of customers can be addressed by SEs [47].

In **AI-performed** encounters large amounts of simple customer requests can be solved. However, as current AI solutions, such as CAs, only reliably answer repetitive and information-intensive requests that require low to high analytical abilities, the risk of service failures for complex customer issues remains [26]. To mitigate the impact of these failures, an optimization of the integration of CA and SE work processes is needed to develop hybrid service recovery solutions [39]. More specifically, in OCS, solutions are required that, on the one hand, meet customers' demands for fast service delivery, as they overestimate the time spent in queue and long waiting time has a negative impact on their satisfaction [18]. On the other hand, SEs should be enabled to avert service failure via handover [40]. To meet these requirements, design approaches are required to create a UI that enables the integration of CA and SE work processes. Related research on the design of UI has shown that features of the interface can help to accommodate humans' limited resources for attention and information processing [48]. As users direct attention to stimulus features, they can be assisted to process task-relevant information by different design elements (e.g., font size, color) [49, 50]. Thus, to enable a timely continuation of the customer encounter, information presentation in a handover UI should be adapted to human factors [51]. To date, however, there is no design knowledge on the subject of handover UI [14, 40].

3   Research Approach

To answer the proposed RQs, we follow the DSR approach, which represents an established research paradigm to construct socio-technical artifacts for prevalent problems [52]. We structure our research project with the methodology of [53], covering two design cycles to ensure evolving maturity of developed design knowledge and created design entities (see Fig. 1).

In the *first cycle*, we established a general understanding of the demand for handovers from CA to SE to avoid service failures based on current findings in literature and interviews with domain experts. Building on these insights, we commenced by generating initial design knowledge in the form of tentative design principles (DPs) for the handover process, the collection and transfer of information by the CA before handover. By demonstrating and evaluating a non-interactive mixed-fidelity mock-up prototype based on these DPs, we provided a proof-of-concept [40].

In the *second cycle*, which is the focus of this paper, the DPs from the first cycle are extended. In this context, as part of **(1) Problem Identification**, the problem relevance was reconsidered by identifying a lack of support for SEs to enable efficient handovers. Hence, within **(2) Objectives of a Solution**, knowledge from applicable kernel theories

DSR activities	Cycle one	Cycle two
(1) Problem Identification	Insufficient recovery strategies for CA failure in service encounters	Lack of support for SEs to enable efficient handover
(2) Objectives of a Solution	Real-time handover from CA to SEs	Handover UI for SEs
(3) Design & Development	Interaction and process design for CA handover	UI prototype based on design principles
(4) Demonstration	Implementation of CA handover with non-interactive mixed-fidelity (mock-up) prototype	Implementation of web-based UI prototype
(5) Evaluation	Qualitative expert evaluation to provide a proof-of-concept	User test for mixed-method evaluation of handover UI
(6) Communication	[40]	This publication

Fig. 1. DSR approach and design cycles.

and insights from application domain experts were used to determine meta-requirements (MRs) for a handover UI that assists SEs in continuing the service encounter instantly after handover. In semi-structured interviews, six experts (E1–6) participated with experience in chat-based service encounters to handle customer requests. The interviews followed a pre-defined structure with questions about their current working reality, a demonstration of the proof-of-concept from cycle one followed by questions about its applicability and requirements for a suitable handover UI. Based on verbatim transcripts, a qualitative analysis of the interviews following the approach of [54] was conducted. Using MAXQDA 2020, two researchers inductively formed code categories by defining and revising rules and categories iteratively working through the transcripts. To ensure objectivity, code sets were continuously harmonized resulting in four main categories (e.g., information requirements handover) and nine sub-categories (e.g., volume of information). Using these insights, MRs were identified and DPs formulated according to [55]. For **(3) Design and Development** and **(4) Demonstration**, the generated DPs were instantiated. Based on defined design features (DFs) that refer to underlying DPs, a web-based prototype was implemented. For the **(5) Evaluation**, we assessed the prototype in user tests. Ten participants (PA) (three female and seven male) from different organizations with experience in handling service- or technology-related requests in OCS from different business fields (e.g., e-commerce, market research) were instructed to seamlessly continue service encounters after handover. In this evaluation setting, the semi-automated technical prototype supported PAs with information whose display was manually triggered by an involved researcher. In addition, detailed information was automatically displayed after button click by PAs. To simulate a natural working situation, the PAs were instructed to handle a customer request referring to a technical problem (laptop battery does not charge) and provided with applicable knowledge prior to the user test to resolve the problem. In subsequent interviews, PAs were asked about the fulfillment of the generated DPs and the impact of the handover UI on their work. To structure the interviews, questions were asked about (1) general impression of handover UI, (2) task processing with handover UI, (3) evaluation of information types and their presentation, and (4) potential for improvement.

4   Design, Development, and Demonstration

To construct a UI for the hybrid service recovery strategy with handover, pertinent theories and practical insights from experts are used to derive a set of MRs to allow optimization of continued interactions with customers after CA failure. We present corresponding DPs and their instantiation via DFs in a web-based prototype.

4.1   Meta-requirements

Theory-Derived MRs. Seamless continuation of interactions with customers after CA failure requires a compilation and presentation of applicable information from the previous CA-customer interaction so that requests can be answered successfully without posing redundant questions. According to Cognitive Load Theory (CLT), the limited human cognitive capacity has to be considered to support individuals during information processing [56, 57]. Individuals' capability to handle task-relevant information can be promoted if the intrinsic, extraneous, and germane loads are balanced and do not overload human working memory [58]. Extraneous and germane load can be influenced by the presentation format [59]. As intrinsic load is high due to the complex requirements of real-time interaction, information should be presented in terms of volume and format that does not overload individuals' capacities to process (extraneous) and comprehend (germane) information. Therefore, the handover UI should comprise a limited amount of information (**MR1**) and present information in a way that supports comprehension building (**MR2**). After handover from CA to SE, the employee has to handle the customer request by executing problem-solving activities. For this purpose, actionable information is required. As the human ability to process information is restricted, problem-solving processes should be supported to limit the invested mental effort [60]. In this regard, Cognitive Fit Theory (CFT) postulates that individuals use information in the problem representation and task to create a mental representation of the problem, which allows them to produce a problem solution [61, 62]. The effectiveness of the problem-solving process can be influenced by the problem-solving task and problem representation. When the task and presentation of the problem match and help the individual to create a corresponding mental representation, problem-solving performance increases via improved accuracy and speed [61]. Accordingly, the handover UI should contain information that adequately represents the customer's problem or request so that SEs can generate a matching mental representation (**MR3**). Besides the type of information, the presentation format is also relevant to support problem-solving behavior. In CFT, symbolic and spatial problem-solving tasks are differentiated. The first type refers to tasks that require the acquisition of discrete data and information to subsequently process via analytical thinking [61, 63]. In spatial tasks, relationships of data and information are established through associative thinking. To support individuals' problem-solving processes and enable them to create a fit between the presented and mental problem, the presentation format should match the task type at hand [63]. As the extraction of specific information is relevant after handover, information should be presented in a tabular format in the handover UI, so that SEs can easily interpret and process information (**MR4**).

Interview-Derived MRs. The adoption of a handover UI to implement a hybrid service recovery strategy for CAs can lead to increased efficiency and effectiveness in continuing the customer encounter through time savings (E2–6) and improved quality in the interaction (E1, E3). To exploit the benefits of a handover UI, requirements in terms of the type and presentation of information should be fulfilled. For the continuation of an interaction, the questions *"what category, what product and what person, and what problem does the person have"* (E4) are essential. The indication of the customer issue and reason for CA failure is important to accurately determine the entry point for the conversation (E1, E3, E4, E6). Therefore, the specification of a request type (e.g., complaint), a summary or possibility to inspect the preceding CA-customer interaction, and overview of proposed solutions by the CA are required (E1–4, E6) (**MR5**). In addition, information about the customer and the object of request should be included: *"I would want to know - when the request is handed over - who this is and what is it about"* (E1). Therefore, information about the product and the customer's name are relevant to conduct a personalized interaction (E3-E5). For the presentation format of information, it is important to be able to *"extract all information at once, if possible at first glance"* (E5). The most important information should be presented in a way that allows quick processing and understanding to keep waiting time for customers short (E1, E3, E4). A prioritization in the arrangement of displayed information is helpful to instantly see the most important information with customer name, object of request, and customer concern (E1, E3, E5) (**MR6**). For conciseness, the amount of presented information should be limited and the possibility should be provided to display further details on request (E3, E4) (**MR7**). Furthermore, a *"structured visual presentation"* (E4) is useful. For this, there should be thematic categories with distances to each other (E3, E6), color differences (E4, E5) and tabular presentation of information with a *"gray-white-gray grid, so that you see rows for each theme"* (E1) (**MR8**). Apart from the presentation of information, the handover needs to be integrated into existing work processes of SEs. To implement handovers effectively, SEs should be informed in a way that minimizes work interruptions (E3–5). Ensuring sufficient preparation, the handover should be announced in advance (E3, E4) (**MR9**).

4.2   Design Principles and Instantiation

DPs. The identified MRs were used to derive three overarching DPs of the type form and function [64]. Based on kernel theories, four MRs emerged, while five were derived through expert interviews. Figure 2 illustrates the mapping of MRs and DPs.

The presentation of information in a handover UI is a prerequisite for the continuation of the service encounter after CA failure. As humans have a limited capacity to process information, the set of information in a handover UI should be limited and more detailed information should be displayed on demand. Thereby, information processing can be supported and negative effects of overload can be avoided (**DP1**). To ensure a goal-directed request processing, information should be presented that allows SEs to quickly comprehend the problem and create a mental representation of it to answer the customer request. Therefore, the object and content of the request as well as identity of the requester should be displayed in a prominent manner (**DP2**). For effortless continuation of request processing after CA failure, information should be visually presented in a way that is easily processable and applicable to facilitate subsequent problem-solving activities of SEs (**DP3**).

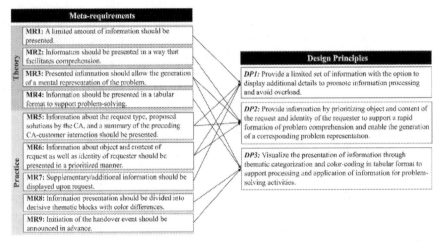

Fig. 2. Derived DPs based on MRs.

Prototype Instantiation. The DPs were instantiated in a prototypical handover UI. To guide the development, DPs were translated into DFs to evaluate the web-based prototype with user tests (see Fig. 3).

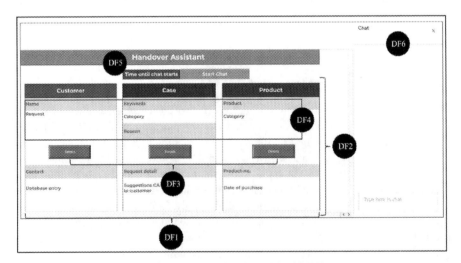

Fig. 3. Web-based handover UI with DFs.

Once the handover has been initiated, the UI is populated with a limited set of information divided into thematic categories (customer, case, and product) (**DF1**: *DP1, 2, 3*) and presented in tabular format with different coloring (**DF2**: *DP2, 3*). Integrated detail-buttons are provided to display additional information for each thematic category (**DF3**: *DP1, 2*). To present inquirer identity, content and object of request, the customer's name, a summary of the previous CA-customer interaction, and product features are displayed (**DF4**: *DP2*) complementary to a chat history in the chat window. To announce an incoming customer interaction via handover, a status indication is presented with changing states (idle, 2 min., 1 min., start chat) (**DF5**: *DP3*). To minimize additional cognitive load and facilitate the use of provided information during customer interaction, the chat window is integrated into the prototype (**DF6**: *DP1*).

5   Evaluation

The handover UI was evaluated with user tests to obtain insights into the usage behavior via screen recordings. In addition, interviews were conducted with ten PAs to assess the influence of the prototype on their behavior and task accomplishment. The analysis of usage behavior showed that PAs sent an initial message to the customer after on average 65 s. One-half (5/10) of the PAs sent a welcome message after on average 33 s, followed by a message with a question and/or problem-solving suggestion after another on average 30 s. The other half sent a combination of welcome message and question or solution proposal after on average 86 s. During the user tests, nine out of ten PAs used all three buttons to view more details. Eight PAs clicked the buttons after their initial message, whereas one person clicked the customer details button before the conversation started. Among these eight PAs, five generated a greeting and then a request-related message. Overall, eight out of ten PAs repeated questions previously asked by the CA. Of four CA questions, four PAs repeated one and four repeated two. All PAs proposed a suitable solution to the customer.

The analysis of the interviews revealed PAs' predominantly positive impression of the handover UI. The handling was rated as simple and presented information were conceived to be concise as they help to comprehend the customer request at hand (PA 1–4, PA6, PA7, PA9) (e.g., *"it is concise and short and not overstimulating, which is why you have a good overview"* (PA2)). The thematic differentiation of the presented information was evaluated positively, as it accentuates where to find which information and allows to determine what is needed (PA1, PA3–7, PA10): *"I also like the structure with these three fields and the overview as it helps to find one missing piece of information – I directly know in which part to look for it"* (PA1) and *"the structuring helps because I can easily filter what is important and what is not"* (PA7). However, the display of CA solution proposals as additional information in the category "Case" was criticized, as this information is important to understand the request and should therefore be visible immediately (PA1–4, PA6–10), e.g., *"I would prefer the suggestions 'chatbot to customer' at the top and not hidden in the detail, because this was the important information that was needed"* (PA6). Overall, the PAs considered the information to be relevant to continue the customer interaction. For problem solving, the category "Case" was rated as most important (PA1, PA2, PA4, PA5, PA8–10), because "[…] *information help to facilitate problem-solving, because I just know where it stopped*" (PA5). In addition to the "Case" summary comprising a category, keywords, and suggested solutions from CA to customer, information about the customer and product was rated to be useful. PAs reported that this information is valuable because no additional effort needs to be invested into collecting customer- or product-specific details. In addition, PAs directly knew how to address the customer, what the product is, and whether a warranty claim is valid (PA1–5, PA7–10). The need for a chat log as information was assessed differently by the PAs. Some preferred a chatlog to reassure themselves about the customer request (PA1, PA5, PA6, PA8) others relied on the summary in "Case" or prefer an optional display of the log (PA3, PA4, PA7, PA10).

For the continuation of the customer interaction, the use of the handover UI initially caused mental effort for the PAs, as displayed information had to be processed and contextualized. Subsequently, the processing of the request became easier (PA2, PA4, PA5, PA6, PA8, PA10), e.g., "*the interface is more complicated at first because I had to understand the interface and you had to figure out where to get what information. And then easier, because I knew where I was and how to proceed*" (PA8). The PAs expressed that request processing without the UI would be more complex and strenuous, as they would have been required to obtain information and evaluate it during customer interaction (PA2, PA4, PA5, PA6, PA8, PA10). In addition, PAs assume that mental demands and errors in the form of repeated questions are reduced by regularly using the handover UI (PA1, PA3, PA4, PA10). The continuation of the customer interaction was quick and goal-directed for the PAs because the initiation of the conversation was facilitated. PAs did not uniformly feel time pressure. For those who experienced it, the interface had a stress-reducing effect (PA1, PA4, PA10). As required information was presented, PAs were able to invest into individualizing customer interaction (e.g., addressing customer by name) (PA2, PA4, PA9). In general, PAs reported that using the handover UI reduced their invested time and workload (PA1, PA3, PA4, PA5, PA10): "*I see advantages in the fact that it reduces time, i.e., it reduces the workload, because you get information about what has previously been asked*" (PA10).

In addition to these findings, the user tests revealed potential for improvement. The continuation of the customer interaction could be improved, if the display of CA solution steps during customer interaction before handover was improved and directly visible (PA1–4, PA6–10). Furthermore, information on customer sentiment either via viewable chatlog or integrated dashboard would be helpful to prepare for the interaction (PA6, PA9). The start of a customer interaction after handover should be determinable by the PA via a button (PA5, PA6, PA9). During interaction, canned responses (e.g., greeting messages) and suggestions for solutions could be useful to speed up problem-solving of PAs (PA6, PA9, PA2).

6 Discussion and Conclusion

In this study, we report on the development of DPs for a handover UI to avert CA failure in OCS and implement a hybrid service recovery strategy. As part of a larger DSR project, design knowledge from the first cycle on the handover process, collection, and transfer of information is supplemented with aspects of designing a UI in the current cycle that enables SEs to continue customer encounters quickly and effortlessly after CA failure. To answer the RQs, we derived three DPs based on practical requirements and theoretical findings and instantiated them in a web-based prototype for evaluation. The conducted user tests showed that the handover UI allows PAs to continue the customer interaction in a goal-directed fashion with limited effort. Therefore, the results suggest that, consistent with CLT, extrinsic cognitive load induced by the amount of presented information was manageable for SEs [56, 59]. The qualitative interviews with PAs revealed that the presented information types are relevant and allowed them to quickly generate an understanding of the problem due to the concise overview (DP1). This perception of the PAs indicates that the tabular presentation of the information in the three thematic categories according to CFT facilitated the quick formation of a mental representation of the problem, i.e., customer request [60, 62]. The importance of the summarized customer concern ("Case") for a seamless continuation of the interaction highlights the relevance of DP2. The integration of design elements (headings, colors, boxes) enabled PAs to easily find and process relevant information (DP3). The partial information display was used by the PAs to initiate the customer interaction promptly after the handover to subsequently view and analyze further details via the buttons. This approach was confirmed by the behavioral analysis based on the screen recordings, which showed that the optional details allow PAs to apply different strategies to start the interaction (greeting vs. greeting and problem-relevant message). However, the hidden display of CA suggestions to customer was obstructive for PAs, as the information remained undetected and customers had to answer redundant questions after handover. The evaluation results indicate that PAs have to invest a limited amount of time to initiate the conversation with the customer due to the handover UI and their workload is reduced. Furthermore, it lowers perceived time pressure and thus enables more customer-centric interactions. Last, the results suggest that benefits from using the UI unfold after repeated use and presupposes SEs' knowledge about the objects of request.

With this study we present a feasible way to advance the hybridization of online customer service. By interlocking CA and SE work processes via handover UI, CA failure can be prevented, SEs can be supported during service recovery, and customers quickly receive a solution. Hence, by presenting DPs and evaluation results, we provide contributions to research and practice. With the prescriptive design knowledge about form and function and explanatory knowledge about effects [55, 65, 66], we contribute insights to address knowledge gaps related to service recovery strategies for AI-based service delivery by incorporating theoretical insights referring to human cognitive functioning to design UIs [14, 21, 40]. Furthermore, we present a designed entity in form of a web-based handover UI, which represents a situational instantiation of our design. Thereby, we deliver guidelines on how to implement an immediate assistance recovery strategy in OCS. In addition, we present a potential solution to advance the hybridization of online service delivery by purposefully combining the strengths of AI and SEs. In practice, the design knowledge can be applied by service companies to implement a hybrid service recovery strategy to avert customer dissatisfaction in the event of CA failure and adequately support SEs to quickly generate a solution after handover.

Despite the promising findings, however, there are a few limitations to consider. The handover UI was artificially evaluated and customers simulated. In addition, the customer request was prepared for the evaluation to allow the involvement of participants from different online service contexts. These aspects limit the generalizability of presented results. Therefore, we propose avenues for future research. In a quantitative-experimental study, time advantages and quality of suggestions of different handover UIs could be compared to a baseline. In this context, the functionality of the UI could be extended by displaying appropriate knowledge items and/or canned responses (e.g., greeting messages) as a complement to the information from the CA customer interaction to support SEs during problem solving. In addition, the hybrid service recovery strategy for CAs could be implemented in an organization to measure (1) SEs' cognitive load induced by handover UI, (2) customers' satisfaction, and (3) operational efficiency in an OCS department with a quantitative longitudinal evaluation setting.

Acknowledgement. The research was financed with funding provided by the German Federal Ministry of Education and Research and the European Social Fund under the "Future of work" program (INSTANT, 02L18A111).

References

1. Bitner, M.J., Brown, S.W., Meuter, M.L.: Technology infusion in service encounters. J. Acad. Mark. Sci. **28**, 138–149 (2000)
2. Larivière, B., et al.: "Service Encounter 2.0": an investigation into the roles of technology, employees and customers. J. Bus. Res. **79**, 238–246 (2017)
3. Chakrabarti, C., Luger, G.F.: Artificial conversations for customer service Chatterbots: architecture, algorithms, and evaluation metrics. Expert Syst. Appl. **42**, 6878–6897 (2015)
4. Bittner, E., Oeste-Reiß, S., Leimeister, J.M.: Where is the bot in our team? Toward a taxonomy of design option combinations for conversational agents in collaborative work. In: 52nd Hawaii International Conference on System Sciences (HICSS). Grand Wailea, USA (2019)
5. Gnewuch, U., Morana, S., Maedche, A.: Towards designing cooperative and social conversational agents for customer service. In: 38th International Conference on Information Systems (ICIS). Seoul, South Korea (2017)
6. Wirtz, J.: Organizational ambidexterity: cost-effective service excellence, service robots, and artificial intelligence. Organ. Dyn. **49**, 100719 (2020)
7. Waizenegger, L., Seeber, I., Dawson, G., Desouza, K.: Conversational agents - exploring generative mechanisms and second-hand effects of actualized technology affordances. In: 53rd Hawaii International Conference on System Sciences (HICSS). Wailea, USA (2020)
8. Janssen, A., Passlick, J., Rodríguez Cardona, D., Breitner, M.H.: Virtual assistance in any context. a taxonomy of design elements for domain-specific Chatbots. Bus. Inf. Syst. Eng. **62**, 211–225 (2020)
9. Corea, C., Delfmann, P., Nagel, S.: Towards intelligent Chatbots for customer care - practice-based requirements for a research agenda. In: 53rd Hawaii International Conference on System Sciences (HICSS). Wailea, USA (2020)
10. Schuetzler, R.M., Grimes, G.M., Giboney, J.S., Rosser, H.K.: Deciding whether and how to deploy Chatbots. MIS Q. Exec. **20**, 1–15 (2021)
11. Smith, A.K., Bolton, R.N., Wagner, J.: A model of customer satisfaction with service encounters involving failure and recovery. J. Mark. Res. **36**, 356–372 (1999)

12. Canhoto, A.I., Clear, F.: Artificial intelligence and machine learning as business tools: a framework for diagnosing value destruction potential. Bus. Horiz. **63**, 183–193 (2020)

13. Sheehan, B., Jin, H.S., Gottlieb, U.: Customer service Chatbots: anthropomorphism and adoption. J. Bus. Res. **115**, 14–24 (2020)

14. Benner, D., Elshan, E., Schöbel, S., Janson. A.: What do you mean? A review on recovery strategies to overcome conversational breakdowns of conversational agents. In: 42nd International Conference on Information Systems. Austin, USA (2021)

15. Følstad, A., Taylor, C.: Conversational repair in Chatbots for customer service: the effect of expressing uncertainty and suggesting alternatives. In: Følstad, A., et al. (eds.) CONVERSATIONS 2019. LNCS, vol. 11970, pp. 201–214. Springer, Cham (2020). https://doi.org/10. 1007/978-3-030-39540-7_14

16. Ashktorab, Z., Jain, M., Liao, Q.V., Weisz, J.D.: Resilient Chatbots: repair strategy preferences for conversational breakdowns. In: 2019 CHI Conference on Human Factors in Computing Systems, pp. 1–12. Glasgow, Scotland (2019)

17. Jylkäs, T., Äijälä, M., Vourikari, T., Rajab, V.: AI assistants as non-human actors in service design. In: 21st DMI: Academic Design Management Conference. London, UK (2018)

18. Wintersberger, P., Klotz, T., Riener, A.: Tell me more: transparency and time-fillers to optimize Chatbots' waiting time experience. In: 11th Nordic Conference on Human-Computer Interaction: Shaping Experiences, Shaping Society. Tallinn, Estonia (2020)

19. Castillo, D., Canhoto, A.I., Said, E.: The dark side of AI-powered service interactions: exploring the process of co-destruction from the customer perspective. Serv. Ind. J. **41**, 1–26 (2020)

20. Kucherbaev, P., Bozzon, A., Houben, G.-J.: Human-aided bots. IEEE Internet Comput. **22**, 36–43 (2018)

21. Bock, D.E., Brown, S.W., Meuter, M.L.: Artificial intelligence: disruption what we know about services. J. Serv. Mark. **34**, 317–334 (2020)

22. Barrett, M., Davidson, E., Prabhu, J., Vargo, S.L.: Service innovation in the digital age: key contributions and future directions. MISQ **39**, 135–154 (2015)

23. Froehle, C.M.: Service personnel, technology, and their interaction in influencing customer satisfaction. Decis. Sci. **37**, 5–38 (2006)

24. Meuter, M.L., Bitner, M.J., Ostrom, A.L., Brown, S.W.: Choosing among alternative service delivery modes: an investigation of customer trial of self-service technologies. J. Mark. **69**, 61–83 (2005)

25. Meuter, M.L., Ostrom, A.L., Roundtree, R.I., Bitner, M.J.: Self-service technologies: understanding customer satisfaction with technology-based service encounters. J. Mark. **64**, 50–64 (2000)

26. Huang, M.-H., Rust, R.T.: Artificial intelligence in service. J. Serv. Res. **21**, 155–172 (2018)

27. Xu, Y., Shieh, C.-H., van Esch, P., Ling, I.-L.: AI customer service: task complexity, problem-solving ability, and usage intention. Australas. Mark. J. **28**, 189–199 (2020)

28. Lu, V.N., et al.: Service robots, customers and service employees: what can we learn from the academic literature and where are the gaps? JSTP **30**, 361–391 (2020)

29. McLean, G., Osei-Frimpong, K.: Examining satisfaction with the experience during a live chat service encounter-implications for website providers. Comput. Hum. Behav. **76**, 494–508 (2017)

30. Diederich, S., Brendel, A.B., Morana, S., Kolbe, L.: On the design of and interaction with conversational agents: an organizing and assessing review of human-computer-interaction research. J. Associat. Inf. Syst. (2022)

31. Gnewuch, U., Morana, S., Adam, M.T.P., Maedche, A.: Faster is not always better: understanding the effect of dynamic response delays in human-Chatbot interaction. In: 26th European Conference on Information Systems (ECIS). Portsmouth, United Kingdom (2018)

32. Nguyen, T.H., Waizenegger, L., Techatassanasoontorn, A.A.: "Don't Neglect the User!" – identifying types of human-Chatbot interactions and their associated characteristics. Inf. Syst. Front. 1–42 (2021).https://doi.org/10.1007/s10796-021-10212-x

33. Poser, M., Bittner, E.: Hybrid teamwork: consideration of teamwork concepts to reach naturalistic interaction between humans and conversational agents. In: 15th International Conference on Wirtschaftsinformatik. Potsdam, Germany (2020)

34. Weiler, S., Matt, C., Hess, T.: Immunizing with information – inoculation messages against conversational agents' response failures. Electron Markets (2021)

35. Lapré, M.A., Tsikriktsis, N.: Organizational learning curves for customer dissatisfaction: heterogeneity across airlines. Manage. Sci. **52**, 352–366 (2006)

36. Diederich, S., Lembcke, T.-B., Brendel, A.B., Kolbe, L.: Not human after all: exploring the impact of response failure on user perception of anthropomorphic conversational service agents. In: 28th European Conference on Information Systems (ECIS). virtual (2020)

37. Chen, N., Mohanty, S., Jiao, J., Fan, X.: To Err is human: tolerate humans instead of machines in service failure. J. Retail. Consum. Serv. **59**, 102363 (2021)

38. Mozafari, N., Schwede, M., Hammerschmidt, M., Weiger, W.H.: Claim success, but blame the bot? User reactions to service failure and recovery in interactions with humanoid service robots. In: 55th Hawaii International Conference on System Sciences. virtual (2021)

39. Ho, T.H., Tojib, D., Tsarenko, Y.: Human staff vs. Service robot vs. Fellow customer: does it matter who helps your customer following a service failure incident? Int. J. Hospital. Manage. **87**, 102501 (2020)

40. Poser, M., Singh, S., Bittner, E.: Hybrid service recovery: design for seamless inquiry handovers between conversational agents and human service agents. In: 55th Hawaii International Conference on System Sciences. Virtual (2021)

41. Xiao, L., Kumar, V.: Robotics for customer service: a useful complement or an ultimate substitute? J. Serv. Res. **24**, 9–29 (2021)

42. van Doorn, J., et al.: Domo Arigato Mr. Roboto: emergence of automated social presence in organizational frontlines and customers service experiences. J. Serv. Res. **20**, 43–58 (2017)

43. Østerlund, C., Jarrahi, M.H., Willis, M., Boyd, K., Wolf, C.: Artificial intelligence and the world of work, a co-constitutive relationship. J Assoc Inf Sci Technol **72**, 128–135 (2021)

44. Lewandowski, T., Grotherr, C., Böhmann, T.: Managing artificial intelligence systems for value co-creation. the case of conversational agents and natural language assistants. In: Edvardsson, B., Tronvoll, B. (eds.) The Palgrave Handbook of Service Management, forthcoming. Springer, Cham (2022)

45. Ostrom, A.L., Fotheringham, D., Bitner, M.J.: Customer acceptance of AI in service encounters: understanding antecedents and consequences. In: Maglio, P.P., Kieliszewski, C.A., Spohrer, J.C., Lyons, K., Patrício, L., Sawatani, Y. (eds.) Handbook of Service Science, Volume II. SSRISE, pp. 77–103. Springer, Cham (2019). https://doi.org/10.1007/978-3-319-98512-1_5

46. Dellermann, D., Ebel, P., Söllner, M., Leimeister, J.M.: Hybrid intelligence. Bus. Inf. Syst. Eng. **61**, 637–643 (2019)

47. Wirtz, J., et al.: Brave new world: service robots in the frontline. J. Serv. Manag. **29**, 907–931 (2018)

48. Ahn, J.-H., Bae, Y.-S., Ju, J., Oh, W.: Attention adjustment, renewal, and equilibrium seeking in online search: an eye-tracking approach. J. Manag. Inf. Syst. **35**, 1218–1250 (2018)

49. Cheung, M., Hong, W., Thong, J.: Effects of animation on attentional resources of online consumers. JAIS **18**, 605–632 (2017)

50. Toreini, P., Langner, M., Maedche, A., Morana, S., Vogel, T.: Designing attentive information dashboards. JAIS (2022)

51. Carroll, J.M.: Human-computer interaction: psychology as a science of design. Annu. Rev. Psychol. **48**, 61–83 (1997)

52. Hevner, A.R., March, S.T., Park, J., Ram, S.: Design science in information systems research. MIS Q. **28**, 75–105 (2004)
53. Peffers, K., Tuunanen, T., Rothenberger, M.A., Chatterjee, S.: A design science research methodology for information systems research. J. Manag. Inf. Syst. **24**, 45–77 (2007)
54. Mayring, P.: Qualitative content analysis: theoretical foundation, basic procedures and software solution (2014)
55. Chandra, L., Seidel, S., Gregor, S.: Prescriptive knowledge in is research: conceptualizing design principles in terms of materiality, action, and boundary conditions. In: 48th Hawaii International Conference on System Sciences (HICSS). Kauai, USA (2015)
56. Sweller, J.: Cognitive load during problem solving: effects on learning. Cogn. Sci. **12**, 257–285 (1988)
57. Paas, F., van Gog, T., Sweller, J.: Cognitive load theory: new conceptualizations, specifications, and integrated research perspectives. Educ Psychol Rev **22**, 115–121 (2010)
58. Pollock, E., Chandler, P., Sweller, J.: Assimilating complex information. Learn. Instr. **12**, 61–86 (2002)
59. Brünken, R., Plass, J.L., Leutner, D.: Direct measurement of cognitive load in multimedia learning. Educ. Psychol. **38**, 53–61 (2003)
60. Teets, J.M., Tegarden, D.P., Russell, R.S.: Using cognitive fit theory to evaluate the effectiveness of information visualizations: an example using quality assurance data. IEEE Trans. Visual Comput. Graphics **16**, 841–853 (2010)
61. Vessey, I., Galletta, D.: Cognitive fit: an empirical study of information acquisition. Inf. Syst. Res. **2**, 63–84 (1991)
62. Shaft, Vessey, Vessey, I.: The Role of cognitive fit in the relationship between software comprehension and modification. MIS Q. **30**, 29–55 (2006)
63. Kelton, A.S., Pennington, R.R., Tuttle, B.M.: The Effects of information presentation format on judgment and decision making: a review of the information systems research. J. Inf. Syst. **24**, 79–105 (2010)
64. Gregor, S., Kruse, L., Seidel, S.: Research perspectives: the anatomy of a design principle. JAIS **21**, 1622–1652 (2020)
65. Gregor, S., Hevner, A.R.: Positioning and presenting design science research for maximum impact. MISQ **37**, 337–355 (2013)
66. vom Brocke, J., Winter, R., Hevner, A., Maedche, A.: special issue editorial –accumulation and evolution of design knowledge in design science research: a journey through time and space. JAIS. **21**, 520–544 (2020)

Virtual Safety Assistant: An Efficient Tool for Ensuring Safety During Covid-19 Pandemic

Manoj Ramanathan[1,2]([✉])[iD], Aalind Singh[1], Arathy Suresh[1],
Daniel Thalmann[1,3], and Nadia Magnenat-Thalmann[1,4]

[1] Dex-Lab Pte. Ltd., Singapore, Singapore
[2] Nanyang Technological University, Singapore, Singapore
mramanathan@ntu.edu.sg
[3] EPFL, Lausanne, Switzerland
[4] Miralab, University of Geneva, Geneva, Switzerland

Abstract. Using intelligent virtual assistants for controlling employee population in workspaces is a research area that remains unexplored. This paper presents a novel application of virtual humans to enforce Covid-19 safety measures in a corporate workplace. For this purpose, we develop a virtual assistant platform, Chloe, equipped with automatic temperature sensing, facial recognition, and dedicated chatbots to act as an initial filter for ensuring public health. Whilst providing an engaging user interaction experience, Chloe minimizes human to human contact, thus reducing the spread of infectious diseases. Chloe restricts the employee population within the office to government-approved safety norms. We experimented with Chloe as a virtual safety assistant in a company, where she interacted and screened the employees for Covid-19 symptoms. Participants filled an online survey to quantify Chloe's performance in terms of interactivity, system latency, engagement, and accuracy, for which we received positive feedback. We performed statistical analysis on the survey results that reveal positive results and show effectiveness of Chloe in such applications. We detail system architecture, results and limitations.

Keywords: Virtual human receptionist · Human computer interaction · Virtual embodied interaction · Covid-19 safety measures

1 Introduction

Artificial intelligence (AI) is a critical technology that has vast potential in the current advanced market. It forms the cornerstone of the scientific community to develop various vision, language and other modality algorithms by which machines can have human-like intelligence. Over the past decade, the animation and graphics industry has seen tremendous progress to create more lifelike and realistic appearance of virtual interfaces. Combining these research avenues has given rise to virtual embodied assistants (VA) in different applications, such as SARA [19], fitness coach (Millie, Ally from TwentyBN, Canada) [32] and Sim Sensei [10].

The current Covid-19 pandemic has disrupted the lives of several people, communities, organizations, companies and countries. With the pandemic still not completely stopped, organizations and companies have had to resort to different technologies to keep the business running. Most companies have opted to have work from home or staggered working hours. Furthermore, in some cases, companies bring a certain percentage of employees back to work. In companies, malls and other public places, it is always necessary for people to be screened for symptoms like fever (temperature measurement) before they are let inside. Most of these screening stations include a temperature measurement device and security guard or receptionist who filters the people entering based on the temperature of the person and premise occupancy. It is required for a guard to be present 24×7 at these stations. Because of this, guards can be exposed to the virus as well.

The above-mentioned VA technology provides a viable alternative for both the guard or receptionist and temperature screening station at public places and work places. With this in mind, we have developed and customized a virtual safety assistant, Chloe, who acts as a covid-19 symptoms screening and virtual office receptionist. Her AI modules are designed to be customized for various applications and can operate as an office receptionist. In this paper, we explore if Chloe can perform the role of an admin or a security guard who allows the entry of employees or guests in a workplace. She recognizes the employees using facial recognition and helps them in entering the workplace hassle-free. Also, Chloe measures the temperature of the employees to make sure that they are safe to enter the office, adhering to Covid-19 safety measures.

Fig. 1. The traditional setup with temperature screening and menu driven kiosk

As a part of safety measures, it is expected that workplaces have a record of employees/visitors who visit. For this purpose, all employees and visitors must manually fill a form or use a menu-driven kiosk to note their official entry. Moreover, the security is expected to make sure that the people make their entries. A sample of the current traditional setup with temperature screening and kiosk is shown in Fig. 1. With our VA, we can automate this process as well. To test the efficacy of this procedure, we conducted a user study comparing Chloe and the traditional method of manually filling the form or menu-driven kiosk to enter a secured premise. In this pandemic situation, usage of this VA breaks the traditional cloud of all other methods by implementing zero physical contact. By having a virtual embodiment, Chloe can also provide a human touch to the whole procedure. Experiments have been conducted to see how the people liked it, and how it compares against traditional methods of screening. This study aims is to observe:

- If Chloe can successfully be deployed as a virtual safety assistant to avoid physical human contact for Covid-19 safety measures.
- If Chloe can identify people by faces and record their temperatures which can be retrieved at any time.
- If employees are comfortable using a VA, such as Chloe, in workplaces.

The paper is organized as follows: Sect. 2 provides a literature review of various virtual embodied assistants and applications. Also, we focus on various methodologies such as face recognition and temperature measurement included in workplaces. In Sect. 3, we introduce our VA, Chloe, her framework and integral AI modules. We provided detailed changes in the overall framework for her to function as a virtual safety assistant at workplaces. Section 4 discusses the experimental setup and survey questionnaire prepared by us for the user study. In Sect. 5, we provide user study results and discuss insights, limitations and possible future scope. We provide conclusions in Sect. 6.

2   Literature Review

With the advent of AI and related deep learning architectures, there has been a wave of research aiming to create algorithms that mimic human-like intelligence and behaviour. We can also observe tremendous progress in graphics with the ability to create several human-like characters in various applications such as gaming, etc. The combination of progress in AI and graphics has led to the development of virtual embodied agents or assistants capable of human-like behaviour, intelligence and movements.

Creating customizable VAs that can be used in various applications has been a vital avenue of research for some time now. Several applications such as virtual human presenter [21], real estate agents [4], virtual tutoring [25], Conference Kiosk handler SARA [19] etc. With the technology in earlier times, VAs like Rea [4], Jacob [13], MACK [5] were rather primitive in realistic appearance or applications or interaction modalities. But now, more and more customizable, sophisticated and realistic VAs are available. For instance, VAs have been implemented and widely used in various healthcare-related applications ranging from answering questions (Olivia and Molly from Sensely, USA), fitness coach (Millie, Ally from TwentyBN, Canada) [32] to therapy (Sim Sensei) [10]. Recently, several other

VAs have been introduced that can be customized for various applications. For instance, 'Rachel from connect to me' [8], 'Cloudia from Cloud minds' [20], 'Millie from TwentyBN' [32] have been customized and used for several applications. Most of the VAs mentioned above can have natural language conversations and can use visual data to understand and behave according to their designed task. In this paper, we focus on our VA, Chloe, whose AI allows her to have a natural language conversation and situation awareness using visual and language cues. Chloe can be customized for various applications. In this paper, we mainly focus on how Chloe can act as Virtual Security Assistant to control the people entering secured premises such as offices/workplaces, malls, hospitals etc.

For this paper, we had installed Chloe at an office lobby as receptionist who can control people's entry based on their face and Covid-19 symptoms screening. Previously, several virtual agents such as Marve [1,2], AVARI [3], Valerie [15], MACK [5] have been used as virtual receptionists. But these methods were mainly focused on rendering the head of the agent only, they either had no bodies [2] or were placed on top of mannequins that did not move [3,15]. In contrast, we render the entire body of Chloe and provide non-verbal behaviors, movements for entire body. [22] provides a detailed survey on the various IVA user studies and considered non-verbal cues to include social behavior, affective behavior and personality traits. Chloe is designed based on these characteristics to work at any work place. The above-mentioned agents work as receptionist in a university or lab setting, where as we have implemented it for workplace or office settings. Also, our architecture is customizable and can be adapted to other applications very easily. For natural language communication, most of these agents are limited as some functionalities are triggered by keywords or phrases only. For instance, Marve [2] requires user to say 'record message' when a user wants to leave a message for another person. Due to recent developments in Natural language processing (NLP), including BERT [11,12], phonetics etc., our agent does not rely on keywords and uses semantic understanding to complete the intended functionality. Similar to the above agents, Chloe can discuss on topics outside her application domain (like jokes, weather etc.) as we have a backend integrated with Google Assistant. But Chloe can learn questions dynamically during conversations and also has a memory of her own for each user. The functionalities of Marve [1,2] are quite similar to ours, which include face detection, handling unknown persons, sending email messages, provide directions etc. But in addition to these functionalities, Chloe is capable of receiving packages, make phone calls, send SMS to known people, book meeting rooms, showing pictures or videos. Apart from this, in this paper, we are mainly focused on Chloe's ability to screen employees and visitors of a work place for Covid-19 symptoms.

Face recognition [6] is a well-researched computer vision problem that aims at recognizing people from video or image data. Researchers have already shown that face can be used as a unique biometric that can be used for restricting the access control to office premises [16,23,27]. Because of the extensive research over the years, face recognition has been linked to several VAs [8,20,25] and robots [24]. In this paper, we integrate face recognition to Chloe to provide door access control to offices/workplaces. It helps her maintain records on employees arrival times and other details that can be retrieved easily whenever needed. It also helps her to customize her conversations according to the person's identity.

Temperature measurement has become an essential component after the Covid-19 pandemic, as fever is one of the most important symptoms. Due to this, all public places, workplaces etc., have some form of temperature measurement system ranging from temperature guns to IR cameras to provide safe access. Recently, Ithermo [7] was introduced as an AI-driven system for temperature screening of people to provide secured access to locations in Singapore. Most of these screenings are required to be manned by a guard or security, who has to check if the person being screened can be let in or not. Due to this, guards have to be hired specifically for this purpose, and they cannot do any other work at that time. Also, these guards can be exposed to Covid-19 as they meet everyone who is being screened. In this paper, we aim at making Chloe, a virtual safety assistant, who can measure the temperature of people and screen them for symptoms such as fever. Using Chloe means guards can do other work if needed and do not have to be exposed to everyone. In this paper, we quantify the functioning of Chloe in recognizing faces (employees), measuring temperature and providing safe access to office premises.

3   Platform Architecture

The capabilities and functionalities of any virtual human or robot are determined by the underlying platform that controls them. Applications/tasks for which a virtual human is made directly influence the way its platform is implemented. For Chloe, our virtual safety assistant, we have developed a platform that focuses on modularity and customization. The platform is designed so that modules can be added/removed; specific functions can be customized according to requirements. This enables Chloe to function in different settings, such as office reception, mall concierge, hospital/health care receptionist, etc. This paper mainly deals with how she can act as a virtual safety assistant for workplaces/organizations controlling people's entry, recognizing symptoms of people and taking necessary actions.

The platform comprises two components, the embodiment (Virtual character) and the mechanism that controls it. Firstly, we will look at the mechanism that controls Chloe's behaviour. The mechanism comprises several AI modules used for sensing information about users and the environment, processing them. The main module involved is the character controller. As the name suggests, it focuses on controlling the behaviour of the character (Chloe). For this purpose, the module houses a separate behaviour tree; an encoded data structure developed to check for various stimuli from the environment and decide how to act according to each of these stimuli. These behaviour trees control four fundamental aspects of the character: animation/gesture, gaze, speech, and emotions. The module receives information from various input devices on the user and environment, which serve as a stimulus. The behaviour trees are encoded with stimulus and weightage for each of them. When any stimulus is received, each behaviour tree will process it separately and act upon it to arrive at a final decision that is to be shown by Chloe (embodiment). For instance, 3D user skeleton position is a stimulus that is handled mainly in gaze tree to change Chloe's eye and neck position.

As mentioned above, the input devices form an essential component of the platform. In this study, we have included four input devices with our platform, namely, 3D Kinect camera (for 3D positions of the user), Web camera or RGB camera (face recognition), Lepton IR camera (for temperature measurement) and microphone (to get user speech). The stimulus received from these devices drives the platform and hence the functioning of Chloe. Interfaces between the Character controller and the other platform components are established using dedicated sockets, and information is passed in JSON format. The usage of JSON format allows for the possibility of web and cloud-hosted embodiment as well. Web sockets can be alternatively used for replacing these dedicated sockets. The JSON format and what is to be sent to the character controller is defined and controlled in the platform architecture. Therefore, any device can be added/replaced/removed based on our requirements. The format and information to be sent can be modified and customized according to the platform architecture.

An essential aspect of a virtual human or robot is the speech interaction capabilities. For this purpose, we have dedicated speech recognition and speech synthesis developed for Chloe. Another important aspect is the natural language understanding and NLP capabilities. For Chloe's speech interaction, we have implemented and integrated a BERT chatbot [11,12]. This chatbot serves as a local database of questions and can be modified according to application/ functionality. The local database is encoded as JSON files, and we include three databases.

- Personal questions - Questions related to Chloe, her personal choices, preferences, outfits etc.
- Application-specific questions - Questions related to the application she is currently employed for, like office receptionist etc.
- Dynamic or on-the-fly learning questions - Questions she is learning during the conversation with users.

For questions outside the chatbot, Chloe is also linked to Google assistant and can pick up answers from it. However, the response time for these cases depends on the network speed. These questions are added to the dynamic question database mentioned above for fast retrieval of responses. The customization of databases allows Chloe to function in different roles. Apart from this, to work in an organizational role, Chloe also has access to employee information.

The second important aspect of the platform is the virtual embodiment of Chloe itself. Chloe's embodiment is completely made in 3DS MAX and ported to Unity 3D, which is used to animate and control her. The hairstyles, appearance, clothes can be customized and changed. Figure 2 shows Chloe in various appearances. Once Chloe is added to the scene in Unity 3D, animations and scripts required for its functioning with the platform can be added to it. After which, an executable can be built in Unity 3D for various platforms. For this study, we have used a High Definition Rendering pipeline[1] as Chloe is installed at the workplace entrance and is rendered on a bigger screen.

Fig. 2. Chloe - Customized with different appearances suitable for various applications.

To function as a Virtual Safety Assistant, Chloe needs to perform the following tasks in a workplace setting:

- Identify if a person entering is an employee or visitor (Face recognition).
- Measure person's temperature to determine if it is safe for him/her to enter the office (Temperature measurement).
- Record the entry of a person with the following information, Name, temperature, time of arrival and telephone number.
- Ensure the employee population at a given time within the office is restricted to the safety norms as suggested by the government. For instance, make sure only 75% of employees are present inside at a given time, etc.

For this purpose, we discuss two components in detail in the following subsections, Face recognition and Temperature Measurement.

---

[1] https://docs.unity3d.com/Packages/com.unity.render-pipelines.high-definition@13.0/manual/index.html.

3.1   Face Recognition

Face recognition allows Chloe to know the person's identity willing to enter the secured premises such as offices/workplaces. For our purpose, we used an open-source Deepface [28] facial recognition and facial attribute analysis model for identifying the person interacting with the virtual system Chloe. To ensure proper recognition and measurement of temperature, we defined a zone where Chloe will interact with the users. This interaction zone is defined based on X, Y, and Z coordinates obtained from the Kinect sensor. Apart from helping to get reliable face image and temperature measurement, the interaction zone also helps us tune the microphone's sensitivity, such that it can pick up speech audio within this range. As soon as the person enters the recognition range (interaction zone), the system checks if it is a known or unknown person based on the employee face database collected. When a known person is recognized, Chloe will note down the arrival time for the corresponding person. For unknown faces, Chloe will take snapshots of the person with arrival time, and these people can be trained at a later stage if needed.

The facial recognition pipeline comprises the four standard stages: detect, align, represent and verify. For the collection of employee face data, we took three face profile photos of employees (Front-facing, Left-facing and Right-facing). We trained the system on employee profiles using the Google FaceNet recognition model [26] available in Deepface [28]. For matching the face profiles, we use the cosine similarity matching distance metric. Based on an initial round of training and testing results, we optimized the various parameters, such as matching threshold distance according to our specific requirements. In few cases, we added a few more face images for certain employees if they are wearing glasses or facial accessories. Initial testing showed that facial accessories and hair could affect facial recognition performance. The final facial recognition system was then connected directly to our character controller and dialogue system to give a personalized response to every employee when they checked in using our system.

3.2   Temperature Measurement

For any person entering the workplace, Chloe is expected to act as a temperature screening device. People showing increased body temperature need to be prevented from entering the premises, and appropriate personnel must be called in to provide proper care. Since each person has to be recognized by face and their temperature measured, Chloe is placed in a kiosk such that each person can be screened separately (using the interaction zone mentioned above). For temperature screening, we have integrated a FLIR Lepton 3.5 camera with the platform. The FLIR lepton 3.5 is a tiny thermal camera with either 160×120 or 80×60 active pixels. Lepton camera captures accurate, calibrated, and non-contact temperature data in every pixel of each image [29]. It can be easily integrated as an IR sensor or thermal imager to mobile devices and other electronics. In our Chloe Kiosk, since the camera is small, we have made a separate holder that houses it, and this can be connected to the kiosk.

Fig. 3. Image from FLIR lepton 3.5 Thermal camera showing the body temperature for an employee

As shown in Fig. 3, we can get temperature data for each pixel in the thermal image. From the Fig. 3, it is necessary to select or average out regions that contain the person only. From the setup shown in Fig. 5, we can see the Microsoft Life Cam used for facial recognition and thermal sensor are placed together. The placement of these cameras helps us get an image with only the person of interest in the image, thus, reducing erroneous temperature measurements. Another essential concern is to calculate the temperature of human skin accurately. For this purpose, we need to consider the effect of emissivity of the object being measured as well. Based on [30,31], we set an emissivity of human skin between 0.95–0.98 for our calculations and find the final temperature for each person being screened. Only when the person's temperature is less than 37.5 °C Celcius, he/she is allowed to enter the premises. Once the person is cleared to enter the premises, the identity of the person (from face recognition), arrival time and the measured temperature are all recorded and maintained by Chloe. The entry is made separately for unknown people; an image of the person is also stored separately with a timestamp. When a person with a temperature of more than 37.5 °C Celcius (showing fever symptoms) is detected, Chloe makes a call to the workplace administrator so that appropriate steps can be taken. For placing phone calls, sending SMS etc., a dedicated account has been made with Twilio API[2].

During the installation and fine-tuning of the thermal camera, we observed certain limitations of our setup. Sometimes, the field of the camera might include other iridescent objects like office lights, etc. The presence of such lights could affect the temperature measurement, especially when they are close to employees. Therefore, we have corrected the placement of the thermal camera to ensure such objects do not appear in the field of view. Also, we observed that employees might have coffee cups in their hands, which could also result in erroneous temperature measurements.

---

[2] Twilio API setup: https://www.twilio.com/.

4   Experimental Study

In order to answer the aim of the study mentioned in Sect. 1 regarding the usability, features, and overall performance of VA, we installed Chloe in an office lobby as a virtual safety assistant and receptionist. This location was chosen so that Chloe can screen employees for Covid-19 symptoms before they enter the premises and can also interact with employees. This will allow her to function both as a virtual safety assistant and receptionist. After their interaction with Chloe, the employees are required to answer a survey questionnaire about how their interaction experience, performance and reliability of Chloe, etc. They can interact with Chloe after they are screened to enter the premises. However, the survey is mainly related to their interaction experience during the screening and maintaining the safety measures for Covid-19. All the participants were required to consent to participate in this study and take photos to train the face recognition module.

4.1   Experiment

The user study was conducted to compare the VA and traditional methods of providing safe access to an office premise. We conducted this experiment with a total of 15 participants. The participants were chosen randomly from different departments of the company who did not have any interaction with the VA before. We conducted the study with a small number of employees. Most of the employees were forced to stay home and could not come to the office because of Covid-19 restrictions and safety measures. For the first phase of the experiments, all 15 participant's faces were trained and added to the facial recognition database of the VA. They were also briefed about the purpose of the study and the protocol that is involved. The questionnaire was not given prior to the experiment to avoid any bias in analysing the VA. The experiment was conducted on the office premises. Each participant was given a week for reporting their usage experiences in the form of a short post-test questionnaire. A 5-point Likert rating and yes/no responses were used for evaluating the user experiences. In addition to these 15 participants, we had collected the face profiles of some more employees who could not be involved in the study as they were mostly home due to covid-19 restrictions. In total, we had 47 employee faces in our database, but only 15 participants were able to use and interact with Chloe as a virtual safety assistant.

4.2   Setup

The user study setup involved the virtual assistant embodiment (Chloe) in the office's reception area with a participant in front of the VA in an interaction zone. This zone is defined with the help of the 3D coordinates provided by the Kinect sensor. Upon entry into the interaction zone, the participant has to initiate the conversation using any greeting as a buzz phrase. This phrase signals the intention of the employee to enter the office. The buzz phrases can

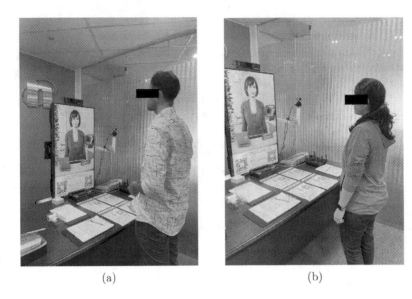

(a)   (b)

Fig. 4. Participants interacting with the Virtual Assistant

be greetings like *'hello'*, *'hi'*, *'good morning'* etc. In response, the VA greets the participant and provides necessary instructions to him/her for a smooth entry to the office by measuring the temperature and recognising the participant's face. These instructions include removing masks and looking into the camera etc. Once a reliable face recognition is done, Chloe will make a database entry of the person, time of arrival and measured temperature of the person for that day. During the procedure, Chloe's dialogue system will greet them by their name and provide information to them about their temperature. For an unknown person, she will inform the workplace administrator about the arrival of visitors. Our VA can also save the images of these visitors with time stamps and temperature. Employees and participants are free to interact with Chloe after she screens them for entry. If the employees come to Chloe again, she will remember them and not screen them as first-time entries. She can still screen them for temperature symptoms. All 15 participants will go through this procedure, followed by filling the questionnaire based on the performance of the VA during the screening procedure. Figure 4 shows employees interacting with Chloe during the study.

Figure 5 shows the setup of Chloe system with various hardware devices included in her system. The system runs on an Intel I7 CPU, 64 GB RAM and Windows 10.

Fig. 5. The virtual safety assistant setup

4.3   Survey Questionnaire

In this subsection, we provide details on the questionnaire used for gauging the performance of our VA. The questionnaire is based upon the Likert Scale [18] and yes/no responses. The objective behind the questionnaire survey is to let the users share their feedback towards Chloe's usability and reliability. The participants were required to use the Chloe system as an entry gateway to the office premises to gauge the same. Chloe would interact with them and determine if the person is authorized and safe to enter. Based on the interaction experience during the screening and entry procedure, participants must fill the survey questionnaire. The ten pointers of the questionnaire are presented in Table 1.

The questionnaire survey is done with the 15 participants from the company who were part of the experiment. The questionnaire was distributed via Google Forms by sending an e-mail to the participants directly. The entire questionnaire is mainly divided into two parts - the usability and the trustability of the VA. The first part focuses on evaluating the usability and satisfaction obtained after using the VA at different levels, starting from the overall performance of the VA to each of its modules seamlessly working, and the second part focuses on the privacy-related questions. The detailed results of the questionnaire survey are presented in the next section.

Table 1. List of questions in Virtual Safety Assistant (VSA) Usability Survey

#	Questions	Options
1	The Virtual Safety Assistant (VSA) is easy to use	Yes/Maybe/No
2	The VSA recognises my face accurately	Yes/Not Sure/No
3	The performance of VSA system is satisfactory	Yes/Maybe/No
4	The responding time is appropriate	Yes/Maybe/No
5	The system can be intrusive or detrimental to privacy	Choose one: – Strongly Agree – Agree – Neutral – Disagree – Strongly Disagree
6	The system will reduce human physical contact during covid-19	Yes/Maybe/No
7	The system can be improved with	Choose one or more: – Quality of Interaction – More empathy – More checking rules – None of the Above
8	Instead of VSA, a voice would have been enough	Yes/Maybe/No
9	Overall, the VSA is better than the traditional methods such as standalone temperature sensors	Yes/Maybe/No
10	Recommendations and comments on the VSA system	Text response from the user

5   Results and Discussion

In this section, we provide the results of the study we conducted with the participants. We use the survey questionnaire and the obtained responses to gauge the usability, accuracy and trustability (security) of Chloe as a virtual safety assistant in an office environment and if Covid-19 safety measures are properly followed when using our VA. Thus, using the survey responses, we intend to determine if the aim proposed in Sect. 1 is valid and Chloe can be successfully deployed in a large scale workplace environment.

5.1   Accurate Detection

The central aspect of Chloe's usage as a virtual safety assistant is her ability to detect employee identity using face recognition and their corresponding temperature accurately. In survey question number 2, we ask the participants in the survey if their face was detected correctly. From Fig. 6(a), we can see 93.3% (14 employees) of the participants were accurately detected. There was one participant who has recorded 'Not sure' response even though he was accurately detected. As mentioned in Subsect. 3.1, the initial trials and parameter tuning conducted resulted in such high accuracy of face recognition. The initial trials helped us fix the distance between the camera and the person's face, cosine matching distance threshold etc.

After recognizing the face of the participant, Chloe measures his/her temperature. Once measured, she will announce the temperature of the individual and if he is cleared to enter or not. Then the information is stored in a secured database that can be retrieved only by the company/ workplace administrator. The participants were required to verify if the temperature given by Chloe is accurate enough or not using a temperature gun placed on the table. If there is any discrepancy, they can record it in the survey as comments. None of the participants reported erroneous temperature detection in the comments section. From the survey, we can clearly see that Chloe is very accurate in face recognition and temperature measurement. This ensures that only authorized and Covid-19 safe employees will be allowed to enter the premises.

5.2   Usability of Chloe

In this subsection, we look at the ease-of-use, comfortability with Chloe etc., from the survey. From Table 1, we can see that questions 1, 2, 3, 4, 7 and 9 are related to the usability of Chloe. But question 2 has already been discussed as a part of accurate face detection.

One important aspect of having a reliable and convincing human embodiment is the response time of the VA. Survey question 4 deals specifically with the response time of Chloe during only the initial screening procedure. From the Fig. 6(a), we can see that there is a mixed response for this question with 40% 'Maybe', 33.3% 'Yes' and 26.7% 'No'. For the screening procedure, we have to complete two primary tasks, recognize the buzz word said by the participant and accurate face and temperature detection. The response time and accurate detections are inversely related because we can greet the participant with an appropriate response only after knowing the employee's identity. To achieve a faster response time, we have to trade-off with the accuracy of face recognition. As we needed a higher accuracy, our response time was larger, around 4–5 s. However, this response time is only during the initial screening procedure; for a normal interaction, this will be reduced to an average of 1–2 s. However, the participants were asked to record their interaction experience with Chloe during the screening procedure alone.

Another important concern is the recognition of buzz phrases spoken by the employees to begin the screening procedure. For speech recognition, we have used a Google cloud console setup[3] with the microphone integrated into Chloe. Specifically, we did not want to use handheld microphones because the same microphone has to be used by every employee. As shown in the Fig. 5, we have used a simple shotgun microphone for our experiments. Speech recognition depends on several parameters, such as microphone sensitivity, microphone direction, noise reduction, etc. We were able to tune these parameters according to the acoustics of the office receptionist area. However, recognizing the speech of employees with

---

[3] Google cloud console setup: https://console.cloud.google.com.

feeble voices would be very difficult. Because of this, recognition of buzz phrases was difficult for some employees resulting in a longer response time.

Questions 1, 3 and 7 specifically are focused on the ease of use and performance of Chloe. From Fig. 6(a) and 6(b), we can see the answers for the questions 1, 3 and 7. None of the participants felt Chloe is not easy to use (80% 'Yes', 20% 'Maybe'). Majority of the participants felt the performance of Chloe was satisfactory with 60% 'Yes', 33.3% 'Maybe' and 6.7% 'No'. We could see from the comments that participants wanted faster response time and more interaction with Chloe than just the initial screening process. Many of the participants could have recorded 'Maybe' or 'No' because they were expecting to have more interaction with Chloe. This is also supported by the response to question 7 illustrated in Fig. 6(b). Most participants have requested for improving quality of interaction with Chloe (60% 'Quality of interaction', 6.7% 'More checking rules' and 33.3% 'None of the above'). From the comments provided, we could see that the participants wanted to have more interaction and functionalities such as 'Chloe as a receptionist to ask questions any time on any subject (multipurpose agent)', 'To recognize the person with the mask on' etc. As mentioned in Sect. 3, Chloe is already integrated with chatbots and google assistant that allows her to interact with participants on any topic and can act as a receptionist. In this survey, participants have recorded only according to interactions in the initial screening procedure and not the speech interaction capabilities. After Covid-19, face recognition technologies needed to be adapted to account for masked faces. Several studies [9,14,17] have shown the effects of masks on face recognition models and how they have been modified. The inclusion of masked face recognition to Chloe would be part of our future work.

Question 1–4 are mainly focused on the usability and performance of Chloe as a VSA. We conducted statistical analysis to determine whether or not there are interactions amongst the variables measured by each of these questions. Since the number of participants were less, a chi-squared test of independence could not be used. Instead we employed either Fisher's exact test (when the contingency tables were 2×2) or the Freeman-Halton extension of the Fisher's exact test (when the contingency tables were 3×3). Among the pairs of questions considered in the analysis, Fisher's exact test showed that the performance of Chloe (Q3) has a marginally significant dependence on face recognition (Q2) ($p = .06$). This result reiterates the importance of accurate face detection for Chloe to be employed in this application. The rest of the pairs did not show any significant dependence.

5.3 Maintaining Safety Protocols for Covid-19 and Comparison to Previous Method

One of our primary goals was to maintain Covid-19 safety protocol by reducing human contact and also replace the traditional method of just having a pen and paper to record the entry of employees. Having a security guard near the entry throughout the day was also difficult as he/she would still come in contact with the people entering the premises. We intended to develop a virtual embodied assistant that can maintain Covid-19 safety by reducing human contact. The virtual embodiment allows us to maintain a human touch to the screening process. To gauge the same, survey questions 6, 8, and 9 were used.

For question 6 related to the reducing human contact, all participants were in favour of Chloe with 86.7% *'Yes'* and 13.3% *'Maybe'* responses. From Fig. 6(a), we can see no participant has said that Chloe will not reduce human physical contact during Covid-19. This is an essential criterion for maintaining the safety of employees. Questions 8 and 9 were specifically related to Chloe embodiment and comparison to the traditional method (pen and paper) discussed earlier in the paper. In question 8, we wanted to know if the participants wanted the embodiment or just the voice would be enough. From Fig. 6(a), we can see most participants (60%) said a voice would not be enough. Rest 40% were equally split between *'Yes'* and *'Maybe'*. Almost all the participants had recorded that the proposed VA (Chloe) is better the traditional methods discussed earlier in the paper (80% *'Yes'* and 20% *'Maybe'* responses, see Fig. 6(a)).

The primary concern for most participants was related to the privacy of the participant (question 5). From Fig. 6(b), we can see that 40% *'Agree'*, 40% *'Neutral'* and 20% *'disagree'* with the statement. This could be mainly because of three reasons. First, Chloe's face recognition module is trained with a database of employee face profiles (can be considered as employee personal data). Second, Chloe records the identity, the temperature measured and the time of arrival of all participants. The participants are unaware that all facial datasets, attributes used for training the model and database of employees making entry into the office are stored as encrypted data that can be accessed only by the company administrator. Due to this, most participants could believe Chloe to be intrusive. Finally, whenever a recognition is made, Chloe calls out the participant name and his/her measured temperature, which others can hear. We had designed this as a feedback mechanism by which employees know that they have been detected correctly and allowed access to the premise. We plan to provide more sophisticated feedback such as sending SMS or secured QR codes in the future for privacy concerns.

From the participants response, we can see an overall positive response to Chloe as a virtual safety assistant that can replace traditional methods. It has been shown to be effective, accurate and reliable to maintain secure access to premises and Covid-19 safety measures at workplaces. One primary benefactor of our proposed VA system is the company administrator responsible for collecting and maintaining the database of individuals entering the workplace. Data of people entering the office with arrival time, temperature measurement are stored in Chloe and can be securely accessed only by the company administrator. It was also necessary for them to ensure that the employee population at a given time within the office is restricted to the government's safety norms. Chloe was able to automate this entire process. The company administrator will be informed immediately if any problem is encountered, like a person with a higher temperature, population more than the government-approved norms etc. Due to the presence of Chloe, no company administrator or security guard have to be present throughout the day at the lobby.

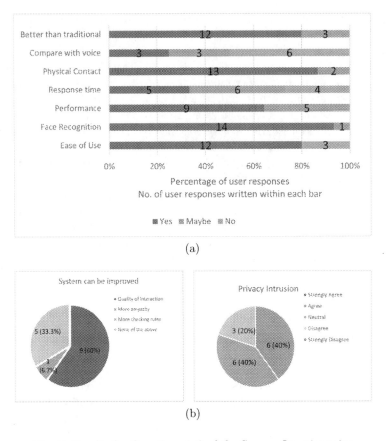

(a)

(b)

Fig. 6. Results for Questions 1–9 of the Survey Questionnaire

6   Conclusion

Covid-19 has changed the ways organizations operate, and there is a requirement to keep workplaces safe and secure. For this reason, it is necessary to screen employees who intend to enter the office. Even though the traditional methods of temperature screening are effective, it still requires a human security guard to be present always (who has a risk of exposure), and administrators are required to keep track of all employees and visitors making entry to the workplace. To provide a secure and safe passage of employees with no human contact, we propose Chloe, a virtual human-embodied safety assistant that can accurately detect faces and measure temperature. Chloe can accurately detect employees and determine if they are safe to enter. She can also detect visitors whose faces can be retrained if needed. Chloe keeps records of employees and visitors with information on the time of arrival, temperature, etc. Chloe can be completely customized according to every organization's needs and can also serve as a virtual receptionist. Having such a virtual receptionist would also help to reduce the work burden on the employee workforce. To test the efficacy and performance of Chloe as a virtual safety assistant, we conducted a user study where Chloe will screen each participant to check if he/she can enter the office. Each participant filled up an online form to record their responses on their interaction during the screening procedure. Based on the results, we can see that Chloe can accurately identify people, check for temperature abnormalities, and provide safe entry to all employees. She can also ensure that Covid-19 safety measures are maintained (employee occupancy at a given time, avoid physical human contact etc.). A few limitations were identified regarding maintaining privacy and response time, which will be done in our future work. But most of the employees gave positive reviews and were comfortable with Chloe as a virtual safety assistant.

References

1. Babu, S., Schmugge, S., Barnes, T., Hodges, L.F.: What would you like to talk about? An evaluation of social conversations with a virtual receptionist. In: Gratch, J., Young, M., Aylett, R., Ballin, D., Olivier, P. (eds.) IVA 2006. LNCS (LNAI), vol. 4133, pp. 169–180. Springer, Heidelberg (2006). https://doi.org/10.1007/11821830_14

2. Babu, S., Schmugge, S., Inugala, R., Rao, S., Barnes, T., Hodges, L.F.: Marve: a prototype virtual human interface framework for studying human-virtual human interaction. In: Panayiotopoulos, T., Gratch, J., Aylett, R., Ballin, D., Olivier, P., Rist, T. (eds.) IVA 2005. LNCS (LNAI), vol. 3661, pp. 120–133. Springer, Heidelberg (2005). https://doi.org/10.1007/11550617_11

3. Cairco, L., Wilson, D.M., Fowler, V., LeBlanc, M.: Avari: animated virtual agent retrieving information. In: Proceedings of the 47th Annual Southeast Regional Conference, pp. 1–6 (2009)

4. Cassell, J.: Embodied conversational interface agents. Commun. ACM **43**(4), 70–78 (2000). https://doi.org/10.1145/332051.332075. https://doi.org/10.1145/332051.332075

5. Cassell, J., et al.: Mack: Media lab autonomous conversational kiosk. In: Proceedings of IMAGINA, January 2002

6. Chen, S., Liu, Y., Gao, X., Han, Z.: Mobilefacenets: efficient CNNs for accurate real-time face verification on mobile devices. CoRR abs/1804.07573 (2018). http://arxiv.org/abs/1804.07573

7. (CNA), C.N.A.: Ai-driven system that speeds up temperature screening piloted at 2 locations (2020). https://www.channelnewsasia.com/news/singapore/wuhan-virus-coronavirus-temperature-ai-tech-12426160

8. Connecttome: Rachel (2021). https://connectome.to/

9. Damer, N., Grebe, J.H., Chen, C., Boutros, F., Kirchbuchner, F., Kuijper, A.: The effect of wearing a mask on face recognition performance: an exploratory study (2020)

10. DeVault, D., et al.: Simsensei kiosk: a virtual human interviewer for healthcare decision support. In: Proceedings of the 2014 International Conference on Autonomous Agents and Multi-Agent Systems, pp. 1061–1068. AAMAS 2014, International Foundation for Autonomous Agents and Multiagent Systems, Richland, SC (2014)

11. Devlin, J., Chang, M.W., Lee, K., Toutanova, K.: Bert: pre-training of deep bidirectional transformers for language understanding. In: NAACL-HLT (2019)

12. Devlin, J., Chang, M.W., Lee, K., Toutanova, K.: Bert: Pre-training of deep bidirectional transformers for language understanding (2019)

13. Evers, M., Nijholt, A.: Jacob - an animated instruction agent in virtual reality. In: Tan, T., Shi, Y., Gao, W. (eds.) ICMI 2000. LNCS, vol. 1948, pp. 526–533. Springer, Heidelberg (2000). https://doi.org/10.1007/3-540-40063-X_69

14. Freud, E., Stajduhar, A., Rosenbaum, R.S., Avidan, G., Ganel, T.: The covid-19 pandemic masks the way people perceive faces. Sci. Rep. 10(22344) (2020). https://doi.org/10.1038/s41598-020-78986-9

15. Gockley, R., et al.: Designing robots for long-term social interaction, pp. 1338–1343 (2005). https://doi.org/10.1109/IROS.2005.1545303

16. Ibrahim, R., Zin, Z.M.: Study of automated face recognition system for office door access control application. In: 2011 IEEE 3rd International Conference on Communication Software and Networks, pp. 132–136 (2011). https://doi.org/10.1109/ICCSN.2011.6014865

17. Libby, C., Ehrenfeld, J.: Facial recognition technology in 2021: masks, bias, and the future of healthcare. J. Med. Syst. 45(4), 1–3 (2021). https://doi.org/10.1007/s10916-021-01723-w

18. Likert, R.: A technique for the measurement of attitudes. Arch. Psychol. no. 140, [s.n.], New York (1932)

19. Matsuyama, Y., Bhardwaj, A., Zhao, R., Romero, O., Akoju, S., Cassell, J.: Socially-aware animated intelligent personal assistant agent. In: Proceedings of the 17th Annual Meeting of the Special Interest Group on Discourse and Dialogue. pp. 224–227 (January 2016). https://doi.org/10.18653/v1/W16-3628

20. Minds, C.: Cloudia (2021). https://www.en.cloudminds.com/home-new/cloud-robots/cloudia/

21. Noma, T., Zhao, L., Badler, N.: Design of a virtual human presenter. IEEE Comput. Graphics Appl. 20(4), 79–85 (2000). https://doi.org/10.1109/38.851755

22. Norouzi, N., et al.: A systematic survey of 15 years of user studies published in the intelligent virtual agents conference. In: Proceedings of the 18th International Conference on Intelligent Virtual Agents, pp. 17–22. IVA 2018, Association for Computing Machinery, New York, NY, USA (2018). https://doi.org/10.1145/3267851.3267901. https://doi.org.remotexs.ntu.edu.sg/10.1145/3267851.3267901

23. Norris, J.S.: Face Detection and Recognition in Office Environments. Master's thesis, Thesis (M.Eng.)-Massachusetts Institute of Technology, Dept. of Electrical Engineering and Computer Science, The address of the publisher (6 1999), uRI: http://hdl.handle.net/1721.1/80108

24. Ramanathan, M., Mishra, N., Thalmann, N.M.: Nadine humanoid social robotics platform. In: Gavrilova, M., Chang, J., Thalmann, N.M., Hitzer, E., Ishikawa, H. (eds.) CGI 2019. LNCS, vol. 11542, pp. 490–496. Springer, Cham (2019). https://doi.org/10.1007/978-3-030-22514-8_49

25. Matsuyama, Y., Bhardwaj, A., Zhao, R., Romero, O., Akoju, S., Cassell, J.: Socially-aware animated intelligent personal assistant agent. In: Proceedings of the 17th Annual Meeting of the Special Interest Group on Discourse and Dialogue, pp. 224–227, January 2016. https://doi.org/10.18653/v1/W16-3628

26. Schroff, F., Kalenichenko, D., Philbin, J.: Facenet: A unified embedding for face recognition and clustering. In: 2015 IEEE Conference on Computer Vision and Pattern Recognition (CVPR), pp. 815–823 (2015). https://doi.org/10.1109/CVPR.2015.7298682

27. Selvi, K., P.Chitrakala, Jenitha, A.: Face recognition based attendance marking system. Int. J. Comput. Sci. Mobile Comput. 3(2), 337–342 (2014)

28. Serengil, S.I., Ozpinar, A.: Lightface: A hybrid deep face recognition framework. In: 2020 Innovations in Intelligent Systems and Applications Conference (ASYU). pp. 23–27. IEEE (2020). https://doi.org/10.1109/ASYU50717.2020.9259802

29. Teledyne FLIR: LWIR micro thermal camera module (2020). https://www.flir.asia/products/lepton/?model=3.5%20Lepton

30. Teledyne FLIR: LWIR micro thermal camera module (2020). https://www.flir.asia/discover/professional-tools/how-does-emissivity-affect-thermal-imaging/

31. Thermo Works: Infrared emissivity table (2020), https://www.thermoworks.com/emissivity-table

32. TwentyBN: Millie (2021). https://20bn.com/

Assisting the Assistant

How and Why People Show Reciprocal Behavior Towards Voice Assistants

Florian Schneider$^{(\boxtimes)}$ and Justus Hagmann

Julius-Maximilians University Würzburg, 97070 Würzburg, Germany
florian.schneider@uni-wuerzburg.de

Abstract. The Computers Are Social Actors (CASA) Paradigm (Nass et al. 1994) describes the interaction between Humans and Computers as fundamentally social. Computers emitting social cues are treated like other humans (Reeves and Nass 1996). This paper aims to evaluate the social norms of reciprocity and politeness in a CASA context using a voice assistant. A 2×2 experimental mixed factorial design with $N = 66$ participants was used. We examined whether participants who have been helped by a voice assistant in a coaching session are more likely to show reciprocal behavior towards the voice assistant compared to participants who have not been helped. In addition, we investigated a possible interviewer-bias (Finkel et al. 1991) when interacting with voice assistants as well as user-sided influencing factors for reciprocal behavior towards voice assistants. Results show that the CASA paradigm can be applied to modern technology. Participants who have been helped complete significantly more tasks for the computer ($M = 7.34$, $SD = 5.11$), than participants who have not been helped ($M = 4.94$, $SD = 3.49$; $t(56.518) = 2.28, p = 0,027, d = .56$). An interviewer bias was not found. Contrary to our expectations a retaliation effect was found. Furthermore, the personality trait *openness to experience* moderates the effect of helpful condition on tasks completed. Future research should consider looking into user-sided influencing factors as personality seems to be a fruitful approach. Moreover, effects of CASA on human-voice assistant interaction need to be considered in practical design and future research.

Keywords: CASA · Media equation · Voice assistants · Reciprocity · Politeness

1 Introduction

Computers, smartphones, voice assistants – technological devices that have the capacity to interact with us in social ways have become ubiquitous in our daily lives. They are there to help users with various tasks, whether at home or at work. To ask the question whether users would in turn also help their devices is nonsensical at first glance. Technological devices are mere tools and not justify such behavior. Compared to other humans, they have no feelings and no conscience. If another person helps us in any task or situation in our lives, we are inclined to also help this person in return. This social norm, the norm of reciprocity, is well studied in human-human interaction and is

© The Author(s), under exclusive license to Springer Nature Switzerland AG 2022
M. Kurosu (Ed.): HCII 2022, LNCS 13304, pp. 566–579, 2022.
https://doi.org/10.1007/978-3-031-05412-9_38

an absolute cornerstone of social psychology (Gouldner 1960). Reeves and Nass asked themselves in the 1990s, whether we apply these social norms, which we know well from various situations in our lives, also in human-computer interaction. In their book *The Media Equation*, Reeves and Nass (1996) describe a series of experiments originally performed in social psychology in which they replaced a human interaction partner with a computer. It is shown that even small social cues are sufficient to trigger social behavior in humans toward computers. Computers are gender stereotyped (Nass et al. 1997), they can be seen as teammates (Nass et al. 1996), we behave politely towards them (Nass et al. 1999) and we help them if they have helped us before (Fogg and Nass 1997). Several years have passed and technologies have evolved significantly compared to the 90s. Experiments then were performed mostly with text-based computers. As modern technology is much more capable of sending social cues, this research needs to be re-validated and extended. Another area that remained largely unexplored is taking a closer look at the user. What user-side variables affect how we respond socially to technological devices? Are there influencing factors that reinforce social behavior or even cause people to behave antisocially toward them? These are exactly the two questions this study attempts to answer based on the experiments performed by Fogg and Nass (1997) and Nass, Moon, and Carney (1999) while including individual differences. In short: when interacting with a voice assistant, do people apply the social norms of politeness and reciprocity? And what influence do personality, anthropocentrism, and suspension of disbelief have on the effects of reciprocity?

2 Theoretical Framework

2.1 The Media Equation and the Computers Are Social Actors Paradigm

Human-computer interaction is fundamentally social. The idea of Reeves' and Nass' research, which started in the 1990s, was that even small social cues in human-computer interaction are sufficient to elicit social reactions usually exclusive to human-human interaction. Reeves and Nass introduced this concept as the media equation, stating that these social reactions to computers or other media entities are not consciously controlled but rather occur unconsciously without deliberate control over one's own behavior (Reeves and Nass 1996). Furthermore, Reeves and Nass assume that media equation can be applied to everyone, can be applied often and as is highly consequential (Reeves and Nass 1996). There are several explanations for this behavior toward computers. One explanation proposed is mindlessness (Langer 1989). Mindlessness refers to a state, in which contextual cues of a situation are neglected due to an overreliance on categories and experiences from the past, and thus leads to "mindless" behavior (Langer 1989). For example, reliance on familiar categories causes contextual cues such as gender, ethnicity, or sense of belonging to a particular group, to elicit mindless social behavior (Langer 1992). The same can be observed even when these cues originate from a technological device like a computer (Nass and Moon 2000). Another explanation proposed by Reeves and Nass (1996) is the evolutionary approach. For almost all human history, the only possible social interaction partners were other humans. There was no need to judge if a social response in interactions was appropriate. Therefore, the human brain has evolved in such a way that social cues are automatically followed by a social response. This behavior, which has evolved over thousands of years, is no longer always appropriate today. Technological devices and media entities have begun to interact with us socially by being able to send social cues or adopt the role of a social actor (Reeves and Nass 1996). However, since our modern brain is still similar to that of our ancestors, social behavior is shown even if the situation does not justify it (Reeves and Nass 1996).

Research which focuses on social reactions towards computers is grouped under the CASA (Computers are Social Actors) paradigm (Nass et al. 1994). The basic assumption of CASA research is that social psychology experiments can be replicated in human-computer interaction by replacing one of the interaction partners with a technological device and that social norms will then be applied when interacting with these devices (Johnson et al. 2004).

2.2 Social Norms in Human-Computer Interaction

This study opted to examine if the social norms of reciprocity and politeness are adopted when interacting with a voice assistant. Generally speaking, social norms can be seen as rules and standards which are understood by members of a group and which guide and/or restrain social behavior (Cialdini and Trost 1998). The norm of reciprocity is essential for human-human interaction. It assumes that people are more willing to help other people if they have already been helped by them in advance (Gouldner 1960).

Based on the politeness theory by Brown and Levinson (1978) and the concept of *face* derived from Goffman (1967), the social norm of politeness is centered around individuals' public images that they are trying to protect. Goffman (1967) defines face as the positive social value a person claims for themselves. It acts as a self-image described in terms of recognized social attributes. Politeness strategies are used to protect one's own face as well as the face of an interaction partner (Brown and Levinson 1978). An example for this is the interviewer-bias. It is assumed that a person rating an interviewer after an interaction does so significantly more positive, when the interviewer directly asks for the rating. However, if the participant is given the opportunity to rate the interviewer with a third, uninvolved person, the rating can be more honest and therefore often worse (Finkel et al. 1991). This is explained by the interviewee being reluctant to commit a face-threatening act. They want to preserve both their own as well as the interviewers face in a direct interaction. As soon as a different person or entity asks about the interviewer's performance the interviewee does not need to be concerned about the interviewer's face anymore.

As they are essential for human-human interaction, both the norm of reciprocity as well as the norm of politeness have been examined in previous HCI research.

2.3 Previous Research

Reciprocity
Fogg and Nass (1997) investigated the extent to which people would help a computer to complete a task if that computer had previously helped them with a task of their own. Subject were first asked to perform an internet search with the help of a computer. The

degree of help the participant received from the computer was experimentally manipulated. Afterwards, the computer asked the participants for help in a separate task. Results confirmed reciprocal behavior: subjects who had received a high level of assistance from the computer performed significantly more optional tasks when asked for help by the same computer. In the condition with low assistance from the computer, a retaliation effect was found. In the subsequent second task, significantly more errors were made when the subjects had worked on the same computer (Fogg and Nass 1997). Reciprocal behavior, as described earlier, is also deeply culturally embedded (Cialdini 2009; Gouldner 1960). To further investigate the application of the social norm of reciprocity in interaction with computers, Katagiri, Nass, and Takeuchi (2001) used a cross-cultural approach. Japan, as a collectivist culture, should apply reciprocity norms differently than the individualistic culture of America. While participants from the United States were only willing to help the exact computer which provided them with help in the first place, Japanese participants were also willing to help a computer which they believed belongs to the same group, in this case the same brand. A computer from a different brand did not receive help.

Another aspect of reciprocity in human-computer interaction is self-disclosure. In an experiment on reciprocal self-disclosure, Moon (2000) had participants interact with a computer that asked them increasingly intimate questions. According to the norm of reciprocity, a computer that discloses seemingly intimate information about itself should lead to the subjects also giving more intimate answers. Participants who were working with a self-disclosing computer did respond to the computer with more intimate responses as well as longer responses compared to participants who worked with a computer that did not reveal details about itself.

Politeness

In an experiment by Nass, Moon, and Carney (1999), subjects were asked to complete a text-based interactive learning unit using a computer. Subjects were told that they would be presented with 20 randomly selected facts from a pool of 1000 facts on the topic of "American culture." These facts were to be rated by the subject on a scale of 1 (know very little about it) to 3 (know very much about it). Based on this rating, subjects were told they would be given appropriate follow-up facts. A multiple-choice test with 12 questions on the previously learned material was then administered. Afterwards, the computer evaluated the subjects' performance. All subjects were told that they answered eight of the twelve questions correctly. In a last step, subjects were asked to evaluate the computer's performance either on the same device, a different computer, or a paper-and-pencil questionnaire. Results indicate an interviewer-bias: subjects who had to submit their evaluation on the same computer rated it significantly better than subjects on a different computer or in the written questionnaire. However, in a debriefing session, all subjects indicated that the condition to which they were assigned had no effect on their responses. Subjects in the condition with the same computer indicated that they would have answered the same way if they had been required to give their feedback on a different computer. All subjects also indicated that they felt it would be unnecessary to show courtesy to a computer. This demonstrates the fundamentally human and social nature of the Media Equation (Reeves and Nass 1996). The experiment was later replicated by Nass et al. (1999) using a speech-based system instead of a text-based one. Once again, subjects rated the assistance significantly worse on a different computer compared to evaluations given on the same computer.

In order to transfer these findings to modern technologies, Carolus, Schmidt, Schneider, Mayr, and Münch (2018) replicated the experiment using smartphones instead of computers. In addition, the paper-and-pencil condition was replaced with an evaluation on the participant's own smartphone. Contrary to previous results, there was no significant difference between the evaluation on the smartphone that had presented the facts and the evaluation on a second, unfamiliar smartphone. However, there was a significant difference between the evaluation of the smartphone that had presented the facts and one's own smartphone, with the latter being significantly worse. With the emergence of intelligent voice assistants as well as the rise of smart home devices, it is of crucial importance to re-examine these findings accordingly.

2.4   Extending the CASA Paradigm

Technology has come a long way since the inception of media equation and CASA research in the 90s. Previous studies mostly employed basic text-based programs and desktop computers. Modern technologies like voice assistants have become ubiquitous and interact with us in social ways that far surpass traditional desktop computers. Voice Assistants are intelligent software agents embedded in designated smart speakers, smartphones, cars or other devices, which can interpret human speech input and respond with a synthesized voice (Hoy 2018). They can be used for a variety of tasks such as search queries, online shopping, gaming, or controlling smart home devices. The number of digital voice assistants in use worldwide grew from 3.25 billion in 2019 to 4.2 billion in 2020 and is expected to double until 2024 to 8.4 billion (Juniper Research 2020). Technologies such as smart home devices and voice assistants use speech as a primary way of interaction. Because speech is the main channel for communication between humans (Schafer 1995) and is an innate human behavior (Pinker 1995), interacting with a voice interface is intuitive (Cohen et al. 2004) and speech output is one of the most powerful ways to evoke social responses in humans when interacting with technology. For example, Moon, Kim and Shin (2016) suggest that there are interaction effects between the user personality and the number of voices which a smart device used. Voice interaction, when compared to text interaction, can also lead to more positive attitudes towards the voice assistant, mediated by perceived human likeness of the voice assistant (Cho et al. 2019). However, little empirical research has been done regarding media equation effects in voice interaction and extending the CASA paradigm to voice assistants in particular.

In addition, Lombard and Xu (2021) propose an extension of the CASA paradigm and emphasize the possible importance of user-side factors influencing media equation effects. Three of those proposed variables are the user's personality, anthropocentrism, and suspension of disbelief.

(1)   Personality has always been part of CASA research. Nass et al. (1995) were able to show that users preferred a computer that matched their own personality resulting in a more satisfying interaction. Furthermore, a computer using a voice that resembles one's own personality is perceived as more competent compared to a voice that does not (Lee et al. 2000).

(2) Anthropocentrism describes the tendency of people to perceive the world as human centered (Nass et al. 1995). Anthropocentrism could therefore suppress CASA effects (Lombard and Xu 2021).

(3) One's ability to suspend disbelief could also influence media equation effects. Duffy and Zawieska (2012) suggest that suspension of disbelief can make a difference in whether people perceive a robot as an entity or as a tool.

As of now there is little empirical research aimed at modernizing the CASA paradigm, even though the importance of voice assistants is growing rapidly. Therefore, this study tries to (1) expand the CASA paradigm to voice assistants and (2) analyze what kind of user-sided factors influence the effects of the media equation.

2.5 Hypothesis

This study adopts the methodological approaches of Fogg and Nass (1997) as well as Nass, Moon and Carney (1999) and transfers them to voice assistants.

People apply the social norm of reciprocity in human-human interactions as well as in human-computer interaction (Fogg and Nass 1997; Katagiri et al. 2001; Moon 2000) Fogg and Nass (1997) could show that people apply significantly more reciprocal behavior towards a computer if the computer helped them in a previous interaction. Therefore, we postulate that:

H1: Participants that interact with a helpful voice assistant show significantly more reciprocal behavior compared to participants that interact with an unhelpful voice assistant.

People have also been shown to adopt the social norm of politeness in human-computer interaction (e.g. Nass et al. 1999; Nass and Moon 2000; Reeves and Nass 1996). Subjects who rate a computer on its performance in a learning scenario do so significantly better when they give feedback to the computer directly. Participants who could give their feedback on a second, but identical computer, rated the coaching-computer significantly worse (Nass et al. 1999). This effect known as the interviewer-based bias (Finkel et al. 1991) is expected to also show in human-voice assistant interaction. We expect that:

H2: Participants rate a voice assistants' performance significantly better on the device itself compared to a second computer.

Following Lombard and Xu (2021), this study also tries to understand how individual differences can impact CASA findings. Therefore, a series of different user characteristics were collected, namely the user's personality, anthropocentrism, and suspension of disbelief. We postulate the following research questions:

RQ: How do individual differences impact reciprocal behavior towards voice assistants?

RQ1: Does user personality influence reciprocal behavior towards a voice assistant?

RQ2: *Does anthropocentrism influence reciprocal behavior towards a voice assistant?*

RQ3: *Does suspension of disbelief influence reciprocal behavior towards a voice assistant?*

3   Method

3.1   Sample

The sample includes $N = 66$ participants aged 18 to 37 years ($M = 22.03$, $SD = 3.44$), with $n = 52$ (78.8%) female and $n = 14$ (21.2%) male participants. 65 participants (98.5%) indicated at least the general higher education entrance qualification as their highest level of education. This results in a final split between conditions of n = 33 in the helpful condition and $n = 33$ in the unhelpful condition. Multiple t-tests for independent samples show no differences between conditions for age ($t_{(64)} = 1.59, p = .116$), gender ($t_{(64)} = .00, p = 1$), neuroticism ($t_{(64)} = -1.6, p = .112$), extraversion ($t_{(59.311)} = -.17$, $p = .864$), openness to experience ($t_{(64)} = 1.05, p = .319$), agreeableness ($t_{(64)} = -.77$, $p = .447$), conscientiousness, ($t_{(64)} = 1.95, p = .056$), suspension of disbelief ($t_{(64)} = -1.20, p = .233$) and anthropocentrism ($t_{(64)} = .48, p = .630$).

3.2   Materials

For this experiment, an Amazon Echo Plus (1. Generation) running a custom-made Skill was used to allow for a controlled human-voice assistant interaction. The Skill was implemented with a codeless backend solution from the provider *Voiceflow* (www.voiceflow.com) and linked to the Amazon Echo via the Amazon Alexa developer interface. The questionnaire was completed on a desktop computer located in the same laboratory using the online questionnaire software *Socisurvey*.

3.3   Procedure

To test the hypotheses, we used 2×2 experimental mixed factorial design. Participants were randomly assigned to one of two conditions (between-factor: helpful voice assistant/unhelpful voice assistant). Every participant also evaluated the conversational agent first on the device itself and a second time on a separate PC (within-factor: evaluation location). The independent variable, helpfulness of the voice assistant, was manipulated via different versions of the custom-made Skill. After a short introduction by the researcher, participants were asked to interact with a voice assistant for about 35 min. The methodological procedure used for this purpose is derived from the previous work of Fogg and Nass (1997) and Nass, Moon, and Carney (1999). The interaction between the participant and the voice assistant consisted of four steps. (1) The participants received a coaching session in which they were presented with twenty facts from a pool of supposedly one thousand possible facts. We gathered obscure facts from different fields of natural sciences such as biology and physics (e.g., "Seahorses do not look like it, but they do belong to the species of fish"). The respondent was asked to rate each of these facts on a scale from 1 (I am not at all familiar with this topic) to 3 (I am completely familiar with this topic). Participants were then told that the following fact would be chosen based on their rating to close as many gaps in their knowledge as possible and to ensure an ideal preparation for the second step of the experiment. All subjects received the same twenty facts, and the rating was added only to give subjects a sense of interaction. (2) In the second step of the experiment, participants took part in a quiz. Here, the voice assistant presented them with ten single-choice questions with three choices each. This quiz, which served as the main manipulation of this experiment, had two different variations. Each participant was randomly assigned to exactly one of the two possible conditions. One of the two quizzes had a high intersection with the coaching facts (the helpful condition), and the other did not (the unhelpful condition). Regardless of their answers, following the quiz subjects in the helpful condition were always told that they answered eight out of ten questions correctly, while subjects in the unhelpful condition were always told they answered two out of ten questions correctly. (3) Participants were then asked to rate additional coaching facts according to their interestingness on a scale of 1 (not at all interesting) to 5 (very interesting). They were told that this step was done on a voluntary basis and after each fact they were given the option to either continue and rate more facts or to move on to the next step of the experiment until they did so. This voluntary behavioral measure is used as one of the dependent variables of this experiment in addition to the traditional questionnaires. A maximum of 15 additional facts could be answered by participants. (4) The final step of the interaction was a rating in which the participants were asked to rate the voice assistant's performance during the interaction. After this evaluation the participants were asked to complete an online questionnaire on a separate desktop computer.

3.4 Measures

Evaluation of the Voice Assistant

The evaluation of the voice assistant, which was used to investigate the interviewer bias, was operationalized both via oral questioning on the device itself and a second time during the online questionnaire with the "valence towards the computer" scale of Nass, Moon and Carney (1999). The scale consists of twelve items (competent, informative, helpful, analytical, knowledgeable, useful, likeable, friendly, warm, enjoyable, fun, and polite) which were rated twice on a 7-point Likert scale from 1 (strongly disagree) to 7 (strongly agree), once on the device itself and again on a separate desktop computer. Reliabilities are $\alpha = .89$ for the verbal query and $\alpha = .82$ for the written query.

Suspension of Disbelief

Suspension of Disbelief was operationalized using the corresponding subscale of the MEC Spatial Presence Questionnaire (Vorderer et al. 2004). The subscale consists of eight items, for example, "I did not pay particular attention to whether there were errors or inconsistencies in my interaction with the voice assistant". All items were asked on a 5-point Likert scale ranging from 1 (strongly disagree) to 5 (strongly agree). The reliability of the scale was $\alpha = .83$.

Personality
Personality was assessed with a Big Five personality questionnaire. For this purpose, a 30-item short version of the NEO Five-Factor Inventory was used (Körner et al. 2008). Each of the five subscales consisted of six items each. All items were rated on a 4-point Likert scale, ranging from 1 (strongly disagree) to 4 (strongly agree) Reliability analysis revealed Neuroticism $\alpha = .85$, Extraversion $\alpha = .77$, Openness to new experiences $\alpha = .81$, Agreeableness $\alpha = .65$, and Conscientiousness $\alpha = .84$.

Anthropocentrism
Anthropocentrism was assessed using an eight-item scale originally developed by Fortuna, Wróblewski, and Gorbaniuk (2021). The items here refer to trait anthropocentrism (e.g., only humans can have a "self" and an "inner life") All items were rated on a 7-point Likert scale, ranging from 1 (strongly disagree) to 7 (strongly agree) A reliability analysis revealed $\alpha = .71$, indicating that the reliability is acceptable.

Reciprocity
The construct of reciprocity was operationalized by means of an objective behavioral measure. Following the quiz, the voice assistant requested participants to help the assistant by evaluating more possible coaching facts with the excuse of extending its database. The prediction was that based on the previous interaction, during which half of the participants were successfully helped by the voice assistant to prepare for the quiz, the number of coaching facts rated additionally would differ between the helpful and unhelpful condition. Thus, the absolute number of facts rated was considered for further analyses.

4 Results

To test Hypothesis 1 a t-test for independent samples was conducted. There was a significant difference in the number of tasks completed between the helpful and the unhelpful condition $t(56.518) = 2.28$, $p = 0,027$, $d = .56$. Participants in the helpful condition completed more optional prompts ($M = 7.34$, $SD = 5.11$) compared to participants in the unhelpful condition ($M = 4.94$, $SD = 3.49$). This confirms Hypothesis 1. Participants in the helpful condition did evaluate significantly more facts than participants in the unhelpful condition thus showing reciprocal behavior towards a voice assistant based on their previous interaction.

Hypothesis 2 postulated that participants will evaluate Alexa better when the evaluation is done on the device itself compared to another device. To test this hypothesis a pair-sampled t-Test was conducted since each participant evaluated Alexa on device as well as on a computer. The results show no significant difference for the location of the evaluation $t(65) = -.644$, $p = .522$. The evaluation on the device ($M = 5.48$, $SD = .66$) was slightly worse than the evaluation on a different computer ($M = 5.55$, $SD = .93$). Further t-Tests were conducted to check whether the condition the participants were in influenced the evaluation. There was also no difference for participants in the helpful condition $t(32) = .303, p = .764$. Participants in the helpful condition did evaluate Alexa slightly better on the device itself ($M = 5.62, SD = .722$) than on a different computer ($M = 5.56, SD = 1.08$). Participants in the unhelpful condition however did show a significant difference $t(32) = -2.93, p = 0.006, d = .39$. But, contrary to the postulated hypothesis, participants rated Alexa significantly better on a separate computer ($M = 5.53, SD = .77$) than on the device itself ($M = 5.34, SD = .57$).

To test RQ1 a series of moderation analyses were conducted. Following Lombard and Xu (2021) the following variables were analyzed: Anthropocentrism, suspension of disbelief and personality. A significant interaction was found for the personality trait openness to experience and the experimental condition on reciprocal behavior with gender as a covariate. The overall model was significant, $R^2 = 17.2\%, F(4, 61) = 2.55, p = .048$. The interaction term was also significant, $\Delta R^2 = 6.8\%, F(1, 62) = 4.91, p = .031$, 95% CI[$-6.813, -0.348$] (Fig. 1). No other significant interactions were found.

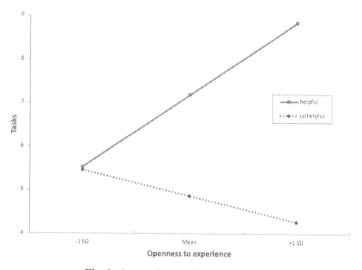

Fig. 1. Interaction condition × openness

5   Discussion

This study tried to investigate if and why people show reciprocal and polite behavior towards voice assistants. We conducted an experiment in which users were free to help the voice assistant in a task after having a helpful or an unhelpful interaction with that assistant.

Participants who have been helped by the voice assistant during their prior interaction showed reciprocal behavior and were willing to complete significantly more additional tasks than participants who were not helped. These results are in line with previous experiments conducted with desktop computers (Fogg and Nass 1997). This study therefore provides empirical evidence that people react socially towards voice assistants. Furthermore, this study also suggests that the CASA paradigm can and should be extended to modern technologies. Contrary to previous research this study did not find evidence for an interviewer-bias and therefore polite social behavior towards voice assistants. In general, there was no difference in rating when the rating was done on the device itself or on a computer afterwards. However, a significant difference in the unhelpful condition was found. Participants in this group rated Alexa's performance significantly worse on the device itself than on the computer. This could indicate a retaliation effect. Fogg and Nass (1997) observed similar behavior within their optional task. As only the number of additional tasks performed was measured, we were unable to assess differences in quality of the help given to the voice assistant. However, it is possible that instead of following politeness norms, participants instead used the oral rating to vent their frustration about the previous unhelpful interaction, which could be considered as an entirely different social reaction. Retaliation towards technological devices is not justified but rather mindless social behavior, in line with the proposed media equation effects. Further research should consider possible retaliation effects in interactions with voice assistants.

This study also aims to understand the psychological mechanisms behind reciprocal behavior towards voice assistants by considering individual differences and whether they moderate the effect of the experimental condition on behavior. Personality provided interesting insight into the psychological mechanisms behind reciprocal behavior towards voice assistants. The personality trait openness to new experiences did moderate the effect the treatment had on the reciprocal behavior. People with low openness for new experiences did not differ in the number of tasks completed between the conditions while participants with medium and high scores in openness did differ significantly. The number of optional tasks completed decreased with rising openness for people in the unhelpful condition while the number of completed optional tasks rose with increasing openness for people in the helpful condition. People with high openness seem might be more disappointed when their interaction with the voice assistant did not meet their expectations and proved unhelpful. Due to the elaborate nature of the Alexa Skill, the lengthy cover story, and a lack of experience with voice assistants which a lot of the participants had, it is also possible that the novelty effect further upped the expectations of those participants and therefore led to an even greater disappointment. People with medium or high openness who experienced a successful interaction which went just as imagined seem to be very satisfied with their interaction, leading to even more completed tasks. Overall openness to new experience seems to be an interesting personality trait for CASA research. Depending on the extent, openness seems to lead to positive as well negative social reactions, depending on whether the user's expectations of the interaction were met or not.

There are a few limitations that need to be addressed. (1) This study focused on the methodological approach of Fogg and Nass (1997) and Nass, Moon, and Carney (1999). Still, some crucial points of the original designs have been changed. Nass et al. (1999) did measure the interviewer-bias as a between subject factor. Due to time constraints during recruitment, this study opted to use a within subject approach instead. (2) The sample needs to be addressed. Because of the way participants were recruited, the sample was rather homogeneous, with participants being predominantly white, highly educated, young and female. There were no significant differences in our experimental groups, but biases could still be found in our results. (3) There are certain technical limitations when it comes to human-voice assistant interaction, resulting in a mostly scripted approach to minimize potential voice recognition errors. The actual inputs given by participants had no influence on the progress of the interaction for the most part.

The results obtained in this study have implications for future research. More attention should be paid to undesirable but nevertheless fundamentally social effects in communication with voice assistants such as retaliation effects. In addition, user-sided individual differences need to be investigated further. Personality seems to provide a fruitful approach for better understanding the underlying psychological mechanisms in CASA research. Furthermore, designers and programmers need to consider the impact of social norms and the corresponding behavior in HCI. Social cues can seemingly trigger both positive (reciprocity) and negative effects (retaliation).

6   Conclusion

In conclusion, this paper provides further evidence that the CASA paradigm can be applied to modern technologies. Participants did exhibit more reciprocal behavior toward voice assistants after a helpful interaction. Contrary to our prediction, an interviewer-bias was not found. However, we did observe a form of retaliation effect towards unhelpful voice assistants, which is still classified as social behavior. In addition, this study also aimed to shed more light on the user and the effect of individual differences. Previous research was focused on different social cues and the resulting social reactions from users. However, it turns out that certain user characteristics can moderate the effects of the media equation. This study provides initial evidence that the personality trait openness to new experiences can have a moderating effect on reciprocal behavior. Thus, in future research, attention should be paid both to the nature of the social cues as well as individual differences in users. As technologies continue to evolve toward a more personalized, user-centric experience, the user should be given more importance in CASA research.

References

1. Brown, P., Levinson, S.C.: Universals in language usage: politeness phenomena. In: Questions and Politeness: Strategies in Social Interaction, pp. 56–311. Cambridge University Press (1978)
2. Carolus, A., Schmidt, C., Schneider, F., Mayr, J., Muench, R.: Are people polite to smartphones? In: Kurosu, M. (ed.) HCI 2018. LNCS, vol. 10902, pp. 500–511. Springer, Cham (2018). https://doi.org/10.1007/978-3-319-91244-8_39
3. Cho, E., Molina, M.D., Wang, J.: The effects of modality, device, and task differences on perceived human likeness of voice-activated virtual assistants. Cyberpsychol. Behav. Soc. Netw. 22(8), 515–520 (2019). https://doi.org/10.1089/cyber.2018.0571
4. Cialdini, R.: Influence: Science and Practice. Harper Collins, New York (2009)
5. Cialdini, R.B., Trost, M.R.: Social Influence: Social Norms, Conformity and Compliance (1998)
6. Cohen, M.H., Cohen, M.H., Giangola, J.P., Balogh, J.: Voice User Interface Design. Addison-Wesley Professional (2004)

7. Duffy, B.R., Zawieska, K.: Suspension of disbelief in social robotics. In: 2012 IEEE RO-MAN: The 21st IEEE International Symposium on Robot and Human Interactive Communication, pp. 484–489 (2012). https://doi.org/10.1109/ROMAN.2012.6343798

8. Finkel, S.E., Guterbock, T.M., Borg, M.J.: Race-of-interviewer effects in a preelection poll: Virginia 1989. Publ. Opin. Q. **55**(3), 313 (1991). https://doi.org/10.1086/269264

9. Fogg, B., Nass, C.: How users reciprocate to computers: an experiment that demonstrates behavior change. In: CHI 1997 Extended Abstracts on Human Factors in Computing Systems, pp. 331–332 (1997)

10. Fortuna, P., Wróblewski, Z., Gorbaniuk, O.: The structure and correlates of anthropocentrism as a psychological construct. Curr. Psychol. (2021). https://doi.org/10.1007/s12144-021-018 35-z

11. Goffman, E.: Interaction Ritual: Essays on Face-to-Face Behavior. Anchor Books (1967)

12. Gouldner, A.W.: The norm of reciprocity: a preliminary statement. Am. Sociol. Rev. **25**(2), 161 (1960). https://doi.org/10.2307/2092623

13. Hoy, M.B.: Alexa, Siri, Cortana, and more: an introduction to voice assistants. Med. Ref. Serv. Q. **37**(1), 81–88 (2018). https://doi.org/10.1080/02763869.2018.1404391

14. Johnson, D., Garndner, J., Wiles, J.: Experience as a moderator of the media equation: the impact of flattery and praise. Int. J. Hum. Comput. Stud. **61**(3), 237–258 (2004)

15. Katagiri, Y., Nass, C., Takeuchi, Y.: Cross-cultural studies of the computers are social actors paradigm: the case of reciprocity. In: Usability Evaluation and Interface Design: Cognitive Engineering, Intelligent Agents, and Virtual Reality, pp. 1558–1562 (2001)

16. Körner, A., et al.: Persönlichkeitsdiagnostik mit dem NEO-Fünf-Faktoren-Inventar: die 30-item-kurzversion (NEO-FFI-30). PPmP Psychother. Psychosomat. Medizin. Psychol. **58**(6), 238–245 (2008). https://doi.org/10.1055/s-2007-986199

17. Langer, E.J.: Mindfulness. Addison-Wesley/Addison Wesley Longman (1989)

18. Langer, E.J.: Matters of mind: mindfulness/mindlessness in perspective. Conscious. Cogn. **1**(3), 289–305 (1992). https://doi.org/10.1016/1053-8100(92)90066-J

19. Lee, E.J., Nass, C., Brave, S.: Can computer-generated speech have gender?: An experimental test of gender stereotype. In: CHI 2000 Extended Abstracts on Human Factors in Computing Systems - CHI 2000, p. 289 (2000). https://doi.org/10.1145/633292.633461

20. Lombard, M., Xu, K.: Social responses to media technologies in the 21st century: the media are social actors paradigm. Hum. Mach. Commun. **2**, 29–55 (2021). https://doi.org/10.30658/hmc.2.2

21. Moon, Y., Kim, K.J., Shin, D.-H.: Voices of the internet of things: an exploration of multiple voice effects in smart homes. In: Streitz, N., Markopoulos, P. (eds.) DAPI 2016. LNCS, vol. 9749, pp. 270–278. Springer, Cham (2016). https://doi.org/10.1007/978-3-319-39862-4_25

22. Moon, Y.: Intimate exchanges: using computers to elicit self-disclosure from consumers. J. Consum. Res. **26**(4), 323–339 (2000). https://doi.org/10.1086/209566

23. Nass, C., Fogg, B.J., Moon, Y.: Can computers be teammates? Int. J. Hum. Comput. Stud. **45**(6), 669–678 (1996). https://doi.org/10.1006/ijhc.1996.0073

24. Nass, C.I., Lombard, M., Henriksen, L., Steuer, J.: Anthropocentrism and computers. Behav. Inf. Technol. **14**(4), 229–238 (1995). https://doi.org/10.1080/01449299508914636

25. Nass, C., Moon, Y.: Machines and mindlessness: social responses to computers. J. Soc. Issues **56**(1), 81–103 (2000). https://doi.org/10.1111/0022-4537.00153

26. Nass, C., Moon, Y., Carney, P.: Are people polite to computers? Responses to computer-based interviewing systems 1. J. Appl. Soc. Psychol. **29**(5), 1093–1109 (1999). https://doi.org/10.1111/j.1559-1816.1999.tb00142.x

27. Nass, C., Moon, Y., Fogg, B.J., Reeves, B., Dryer, C.: Can computer personalities be human personalities? In: Conference Companion on Human Factors in Computing Systems (CHI 1995), pp. 228–229 (1995). https://doi.org/10.1145/223355.223538

28. Nass, C., Moon, Y., Green, N.: Are machines gender neutral? Gender-stereotypic responses to computers with voices. J. Appl. Soc. Psychol. **27**(10), 864–876 (1997). https://doi.org/10.1111/j.1559-1816.1997.tb00275.x

29. Nass, C., Steuer, J., Tauber, E.R.: Computers are Social Actors. In: Proceedings of the SIGCHI Conference on Human Factors in Computing (CHI 1994), pp. 72–78 (1994)

30. Juniper Research. Number of Voice Assistant Devices in Use to Overtake World Population by 2024. (2020). https://www.juniperresearch.com/press/press-releases/number-of-voice-assistant-devices-in-use

31. Pinker, S.: The language instinct (1st HarperPerennial ed). HarperPerennial (1995)

32. Reeves, B., Nass, C.: The media equation (1. paperback ed., [Nachdr.]). CSLI Publ. [u.a.] (1996)

33. Schafer, R.W.: Scientific bases of human-machine communication by voice. Proc. Natl. Acad. Sci. **92**(22), 9914–9920 (1995). https://doi.org/10.1073/pnas.92.22.9914

34. Vorderer, P., et al.: MEC Spatial Presence Questionnaire (MEC-SPQ), p. 15 (2004)

Toward Charismatic Virtual Agents: How to Animate Your Speech and Be Charismatic

Ning Wang[✉], Abhilash Karpurapu, Aditya Jajodia, and Chirag Merchant

Institute for Creative Technologies, University of Southern California,
Los Angeles, USA
nwang@ict.usc.edu

Abstract. Charisma is a powerful device of communication and persuasion. Researchers have pinpointed specific behaviors that contribute to the perception of charisma. How can we realize such behaviors in a virtual character? In this paper, we discuss our work in the design of charismatic behavior for a virtual human. We developed a series of verbal charismatic strategies based on the research on charismatic leaders, which was then used to re-write an existing tutorial on the human circulatory system to express charisma. We then collected voice recordings of the tutorial in both charismatic and non-charismatic voices using actors from a crowd-sourcing platform. In this paper, we present the analysis of the charismatic and non-charismatic voice recordings, and discuss what nonverbal behaviors in speeches contribute to perceived charisma. Results can shed light on the synthesis of charismatic speeches for virtual characters.

Keywords: Charisma · Prosody analysis · Speech synthesis

1 Introduction

Charisma is a powerful device of persuasion [18]. Leaders have used charisma to make their messages memorable and inspiring [14,16,23,28]. Contrary to the idea that charisma is a personal quality [53], researchers have pinpointed the specific verbal and nonverbal behaviors that contribute to the perception of charisma [4,5,15,20,26,40,49,52].

An important aspect of charismatic nonverbal behavior is the use of animated voice. While different speech features might have different affective effects in different languages [37], researchers in expressive speech generally consider pitch [54], loudness [21], spectral structure [31], voice quality [8,24], etc. as features relevant to perceived expressiveness (e.g., emotional states) in speech. Specific to perceived charisma, previous research indicates that variations in pitch range and standard deviations are correlated with charisma [48]. Additionally, speech rate (speed and variation), intensity (loudness and variation), intonation (e.g., phrasal ending patterns, shape, variations), and vocal clarity also play a role in perception of charisma [14,38].

M. Kurosu (Ed.): HCII 2022, LNCS 13304, pp. 580–590, 2022.
https://doi.org/10.1007/978-3-031-05412-9_39

How can we realize charismatic behaviors in a virtual character? Given the broad range of applications of virtual characters in, for example, health care [6], energy conservation [1], and education [32], being able to employ charismatic behaviors in virtual characters can have great potential in influencing the learning and decision-making of their human interactants. In this paper, we discuss the design of nonverbal behaviors for a virtual human, particularly the synthesis of pauses in charismatic speech. We developed a series of verbal charismatic strategies and implemented them in a tutorial on the human circulatory system. We then collected recordings of the tutorial in both charismatic and noncharismatic voice using actors from a crowd-sourcing platform. We conducted analyses to compare the charismatic and non-charismatic voice recordings and shed light on what types of nonverbal behaviors in speeches contribute to perceived charisma, and how such behaviors can be realized in virtual characters.

2   Related Work

2.1   Charisma

Much progress has been made in understanding the behavioral makeup of charisma, particularly in the study of charismatic leadership in organizational science. Verbally, charisma is often expressed through the use of metaphors, which are very effective persuasion devices that affect information processing and framing by simplifying the message, stirring emotions, invoking symbolic meanings, and aiding recall [11,18,33]. Stories and anecdotes are also often employed as devices of charisma [20,49], by making the message understandable and easy to remember [7]. Rhetorical devices, such as contrasts (to frame and focus the message), lists (to give the impression of completeness), rhetorical questions [4], are often used in charismatic communications as well. In addition, charismatic speakers are skilled at expressing empathy [39], setting high expectations, and communicating confidence that the expectations can be met [26]. Theoretically, these charismatic behaviors are catalysts of motivation [17] and increase self-efficacy belief [41].

On a nonverbal level, of most relevance to this paper, charismatic speakers speak with varied pitch, amplitude, rate, fluency, emphasis, and an overall animated voice tone [20,49]—all aspects of speech commonly associated with a more engaged and lively style of speech and all predicting higher ratings of charisma [38]. Both the verbal and nonverbal behaviors make the message more memorable [7,18,33,52] and increase self-efficacy [3,20,49].

2.2   Speech Synthesis

Text-to-speech and speech synthesis have come a long way in generating natural-sounding speech [43,46,47,55]. Recent trends in research in spontaneous and conversational speech synthesis have added non-speech behaviors such as breathing to make the synthesized speech even more realistic, particularly in conversational settings [22,44]. More recent advances in synthesized speech have created voices that are increasingly challenging to distinguish from real human speakers [42,51]. In addition to synthesizing speech that aims to be natural or spontaneous, researchers have sought to generate speech that is expressive, for example, speech that expresses different emotions and speaking styles [9,19,35,45]. Often, the expressive information can be incorporated, either before or after the synthesis of neutral speech [9,45]. However, there is very little work on synthesizing charismatic speech, even though charismatic nonverbal behaviors in speech (such as those of charismatic leaders) are well studied in the organizational sciences. Additionally, most of the methods in speech synthesis take the big data, deep-learning approach, while employing machine-learning algorithms that are hard to explain. While such synthesis methods have generated great end-to-end outcomes, it is challenging to distill explainable outcomes that can contribute to the knowledge of, for example, what is important to synthesize charismatic speech and how the existing theoretical framework on charisma performs in generating charismatic speeches.

3   Charismatic Speech Dataset

3.1   Charismatic Verbal Strategies

Based on the research on charismatic speech, we developed a series of verbal strategies to express charisma, for example, the use of metaphor and analogies [20], stories [20,49], rhetorical questions [4], etc. Using these strategies, we re-wrote an existing tutorial on the human circulatory system [12]. For example, instead of saying "The major function of the blood is to transport nutrients and oxygen to the cells and to carry away carbon dioxide and nitrogenous wastes from the cells", we rephrased it using the strategy of "metaphors" - "The major function of the blood is to be both the body's mailmen, delivering nutrients and oxygen to the cells, and its garbagemen, carrying away carbon dioxide and nitrogenous wastes from the cells". A previous human-subject study comparing the tutorial text with and without the use of charismatic strategies showed that the use of charismatic strategies significantly improved the perceived charisma [50].

3.2   Data Collection

Using the "charismatic" version of the tutorial (106 sentences, 1824 words), we gathered voice recordings from 13 participants, who read the tutorial out loud in both charismatic (e.g., animated) and non-charismatic (e.g., monotone) voice. To gather the data, we first recruited 95 participants through a crowd-sourcing platform to record a snippet of the tutorial in charismatic and non-charismatic voices. Participants were given instructions that explain what is considered a charismatic vs. non-charismatic voice. For example,

– *"A voice conveys charisma is often considered to be varying in speed (e.g., sometimes fast, sometimes with pause), varying in energy (e.g., stress certain* word or phrase), and varying in pitch (e.g., a more animated voice), compared to a mono-tone and mono-speed voice that often puts one to sleep. A charismatic speech inspires and motivates."

– "A voice in contrast with a voice that conveys charisma is, for example, mono-tone, lack of emphasis, without changes in speed or pauses. And generally a voice that's boring and puts one to sleep."

Two members of the research team then selected the 13 participants whose recordings more closely followed the instructions, out of the 95 participants. The 13 participants then went on to create voice recordings of the tutorial in full length, in both charismatic and non-charismatic voices.

4   Results

The body of work on charismatic speakers indicates that charismatic speeches are spoken with varied pitch, amplitude, rate, fluency, emphasis, and an overall animated voice tone [20,49]. Thus, our analysis focused on measurable variables such as pitch, energy (i.e., amplitude), and speed (i.e., rate), in the comparison between charismatic and non-charismatic speeches. To study the dynamics in charismatic speech, we zoomed in on pauses (an indication of varied speech rate) and emphasis. Both pauses and emphasis can to draw listeners' attention to specific parts of the speech. Thus they can be effective devices employed by charismatic speakers to make their messages more memorable. Because our data consist of "prepared speech" (as opposed to spontaneous speeches), we did not examine the fluency variable in our data. In this paper, we will discuss the analysis on pauses.

4.1   Charismatic vs. Non-charismatic Speeches

Using Paired Sample T-Test, we compared the charismatic (C) and non-charismatic (NC) recordings in pitch, energy and speed - three factors that are key to charismatic speech [14,38]. Results show that charismatic speeches are spoken with significantly low speed ($M_C = 7.3, M_{NC} = 7.01, p < .0001$, duration in seconds for a sentence), higher energy ($M_C = .073, M_{NC} = .068, p < .0001$, in dB) and higher pitch ($M_C = 2414.8, M_{NC} = 2209.2, p < .0001$, in Hz). As an overall indication of how "animated" a speech is, we also compared the variations in pitch, energy, and speed. Results show that there are significantly greater variations in energy and pitch (Levene's test, $p < .001$ for both comparisons), but not speed, in charismatic recordings compared to non-charismatic ones.

4.2   Pauses in Charismatic Speech

The use of pauses is one of the ways to vary speed in speech and draw attention to the messages to follow.

Pause Duration. Pauses in speech are often categorized into silent pauses, filler pauses, and breath pauses. Breath pauses are regular natural pauses caused by respiration activity. Filler pauses are pseudo-words, such as "Mmmm" and "Hmmmm", that do not affect the meaning of the sentence [27]. Because our dataset consists of only prepared speeches, we did not include analysis of filler pauses, which primarily occur in spontaneous speeches. While silent pauses can be indications of disfluencies, uncertainty, and hesitation, which occur more often in spontaneous speeches, they are primarily intentional stylistic pauses used purposely by professional speakers and the like [27]. There has been great debate since the 1970s s about the duration of silence that defines a silent pause [29]. Previous work has often adopted the convention of .2 to .25 s of silence (or longer) as indication of silent pauses, while those that fall below this threshold are often considered breath pauses [10,25,36]. In automated puncture detection in speech, it has been shown that over 95% of the pauses of .35 s or longer are the sentence boundaries [30]. Thus, in our analysis, we focused our analysis on silent pauses of .2 s or longer.

We extracted the pauses (e.g., a silence of at least .2 s long) from the charismatic and non-charismatic speech recordings. We first conducted a paired t-test to compare the number of silent pauses in charismatic and non-charismatic speech. Results show that there is no significant differences in the number of pauses between charismatic and non-charismatic speech ($M_C = 228.6, M_{NC} = 277.2, p = .214$).

Pause Locations. To synthesize charismatic speech, it is important to know where the pauses occur in addition to how long the pauses should be. Given that we have a unique dataset where all the recordings are based on the same text, we tabulated where the silent pauses occurred in each participant's recording and examined whether there was consensus among the participants on where to place silent pauses. Figure 1 shows that there are a total of 589 silent pauses (made by the 13 participants) of a duration of .2 s or longer. Additionally, Fig. 1 suggests that there is great variance in where participants placed the pauses. For example, there are only 208 cases where 3 or more participants paused at the same place. For consensus among half or more speakers (e.g., 6 or more participants), the number of "commonly agreed" pauses dropped to 57.

We then annotated the tutorial text using part-of-speech (POS) tags (e.g., verb, noun, [34]). We then analyzed the pairs of POS tags where the pauses most frequently occur (e.g., between a verb and a noun). Table 1 shows that, of the silence pauses of .2 s and longer, the most common places where a pause happens are between a noun (NN) and a preposition (IN, e.g., "in", "of", "to"), a noun (NN) and a coordinating conjunction (CC, e.g., "and", "but"), a noun (NN) and a determiner (DT, e.g., "the", "my", "some"). Table 2 shows the part-of-speech pairs that have the highest percentage of occurrence of pause. Descriptions and examples of POS tags are shown in Table 3.

From Table 2, we can see that 92% of NNS-CD POS pairs have a pause in between, which indicates a high consensus among the participants. However,

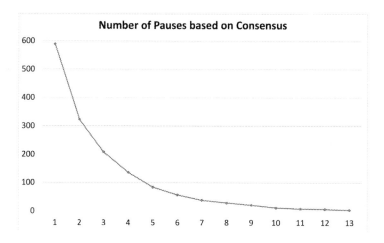

Fig. 1. Number of pauses based on consensus among the speakers, for example, for 84 pauses, 5 or more speakers paused at the same place. The x-axis indicates the number of consensus. The y-axis indicates the number of pauses.

Table 1. Part-of-speech (POS) tag pairs where there are most pauses.

POS pair	Total # in text	# with a pause
('NN', 'IN')	117	20
('NN', 'CC')	37	17
('NN', 'DT')	27	14
('NN', 'NNS')	63	11
('NN', 'NN')	115	10

Table 2. Part-of-speech (POS) tag pairs with the highest percentage of pauses. For example, 92% of the ('NNS', 'CD') POS pair in the charismatic text has a pause in between.

POS pair	Total # in text	% with a pause
('NNS', 'CD')	1	92%
('NN', 'WDT')	1	85%
('DT', 'WP')	1	77%
('VBN', 'VBG')	1	77%
('VBZ', 'CC')	1	77%

for all the top pairs listed here, each only occurred in the charismatic tutorial once. Table 4 lists more commonly seen POS pairs (with at least 10 occurrences in the tutorial) and how often there is a pause in between. This gives a more realistic view of how often more frequently-occurring POS tag pairs have a pause in between. Data on these POS tag pairs may better inform how to synthesize

Table 3. Descriptions and examples of Part-of-speech (POS) tags.

POS	Description	Example
CC	Coordinating conjunction	and, but
CD	Cardinal digit	1, 3, 8
DT	Determiner	the, my, some
IN	Preposition	in, of , to
NN	Noun, singular	cat, tree
NNS	Noun, plural	cats, trees
RB	Adverb	slowly, softly
VBG	Verb gerund	judging
VBN	Verb past participle	judged
VBZ	Verb, present tense with 3rd person singular	judges
WDT	wh-determiner	that, what
WP	wh- pronoun	who

pauses, e.g., where to insert them. Interestingly, our data show that, only NN-VBG and NN-DT pairs have a better than chance ($>50\%$) percentage of having a pause in between.

Table 4. Similar to Table 2, this table shows the part-of-speech (POS) tag pairs with the highest percentage of pauses. However, here, we only focus on these POS pairs have 100 or more occurrences in the text.

POS pair (>100 in text)	Total # in text	% with a pause
('NN', 'VBG')	10	62%
('NN', 'DT')	27	52%
('NN', 'CC')	37	46%
('NN', 'RB')	12	40%
('NNS', 'CC')	16	37%

5   Discussion

In this paper, we discussed a study to collect charismatic and non-charismatic speech samples. Analysis of the data revealed that charismatic speeches are spoken at lower speed, higher energy, and higher pitch. There was also more variance in energy and pitch in charismatic speeches compared to non-charismatic ones. These results are in line with existing research findings that charismatic speeches are more animated and less monotone.

We then furthered our analysis to explore, for example, how speech, energy and pitch vary, in the hope of deriving design principles to synthesize charismatic speech. In this paper, we focused our analysis on pauses. Our data show that charismatic speeches contained significantly more silence pauses, compared to non-charismatic ones. We further identified the linguistic features, i.e. the POS tag pairs, that are more frequently related to pauses.

Pause Synthesis. Based on the analysis of pauses in our dataset, we have begun to experiment with a number of ways to synthesis pauses to express charisma. We first used a commercial speech synthesizer (Amazon Polly, [2]) to generate a baseline or neutral recording of the tutorial. Given that we used .2 s of silence as the threshold to extract pauses in our data, we plan to insert silent pauses of .2 s into the baseline speech.

There are a number of methods we plan to explore and experiment with in where to insert the pauses. First, we can insert pauses between POS tags that our data suggest are more likely to have a pause. A probability distribution can be employed to determine how often pauses should be inserted. Second, we can take a consensus-based approach and insert pauses where, for example, more than half of the speakers in our data paused. Ultimately, it's a balance between precision and recall [13]: we can generate fewer pauses with high confidence or fill the speech with more pauses while lowering the threshold of certainty. One of the immediate next steps is to carry out human-subject studies with the synthesized speech to study its impact on perceived charisma.

Limitations. While the balance between precision and recall is a general approach, the method to synthesize, for example, pauses in charismatic speech is specific to the tutorial text of interest to this project. This is largely due to the nature of the dataset, e.g., multiple recordings of the same text, and the small size of the dataset. To generalize the approach, we plan to extend the POS-based analysis to POS dependencies based on sentence structures. Such an approach is not applicable to our existing dataset, given that the charismatic text used for speech data recording has very limited representation of sentence structures. Thus, as one of the next steps, we plan to extend the analysis to large publicly available speech datasets of charismatic speakers (e.g., speeches from past presidents, motivational speakers, etc.).

Acknowledgement. This research was supported by the National Science Foundation under Grant #1816966. Any opinions, findings, and conclusions expressed in this material are those of the authors and do not necessarily reflect the views of the National Science Foundation.

References

1. Al Mahmud, A., Dadlani, P., Mubin, O., Shahid, S., Midden, C., Moran, O.: iParrot: towards designing a persuasive agent for energy conservation. In: de Kort, Y., IJsselsteijn, W., Midden, C., Eggen, B., Fogg, B.J. (eds.) Persuasive 2007. LNCS, vol. 4744, pp. 64–67. Springer, Heidelberg (2007). https://doi.org/10.1007/978-3-540-77006-0_8

2. Amazon. Amazon Polly (2022). https://aws.amazon.com/polly/

3. Antonakis, J., Fenley, M., Liechti, S.: Can charisma be taught? tests of two interventions. Acad. Manag. Learn. Educ. **10**(3), 374–396 (2011)

4. Atkinson, J.M.: Lend me your ears: all you need to know about making speeches and presentations. Oxford University Press on Demand (2005)

5. Awamleh, R., Gardner, W.L.: Perceptions of leader charisma and effectiveness: the effects of vision content, delivery, and organizational performance. Leadersh. Quart. **10**(3), 345–373 (1999)

6. Bickmore, T.W., Pfeifer, L.M., Jack, B.W.: Taking the time to care: empowering low health literacy hospital patients with virtual nurse agents. In: Proceedings of the SIGCHI Conference on Human Factors in Computing Systems, pp. 1265–1274 (2009)

7. Bower, G.H.: Experiments on story understanding and recall. Quart. J. Exp. Psychol. **28**(4), 511–534 (1976)

8. Burkhardt, F., Sendlmeier, W.F.: Verification of acoustical correlates of emotional speech using formant-synthesis. In: ISCA Tutorial and Research Workshop (ITRW) on Speech and Emotion (2000)

9. Campbell, N., Hamza, W., Hoge, H., Tao, J., Bailly, G.: Editorial special section on expressive speech synthesis. IEEE Trans. Audio Speech Lang. Process. **14**(4), 1097–1098 (2006)

10. Campione, E., Véronis, J.: A large-scale multilingual study of silent pause duration. In: Speech Prosody 2002, International Conference (2002)

11. Charteris-Black, J.: Politicians and Rhetoric: The Persuasive Power of Metaphor. Springer, London (2011). https://doi.org/10.1057/9780230319899

12. Chi, M.T., Siler, S.A., Jeong, H., Yamauchi, T., Hausmann, R.G.: Learning from human tutoring. Cogn. Sci. **25**(4), 471–533 (2001)

13. Davis, J., Goadrich, M.: The relationship between precision-recall and roc curves. In: Proceedings of the 23rd International Conference on Machine Learning, pp. 233–240 (2006)

14. DeGroot, T., Aime, F., Johnson, S.G., Kluemper, D.: Does talking the talk help walking the walk? An examination of the effect of vocal attractiveness in leader effectiveness. Leadership Quart. **22**(4), 680–689 (2011)

15. Den Hartog, D.N., Verburg, R.M.: Charisma and rhetoric: communicative techniques of international business leaders. Leadership Quart. **8**(4), 355–391 (1997)

16. Dumdum, U.R., Lowe, K.B., Avolio, B.J.: A meta-analysis of transformational and transactional leadership correlates of effectiveness and satisfaction: an update and extension. In: Transformational and Charismatic Leadership: The Road Ahead 10th Anniversary Edition, pp. 39–70. Emerald Group Publishing Limited (2013)

17. Eden, D., et al.: Implanting pygmalion leadership style through workshop training: seven field experiments. Leadership Quart. **11**(2), 171–210 (2000)

18. Emrich, C.G., Brower, H.H., Feldman, J.M., Garland, H.: Images in words: presidential rhetoric, charisma, and greatness. Admin. Sci. Quart. **46**(3), 527–557 (2001)

19. Erickson, D.: Expressive speech: production, perception and application to speech synthesis. Acoust. Sci. Technol. **26**(4), 317–325 (2005)

20. Frese, M., Beimel, S., Schoenborn, S.: Action training for charismatic leadership: two evaluations of studies of a commercial training module on inspirational communication of a vision. Person. Psychol. **56**(3), 671–698 (2003)

21. Frick, R.W.: Communicating emotion: the role of prosodic features. Psychol. Bull. **97**(3), 412 (1985)

22. Fujisaki, H.: Prosody, models, and spontaneous speech. In: Computing Prosody, pp. 27–42. Springer, New York (1997). https://doi.org/10.1007/978-1-4612-2258-3_3

23. Gasper, J.M.: Transformational leadership: an integrative review of the literature. Western Michigan University (1992)

24. Gobl, C., Bennett, E., Chasaide, A.N.: Expressive synthesis: how crucial is voice quality? In: Proceedings of 2002 IEEE Workshop on Speech Synthesis, 2002, pp. 91–94. IEEE (2002)

25. Goldman-Eisler, F.: The distribution of pause durations in speech. Lang. Speech **4**(4), 232–237 (1961)

26. House, R.J.: A 1976 theory of charismatic leadership. Working Paper Series 76–06 (1976)

27. Igras-Cybulska, M., Ziółko, B., Żelasko, P., Witkowski, M.: Structure of pauses in speech in the context of speaker verification and classification of speech type. EURASIP J. Audio Speech Music Process. **2016**(1), 1–16 (2016). https://doi.org/10.1186/s13636-016-0096-7

28. Judge, T.A., Piccolo, R.F.: Transformational and transactional leadership: a meta-analytic test of their relative validity. J. Appl. Psychol. **89**(5), 755 (2004)

29. Kirsner, K., Dunn, J., Hird, K.: Language production: a complex dynamic system with a chronometric footprint (2005)

30. Lea, W.A.: Trends in Speech Recognition. Prentice Hall PTR (1980)

31. Lee, C.M., et al.: Emotion recognition based on phoneme classes. In: Eighth International Conference on Spoken Language Processing (2004)

32. Martha, A.S.D., Santoso, H.B.: The design and impact of the pedagogical agent: a systematic literature review. J. Educat. Online **16**(1), n1 (2019)

33. Mio, J.S., Riggio, R.E., Levin, S., Reese, R.: Presidential leadership and charisma: the effects of metaphor. Leadership Quart. **16**(2), 287–294 (2005)

34. Petrov, S., Das, D., McDonald, R.: A universal part-of-speech tagset. arXiv preprint arXiv:1104.2086 (2011)

35. Pitrelli, J.F., Bakis, R., Eide, E.M., Fernandez, R., Hamza, W., Picheny, M.A.: The IBM expressive text-to-speech synthesis system for American English. IEEE Trans. Audio Speech Lang. Process. **14**(4), 1099–1108 (2006)

36. Rochester, S.R.: The significance of pauses in spontaneous speech. J. Psycholinguist. Res. **2**(1), 51–81 (1973)

37. Roehling, S., MacDonald, B., Watson, C.: Towards expressive speech synthesis in English on a robotic platform. In: Proceedings of the Australasian International Conference on Speech Science and Technology, pp. 130–135 (2006)

38. Rosenberg, A., Hirschberg, J.: Charisma perception from text and speech. Speech Commun. **51**(7), 640–655 (2009)

39. Shamir, B., Arthur, M.B., House, R.J.: The rhetoric of charismatic leadership: a theoretical extension, a case study, and implications for research. Leadership Quart. **5**(1), 25–42 (1994)

40. Shamir, B., Arthur, M.B., House, R.J.: The rhetoric of charismatic leadership: A theoretical extension, a case study, and implications for research. In: Leadership Now: Reflections on the Legacy of Boas Shamir, pp. 31–49. Emerald Publishing Limited (2018)

41. Shamir, B., House, R.J., Arthur, M.B.: The motivational effects of charismatic leadership: a self-concept based theory. Organ. Sci. **4**(4), 577–594 (1993)

42. Shen, J., et al.: Natural TTS synthesis by conditioning Wavenet on Mel spectrogram predictions. arXiv preprint arxiv:1712.05884 (2017)

43. Stylianou, Y.: Applying the harmonic plus noise model in concatenative speech synthesis. IEEE Trans. Speech Audio Process. **9**(1), 21–29 (2001)
44. Székely, É., Henter, G.E., Beskow, J., Gustafson, J.: Spontaneous conversational speech synthesis from found data. In: Interspeech, pp. 4435–4439 (2019)
45. Tao, J., Kang, Y., Li, A.: Prosody conversion from neutral speech to emotional speech. IEEE Trans. Audio Speech Lang. Process. **14**(4), 1145–1154 (2006)
46. Tokuda, K., Nankaku, Y., Toda, T., Zen, H., Yamagishi, J., Oura, K.: Speech synthesis based on hidden Markov models. Proc. IEEE **101**(5), 1234–1252 (2013)
47. Tokuda, K., Zen, H., Black, A.W.: An HMM-based speech synthesis system applied to English. In: IEEE Speech Synthesis Workshop, pp. 227–230. IEEE Santa Monica (2002)
48. Touati, P.: Prosodic aspects of political rhetoric. In: ESCA Workshop on Prosody (1993)
49. Towler, A.J.: Effects of charismatic influence training on attitudes, behavior, and performance. Person. Psychol. **56**(2), 363–381 (2003)
50. Wang, N., Pacheco, L., Merchant, C., Skistad, K., Jethwani, A.: The design of charismatic behaviors for virtual humans. In: Proceedings of the 20th ACM International Conference on Intelligent Virtual Agents, pp. 1–8 (2020)
51. Wang, Y., et al.: Tacotron: a fully end-to-end text-to-speech synthesis model. arXiv preprint arxiv:1703.10135 (2017)
52. Wasielewski, P.L.: The emotional basis of charisma. Symbol. Interact. **8**(2), 207–222 (1985)
53. Weber, M.: The Theory of Social and Economic Organization. Simon and Schuster (2009)
54. Williams, C.E., Stevens, K.N.: Emotions and speech: some acoustical correlates. J. Acoust. Soc. Am. **52**(4B), 1238–1250 (1972)
55. Ze, H., Senior, A., Schuster, M.: Statistical parametric speech synthesis using deep neural networks. In: 2013 IEEE International Conference on Acoustics, Speech and Signal Processing, pp. 7962–7966. IEEE (2013)

Enabling Embodied Conversational Agents to Respond to Nonverbal Behavior of the Communication Partner

Matthias Wölfel[✉], Christian Felix Purps, and Noah Percifull

Faculty of Computer Science and Business Information Systems,
Karlsruhe University of Applied Sciences, Karlsruhe, Germany
{matthias.woelfel,christian_felix.purps}@h-ka.de

Abstract. Humans communicate on three levels: words, paralanguage, and nonverbal. While conversational agents focus mainly on the interpretation of words that are being spoken, recently the focus has also shifted to how we say those words with our tone, pace, and intonation. Nonverbal communication, including facial expression, eye contact, posture, and proximity, has been largely ignored in human-agent interactions.

In this work, we propose to incorporate nonverbal behavior into conversations between humans and agents by displaying a human-like embodied agent on a large screen and by responding appropriately to nonverbal cues from the interlocutors. In a user study with 19 volunteers, we investigated the influence on the participants for different behaviors (mimicry, positively biased mimicry, negatively biased mimicry, random) of the embodied conversation agents. The results indicate that goal-directed behavior is perceived significantly better concerning likability, social competence, attitude, and responsiveness in comparison to random behavior. This indicates that already simple nonverbal methods of building rapport can be used to improve the perceived conversational quality with an embodied conversational agent.

Keywords: Embodied agent · Nonverbal communication ·
Human-agent interaction · Large screen · Rapport

1 Introduction

Conversational agents have become commonplace in two forms, either as chatbots or voice assistance. While both forms are capable of processing natural language, the first works only with text, while the second can process speech in its spoken form. Although conversational agents try to mimic conversations between real people, they usually do so without embodiment. Adding embodiment and functionalities to simulate human nonverbal behavior could improve the perceived quality of a user's conversation with the agent. We will refer to *embodied conversational agents* (ECAs) as automated agents with a three-dimensional human-like body that can speak, understand, reason, express emotions, and perform tasks. Note that, in contrast to our definition, the general use

© The Author(s), under exclusive license to Springer Nature Switzerland AG 2022
M. Kurosu (Ed.): HCII 2022, LNCS 13304, pp. 591–604, 2022.
https://doi.org/10.1007/978-3-031-05412-9_40

of embodiment refers to a digital or physical manifestation of an agent, which typically does not require a replica of a human appearance. In addition, we would like to note that the term "embodied agent" should not be confused with other forms of human-like representations such as avatars, which usually do not behave autonomously.

Bodily communication takes place whenever a person influences others through facial expressions, poses, gestures, and so on. Therefore, the embodiment of an agent must respond to the user in one way or another. The basic encoding-decoding paradigm follows the pattern that a state of person A, such as an emotion, is encoded into a nonverbal signal, which in turn is decoded by person B. Bodily communication is rich in fundamentally different signals. Therefore, the implementation of embodied agent's behavioral logic has to focus on a reasonable number of bodily gestures (focusing mainly on rapport, which is characterized by agreement, mutual understanding, or empathy between two people and plays an important role in building human relationships) including:

- *Behavioral mimicry*, which is the adoption of another person's mannerisms, posture, gestures, and motor movements.
- *Proximity*, which defines the distance between two people as a function of their interpersonal relationship.
- *Back-channel feedback*, which consists largely of small but strong reinforcing signals, such as head nods. The absence of these signals can be interpreted as a negative response.
- *Gaze direction*, which is a strong indicator of where attention is focused.

2   Related Work

Successful communication is largely determined by the social awareness of the interlocutors, which opened the field for socially-aware computing that takes social intelligence into account and aims to create more natural, flexible computing technologies [26,31]. The adoption of agents aims to enable more intuitive human-computer interaction [1,29]. Conversational user interfaces integrate computational linguistics with a communication channel to interpret and respond to user utterances in natural language [21]. Conversational agents can be embodied to use visible speech, facial expressions, or body language, adding supplementary modalities [24]. These types of social cues allow for synchronicity and fluency between the speaker and the listener, increasing conversational quality and facilitating the development of a social relationship [9,13]. Several works show, that users interact with ECAs as they would with other humans, as the agents are able to elicit the same responses as real people [25]. However, while ECAs are inspired by interpersonal conversations, they do not necessarily need to be an exact copy, but can be seen as a new genre following own rules of interaction [10].

New approaches enabled by artificial intelligence are already improving the agent's awareness of its environment [11]. Representations of ECAs are diverse, ranging from talking heads to realistically looking virtual humans, but can also take the form of a fantasy character, an animal, or other entities [6]. Talking heads have been developed for versatile purposes, aiming to express emotions through facial expressions and articulated language to user responses, and more recently provide a very naturalistic appearance [2,14,33]. Talking heads, however, miss the opportunity to include aspects of nonverbal communication besides facial expressions, such as social behaviors manifested in postures, hand gestures, or proximity. These unconscious behaviors (e.g., behavioral imitation, feedback, or spatial positioning) create a sense of connectedness, agreement, greater liking, and trust that should be considered in ECA [13,15,18].

Hoque et al. presented a system that provided embodied interaction and real-time feedback through virtual humans, as well as post-interaction feedback on the user's performance. Their ECA reads facial expressions, speech, and prosody, and responds in a rule-based manner with verbal and nonverbal behavior by informing a trainee about verbal (pauses, speech rate, filler words, etc.) and nonverbal (smiles, head nods, shakes, etc.) performance [19]. Most participants, in this study, perceived the character's behavior as natural. Because of the given interview situation in a sitting position, the agent did not have the possibility to include spatial behavior. Bickmore et al. were among the first to develop an application that links an ECA to a large screen [4]. Their wide-ranging research included many aspects and applications for ECAs, such as their use in health care and the implementation of Rea, an embodied conversational agent for social dialogues that can respond to visual, auditory, and linguistic cues typically used in face-to-face conversations [7]. Although Rea's implementation was very sophisticated for the time, some capabilities remained unused (likely due to hardware limitations), such as intelligent spatial behavior.

3 Embodied Agent System

To test our hypothesis, we needed to design an ECA capable of perceiving a range of social signals from its human interlocutor and responding nonverbally to gestures, postures and spatial behaviors. We developed our agent entirely in the multi-platform environment *Unity* (v. 2020.3), which allows comparatively easy access to a 3D engine, scripting of the contained game objects, animation of rigged characters, and product deployment [30], accompanied by a basic rapport logic that can mimic trained gestures using motion sensed movements. The ECA was projected in life-size on a large screen. Based on the gestures of the conversational partner, the agent can react accordingly based on self-developed program logic. Getting the ECA to mimic a gesture, essentially requires two components: the detection of gestures and the action of the agent that corresponds to the gesture.

3.1 Embodiement

The selected visual representation for our agent comes from Mixamo[1] (Character Joe), as it allows independently created characters to be rigged with a human

---

[1] www.mixamo.com.

skeleton. Since our system focuses on nonverbal behavior, we chose a generic human-like character. In order not to influence the evaluation by facial expressions, the character was fitted with a surgical face mask covering the agent's face (see Fig. 1). Since the year 2021 was heavily influenced by the pandemic, the use of face masks is common and did not cause irritation among participants. To avoid irritating behavior of the embodied agent by leg motions that do not correspond to the character's movements, only the upper body, the hands, and the head are displayed. This representation is not uncommon in social virtual environments.

Fig. 1. Agent Representation: virtual human (Joe by Mixamo) equipped with a surgical face mask without lower body

3.2   Perception

To enable the embodied agent to perceive and understand its environment and, in particular, to be able to observe and interpret the nonverbal cues of its interlocutors, optical sensors are required. Since depth sensors have shown promising results in recognizing the shape of people, matching skeletons, and to recognize gestures, we decided to use Microsoft Azure Kinects. The Kinect comes with a full body-tracking SDK[2] that allows for real-time extraction of joint information from the depth image. To access data from an Azure Kinect array that covers a large area, we use a self-developed middleware that seamlessly integrates the *Kinetic Space*[3] gesture recognition module. Using Kinetic Space, we recorded

---

[2] Body Tracking SDK for Azure Kinect enables segmentation of exposed instances and both observed and estimated 3D joints and landmarks for fully articulated, uniquely identified body tracking of skeletons. (www.azure.microsoft.com/en-us/services/kinect-dk).

[3] Kinetic Space is an open-source tool that enables training, analysis, and recognition of individual gestures with a depth camera like Microsoft's Kinect family [32].

various postures and gestures to be used later for recognition. Due to its underlying algorithm, Kinetic Space is able to learn and recognize gestures from a single example. The skeleton data is normalized (size, position, and rotation) so that individual features and location do not affect recognition accuracy. The detected social signals and the spatial coordinates of the participants are then transmitted by the middleware to Unity for further processing.

3.3 Social Signals

Nonverbal signals are manifold and gestures or postures must always be interpreted in their entirety of interaction, cultural environment, and context to avoid miscommunication and misunderstanding. However, within the broad spectrum of human social signals, we have limited the agent's action space to specific gestures, spatial behavior, and gaze direction. The integrated gestures, as well as spatial behavior and gaze direction, were selected based on their relative clarity of interpretation, their quality for expressing interpersonal relationships, and the likelihood that a participant would actually use them. For the action space of the agent, different postures and gestures were selected that are associated with either agreement or disagreement.

Table 1. Social signals recognized and emitted by the agent: the symbols indicate if the agent is capable (filled circle) or incapable (without filling) of sensing/emitting the specific type of social signal.

Social Signal	Type	Rapport	Sensing	Emitting
Head nod	Gesture	Positive	●	●
Wave	Gesture	Positive	●	●
Lateral head tilt	Posture	Positive	●	●
Look towards	Gaze	Positive	○	●
Turn towards	Proximity	Positive	○	●
Spacial approach	Proximity	Positive	●	●
Follow	Proximity	Positive	●	●
Hands behind back	Posture	Neutral	●	●
Arms neutral	Posture	Neutral	●	●
Arms folded	Posture	Negative	●	●
Arms akimbo	Posture	Negative	●	●
Look away	Gaze	Negative	○	●
Turn away	Proximity	Negative	○	●
Spacial retreat	Proximity	Negative	●	●

To establish a positive connection with the agent during the conversation, we chose the following gestures: nodding the head (agreement, confirmation), waving (greeting, bonding), and lateral head tilting (friendliness, conciliation) [23,27,28]. To establish a negative connection, we chose folding the arms (withdrawal, disagreement) and placing the hands on the hips (dominance, authoritarianism) [3,5,17].

As another feature of a positive or negative interpersonal relationship, the agent is able to turn its direction of gaze as well as the orientation of its body toward or away from the interlocutor [16]. The agent is also able to adjust its interpersonal distance by moving closer or further away from its interlocutor. Within the tracking area the agent can follow the participant maintaining an appropriate interpersonal distance (never approaching closer than one meter to avoid discomfort). This behavior is not applied in reverse, i.e. if the participant moves away from the agent, the agent will not follow the user unless the participant moves too far away.

3.4 Animations

To create customized postures and gestures for the embodied agent, we recorded Azure Kinect tracking data. Since the recorded data was quite noisy, we had to post-process the animations to remove artifacts and jitter to make the movements look more organic and natural. All animations were manually adjusted to be loopable by making the last frame of the animation congruent with the first frame. This way, no interruption of the animation can be observed when the animation is played continuously. Similarly, the transitions between different animations were interpolated and smoothed using the automatic animation blending mechanism of Unity (Fig. 2).

Fig. 2. Examples of recorded and post-processed embodied agent animations (left to right): custom idle, arms folded, hands behind back, hands on hips, wave, lateral head tilt

4   Methodology

To investigate the responsiveness of the embodied agent, we adopted four different behavioral logics: mimicry, positive bias, negative bias, and random. All rapport modes are based on the phenomenon of behavioral imitation, which has been shown to increase sympathy for the mimicker, improve the flow of the interaction, increase feelings of belonging and connectivity, and foster prosocial behavior [12].

4.1   Study Design

Each behavioral scenario of the agent has access to the entire array of implemented nonverbal signals (see Table 1) and their recognition. Different behavioral logics determine when and with which behavior the agent responds. Specifically, four nonverbal behavioral modes were developed for the study, each as a condition for a within-subjects experimental design.

In the *mimicry* condition, the agent detects the participant's nonverbal behavior and mimics the exact same pose or gesture after it is recognized (delay of 1.5 s [20]), and follows the participant while maintaining its spatial distance and gaze direction towards the participant. If a new gesture is detected while the animation is still running, the novel gesture is queued and then executed.

In the condition *mimicry + positive bias*, the mimicry performed by the embodied agent executes behaviors that are expected to increase the rapport of the interlocutor. Artificially enhanced behaviors include head nodding, waving, lateral head tilting, and spatial approach. When the agent has not detected a social signal to imitate within 10 s and thus been idle, it performs a randomly selected gesture with positive rapport.

In the condition *mimicry + negative bias*, the mimicry performed by the embodied agent executes behaviors that are expected to reduce the rapport of the interlocutor. Artificially reinforced behaviors include crossing arms, arms akimbo, clasping hands behind back, looking away, and spatial retreat. If the agent has not detected a social signal to mimic and thus been inactive for 10 s, it triggers a randomly selected gesture with negative rapport.

In the *random* condition, the participant does not influence the agent's behavior-it does not follow or mimic, and proximity to the user is disregarded. Instead, the agent exhibits random behavior (a random activity from Table 1 is performed) after a random period between 6 s and 16 s of inactivity.

To engage participants in our study in a verbal conversation, we hid a confederate interlocutor behind the screen. During the conversation with the hidden interlocutor, the participant interacted with the embodied agent. To provide enough conversation topics, we talked about weather, sports, vacations, and work. The topic was randomly assigned to each of the four rapport modes. The general setup of the experiment is shown in Fig. 3. The embodied agent was projected life-size onto a curved 180° screen with a projection area of 2.5 x 10 m^2. An Azure Kinect array tracked the participant's social cues, location, and orientation.

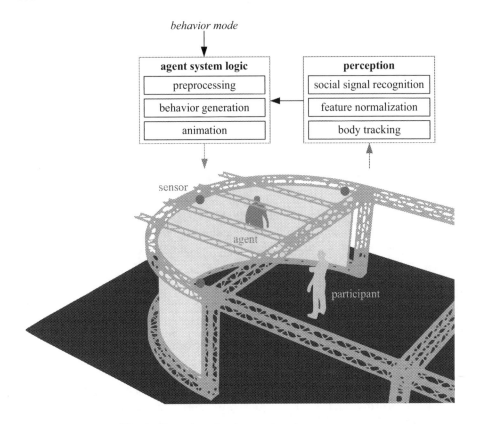

Fig. 3. Experiment setup and system process

4.2   Participants

In the study 19 individuals (4 females, 15 males, average age 30) participated without compensation for their effort. 14 participants have a background in engineering. The majority had little to no experience with mixed reality applications (11 participants < 1 h, 2 participants > 10 h). A photo of a participant interacting with the embodied agent is given in Fig. 3.

4.3   Procedure

Before the experiment participants got informed about the setup of the lab (tracking, camera recordings, trial duration, number of trials) and then asked to fill in the pre-experiment questionnaire. Before the first trial began for each participant, the agent system logic generated a random order of the agent's four behaviors, which were randomly combined with one of the four conversation topics. The participant then discussed each given topic with the confederate (hidden behind the screen) during an approximately three-minute conversation while communicating nonverbally with the embodied agent projected on the

Fig. 4. Participant during interaction with the embodied agent

180° canvas. After each trial, the participant was asked to complete the post-trial questionnaire assessing dependent measures. After all scenarios and formal questions were completed, participants were debriefed and interviewed for qualitative analysis (Fig. 4).

4.4 Dependent Measures

In the post-trial questionnaire, participants were asked to judge the agent's responsiveness (1 = non-responsive, 5 = responsive), perceived social competence (consisting of the four questions each judged from 1 = not to 7 = very: "How well could the agent express itself in body language?", "How would you rate the agent's social skills?", "How plausibly did the agent move around the room?", "How intelligent did you find the agent?", Cronbach's $\alpha = 0.831$) and likability (consisting of the five questions with ratings each from 1 = not to 7 = very: "How polite did the agent behave towards you?", "How sympathetic did you find the agent?", "Has the agent been more open than reserved?", "Did you feel attached to the agent?", "Did you find the agent's behavior off-putting?", Cronbach's $\alpha = 0.904$) derived according to the questionnaires from Lucas et al. and Cerekovic et al. [8,22]. Additionally, the participants were asked to rate the perceived agent's attitude (1 = negative, 2 = neutral, 3 = positive).

5   Findings

The presented embodied agent provided reliable results during the study. For each participant the agent mimicked in average 14 distinct social signals (waving was performed in average 6 times, closely followed by hands behind the back in average 5 times) and changed spacial position in average 3 times. The agent's mimicking duration for folding arms (mimicry: 11.0 s, pos. bias: 5.9 s, neg. bias: 23.8 s), arms akimbo (mimicry: 6. 5 s, pos. bias: 6.3 s, neg. bias: 21.8 s) and hands behind the back (mimicry: 56.6 s, pos. bias: 42.5 s, neg. bias: 25.15 s) were quite variable for the different conditions. No lateral head tilts or nods were detected. The positive and negative bias conditions produced 8 more social signals compared to the mimicry condition. The random behavior performed an average of 16 social signals per trial.

A within-subjects one-way ANOVA was performed to compare the effect of the agent's behavioral patterns on the perceived agent responsiveness, social competence, likability, and attitude. The results are summarized in Fig. 5.

There was a statistically significant difference and a large effect size between at least two conditions for agent responsiveness ($F = 14.48, p = 0.001, \eta_p^2 = 0.446$), social competence ($F = 14.32, p = 0.001, \eta_p^2 = 0.443$), likability ($F = 49.91, p < 0.001, \eta_p^2 = 0.735$), and attitude ($F = 30.06, p < 0.001, \eta_p^2 = 0.601$). Pairwise comparisons revealed that the values were significantly different between random behavior and all other conditions: mimicry (responsiveness: $p = 0.002$, likability and attitude: $p < 0.001$, social competence: $p = 0.003$), positive bias (responsiveness, likability, attitude, and social competence: $p < 0.001$), negative bias (responsiveness, likability, and social competence: $p < 0.001$, attitude: $p = 0.002$). A significant difference was also found in pairwise comparisons between mimicry and positive bias in likability ($p = 0.015$) and social competence ($p = 0.008$) and between positive and negative bias (likability: $p < 0.001$, social competence: $p = 0.048$).

A within-subjects one-way ANOVA between conversational topic and responsiveness, social competence, likability, or attitude was not significant. Neither estimated screen time nor participant age correlated with responsiveness, social competence, likability, or attitude.

6   Discussion and Future Work

The results demonstrate that any goal-directed behavior pattern of the agent is perceived significantly better in comparison to random behavior. Social competence and likability yielded similar results. However, it is possible that the chosen indices measure largely the same effects. The measures of responsiveness suggest that participants were able to grasp that the agent did not respond randomly. Augmenting positive and negative behavior to pure mimicry did not seem to have had any effect on the perceived responsiveness of the agent. This could be a significant factor and a reason why social competence and liking were also rated significantly lower for this condition and can be explained in terms of unwillingness to interact with the agent. Mimicry and negatively biased mimicry were not

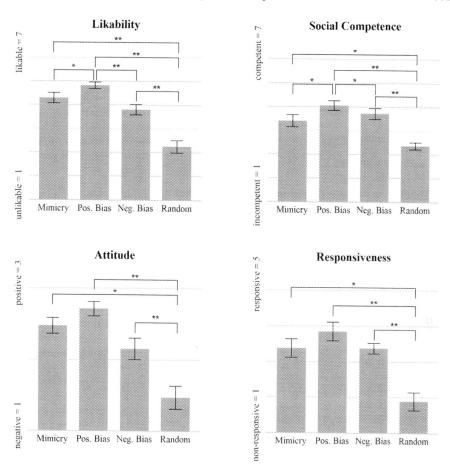

Fig. 5. Comparison of the different agent behaviors in terms of perceived agent responsiveness, social competence, likability, and attitude.

perceived as significantly different, but the positively biased behavior resulted in remarkably higher ratings of social competence and likability compared to (negatively biased) mimicry. The reason why the negatively biased behavior did not result in lower likability could be that the negative gestures were not expressive or powerful enough, or that participants did not interpret them as intended. Thus, the supposed negatively associated social cues need to be reconsidered. Lateral head tilts and head nods were not detected by our social signal recognition algorithms. This may be due to participants not performing these social signals or that these signals were too subtle to be reliably detected.

The debriefings revealed that participants were somewhat afraid of behaving ridiculously. Being not directly observed by an operator somewhat reduced these concerns. To improve a more natural behavior it might be helpful to place the potential interlocutor in a different room and have participants believe that the system has full speech integration. It was sometimes observed that if expectations, on how the embodied agent has to act according to a performed gesture of the participant, were not fulfilled led to an exaggeration of the very same gesture, e.g., participants waving with both hands to receive a wave back. This suggests that an unanticipated response to a purposely performed gesture may lead to social dissonance between the human and the agent.

Hiding the agent's facial expressions with a face mask-while fitting in today's world-is not a permanent solution, as facial expressions are essential for recognizing emotions and thus for building relationships. Therefore, facial expressions should be integrated into future applications. The robustness of the presented solution for agent interaction proved to be reliable. The custom embodied agent behavior animations run quite smoothly, yet the integration of a Bayes filter would have the ability to almost completely eliminate the remaining jitter and artifacts. Nonverbal behavior in general, however, needs further investigation in terms of interactions on a 180° screen. In particular, the movements of the agent following the participant around the room cannot be considered natural. Also, the integration of nonverbal behaviors such as turn-taking or eye-tracking, which have not been implemented due to complexity and technical limitations, should be considered in more sophisticated systems.

7   Conclusion

We have presented a system for embodied agent interactions on a large projection surface, such as a 180° screen, that provides the basic logic for an agent to generate nonverbal rapport. As of now, the embodied agent can mimic gestures by replaying motion-captured animation or respond with a different gesture if desired. It can change smoothly between these different gesture animations. To some extent, the agent can autonomously-according to some predefined logic-move within the interaction space. It can move sideways, forward, and backward, follow the user and rotate to look at the user. The results of our user study show that our agent's directed behavioral logic performs significantly better than randomly generated behavior. We hypothesize that supplementing purely imitative agent behavior with positively associated nonverbal signals can improve rapport without feeling less responsive. This can facilitate communication and contribute to positive impression formation. Our system provides initial insights and can serve as a research platform, in different media, on large screens, but also in head-mounted augmented reality and virtual reality environments.

References

1. AbuShawar, B., Atwell, E.: Alice chatbot: trials and outputs. Computación y Sistemas 19(4), 625–632 (2015)
2. Albrecht, I., Schröder, M., Haber, J., Seidel, H.P.: Mixed feelings: expression of nonbasic emotions in a muscle-based talking head. Virt. Real. 8(4), 201–212 (2005)
3. Argyle, M.: Bodily Communication, 2nd edn, pp. 1–111. Routledge, London (1986)

4. Bickmore, T., Cassell, J.: Small talk and conversational storytelling in embodied conversational interface agents. In: AAAI Fall Symposium on Narrative Intelligence, pp. 87–92 (1999)
5. Bull, P.: Gesture and Posture. Pergamon Press, Oxford (1987)
6. Butz, M., Hepperle, D., Wölfel, M.: Influence of visual appearance of agents on presence, attractiveness, and agency in virtual reality. In: Wölfel, M., Bernhardt, J., Thiel, S. (eds.) 10th EAI International Conference, ArtsIT 2021. LNICS, vol. 422, p. 44. Springer, Cham (2021). https://doi.org/10.1007/978-3-030-95531-1_4
7. Cassell, J., et al.: Embodiment in conversational interfaces: Rea. In: Proceedings of the SIGCHI Conference on Human Factors in Computing Systems, pp. 520–527 (1999)
8. Cerekovic, A., Aran, O., Gatica-Perez, D.: Rapport with virtual agents: what do human social cues and personality explain? IEEE Trans. Affect. Comput. 8(3), 382–395 (2017)
9. Chartrand, T.L., Bargh, J.A.: The chameleon effect: the perception-behavior link and social interaction. J. Pers. Soc. Psychol. 76(6), 893–910 (1999)
10. Clark, L., et al.: What makes a good conversation? Challenges in designing truly conversational agents. In: Proceedings of the 2019 CHI Conference on Human Factors in Computing Systems, pp. 1–12. Association for Computing Machinery, New York (2019)
11. Das, A., Datta, S., Gkioxari, G., Lee, S., Parikh, D., Batra, D.: Embodied question answering. In: Proceedings of the IEEE Conference on Computer Vision and Pattern Recognition, pp. 1–10 (2018)
12. Duffy, K.A., Chartrand, T.L.: Mimicry: causes and consequences. Curr. Opin. Behav. Sci. 3, 112–116 (2015)
13. Duncan, S., Fiske, D.W.: Face to Face Interaction Research. Methods and Theory (1977)
14. Gong, L.: Is happy better than sad even if they are both non-adaptive? Effects of emotional expressions of talking-head interface agents. Int. J. Hum. Comput. Stud. 65(3), 183–191 (2007)
15. Gratch, J., et al.: Virtual Rapport. In: Gratch, J., Young, M., Aylett, R., Ballin, D., Olivier, P. (eds.) IVA 2006. LNCS (LNAI), vol. 4133, pp. 14–27. Springer, Heidelberg (2006). https://doi.org/10.1007/11821830_2
16. Harrigan, J.A., Oxman, T.E., Rosenthal, R.: Rapport expressed through nonverbal behavior. J. Nonverbal Behav. 9(2), 95–110 (1985)
17. Harrigan, J.A., Rosenthal, R.: Physicians' head and body positions as determinants of perceived rapport. J. Appl. Soc. Psychol. 13(6), 496–509 (1983)
18. Heylen, D.: Challenges ahead: head movements and other social acts in conversations. Virt. Soc. Agents, 45–52 (2005)
19. Hoque, M.E., Courgeon, M., Martin, J.C., Mutlu, B., Picard, R.W.: MACH: my automated conversation coach. In: Proceedings of the 2013 ACM International Joint Conference on Pervasive and Ubiquitous Computing, UbiComp 2013, pp. 697–706. Association for Computing Machinery, New York (2013)
20. Huang, L., Morency, L.-P., Gratch, J.: Virtual Rapport 2.0. In: Vilhjálmsson, H.H., Kopp, S., Marsella, S., Thórisson, K.R. (eds.) IVA 2011. LNCS (LNAI), vol. 6895, pp. 68–79. Springer, Heidelberg (2011). https://doi.org/10.1007/978-3-642-23974-8_8
21. Lester, J., Branting, K., Mott, B.: Conversational Agents. The Practical Handbook of Internet Computing, pp. 220–240 (2004)

22. Lucas, G.M., et al.: Getting to know each other: the role of social dialogue in recovery from errors in social robots. In: Proceedings of the 2018 ACM/IEEE International Conference on Human-Robot Interaction, pp. 344–351. ACM, Chicago (2018)

23. Mara, M., Appel, M.: Effects of lateral head tilt on user perceptions of humanoid and android robots. Comput. Hum. Behav. **44**, 326–334 (2015)

24. Massaro, D.W., Cohen, M.M., Daniel, S., Cole, R.A.: Developing and evaluating conversational agents. In: Human Performance and Ergonomics, pp. 173–194. Elsevier (1999)

25. Nass, C., Moon, Y.: Machines and mindlessness: social responses to computers. J. Soc. Issues **56**(1), 81–103 (2000)

26. Pentland, A.: Socially aware, computation and communication. Computer **38**(3), 33–40 (2005)

27. Poggi, I., D'Errico, F., Vincze, L.: Types of nods. The polysemy of a social signal. In: Proceedings of the Seventh International Conference on Language Resources and Evaluation (LREC 2010) (2010)

28. Salem, B., Earle, N.: Designing a non-verbal language for expressive avatars. In: Proceedings of the Third International Conference on Collaborative Virtual Environments, CVE 2000, pp. 93–101. Association for Computing Machinery, New York (2000)

29. Schiaffino, S., Amandi, A.: User-interface agent interaction: personalization issues. Int. J. Hum. Comput. Stud. **60**(1), 129–148 (2004)

30. Technologies, U.: Unity—2D 3D Game Creator & Editor—Augmented. Virtual Reality Software—Game Engine. https://unity.com/products/unity-platform

31. Wang, F.Y., Carley, K.M., Zeng, D., Mao, W.: Social computing: from social informatics to social intelligence. IEEE Intell. Syst. **22**(2), 79–83 (2007)

32. Wölfel, M.: Kinetic Space - 3D Gestenerkennung für Dich und Mich. Konturen **32**, 58–63 (2012)

33. Zakharov, E., Shysheya, A., Burkov, E., Lempitsky, V.: Few-shot adversarial learning of realistic neural talking head models. In: Proceedings of the IEEE/CVF International Conference on Computer Vision, pp. 9459–9468 (2019)

Giving Alexa a Face - Implementing a New Research Prototype and Examining the Influences of Different Human-Like Visualizations on the Perception of Voice Assistants

Carolin Wienrich[✉], Felix Ebner, and Astrid Carolus[ID]

Julius-Maximilians-Universität Würzburg, Human-Technology-Systems, Sanderring 2, 97070 Würzburg, Germany
carolin.wienrich@uni-wuerzburg.de

Abstract. Since the introduction of the Amazon Echo, smart speakers have increasingly found their way into private households. What if the voice assistant could not only be heard but also seen? How would people then evaluate smart speakers? Based on the trend that smart speakers will start to integrate or even become displays, this article (1) presents a research prototype of a visualized smart speaker and (2) investigates how people perceive a visualized voice assistant (VA) by comparing three different human-like visualizations of the prototype. A software solution using Unity combined with a commercial smart speaker makes it possible to visualize the speech assistant. The prototype can record the interaction with the VA without sending sensitive data to the VA provider. We created three visualizations of a VA differing in their amount of human-like facial features based on this prototype. The online study with 51 participants reveals that visualizations with more facial features were perceived significantly more human-like than visualizations with fewer features. Furthermore, our results indicate that perceived anthropomorphism significantly influences how other human-like characteristics are attributed to the visualizations. Overall, our study gives initial insights into the growing segment of visualized VAs with implications for future cases of use and design.

Keywords: Voice assistant · Media equation · Smart speaker · Human-centered · AI · Anthropomorphism

1 Introduction

Since their introduction seven years ago, smart speakers have steadily increased in popularity. In 2021, 35% of American adults owned smart speakers, with Great Britain boasting an even higher 38% of smart speaker ownership [1]. Although smart speakers are becoming more popular, the devices have changed little in their appearance and structure. Most of them still resemble cylindrical or spherical speakers with lights to indicate their current state of activity. However, smart speakers are more than just speakers with an Internet connection. Various studies have shown that people quickly tend to personalize their devices in recent years. People attribute human characteristics to the devices, although they are well aware that they are purely technical devices [2, 3]. The present contribution focuses on what would happen if smart speakers had a "face" and thus visualized the voice assistant. The question is motivated by a new generation of smart speakers and smart products, such as the Amazon Astro and the Amazon Echo Show 10. According to these new products, smart speakers will soon ditch their traditional structure as speakers and start taking on more diverse shapes such as displays or robots. While the new generation still provides the hands-free advantages of the conventional smart speaker structure, it also allows for visual interaction. Since voice already triggers human-like attribution, the visual interface may either reinforce or contradict previous findings concerning smart speakers. Would people identify more with the smart speaker if the voice assistant had a face? What consequences would various visualizations have on the use of the devices? Would people find the visualization creepy or feel observed by it?

Based on the trend that smart speakers will start to integrate or even become displays, this article (1) presents a research prototype of a visualized smart speaker, allowing various investigations independently of commercial products and in line with privacy regulations. Further, (2) it investigates how people perceive a visualized voice assistant by comparing three different anthropomorphic visualizations.

Fig. 1. Three visualization prototypes. A: No facial human-like features (*control condition*); B: Few facial human-like features (*few features condition*); C: Many human-like features (*many features condition*)

2 Related Work

2.1 Research on Voice-Based Assistants

With the increasing popularity of VAs, research regarding the devices has also become more important. Up to now research regarding VAs has mostly focused on their acceptance and users' privacy concerns. Although concerns regarding the devices are an important topic, the underlying psychological effects of VAs should not be overlooked. Thus, more recently researchers have started to focus on how people perceive and engage with VAs.

One important part of VA perception is the topic of anthropomorphism. Anthropomorphism describes the tendency of humans to attribute human characteristics to nonhuman entities [4]. In the context of HCI, anthropomorphism has already been researched in many experiments and theories (e.g., [5, 6], see for an overview [7]). The Media Equation Theory is one of the most influential theories explaining this tendency to attribute human characteristics. It states that people tend to treat technical devices like real social actors even though they are aware of their technical nature (for an overview see [8]). A series of experiments applying the CASA paradigm (Computers As Social Actors) revealed that humans mindlessly apply social norms (e.g., being polite) rather than believing the computer or digital device to be human (e.g., [9–11]).

In contrast, VAs employ a lot more human-like features than computers or other technical devices. For users to interact with the device, the VA has a concrete name and human voice [12]. Users are therefore also able to identify the gender of the VA as well as ascribe a personality to the VA. These features suggest that VAs are likely to be perceived as more anthropomorphic and treated more as social actors [13].

Multiple studies have been conducted evaluating the anthropomorphism of VAs. Purington et al. [2] used Amazon reviews in order to investigate how users perceive their VAs. The authors defined anthropomorphization as cases where people used the VA's name ("Alexa") or personal pronouns (e.g., "she" or "it") to refer to the VA. Results showed that more than half of the investigated reviews used the personified name of the VA and that members in multi-user households are more likely to personify the device. In a follow-up study by Gao et al. [14] a similar approach was used for evaluating Amazon reviews regarding users' relationship with the VA. In a review of over 55,000 samples, the authors showed that over 30% of the analyzed reviews showed personification behavior. Furthermore, some users even developed a close relationship with their device, referring to the VA as best friend or wife. Lopatovska and Williams [15] reported similar findings in their diary study. Participants also used personal pronouns to refer to the VA as well as greet or thank it. The authors characterized most personification behavior as mindless politeness and overlearned social responses, with only two participants reporting deeper personification. A recent study by Pradhan, Findlater & Lazar [3] gives further insight into how older adults categorize VAs. The study shows that older adults fluidly move between categorizing the VA as "human-like" or "object-like" depending on factors such as the users' desires or the location and moment of interaction.

In summary, research on the anthropomorphism/personification of VAs shows that users tend to personify the agent and categorize the VA to be a "companion" or "friend". Although smart speakers with displays are becoming more popular, little to no research has been conducted on visualized VAs. Our work aims to provide initial insights into how these new devices are perceived, by systematically varying the amount of human-like features of a visualized VA. For example, indicators for the devices' perception are the degree of anthropomorphism, social presence, acceptance, and trust.

2.2   Research on Combinations of Voice-Based Assistants

Since current smart speakers don't visualize the voice assistant, there is little to no research regarding the perception and effects of visualized VAs. However, in the linked field of social robotics, researchers have long been investigating the impact of human-like features on the perception of the social counterpart. Recently robots are increasingly being designed with displays as faces with dynamic facial expressions [16, 17]. For example, Song, Luximon & Luximon [18] investigated the effect of different combinations of schematic baby facial features on the perceived trustworthiness of the robot. The results showed that eye size, eye position and mouth position have a significant impact on perceived trustworthiness. Other studies have focused their investigations on the effect of specific facial features. In a study by Luria, Hodgins & Forlizzi [19], the impact of variations in eye design using low-fidelity paper prototypes has been investigated. The authors showed that more lifelike eye designs were rated higher on personable qualities and were perceived more suitable for use at home.

Overall, studies in the field of social robotics show that the design and presence of facial features have significant effects on the perception of the robot (e.g., [17, 20]; for a recent review see [21]). Based on these results, we can assume that by giving the VA a "face", the perception of the device can be heavily influenced. However, most social robots have a body where different body parts such as the face and arms are easily discernible. In contrast, Goudey & Bonnin [22] investigated the effect of anatomical anthropomorphism on the perception of social robots. To vary the amount of anatomical anthropomorphism of social robots, the authors defined indicators that refer to human anatomy. Based on these indicators, three social robots were chosen and evaluated in an online survey using a picture of the robot and a written scenario. The results of the study indicate that the perceived anthropomorphism of the robot can partially be manipulated by the amount of human anatomical indicators, whereby the robot with the most indicators is perceived as significantly more human than the other two robots. Furthermore, a significant effect of perceived anthropomorphism on the acceptance of the robot could be observed when controlling for technology experience.

In order to investigate how people perceive visualized VAs we combined the results of social robotics literature on facial design and the approach taken in the study of Goudey & Bonnin [22]. We, therefore, created a new research prototype including three visualizations of the VA. The visualizations vary in the extent of their human-like facial features, from no features to a lot of features (Contribution 1). Using these visualizations, we investigate the perceived anthropomorphism and examine the effect of trait attribution of the VA as a function of the perceived anthropomorphism (Contribution 2).

3   Contribution 1: The Implementation of a New Research Prototype

The first contribution of the present article concerns the analysis and implementation of the technical basis required for researching the questions mentioned above. Of course, some products are already available: Vector [23], Jibo [24], or Amazon Echo Show 10 [25]. The former examples differ in two respects: they can move and use specially developed speech recognizers and speech models. On the other hand, for our research prototype, it was decided to use a commercially successful device, which has several advantages. Commercial devices have better-trained speech recognition and natural speech output. Another advantage of using commercially available smart speakers is that existing literature on the devices can be compared to the fact of visualization. Smart speakers from major manufacturers, such as Amazon or Google, have been evaluated in recent years with regard to a wide variety of aspects, such as voice gender [26] and trust in the device [27]. New research findings can then be compared and drawn upon to better explain the observed phenomena. However, the Amazon Echo Show display is limited to the default features; systematic manipulation of visual features is not possible. In addition, commercial smart speakers are associated with privacy concerns. Thus, a product that uses well-trained speech recognition to understand requests from the user and displays suitable visualizations with different amounts of human-like features was not yet available. For ethically conform research, such a product should record and save the users' reactions independently of the provider. The following Table 1 summarizes the requirements and corresponding solution ideas guiding the implementation of our research prototype.

Table 1. Requirements and corresponding solution ideas of the research prototype, the visualized voice assistant.

Requirements	Example
Ability to show continuous and manipulatable visualization	Use a separate display applying a Unity application
Ability to record and save the interaction independently of the VA provider	Implementation of an external microphone and recorder at the place of interaction
Ability to record and save long user reactions (>30 s)	Implementation of a special VA skill
Prevention of data transfer to the VA provider	Implementation of a special VA skill
High-quality speech recognition	Use of existing and well-trained VAs

3.1   Implementation

Based on the identified requirements, we created a prototype that consists of three main components. The first component is a third generation Amazon Echo. The smart speaker serves as the basis of the prototype and enables high-quality verbal interaction with the VA. The second component is represented by a Unity [28] application and an external display. Since current Smart Speakers are not able to continuously visualize the VA, we created a Unity application that is able to communicate with the VA and permanently display the VA using an external display. The Unity application runs on a separate computer and is connected to the external display via HDMI. Thus, the application and the display serve the purpose of visually displaying the VA. The third and last component consists of a particular skill for the VA. The skill ties all components together to allow for verbal and visual interaction with the VA. Thus, the skill receives incoming commands from the user and processes them. Afterwards the response to the command is sent back to the VA and simultaneously a short message containing the correspondent visualization is sent to the Unity application. Thus, the VA can respond both verbally and visually to the users' commands.

To prevent the transfer of user information to the VA manufacturer and permit longer recordings of user reactions, the skill follows a specific structure. Basically, every command sent to the VA restarts the skill. The skill then returns from the last point of interaction, answers (or asks) and shuts down again. Afterwards, users can answer without a time limit and without sending the response to the VA provider, since the skill is turned off. Therefore, the prototype can be used, for example as an interview tool in a privacy-sensitive context, something which current VAs cannot fulfil.

4   Contribution 2: Empirical Evaluation of the Research Prototype

As mentioned above, new challenges emerge with new design features of the voice assistant and the corresponding user experience. For example, how should the voice assistant and its information best be visualized? What effects could the visualization have on users' perceptions? Although the new generation of voice assistants appears more human-like than its predecessors, the current devices do not systematically offer different visualizations or design interfaces to investigate the impact of new features. To bridge this gap, we evaluated three different display visualizations of a voice assistant, varying in the extent of their human likeness on the perception of the voice assistant.

4.1   Method

Participants. The participants included 54 students at a German university. Three participants had to be excluded from the sample since they did not watch the whole video of the voice assistant thus reducing the final sample size to 51 participants (average age: $M = 21.33$, $SD = 1.60$; 35 females). The study was advertised through the university's recruitment system. Participants were self-selected and received course credits for their time in the half-hour-long online study.

Overall VA experience was high, with more than half of the sample ($n = 27$) indicating that they use a VA often. On the other hand, smart speaker ownership was low, with only nine participants owning a smart speaker.

Material
The Visualizations. To investigate the effect of different human-like visualizations on the perception of the voice assistant, we created three visualizations for the voice assistant applying the research prototype introduced above. since the voice assistant already has a "body" in the form of the smart speaker, we chose to focus on the "face" of the voice assistant. Therefore, we adopted the approach used by Goudey & Bonnin [22] to create three visualizations varying in the amount of human-like facial features (Fig. 1). The first visualization (a, *control* condition) incorporates no human-like facial features and resembles the light circle found on Amazon smart speakers. The second visualization (B, *few features* condition) employs few human-like facial features by displaying two stylized eyes. The eyes can blink to appear more human-like and explicitly show that

they portray eyes. lastly, a visualization with many human-like facial features (C, *many features* condition) was realized using Apple's Memoji function and had a lot of human-like facial features. The visualization shows an entirely stylized head of a neutral female avatar that can blink and move naturally.

The Video Stimuli. The visualizations were presented to participants in a short video lasting about two minutes. The picture of an Amazon Echo Show 10 was used as a background for the video. The visualization of the voice assistant was then overlaid onto the display portion of the smart speaker to simulate the visualized voice assistant. During the video, different commands were sent to the smart speaker. The commands were only presented visually as subtitles, to eliminate the effects of the speaker's voice and aid understandability. After a command was given, the voice assistant responded both verbally and visually.

As for the commands given to the voice assistant, the most popular functions of voice assistants such as weather forecast and information [29] were used to evaluate the visualizations using a realistic use case. We chose not to give commands regarding the voice assistant's alarm, automation and video functions since they would have been difficult to present in the form of a video. All voice assistant visualizations were shown using the same commands at identical timestamps to aid comparability.

4.2   The Measurements

Demographic Measures. To investigate the demography of participants, we asked questions regarding their age ("How old are you?"), sex ("Which gender do you identify as?"), education ("What is your educational background?") and native language ("What is your native language?").

Control Measures. Control measures were assessed during the pre-questionnaire and referred to concepts such as media usage, VA ownership, VA usage, individual anthropomorphic tendencies, need to belong, online trust, attitudes towards VAs and technology commitment. The collected questionnaires are presented below.

Media Usage. General media usage was measured using nine items referring to different media (e.g., "notebook/desktop PC" or "printed books"). Participants were instructed to indicate how often they used the devices, and responses could be given on a 9-point scale ranging from "never" to "several times an hour".

VA Ownership and Usage. VA ownership and usage were assessed based on seven devices (e.g., "Alexa/Amazon Echo" or "Google Home"). To measure VA usage, participants were instructed to answer how often they used the respective device on a 5-point scale ranging from "never" to "very often". As for VA ownership, participants were asked to indicate which of the seven VAs they owned using a binary scale.

Individual Anthropomorphic Tendencies. The Individual Differences in Anthropomorphism Questionnaire [30] was used to measure participants' differences in anthropomorphism. The questionnaire consists of 30 Likert scale items with anthropomorphic subscales (e.g., "To what extent does the average fish have free will?") and non-anthropomorphic attribution (e.g., "To what extent is the desert lethargic?"). In addition, participants were asked to rate the extent to which they possess the capacity to stimulate on an 11-point Likert scale ranging from "not at all" to "very much". Cronbach's alpha was satisfactory (above .70) for each subscale, indicating sufficient internal consistency.

Need to Belong. The need to belong was measured using the Need to Belong Scale [31]. The scale consists of 10 questions (e.g., "If other people don't seem to accept me, I don't let it bother me."). Participants indicated their level of agreement on a 5-point Likert scale ranging from "not at all" to "extremely". Internal consistency of the questionnaire was high with Cronbach's alpha = .80.

Online Trust. The Scale for Online User's Trust was used to assess users' trust in online resources [32]. The scale consists of 15 Likert scale questions with subscales for perceived trustworthiness, perceived risk, trust disposition and institutional trust. For the pre-questionnaire, we only used the subscale for measuring trust disposition (e.g., "I tend to trust people or things quickly"). Participants indicated their level of agreement on a 5-point Likert scale ranging from "strongly disagree" to "strongly agree". Cronbach's alpha was high for the subscale (above .90), ensuring internal consistency.

Negative Attitudes Towards VA. Negative attitudes towards VA were measured using the Negative Attitudes toward Robot Scale [33]. The scale consists of 14 Likert scale questions with subscales for negative attitudes towards situations of interaction with robots, the social influence of robots, and emotions in interaction with robots. To assess the negative attitudes towards VAs instead of robots, we replaced the word robot/robots in the items with VA/VAs (e.g., "I would feel relaxed talking with robots" was changed to "I would feel relaxed talking with voice assistants"). Participants indicated their level of agreement on a 5-point Likert scale ranging from "strongly disagree" to "strongly agree". Internal consistency of the subscales was low, with Cronbach's alpha being around .50. The scale, therefore, seems unsuitable for modification to assess VAs. Due to the low internal consistency, no statistical tests were performed on the questionnaire's results.

Technology Commitment. The Kurzskala Technikbereitschaft [34] was used to measure technology commitment. The scale consists of 12 Likert scale questions with subscales for technology acceptance, technology competence and technology control convictions (e.g., "I'm always interested in using the latest technological devices"). Participants indicated their level of agreement on a 5-point Likert scale ranging from "strongly disagree" to "strongly agree". Cronbach's alpha was acceptable (around .70) for each subscale, indicating sufficient internal consistency.

Measuring the Perceived Anthropomorphism.
Uncanny Valley Indices. The Uncanny Valley Indices [35] were used to measure the visualization's perceived humanness, eeriness and attractiveness. The scale consists of 21 semantic differential items with three subscales for humanness (e.g., "synthetic – real"), eeriness (e.g., "plain – weird") and attractiveness (e.g., "ugly – beautiful"). Participants rated their impression of the VA on a 7-point semantic differential scale. Internal consistency for each subscale was high, with Cronbach's alpha above .75.

Measuring Human-Like Attributions

Godspeed Indices. The Godspeed Questionnaire Series was used to measure the overall perception of the VA [36]. The questionnaire series consists of 24 semantic differential items with subscales for anthropomorphism (e.g., "machine-like – human-like"), animacy (e.g., "dead - alive"), likeability (e.g., "dislike - like"), perceived intelligence (e.g., "incompetent - competent") and perceived safety (e.g., "anxious - relaxed"). Participants rated their impression of the VA on a 5-point semantic differential scale.

Due to high correlations between humanness (Uncanny Valley Indices) and the subscales anthropomorphism ($r = .85$, $p < .001$) as well as animacy ($r = .80$, $p < .001$), these subscales were excluded from further analyses. Cronbach's alpha was high ($> .7$) for all subscales except perceived safety (alpha $= .46$). Therefore, no statistical tests were performed for perceived safety.

VA Acceptance. The acceptance of the VA was measured using the Robot Acceptance Questionnaire [37]. The questionnaire consists of 41 Likert scale questions that can be answered on a 7-point Likert scale running from "strongly disagree" to "strongly agree". To measure the acceptance of the VA instead of a robot, we reformulated the items to measure the VA. Furthermore, we followed the limited model for studies on social abilities or social presence and only collected the subscales intention to use (e.g., "I am certain to use the VA during the next few days."), perceived enjoyment (e.g., "I enjoy the VA talking to me."), perceived ease of use (e.g., "I find the VA easy to use."), perceived sociability (e.g., "I feel the VA understands me."), social presence (e.g., "I often think the VA is not a real person.") and trust (e.g., "I would trust the robot if it gave me advice"). Internal consistency was satisfactory for the subscales intention to use (alpha $= .97$), perceived enjoyment (alpha $= .83$), social presence (alpha $= .73$) and trust (alpha $= .69$). The subscales perceived ease of use and perceived sociability did not yield sufficient internal consistency (below .60) and were therefore excluded from further analyses.

VA Usability. The Voice Usability Scale [38] was used to measure the VA's perceived usability. The scale consists of 10 Likert scale questions (e.g., "I thought the response of the VA was easy to understand."). Participants stated their level of agreement on a 7-point Likert scale ranging from "strongly disagree" to "strongly agree". Cronbach's alpha was sufficient (above .60) for each subscale, indicating internal consistency.

Mind Attribution. The Mind Attribution Scale [39] was used to measure the mind attribution of the VA. The scale consists of 10 Likert scale items with subscales for emotion (e.g., "This VA has complex feelings."), intention (e.g., "This VA has goals.") and cognition (e.g., "This VA is highly conscious."). Instructions were changed from referring to a person to referring to the VA. Participants rated their level of agreement on a 7-point Likert scale ranging from "strongly disagree" to "strongly agree". Internal consistency was satisfactory for each subscale, with Cronbach's alpha above .60.

Additional Measures. In addition to the measures mentioned already, we also asked six additional Likert scale questions. Four questions were adapted from the Human-Computer Trust Model [40] and measured the perceived trustworthiness of the VA (e.g., "I believe that there could be negative consequences when using the VA."). The other two questions consisted of a question measuring the overall trustworthiness of the VA ("I feel that I can trust the VA.") and a question assessing to what extent participants felt watched by the VA ("I felt as if the VA was watching me."). Participants indicated their level of agreement on a 7-point Likert scale ranging from "strongly disagree" to "strongly agree".

4.3 Procedure

To investigate the effect of different voice assistant visualizations, we conducted an online survey using SoSci Survey [41]. After arriving at the online survey, they first assured confidentiality and then provided informed consent. First, participants filled out questions regarding their demography and the control variables. Participants were then presented with a video of one of the three anthropomorphic visualizations. Participants were asked to watch the whole video in quiet surroundings with the sound of the video turned on. After watching the video, participants were presented with different questionnaires regarding the perception of the voice assistant.

4.4 Design, Assumptions and Data Analyses

The study uses a between-subjects design with one factor (*amount of human-like facial features*) varying in three levels (*control condition* with no facial features, *few features* showing few facial features or *many features* showing many facial features). Accordingly, participants were randomly assigned to one of the three visualizations (control condition: $n = 17$; few features condition: $n = 18$; many features condition: $n = 16$).

Since previous research in other fields revealed an impact of human-like features on the perception of digital devices, we assumed that human-like facial features lead to more perceived anthropomorphism of our research prototypes (Assumption 1). Furthermore, we assumed that higher levels of perceived anthropomorphism mediated the impact of human-like facial features and the attribution measures (Assumption 2).

To investigate the first assumption, we conducted a one-way ANOVA and subsequent pairwise comparisons on an alpha level of .05. The second assumption was investigated by conducting mediational analyses to explore to what extent the perceived anthropomorphism mediates the relationship between experimental conditions and attribution measures. Figure 2 illustrates the design, assumptions, and analyses.

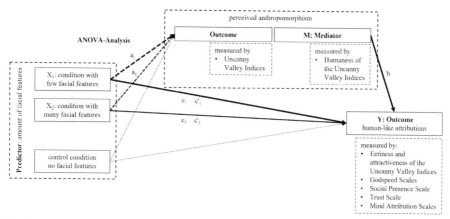

Fig. 2. Illustrates the design, assumptions and analyses. The thicker the arrows, the more impact was assumed. The dotted lines show the assumption that more human-like facial features (X_1; X_2) lead to more perceived anthropomorphism. Perceived anthropomorphism is the outcome variable in the corresponding ANOVA analyses. Mediator analyses investigate the mediating impact of the perceived anthropomorphism (M) on the other outcome variables (Y) reported by the indirect effect ($c - c' = a * b$). The total effect (c) described the impact of our experimental conditions on the other outcome variables ($c = c' + a * b$) The direct effect (c') is the extent to which the dependent variable changes when the independent variable increases by one unit and the mediator variable remains unaltered ($c' = c - a * b$) [42].

4.5   Results and Short Discussion

Control Measures. No significant differences could be found between the three experimental conditions regarding demographics or the pre-questionnaire, except for the ownership of the VA "Siri", $X^2(2, N = 51) = 8.44, p = .015, V = .41$. Although participants differed in their ownership of "Siri", no significant differences could be found regarding its usage, $H(2) = 4.20, p = .122$. The difference in ownership was thus neglected in the following analyses.

Assumption 1: Anthropomorphism Measures as Outcome Variables. First, the assumption that the amount of human-like facial features could affect the perceived anthropomorphism was confirmed. Accordingly, a one-way ANOVA showed significant differences between experimental conditions ($F(2, 48) = 17.68, p < .001, \eta^2 = .424$) with post-hoc tests showing differences between all three experimental conditions on the humanness subscale (see Table 2). As expected, the control condition was considered least human ($M = 2.06, SD = .64$), followed by the few features condition ($M = 2.78, SD = .84$); lastly the many features condition was rated most human ($M = 3.57, SD = .68$).

Table 2. Post-hoc table (Tukey-HSD) for perceived humanness

Comparison				
Condition	Condition	Mean difference	SE	Sig.
Control	Few features	−0.72	.25	.015
	Many features	−1.51	.25	<.001
Few features	Control	0.72	.25	.015
	Many features	−0.80	.25	.007
Many features	Control	1.51	.25	<.001
	Few features	0.80	.25	.007

In addition to perceiving visualizations with increasing features as more human-like, significant differences were observed for eeriness ($F(2, 48) = 6.128$, $p < .004$, $\eta^2 = .203$) and attractiveness ($F(2, 48) = 3.694$, $p = .032$, $\eta^2 = .133$). For the perceived eeriness, post-hoc tests revealed that the many features condition ($M = 3.42$, $SD = .63$) was rated significantly more eerie ($p = .004$) than the control condition ($M = 2.64$, $SD = .72$; .78, 95% CI [0.23, 1.34]). Between the control condition and the few features condition ($M = 3.16$, $SD = .62$) there was no significant difference (−.26, 95% CI [−0.80, 0.29]).

Similar results could be observed for the attractiveness of the visualization. Post-hoc tests revealed that the condition with many features ($M = 5.31$, $SD = .66$) was perceived significantly more attractive ($p < .05$) than the control condition ($M = 4.60$, $SD = .74$; .71, 95% CI [0.01, 1.42]). Between the control condition and the few feature condition ($M = 4.64$, $SD = 1.05$) there was no significant difference (.04, 95% CI [−0.64, 0.73]).

Assumption 2: Anthropomorphism Measures as Mediator Variables. For the mediational analyses, the perceived anthropomorphism was used as a mediator. To reduce the number of analyses, we only used the humanness subscale of the Uncanny Valley Indices as an indicator for perceived anthropomorphism. The factor amount of human-like facial features serves as a predictor. since the predictor has three levels, we conducted mediational analyses with a multi-categorical antecedent following the approach of Hayes [42] (see Fig. 2). We set the control condition as the reference group and used indicator coding for the other two conditions. Thus, the reported effects are relative effects, explaining the impact of the facial feature conditions compared to the control group respectively.

The eeriness and attractiveness of the Uncanny Valley Indices and the attribution measures serve as outcome variables (see Fig. 2).

Analyses revealed significant relative total effects on eeriness, attractiveness, social presence, attributed cognition and perceived negative consequences. Additional mediations of perceived anthropomorphism were found for eeriness, attractiveness, likeability, intention to use, enjoyment, social presence, trust and attributed emotion. The results are presented in the following.

Eeriness and Attractiveness. In order to check whether the significant differences in eeriness and attractiveness are mediated by the perceived anthropomorphism, two mediational analyses were carried out. For eeriness, significant relative total effects could be observed for both experimental conditions ($c_1 = .53$, $p = .022$; $c_2 = .78$, $p = .001$). In addition, relative indirect effects were found for both experimental conditions ($a_1b = .38$, 95% CI [0.15, 0.63]; $a_2b = .80$, 95% CI [0.52, 1.18]), showing that perceived anthropomorphism (humanness subscale) fully mediates the effect of the experimental conditions on eeriness.

Similar results were observed for attractiveness. A significant relative total effect was found for the many features condition, $c_2 = .71$, $p = .019$. Additionally, relative indirect effects could be observed for both experimental conditions ($a_1b = .42$, 95% CI [0.07, 0.87]; $a_2b = .88$, 95% CI [0.25, 1.47]). The relationship between experimental condition and attractiveness is therefore mediated by the perceived anthropomorphism.

Attribution Measures. First, relative indirect effects were found for the likeability of the VA in both experimental conditions, $a_1b = .29$, 95% CI [0.08, 0.60]; $a_2b = .60$, 95% CI [0.28, 0.97]. No significant relative total or relative direct effects could be observed. The likeability of the VA is therefore completely mediated by the perceived anthropomorphism of the visualization.

Similar results were observed for the intention to use the device, with both experimental conditions showing relative indirect effects, $a_1b = .64$, 95% CI [0.13, 1.35]; $a_2b = 1.34$, 95% CI [0.44, 2.40]. In addition, the mediational analysis also showed significant relative direct effects for both experimental conditions, $c_1' = -1.31$, $p = .038$; $c_2' = -2.00$, $p = .012$. The effect of the amount of features on the intention to use is thus only partially mediated by the perceived anthropomorphism.

Analysis of the perceived enjoyment of the VA revealed relative indirect effects, $a_1b = .47$, 95% CI [0.09, 0.97]; $a_2b = 1.00$, 95% CI [0.32, 1.67]. Since no other significant effects were observed, the effect of the experimental conditions on the perceived enjoyment is completely mediated by the perceived anthropomorphism.

Mediational analysis regarding social presence initially showed significant relative total effects of experimental conditions on social presence, $c_1 = .82$, $p = .021$; $c_2 = 1.08$, $p = .004$. In addition, relative indirect effects were found for both experimental conditions, $a_1b = .61$, 95% CI [0.21, 1.09]; $a_2b = 1.29$, 95% CI [0.84, 1.81]. The relationship between experimental conditions and social presence is therefore fully mediated by the perceived anthropomorphism.

Regarding the trust subscale of the robot acceptance questionnaire, firstly a significant relative direct effect could be observed for the many features condition, $c_2' = -1.16$, $p = .046$. Additionally, relative indirect effects were found for both experimental conditions, $a_1b = .45$, 95% CI [0.02, 1.01]; $a_2b = .94$, 95% CI [0.07, 1.83]. The relationship between experimental conditions and trust is partially mediated by the perceived anthropomorphism.

We also found that for the emotion subscale of the mind attribution scale, the relationship between the experimental conditions and the attribution of emotion is fully mediated by the perceived anthropomorphism, $a_1b = .41$, 95% CI [0.11, .86]; $a_2b = .86$, 95% CI [0.33, 1.71].

Lastly mediational analysis revealed significant total effects for attributed cognition $(c_1 = .87, p = .033; c_2 = .85, p = .044)$, and in the few features condition for perceived negative consequences $(c_1 = 1.30, p = .01)$. Attributed cognition and perceived negative consequences are therefore not mediated by perceived anthropomorphism.

5   General Discussion

5.1   Motivation and Aim of Research

The present contribution focuses on what would happen if the smart speaker got a "face" and thus visualized the voice assistant. The question is motivated by a new era of smart speakers that still provide the hands-free advantages of the conventional smart speaker structure and allow for additional visual interaction. Since voice already triggers human-like attribution, the visual interface might reinforce or contradict the previous findings on smart speakers. Based on the trend that smart speakers will start to integrate or even become displays, the present article (1) presents a research prototype of a visualized smart speaker recording and understanding requests from the user and displaying suitable visualizations of the voice assistant on a display. Furthermore, (2) we have extended the current state of research in the field of smart speakers by investigating how people perceive three versions of the prototype that resemble visualized voice assistants.

5.2   Implications of Results

Anthropomorphism. In line with the study from Goudey & Bonnin [22], the manipulation of the amount of human-like features showed a difference in perceived anthropomorphism. Although Goudey & Bonnin only found a significant difference between the group with the most and the least features, our findings showed significant differences between each experimental condition. Moreover, the results reveal that the perceived anthropomorphism could successfully be manipulated by the amount of human-like facial features presented on our research prototypes. The difference in the results of our findings to those of Goudey & Bonnin can most likely be attributed to the difference in stimulus presentation. In the study by Goudey & Bonnin, participants were presented with an image of the social robot, whereas we chose to show the visualized VA using a video. Since participants in our study were also able to perceive the movement and functionality of the VA, a greater amount of information about the VA was given in comparison to an image. Participants therefore had more information available on which to base their judgment of the VA, leading to an amplified impact on perception. Another reason for the differing results could also have been the length of the stimulus presentation. The video was around two minutes long, which may have created a stronger impression of the visualized VA. Again, the length of stimulus presentation might increase the impact of our stimuli compared to Goudey & Bonnin [22].

Extending the findings of Goudey & Bonnin, we also investigated the effect of anthropomorphism on the eeriness and attractiveness of the VA. Regarding eeriness, the many features condition was perceived significantly more eerie than the control condition. One reason might be the uncanny valley effect [43]. The uncanny valley hypothesis describes a graph showing the relationship between human-likeness and familiarity. With increasing human-likeness, familiarity increases up to a point where something looks so human that nonhuman imperfections are perceived as unsettling [44]. Following this graph, our results would appear to indicate that the control condition was perceived as less eerie, since human-likeness is low. The many features condition, on the other hand, was perceived as human-like enough that imperfections became noticeable, and the visualization falls into the valley, thereby being perceived as eerier.

One aspect of our results that goes against this explanation is the means of the experimental conditions. Taking a look at participants' ratings of eeriness, we can see that with increasing human-like facial features, eeriness also increases. Following the uncanny valley hypothesis in order to achieve this relation, both few and many features conditions would need to be close together and located in the uncanny valley. Since the mean eeriness score of the many features condition (rated "most eerie") is just below the middle of the scale ($M = 3.42$), the uncanny valley hypothesis does not on its own explain the observed results.

Another explanation that also builds on the uncanny valley hypothesis could lie in the interplay between the humanness of the face and the voice. Although current VAs have become very good in natural speech synthesis, results of additional open-questions during our study indicate that users still perceive the VA's voice as "computer-like" or "unnatural". A study by Mitchell et al. [45] showed that a mismatch between the human realism of the face and the voice can elicit feelings of eeriness. Since participants perceived the voice of the VA more machine-like than human-like, a mismatch could have occurred in the few and many feature conditions, thereby leading to the visualization being rated eerier. To test this assumption, future studies should therefore also assess the human-likeness of the voice in addition to the visualization.

As for the attractiveness of the visualization, our results show a significant difference between the many features condition and the control condition, with the former being perceived as more attractive. The most likely explanation for these results is that to judge attractiveness, a high level of anthropomorphism must exist, since the concept is specific to humans. This explanation is further supported by the fact that the mean attractiveness score between the control condition and the few features condition is very similar.

Human-Like Attribution. The second aim of this study was to explore the impact of anthropomorphism on the relationship between the amount of human-like facial features and human-like attribution measures and perceived consequences. Mediation analyses showed multiple mediations of anthropomorphism on attribution measures and significant relative overall effects.

Firstly, the results show that anthropomorphism completely mediates the relationship between experimental conditions and likeability. This finding is in line with recent studies regarding the anthropomorphism of intelligent devices. Niu, Terken & Eggen [46] observed significant positive correlations between perceived anthropomorphism and liking in a study comparing symbolic only vs. symbolic and anthropomorphic information in an autonomous car. Similar results were found by Wagner, Nimmermann & Schramm-Klein [47] in the field of voice assistance. The results of an online survey assessing participants' VA perception showed a positive impact of anthropomorphism on the likeability of VAs. Our results thus confirm previous findings regarding the positive effect of anthropomorphism on likeability.

Secondly, a partial mediation of anthropomorphism for the relationship between the experimental condition and the intention to use was found. Significant relative direct effects indicate that the amount of human-like facial features has a negative impact on the intention to use that is not explained by the perceived anthropomorphism. Nonetheless, a positive relatively indirect effect could be observed for anthropomorphism. Although increasing amounts of human-like facial features lead to a lesser intention to use, this effect is suppressed by the positive mediation of anthropomorphism. While most studies show a significant effect of anthropomorphism on the intention to use, the direction of the impact varies [7]. Although our results indicate a positive relationship between anthropomorphism and the intention to use, further investigation is needed in order to explain the negative effect of more human-like visualizations.

Perceived enjoyment is another concept closely related to the intention to use the device. Our results show a completely positive mediation of anthropomorphism for the relationship between experimental condition and perceived enjoyment. This result is in line with the findings of Moussawi, Koufaris & Benbunan-Fich [48]. In a lab-based interaction session, participants with no to little prior VA experience were introduced to a VA and asked to complete multiple tasks with the assistant. Afterwards, participants were questioned about the research model. The results of this study revealed significant positive effects of perceived anthropomorphism on perceived enjoyment and thus the intention to use. Our findings, therefore, confirm the results of Moussawi, Koufaris & Benbunan-Fich by also revealing a positive mediation of anthropomorphism for perceived enjoyment.

In addition, our results also show a significant relative total effect of the experimental conditions on the perceived social presence of the VA. Visualizations with more human facial-like features were thereby perceived as more socially present than visualizations with less features. Moreover, this relation is completely mediated by the perceived anthropomorphism. As in the study by Lee, Kim & Shin [49], it can be assumed that visualizations employing more anthropomorphic cues such as gender, personality or facial expressions make the interaction seem more socially meaningful, thereby increasing the perceived social presence.

Trust is an important concept when it comes to smart speakers and VAs. Since most devices are used in private households and are always listening to users, trust can play a significant role in their usage and adoption. Although research concerning the trust in VAs has received a lot of attention, results regarding the concept vary [7]. Our results showed a significant negative relative direct effect of the many features condition on perceived trust. Accordingly, the many features condition was perceived as more untrustworthy than the other experimental conditions. In addition, a partial positive mediation could be observed for anthropomorphism. Niu, Terken & Eggen [46] argue that presenting information in a more human way facilitates understanding of the information and thus increases trust. Another explanation for increased trust through anthropomorphism is given by Waytz, Heafner & Epley [50]. The authors argue that more anthropomorphic agents appear capable of controlling their actions, thereby also appearing more responsible and trustworthy. The second explanation is supported by the fact that we also observed a significant positive relative total effect for the attribution of cognition. Participants perceived visualizations with a greater amount of features to be more capable of cognitive processing, which might lead to greater perceptions of responsibility and trust.

In addition to higher cognition attribution of more human-like visualizations, we also observed a complete mediation of anthropomorphism for emotion attribution. This result should come as no surprise, with Epley, Waytz & Cacioppo [4] even defining anthropomorphism as a tendency to imbue nonhuman agents with emotions, amongst other things. Thus, the attribution of emotion and perception of anthropomorphism are closely related, and emotion is often regarded as antecedent to anthropomorphism [7]. Similar to the facilitated cognition processing with an increasing amount of human-like facial features and perceived anthropomorphism, it can be assumed that it becomes easier for users to discern emotions and therefore judge emotional attribution higher.

Lastly, a significant relative total effect was found for the few features condition concerning perceived negative consequences by using the VA. This result seems surprising since the few features condition was neither perceived as most human-like nor most eerie. Looking at the descriptive data helps us gain initial insights into this result. Although information given by the few features condition was trusted the most, participants also felt the most watched by this condition as well as attributed it the most intention (no significant differences for each scale). The results therefore indicate that while participants trust the information given by the few features condition the most, they don't trust the VA with their personal data, since they perceive intentionality behind the VAs' actions. A possible reason for this result could be the lack of human-like features. Although the few features condition is perceived slightly human, the amount of features isn't sufficient in order for participants to fully interpret the VAs' face. Participants could therefore be uncertain about the VAs' actions and intentions leading to a higher perception of negative consequences. In order to better understand this relationship future studies should assess trust more specifically and investigate privacy concerns of visualized VAs.

5.3 Limitations of Results

This study was conducted with a particular user group and a relatively small sample size. Given the future importance of VAs, the study should be replicated with a larger and more diverse user group, in order to aid the generalizability of our findings.

The most significant limitation of the current study is that users were not able to interact with the visualized VA itself. The usage of a video stimulus meant that users were only able to observe the interaction with the device but not actively participate in it. We chose to follow this approach to quickly gain initial insights into people's perceptions of different visualizations. Nonetheless, the missing interaction with the VA could have a great impact on how users perceive the device, especially where sensitive issues like surveillance or acceptance are concerned. Therefore, future studies should evaluate visualized VAs in presence studies which enable active interaction with the device.

Another limitation of this study was the context in which the visualized VA was shown. We chose to present the most commonly used functions of VAs, in order to evaluate the visualizations in the most realistic context possible. Although this approach was appropriate for an initial evaluation of the VA, it may be that important concepts like safety and trust cannot be accurately evaluated using such a general context. Therefore, future analysis should consider visualized VAs in more sensitive and diverse contexts to gain further insights.

Lastly, the visualizations used in the study differ strongly from each other. Although one of the main goals of this study was to examine the effect of different amounts of human-like facial features on the perception of the VA, the approach we chose resulted in strongly differing visualizations (see [22]). The issue here is that we cannot pinpoint the specific parts of the visualization that led to the differences in anthropomorphism due to the considerable differences between the visualizations. Furthermore, the comparability of the visualizations should be seen rather critically. Thus, our study only gives a reference point as to what visualized VAs could look like. Therefore, future studies should examine more comparable visualizations to build on our findings.

6 Conclusion

Since their introduction seven years ago, smart speakers have steadily gained in popularity. The present contribution focuses on what would happen if smart speakers had a "face" and thus visualized the voice assistant. Based on the trend that smart speakers will increasingly include a display or even be fully integrated in one, this article (1) presents a research prototype of a visualized smart speaker and (2) investigates how people perceive a visualized voice assistant by comparing three different human-like visualizations of the prototype. The prototype continuously visualizes the VA and allows for experimental manipulation of the display content; a requirement that commercial smart speakers do not meet at present. Furthermore, the prototype can record the interaction with the VA for study purposes (in line with privacy regulations). Additionally, it overcomes limitations such as limited answering time by using a particular function without sending sensitive data to the VA provider. We created three visualizations of a VA differing in their amount of human-like facial features based on this prototype. We conducted an online study with 51 participants to investigate the effect of the visualizations on the perceived anthropomorphism of the VA and explored the influence of anthropomorphism on the attribution of other human-like characteristics (such as eeriness, likeability, intelligence, social presence, etc.). Our findings show that visualizations with more facial features were perceived as significantly more human-like than visualizations with fewer features.

Furthermore, our results indicate that perceived anthropomorphism substantially influences the relationship between the experimental conditions and attribution measures. Although anthropomorphism had a considerable impact on attribution measures, some relationships were only partially (e.g., intention to use) or not at all (e.g., cognition attribution, perception of negative consequences) mediated by anthropomorphism. The results show that next to anthropomorphism, other concepts could influence the perception of visualized VAs, and that further research is needed to get a complete overview.

Overall, our study gives initial insights into the growing segment of visualized VAs. Results show that even when the voice of the VA remains the same, visualizations can have substantial effects on how VAs are perceived and the intention to use. Future research should further investigate the perception of visualized VAs, especially for sensitive and safety-critical domains, and lead to guidelines for designing these new kinds of VAs.

References

1. Kinsella, B.: UK smart speaker adoption surpasses U.S. in 2020 - new report with 33 charts. https://voicebot.ai/2021/06/18/uk-smart-speaker-adoption-surpasses-u-s-in-2020-new-report-with-33-charts/
2. Purington, A., Taft, J.G., Sannon, S., Bazarova, N.N., Taylor, S.H.: Alexa is my new BFF. In: Proceedings of the 2017 CHI Conference Extended Abstracts on Human Factors in Computing Systems (2017)
3. Pradhan, A., Findlater, L., Lazar, A.: Phantom friend or just a box with information. Proc. ACM Hum.-Comput. Interact. **3**, 1–21 (2019)
4. Epley, N., Waytz, A., Cacioppo, J.T.: On seeing human: a three-factor theory of anthropomorphism. Psychol. Rev. **114**, 864–886 (2007)
5. Epley, N., Waytz, A., Akalis, S., Cacioppo, J.T.: When we need a human: motivational determinants of anthropomorphism. Soc. Cogn. **26**, 143–155 (2008)
6. Lemaignan, S., Fink, J., Dillenbourg, P., Braboszcz, C.: The cognitive correlates of anthropomorphism. In: Human-Robot-Interaction Conference, Workshop "HRI: A Bridge Between Robotics and Neuroscience" (2014)
7. Li, M., Suh, A.: Machinelike or humanlike? A literature review of anthropomorphism in AI-Enabled Technology. In: Proceedings of the Annual Hawaii International Conference on System Sciences (2021)
8. Nass, C., Moon, Y.: Machines and mindlessness: social responses to computers. J. Soc. Issues **56**, 81–103 (2000)
9. Nass, C., Fogg, B.J., Moon, Y.: Can computers be teammates? Int. J. Hum. Comput. Stud. **45**, 669–678 (1996)
10. Nass, C., Moon, Y., Carney, P.: Are people polite to computers? Responses to computer-based interviewing systems 1. J. Appl. Soc. Psychol. **29**, 1093–1109 (1999)
11. Carolus, A., Binder, J.F., Muench, R., Schmidt, C., Schneider, F., Buglass, S.L.: Smartphones as digital companions: characterizing the relationship between users and their phones. New Media Soc. **21**, 914–938 (2018)
12. Wienrich, C., Carolus, A.: Development of an instrument to measure conceptualizations and competencies about conversational agents on the example of Smart Speakers. Front. Comput. Sci. **3** (2021)
13. Wienrich, C., Reitelbach, C., Carolus, A.: The trustworthiness of voice assistants in the context of healthcare investigating the effect of perceived expertise on the trustworthiness of voice assistants, providers, data receivers, and automatic speech recognition. Front. Comput. Sci. 3 (2021)
14. Gao, Y., Pan, Z., Wang, H., Chen, G.: Alexa, my love: analyzing reviews of amazon echo. In: 2018 IEEE SmartWorld, Ubiquitous Intelligence & Computing, Advanced & Trusted Computing, Scalable Computing & Communications, Cloud & Big Data Computing, Internet of People and Smart City Innovation (SmartWorld/SCALCOM/UIC/ATC/CBDCom/IOP/SCI). (2018)
15. Lopatovska, I., Williams, H.: Personification of the Amazon Alexa. In: Proceedings of the 2018 Conference on Human Information Interaction & Retrieval - CHIIR 2018, pp. 265–268 (2018)

16. McGinn, C.: Why do robots need a head? The role of social interfaces on Service Robots. Int. J. Soc. Robot. **12**, 281–295 (2019)

17. Kalegina, A., Schroeder, G., Allchin, A., Berlin, K., Cakmak, M.: Characterizing the design space of rendered Robot Faces. In: Proceedings of the 2018 ACM/IEEE International Conference on Human-Robot Interaction (2018)

18. Song, Y., Luximon, A., Luximon, Y.: The effect of facial features on facial anthropomorphic trustworthiness in social robots. Appl. Ergon. **94**, 103420 (2021)

19. Luria, M., Forlizzi, J., Hodgins, J.: The effects of eye design on the perception of Social Robots. In: 2018 27th IEEE International Symposium on Robot and Human Interactive Communication (RO-MAN), pp. 1032–1037 (2018)

20. Pollmann, K., Tagalidou, N., Fronemann, N.: It's in your eyes: which facial design is best suited to let a robot express emotions? In: Proceedings of Mensch und Computer 2019, pp. 639–642 (2019)

21. Song, Y., Luximon, Y.: The face of trust: the effect of robot face ratio on consumer preference. Comput. Hum. Behav. **116**, 106620 (2021)

22. Goudey, A., Bonnin, G.: Must smart objects look human? Study of the impact of anthropomorphism on the acceptance of companion robots. Recherche et Applications en Marketing (English Edition). **31**, 2–20 (2016)

23. Meet Vector. https://www.digitaldreamlabs.com/pages/meet-vector

24. Together for you. https://jibo.com/

25. Echo show 10 (3. generation): Hochauflösendes smart display MIT Bewegungsfunktion und Alexa, Anthrazit : Amazon.de: Amazon-Geräte & Zubehör. https://www.amazon.de/der-neue-echo-show-10-hochauflosendes-smart-display-mit-bewegungsfunktion-und-alexa-ant hrazit/dp/B084P3KP2S

26. Cambre, J., Kulkarni, C.: One voice fits all? Social implications and research challenges of designing voices for smart devices. Proc. ACM Hum.-Comput. Interact. **3**, 1–19 (2019)

27. Lau, J., Zimmerman, B., Schaub, F.: Lexa, are you listening? Privacy perceptions, concerns and privacy-seeking behaviors with smart speakers. Proc. ACM Hum.-Comput. Interact. **2**, 1–31 (2018)

28. Willkommen bei den Unity Gaming Services. https://unity.com/de

29. Bentley, F., Luvogt, C., Silverman, M., Wirasinghe, R., White, B., Lottridge, D.: Understanding the long-term use of smart speaker assistants. Proc. ACM Interact. Mobile Wearable Ubiquit. Technol. **2**, 1–24 (2018)

30. Waytz, A., Cacioppo, J., Epley, N.: Who sees human? The stability and importance of individual differences in anthropomorphism. Perspect. Psychol. Sci. **5**, 219–232 (2010)

31. Leary, M.R., Kelly, K.M., Cottrell, C.A., Schreindorfer, L.S.: Construct validity of the need to belong scale: Mapping the nomological network. J. Pers. Assess. **95**, 610–624 (2013)

32. Bär, N., Hoffmann, A., Krems, J.: Entwicklung von Testmaterial zur experimentellen Untersuchung des Einflusses von Usability auf Online-Trust. Reflexionen und Visionen der Mensch-Maschine-Interaktion–Aus der Vergangenheit lernen, Zukunft gestalten. 9 (2011)

33. Nomura, T., Suzuki, T., Kanda, T., Kensuko Kato: Altered attitudes of people toward robots: investigation through the negative attitudes toward robots scale. In: AAAI 2006 Workshop on Human Implications of Human-Robot Interaction 2006, pp. 29–35 (2006)

34. Neyer, F.J., Felber, J., Gebhardt, C.: Entwicklung und Validierung einer Kurzskala zur Erfassung von Technikbereitschaft. Diagnostica **58**, 87–99 (2012)

35. Ho, C.-C., MacDorman, K.F.: Revisiting the uncanny valley theory: developing and validating an alternative to the godspeed indices. Comput. Hum. Behav. **26**, 1508–1518 (2010)

36. Bartneck, C., Kulić, D., Croft, E., Zoghbi, S.: Measurement instruments for the anthropomorphism, animacy, likeability, perceived intelligence, and perceived safety of Robots. Int. J. Soc. Robot. **1**, 71–81 (2008)

37. Heerink, M., Krose, B., Evers, V., Wielinga, B.: Measuring acceptance of an assistive social robot: a suggested toolkit. In: RO-MAN 2009 - The 18th IEEE International Symposium on Robot and Human Interactive Communication, pp. 528–533 (2009)

38. Zwakman, D.S., Pal, D., Triyason, T., Arpnikanondt, C.: Voice usability scale: measuring the user experience with voice assistants. In: 2020 IEEE International Symposium on Smart Electronic Systems (iSES) (Formerly iNiS), pp. 308–311 (2020)

39. Kozak, M.N., Marsh, A.A., Wegner, D.M.: What do I think you're doing? Action identification and mind attribution. J. Pers. Soc. Psychol. **90**, 543–555 (2006)

40. Gulati, S., Sousa, S., Lamas, D.: Design, development and evaluation of a human-computer trust scale. Behav. Inf. Technol. **38**, 1004–1015 (2019)

41. Sosci Survey: Die Lösung für eine Professionelle Onlinebefragung. https://www.soscisurv ey.de/

42. Hayes, A.F.: Introduction to Mediation, Moderation, and Conditional Process Analysis. A Regression-Based Approach, 2nd edn. Guilford Press (2018)

43. Mori, M.: Bukimi no tani (the uncanny valley). Energy **7**, 33–35 (1970)

44. MacDorman, K.F., Green, R.D., Ho, C.-C., Koch, C.T.: Too real for comfort? Uncanny responses to computer generated faces. Comput. Hum. Behav. **25**, 695–710 (2009)

45. Mitchell, W.J., Szerszen, K.A., Lu, A.S., Schermerhorn, P.W., Scheutz, M., MacDorman, K.F.: A mismatch in the human realism of face and voice produces an Uncanny Valley. i-Perception. **2**, 10–12 (2011)

46. Niu, D., Terken, J., Eggen, B.: Anthropomorphizing information to enhance trust in autonomous vehicles. Hum. Fact. Ergon. Manuf. Serv. Ind. **28**, 352–359 (2018)

47. Wagner, K., Nimmermann, F., Schramm-Klein, H.: Is it human? The role of anthropomorphism as a driver for the successful acceptance of Digital Voice assistants. In: Proceedings of the Annual Hawaii International Conference on System Sciences (2019)

48. Moussawi, S., Koufaris, M., Benbunan-Fich, R.: How perceptions of intelligence and anthropomorphism affect adoption of personal intelligent agents. Electron. Mark. **31**(2), 343–364 (2020). https://doi.org/10.1007/s12525-020-00411-w

49. Lee, J.-G., Kim, K.J., Lee, S., Shin, D.-H.: Can autonomous vehicles be safe and trustworthy? Effects of appearance and autonomy of unmanned driving systems. Int. J. Hum.-Comput. Interact. **31**, 682–691 (2015)

50. Waytz, A., Heafner, J., Epley, N.: The mind in the machine: anthropomorphism increases trust in an autonomous vehicle. J. Exp. Soc. Psychol. **52**, 113–117 (2014)

Author Index

Printed in the United States
by Baker & Taylor Publisher Services